Genealogical & Local History Books in Print

5th Edition

Family History Volume

GENEALOGICAL & LOCAL HISTORY BOOKS IN PRINT

5th Edition

Family History Volume

Compiled and Edited by
Marian Hoffman

929.1

Published by Genealogical Publishing Co., Inc.
1001 N. Calvert St., Baltimore, MD 21202
Library of Congress Catalogue Card Number 96-75602
International Standard Book Number 0-8063-1513-X
Made in the United States of America

Contents

Introduction vii

List of Vendors (organized numerically) ix

List of Vendors (organized alphabetically) xxiii

Family Histories 1

Compiled Genealogies 373

Surname Index 405

Index to Advertisers 449

Introduction

This *Family History Volume*, part of the entirely new 5th edition of *Genealogical & Local History Books in Print*, contains listings of available family histories as well as listings of pedigrees, biographies, and family newsletters in print. With the aid of this volume, researchers will know instantly what family histories are available for sale and where they can be bought.

Divided into two parts—family histories and compiled genealogies—the *Family History Volume* contains a total of 4,634 entries. Alphabetically arranged by family name, each entry identifies a published family history that is available and in print. Typically, entries give the full title of the work, the author, date of publication, whether indexed or illustrated, in cloth or paper, number of pages, selling price, and vendor number.

Each publication listed has been assigned a book number, which appears in the left margin. All surnames cited in the title and/or the body of the entry appear in the surname index in the back of the book, where they are keyed to this book number.

To order any of the listed publications, locate the vendor number at the bottom right of each listing. The names and addresses of these vendors, and any special ordering information, are listed on page ix. Send your order to the vendor and include the proper fee. Be sure to mention that you saw their work advertised in *Genealogical & Local History Books in Print*. The prices given in this volume include shipping and handling costs unless otherwise stated. They do not, however, include sales tax. *You must pay the state sales tax required by the government of the state in which you reside if you order books from vendors operating in your state.*

All the information included for each listing has been provided by the vendor. The books listed in this volume have not been examined or evaluated by the editor, and no comment on genealogical value can be made. Many of the vendors have descriptive literature concerning their works, which they will provide on request.

Compilation of the next edition of the *Family History Volume* will begin almost as soon as this volume is published. All authors or publishers of family histories are invited to list their publications. There is a small fee to do so. Write for information to Genealogical & Local History Books in Print, 1001 N. Calvert Street, Baltimore, MD 21202. Authors and publishers are also encouraged to send in listings for the other volumes of *Genealogical & Local History Books in Print,* which contain lists of general reference books and locality sourcebooks in print.

List of Vendors
(organized numerically)

G0001 Beatrice West Seitz, 2608 E. Racine Street, Apt 11, Janesville, WI 53545-5227

G0003 Alligator Book Co., 314 Seabrook Drive, Hilton Head, SC 29926; tel. 803-689-2655

G0004 William S. Farley, 6592 E. Jackson Court, Highlands Ranch, CO 80126

G0005 Jane McMurtry Allen, 4564 Holly Lake Drive, Lake Worth, FL 33463-5301

G0006 Madrue Chavers-Wright, 2410 Barker Avenue, Suite 14-G, Bronx, New York 10467-7634; tel. 718-654-9445

G0007 Randall C. Maydew, 6908 Brandywine Loop NE, Albuquerque, NM 87111; tel. 505-821-0102

G0008 Paul F. Burgess, 12305 Harbor Drive, Woodbridge, VA 22192; or c/o G. Pillsbury, RR-01, Box 1645, Springvale, ME 04083

G0009 Virginia Carlisle d'Armand, 3636 Taliluna Avenue, Apt. #235, Knoxville, TN 37919

G0010 Genealogical Publishing Co., Inc., 1001 N. Calvert Street, Baltimore, MD 21202-3879; tel. 410-837-8271; fax: 410-752-8492

> *Postage & handling. On orders over $10.00: one book $3.50, each additional book $1.25; on orders totaling $10.00 or less: $1.50. When ordering sets: First volume $3.50, each additional volume, $1.25. Maryland residents add 5% sales tax; Michigan residents add 6% sales tax.*

G0011 Clearfield Company, 1001 N. Calvert Street, Baltimore, MD 21202; tel. 410-625-9004; fax: 410-752-8492

> *Postage & handling. One book $3.50; each additional book $1.25. Maryland residents add 5% sales tax; Michigan residents add 6% sales tax*

G0012 Reta M. Evans, 5605 Westcreek Drive, Fort Worth, TX 76133-2246

G0017 Mary Ann Thompson, 2721 Knollwood Court, Plano, TX 75075-6424

G0018 Lois L. Hupfer, 3087 South Harlan, Denver, CO 80227-3818

G0020 Vernon Stiver, 501 West Loveland Avenue, Loveland, OH 45140

G0022 Ralph W. Morton, 4867 Chambersburg Road, Dayton, OH 45424; or John H. Warvel, 10951 E. Mallard Way, Indianapolis, IN 46278

G0023 Goldenwest Marketing, 10528 Lower Azusa Road #162, El Monte, CA 91731-1296; tel. 818-309-0764

G0024 Hilde Shuptrine Farley, 10325 Russell Street, Shawnee Mission, KS 66212-1736

G0025 Anne Morrow Nees, 6612 W. 93rd Street Apt. B, Overland Park, KS 66212

G0027 Virginia A. Stuhr, 8531 Glenwood, Overland Park, KS 66212-1125; tel. 913-642-7596

G0028 Susan R. Alexander, PO Box 460614, Houston, TX 77056-8614

G0029 Jack R. Hutchins, 23 Orchard Way South, Rockville, MD 20854; tel. 301-762-3251

G0030 Blanche W. Jernigan, PO Box 486, Pewee Valley, KY 40056; tel. 502-241-1606

G0032 Linda Berg Stafford, PO Box 5261, Bloomington, IN 47407

G0033 Victor H. Walworth, PO Box 924, Columbia, SC 29202; tel. 803-781-7886

G0034 Gayle King Blankenship, 24 Roberts Landing, Poquoson, VA 23662; tel. 804-868-8022

G0035 James W. Lowry, 13531 Maugansville Road, Hagerstown, MD 21740

G0037 Katherine Lytle Sharp, 2008 Forest Dale Drive, Silver Spring, MD 20903-1529; tel. 301-434-7751

G0038 Ken Stevens, PO Box 118, Walpole, NH 03608

G0041 Clarence D. Stephenson, PO Box 236, Marion Center, PA 15759-0236

G0043 Kimball Family Association, 14 Manson Road, Kittery, ME 03904-5534

G0044 Ward Publishing Company, 42 Larchmont Road, Asheville, NC 28804

G0045 Stephen L. Lawton, 620 Howard Avenue, Pitman, NJ 08071

G0047 Townsend Family Missing Links Assoc., 5721 Antietam Drive, Sarasota, FL 34231-4903

G0049 Harry D. Zook, 110 Village Lane, Winter Park, FL 32792-3412; tel. 407-678-2372

G0050 Sandra Johnson, Marketing Manager, University of Nebraska Press, 312 N. 14th St., Lincoln, NE 68588-0484

G0051 Dale C. Kellogg, 221 Lexington Avenue, Elyria, OH 44035-6219

G0052 Nannie E. Houser, 6601 NW 97th Avenue, Tamarac, FL 33321

G0053 Valentine T. Petersheim, RD #2, Box 1000, Mifflintown, PA 17059

G0054 E.L. Woodworth-Barnes, 150 Downs Boulevard, Apt B-209, Clemson, SC 29631-2046

G0056 Herman W. Ferguson, 600 Chad Drive, Rocky Mount, NC 27803; tel. 919-443-2258

G0059 Broken Arrow Genealogical Society, PO Box 1244, Broken Arrow, OK 74013-1244

G0060 Linda Dubé, 39 Birch Street, Madawaska, ME 04756; tel. 207-728-4082

G0061 Family Publications—Rose Caudle Terry, 5628 60th Drive NE, Marysville, WA 98270-9509; e-mail: cxwp57@prodigy.com

G0062 Roger Williams Family Association, PO Box 24, East Greenwich, RI 02818; tel. 401-246-0246

G0063 Bonnie J. Feldhausen, Sec.-Treas., Feldhausen Reunion, 1880 Utah Road, Frankfort, KS 66427

G0066 Torkwood, Inc., 5 Court of Bucks County, Lincolnshire, IL 60069

G0068 Susan L. Mitchell, 34233 Shawnee Trail, Westland, MI 48185

G0069 Gloucester County Historical Society, 17 Hunter Street, Woodbury, NJ 08096-4605

G0073 Mrs. Jane Kyhl Beekman, 4404 W. Kings Row Street, Muncie, IN 47304-2438

G0077 Roy F. Olson, Jr., 360 Watson Road, Paducah, KY 42003-8978

G0078 Patricia Hewitt Morrison, 9611 Westbourne Court, Cypress, CA 90630-2760

G0082 Picton Press, PO Box 250, Rockport, ME 04856; tel. 207-236-6565: fax: 207-236-6713; e-mail: Picton@midcoast.com

G0086 Jeanne W. Strong, 26969 Beaver Lane, Los Altos Hills, CA 94022; tel. 415-493-3322

G0090 Valerie Giorgi, 4168 Woodland Street, Santa Maria, CA 93455-3356

G0091 Marie Wright, RT 1, Box 7, Bonnerdale, AR 71933; tel. 501-356-3488

G0092 Southern Tier Genealogical Society, PO Box 680, Vestal, NY 13850-0680

G0093 Heart of the Lakes Publishing, PO Box 299, Interlaken, NY 14847-0299; tel. 800-782-9687; fax: 607-532-4684; e-mail: HLP Books@AOL.com
Visa & MasterCard accepted. Shipping additional: $4.00 for first book; $1.00 for each additional book; most shipping via UPS—provide appropriate delivery address.

G0094 Glyndwr Resources, 43779 Valley Rd, Decatur, MI 49045

G0096 Ronald R. Templin, 2256 River Oak Lane SE, Fort Myers, FL 33905; tel. 813-694-8347

G0097 William S. Borders, 235 Sotir Street, Fort Walton Beach, FL 32548; tel. 904-862-1500

G0098 Powell Genealogical Services, 720 Highpoint Drive, Wexford, PA 15090-7571

G0099 Wilton M. Whisler, 121 South 168, Seattle, WA 98148-1611

G0100 Edmund K. Swigart, PO Box 1134, Washington, CT 06793

G0101 Gene S. Kuechmann, 8113 NE 25th Avenue, Vancouver, WA 98665-9726

G0102 International Forum, PO Box 7000-350, Palos Verdes Peninsula, CA 90274-3218

G0104 Sarah S. Splaun, 25 Troxell Lane, Staunton, VA 24401

G0105 Martha Ashcraft Neal, PO Box 989, Washington, PA 15301

G0106 Mary Lynch Young, 2470 Plata Drive, Santa Rosa, CA 95403; tel. 707-527-8388

G0107 Jane Gray Buchanan, 114 Berwick Drive, Oak Ridge, TN 37830

G0111 Robert Serré, 1057 Riviera Drive, Ottawa, Ontario, Canada K1K 0N7

G0112 W.E. Morrison & Co., Ovid, NY 14521; tel. 607-869-2561

G0114 M.E. Conover, 300 Strasbourg Drive, Lafayette, LA 70506

G0115 Mrs. Barbara Knott Horsman, 14704 Jefferson Avenue, Chester, VA 23831

G0116 Goodenow Family Association, RT 2, Box 718, Shepherdstown, WV 25443; tel. 304-876-2008

G0119 Granville W. Hough, 3438 Bahia Blanca W., Apt. B, Laguna Hills, CA 92653-2830

G0120 James C. Starbuck, 3266 Poplar Ridge Drive, Rex, GA 30273-2459; tel. 404-961-6618

G0121 Donald Lewis Osborn, 322 SE Willow Way, Lee's Summit, MO 64063-2928; tel. 816-524-5785

G0122 Joan Kusek, 9640 Walmer, Overland Park, KS 66212-1554

G0124 Arapacana Press, PO Box 193685, San Francisco, CA 94119-3685; tel. 415-648-3460

G0125 Lucile Novak, 16 Smith Garrison Road, Newmarket, NH 03857

G0126 Catoctin Press, PO Box 505, New Market, MD 21774-0505; fax: 301-620-1817

G0127 Mrs. Ellen Brzoska, 402 W. Nob Hill Boulevard, Yakima, WA 98902-4635

G0133 Judge Noble K. Littell, PO Box 1019, Sebring, FL 33871; tel. 813-471-9387

G0135 Kenneth Luttner, Ohio Genealogy Center, PO Box 395, St. Peter, MN 56082; tel. 507-388-7158

G0137 Alexander L. Wiatt, 24 Madison Lane South, Newport News, VA 23606-2855

G0143 Quirke, Quirke & Assoc., 2310 Juniper Court, Golden, CO 80401-8087; tel. 303-526-1319

G0145 Mildred S. Wright, 140 Briggs, Beaumont, TX 77707-2329; tel. 409-832-2308

G0146 Genealogical Services, Rte. 7, Box 250, Re: Craig, Bassett, VA 24055; tel. 540-629-9191

G0146A Genealogical Services, Rte. 7, Box 250, Re: Rakestraw, Bassett, VA 24055; tel. 540-629-9191

G0150 Lancaster Mennonite Historical Society, 2215 Millstream Road, Lancaster, PA 17602-1499; tel. 717-393-9745

G0153 Mary Dudley-Higham, c/o Genesis Publications, 5272 Williams Road, Suisun, CA 94585

G0154 Pau Hana Press, 1116 Kealaolu Avenue, Honolulu, HI 96816-5419

G0158 Carol J. Snow, PO Box 31, Del Mar, CA 92014

G0159 James W. Thompson, PO Box 1032, Stevensville, MD 21666

G0161 The Cuthbertson Family History, c/o Thomas H. Aldridge, 7605 Water Oak Lane, Monroe, NC 28110; tel. 704-753-4487

G0162 William A. Fox, 112 Colonel's Way, Williamsburg, VA 23185

G0166 Lois B. Goff, 1625 Elmwood Avenue, Wilmette, IL 60091-1553

G0168 Mrs. Manly Yielding, 2300 Brookshire Place, Birmingham, AL 35213

G0169 C.R. Stewart, PO Box 3011, Long Beach, CA 90803-0011; tel. 218-963-3259

G0171 Hosford Books, 1 Binney Road, Old Lyme, CT 06371-1401; tel. 203-434-2907

G0173 James C. Van Winkle, PO Box 683, Tybee Island, GA 31328-0683

G0178 Phyllis W. Johnson, 2830 N. Westmoreland Street, Arlington, VA 22213; tel. 703-532-0144

G0182 New York Genealogical and Biographical Society, 122 East 58th Street, New York, NY 10022; tel. 212-755-8532

G0183 Tennessee Valley Publishing, PO Box 52527, Knoxville, TN 37950-2527; tel. 800-762-7079; fax: 423-584-0113; e-mail: tvp1@ix.netcom.com

G0184 Solano County Genealogical Society, Inc., PO Box 2494, Fairfield, CA 94533

G0185 Carol W. Brown, 32 Everett Drive, Rochester, NY 14624-3904; tel. 716-247-5689

G0186 Herbert L. McMillan, 29378 Gillette Court, Sun City, CA 92586; or Lorna M. Stewart, 5539 Columbia Pike, Apt 701, Arlington, VA 22204-5812

G0191 The Ancestor Shoppe, 5501 Duncan Road #315, Fort Smith, AR 72903

G0192 Dr. Larry D. Crummer, 2649 Mission Greens Drive, San Jose, CA 95148-2568; tel. 408-270-4113

G0194 Marjorie Dikeman Chamberlain, 13650 N. Frontage Road #334, Yuma, AZ 85367

G0194A Dyckman/Dikeman/Dykeman Family Association, 13650 N. Frontage Road #334, Yuma, AZ 85367

G0196 Kenneth V. Graves, 261 South Street, Wrentham, MA 02093-1504; tel. 508-384-8084

G0198 Carl Boyer, 3rd, PO Box 220333, Santa Clarita, CA 91322-0333

G0200 Ken Haughton, 16200 Kennedy Road, Los Gatos, CA 95032

G0201 Doris Bankes Kent, 2 N. West Street, Green City, MO 63545

G0202 The Genealogical Society of Pennsylvania, Herbert K. Zearfoss, Pres., 1300 Locust Street, Philadelphia, PA 19107-5661; tel. 215-545-0391

G0205 J. Raymond Gourdin, PO Box 648, Columbia, MD 21045-0648; tel. 410-381-2816

G0206 William B. Fetters, 12814 Brunswick Lane, Bowie, MD 20715-2403; tel. 301-262-3925

G0207 William L. Forst, PO Box 5, Foristell, MO 63348-0005

G0208 Mrs. Helen D. Woodman, 207 Balsam Road, Hendersonville, NC 28792

G0209 John A. Blazer, PO Box 309, Hendersonville, TN 37077

G0210 Jean M. Rand, 209-07 Whitehall Terrace, Queens Village, NY 11427; tel. 718-468-1674

G0211 Kenneth W. Faig, Jr., 2311 Swainwood Drive, Glenview, IL 60025-2741

G0212 Sara Hunter Kellar, 3736 Chiara Drive, Titusville, FL 32796; tel. 407-268-2924

G0213 Hugh Coffman, Rt 2, Box 177, Marietta, OH 45750; tel. 614-374-6718

G0214 Dr. James O. Bond, 17305 Quaker Lane, Sandy Spring, MD 20860; tel. 301-570-1725; e-mail: JQUAKE@AOL.COM

G0215 Patricia Wilkinson Weaver Balletta, 26 Sunset Road, Bay Shore, L.I., NY 11706; tel. 516-666-9506

G0216 Carolyn C. Volpe, 4025 Pulitzer Place #135, San Diego, CA 92122; tel. 619-457-8058

G0217 Charles R. Barr, 800 S. FM 1417, Apt. 323, Sherman, TX 75092; tel. 903-813-0132

G0219 Mr. E.R. Van Etten, 12 Suburban Drive, PO Box 95, Big Flats, NY 14814-0095; tel. 607-562-8613

G0220 Dr. Joan S. Guilford, 2710 E. Adams Avenue, Orange, CA 92667-6240

G0221 Sue Ann Gardner Shreve, 5 Anderson Court, W. Bay Shore, L.I., NY 11706-7701; tel. 516-665-7693

G0222 Arlene F. Mansfield, 498 Quartz Street, Los Alamos, NM 87544; tel. 505-662-2115; fax: 505-662-5781

G0223 Genealogy Publishing Service, 448 Ruby Mine Road, Franklin, NC 28734; tel. 704-524-7063

   Make checks payable to the author, Joan S. Guilford.

G0224 Jackson Genealogy—Michael Stephen Jackson, 202 E. St. Clair Street, Freeburg, IL 62243-1243

G0225 Patricia O'Boyle, 5802 North 42nd Avenue, Phoenix, AZ 85019-1820

G0226 Fern Maynard, 801 Gillaspie Drive, Apt. 130, Boulder, CO 80303-6549

G0228 COMPU-CHART, c/o Paula Perkins Mortensen, 363 So. Park Victoria Drive, Milpitas, CA 95035-5708

G0229 Margaret E. Sheaffer/Carol M. Sheaffer, M.D., 10 Wexford Drive, Lawrenceville, NJ 08648; tel. 609-896-0286

G0230 Dr. Holland D. Warren, 207 Nottingham Circle, Lynchburg, VA 24502

G0231 Roy Crego, 12 Mt. Airy Road, Basking Ridge, NJ 07920

G0232 Charles Mathieson Otstot, 5124 North 33rd Street, Arlington, VA 22207-1854;

tel. 703-538-5446

G0233 Mr./Mrs. John Pattee Wallach, 19 Allen Street, Harwich, MA 02645

G0234 Marie Bowen Canterbury, 5117 N. 26th Road, Arlington, VA 22207

G0235 Shirley Jennings Weber, N. 410 E. Fairway Drive, Hoodsport, WA 98548-9632; tel. 360-877-9696

G0236 Mrs. Jo Ann De Board Touchstone, 815 West Frantz, Enid, OK 73701-8091

G0237 Robinson Family Association, Hewick Plantation, Box 82, Urbanna, VA 23175-0082; tel. 804-758-4214; fax: 804-758-4214

G0238 Family History & Genealogy Center, 1300 E. 109th Street, Kansas City, MO; tel. 64131-3585; fax: 816-943-0477

G0239 Joseph H. Vance, 310 North Garfield Street, Lombard, IL 60148-2042; tel. 708-629-0581

G0240 Allen Books, Corben E. Allen, 8439 Terradell Street, Pico Rivera, CA 90660

G0241 Snackerty Enterprises, RFD 2, Box 668, Center Barnstead, NH 03225; fax: 603-269-4524

G0242 Shields' Valley Publishing Co., HC 85, Box 4275, Livingston, MT 59047; tel. 406-222-2725

G0243 Cecelia E. Casey, 4110 Pleasant Meadow Court, Chantilly, VA 22021; tel. 703-222-9735; or Box 372, Elk Rapids, MI 49629

G0244 Nan Overton West, West Printing Co., 4207 34th Street, Lubbock, TX 79410; tel. 806-794-3687; fax: 806-793-3207

If ordering in Texas, please add sales tax to price of book.

G0245 Rosamond Houghton Van Noy, 4700 Hwy. K East, Conover, WI 54519; tel. 715-479-5044

G0246 Bakeman's Books, 1178 County Road B West, Roseville, MN 55113-4301; tel. 612-488-4416; fax: 612-488-2653

G0247 William M. Gage, 4001 Garrison Street NW, Washington, DC 20016

G0248 Janet Bradham, 316 Brockington Street, Manning, SC 29102; tel. 803-435-4016

G0249 Marcus V. Brewster, 316 Brockington Street, Manning, SC 29102; tel. 803-435-4016

G0250 Wilmer L. Kerns, 4715 North 38th Place, Arlington, VA 22207-2914; tel. 703-533-1040

G0251 Janet S. Welsh, 7416 Cliffbourne Court, Derwood, MD 20855-1101

G0252 James G. Faulconer, 5200 Oakbrooke Drive, Kettering, OH 45440; tel. 513-439-2029

G0253 Whitfield Books, Vallie Jo Whitfield, 1841 Pleasant Hill Road, Pleasant Hill, CA 94523. Branch Office: Joanne Whitfield, 13 Costa Street, San Francisco, CA 94110. e-mail: Jotea@aol.com.

G0254 Bettina P.H. Burns, PO Box 325, Cullman, AL 35056-0325

G0255 Dolores Graham Doyle, 765 E. Wood Duck Circle, Fresno, CA 93720-0806; tel. 209-434-5212; e-mail: JSJT14A@Prodigy.Com

G0256 Arthur Louis Finnell Books, 9033 Lyndale Avenue S., Suite 108, Bloomington, MN 55420-3535

G0258 Mrs. Paula P. Mortensen, 363 So. Park Victoria Drive, Milpitas, CA 95035-5708; tel. 408-262-1051; e-mail: 103137.3321@compuserve.com

G0259 Higginson Book Company, Publishers and reprinters of genealogy and local history,148-BP Washington Street, PO Box 778, Salem, MA 01970; tel. 508-745-7170; fax: 508-745-8025

Complete catalogs are available free with your order, or $4.00 separately. To order: We accept checks or money order, or MC/Visa. Please add $3.50 for the first book and $1.00 for each additional book. We bind our books to order; please allow six to eight weeks for delivery, plus two additional weeks for hardcover books.

G0260 Decatur Genealogical Society, PO Box 1548, Decatur, IL 62525-1548

G0261 Betty R. Darnell, 204 Hartford Drive, Mount Washington, KY 40047; tel. 502-538-8743; fax: 502-538-8743

G0262 Catherine M. Rhoads, 10435 Tullymore Drive, Adelphi, MD 20783

G0263 Hazel N. Hassan, 19549 County Road 38, Goshen, IN 46526; tel. 219-534-1527

G0264 Marianne Elizabeth Hall Little, RR2, Box 148A, Yorktown, TX 78164-9538

G0265 Alan J. Lamb, PO Box 5360, Santa Fe, NM 87502-5360

G0266 Betty V. Dearing, 3444 N. Wolters, Fresno, CA 93726-5922; tel. 209-224-9503

G0267 Howard J. Dean, PO Box 115, Westernville, NY 13486; tel. 315-827-4606

G0268 Honakers, PO Box 3636, Alexandria, VA 22302-9998; tel. 703-751-7321

G0269 First Genealogical Research Center (FGRC), 2108 Champagne Circle, Salt Lake City, UT 84118; tel. 801-967-6687

G0270 Patricia Brown Darling, PO Box 71, Akutan, AK 99553

G0271 Willett Books, PO Box 5871, Kingsport, TN 37663; tel. 615-239-7912

G0272 Albert Armington, c/o Genealogical Publishing Service, 448 Ruby Mine Road, Franklin, NC 28734; fax: 860-345-3013; e-mail: BERT1@AOL.COM

G0273 Mrs. Ethel M. Woelfel, 1052 Cumberland Street, Bethlehem, PA 18017; tel. 610-868-6565

G0275 John D. Roberts, 1 Melrose Street, Dunedin, New Zealand

G0276 Mrs. Mary Jo Hunavy, 108 Sea Grape Drive, Jacksonville Beach, FL 32250

G0277 Fred J. Riffe, 154 Indies Drive North, Marathon, FL 33050; tel. 305-743-7465; fax: 305-743-9140

G0279 Ruth Bailey Allen, PO Box 1585, Clayton, GA 30525

G0280 James H. Shaw, 260 Thornton Road, Brownsville, PA 15417-0012

G0281 Kathryn B. Fischer, 70 Hyacinth Drive, Covington, LA 70433; 504-892-4365

G0282 Elberta Price Griffiths, 2555 N. Price Road, Apt. 282, Chandler, AZ 85224

G0283 William Gerade, 5222 Mitchell Street, Alexandria, VA 22312; tel. 703-354-3830; fax: 703-354-3830 (call first)

G0284 Mrs. Richard G. Askew, 2617 Regency Road, Bartlesville, OK 74006-7540

G0285 Von Gail Hamilton, 148 S. 90th Place, Mesa, AZ 85208; tel. 602-986-7180

G0286 Louise Burt, 9935 Kingston Farm Road, Kingston, WA 98346; tel. 360-297-7084

G0287 Larry G. Shuck, 164 Julep Lane, Cincinnati, OH 45218-1206

G0288 Lenore B. Stevenson, Box 660, Beaufort, SC 29901

G0289 Frances Lane Harris, 3008 SE 154th Avenue, Vancouver, WA 98684-5188

G0290 Rudd Family Research Association, 461 Emerson Street, Chula Vista, CA 91911; tel. 619-422-4445

G0291 Raymond L. Olson, 763 South Crescent Avenue, Lodi, CA 95240-4630; tel. 209-368-8071

G0292 Mrs. Jean Fairchild Gilmore, 1300 N. Horse Prairie Road, Inverness, FL 34450-1875

G0293 Melvin L. Bock, 2807 Spanish Oak Court, Clearwater, FL 34621

G0294 Carol R. Austin, 9726 Mirage Circle, Garden Grove, CA 92644; tel. 714-537-3139

G0295 Joyce J. Parris, 220 Northwest Avenue, Swannanoa, NC 28778-2618

G0296 Dr. Jim Fenner, 2611 Avenue "S," Brooklyn, NY 11229; tel. 718-998-8593

G0297 Judy B. Anderson, 4485 South 2025 West, Roy, UT 84067; tel. 801-731-2275

G0298 Al B. Cory, 11056 Orange Cart Way, Jacksonville, FL 32223-7336; tel. 904-886-9404

G0299 Margarette Hall Wood, 2234 Pinoak Knolls, San Antonio, TX 78248-2303

G0300 Joann H. Nichols, 46 Chestnut Street, Brattleboro, VT 05301-3152; tel. 802-254-9554

G0301 Lynn Berry Hamilton, 2101 Treasure Hills #606, Harlingen, TX 78550; tel. 210-423-1330; fax: 210-425-5078; e-mail: FDTV62a (Prodigy)

G0302 Genealogical Services, 1001 S. Marshall Street, Suite 53, Winston-Salem, NC 27101; fax: 910-777-3603

G0303 Solo Press, PO Box 507, Keno, OR 97627

G0304 Leallah Franklin, 822 Camino De Los Padres, Tucson, AZ 85718

G0306 Rana Research, Attn: Nadine, 706 Pershing, College Station, TX 77840; tel. 409-696-2929

G0307 Margaret B. Kinsey, PO Box 459, Lamesa, TX 79331; tel. 806-872-3603

G0308 William S. West, 1707 Front Street, Beaufort, NC 28516-9307

G0309 Holland Family Association, Rt. 1, Box 38, Garden City, MN 56034

G0310 Louise Biles Memorial Fund, 1730 East Gate Drive, Stone Mountain, GA 30087

G0311 Faye M. Lightburn, 1137 - 6th Avenue North, Jacksonville Beach, FL 32250; tel. 904-249-4263

G0312 Mrs. Michal Martin Farmer, PO Box 140880, Dallas, TX 75214-0880

G0313 Cobb County GA Genealogical Society, Inc., PO Box 1413, Marietta, GA 30061-1413

G0315 Patricia Kinney Kaufman, 155 SE Norton, Sherwood, OR 97140; tel. 503-625-6563

G0316 Marion Mann, 1453 Whittier Place NW, Washington, DC 20012; tel. 202-291-4409

G0317 Joan P. Fortune, 1039 Trickham Bridge Road, Brandon, MS 39042-9644; e-mail: joanf@netdoor.com

G0318 Thomas R. Moore, Esq., 1170 Fifth Avenue, Suite 2A, New York, NY 10029

G0319 John H. Stoddard, PO Box 434, Elmhurst, IL 60126; tel. 708-617-4906

G0320A Mildred Stout, NE 1115 Orchard Drive, Pullman, WA 99163; tel. 509-332-5612

G0320B Kemble Stout, NE 1115 Orchard Drive, Pullman, WA 99163; tel. 509-332-5612

G0321 Warren A. Brannon, 48 Laurel Place, Fanwood, NJ 07023-1315; tel. 908-889-4988

G0322 Rhoda J. Morley, 3215 Hwy 441-N, Okeechobee, FL 34972-1854; tel. 941-467-2482

G0323 Mildred S. Ezell, 4416 Briers Place, Stone Mountain, GA 30083; tel. 404-292-5699; e-mail: ME2ATL@MEGAWEB.COM; ME2ATL@ICHANGE.COM

G0324 Virginia Easley De Marce, 5635 N. 25th Road, Arlington, VA 22207-1403

G0325 Hallock Family Association, c/o Marion H. Adams, 4 Woodland Drive, Severna Park, MD 21146

Make checks payable to Hallock Family Association.

G0326 Mrs. Bev Jesse Shuptrine, 4851 Royce Road, Irvine, CA 92715-2233

G0327 Paul J. Curtin, 11007 Legends Lane, Austin, TX 78747-1222; tel. 512-282-8462

G0328 William B. Saxbe, C.G., 346 Reamer Place, Oberlin, Ohio 44074

G0329 Glenn Kilmer, 34 Rosehill Avenue, Brantford, Ontario, Canada N3T 1R8; tel. 519-753-8265

Payment may be made by any U.S. postal or bank money order.

G0330 William T. Tuley, c/o Minuteman Press, 2313 Wicker Avenue, Schererville, IN 46375; tel. 219-322-6677; fax: 219-322-7400

G0331 Willard J. Prentice, 2419 Chetwood Circle, Timonium, MD 21093-2533

G0332 Virginia B. Fletcher, 721 NW 73 Avenue, Ft. Lauderdale, FL 33317-1140; e-mail: VBFletcher@AOL.com

G0334 Carl Gwynn, 605 Fir Street, Coulee Dam, WA 99116

G0335 Warren Co. (OH) Genealogical Society, 300 East Silver Street, Lebanon, OH 45036; tel. 513-933-1144

G0336 David Bellhouse, 905 Maitland Street, London, Ontario, Canada N5Y 2X2; tel. 519-661-3614; fax: 519-661-3813; e-mail: bellhouse@stats.uwo.ca

G0337 Nancie Todd Weber, 22309 Canyon Lake Drive South, Canyon Lake, CA 92587; e-mail: HJDR04B@prodigy.com

G0338 Glenna W. Wilding, 606 Riverwood Drive, Louisville, KY 40207-1346

G0339 Ms. Tiger Gardiner, 9653 Whiteacre Road, #C-4, Columbia, MD 21045-3571

G0340 Hauk Data Services, PO Box 1577, Anderson, IN 46014; e-mail: ChrisHauk@aol.com

G0341 Arthur F. Maes, 4801 Hackamore Drive N., Colorado Springs, CO 80918; tel. 719-598-7806

G0342 Thomas R. Topping, 1201 Berry Ridge Road, Charlotte, NC 28270-1463; tel. 704-847-8648

G0343 Henry F. Ball, 3120 Bellaire Drive W., Fort Worth, TX 76109; tel. 817-926-5118

G0344 Thomas D. Ayres, 3 Windham Drive, Simsbury, CT 06070

G0345 Floyd R. Mason, 115 E. Rainbow Drive, Bridgewater, VA 22812

G0346 Louis E. LeGrand, 8100 Colebrook Road, Richmond, VA 23227-1613

G0347 Leland E. Wilson, PO Box 893, Lindale, TX 75771; tel. 903-882-5915

G0348 Charles F. Berg, 5025 Shooting Range Road, Phelps, WI 54554; tel. 715-545-3406

G0349 Dean H. Roe, 9240 Werner Drive, Kewaskum, WI 53040; tel. 414-626-2696

G0350 Inez Taylor, 969 N. Reed Station Road, Carbondale, IL 62901; tel. 618-549-2004

G0351 Harry T. Dolan, Jr., PO Box 68, Cutchogue, NY 11935-0068

G0352 Jay Hobson, 5805 Warwick Place, Columbus, GA 31904; tel. 706-323-6273

G0353 Paul A. Schwabe, 1004 NW Second Street, Washington, IN 47501; tel. 812-254-7290

G0354 Phyllis Smith Oyer, 263 Bakerdale Road, Rochester, NY 14616-3654; tel. 716-663-1735

G0355 Raymond K. Donner, 2650 N. Lakeview #1010, Chicago, IL 60614; tel. 312-281-2432; fax: 312-281-2432

G0356 Honeywell Family Association, A. Parks Honeywell, Editor, 785 Island Way, Clearwater, FL 34630-1816; tel. 813-461-4244; fax: 813-461-4244; e-mail: PARKSHONEY@AOL.COM

G0357 Richard C. Harris, 701 Hard Scuffle Court, Bowling Green, KY 42103

G0358 Larry Wright, Inc., Route 7, Box 3-5, Amarillo, TX 79118; tel. 806-622-1819

G0359 Kenneth F. Haas, 1730 Fairmeadows Drive, Bettendorf, IA 52722; tel. 319-355-7942

G0360 Gloria Shipp Frazier, 3007 Paula Drive, West Plains, MO 65775

G0361 John Steinbrugge, 4072 Ondine Circle, Huntington Beach, CA 92649

G0362 Dr. Dave Auxier, 2034 Elvis Presley Boulevard, Memphis, TN 38106; tel. 901-396-4979; fax: 901-345-0551

G0363 Wm. E. Wright, 11710 Green Bay, Houston, TX 77024; tel. 713-975-1188

G0364 George S. Robbins, 97 Burns Street, Marinette, WI 54143; tel. 715-735-5236

G0365 Patricia Turner Ritchie, 1559 Moffett Drive, Winchester, VA 22601

G0366 Lyle B. Marquess, 761 Lincoln Avenue, Bentleyville, PA 15314

G0367 Linda Lightholder Kmiecik, 431 S. Center Street, Bensenville, IL 60106-2642

G0368 Barbara B. Ford, 313 Henry Lane, Wallingford, PA 19086; tel. 610-566-4888

G0369 Jean A. Sargent, 12217 Shadetree Lane, Laurel, MD 20708-2814

G0370 Morris N. Sherk, 924 Williams Grove Road, Mechanicsburg, PA 17055-8000

G0372 Robert Haydon, 12 Fenchley Court, Little Rock, AR 72212; tel. 501-224-1313; fax: 501-224-7081

G0373 Philip W. Allen, 2655 S. Rosanna Street, Las Vegas, NV 89117-3043

G0374 Ann Blomquist, 427 E. Richmond Street, Orlando, FL 32806; tel. 407-423-3738; e-mail: blomq@ix.netcom.com

G0375 Dorothy N. Perkins, 4895 Avion Way, San Diego, CA 92115; tel. 619-583-6430

G0376 Frederic W. Barnes, 794 Chestnut Drive, Fairfield, CA 94533-1465; e-mail: FWBARNES@AOL.COM

G0377 James Bestman, Box 517, Addison, IL 60101-0517; 708*-543-7899
*Area code changes to 630 after August 3, 1996.

G0378 Carl W. Troyer, 3623 Pebble Beach Drive, Dallas, TX 75234-2545; tel. 214-241-5777; e-mail: WBDS18A@PRODIGY.COM

G0379 Ruth Erwin Moore, 2908 Cobbs Way, Anderson, SC 29621; tel. 864-226-7212; e-mail: smokeypup@aol.com

G0380 Henry Teer, 1416 Colony Drive, Irving, TX 75061; tel. 214-254-1162

G0381 Glenn H. Morrison, 3319 Bedford Forrest Drive, Missouri City, TX 77459-4904; tel. 713-438-4808; e-mail: kmwe81a@prodigy.com

G0382 Shirley B. Adair, 309 Dartbrook, Rockwall, TX 75087; tel. 214-771-2662

G0383 Robert E. Pitts, 10020 Artesia Drive, Shreveport, LA 71115-3405; tel. 318-797-0442

G0384 Blair Society for Genealogical Research, 20 W. College Avenue, Brownsburg, IN 46112-1253; tel. 317-852-5078; fax: 317-852-9637; e-mail: EPBlair@aol.com

G0385 Love Letters, Pat Love Stubblefield, Editor, 1300 Arbolita Drive, La Habra, CA 90631-3206; tel. 310-697-9902

G0386 Rick Crume, RR2 Box 169, Glyndon, MN 56547-9651; tel. 218-498-0235; fax: 218-498-2901; e-mail: 71161.2632@compuserve.com

G0387 Bland Books, R5, Box 412 "Dreamwood," Fairfield, IL 62837-8903

G0388 Judy Montgomery, 3858 W. 226 Street #109, Torrance, CA 90505

G0389 Pat Frappier, Box 46, Evergreen Point Road, Jonesboro, ME 04648

G0390 Lomar Research, PO Box 931, Lyman, WY 82937

G0391 Thomas A. Ryerson, PO Box 262, Ingersoll, Ontario, Canada N5C 3K5; tel. 519-421-3621; fax: 519-539-7335

G0392 Elder Family Newsletter, PO Box 340, Hancock, MD 21750-0340; tel. 301-678-6999; e-mail: DonnaL3@aol.com; fanfare@intrepid.net

G0392A Younkin Family News Bulletin, PO Box 340, Hancock, MD 21750-0340; tel. 301-678-6999; e-mail: DonnaL3@aol.com; fanfare@intrepid.net

G0392B Crippen-Crippin Family Journal, PO Box 340, Hancock, MD 21750-0340; tel. 301-678-6999; e-mail: DonnaL3@aol.com; fanfare@intrepid.net

G0393 Fay Louise Smith Arellano, 3628 West Earll Drive, Phoenix, AZ 85019-4243

G0394 Betty King, 2820 34th Place, NW, Washington, DC 20007; tel. 202-338-4424

G0395 Rodney L. Arroyo, 3248 Greenfield Road, Berkley, MI 48072; e-mail: ArroyoR@AOL.COM

G0396 Lela Brooks Fennell, 100 Wynnwood Drive, Windybush, Wilmington, DE 19810-4428; tel. 302-475-5969

G0397 Donald S. Barber, 6 Edgewood Court Ext., Middlefield, CT 06455

G0398 The Queenstown Press, PO Box 151, Pennington, NJ 08534

G0399 Nathan Mathews, PO Box 1975, Fayetteville, GA 30214; e-mail: Prodigy KNHK84A

G0400 Ronald L. Roberts, PO Box 7086, South Lake Tahoe, CA 96158-0086; tel. 916-541-3562

G0401 Warren L. Forsythe, Box 1299, Ellensburg, WA 98926-1299

G0402 Mae Gean Pettit, Route 1, Box 149, Alto, TX 75925

G0403 Paca Associates, 400 Shoreline Drive, Belhaven, NC 27810; tel. 919-964-2233

G0404 Robert N. Grant, 15 Campo Bello Court, Menlo Park, CA 94025; tel. 415-854-0895

G0405 Young & Sons Enterprises, PO Box 759, Apache, OK 73006-0759; tel. 405-588-2093

G0406 New England Historic Genealogical Society Sales Dept., 160 N. Washington Street, 4th floor, Boston, MA 02114-2120; tel. 617-536-5740; fax: 617-624-0325; e-mail: 74777.3612@compuserve.com

G0407 Mrs. George F. Bertine, PO Box 2965, Denton, TX 76202; tel. 817-387-9993

G0408 Robert L. Downen, 4009 Terrace Drive, Annandale, VA 22003

G0409 Dr. John F. Byerly, Jr., 8503 Spring Hollow Drive, Richmond, VA 23227; tel. 804-262-8855

G0410 Timothy D. Booth, 6620 White Post Road, Centreville, VA 22020-2147; tel. 703-968-8685; fax: Call for fax; e-mail: TimBooth99@aol.com

G0411 The Bingham Association, 19 East 72nd Street, New York, NY 10021; fax: 212-628-5358

G0412 Judith E. FitzPatrick, 8273 Theisen, Center Line, MI 48015; tel. 810-757-7560

G0413 Gary and Lynn Marks, 5117 North 18th Place, Phoenix, AZ 85016

G0414 Frank L. and Odette J. Kaufman, 2794 Hyannis Way, Sacramento, CA 95827-1343; tel. 916-362-2462

G0415 Dorothy P. Brawley, 1001 Sierra Road, Newport, TN 37821-6006; tel. 423-625-9325

G0416 Evejean Fortney McKnight, 379 Two Ponds Drive, Coolville, OH 45723-9531; tel. 614-667-3736

G0417 William P. Brothers, 430 Maple Way, Woodside, CA 94062; tel. 415-365-4644; e-mail: wbroth7485@aol.com

G0418 Janice B. Palmer, 6302 Fairview Drive, Pensacola, FL 32505-2057; tel. 904-432-5291

G0419 Patricia Wright Strati, 47 Rose Drive, Cragston, Highland Falls, NY 10928-9801

G0420 Marvin T. Jones, 7890-158 R Avenue SE, Wyndmere, ND 58081; tel. 701-439-2528

G0421 Historical Data Services, 14 Clark Street, Glens Falls, NY 12804

G0422 Warren W. Perney, 10121 Orchard Park, West Drive, Indianapolis, IN 46280-1516; tel. 317-846-7164

G0423 Alma Usher Barclay, PO Box 174, Newton Grove, NC 28366

G0424 James R. Sisson, PO Box 158, Manitowish Waters, WI 54545; e-mail: 73621.2523@cserve.com

G0425 Dudley Herndon, 825 Ketch Drive, Apt. 301, Naples, FL 33940; tel. 941-434-7732

G0426 Paddleford Publishing Company, 4484 Pitch Pine Court, Concord, CA 94521-4406; tel. 510-827-0571; fax: 510-680-1312

G0427 Avis E. Cox and Marion R. Cox, Route #2, Box 134, Winona, MN 55987-9631; tel. 507-454-1172

G0429 Martha A. Cieglo, 6854 Cedarbrook, Bloomfield Hills, MI 48301; e-mail: WJJP15A@Prodigy.com

G0430 Barbara Stacy Mathews, 1420 D Street, Marysville, CA 95901; tel. 916-741-2967

G0431 Allen W. Bernard, 1011 Jerome Street, Cincinnati, OH 45202-1736; tel. 513-381-5558

G0432 Wanda Colvin, 202 S. Roosevelt, Cleveland, TX 77327; tel. 713-592-7017

G0433 Beverley Book Reprint, c/o Shenandoah Seasons, 989 Black Bear Road, Maurertown, VA 22644; tel. 800-233-3836; fax: 540-436-8115
    For each book, add $4.00 for postage and handling, and VA residents add 4.5% VA sales tax.

G0434 Freddie L. Brinkley, 100 Litton Dale Lane, Pasadena, MD 21122-4058; tel. 410-544-0084

G0435 Claiborne T. Smith, Jr., MD, E-3 N. St. George's Apts., 119 Mill Creek Road, Ardmore, PA 19003; tel. 610-649-5920

G0436 Virginia Westfall, 205 Rice Lane, Amity, OR 97101

G0437 Marjorie Stubbs Heaney, 2596 Whitehurst Road, DeLand, FL 32720-2032

G0438 Janice Cale Sisler, PO Box 113, Bruceton Mills, WV 26525-0113

G0439 Lewis G. Proper, 155 Seville Drive, Rochester, NY 14617; tel. 716-544-6546

G0441 Fred A. Rutledge, 1208 Argonne Drive, Baltimore, MD 21218-1429; tel. 410-889-0035

G0442 Robert H. (Bob) Henderson, 119 Pinewood Drive, Greer, SC 29651-1441; tel. 864-877-2424

G0443 Betty H. Vollenweider, 1520 Mt. Tabor Church Road, Dallas, GA 30132; tel. 770-445-7689

G0444 L. Welch Pogue, 5204 Kenwood Avenue, Chevy Chase, MD 20815-6604; tel. 301-654-7233

G0445 Harry Leon Sellards, Jr., 4031 Grand Avenue, DeLand, FL 32720; tel. 904-985-4046

G0446 National Stanley Family Association, 10236 Luman Lane, Twinsburg, OH 44087

G0447 Mary Ann Tschopp, RD 3, Box 307, Stewartstown, PA 17363; tel. 717-993-6094

G0448 Dr. Lawrence Kent, 608 South Conway Road, Suite G, Orlando, FL 32807-104408

G0450 Kinship, 60 Cedar Heights Road, Rhinebeck, NY 12572; tel. 914-876-4592; e-mail: 71045.1516@compuserve.com

G0451 Bruce A. Breeding, 8311 Braesview Lane, Houston, TX 77071-1231

G0452 Anneke JANS and Everardus BOGARDUS Descendants Assoc., 1121 Linhof Road, Wilmington, OH 45177-2917

G0453 Joseph P. Beierschmitt, 3700 Mill Way, Bowie, MD 20715

G0454 Sayre A. Schwarztrauber, 60 Old Mill Road, PO Box 589, Osterville, MA 02655-0589; tel. 508-428-8350

G0455 Irish Genealogical Foundation, PO Box 7575, Kansas City, MO 64116 USA; tel. 816-454-2410; fax: 816-454-2410.

List of Vendors
(organized alphabetically)

Shirley B. Adair, 309 Dartbrook, Rockwall, TX 75087; tel. 214-771-2662 [Vendor G0382]

Susan R. Alexander, PO Box 460614, Houston, TX 77056-8614 [Vendor G0028]

Allen Books, Corben E. Allen, 8439 Terradell Street, Pico Rivera, CA 90660 [Vendor G0240]

Jane McMurtry Allen, 4564 Holly Lake Drive, Lake Worth, FL 33463-5301 [Vendor G0005]

Philip W. Allen, 2655 S. Rosanna Street, Las Vegas, NV 89117-3043 [Vendor G0373]

Ruth Bailey Allen, PO Box 1585, Clayton, GA 30525 [Vendor G0279]

Alligator Book Co., 314 Seabrook Drive, Hilton Head, SC 29926; tel. 803-689-2655 [Vendor G0003]

The Ancestor Shoppe, 5501 Duncan Road #315, Fort Smith, AR 72903 [Vendor G0191]

Judy B. Anderson, 4485 South 2025 West, Roy, UT 84067; tel. 801-731-2275 [Vendor G0297]

Arapacana Press, PO Box 193685, San Francisco, CA 94119-3685; tel. 415-648-3460 [Vendor G0124]

Fay Louise Smith Arellano, 3628 West Earll Drive, Phoenix, AZ 85019-4243 [Vendor G0393]

Albert Armington, c/o Genealogical Publishing Service, 448 Ruby Mine Road, Franklin, NC 28734; fax: 860-345-3013; e-mail: BERT1@AOL.COM [Vendor G0272]

Rodney L. Arroyo, 3248 Greenfield Road, Berkley, MI 48072; e-mail: ArroyoR@AOL.COM [Vendor G0395]

Mrs. Richard G. Askew, 2617 Regency Road, Bartlesville, OK 74006-7540 [Vendor G0284]

Carol R. Austin, 9726 Mirage Circle, Garden Grove, CA 92644; tel. 714-537-3139 [Vendor G0294]

Dr. Dave Auxier, 2034 Elvis Presley Boulevard, Memphis, TN 38106; tel. 901-396-4979; fax: 901-345-0551 [Vendor G0362]

Thomas D. Ayres, 3 Windham Drive, Simsbury, CT 06070 [Vendor G0344]

Bakeman's Books, 1178 County Road B West, Roseville, MN 55113-4301; tel. 612-488-4416; fax: 612-488-2653 [Vendor G0246]

Henry F. Ball, 3120 Bellaire Drive W., Fort Worth, TX 76109; tel. 817-926-5118 [Vendor G0343]

Patricia Wilkinson Weaver Balletta, 26 Sunset Road, Bay Shore, L.I., NY 11706; tel. 516-666-9506 [Vendor G0215]

Donald S. Barber, 6 Edgewood Court Ext., Middlefield, CT 06455 [Vendor G0397]

Alma Usher Barclay, PO Box 174, Newton Grove, NC 28366 [Vendor G0423]

Frederic W. Barnes, 794 Chestnut Drive, Fairfield, CA 94533-1465; e-mail: FWBARNES@AOL.COM [Vendor G0376]

Charles R. Barr, 800 S. FM 1417, Apt. 323, Sherman, TX 75092; tel. 903-813-0132 [Vendor G0217]

Mrs. Jane Kyhl Beekman, 4404 W. Kings Row Street, Muncie, IN 47304-2438 [Vendor G0073]

Joseph P. Beierschmitt, 3700 Mill Way, Bowie, MD 20715 [Vendor G0453]

David Bellhouse, 905 Maitland Street, London, Ontario, Canada N5Y 2X2; tel. 519-661-3614; fax: 519-661-3813; e-mail: bellhouse@stats.uwo.ca [Vendor G0336]

Charles F. Berg, 5025 Shooting Range Road, Phelps, WI 54554; tel. 715-545-3406 [Vendor G0348]

Allen W. Bernard, 1011 Jerome Street, Cincinnati, OH 45202-1736; tel. 513-381-5558 [Vendor G0431]

Mrs. George F. Bertine, PO Box 2965, Denton, TX 76202; tel. 817-387-9993 [Vendor G0407]

James Bestman, Box 517, Addison, IL 60101-0517; 708*-543-7899 (*area code changes to 630 after August 3, 1996) [Vendor G0377]

Beverley Book Reprint, c/o Shenandoah Seasons, 989 Black Bear Road, Maurertown, VA 22644; tel. 800-233-3836; fax: 540-436-8115 [Vendor G0433]

Louise Biles Memorial Fund, 1730 East Gate Drive, Stone Mountain, GA 30087 [Vendor G0310]

The Bingham Association, 19 East 72nd Street, New York, NY 10021; fax: 212-628-5358 [Vendor G0411]

Blair Society for Genealogical Research, 20 W. College Avenue, Brownsburg, IN 46112-1253; tel. 317-852-5078; fax: 317-852-9637; e-mail: EPBlair@aol.com [Vendor G0384]

Bland Books, R5, Box 412 "Dreamwood," Fairfield, IL 62837-8903 [Vendor G0387]

Gayle King Blankenship, 24 Roberts Landing, Poquoson, VA 23662; tel. 804-868-8022 [Vendor G0034]

John A. Blazer, PO Box 309, Hendersonville, TN 37077 [Vendor G0209]

Ann Blomquist, 427 E. Richmond Street, Orlando, FL 32806; tel. 407-423-3738; e-mail: blomq@ix.netcom.com [Vendor G0374]

Melvin L. Bock, 2807 Spanish Oak Court, Clearwater, FL 34621 [Vendor G0293]

Dr. James O. Bond, 17305 Quaker Lane, Sandy Spring, MD 20860; tel. 301-570-1725; e-mail: JQUAKE@AOL.COM [Vendor G0214]

Timothy D. Booth, 6620 White Post Road, Centreville, VA 22020-2147; tel. 703-968-8685; fax: Call for fax; e-mail: TimBooth99@aol.com [Vendor G0410]

William S. Borders, 235 Sotir Street, Fort Walton Beach, FL 32548; tel. 904-862-1500 [Vendor G0097]

Carl Boyer, 3rd, PO Box 220333, Santa Clarita, CA 91322-0333 [Vendor G0198]

Janet Bradham, 316 Brockington Street, Manning, SC 29102; tel. 803-435-4016 [Vendor G0248]

Warren A. Brannon, 48 Laurel Place, Fanwood, NJ 07023-1315; tel. 908-889-4988 [Vendor G0321]

Dorothy P. Brawley, 1001 Sierra Road, Newport, TN 37821-6006; tel. 423-625-9325 [Vendor G0415]

Bruce A. Breeding, 8311 Braesview Lane, Houston, TX 77071-1231 [Vendor G0451]

Marcus V. Brewster, 316 Brockington Street, Manning, SC 29102; tel. 803-435-4016 [Vendor G0249]

Freddie L. Brinkley, 100 Litton Dale Lane, Pasadena, MD 21122-4058; tel. 410-544-0084 [Vendor G0434]

Broken Arrow Genealogical Society, PO Box 1244, Broken Arrow, OK 74013-1244 [Vendor G0059]

William P. Brothers, 430 Maple Way, Woodside, CA 94062; tel. 415-365-4644; e-mail: wbroth7485@aol.com [Vendor G0417]

Carol W. Brown, 32 Everett Drive, Rochester, NY 14624-3904; tel. 716-247-5689 [Vendor G0185]

Mrs. Ellen Brzoska, 402 W. Nob Hill Boulevard, Yakima, WA 98902-4635 [Vendor G0127]

Jane Gray Buchanan, 114 Berwick Drive, Oak Ridge, TN 37830 [Vendor G0107]

Paul F. Burgess, 12305 Harbor Drive, Woodbridge, VA 22192; or c/o G. Pillsbury, RR-01, Box 1645, Springvale, ME 04083 [Vendor G0008]

Bettina P.H. Burns, PO Box 325, Cullman, AL 35056-0325 [Vendor G0254]

Louise Burt, 9935 Kingston Farm Road, Kingston, WA 98346; tel. 360-297-7084 [Vendor G0286]

Dr. John F. Byerly, Jr., 8503 Spring Hollow Drive, Richmond, VA 23227; tel. 804-262-8855 [Vendor G0409]

Marie Bowen Canterbury, 5117 N. 26th Road, Arlington, VA 22207 [Vendor G0234]

Cecelia E. Casey, 4110 Pleasant Meadow Court, Chantilly, VA 22021; tel. 703-222-9735; or Box 372, Elk Rapids, MI 49629 [Vendor G0243]

Catoctin Press, PO Box 505, New Market, MD 21774-0505; fax: 301-620-1817 [Vendor G0126]

Marjorie Dikeman Chamberlain, 13650 N. Frontage Road #334, Yuma, AZ 85367 [Vendor G0194]

Madrue Chavers-Wright, 2410 Barker Avenue, Suite 14-G, Bronx, New York 10467-7634; tel. 718-654-9445 [Vendor G0006]

Martha A. Cieglo, 6854 Cedarbrook, Bloomfield Hills, MI 48301; e-mail: WJJP15A@Prodigy.com [Vendor G0429]

Clearfield Company, 1001 N. Calvert Street, Baltimore, MD 21202; tel. 410-625-9004; fax: 410-752-8492 [Vendor G0011]

Cobb County GA Genealogical Society, Inc., PO Box 1413, Marietta, GA 30061-1413 [Vendor G0313]

Hugh Coffman, Rt 2, Box 177, Marietta, OH 45750; tel. 614-374-6718 [Vendor G0213]

Wanda Colvin, 202 S. Roosevelt, Cleveland, TX 77327; tel. 713-592-7017 [Vendor G0432]

COMPU-CHART, c/o Paula Perkins Mortensen, 363 So. Park Victoria Drive, Milpitas, CA 95035-5708 [Vendor G0228]

M.E. Conover, 300 Strasbourg Drive, Lafayette, LA 70506 [Vendor G0114]

Al B. Cory, 11056 Orange Cart Way, Jacksonville, FL 32223-7336; tel. 904-886-9404 [Vendor G0298]

Avis E. Cox and Marion R. Cox, Route #2, Box 134, Winona, MN 55987-9631; tel. 507-454-1172 [Vendor G0427]

Roy Crego, 12 Mt. Airy Road, Basking Ridge, NJ 07920 [Vendor G0231]

Crippen-Crippin Family Journal, PO Box 340, Hancock, MD 21750-0340; tel. 301-678-6999; e-mail: DonnaL3@aol.com; fanfare@intrepid.net [Vendor G0392B]

Rick Crume, RR2 Box 169, Glyndon, MN 56547-9651; tel. 218-498-0235; fax: 218-498-2901; e-mail: 71161.2632@compuserve.com [Vendor G0386]

Dr. Larry D. Crummer, 2649 Mission Greens Drive, San Jose, CA 95148-2568; tel. 408-270-4113 [Vendor G0192]

Paul J. Curtin, 11007 Legends Lane, Austin, TX 78747-1222; tel. 512-282-8462 [Vendor G0327]

The Cuthbertson Family History, c/o Thomas H. Aldridge, 7605 Water Oak Lane, Monroe, NC 28110; tel. 704-753-4487 [Vendor G0161]

Patricia Brown Darling, PO Box 71, Akutan, AK 99553 [Vendor G0270]

Virginia Carlisle d'Armand, 3636 Taliluna Avenue, Apt. #235, Knoxville, TN 37919 [Vendor G0009]

Betty R. Darnell, 204 Hartford Drive, Mount Washington, KY 40047; tel. 502-538-8743; fax: 502-538-8743 [Vendor G0261]

Howard J. Dean, PO Box 115, Westernville, NY 13486; tel. 315-827-4606 [Vendor G0267]

Betty V. Dearing, 3444 N. Wolters, Fresno, CA 93726-5922; tel. 209-224-9503 [Vendor G0266]

Decatur Genealogical Society, PO Box 1548, Decatur, IL 62525-1548 [Vendor G0260]

Virginia Easley De Marce, 5635 N. 25th Road, Arlington, VA 22207-1403 [Vendor G0324]

Harry T. Dolan, Jr., PO Box 68, Cutchogue, NY 11935-0068 [Vendor G0351]

Raymond K. Donner, 2650 N. Lakeview #1010, Chicago, IL 60614; tel. 312-281-2432; fax: 312-281-2432 [Vendor G0355]

Robert L. Downen, 4009 Terrace Drive, Annandale, VA 22003 [Vendor G0408]

Dolores Graham Doyle, 765 E. Wood Duck Circle, Fresno, CA 93720-0806; tel. 209-434-5212; e-mail: JSJT14A@Prodigy.Com [Vendor G0255]

Linda Dubé, 39 Birch Street, Madawaska, ME 04756; tel. 207-728-4082 [Vendor G0060]

Mary Dudley-Higham, c/o Genesis Publications, 5272 Williams Road, Suisun, CA 94585 [Vendor G0153]

Dyckman/Dikeman/Dykeman Family Association, 13650 N. Frontage Road #334, Yuma, AZ 85367 [Vendor G0194A]

Elder Family Newsletter, PO Box 340, Hancock, MD 21750-0340; tel. 301-678-6999; e-mail: DonnaL3@aol.com; fanfare@intrepid.net [Vendor G0392]

Reta M. Evans, 5605 Westcreek Drive, Fort Worth, TX 76133-2246 [Vendor G0012]

Mildred S. Ezell, 4416 Briers Place, Stone Mountain, GA 30083; tel. 404-292-5699; e-mail: ME2ATL@MEGAWEB.COM; ME2ATL@ICHANGE.COM [Vendor G0323]

Kenneth W. Faig, Jr., 2311 Swainwood Drive, Glenview, IL 60025-2741 [Vendor G0211]

Family History & Genealogy Center, 1300 E. 109th Street, Kansas City, MO; tel. 64131-3585; fax: 816-943-0477 [Vendor G0238]

Family Publications—Rose Caudle Terry, 5628 60th Drive NE, Marysville, WA 98270-9509; e-mail: cxwp57@prodigy.com [Vendor G0061]

Hilde Shuptrine Farley, 10325 Russell Street, Shawnee Mission, KS 66212-1736 [Vendor G0024]

William S. Farley, 6592 E Jackson Court, Highlands Ranch, CO 80126 [Vendor G0004]

Mrs. Michal Martin Farmer, PO Box 140880, Dallas, TX 75214-0880 [Vendor G0312]

James G. Faulconer, 5200 Oakbrooke Drive, Kettering, OH 45440; tel. 513-439-2029 [Vendor G0252]

Bonnie J. Feldhausen, Sec.-Treas., Feldhausen Reunion, 1880 Utah Road, Frankfort, KS 66427 [Vendor G0063]

Lela Brooks Fennell, 100 Wynnwood Drive, Windybush, Wilmington, DE 19810-4428; tel. 302-475-5969 [Vendor G0396]

Dr. Jim Fenner, 2611 Avenue "S," Brooklyn, NY 11229; tel. 718-998-8593 [Vendor G0296]

Herman W. Ferguson, 600 Chad Drive, Rocky Mount, NC 27803; tel. 919-443-2258 [Vendor G0056]

William B. Fetters, 12814 Brunswick Lane, Bowie, MD 20715-2403; tel. 301-262-3925 [Vendor G0206]

Arthur Louis Finnell Books, 9033 Lyndale Avenue S., Suite 108, Bloomington, MN 55420-3535 [Vendor G0256]

First Genealogical Research Center (FGRC), 2108 Champagne Circle, Salt Lake City, UT 84118; tel. 801-967-6687 [Vendor G0269]

Kathryn B. Fischer, 70 Hyacinth Drive, Covington, LA 70433; 504-892-4365 [Vendor G0281]

Judith E. FitzPatrick, 8273 Theisen, Center Line, MI 48015; tel. 810-757-7560 [Vendor G0412]

Virginia B. Fletcher, 721 NW 73 Avenue, Ft. Lauderdale, FL 33317-1140; e-mail: VBFletcher@AOL.com [Vendor G0332]

Barbara B. Ford, 313 Henry Lane, Wallingford, PA 19086; tel. 610-566-4888 [Vendor G0368]

William L. Forst, PO Box 5, Foristell, MO 63348-0005 [Vendor G0207]

Warren L. Forsythe, Box 1299, Ellensburg, WA 98926-1299 [Vendor G0401]

Joan P. Fortune, 1039 Trickham Bridge Road, Brandon, MS 39042-9644; e-mail: joanf@netdoor.com [Vendor G0317]

William A. Fox, 112 Colonel's Way, Williamsburg, VA 23185 [Vendor G0162]

Leallah Franklin, 822 Camino De Los Padres, Tucson, AZ 85718 [Vendor G0304]

Pat Frappier, Box 46, Evergreen Point Road, Jonesboro, ME 04648 [Vendor G0389]

Gloria Shipp Frazier, 3007 Paula Drive, West Plains, MO 65775 [Vendor G0360]

William M. Gage, 4001 Garrison Street NW, Washington, DC 20016 [Vendor G0247]

Ms. Tiger Gardiner, 9653 Whiteacre Road, #C-4, Columbia, MD 21045-3571 [Vendor G0339]

Genealogical Publishing Co., Inc., 1001 N. Calvert Street, Baltimore, MD 21202-3879; tel. 410-837-8271; fax: 410-752-8492 [Vendor G0010]

Genealogical Services, 1001 S. Marshall Street, Suite 53, Winston-Salem, NC 27101; fax: 910-777-3603 [Vendor G0302]

Genealogical Services, Rte. 7, Box 250, Bassett, VA 24055; tel. 540-629-9191 [Vendor G0146 and G0146A]

The Genealogical Society of Pennsylvania, Herbert K. Zearfoss, Pres., 1300 Locust Street, Philadelphia, PA 19107-5661; tel. 215-545-0391 [Vendor G0202]

Genealogy Publishing Service, 448 Ruby Mine Road, Franklin, NC 28734; tel. 704-524-7063 [Vendor G0223]

William Gerade, 5222 Mitchell Street, Alexandria, VA 22312; tel. 703-354-3830; fax: 703-354-3830 (call first) [Vendor G0283]

Mrs. Jean Fairchild Gilmore, 1300 N. Horse Prairie Road, Inverness, FL 34450-1875 [Vendor G0292]

Valerie Giorgi, 4168 Woodland Street, Santa Maria, CA 93455-3356 [Vendor G0090]

Gloucester County Historical Society, 17 Hunter Street, Woodbury, NJ 08096-4605 [Vendor G0069]

Glyndwr Resources, 43779 Valley Rd, Decatur, MI 49045 [Vendor G0094]

Lois B. Goff, 1625 Elmwood Avenue, Wilmette, IL 60091-1553 [Vendor G0166]

Goldenwest Marketing, 10528 Lower Azusa Road #162, El Monte, CA 91731-1296; tel. 818-309-0764 [Vendor G0023]

Goodenow Family Association, RT 2 Box 718, Shepherdstown, WV 25443; tel. 304-876-2008 [Vendor G0116]

J. Raymond Gourdin, PO Box 648, Columbia, MD 21045-0648; tel. 410-381-2816 [Vendor G0205]

Robert N. Grant, 15 Campo Bello Court, Menlo Park, CA 94025; tel. 415-854-0895 [Vendor G0404]

Kenneth V. Graves, 261 South Street, Wrentham, MA 02093-1504; tel. 508-384-8084 [Vendor G0196]

Elberta Price Griffiths, 2555 N. Price Road, Apt. 282, Chandler, AZ 85224 [Vendor G0282]

Dr. Joan S. Guilford, 2710 E. Adams Avenue, Orange, CA 92667-6240 [Vendor G0220]

Carl Gwynn, 605 Fir Street, Coulee Dam, WA 99116 [Vendor G0334]

Kenneth F. Haas, 1730 Fairmeadows Drive, Bettendorf, IA 52722; tel. 319-355-7942 [Vendor G0359]

Hallock Family Association, c/o Marion H. Adams, 4 Woodland Drive, Severna Park, MD 21146 [Vendor G0325]

Lynn Berry Hamilton, 2101 Treasure Hills #606, Harlingen, TX 78550; tel. 210-423-1330; fax: 210-425-5078; e-mail: FDTV62a (Prodigy) [Vendor G0301]

Von Gail Hamilton, 148 S. 90th Place, Mesa, AZ 85208; te. 602-986-7180 [Vendor G0285]

Frances Lane Harris, 3008 SE 154th Avenue, Vancouver, WA 98684-5188 [Vendor G0289]

Richard C. Harris, 701 Hard Scuffle Court, Bowling Green, KY 42103 [Vendor G0357]

Hazel N. Hassan, 19549 County Road 38, Goshen, IN 46526; tel. 219-534-1527 [Vendor G0263]

Ken Haughton, 16200 Kennedy Road, Los Gatos, CA 95032 [Vendor G0200]

Hauk Data Services, PO Box 1577, Anderson, IN 46014; e-mail: ChrisHauk@aol.com [Vendor G0340]

Robert Haydon, 12 Fenchley Court, Little Rock, AR 72212; tel. 501-224-1313; fax: 501-224-7081 [Vendor G0372]

Marjorie Stubbs Heaney, 2596 Whitehurst Road, DeLand, FL 32720-2032 [Vendor G0437]

Heart of the Lakes Publishing, PO Box 299, Interlaken, NY 14847-0299; tel. 800-782-9687; fax: 607-532-4684; e-mail: HLP Books@AOL.com [Vendor G0093]

Robert H. (Bob) Henderson, 119 Pinewood Drive, Greer, SC 29651-1441; tel. 864-877-2424 [Vendor G0442]

Dudley Herndon, 825 Ketch Drive, Apt. 301, Naples, FL 33940; tel. 941-434-7732 [Vendor G0425]

Higginson Book Company, Publishers and reprinters of genealogy and local history, 148-BP Washington Street, PO Box 778, Salem, MA 01970; tel. 508-745-7170; fax: 508-745-8025 [Vendor G0259]

Historical Data Services, 14 Clark Street, Glens Falls, NY 12804 [Vendor G0421]

Jay Hobson, 5805 Warwick Place, Columbus, GA 31904; tel. 706-323-6273 [Vendor G0352]

Holland Family Association, Rt. 1, Box 38, Garden City, MN 56034 [Vendor G0309]

Honakers, PO Box 3636, Alexandria, VA 22302-9998; tel. 703-751-7321 [Vendor G0268]

Honeywell Family Association, A. Parks Honeywell, Editor, 785 Island Way, Clearwater, FL 34630-1816; tel. 813-461-4244; fax: 813-461-4244; e-mail: PARKSHONEY@AOL.COM [Vendor G0356]

Mrs. Barbara Knott Horsman, 14704 Jefferson Avenue, Chester, VA 23831 [Vendor G0115]

Hosford Books, 1 Binney Road, Old Lyme, CT 06371-1401; tel. 203-434-2907 [Vendor G0171]

Granville W. Hough, 3438 Bahia Blanca W., Apt. B, Laguna Hills, CA 92653-2830 [Vendor G0119]

Nannie E. Houser, 6601 NW 97th Avenue, Tamarac, FL 33321 [Vendor G0052]

Mrs. Mary Jo Hunavy, 108 Sea Grape Drive, Jacksonville Beach, FL 32250 [Vendor G0276]

Lois L. Hupfer, 3087 South Harlan, Denver, CO 80227-3818 [Vendor G0018]

Jack R. Hutchins, 23 Orchard Way South, Rockville, MD 20854; tel. 301-762-3251 [Vendor G0029]

International Forum, PO Box 7000-350, Palos Verdes Peninsula, CA 90274-3218 [Vendor G0102]

Irish Genealogical Foundation, PO Box 7575, Kansas City, MO 64116 USA; tel. 816-454-2410; fax: 816-454-2410 [Vendor G0455]

Jackson Genealogy—Michael Stephen Jackson, 202 E. St. Clair Street, Freeburg, IL 62243-1243 [Vendor G0224]

Anneke JANS and Everardus BOGARDUS Descendants Assoc., 1121 Linhof Road, Wilmington, OH 45177-2917 [Vendor G0452]

Blanche W. Jernigan, PO Box 486, Pewee Valley, KY 40056; tel. 502-241-1606 [Vendor G0030]

Phyllis W. Johnson, 2830 N. Westmoreland Street, Arlington, VA 22213; tel. 703-532-0144 [Vendor G0178]

Marvin T. Jones, 7890-158 R Avenue SE, Wyndmere, ND 58081; tel. 701-439-2528 [Vendor G0420]

Frank L. and Odette J. Kaufman, 2794 Hyannis Way, Sacramento, CA 95827-1343; tel. 916-362-2462 [Vendor G0414]

Patricia Kinney Kaufman, 155 SE Norton, Sherwood, OR 97140; tel. 503-625-6563 [Vendor G0315]

Sara Hunter Kellar, 3736 Chiara Drive, Titusville, FL 32796; tel. 407-268-2924 [Vendor G0212]

Dale C. Kellogg, 221 Lexington Avenue, Elyria, OH 44035-6219 [Vendor G0051]

Doris Bankes Kent, 2 N. West Street, Green City, MO 63545 [Vendor G0201]

Dr. Lawrence Kent, 608 South Conway Road, Suite G, Orlando, FL 32807-104408 [Vendor G0448]

Wilmer L. Kerns, 4715 North 38th Place, Arlington, VA 22207-2914; tel. 703-533-1040 [Vendor G0250]

Glenn Kilmer, 34 Rosehill Avenue, Brantford, Ontario, Canada N3T 1R8; tel. 519-753-8265 [Vendor G0329]

Kimball Family Association, 14 Manson Road, Kittery, ME 03904-5534 [Vendor G0043]

Betty King, 2820 34th Place, NW, Washington, DC 20007; tel. 202-338-4424 [Vendor G0394]

Margaret B. Kinsey, PO Box 459, Lamesa, TX 79331; tel. 806-872-3603 [Vendor G0307]

Kinship, 60 Cedar Heights Road, Rhinebeck, NY 12572; tel. 914-876-4592; e-mail: 71045.1516@compuserve.com [Vendor G0450]

Linda Lightholder Kmiecik, 431 S. Center Street, Bensenville, IL 60106-2642 [Vendor G0367]

Gene S. Kuechmann, 8113 NE 25th Avenue, Vancouver, WA 98665-9726 [Vendor G0101]

Joan Kusek, 9640 Walmer, Overland Park, KS 66212-1554 [Vendor G0122]

Alan J. Lamb, PO Box 5360, Santa Fe, NM 87502-5360 [Vendor G0265]

Lancaster Mennonite Historical Society, 2215 Millstream Road, Lancaster, PA 17602-1499; tel. 717-393-9745 [Vendor G0150]

Stephen L. Lawton, 620 Howard Avenue, Pitman, NJ 08071 [Vendor G0045]

Louis E. LeGrand, 8100 Colebrook Road, Richmond, VA 23227-1613 [Vendor G0346]

Faye M. Lightburn, 1137 - 6th Avenue North, Jacksonville Beach, FL 32250; tel. 904-249-4263 [Vendor G0311]

Judge Noble K. Littell, PO Box 1019, Sebring, FL 33871; tel. 813-471-9387 [Vendor G0133]

Marianne Elizabeth Hall Little, RR2, Box 148A, Yorktown, TX 78164-9538 [Vendor G0264]

Lomar Research, PO Box 931, Lyman, WY 82937 [Vendor G0390]

Love Letters, Pat Love Stubblefield, Editor, 1300 Arbolita Drive, La Habra, CA 90631-3206; tel. 310-697-9902 [Vendor G0385]

James W. Lowry, 13531 Maugansville Road, Hagerstown, MD 21740 [Vendor G0035]

Kenneth Luttner, Ohio Genealogy Center, PO Box 395, St. Peter, MN 56082; tel. 507-388-7158 [Vendor G0135]

Arthur F. Maes, 4801 Hackamore Drive N., Colorado Springs, CO 80918; tel. 719-598-7806 [Vendor G0341]

Marion Mann, 1453 Whittier Place NW, Washington, DC 20012; tel. 202-291-4409 [Vendor G0316]

Arlene F. Mansfield, 498 Quartz Street, Los Alamos, NM 87544; tel. 505-662-2115; fax: 505-662-5781 [Vendor G0222]

Gary and Lynn Marks, 5117 North 18th Place, Phoenix, AZ 85016 [Vendor G0413]

Lyle B. Marquess, 761 Lincoln Avenue, Bentleyville, PA 15314 [Vendor G0366]

Floyd R. Mason, 115 E. Rainbow Drive, Bridgewater, VA 22812 [Vendor G0345]

Barbara Stacy Mathews, 1420 D Street, Marysville, CA 95901; tel. 916-741-2967 [Vendor G0430]

Nathan Mathews, PO Box 1975, Fayetteville, GA 30214; e-mail: Prodigy KNHK84A [Vendor G0399]

Randall C. Maydew, 6908 Brandywine Loop NE, Albuquerque, NM 87111; tel. 505-821-0102 [Vendor G0007]

Fern Maynard, 801 Gillaspie Drive, Apt. 130, Boulder, CO 80303-6549 [Vendor G0226]

Herbert L. McMillan, 29378 Gillette Court, Sun City, CA 92586; or Lorna M. Stewart, 5539 Columbia Pike, Apt 701, Arlington, VA 22204-5812 [Vendor G0186]

Evejean Fortney McKnight, 379 Two Ponds Drive, Coolville, OH 45723-9531; tel. 614-667-3736 [Vendor G0416]

Susan L. Mitchell, 34233 Shawnee Trail, Westland, MI 48185 [Vendor G0068]

Judy Montgomery, 3858 W. 226 Street #109, Torrance, CA 90505 [Vendor G0388]

Ruth Erwin Moore, 2908 Cobbs Way, Anderson, SC 29621; tel. 864-226-7212; e-mail: smokeypup@aol.com [Vendor G0379]

Thomas R. Moore, Esq., 1170 Fifth Avenue, Suite 2A, New York, NY 10029 [Vendor G0318]

Rhoda J. Morley, 3215 Hwy 441-N, Okeechobee, FL 34972-1854; tel. 941-467-2482 [Vendor G0322]

Glenn H. Morrison, 3319 Bedford Forrest Drive, Missouri City, TX 77459-4904; tel. 713-438-4808; e-mail: kmwe81a@prodigy.com [Vendor G0381]

Patricia Hewitt Morrison, 9611 Westbourne Court, Cypress, CA 90630-2760 [Vendor G0078]

W.E. Morrison & Co., Ovid, NY 14521; tel. 607-869-2561 [Vendor G0112]

Mrs. Paula P. Mortensen, 363 So. Park Victoria Drive, Milpitas, CA 95035-5708; tel. 408-262-1051; e-mail: 103137.3321@compuserve.com [Vendor G0258]

Ralph W. Morton, 4867 Chambersburg Road, Dayton, OH 45424; or John H. Warvel, 10951 E. Mallard Way, Indianapolis, IN 46278 [Vendor G0022]

Martha Ashcraft Neal, PO Box 989, Washington, PA 15301 [Vendor G0105]

Anne Morrow Nees, 6612 W. 93rd Street, Apt. B, Overland Park, KS 66212 [Vendor G0025]

New England Historic Genealogical Society Sales Dept., 160 N. Washington Street, 4th floor, Boston, MA 02114-2120; tel. 617-536-5740; fax: 617-624-0325; e-mail: 74777.3612@compuserve.com [Vendor G0406]

New York Genealogical and Biographical Society, 122 East 58th Street, New York, NY 10022; tel. 212-755-8532 [Vendor G0182]

Joann H. Nichols, 46 Chestnut Street, Brattleboro, VT 05301-3152; tel. 802-254-9554 [Vendor G0300]

Lucile Novak, 16 Smith Garrison Road, Newmarket, NH 03857 [Vendor G0125]

Patricia O'Boyle, 5802 North 42nd Avenue, Phoenix, AZ 85019-1820 [Vendor G0225]

Raymond L. Olson, 763 South Crescent Avenue, Lodi, CA 95240-4630; tel. 209-368-8071 [Vendor G0291]

Roy F. Olson, Jr., 360 Watson Road, Paducah, KY 42003-8978 [Vendor G0077]

Donald Lewis Osborn, 322 SE Willow Way, Lee's Summit, MO 64063-2928; tel. 816-524-5785 [Vendor G0121]

Charles Mathieson Otstot, 5124 North 33rd Street, Arlington, VA 22207-1854; tel. 703-538-5446 [Vendor G0232]

Phyllis Smith Oyer, 263 Bakerdale Road, Rochester, NY 14616-3654; tel. 716-663-1735 [Vendor G0354]

Paca Associates, 400 Shoreline Drive, Belhaven, NC 27810; tel. 919-964-2233 [Vendor G0403]

Paddleford Publishing Company, 4484 Pitch Pine Court, Concord, CA 94521-4406; tel. 510-827-0571; fax: 510-680-1312 [Vendor G0426]

Janice B. Palmer, 6302 Fairview Drive, Pensacola, FL 32505-2057; tel. 904-432-5291 [Vendor G0418]

Joyce J. Parris, 220 Northwest Avenue, Swannanoa, NC 28778-2618 [Vendor G0295]

Pau Hana Press, 1116 Kealaolu Avenue, Honolulu, HI 96816-5419 [Vendor G0154]

Dorothy N. Perkins, 4895 Avion Way, San Diego, CA 92115; tel. 619-583-6430 [Vendor G0375]

Warren W. Perney, 10121 Orchard Park, West Drive, Indianapolis, IN 46280-1516; tel. 317-846-7164 [Vendor G0422]

Valentine T. Petersheim, RD #2, Box 1000, Mifflintown, PA 17059 [Vendor G0053]

Mae Gean Pettit, Route 1, Box 149, Alto, TX 75925 [Vendor G0402]

Picton Press, PO Box 250, Rockport, ME 04856; tel. 207-236-6565: fax: 207-236-6713; e-mail: Picton@midcoast.com [Vendor G0082]

Robert E. Pitts, 10020 Artesia Drive, Shreveport, LA 71115-3405; tel. 318-797-0442 [Vendor G0383]

L. Welch Pogue, 5204 Kenwood Avenue, Chevy Chase, MD 20815-6604; tel. 301-654-7233 [Vendor G0444]

Powell Genealogical Services, 720 Highpoint Drive, Wexford, PA 15090-7571 [Vendor G0098]

Willard J. Prentice, 2419 Chetwood Circle, Timonium, MD 21093-2533 [Vendor G0331]

Lewis G. Proper, 155 Seville Drive, Rochester, NY 14617; tel. 716-544-6546 [Vendor G0439]

The Queenstown Press, PO Box 151, Pennington, NJ 08534 [Vendor G0398]

Quirke, Quirke & Assoc., 2310 Juniper Court, Golden, CO 80401-8087; tel. 303-526-1319 [Vendor G0143]

Rana Research, Attn: Nadine, 706 Pershing, College Station, TX 77840; tel. 409-696-2929 [Vendor G0306]

Jean M. Rand, 209-07 Whitehall Terrace, Queens Village, NY 11427; tel. 718-468-1674 [Vendor G0210]

Catherine M. Rhoads, 10435 Tullymore Drive, Adelphi, MD 20783 [Vendor G0262]

Fred J. Riffe, 154 Indies Drive North, Marathon, FL 33050; tel. 305-743-7465; fax: 305-743-9140 [Vendor G0277]

Patricia Turner Ritchie, 1559 Moffett Drive, Winchester, VA 22601 [Vendor G0365]

George S. Robbins, 97 Burns Street, Marinette, WI 54143; tel. 715-735-5236 [Vendor G0364]

John D. Roberts, 1 Melrose Street, Dunedin, New Zealand [Vendor G0275]

Ronald L. Roberts, PO Box 7086, South Lake Tahoe, CA 96158-0086; tel. 916-541-3562 [Vendor G0400]

Robinson Family Association, Hewick Plantation, Box 82, Urbanna, VA 23175-0082; tel. 804-758-4214; fax: 804-758-4214 [Vendor G0237]

Dean H. Roe, 9240 Werner Drive, Kewaskum, WI 53040; tel. 414-626-2696 [Vendor G0349]

Rudd Family Research Association, 461 Emerson Street, Chula Vista, CA 91911; tel. 619-422-4445 [Vendor G0290]

Fred A. Rutledge, 1208 Argonne Drive, Baltimore, MD 21218-1429; tel. 410-889-0035 [Vendor G0441]

Thomas A. Ryerson, PO Box 262, Ingersoll, Ontario, Canada N5C 3K5; tel. 519-421-3621; fax: 519-539-7335 [Vendor G0391]

Jean A. Sargent, 12217 Shadetree Lane, Laurel, MD 20708-2814 [Vendor G0369]

William B. Saxbe, C.G., 346 Reamer Place, Oberlin, Ohio 44074 [Vendor G0328]

Paul A. Schwabe, 1004 NW Second Street, Washington, IN 47501; tel. 812-254-7290 [Vendor G0353]

Sayre A. Schwarztrauber, 60 Old Mill Road, PO Box 589, Osterville, MA 02655-0589; tel. 508-428-8350 [Vendor G0454]

Beatrice West Seitz, 2608 E Racine Street, Apt. 11, Janesville, WI 53545-5227 [Vendor G0001]

Harry Leon Sellards, Jr., 4031 Grand Avenue, DeLand, FL 32720; tel. 904-985-4046 [Vendor G0445]

Robert Serré, 1057 Riviera Drive, Ottawa, Ontario, Canada K1K 0N7 [Vendor G0111]

Katherine Lytle Sharp, 2008 Forest Dale Drive, Silver Spring, MD 20903-1529; tel. 301-434-7751 [Vendor G0037]

James H. Shaw, 260 Thornton Road, Brownsville, PA 15417-0012 [Vendor G0280]

Margaret E. Sheaffer/Carol M. Sheaffer, M.D., 10 Wexford Drive, Lawrenceville, NJ 08648; tel. 609-896-0286 [Vendor G0229]

Morris N. Sherk, 924 Williams Grove Road, Mechanicsburg, PA 17055-8000 [Vendor G0370]

Shields' Valley Publishing Co., HC 85, Box 4275, Livingston, MT 59047; tel. 406-222-2725 [Vendor G0242]

Sue Ann Gardner Shreve, 5 Anderson Court, W. Bay Shore, L.I., NY 11706-7701; tel. 516-665-7693 [Vendor G0221]

Larry G. Shuck, 164 Julep Lane, Cincinnati, OH 45218-1206 [Vendor G0287]

Janice Cale Sisler, PO Box 113, Bruceton Mills, WV 26525-0113 [Vendor G0438]

James R. Sisson, PO Box 158, Manitowish Waters, WI 54545; e-mail: 73621.2523@cserve.com [Vendor G0424]

Claiborne T. Smith, Jr., MD, E-3 N. St. George's Apts., 119 Mill Creek Road, Ardmore, PA 19003; tel. 610-649-5920 [Vendor G0435]

Snackerty Enterprises, RFD 2, Box 668, Center Barnstead, NH 03225; fax: 603-269-4524 [Vendor G0241]

Carol J. Snow, PO Box 31, Del Mar, CA 92014 [Vendor G0158]

Solano County Genealogical Society, Inc., PO Box 2494, Fairfield, CA 94533 [Vendor G0184]

Solo Press, PO Box 507, Keno, OR 97627 [Vendor G0303]

Southern Tier Genealogical Society, PO Box 680, Vestal, NY 13850-0680 [Vendor G0092]

Sarah S. Splaun, 25 Troxell Lane, Staunton, VA 24401 [Vendor G0104]

Linda Berg Stafford, PO Box 5261, Bloomington, IN 47407 [Vendor G0032]

National Stanley Family Association, 10236 Luman Lane, Twinsburg, OH 44087 [Vendor G0446]

James C. Starbuck, 3266 Poplar Ridge Drive, Rex, GA 30273-2459; tel. 404-961-6618 [Vendor G0120]

John Steinbrugge, 4072 Ondine Circle, Huntington Beach, CA 92649 [Vendor G0361]

Clarence D. Stephenson, PO Box 236, Marion Center, PA 15759-0236 [Vendor G0041]

Ken Stevens, PO Box 118, Walpole, NH 03608 [Vendor G0038]

Lenore B. Stevenson, Box 660, Beaufort, SC 29901 [Vendor G0288]

C.R. Stewart, PO Box 3011, Long Beach, CA 90803-0011; tel. 218-963-3259 [Vendor G0169]

Vernon Stiver, 501 West Loveland Avenue, Loveland, OH 45140 [Vendor G0020]

John H. Stoddard, PO Box 434, Elmhurst, IL 60126; tel. 708-617-4906 [Vendor G0319]

Mildred and Kemble Stout, NE 1115 Orchard Drive, Pullman, WA 99163; tel. 509-332-5612 [Vendors G0320A & G0320B]

Patricia Wright Strati, 47 Rose Drive, Cragston, Highland Falls, NY 10928-9801 [Vendor G0419]

Jeanne W. Strong, 26969 Beaver Lane, Los Altos Hills, CA 94022; tel. 415-493-3322 [Vendor G0086]

Virginia A. Stuhr, 8531 Glenwood, Overland Park, KS 66212-1125; tel. 913-642-7596 [Vendor G0027]

Edmund K. Swigart, PO Box 1134, Washington, CT 06793 [Vendor G0100]

Inez Taylor, 969 N. Reed Station Road, Carbondale, IL 62901; tel. 618-549-2004 [Vendor G0350]

Henry Teer, 1416 Colony Drive, Irving, TX 75061; tel. 214-254-1162 [Vendor G0380]

Ronald R. Templin, 2256 River Oak Lane SE, Fort Myers, FL 33905; tel. 813-694-8347 [Vendor G0096]

Tennessee Valley Publishing, PO Box 52527, Knoxville, TN 37950-2527; tel. 800-762-7079; fax: 423-584-0113; e-mail: tvp1@ix.netcom.com [Vendor G0183]

James W. Thompson, PO Box 1032, Stevensville, MD 21666 [Vendor G0159]

Mary Ann Thompson, 2721 Knollwood Court, Plano, TX 75075-6424 [Vendor G0017]

Thomas R. Topping, 1201 Berry Ridge Road, Charlotte, NC 28270-1463; tel. 704-847-8648 [Vendor G0342]

Torkwood, Inc., 5 Court of Bucks County, Lincolnshire, IL 60069 [Vendor G0066]

Mrs. Jo Ann De Board Touchstone, 815 West Frantz, Enid, OK 73701-8091 [Vendor G0236]

Townsend Family Missing Links Assoc., 5721 Antietam Drive, Sarasota, FL 34231-4903 [Vendor G0047]

Carl W. Troyer, 3623 Pebble Beach Drive, Dallas, TX 75234-2545; tel. 214-241-5777; e-mail: WBDS18A@PRODIGY.COM [Vendor G0378]

Mary Ann Tschopp, RD 3, Box 307, Stewartstown, PA 17363; tel. 717-993-6094 [Vendor G0447]

William T. Tuley, c/o Minuteman Press, 2313 Wicker Avenue, Schererville, IN 46375; tel. 219-322-6677; fax: 219-322-7400 [Vendor G0330]

University of Nebraska Press, Sandra Johnson, Marketing Manager, 312 N. 14th St., Lincoln, NE 68588-0484 [Vendor G0050]

Joseph H. Vance, 310 North Garfield Street, Lombard, IL 60148-2042; tel. 708-629-0581 [Vendor G0239]

Mr. E.R. Van Etten, 12 Suburban Drive, PO Box 95, Big Flats, NY 14814-0095; tel. 607-562-8613 [Vendor G0219]

Rosamond Houghton Van Noy, 4700 Hwy. K East, Conover, WI 54519; tel. 715-479-5044 [Vendor G0245]

James C. Van Winkle, PO Box 683, Tybee Island, GA 31328-0683 [Vendor G0173]

Betty H. Vollenweider, 1520 Mt. Tabor Church Road, Dallas, GA 30132; tel. 770-445-7689 [Vendor G0443]

Carolyn C. Volpe, 4025 Pulitzer Place #135, San Diego, CA 92122; tel. 619-457-8058 [Vendor G0216]

Mr./Mrs. John Pattee Wallach, 19 Allen Street, Harwich, MA 02645 [Vendor G0233]

Victor H. Walworth, PO Box 924, Columbia, SC 29202; tel. 803-781-7886 [Vendor G0033]

Ward Publishing Company, 42 Larchmont Road, Asheville, NC 28804 [Vendor G0044]

Dr. Holland D. Warren, 207 Nottingham Circle, Lynchburg, VA 24502 [Vendor G0230]

Warren Co. (OH) Genealogical Society, 300 East Silver Street, Lebanon, OH 45036; tel. 513-933-1144 [Vendor G0335]

Nancie Todd Weber, 22309 Canyon Lake Drive South, Canyon Lake, CA 92587; e-mail: HJDR04B@prodigy.com [Vendor G0337]

Shirley Jennings Weber, N. 410 E. Fairway Drive, Hoodsport, WA 98548-9632; tel. 360-877-9696 [Vendor G0235]

Janet S. Welsh, 7416 Cliffbourne Court, Derwood, MD 20855-1101 [Vendor G0251]

Nan Overton West, West Printing Co., 4207 34th Street, Lubbock, TX 79410; tel. 806-794-3687; fax: 806-793-3207 [Vendor G0244]

William S. West, 1707 Front Street, Beaufort, NC 28516-9307 [Vendor G0308]

Virginia Westfall, 205 Rice Lane, Amity, OR 97101 [Vendor G0436]

Wilton M. Whisler, 121 South 168, Seattle, WA 98148-1611 [Vendor G0099]

Whitfield Books, Vallie Jo Whitfield, 1841 Pleasant Hill Road, Pleasant Hill, CA 94523. Branch Office: Joanne Whitfield, 13 Costa Street, San Francisco, CA 94110. e-mail: Jotea@aol.com. [Vendor G0253]

Alexander L. Wiatt, 24 Madison Lane South, Newport News, VA 23606-2855 [Vendor G0137]

Glenna W. Wilding, 606 Riverwood Drive, Louisville, KY 40207-1346 [Vendor G0338]

Willett Books, PO Box 5871, Kingsport, TN 37663; tel. 615-239-7912 [Vendor G0271]

Roger Williams Family Association, PO Box 24, East Greenwich, RI 02818; tel. 401-246-0246 [Vendor G0062]

Leland E. Wilson, PO Box 893, Lindale, TX 75771; tel. 903-882-5915 [Vendor G0347]

Mrs. Ethel M. Woelfel, 1052 Cumberland Street, Bethlehem, PA 18017; tel. 610-868-6565 [Vendor G0273]

Margarette Hall Wood, 2234 Pinoak Knolls, San Antonio, TX 78248-2303 [Vendor G0299]

Mrs. Helen D. Woodman, 207 Balsam Road, Hendersonville, NC 28792 [Vendor G0208]

E.L. Woodworth-Barnes, 150 Downs Boulevard, Apt B-209, Clemson, SC 29631-2046 [Vendor G0054]

Larry Wright, Inc., Route 7, Box 3-5, Amarillo, TX 79118; tel. 806-622-1819 [Vendor G0358]

Marie Wright, RT 1, Box 7, Bonnerdale, AR 71933; tel. 501-356-3488 [Vendor G0091]

Mildred S. Wright, 140 Briggs, Beaumont, TX 77707-2329; tel. 409-832-2308 [Vendor G0145]

Wm. E. Wright, 11710 Green Bay, Houston, TX 77024; tel. 713-975-1188 [Vendor G0363]

Mrs. Manly Yielding, 2300 Brookshire Place, Birmingham, AL 35213 [Vendor G0168]

Mary Lynch Young, 2470 Plata Drive, Santa Rosa, CA 95403; tel. 707-527-8388 [Vendor G0106]

Young & Sons Enterprises, PO Box 759, Apache, OK 73006-0759; tel. 405-588-2093 [Vendor G0405]

Younkin Family News Bulletin, PO Box 340, Hancock, MD 21750-0340; tel. 301-678-6999; e-mail: DonnaL3@aol.com; fanfare@intrepid.net [Vendor G0392A]

Harry D. Zook, 110 Village Lane, Winter Park, FL 32792-3412; tel. 407-678-2372 [Vendor G0049]

Genealogical & Local History Books in Print

5th Edition

Family History Volume

FAMILY HISTORIES

1   **ABBE–ABBEY GEN., IN MEMORY OF JOHN ABBE & HIS DESC.**, by
C. Abbe and J.G. Nichols. 1916.
Cloth, $92.00. Paper, $82.00. 525pp. .... Vendor G0259

2   **MEM. OF CAPT. THOMAS ABBEY; ANC. & DESC. OF THE ABBEY
FAM.: PATHFINDERS, SOLDIERS, PIONEERS OF CT., ITS WEST.
RESERVE IN OH. & THE GREAT WEST.** 2nd ed., 1917.
Cloth, $36.50. Paper, $26.50. 175pp. .... Vendor G0259

3   **A GEN. REGISTER OF THE DESC. OF GEORGE ABBOT OF
ANDOVER, GEORGE OF ROWLEY, THOMAS OF ANDOVER,
ARTHUR OF IPSWICH, ROBERT OF BRANFORD, CONN., AND
GEORGE OF NORWALK, CONN.**, by A. and E. Abbot. 1847.
Cloth, $42.50. Paper, $32.50. 217pp. .... Vendor G0259

4   **DESC. OF GEO. ABBOTT OF ROWLEY, MA., & GEO. ABBOTT, JR.
OF ANDOVER**, by L. Abbott. 2 vols. 1906.
Cloth, $166.00. Paper, $156.00. 1,232pp. .... Vendor G0259

5   **F.C. ABBOTT 1856–1936**, by David L. Zolman. 1994. Indexed. Illus.
History of the **Abbott** family who moved from New Hampshire to Kansas to
Washington.
Cloth. $45.00, incl. p&h. 228pp. .... Vendor G0269

6   **JAMES SMITH ABBOTT**, by Ronald B. McIntire and David L. Zolman.
Indexed. Illus.
History of the first postmaster of Bunkerville, Nevada; includes his diaries,
collection of family photos, and excellent supporting information.
Cloth. $33.00, incl. p&h. 201pp. .... Vendor G0269

7   **WILLIAM ELIAS ABBOTT (1869–1949)**, by Ronald B. McIntire and David
L. Zolman. 1993. Indexed. Illus.
History of the first mayor of Mesquite, Nevada, and family stories of his
large family.
Cloth. $33.00. 265pp. .... Vendor G0269

8   **ABELL FAMILY IN AMERICA: ROBERT ABELL OF REHOBETH, MA.,
HIS ENGLISH ANC. & IMMIGR.; ABELL FAMS. IN ENGLAND**, by
H.A. Abell and L.P. Abell. 1940.
Cloth, $61.00. Paper, $51.00. 339pp. .... Vendor G0259

9   **ANC. & DESC. OF JONATHAN ABELL, WHO CAME FROM CONN. &
SETTLED IN SCHENECTADY CO., NY, ABOUT 1812**, by H.A. Abell.
1933.
Paper. $12.00. 61pp. .... Vendor G0259

10   **THE ABERCROMBIES OF BALTIMORE: GENEALOGICAL & BIO-
GRAPHICAL SKETCH OF THE FAMILY OF DAVID ABERCROMBIE**

WHO SETTLED IN BALTIMORE, MD., IN 1848, by R.T. Abercrombie. 1940.
Paper. $7.00. 35pp. .... Vendor G0259

11   **ADAIR HISTORY & GENEALOGY**, by J.B. Adair. 1924.
Cloth, $61.50. Paper, $51.50. 330pp. .... Vendor G0259

12   **ROBERT ADAIR (1770–1845), SOUTH CAROLINA TO MISSISSIPPI**, by Shirley B. Adair. 1995. Indexed. Illus.
Reid, Emerson, Hobbs, Worley, Thompson.
Paper. $16.50. 170pp. .... Vendor G0382

13   **ADAMS FAM. OF IPSWICH & NEWBURY, MASS. (Extr. Essex Antiq.).**
Paper. $8.50. 43pp. .... Vendor G0259

14   **ADAMS FAM. RECORDS, A GEN. AND BIOGR. HIST.: VOL. I, NO. 1**, by J.T. Adams. 1929.
Paper. $19.50. 108pp. .... Vendor G0259

15   **ANC. & DESC. OF ELIAS ADAMS, THE PIONEER, 600–1930**, by F.D. Adams. 1930.
Cloth, $51.00. Paper, $41.00. 274pp. .... Vendor G0259

16   **ANCESTORS OF CORA BELLE ADAMS 1881–1957—MY WORKING NOTEBOOK**, by William Sheperd West.
Adams family members include: John Emory, 1844–1935; Isaac, 1809–1877; Isaac, ca. 1790. Related families include **Gordy, Dashiell, Jones, Magee, Mcgee, Ward, Winder, Wootten, Cordry, Cordray, Crewe, Sterling, Hearn, Jones, Carter, Walters, Cannon, Inglis, Davis, Frizzell, Southern, de Chiel, Waters, Foxcroft, Robesoume** primarily in Sussex County, Delaware and in nearby counties on Maryland's Eastern Shore. Interesting charts, photographs, etc. planned. Your information welcome.
Cloth. $35.00. Approx. 200pp. .... Vendor G0308

17   **DESC. OF JAMES & WM. ADAMS OF LONDONDERRY, NOW DERRY, N.H.**, by A.N. Adams. 1894.
Paper. $15.00. 87pp. .... Vendor G0259

18   **GEN. & HIST. OF PART OF THE NEWBURY ADAMS FAM., FORMERLY OF DEVONSHIRE, ENG., DESC. OF ROBERT ADAMS & WIFE ELEANOR**, by S. Adams. 1895.
Paper. $12.50. 61pp. .... Vendor G0259

19   **GEN. HIST. OF HENRY ADAMS OF BRAINTREE MA & HIS DESC.; ALSO JOHN OF CAMBRIDGE**, by A. Adams. 1898.
Cloth, $165.00. Paper, $155.00. 1,246pp. .... Vendor G0259

20   **GEN. HIST. OF ROBERT ADAMS OF NEWBURY, MASS. & HIS DESC., 1675–1900**, by A. Adams. 1900.
Cloth, $82.50. Paper, $72.50. 564pp. .... Vendor G0259

21   **GEN. OF THE ADAMS FAM. OF KINGSTON, MASS.**, by G. Adams. 1861.
Paper. $12.50. 64pp. .... Vendor G0259

22 HENRY ADAMS OF SOMERSET, ENG. & BRAINTREE, MA.; ENG. ANCESTORS & SOME DESC., by J.G. Bartlett. 1927.
Cloth, $35.00. Paper, $25.00. 185pp. .... Vendor G0259

23 HIST. OF THE ADAMS FAM., by H. Whittemore. 1893.
Paper. $17.00. 84pp. .... Vendor G0259

24 HISTORY OF THE ADAMS FAMILY OF NO. STAFFORDSHIRE . . . WITH NUMEROUS PEDIGREE CHARTS & NOTES ON ALLIED FAMILIES, by Percy W.L. Adams. 1914 (London).
Cloth, $82.00. Paper, $72.00. 417+63pp. .... Vendor G0259

25 HISTORY OF THE THOMAS ADAMS & THOMAS HASTINGS FAMS. OF AMHERST, MASS., by H. Adams. 1880.
Paper. $12.50. 66pp. .... Vendor G0259

26 JEREMY ADAMS OF CAMBRIDGE, MASS. & HARTFORD, CONN. & HIS DESC., by A. Adams. 1955.
Paper. $9.00. 45pp. .... Vendor G0259

27 THE ADAMS FAMILY OF MARTHA'S VINEYARD, by Henry E. Scott, Jr. 1987. Illus.
Cloth. $23.50. 64pp. .... Vendor G0406

28 HISTORY OF ADDINGTON FAMILY IN U.S. AND ENGLAND, by H.M. Addington. 1931.
Cloth, $30.00. Paper, $20.00. 101pp. .... Vendor G0259

29 A RECORD OF THE AGEE FAMILY, by P.M. Agee. 1937.
Cloth, $62.50. Paper, $52.50. 330pp. .... Vendor G0259

30 [Agnew]. HEREDITARY SHERIFFS OF GALLOWAY, THEIR FOREBEARS & FRIENDS, THEIR COURTS & CUSTOMS OF THEIR TIMES WITH NOTES OF THE EARLY HIST., by Sir Andrew Agnew. 2 vols. 1893 (Scotland).
Cloth, $81.50/vol. Paper, $71.50/vol. 474+477pp. .... Vendor G0259

31 THE BOOK OF THE AGNEWS. JAMES AGNEW OF PA.; HIS RACE, ANC. & DESC., by M.V. Agnew, et al. 1926.
Cloth, $99.50. Paper, $89.50. 607pp. .... Vendor G0259

32 GEN. OF THE AINSWORTH FAMILIES IN AMERICA, by F.J. Parker. 1894.
Cloth, $42.00. Paper, $32.00. 212pp. .... Vendor G0259

33 OUR KINSFOLK (DESCENDANTS OF WM. AKERS OF NJ, CA. 1698), by W.R. Akers. 1957.
Paper. $19.50. 114pp. .... Vendor G0259

34 ALBEE FAMILY RECORDS, by R.S. Albee. 1920.
Cloth, $40.00. Paper, $30.00. 221pp. .... Vendor G0259

35 ALBRIGHT, CLAPP, BURK FAMILIES; INCLUDING: PHILIP AND ANNA CHRISTINA (CLAPP) ALBRIGHT, THEIR ANCESTORS AND DESCENDANTS, by Joseph H. Vance. 1988. Indexed. Illus.
Big page size: 8^1/2 x 11 inches. New genealogical discoveries in recent years make this the most up-to-date, accurate, comprehensive book on these families.

ALBRIGHT. Immigrant ancestor: Johannes **Albrecht** (John **Albright**), born 1695, in what is now western Germany. Arrived Philadelphia 8 Sep 1732 aboard ship *Johnson* with wife, Anna Barbara, and five minor children. A sixth child, Judith, was born in Pennsylvania. CLAPP. Immigrant ancestor: Johann Jost **Klapp** (Joseph **Clapp**), born 1669, Istha, Hesse. Family of fourteen, including wife, Anna Margaretha, arrived Philadelphia 27 Sep 1727 aboard ship *James Goodwill*. Settled in what is now Berks County, Pennsylvania. Two sons moved to North Carolina. BURK. Earliest known progenitor: Isaac **Burk**. Will dated 31 Dec 1833, filed Preble County, Ohio. Married Mrs. Esther (**Clapp**) **Albright,** about 1793 in North Carolina. Esther was daughter of John Ludwig and Anna Margaret **Clapp** and widow of John Rick **Albright.**

Write or call author for free brochure.

Cloth, $37.50. Paper, $29.00. 362pp. . . . . Vendor G0239

36 **THE ALBRITE–ALBRIGHT FAMILY IN SHENANDOAH & ROCKINGHAM COUNTIES, VA & HARDY CO., WV,** by Patricia Turner Ritchie. 1990. Indexed.
Paper. $17.00. 120pp. . . . . Vendor G0365

37 **DESCENDANTS OF POLLY & EBENEZER ALDEN, WHO WERE 6TH IN DESCENT FROM JOHN ALDEN, THE PILGRIM,** by E. Alden & H. Shaw. 1903.
Paper. $19.50. 100pp. . . . . Vendor G0259

38 **ELIAB ALDEN OF MIDDLEBOROUGH, MASS. & CAIRO, NY: HIS ALDEN ANCESTORS & HIS DESCENDANTS,** by Charles Henry Alden. 1905.
Paper. $11.00. 55pp. . . . . Vendor G0259

39 **GEN. OF FOURTEEN FAMS. OF THE EARLY SETTLERS OF NEW ENGLAND, OF THE NAMES OF ALDEN, ADAMS, ARNOLD, BASS, BILLINGS, CAPEN ET AL,** by E. Thayer. 1835.
Cloth, $38.00. Paper, $28.00. 180pp. Vendor G0259

40 **MEM. OF THE DESC. OF THE HON. JOHN ALDEN, INCL. SUPPL. TO 1869,** by E. Alden. 1867.
Cloth, $32.50. Paper, $22.50. 184pp. Vendor G0259

41 **THE ANC. AND DESC. OF ISAAC ALDEN AND IRENE SMITH, HIS WIFE, 1599–1903,** by H.C. Fielding. 1903.
Cloth, $31.50. Paper, $21.50. 144pp. Vendor G0259

42 **THE DESC. OF DANIEL ALDEN, 6TH IN DESC. FROM JOHN ALDEN, THE PILGRIM,** by F. Alden. 1923.
Paper. $17.00. 113pp. . . . . Vendor G0259

43 **[Alden]. THE STORY OF A PILGRIM FAMILY FROM THE MAYFLOWER TO THE PRESENT TIME (1899), WITH AUTOBIOGRAPHY, RECOLLECTIONS, LETTERS, INCIDENTS AND GENEALOGY,** by Rev. John Alden. 1889.
Cloth, $78.00. Paper, $68.00. 441pp. Vendor G0259

44 **"HI, COUSIN": THE MASON J. ALDRICH FAM. HIST.,** by M. Aldrich. 1967.
Cloth, $31.00. Paper, $21.00. 125pp. t.s. . . . . Vendor G0259

45   ALDWORTH–ELBRIDGE FAM., **1590–1811**, by E. Salisbury. 1885.
Paper. $8.00. 40pp. .... Vendor G0259

46   **ALEXANDER AND PHILLIPS WITH ALLIED FAMILIES,** by Everett L.
Alexander. 1982. Indexed. Illus.
Cloth, $17.50. Paper, $14.00. 191pp. .... Vendor G0260

47   **DESCENT OF THE SCOTTISH ALEXANDERS; GEN. SKETCH, WITH
DISCUSSIONS OF SOME HIST. MATTERS,** by F.A. Sondley. 1912.
Paper. $15.00. 73pp. .... Vendor G0259

48   **EARLIER GEN. OF THE ALEXANDER FAM. OF VA.,** by S.M. Culbertson.
1934.
Paper. $9.50. 46pp. .... Vendor G0259

49   **FAMILY BIOGRAPHIES OF THE FAMILIES OF ALEXANDER,
WILKINSON, SPARR & GUTHRIE, WITH SKETCHES & MEMORI-
ALS,** by Wm. G. Alexander. 1892.
Cloth, $39.00. Paper, $29.00. 180pp. .... Vendor G0259

50   **NOTES ON THE ALEXANDER FAM. OF S.C. & GA. & CONNECTIONS,**
by H.A. Alexander. 1954.
Cloth, $33.00. Paper, $23.00. 142pp. .... Vendor G0259

51   **RECORD OF THE DESCENDANTS OF JOHN ALEXANDER OF
LANARKSHIRE, SCOTLAND, & HIS WIFE MARGARET GLASSON,
WHO EMIGRATED FROM CO. ARMAGH, IRELAND, TO CHESTER
CO. PA.,** by J.A. Alexander. 1878.
Cloth, $46.00. Paper, $36.00. 220pp. .... Vendor G0259

52   **THE ALEXANDERS OF ME.,** by D. Alexander. 1908.
Paper. $19.00. 129pp. .... Vendor G0259

53   **GEN. HIST. OF FAM. OF THOMAS ALGER OF TAUNTON &
BRIDGEWATER,** by A.M. Alger. 1876.
Paper. $12.00. 60pp. .... Vendor G0259

54   **THE THOMAS ALGER FAMILY, JABEZ ALGER LINE, 1645–1994, OF
TAUNTON, MA.,** by Eleanor M. Crouch. 1994.
Paper. $19.50. 165pp. .... Vendor G0259

55   **A BRIEF HIST. OF LEWIS ALLEN OF FISHER'S IS. & NEW LON-
DON, CONN., & HIS DESC., FROM 1699–1954,** by M.A. Phinney. 1954.
Cloth, $44.50. Paper, $34.50. 207pp. .... Vendor G0259

56   **ALLEN FAMILY HISTORY,** by J. Montgomery Seaver. Illus.
Paper. $9.00. 86pp. .... Vendor G0011

57   **ALLEN FAMILY HISTORY,** by J.M. Seaver.
Paper. $17.50. 86pp. .... Vendor G0259

58   **ALLEN FAM. OF KENTUCKY. EXTR. FROM "HIST. FAMS. OF KY.,"**
by T.M. Green.
Paper. $11.00. 55pp. .... Vendor G0259

59   **ALLEN FAMILY OF MANCHESTER, MASS., TO 1886,** by J. Price. 1888.
Paper. $9.50. 47pp. .... Vendor G0259

60   **ALLEN MEM. (1ST SERIES) DESC. OF EDW. ALLEN OF NANTUCKET, MASS., 1690–1905**, by O.P. Allen. 1905.
Cloth, $31.50. Paper, $21.50. 123pp. .... Vendor G0259

61   **ALLEN MEMORIAL, 2ND SERIES. DESC. OF SAMUEL ALLEN OF WINDSOR, CT., 1640–1907**, O.P. Allen. 1907.
Cloth, $49.50. Paper, $39.50. 303pp. .... Vendor G0259

62   **ANCESTORS OF PHILIP & JEAN ALLEN**, by Philip W. Allen. 1995.
Includes **McEwen, Creighton, Ott, Luers, Sowash, Gaumer, Estep, Wymer, Werts, Polhemus, Cornell, Rapalje, Nyssen, Bergen, Vanderveer, Haring, Gulick, Quick, Cortelyou, Vanderbeek, Haff, De Motte, Smith, Van Nice, Stout.**
Paper. $15.00. 47pp. .... Vendor G0373

63   **DESCENDANTS OF WILLIAM ALLEN OF PRUDENCE ISLAND, RHODE ISLAND, b. 1640 (ENGLAND), EMIGR. TO RHODE ISLAND ca. 1660**, by Devere Allen. 1942–7.
Allen/Allin.
Cloth, $63.00. Paper, $53.00. 338pp. t.s. .... Vendor G0259

64   **GEN. & HIST. OF THE ALLEN FAM. OF DEDHAM & MEDFIELD, MA., 1637–1898**, by F. Hutchinson. 1896.
Paper. $16.00. 80pp. .... Vendor G0259

65   **GEN. HIST. OF THE ALLEN FAM. AND SOME OF THEIR CONNEC-TIONS**, by F.M. Stoddard. 1891.
Cloth, $33.00. Paper, $23.00. 136pp. .... Vendor G0259

66   **GEN. OF SAMUEL ALLEN OF WINDSOR, CONN., AND SOME OF HIS DESC.**, by W.S. Allen. 1876.
Paper. $15.00. 76pp. .... Vendor G0259

67   **GEN. OF THE ALLEN & WITTER FAM. AND THEIR DESC.**, by A.W. Allen. 1872.
Cloth, $47.50. Paper, $37.50. 251pp. .... Vendor G0259

68   **THE ALLENS OF LITTLE EGYPT**, by Hardy Lee Hiram Allen and Corben E. Allen, Editor. 1995. Indexed. Illus.
Allan, Allen, Allin, Allon. The oldest Allen we have discovered in our direct line during our research is Robert Allin who was born in 1664 in Ulster County, North Ireland. We found that his forefathers came from the Island of Bute which is located in the Firth of the Clyde River, just off the southeast coast of the mainland of Scotland. Robert arrived in America on the ship Charles at Port Tobacco, Maryland in 1690 as an indentured servant. Thomas was the only child we have discovered who was born to Robert and NN Allin. Robert taught Thomas the family trade, a worker-in-wood. Thomas died in Virginia in 1770. Three sons are known to be born to him and NN Allin. They are: Rhoda/Rhody Allin, born 1742 in Charles County, Maryland, and died in Jefferson County, Illinois in 1820, and is buried there in Old Union Cemetery. George was born in 1751; he lived in Pennsylvania and moved to Sumner County, Tennessee, ND. Reuben was born ND, and he settled in Shenandoah County, Virginia. We have not researched the offsprings of the last two brothers, George and Reuben.
Rhoda/Rhody Allen is the "high priest" of our Allen line. His children by his

first wife (Mary Emile [**Ransom**]) are: Theopholus was born in 1770; Mary Emily, Jr. was born in 1773; Sarah was born in 1775, the same year the Revolutionary War broke out, Henry Davis was born 26 March 1782; Rhodam was born 10 April 1785; and Elizabeth was born in 1787. The three sons were born in North Carolina. Rhoda/Rhody and his second wife, Lucinda (**Overby**) produced at least three children; Margaret N., born in Sumner County, Tennessee in 1810; John Wesley, born 4 August 1813, and married Sarah (**Owens**) 24 November 1833 in Jefferson County, Illinois. John Wesley died February 1889 in Jefferson County, Illinois and was buried there in Old Shiloh Cemetery in the plot of his brother-in-law Captain Peter Owens. The third child of Rhoda and Lucinda is William S. Allen who inherited land in Illinois from Rhoda/Rhody Allen 2 June 1837. We know very little about his son. We were more interested in John Wesley, Methodist Minister, wheelwright, and blacksmith because he is in our direct line to Rhoda/Rhody Allen.

John Wesley and Sarah (Owens) Allen's children are: Hiram Richard born 18 January 1834, and died February 1917; William Burton, born 30 January 1836, and died 5 November 1896; Edward V.C., born 1838, and died in 1846; John Robert, born 1840, and died in 1907; Rhodah E., born 5 January 1845, and died 20 May 1846. All of the above were born in Jefferson County, Illinois. Edy D was born 29 September 1843; Jane F. was born 3 May 1847; Mary L. was born 25 August 1849, and died 25 August 1931. (All the girls were born in Washington County, Illinois.) Harvey N. was born 22 September 1855, and died 15 November 1926 in Montgomery County, Illinois.

We have researched Captain Henry Davis Allen's line down to the present. He spent much of his life in Northern Alabama, near the northern border of Tennessee. William Burton's life has been researched down to the present. Hiram Richard Allen's line, the author's line, has been thoroughly researched.

Your family line probably fits in the picture somewhere—use your family's Oral Traditional information as your base from which to start your search. Notice all the places the Allens have lived as described in The Allens of Little Egypt, and look for resemblances of the photographs to those of your immediate family. Sometimes the resemblances are striking. Don't forget that Thomas Allen had two sons, one who lived in Pennsylvania and one in Virginia, whom we know nothing about. Could you have been a descendant of one of them? You are an Allen and you need this book. If you fail to get it, you will kick yourself later. The older you get, the more you need to know exactly who you are. We hope you have a happy search on your own line.

The book is 8¹/₂ x 11 inches, weighs almost four pounds, and its 33 two-column pages contain the first names of 330 Allens, the first names of more than 9,600 non-Allens, and 1,300 non-Allen family names. One chapter contains more than 260 photographs, some in color. The title and author's name are imprinted in gold on the front and spine of the blue back.

Compiler and Editor of this book
The Allens of Little Egypt
Corben E. Allen

Cloth. $45 for the standard book, $60 for the deluxe edition with golden edges. 450pp. .... Vendor G0240

69 GEN. SKETCHES OF THE ALLEN FAM. OF MEDFIELD; WITH AN ACCOUNT OF THE GOLDEN WEDDING OF ELLIS AND LUCY

ALLEN, ALSO OF GERSHOM AND ABIGAIL (ALLEN) ADAMS, by J. Allen. 1869.
Paper. $15.00. 88pp. .... Vendor G0259

70   MEMORIAL OF JOSEPH & LUCY CLARK ALLEN (NORTH-BOROUGH, MASS.), by E.W. Allen. 1891.
Cloth, $47.00. Paper, $37.00. 246pp. .... Vendor G0259

71   THE TANDY & JOANNA ALLEN FAMILY HISTORY, by Philip W. Allen and Neva L. Callison. 1990. Indexed.
Includes descendants (Cassity, Prather, Goltry, Johnson, Wortman, etc.) of Allens.
Paper. $13.00. 148pp. .... Vendor G0373

72   WALTER ALLEN OF NEWBURY, MASS., 1640, & SOME DESCEN-DANTS, by A.H. Bent. 1896.
Paper. $13.00. 66pp. .... Vendor G0259

73   HIST. OF THE ALLERTON FAM. IN THE U.S., 1585–1885, & DESC. OF ISAAC ALLERTON, by Allerton & Currier. 1900.
Cloth, $37.50. Paper, $27.50. 149pp. .... Vendor G0259

74   ABRAHAM ALLING OF OYSTER BAY, NEW YORK (abt. 1630–post 1711), by Jane McMurtry Allen. 1993. Indexed. Illus.
Some of his descendants and related families: Allyn, Clapp, Couch, Feake, Golder, Harcourt, Hunt, Ludlam/Ludlum, Ludlow, Shadbolt, Thorne, Van Nostrand, Whaley.
Cloth. $35.00. 377pp. .... Vendor G0005

75   HIST. & GEN. RECORD OF THE ALLING–ALLENS OF NEW HAVEN, CONN., THE DESC. OF ROGER ALLING, 1ST, & JOHN ALLING, SR., FROM 1639, by G.P. Allen. 1899.
Cloth, $57.50. Paper, $47.50. 317pp. .... Vendor G0259

76   HIST. OF THE ALISON–ALLISON FAM. IN EUR. & AMER., 1135–1893, by L. Morrison. 1893.
Cloth, $51.00. Paper, $41.00. 328pp. .... Vendor G0259

77   HIST. OF THE ALLISON FAM. OF PENN., 1750–1912, by J.L. Allison. 1912.
Cloth, $32.50. Paper, $22.50. 115pp. .... Vendor G0259

78   [Allyn]. ANC. & DESC. OF NANCY ALLYN (FOOTE) WEBB, REV. EDW. WEBB, & JOSEPH WILKINS COOCH, by M.E.W. Cooch. 1919.
Cloth, $35.00. Paper, $25.00. 157pp. .... Vendor G0259

79   SKETCH OF MATTHEW ALLYN OF CAMBRIDGE, MASS., by J. Allyn. 1884.
Paper. $7.50. 37pp. .... Vendor G0259

80   ALSTON–ALSTONS OF N. & S. CARO., COMP. FROM ENG., COL. & FAM. REC., WITH PERSONAL REMINISCENCES & NOTES OF SOME ALLIED FAMS., by J.A. Groves. 1901.
Cloth, $68.50. Paper, $58.50. 367pp. .... Vendor G0259

81   ALTEN–VON ALTEN: PROOF OF THE 400 YEAR-OLD FAMILY RU-MOR, by James F. Bestman. 1991. Illus.
Genealogical interpretation of facts and surviving evidence that show the

connection between the Hannover, Germany **Von Alten** family and the Lathwehren, Germany **Alten** Family. (25 years of research.)
Paper. $35.00. 86pp. .... Vendor G0377

82 **DESC. OF ALEXANDER ALVORD OF WINDSOR, CONN., & NORTHAMPTON, MASS.**, by S.M. Alvord. 1905.
Cloth, $113.00. Paper, $103.00. 823pp. .... Vendor G0259

83 **A RECORD OF THE DESCENDANTS OF ROGER AMADOWNE OF REHOBETH, MASS.**, by Frank E. Best. 1904.
Cloth, $36.00. Paper, $26.00. 165pp. .... Vendor G0259

84 **GEN. MEM. OF DESC. OF SAMUEL AMES OF CANTERBURY, N.H.**, by J. Kimball. 1890.
Paper. $11.00. 55pp. .... Vendor G0259

85 **THE DESC. OF HUGH AMORY, 1605–1805**, by G. Meredith. 1901.
Cloth, $68.50. Paper, $58.50. 385pp. .... Vendor G0259

86 **"OUR ANCESTRY" [AMOS, BEVERLY, GOODALE, GRAHAM, KEENEY, MILLER, WALTON]**, by Hazel Crane Amos. 1955.
Cloth, $42.00. Paper, $32.00. 202pp. .... Vendor G0259

87 **ANDERSON GEN., IN PART, OF THE ANDERSON-OWEN-BEALL FAMILIES**, by G.J. Anderson. 1909.
Cloth, $34.00. Paper, $24.00. 159pp. .... Vendor G0259

88 **ANDERSON–KROGH GENEALOGY: ANC. LINES & DESC.**, by L.W. Hansen. 1956.
Cloth, $61.50. Paper, $51.50. 323pp. .... Vendor G0259

89 **ANDERSON–OVERTON GENEALOGY. A CONTINUATION OF "ANDERSON FAM. RECORDS" (1936) & "EARLY DESC. OF WM. OVERTON & ELIZABETH WATERS OF VA." (1938)**, by W.P. Anderson. 1945.
Cloth, $69.50. Paper, $59.50. 376pp. .... Vendor G0259

90 **ANDERSONS OF GOLDMINE, HANOVER COUNTY, VA.**, by E.L. Anderson.
Paper. $7.00. 36pp. .... Vendor G0259

91 **THOMAS ANDREW, IMMIGRANT. A GEN. OF THE POSTERITY OF THOMAS ANDREW, ONE OF THE EARLY SETTLERS OF NEW ENGLAND**, by L.C. Andrew. 1971.
Cloth, $36.50. Paper, $26.50. 166pp. .... Vendor G0259

92 **ANDREWS MEM.; GEN. OF THE ANDREWS OF TAUNTON & STOUGHTON, MASS., DESC. OF JOHN & HANNAH ANDREWS OF BOSTON, 1656–1886**, by G. Andrews. 1887.
Paper. $17.00. 86pp. .... Vendor G0259

93 **GEN. HIST. OF JOHN AND MARY ANDREWS, WHO SETTLED IN FARMINGTON, CONN., 1640, DESC. TO 1872**, by A. Andrews. 1872.
Cloth, $92.00. Paper, $82.00. 652pp. .... Vendor G0259

94   HIST. OF THE ANDREWS FAM. A GEN. OF ROBERT ANDREWS &
     DESC., **1635–1890**, by H. Andrews. 1890.
     Cloth, $45.00. Paper, $35.00. 234pp. .... Vendor G0259

95   **"POSTMARKED HUDSON": LETTERS OF SARAH ANDREWS TO
     HER BROTHER JAMES A. ANDREWS, 1864–5, WITH GEN. OF THE
     ANDREWS FAM.**, edited by W. Miller. 1955.
     Paper. $15.00. 76pp. .... Vendor G0259

96   WM. ANDREWS OF HARTFORD, CT. & HIS DESC. IN THE DIRECT
     LINE TO ASA ANDREWS OF HARTLAND, CT. & HARTFORD, OHIO,
     by F. Andrews. 1938.
     Paper. $14.00. 69pp. .... Vendor G0259

97   A FEW FACTS ABOUT THE ANDRUS FAMILY, ITS RELATIVES &
     ANCESTORS (SOME DESCENDANTS OF WM. OF WALLINGFORD,
     CT.), by L.R. Andrus. 1932.
     Paper. $12.00. 58pp. .... Vendor G0259

98   SUPPLEMENT TO THE ABOVE, by L.R. Andrus. 1933.
     Cloth, $49.00. Paper, $39.00. 379pp. .... Vendor G0259

99   THE ANCESTRY OF EMILY JANE ANGELL, **1844–1910**, by Dean
     Crawford Smith; edited by Melinde Lutz Sanborn. 1992. Indexed. Illus.
     Cloth. $43.50. 680pp. .... Vendor G0406

100 SKETCH OF THE LIFE & SOME DESCENDANTS OF DEWALD
     ANKENY: b. GERMANY, 1728; CAME TO AMERICA, 1746, & SETTLED
     IN LANCASTER CO.; MOVED, 1762 TO MD. & DIED IN 1781; WITH
     SKETCH OF DESC. OF MICHAEL WALTER & CATHERINE ANKENY,
     by C. Shultz. 1948.
     Cloth, $38.00. Paper, $28.00. 100+82pp. .... Vendor G0259

101 ANTHON GENEALOGY, by S. Fish. 1930.
     Cloth, $49.50. Paper, $39.50. 214+xlpp. .... Vendor G0259

102 GEN. OF THE ANTHONY FAM., **1495–1904**, by C.L. Anthony. 1904.
     Cloth, $59.00. Paper, $49.00. 379pp. .... Vendor G0259

103 GEN. OF THE DESC. OF LAWRENCE & MARY ANTISELL OF NOR-
     WICH & WILLINGTON, CT: INCL. SOME RECORDS OF CHRISTO-
     PHER ANTISELL OF SRADUFF, BIRR, (KING'S CO.) IRE., by M.
     Wyman. 1908.
     Cloth, $63.00. Paper, $53.00. 335pp. .... Vendor G0259

104 RECORDS OF THE ANTRIM FAM. OF AMERICA, by H.S. Antrim. 1899.
     Cloth, $45.00. Paper, $35.00. 232pp. .... Vendor G0259

105 APPLER FAMILY HISTORY, by Charles Ross Appler. 1976.
     Cloth, $54.00. Paper, $44.00. 280pp. .... Vendor G0259

106 APPLETON FAMILY GENEALOGY, by W.S. Appleton. 1874.
     Paper. $10.00. 54pp. .... Vendor G0259

107 THE DESC. OF JAMES ARDERY OF FRANKLIN CO., PENN., INCL.

ALLIED FAMILIES READ, ELDER, MCNUTT, MCGRIFFIN AND OTHERS, by E.C. Floyd. 1984.
Paper. $14.00. 112pp. .... Vendor G0259

108 **RICHARD AREY OF MARTHA'S VINEYARD & SOME OF HIS DESC.**, by R.V. Chamberlin. 1932–3.
Paper. $10.00. 51pp. .... Vendor G0259

109 **THE FAMILY OF JOSEPH ARMINGTON IN AMERICA, 1713 TO 1994**, by Albert A. Armington and Walker Craig Armington. 1994. Indexed. Illus.
Cloth. $26.00. 183pp. .... Vendor G0272

110 **ARMISTEAD FAMILY, 1635–1910**, by V.A. Garber. 1910.
Cloth, $59.50. Paper, $49.50. 319pp. .... Vendor G0259

111 **DESCENDANTS OF WILLIAM ARMISTEAD OF VIRGINIA**, by Carol A. Hauk. 1995. Indexed.
Paper. $60.00. 704pp. .... Vendor G0340

112 **A GEN. RECORD OF THE ARMS FAM. IN THIS COUNTRY, EMBRACING ALL THE KNOWN DESC. OF WILLIAM 1ST**, by E.W. Arms. 1877.
Paper. $11.00. 57pp. .... Vendor G0259

113 **CHRONICLES OF THE ARMSTRONGS**, by J.L. Armstrong. 1903.
Cloth, $62.00. Paper, $52.00. 407pp. .... Vendor G0259

114 **HISTORY OF THE ARMSTRONG FAMILY, 980–1939, & GENEALOGY OF DAVID ARMSTRONG & SARAH HARRIS ARMSTRONG, 1746–1939**, by T.E. Armstrong & J.H. Moyer. 1939.
Cloth, $53.00. Paper, $43.00. 270pp. .... Vendor G0259

115 **THE STORY OF THE ARNDTS. THE LIFE, ANTECEDANTS & DESC. OF BERNHARD ARNDT, WHO EMIGR. TO PA. IN 1731**, by J.S. Arndt. 1922.
Cloth, $77.50. Paper, $67.50. 428pp. .... Vendor G0259

116 **ARNOLD–LUCKEY FAMILY TIES: AUTHORIZED HIST. & GEN., COMPLETE**, by L.W. Arnold & E.Z. Luckey. 1931.
Cloth, $35.00. Paper, $25.00. 168pp. .... Vendor G0259

117 **ARNOLD MEM.; WM. ARNOLD OF PROVIDENCE & PAWTUXET, 1587–1675, & GEN. OF HIS DESC.**, by E. Arnold. 1935.
Cloth, $59.50. Paper, $49.50. 311pp. .... Vendor G0259

118 **DESC. OF WM. ARNOLD OF HINGHAM, MA., WITH COOKE, HARRIS & MOWRY FAMS.**, by E. Richardson. 1876.
Paper. $14.00. 69pp. .... Vendor G0259

119 **ARROYO AND VELOZ: A FAMILY HISTORY**, by Rodney L. Arroyo. 1993. Illus.
Paper. $29.95. 87pp. .... Vendor G0395

120 **ASHCRAFT FAMILY DESCENDANTS OF DANIEL**, by Martha Ashcraft Neal. 1994. Indexed. Illus.
Four centuries of **Ashcraft** history and almost 4,000 descendants of the original Ashcraft immigrant. Well-documented and comprehensive Appendix.
Cloth. $34.00. 665pp. .... Vendor G0105

121 **ASHLEY GEN. A HIST. OF THE DESC. OF ROBERT ASHLEY OF SPRINGFIELD, MA.**, by F.B. Trowbridge. 1896.
Cloth, $70.00. Paper, $60.00. 483pp. . . . . Vendor G0259

122 **JOSIAH ASKEW OF EDGECOMBE COUNTY, NORTH CAROLINA**, by Alice Ann Askew. 1988. Indexed. Illus.
Includes other surnames of **Blackstock, Burch, Carroll, Cathey, Dickinson, Dupree, Hearne, Jernigan, Oglethorpe, Russell**, and many others.
Cloth. $25.00. 200pp. . . . . Vendor G0284

123 **ASPINWALL GENEALOGY [PETER ASPINWALL OF BROOKLINE, MA]**, by A.A. Aspinwall. 1901.
Cloth, $44.50. Paper, $34.50. 262pp. . . . . Vendor G0259

124 **JOSEPH ATKINS: STORY OF A FAMILY**, by F.H. Atkins. 1891.
Cloth, $35.00. Paper, $25.00. 158pp. . . . . Vendor G0259

125 **GEN. RECORD OF ATLEE FAM. OF LANCASTER CO., PENN.**, by E. A. Barber. 1884.
Cloth, $32.00. Paper, $22.00. 130pp. . . . . Vendor G0259

126 **A GEN. REGISTER OF THE DESC. IN THE MALE LINE OF DAVID ATWATER, OF NEW HAVEN, CONN., TO THE 6TH GENERATION**, by E.E. Atwater. 1873.
Paper. $12.50. 64pp. . . . . Vendor G0259

127 **[Atwater]. HIST. & GEN.**, by F. Atwater. Vol. I, 1901.
Cloth, $86.50. Paper, $76.50. 492pp. . . . . Vendor G0259

128 **[Atwater]. HIST. & GEN.**, by F. Atwater. Vol. II, 1907.
Cloth, $58.00. Paper, $48.00. 304pp. . . . . Vendor G0259

129 **[Atwood]. YE ATTE WODE ANNALS, 1–4**, by E. Atwood. 1928.
Paper. $16.50. 90pp. . . . . Vendor G0259

130 **JOHN & ELIZABETH AUCHINCLOSS; THEIR ANC. & DESC.**, by J.R. Auchincloss & C.A. Fowler. 1957.
Paper. $13.50. 67pp. . . . . Vendor G0259

131 **FAM. HIST. AND GEN. OF THE DESC. OF ROBERT AUGUR OF NEW HAVEN COLONY**, by E.P. Augur. 1904.
Cloth, $49.00. Paper, $39.00. 260pp. . . . . Vendor G0259

132 **AULL AND MARTIN GENEALOGY**, by W.F. Aull. 1920.
Cloth, $38.50. Paper, $28.50. 189pp. . . . . Vendor G0259

133 **A GEN. OF THE DESC. OF ROBERT AUSTIN OF KINGSTOWN, R.I.**, by E.A. Moore. 1951.
Cloth, $119.00. Paper, $109.00. 738pp. . . . . Vendor G0259

134 **THE DESC. OF RICHARD AUSTIN OF CHARLESTOWN, MASS., 1638**, by E.A. Moore & W.A. Day. 1951 (?).
Cloth, $99.50. Paper, $89.50. 608pp. . . . . Vendor G0259

135 **FAM. & DESC. OF CAPT. JOHN AUTRY**, by M.B. Autry. 1964.
Cloth, $41.00. Paper, $31.00. 209pp. . . . . Vendor G0259

136 **THE AUXIER FAMILY**, by Dr. Dave Auxier. 1995. Indexed. Illus.
A genealogy containing 17,200 names and 6,300 marriages in 12 generations
dating back to 1685 in France.
Cloth. $60.00. 704pp. .... Vendor G0362

137 **AVERELL–AVERY FAM. A RECORD OF DESC. OF WM. & ABIGAIL
AVERELL OF IPSWICH, MA.**, by C.A. Avery. 2 vols. 1906 & 1914.
Cloth, $159.00. Paper, $149.00. 1,094pp. .... Vendor G0259

138 **AVERY, FAIRCHILD & PARK FAMS. OF MA., CT. & R.I.**, by S.P. Avery.
1919.
Cloth, $35.00. Paper, $25.00. 169pp. .... Vendor G0259

139 **AVERY NOTES & QUERIES. A QUARTERLY MAGAZINE DEVOTED
TO THE HIST. OF THE GROTON AVERYS, # 1–18**, edited by E.M. Avery.
1898–1902.
Cloth, $47.00. Paper, $37.00. 246pp. .... Vendor G0259

140 **AVERY (OF DEDHAM MA) GEN. RECORD OF THE DEDHAM
BRANCH OF THE AVERY FAM. IN AMER., WITH 1987 INDEX**, by
Carter and Holmes. 1893.
Cloth, $68.00. Paper, $58.00. 366pp. .... Vendor G0259

141 **CAPT. JOHN AVERY, PRES. JUDGE AT THE WHOREKILL IN DELA.
BAY & HIS DESC.**, by E.J. Sellers. 1908.
Paper. $11.00. 55pp. .... Vendor G0259

142 **THE AVERYS OF GROTON, CT., GEN. & BIOGR.**, by H.D. Sweet. 1894.
Cloth, $98.00. Paper, $88.00. 698pp. .... Vendor G0259

143 **THE GROTON AVERY CLAN**, by E.M. and C.H. Avery. 2 vols. 1912.
Cloth, $119.00/vol. Paper, $109.00/vol. 785+740pp. .... Vendor G0259

144 **[Avery]. WARREN, LITTLE, LOTHROP, PARK, DIX, WHITMAN,
FAIRCHILD, PLATT, WHEELER, LANE & AVERY PED. OF SAM'L
PUTNAM AVERY**, by S. Avery. 1925.
Cloth, $54.00. Paper, $44.00. 292pp. .... Vendor G0259

145 **THE AXFORDS OF OXFORD, NJ: A GENEALOGY BEGINNING IN
1725**, by Wm. C. Armstrong. 1931.
Paper. $16.00. 78pp. .... Vendor G0259

146 **AXTELL RECORD: DESC. OF HENRY AXTELL, OF MORRIS CO.,
N.J.**, by E.S. Axtell. 1886.
Paper. $14.00. 68pp. .... Vendor G0259

147 **ARTHUR AYLSWORTH & HIS DESC. IN AMER.**, by H.E. Aylsworth;
edited by J.N. Arnold. 1887.
Cloth, $105.00. Paper, $95.00. 632pp. .... Vendor G0259

148 **AYMAR FAM. OF N.Y.** (extr. from "Huguenot Soc. of Amer."), by B. Aymar.
1903.
Paper. $13.00. 63pp. .... Vendor G0259

149 **AYRES GENEALOGY**, by Thomas D. Ayres. (1972) reprint 1995. Indexed.
Some of the descendants of Captain John **Ayres** of Brookfield, Massa-
chusetts.
Paper. $20.00. 66pp. .... Vendor G0344

150 GEN. OF THE AYRES FAM. OF FAIRFIELD CO., CONN., by J.N. States. 1916.
Cloth, $32.50. Paper, $22.50. 127pp. .... Vendor G0259

151 RECORD OF DESC. OF CAPT. JOHN AYRES OF BROOKFIELD, MASS., by W.H. Whitmore. 1870.
Paper. $11.00. 55pp. .... Vendor G0259

152 BABB FAMILIES OF AMERICA, by Jean A. Sargent. 1994. Indexed. Illus.
Cloth. $49.00. 624pp. .... Vendor G0369

153 BABBITT FAM. HIST., 1643–1900, by W.B. Browne. 1912.
Cloth, $111.00. Paper, $101.00. 761pp. .... Vendor G0259

154 BABCOCK AND ALLIED FAMILIES, by L.E. de Forest. 1928.
Cloth, $33.50. Paper, $23.50. 137pp. .... Vendor G0259

155 BABCOCK GENEALOGY, by S. Babcock. 1903.
Cloth, $91.00. Paper, $81.00. 670pp. .... Vendor G0259

156 GEN. RECORD OF NATHANIEL BABCOCK, SIMEON MAIN, ISAAC MINER, EZEKIEL MAIN, by C.H. Brown. 1909.
Cloth, $58.00. Paper, $57.00. 362pp. .... Vendor G0259

157 ISAIAH BABCOCK, SR., & DESC., by A.E. Babcock. 1903.
Paper. $19.50. 119pp. .... Vendor G0259

158 BACKENSTOSS FAMILY ASSOCIATION OF AMERICA [GENEAL-OGY], compiled by the Family. 1949.
Cloth, $39.50. Paper, $29.50. 188pp. .... Vendor G0259

159 BACKUS FAMILIES OF EARLY NEW ENGLAND, by Reno W. Backus. 1966.
Cloth, $42.50. Paper, $32.50. 199pp. .... Vendor G0259

160 GEN. MEM. OF THE BACKUS FAM., WITH PRIVATE JOURNAL OF JAMES BACKUS BEARING ON 1ST SETTLEMENT OF OHIO AT MARIETTA, by W. Backus. 1889.
Cloth, $70.00. Paper, $60.00. 392pp. .... Vendor G0259

161 BACON & ALLIED FAMILIES: A FAMILY DIRECTORY. 1958.
Cloth, $66.00. Paper, $56.00. 370pp. .... Vendor G0259

162 BACON GEN. MICHAEL BACON OF DEDHAM, 1640, AND HIS DESC., by T.W. Baldwin. 1915.
Cloth, $54.00. Paper, $44.00. 422pp. .... Vendor G0259

163 "BACON'S ADVENTURE", WITH BACON & WOOD GENEALOGIES, by Herbert M. Bacon. 1948.
Cloth, $39.50. Paper, $29.50. 197pp. .... Vendor G0259

164 GILES BADGER & HIS DESC., by J.C. Badger. 1909.
Paper. $12.50. 64pp. .... Vendor G0259

165 GEN. OF JOHANNES BAER, 1749–1910, by D.M.and R.B. Bare. 1910.
Cloth, $54.00. Paper, $44.00. 288pp. .... Vendor G0259

166 ACCTS. OF 2ND, 3RD AND 12TH ANNUAL GATHERINGS OF THE

BAILEY-BAYLEY FAM. ASSOC. 1894–1908.
Paper. $18.75. 123pp. .... Vendor G0259

167 **BAILEY GEN. JAMES, JOHN & THOMAS & THEIR DESC., IN THREE PARTS,** by H.R. Bailey. 1899.
Cloth, $71.00. Paper, $61.00. 479pp. .... Vendor G0259

168 **REC. OF THE BAILEY FAM., DESC. OF WM. BAILEY OF NEWPORT, R.I., CHIEFLY THE LINE OF HIS SON HUGH, E. GREENWICH, R.I.,** by H. Hopkins. 1895.
Cloth, $41.00. Paper, $31.00. 207pp. .... Vendor G0259

169 **BAILLIES OF INVERNESS, SCOTLAND, & SOME OF THEIR DESCENDANTS IN THE U.S.,** by J.G.B. Bulloch. 1923.
Paper. $17.00. 86pp. .... Vendor G0259

170 **BAIRD & BEARD FAMS.; A GEN., BIOGR. & HIST. COLLECTION OF DATA,** by F.B. Catchings. 1918.
Cloth, $46.00. Paper, $36.00. 230pp. .... Vendor G0259

171 **THE DESCENDANTS OF JOHN BAKEMAN ESQ. AND CHRISTIAN SMART OF CAPE ROSIER, HANCOCK COUNTY, MAINE AND OTHER BAKEMAN FAMILIES,** by Mary Hawker Bakeman. 1993. Indexed. Illus.
Paper. $20.00. 160pp. .... Vendor G0246

172   **ANC. OF PRISCILLA BAKER, WIFE OF ISAAC APPLETON OF IPSWICH**, by W.S. Appleton. 1870.
Cloth, $31.50. Paper, $21.50. 143pp. .... Vendor G0259

173   **BAKER FAMILY GEN.: DESC. OF JOHN NICHOLAS BAKER, 1701–63 (NATIVE OF GERMANY; CAME TO U.S. IN 1754) WITH SOME CONNECTING LINES**, by R.H. Baker. 1955.
Cloth, $48.00. Paper, $38.50. 233pp. .... Vendor G0259

174   **GEN. OF THE DESC. OF EDWARD BAKER OF LYNN, MASS., 1630**, by N.M. Baker. 1867.
Paper. $13.00. 99pp. .... Vendor G0259

175   **BALCH GENEALOGICA**, by T.W. Balch. 1907.
Cloth, $61.50. Paper, $51.50. 410pp. .... Vendor G0259

176   **BALCH LEAFLETS. VOL. I, # 1–12**, by E. Putnam. 1897.
Paper. $15.00. 75pp. .... Vendor G0259

177   **GEN. OF THE BALCH FAM. IN AMER.**, by G.B. Balch. 1897.
Cloth, $80.00. Paper, $70.00. 585pp. .... Vendor G0259

178   **FIRST BOOK OF THE BALCOMBE FAMILY**, by F.W. Balcomb. 1942.
Paper. $17.00. 95pp. .... Vendor G0259

179   **BALDWIN GENEALOGY, 1500–1881**, by C.C. Baldwin. 1881.
Cloth, $156.00. Paper, $146.00. 974pp. .... Vendor G0259

180   **BALDWIN GEN. SUPPLEMENT**, by C.C. Baldwin. 1889.
Cloth, $65.00. Paper, $55.00. 398pp. .... Vendor G0259

181   **BALL COUSINS, DESCENDANTS OF JOHN AND SARAH BALL AND OF WILLIAM AND ELIZABETH RICHARDS OF COLONIAL PHILADELPHIA COUNTY, PENNSYLVANIA**, by Margaret B. Kinsey. 1981. Indexed. Illus.
Documents estate of Joseph **Ball** (died 1821 Pennsylvania), its 955 beneficiaries, their ancestors and descendants. Some other families: **Campbell, Chilton, Cleaver, Compton, Custer, Daniels, Dewees, Fisher, Frank, Green, Hafer, Holloway, Kemper, Kunzman, McWilliams, Mountjoy, Munford, Pate, Porter, Reeder, Rhoads, Sailer, Stewart, Supplee, Yocum.**
Cloth. $20.00. 366pp. .... Vendor G0307

182   **BALL FAM. RECORDS; GEN. MEM. OF SOME BALL FAM. OF GR. BRIT., IRELAND & AMER.**, by W.B. Wright. 1908.
Cloth, $52.00. Paper, $42.00. 284pp. .... Vendor G0259

183   **BARTHOLOMEW'S CHILDREN—A SOUTHERN BALL FAMILY**, by Henry Fletcher Ball, Jr. 1992. Indexed. Illus.
Cloth. $33.00. 259pp. .... Vendor G0343

184   **COL. WILLIAM BALL OF VA., THE GREAT-GRANDFATHER OF WASHINGTON**, by E.L.W. Heck. 1928 (London).
Paper. $9.50. 47pp. .... Vendor G0259

185   **CONQUERING THE FRONTIERS, A BIOGRAPHY & HISTORY OF ONE BRANCH OF THE BALL FAMILY**, by R.H. Ball. 1956.
Paper. $18.50. 102pp. .... Vendor G0259

186 **DESC OF JOHN BALL, WATERTOWN, MASS., 1630–1635**, by F.D. Warren and G.H. Ball. 1932.
Cloth, $36.00. Paper, $26.00. 161pp. Vendor G0259

187 **DESCENDANTS OF WILLIAM BALL OF VIRGINIA**, by Carol A. Hauk. 1995. Indexed.
Paper. $45.00. 305pp. . . . . Vendor G0340

188 **BALL (EXTR. FROM VIRGINIA GEN.)**.
Paper. $18.50. 102pp. . . . . Vendor G0259

189 **HIST. OF THE BALL FAM. GEN. OF THE NEW HAVEN BRANCH; ALLEN BALL & SOME OF HIS DESC., 1638–1864**, by L.A. Bradley. 1916.
Paper. $12.00. 59pp. . . . . Vendor G0259

190 **BALLARD GEN.: DESC. OF ISRAEL BALLARD (1748–1810) & ALICE FULLER, HIS WIFE (1751–1796)**, by M.G. Dodge. 1942.
Cloth, $68.00. Paper, $58.00. 375pp. Vendor G0259

191 **BALLARD GEN. WM. BALLARD (1603–1639) OF LYNN, MA., & WM. BALLARD (1617–1689) OF ANDOVER, MA. & THEIR DESC.**, by Farlow and Pope. 1911.
Cloth, $40.00. Paper, $30.00. 203pp. Vendor G0259

192 **BALLARD NEWS.** 1994.
Published quarterly. Master index. **Ballard**s anywhere in the U.S. or Canada. Subscription. $15.00/year. 70pp per issue . . . . Vendor G0429

193 **[Ballard]. FROM THE "EDWARD PLEASANTS VALENTINE PAPERS", ABSTR. OF REC. IN THE LOCAL & GENERAL ARCHIVES OF VA.**, compiled by The Valentine Museum.
Paper. $13.50. 67pp. . . . . Vendor G0259

194 **AN ELABORATE HIST. AND GEN. OF THE BALLOUS IN AMERICA**, by A. Ballou. 1888.
Cloth, $176.00. Paper, $166.00. 1,338pp. . . . . Vendor G0259

195 **BANGS FAM. IN AMER. HIST. & GEN.; THE DESC. OF EDW. BANGS OF PLYMOUTH & EASTHAM**, by D. Dudley. 1896.
Cloth, $56.50. Paper, $46.50. 360pp. Vendor G0259

196 **PARTIAL HIST. & GEN. RECORD OF THE BANKER OR BANKOR FAMILIES OF AMERICA, IN PARTICULAR THE DESC. OF LAURENS MATTYSE BANKER.** 1909.
Cloth, $80.00. Paper, $70.00. 458pp. Vendor G0259

197 **THE GEN. REC. OF THE BANKS FAM. OF ELBERT CO., GA.**, coll. by E.A. Banks (2nd ed.); compiled and edited by G.B. Young and S.B. Franklin. 1934.
Cloth, $42.50. Paper, $32.50. 215pp. Vendor G0259

198 **GEN. & BIOGR. RECORDS OF THE BANNING & ALLIED FAM. FROM THE AMER. HIST. SOC.** 1924.
Cloth, $34.00. Paper, $24.00. 161pp. Vendor G0259

199 **A FRISIAN FAM., THE BANTA GEN. DESC. OF EPKE JACOBSE WHO**

CAME FROM FRIESLAND, NETHERLANDS TO NEW AMSTERDAM, FEBRUARY 1659, by T.M. Banta. 1893.
Cloth, $77.00. Paper, $67.00. 427pp. .... Vendor G0259

200 **BARBER GENEALOGY. PT. 1. DESC. OF THOMAS BARBER OF WINDSOR, CT., 1614–1909. PT 2. DESC. OF JOHN BARBER OF WORCESTER, MASS., 1714–1909,** by J.B. White and L.M. Wilson. 1909.
Cloth, $113.00. Paper, $103.00. 826pp. .... Vendor G0259

201 **GEN. OF DESC. OF LYMAN BARBER OF NEWARK VALLEY, N.Y.,** by L.B. Barber. 1944.
Paper, $12.00. 60pp. .... Vendor G0259

202 **GEN. OF THE BARBER FAM.: DESC. OF ROBT. BARBER, LANCASTER CO., PA.,** by E. Barber. 1890.
Cloth, $35.00. Paper, $25.00. 166pp. .... Vendor G0259

203 **RECORD OF ANC. & DESC. OF EDWARD BARBER OF HOPKINTON, R.I., AND WIFE PHOEBE TILLINGHAST,** by D.W. Matteson. 1892.
Paper. $16.00. 80pp. .... Vendor G0259

204 **THE CONNECTICUT BARBERS. A GENEALOGY OF THE DESCENDANTS OF THOMAS BARBER OF WINDSOR, CONN.,** by Donald S. Barber, M.D. 1992. Indexed.
Thomas had 6 children, who had 54 more. 13 generations are followed throughout the country. Years of research make this genealogy 4 times as extensive as the White–Wilson 1909 version: 1,800 **Barber** and daughters' families. Index: 22,000 names. Correspondents list. Completely referenced. 6" x 9".
Cloth. $42.00. 544pp. .... Vendor G0397

205 **BARCLAYS OF N.Y.: WHO THEY ARE & WHO THEY ARE NOT, & OTHER BARCLAYS,** by R.B. Moffat. 1904.
Cloth, $85.00. Paper, $75.00. 481pp. .... Vendor G0259

206 **BARCROFT FAMILY REC. ACCT. OF THE FAM. IN ENG. & DESC. OF AMBROSE BARCORFT THE EMIGR. OF SOLEBURY, PA.,** by E.T. Runk. 1910.
Cloth, $63.00. Paper, $53.00. 334pp. .... Vendor G0259

207 **BARD FAM.; HIST. & GEN. OF THE BARDS OF "CARROLL'S DELIGHT" & GEN. OF THE BARD KINSHIP,** by G. Seilhamer. 1908.
Cloth, $89.50. Paper, $79.50. 515pp. .... Vendor G0259

208 **BARGER JOURNAL; BARGERS AND ALLIED KINDRED,** by A.L. Barger. 1924.
Cloth, $39.00. Paper, $29.00. 144pp. .... Vendor G0259

209 **BARKER FAMILY,** by E.F. Barker. 1927.
Cloth, $88.50. Paper, $78.50. 553pp. .... Vendor G0259

210 **BARKER FAM. OF PLYMOUTH COL. & CO.,** by B. Newhall.
Paper. $19.00. 102pp. .... Vendor G0259

211 **THE BARKLEY BRIGADE: THE STORY OF JOHN BARKLEY OF SMITH CO., TN AND HIS DESCENDANTS, 1753–1994,** by Kathryn Barkley Fischer. 1994. Indexed. Illus.

```
B        12 Generations              B
A     THOMAS BARNES                  A
R     OF HARTFORD/FARMINGTON, CT     R
      Plus 1,766 Descendants (1615-1994)
R     HARDBOUND 8.5" X 11" GREEN/GOLD TOOLING   R
N     READY FOR SHIPMENT - 175+ SOLD            N
E     $35. (Includes S & H.)  CA address-add $2.54 tax.   E
      FRED W. BARNES, 794 CHESTNUT DR.
S     FAIRFIELD, CA 94533-1465       S
```

The book concerns these additional families: **Anderson, Atchisons, Bennett, Brown, Butler, Cagle, Crain, Hatch, Lancaster, Spain, Tannehill, Ward.** Cloth. $22.50. 306pp. .... Vendor G0281

212 **BARKSDALE FAMILY HISTORY & GENEALOGY (WITH COLLATERAL LINES)**, by Capt. J.A. Barksdale. 1940. Cloth, $105.00. Paper, $95.00. 634pp. .... Vendor G0259

213 **BARLOW FAM. GEN., COMPRISING THE ANC. & DESC. OF JONATHAN BARLOW & PLAIN ROGERS, OF DELAWARE CO., NY**, by G. Barlow. 1891. Cloth, $86.00. Paper, $76.00. 508pp. .... Vendor G0259

214 **ROBERT BARNARD OF ANDOVER, MASS., AND HIS DESC.**, by R.M. Barnard. 1899. Paper. $9.00. 40pp. .... Vendor G0259

215 **BARNES FAMILY YEAR BOOK, VOLS. I–III**, by Trescott C. Barnes. 1907–10. Cloth, $35.00. Paper, $25.00. 64+44+49pp. .... Vendor G0259

216 **BARNES GEN., INCL. A COLL. OF ANC., GEN., & FAM. RECORDS & BIOGR. SKETCHES OF BARNES PEOPLE**, by G.N. Barnes. 1903. Cloth, $44.00. Paper, $34.00. 226pp. .... Vendor G0259

217 **TEN GENERATIONS OF THE BARNES FAMILY IN BRISTOL, CT.**, by F.F. Barnes. 1946. Cloth, $54.00. Paper, $44.50. 280pp. .... Vendor G0259

218 **THOMAS BARNES OF HARTFORD, CT + 1,766 DESCENDANTS (1615–1994)**, by Frederic Wayne Barnes and Edna Cleo (Bauer) Barnes. 1994. Indexed. Illus. Allied surnames frequently appearing include: **Adams, Andrews, Avery, Beall, Beavens, Beebe, Bement, Bronson, Brown, Clark, Day, Foote, Gaylord, Hart, Hayes, Heist, Johnson, Jones, Langdon, Lee, Lewis, Miller, Moore, Munson, Neal, Painter, Potter, Rice, Ripley, Root, Scoville, Smith, Tuttle, Warner, Webster, Williams, Wing, Woodruff.** Hardbound. $35.00, CA tax $2.54. 327pp. .... Vendor G0376

219 **BARNEY (1634)–HOSMER (1635) [FAMILY RECORDS]**, by W.F. Adams. 1912.
Cloth, $31.00. Paper, $21.00. 133pp. Vendor G0259

220 **MANY INTERESTING FACTS CONNECTED WITH THE LIFE OF COMMODORE JOSHUA BARNEY, HERO OF U.S. NAVY, 1776–1812; ALSO A COMP. OF GEN. MATERIAL REL. TO HIS ANC. & DESC., WITH VALUABLE REC. OF BARNEY FAM. CONNECTIONS**, by W.F. Adams. 1912.
Cloth, $46.00. Paper, $36.00. 228pp. Vendor G0259

221 **THE DESCENDANTS OF JOHN & MARIAH (HIVELEY) BARNHART: A GENEALOGY OF THE ANCESTORS & DESCENDANTS OF JOHN BARNHART & MARIAH HIVELY OF EASTERN OHIO TO THE PRESENT**, by James K. Raywalt. 1990.
Paper. $19.00. 109pp. . . . . Vendor G0259

222 **A BARR FAMILY HISTORY: DESCENDANTS OF ROBERT BARR (ca. 1725–1808), AND HIS WIFE MARY WILLS, OF McALEVYS FORT, PENNSYLVANIA**, by Charles R. Barr. 1995. Indexed.
Cloth. $30.00. 217pp. . . . . Vendor G0217

223 **HIST. OF THE BARR FAM., BEGINNING WITH GR-GRANDFATHER ROBT BARR & MARY WILLS: THEIR DESC. DOWN TO THE LATEST CHILD**, by W.B. Barr. 1901.
Cloth, $42.00. Paper, $32.00. 216pp. Vendor G0259

224 **GENEALOGY OF SOME OF THE DESCENDANTS OF THOMAS BARRETT, SR., OF BRAINTREE, MA., 1635**, by Wm. Barrett. 1888.
Cloth, $52.50. Paper, $42.50. 295pp. Vendor G0259

225 **BARRY FAMILY RECORDS, VOL. I: CAPT. CHARLES BARRY & HIS DESC.**, by L.H. Parker. 1951.
Cloth, $35.00. Paper, $25.00. 148pp. Vendor G0259

226 **BARRYMORE: RECORDS OF THE BARRYS OF CO. CORK, FROM THE EARLIEST TO THE PRESENT TIME, WITH PEDIGREES**, by Rev. E. Barry. 1902.
Cloth, $45.00. Paper, $35.00. 214pp. Vendor G0259

227 **RECORD OF THE BARTHOLOMEW FAM.: HIST., GEN. & BIOGR.**, by G.W. Bartholomew, Sr. 1885.
Cloth, $104.00. Paper, $94.00. 769pp. Vendor G0259

228 **A GENEALOGY OF THE DESCENDANTS OF JOSEPH BARTLETT OF NEWTON, MASS, FOR SEVEN GENERATIONS**, by Aldis E. Hibner. 1934.
Cloth, $67.00. Paper, $57.00. 291+78pp. . . . . Vendor G0259

229 **ANC., GEN., BIOGR., HIST.: ACCT. OF THE AMER. PROGENITURES OF THE BARTLETT FAM. WITH SPECIAL REF. TO THE DESC. OF JOHN BARTLETT OF WEYMOUTH & CUMBERLAND**, by T.E. Bartlett. 1892.
Paper. $19.00. 112pp. . . . . Vendor G0259

230 **FOREFATHERS & DESCENDANTS OF WILLARD & GENEVIEVE**

WILSON BARTLETT, & ALLIED FAMILIES MOULTON–MCGEHEE–ENDRESS, by G.W. Bartlett. 1952.
Cloth, $52.00. Paper, $42.00. 270pp. . . . . Vendor G0259

231 **GEN. & BIOGR. SKETCHES OF THE BARTLETT FAM. IN ENGLAND & AMERICA**, by L. Bartlett. 1876.
Paper. $19.50. 114pp. . . . . Vendor G0259

232 **LT. WILLIAM BARTON OF MORRIS CO., N.J., & HIS DESC.**, by W.E. Barton. 1900.
Cloth, $32.00. Paper, $22.00. 148pp. Vendor G0259

233 **BARTOW GEN; PARTS 1 & 2, WITH SUPPL.**, by E. Bartow. 1878–9.
Cloth, $59.50. Paper, $49.50. 318pp. Vendor G0259

234 **GEN. RECORD OF THOS. BASCOM & HIS DESC.**, by E.D. Harris. 1870.
Paper. $16.00. 79pp. . . . . Vendor G0259

235 **JERIAH BASS & HIS DESCENDANTS: LEAVES FROM MEMORY'S SCRAPBOOK & FACTS FROM AUTHENTIC SOURCES**, by L.E. Bass. 1940.
Cloth, $39.50. Paper, $29.50. 195pp. Vendor G0259

236 **BASSETT–PRESTON ANCESTORS: HISTORY OF ANCESTORS IN AMERICA OF THE CHILDREN OF EDWARD M. & ANNIE PRESTON BASSETT**, by B. Preston. 1930.
Cloth, $59.00. Paper, $49.00. 359pp. Vendor G0259

237 **ONE BASSETT FAM. IN AMERICA WITH ALL CONNECTIONS IN AMERICA AND MANY IN GREAT BRITAIN AND FRANCE**, by B.B. Bassette. 1926.
Cloth, $129.00. Paper, $119.00. 867pp. . . . . Vendor G0259

238 **BASYE FAMILY IN THE U.S.**, by O. Basye. 1950.
Cloth, $145.00. Paper, $135.00. 987pp. . . . . Vendor G0259

239 **ANC. & DESC. OF DEACON DAVID BATCHELDER OF HAMPTON FALLS, N.H.**, by M.J. Greene. 1902.
Paper. $16.00. 80pp. . . . . Vendor G0259

240 **BATCHELDER–BATCHELLER; DESC. OF REV. STEPHEN BACHILAR OF ENG., LEADING NON-CONFORMIST WHO SETTLED THE TOWN OF NEW HAMPTON, NH, & JOSEPH, HENRY, JOSHUA & JOHN BATCHELLER OF ESSEX CO., MASS.**, by F.C. Pierce. 1898.
Cloth, $103.00. Paper, $93.50. 623pp. Vendor G0259

241 **BATES & FLETCHER GEN. REGISTER**, by T.C. Bates. 1892.
Paper. $12.50. 60pp. . . . . Vendor G0259

242 **BATES, BEARS, AND BUNKER BILL**, by E. Deacon. 1911.
Paper. $18.00. 90pp. . . . . Vendor G0259

243 **BATES BULLETIN, SERIES 1 THROUGH 5**. 1907–1932.
Cloth, $81.00. Paper, $71.00. 574pp. Vendor G0259

244 **GEN. OF THE DESC. OF EDWARD BATES OF WEYMOUTH, MA.**, by S.A. Bates; edited by F. Bates. 1900.
Cloth, $34.00. Paper, $24.00. 145pp. Vendor G0259

245   **DESCENDANTS OF JOHN BATTAILE OF VIRGINIA**, by Carol A. Hauk. 1995. Indexed.
Paper. $30.00. 103pp. .... Vendor G0340

246   **THE BATTEN FAMILY DESCENDANTS OF FRANCIS BATTEN AND ANN CHEESMAN**, by Retha Batten. 1993. Indexed. Illus.
Thousands of names cover ten detailed generations of this excellent genealogy.
Paper. $27.50. 396pp. .... Vendor G0069

247   **SAMSON BATTEY OF RHODE ISLAND, THE IMMIGRANT ANCESTOR & HIS DESCENDANTS**, by H.V. Battey. 1932.
Cloth, $71.00. Paper, $61.00. 400pp. .... Vendor G0259

248   **BATTLE BOOK: GENEALOGY OF THE BATTLE FAMILY IN AMERICA**, by Herbert Bemerton Battle and Lois Yelverton. 1930.
Cloth, $109.00. Paper, $99.50. 768pp. .... Vendor G0259

249   **[Baughman]. HARVEST TIME . . . HISTORY OF THE SWISS, GERMAN & DUTCH FOLK IN EARLY AMERICA**, by J. Ross Baughman. 1994.
Paper. $31.00. 256pp. .... Vendor G0150

250   **SOME ANCESTORS OF THE BAUGHMAN FAMILY**, by J. Ross Baughman. 1989.
Paper. $31.00. 188pp. .... Vendor G0150

251   **THE BAUMAN/BOWMAN FAMILY OF THE COCALICO VALLEY**, by Clarence Edwin Spohn and Cynthia Marquet. 1994.
Paper. $19.00. 94pp. .... Vendor G0150

252   **BAXTER FAMILY: DESC. OF GEORGE & THOMAS BAXTER OF WESTCHESTER CO., N.Y., AS WELL AS SOME W.V. & S.C. LINES**, by F. Baxter. 1913.
Cloth, $35.00. Paper, $25.00. 157pp. .... Vendor G0259

253   **MEM. OF THE BAXTER FAM.**, by J. Baxter. 1879.
Paper. $16.50. 114pp. .... Vendor G0259

254   **SOME MARYLAND BAXTERS & THEIR DESC., INCLUDNG FAMS. WITH SURNAMES ANDERSON, BAKER, BONNER, BROWN, BUTLER, ET AL**, by A.S. Humphreys. 1948.
Cloth, $32.50. Paper, $22.50. 139pp. .... Vendor G0259

255   **ANCESTORS AND DESCENDANTS OF KASPAR BAYERSCHMITT (b. 1681–d. 1763)**, by Joseph P. Beierschmitt. 1994. Indexed. Illus.
Baierschmidt–Baierschmitt–Beierschmitt–Biersmith–Boyersmith–Byersmith. Fourteen generations, 1540s to present. Over 700 lineal descendants; more than 900 collateral families.
Cloth. $49.50. 464pp. G0453

256   **BAYLES FAMILIES OF LONG ISLAND & N.J., & THEIR DESCENDANTS; ALSO ANCESTORS OF JAMES BAYLES & JULIA HALSEY DAY**, by H.G. Bayles and F.P. Bayles. 1944.
Cloth, $52.00. Paper, $42.00. 270pp. .... Vendor G0259

257 **[Bayley]. BAILLEULS OF FLANDERS & BAYLEYS OF WILLOW HALL**, by F. Bayley. 1881 (London).
Cloth, $53.00. Paper, $43.00. 272pp. .... Vendor G0259

258 **BAYLIS FAMILY OF VA., WITH SUPPLEMENTS ON THE CHUNN, FAWCETT, HAWKINS & TURNER FAMILIES AND A BAYLIS FAMILY IN ENGLAND**, by W.B. Blum and Wm. Blum, Sr. 1958.
Cloth, $109.00. Paper, $99.00. 669pp. .... Vendor G0259

259 **HIST. GEN. OF THE FAM. OF BAYNE OF NIDDERDALE, SHOWING ALSO HOW BAYEUX BECAMES BAYNES**, by J. Lucat. 1896.
Cloth, $90.00. Paper, $80.00. 635pp. .... Vendor G0259

260 **REV. JOHN BEACH & DESC., WITH HIST. & BIOGR. SKETCHES, & ANC. & DESC. OF JOHN SANFORD OF REDDING, CONN.**, by Beach and Gibbons. 1898.
Cloth, $71.00. Paper, $61.00. 397pp. .... Vendor G0259

261 **THE DESC. OF THOMAS BEACH OF MILFORD, CONN.**, by M.E. Beach. 1912.
Paper. $10.00. 51pp. .... Vendor G0259

262 **BEAL FINDINGS: SOME DESCENDANTS OF WILLIAM BEAL OF GLOUCESTER, ENGLAND**, by Jeanne Waters Strong. 1992. Indexed. Illus.
Cloth. $25.00. 79pp. .... Vendor G0086

263 **BEALE FAMILY OF VIRGINIA, 1399–1956**, by Frances Beal S. Hodges. 1956.
Cloth, $61.00. Paper, $51.00. 391pp. .... Vendor G0259

264 **DESCENDANTS OF THOMAS BEALE OF VIRGINIA**, by Carol A. Hauk. 1995. Indexed.
Paper. $35.00. 176pp. .... Vendor G0340

265 **THE BEALES OF CHESTER CO., PA.**, by M.B. Hitchens. 1957.
Paper. $12.00. 58pp. .... Vendor G0259

266 **BEAMAN & CLARK GEN.: A HIST. OF THE DESC. OF GAMALIEL BEAMAN & SARAH CLARK OF DORCHESTER & LANCASTER, MASS., 1635–1909**, by E.B. Wooden. 1909.
Cloth, $45.00. Paper, $35.00. 219pp. .... Vendor G0259

267 **JOSHUA BEAN OF EXETER, BRENTWOOD & GILMANTON, N. H. & SOME OF HIS DESC.**, by J.H. Drummond. 1903.
Cloth, $30.50. Paper, $20.50. 116pp. .... Vendor G0259

268 **A GEN. OF THE BEAR FAM. AND BIOGR. RECORD OF THE DESC. OF JACOB BEAR**, by W.S. Bear. 1906.
Cloth, $42.00. Paper, $32.00. 216pp. .... Vendor G0259

269 **GEN. OF DESC. OF WIDOW MARTHA BEARD OF MILFORD, CONN.**, by R. Beard. 1915.
Paper. $19.50. 99pp. .... Vendor G0259

270 **HISTORY OF ADAM BEARD AND HIS DESCENDANTS**, by Irene Beard. 1952.
Paper. $18.50. 93pp. .... Vendor G0259

271 **GEN. HIST. OF BEARDSLEY–LEE FAM. IN AMER., 1635–1902**, by I.H. Beardsley. 1902.
Cloth, $79.50. Paper, $69.50. 453pp. .... Vendor G0259

272 **WILLIAM BEARDSLEY OF STRATFORD, CONN., & DESC.**, by H.F. Johnston.
Cloth, $30.00. Paper, $20.00. 108pp. .... Vendor G0259

273 **BEATTY–ASFORDBY, THE ANCESTRY OF JOHN BEATTY & SUSANNA ASFORDBY, WITH SOME OF THEIR DESCENDANTS**, by S.R. Turk. 1909.
Cloth, $39.50. Paper, $29.50. 183pp. .... Vendor G0259

274 **GEN. RECORD OF THE FAM. OF BEATTY, EGLE, MULLER, MURRAY, OUTH & THOMAS**, by W.H. Egle. 1886.
Cloth, $31.00. Paper, $21.00. 129pp. .... Vendor G0259

275 **DESCENDENTS OF ASHER B. BEAUCHAMP AND JOHN CASEY**, by Shirley B. Adair. 1995. Indexed. Illus.
Kentucky to Missouri. **Nave, Ball, Bingham**.
Paper. $16.50. 160pp. .... Vendor G0382

276 **A HIST. OF THE BECK FAM. TOGETHER WITH A GEN. RECORD OF THE ALLEYNES & THE CHASES FROM WHOM THEY ARE DESC.**, by C.R. Conover. 1907.
Cloth, $49.00. Paper, $39.00. 259pp. .... Vendor G0259

277 **BECKHAM FAM. IN VA.**, by J.M. Beckham. 1910.
Paper. $19.00. 98pp. .... Vendor G0259

278 **DESC. OF RICHARD BECKLEY OF WETHERSFIELD, CONN.**, by C.B. Sheppard. 1948.
Cloth, $71.50. Paper, $61.50. 406pp. .... Vendor G0259

279 **BECKWITH NOTES, NOS. 1–6. MARVIN BECKWITH & HIS WIFE ABIGAIL CLARK; THEIR COLONIAL ANCESTORS & DESC., WITH SOME NOTES ON ALLIED FAMS.** 1899–1907.
Cloth, $67.00. Paper, $57.00. 378pp. .... Vendor G0259

280 **ADDITIONAL BECKWITH NOTES, INCLUDING AVERY, ELY, GILBERT, HOLMES, LEE, SMITH, SOUTHERLAND, WIGHTMAN & WILLIAMS FAMILIES**, by F.W. Beckwith. 1956.
Paper. $10.00. 49pp. .... Vendor G0259

281 **THE BECKWITHS**, by P. Beckwith. 1891.
Cloth, $61.50. Paper, $51.50. 384pp. .... Vendor G0259

282 **BEDON FAM. OF SO. CAROLINA.**
Cloth, $13.50. Paper, $3.50. 4pp. .... Vendor G0259

283 **HUGH M. BEDWELL AND RELATED FAMILIES**, by William Talbert Bedwell, Ruth Lucas Bedwell, and Judith Bedwell FitzPatrick. 1993. Indexed. Illus.
Related families include William Armstrong **Smith** Jr., Caleb Davis **Williams**, and James Wesley **Brown** from the Calloway County, Kentucky area.
Cloth. $28.00. 167pp. .... Vendor G0412

284 GENEALOGY OF THE FAMILY OF BEEBE, FROM THE EARLIEST KNOWN IMMIGRANT, JOHN BEEBE OF BROUGHTON, ENG., 1650, compiled and edited by Clifford Beebe. 1991.
Cloth, $41.00. Paper, $31.00. 217pp. .... Vendor G0259

285 GENEALOGY OF THE FAMILY OF BEEBE, VOL. II: THE SECOND EMIGRATION, by J.B. Fisher and C. Beebe. 1993.
Cloth, $52.50. Paper, $42.50. 282pp. t.s. .... Vendor G0259

286 LUCIUS BEEBE OF WAKEFIELD & SYLENDA MORRIS, HIS WIFE: FOREBEARS & DESC., by L. Wilder. 1930.
Cloth, $48.00. Paper, $38.00. 255pp. .... Vendor G0259

287 MONOGRAPH OF DESC. OF BEEBE FAM., by C. Beebe. 1904.
Cloth, $35.00. Paper, $25.00. 127pp. .... Vendor G0259

288 HISTORY OF THE DESCENDANTS OF ABRAHAM BEERY . . . SWITZERLAND TO PENNSYLVANIA . . . 1736, by Joseph H. Wenger. (1905) reprint 1989.
Cloth. $29.00. 328pp. .... Vendor G0150

289 HIST. OF THE DESC. OF ABRAHAM BEERY, b. IN 1718, EMIGR. TO PENN. IN 1736, & COMP. GEN. FAM. REGISTER, by J.H. Wenger. 1905.
Cloth, $61.50. Paper, $51.50. 328pp. .... Vendor G0259

290 BEESON GENEALOGY, by Jasper L. Beeson. 1925.
Cloth, $35.00. Paper, $25.00. 144pp. .... Vendor G0259

291 BOOK OF BEGGS; GEN. STUDY OF THE BEGGS FAM. IN AMER., by R. and C. Beggs. 1928.
Cloth, $37.00. Paper, $27.00. 135pp. .... Vendor G0259

292 BEHARRELL FAMILY HISTORY, by N.C. Messenger with V.B. Chapman. 1974.
Cloth, $34.00. Paper, $24.00. 130pp. .... Vendor G0259

293 GEN. REC. OF THE DESC. OF JACOB BEIDLER OF LOWER MILFORD TWP., BUCKS CO., PA., by A.J. Fretz. 1903.
Cloth, $94.50. Paper, $84.50. 565pp. .... Vendor G0259

294 THE WEDGE: BEISEL/BEISSEL INTERNATIONAL GENEALOGY, by James D. Beissel, Sr. 1990.
Cloth. $74.00. 462pp. .... Vendor G0150

295 BELCHER FAM. IN ENG. & AMER., COMPREHENDING A PERIOD OF 765 YEARS WITH PART. REF. TO DESC. OF ADAM BELCHER OF SOUTHFIELDS, ORANGE CO., N.Y., by W. and J. Belcher. 1941.
Cloth, $85.00. Paper, $75.00. 481pp. .... Vendor G0259

296 [Belden]. SOME OF THE ANC. & DESC. OF ROYAL DENISON & OLIVE CADWELL BELDEN, by J.P. Belden. 1898.
Cloth, $47.00. Paper, $37.00. 248pp. .... Vendor G0259

297 BELL FAM. IN AMERICA, by W. Clemens. 1913.
Paper. $9.00. 45pp. .... Vendor G0259

298   **BELL FAMILY RECORDS**, by J. Montgomery Seaver. 1929.
Paper. $7.50. 36pp. .... Vendor G0259

299   **THE BELLAMYS AND CORNISH COUSINS OF NORTH CORNWALL, ENGLAND**, by Mary Dudley-Higham. 1994. Indexed. Illus.
Baker, Ballamy/Bellamy, Barrett, Bines, Bray, Collacutt, Cornish, Dennis, Dyer, Featherstone, Greenaway, Gregory, Hacker, Ham, Hicks, Male, Mark, Marshall, Oliver, Pearce, Sandercock, Sanders, Spry, Tamblyn, Treweek, Tucker, Venner, Warfield, Wells/Wills, Wickett. Over 5,000 indexed names.
Cloth. $40.00 tax included. 200pp. .... Vendor G0153

300   **JEAN BELLEVILLE THE HUGUENOT, HIS DESCENDANTS**, by Paul Belville Taylor. 1973.
Cloth, $99.00. Paper, $89.00. 610pp. .... Vendor G0259

301   **DAVID BELLHOUSE AND SONS, MANCHESTER**, by D.R. Bellhouse. 1992. Illus.
The eighteenth-century origins and impact to the present day of a family business in timber, building construction, iron founding, and cotton spinning is described. Biographical material of the ancestors and descendants of David **Bellhouse** (1764–1840) is also given.
Paper. $20.00. 130pp. .... Vendor G0336

302   **THE BELLOWS GEN.; OR, JOHN BELLOWS THE BOY EMIGRANT OF 1635 AND HIS DESC.**, by T.B. Peck. 1898.
Cloth, $93.50. Paper, $83.50. 673pp. .... Vendor G0259

303   **BELSER FAM. OF SO. CARO.**, by W.G. Belser, et al. 1941.
Paper. $13.50. 67pp. .... Vendor G0259

304   **BEMIS HIST. & GEN.; AN ACCT. OF THE DESC. OF JOS. BEMIS OF WATERTOWN, MASS.**, by T. Draper. 1900.
Cloth, $47.50. Paper, $37.50. 295pp. .... Vendor G0259

305   **GEN. OF THE BENEDICTS IN AMERICA**, by H.M. Benedict. 1870.
Cloth, $70.00. Paper, $60.00. 494pp. .... Vendor G0259

306   **GEN. OF THE BENJAMIN FAM. IN U.S.A. 1632–1898**, by E.B. Baker. 1898.
Paper. $17.50. 88pp. .... Vendor G0259

307   **BENNAGE–BENNETCH FAMILY HISTORY**, by Betty Jane B. Wise and David Lee Wise. 1985.
Cloth. $24.50. 230pp. .... Vendor G0150

308   **ANCESTORS AND DESCENDANTS OF LUCY ANN AND GEORGE EPHRAIM CLEAVER BENNETT. 2 VOL. SET**, by Dorothy Wilkerson Bertine and Nina K. Bennett Wilkerson. 1988. Indexed. Illus.
Comprehensive genealogies of: **DeHaven, Supplee, Rambo, Levering, Cleaver, Wilkerson, McGlathery, Koch, Wentz, Coulston**. Maps, charts, documents, photos, archival paper.
Cloth. $175.00. 1,296pp. .... Vendor G0407

309   **BENNETT & ALLIED FAMILIES. ADDENDA TO BULLARD & ALLIED FAMILIES**, by E.J. Bullard. 1931.
Paper. $8.50. 43pp. .... Vendor G0259

310 **BENNETT FAMILY, 1628–1910**, by E.B. Bennett. 1910.
Paper. $10.00. 50pp. .... Vendor G0259

311 **BENNETT FAM. OF SUSSEX CO., DELAWARE, 1680–1860, WITH BRANCHES INTO THE WARREN, SHOCKLEY & OTHER FAMS.**, by J.B. Hill. 1970.
Paper. $14.00. 71pp. .... Vendor G0259

312 **ORIGIN & HIST. OF THE NAME BENNETT, WITH BIOGR. OF THE MOST NOTED PERSONS OF THE NAME.** 1905.
Paper. $19.50. 112pp. .... Vendor G0259

313 **BENSON FAMILY OF NEWPORT, R.I., WITH AN APPENDIX CONCERNING THE BENSONS IN AMERICA OF ENGLISH DESC.**, by W.P. Garrison. 1872.
Paper. $13.00. 65pp. .... Vendor G0259

314 **JACOB BENSON, PIONEER & HIS DESC. IN DOVER & AMENIA, N.Y.**, by A.T. Benson. 1915.
Cloth, $36.00. Paper, $26.00. 130pp. .... Vendor G0259

315 **THE BENSON FAM. RECORDS**, by F.H. Benson. 1920.
Cloth, $41.00. Paper, $31.00. 207pp. .... Vendor G0259

316 **BENT FAMILY IN AMERICA, BEING MAINLY A GEN. OF THE DESC.**

OF JOHN BENT, WHO SETTLED IN SUDBURY, MASS. IN 1638, by A.H. Bent. 1900.
Cloth, $59.50. Paper, $49.50. 313pp. .... Vendor G0259

317 **BENTLEY GLEANINGS**, by J.H. Lobdell; **FAM. OF JOHN WITHERSTINE**, by W. Witherstine. 1905.
Cloth, $31.00. Paper, $21.00. 128pp. .... Vendor G0259

318 **SAMUEL BLADE BENTON, HIS ANC. & DESC., 1620–1901**, by J.H. Benton, Jr. 1901.
Cloth, $68.00. Paper, $58.00. 366pp. .... Vendor G0259

319 **BERGEN FAMILY; OR, THE DESC. OF HANS HANSEN BERGEN OF NEW YORK & BROOKLYN, WITH NOTES ON OTHER LONG IS-LAND FAMILIES**, by T.G. Bergen. 1876.
Cloth, $93.50. Paper, $83.50. 658pp. .... Vendor G0259

320 **BERGEY GEN.; A RECORD OF THE DESC. OF JOHN ULRICH BERGEY & HIS WIFE MARY**, by D. Bergey. 1925.
Cloth, $178.00. Paper, $168.00. 1,166pp. .... Vendor G0259

321 **THE BERKELEYS OF BARN ELMS**, F.B. Young. 1954.
Cloth, $31.00. Paper, $21.00. 123pp. .... Vendor G0259

322 **THE BERKEY BOOK**, by William Albert Berkey and Ruth Berkey Reichley. (1984) 2nd ed. 1995.
Cloth. $30.00. 527pp. .... Vendor G0150

323 **THE FRENCH CONNECTION: THE LEON AND CATHERINE BER-NARD FAMILY AND THEIR DESCENDANTS 1789–1994**, by Allen W. Bernard. 1994. Indexed. Illus.
French origins and over 800 descendants of these Mercer County, Ohio pio-neers are featured in this carefully researched book. Leon and Catherine (**Kilker**) **Bernard**, French immigrants from the Territory of Belfort, came to Perry County, Ohio in 1828 and later moved to Mercer County in 1836. Numerous maps, photos, and documents are illustrated. Register System format. Fine quality acid-free paper.
Includes the **Hoying, Rolfes, Goecke, Vehorn**, and **Brockman** families.
Cloth. $34.00. 344+xvpp. .... Vendor G0431

324 **BERRY/BERREY FAMILY, THE FAMILY OF ELIJAH BERRY VA., GA., ALA. AND TEX., 1700–1980**, by Lynn Berry Hamilton. 1980. Indexed. Illus.
Cloth. $25.00. 300pp. .... Vendor G0301

325 **PIERRE BERTINE—1686, DESCENDANTS AND ALLIED FAMILIES**, by Dorothy Wilkerson Bertine. 1994. Indexed. Illus.
Comprehensive family genealogies of: **Brewer, Coutant, Drake, Ernst, Hunt, LeRoy, Logan, Murray, Renaud, Rodman, Vermilyea, Vincent, Seacord**. Maps, charts, photos, archival paper.
Cloth. $110.00. 504pp. .... Vendor G0407

326 **GENEALOGICAL HIST. OF THE BERTOLET FAM.; DESCENDANTS OF JEAN BERTOLET**, by D.H. Bertolet. 1914.
Cloth, $51.00. Paper, $41.00. 260pp. .... Vendor G0259

327 **THE BESTMAN HOUSE ON BALLARD ROAD**, by James F. Bestman. 1991. Illus.

The Beverley Family of Virginia. A Genealogy

Descendants, Allied Families of Major Robert Beverley (1641–1687)
John McGill, [1956] **1995 Reprint** Thomas Turner Association
Contact Vendor G0433 for information

History of the 22-acre truck farm that today is part of eastern Des Plaines, Illinois. The original farmhouse still stands on its original foundation at its original location.
Paper. $18.00. 22pp. .... Vendor G0377

328 **BETTS FAM. HIST., 1634–1958**, by W. Robbins. 1959.
Cloth, $32.00. Paper, $22.00. 122pp. .... Vendor G0259

329 **THOMAS BETTS & DESC.**, by C.W. and F. Betts. 1888.
Cloth, $34.50. Paper, $24.50. 136pp. .... Vendor G0259

330 **THE BEVERLEY FAMILY OF VIRGINIA—A GENEALOGY—DE-SCENDANTS & ALLIED FAMILIES OF MAJOR ROBERT BEVERLEY (1641–1687)**, by John McGill (1956). Reprinted by The Thomas Turner Association, 1995. Indexed.
110 page index, 21,000 names, 12 generations. **Beverley, Turner, Carter, Nelson, Page, Randolph, Robinson, Taylor, Washington, Whiting, Williams,** and many others.
Cloth. $49.95 plus $5.95 s&h. 1,117+pp. .... Vendor G0433

331 **BEVIER FAMILY. A HIST. OF THE DESC. OF THE DESC. OF LOUIS BEVIER, WHO CAME FROM FRANCE & SETTLED IN NEW PALTZ, N.Y.**, by K. Bevier. 1916.
Cloth, $51.00. Paper, $41.00. 291pp. .... Vendor G0259

332 **BEVILLE FAM. OF VA., GA., & FLA., & SEVERAL ALLIED FAMI-LIES, NORTH & SOUTH**, by A.B.V. Tedcastle. 1917.
Cloth, $44.00. Paper, $34.00. 212pp. .... Vendor G0259

333 **BIBB FAMILY IN AMERICA, 1640–1940**, by C.W. Bibb. 1941.
Cloth, $34.00. Paper, $24.00. 149pp. .... Vendor G0259

334 **A MEM. OF A RESPECTABLE & RESPECTED FAM., ESP. OF JOSHUA BICKNELL. WITH TOMBSTONES INSCRP. IN SARRINGTON, R.I.**, by T. Bicknell. 1880.
Paper. $9.50. 48pp. .... Vendor G0259

335 **HIST. & GEN. OF THE BICKNELL FAM. & SOME COLLATERAL LINES, OF NORMANDY, GREAT BRITAIN AND AMERICA**, by T.W. Bicknell. 1913.
Cloth, $103.00. Paper, $93.00. 620pp. .... Vendor G0259

336 **A SKETCH OF OWEN BIDDLE, TO WHICH IS ADDED A SHORT ACCOUNT OF THE PARKE FAM., TOGETHER WITH A LIST OF HIS DESC.**, by H.D. Biddle. 1892.
Paper. $17.50. 87pp. .... Vendor G0259

337 A SKETCH OF OWEN BIDDLE, TO WHICH IS ADDED A SHORT
     ACCT. OF THE PARKE FAM., WITH A LIST OF HIS DESC., by H.D.
     Biddle. Rev. & enl. ed. 1927.
     Cloth, $31.00. Paper, $21.00. 111pp. .... Vendor G0259

338 GEN. TO THE 7TH GEN. OF BIDWELL FAM. IN AMERICA, by E. M.
     Bidwell. 1884.
     Cloth, $35.00. Paper, $25.00. 123pp. .... Vendor G0259

339 ANCESTORS IN THE U.S. OF BYRON BIERCE & HIS WIFE MARY
     IDA COTTRELL, OF CORTLAND CO., NY, by T.H. Bierce & L. Cottrell.
     1962.
     Cloth, $54.00. Paper, $44.00. 289pp. .... Vendor G0259

340 GEN. OF THE BIGELOW FAM. OF AMER., FROM THE MARR. IN
     1642 OF JOHN BIGELOW & MARY WARREN TO THE YEAR 1890, by
     G.B. Howe. 1890.
     Cloth, $75.00. Paper, $65.00. 517pp. .... Vendor G0259

341 FIVE GENERATIONS OF THE BIGNOLD FAM., 1761–1947, & THEIR
     CONNECTION WITH NORWICH UNION [INSURANCE], by Sir Robert
     Bignold. 1948
     Cloth, $59.50. Paper, $49.50. 320pp. .... Vendor G0259

342 HIST. OF THE BILL FAM., by L. Bill. 1867.
     Cloth, $57.50. Paper, $47.50. 368pp. .... Vendor G0259

343 GEN. OF SOME DESC. OF WILLIAM BILLING(S) OF STONINGTON,
     CONN., by F. Billings.
     Paper. $10.00. 49pp. .... Vendor G0259

344 BILYEU BY YOU, VOLUME 1 (ALL SPELLINGS), by Rose Caudle Terry.
     1993. Indexed. Illus.
        Includes **Balew, Ballou, Belew, Belieu, Bellew, Belue, Bilieu, Bilyeu, Blue,**
     Boileau. Queries published free.
     Paper. $10.45. 35pp. .... Vendor G0061

345 BILYEU BY YOU, VOLUME 2 (ALL SPELLINGS), by Rose Caudle Terry.
     1994. Indexed. Illus.
        Queries published free. Future volumes expected or may already be com-
     pleted.
     Paper. $10.45. 36pp. .... Vendor G0061

346 BINFORD FAMILY GENEALOGY, by Mary L. Bruner. 1925?
     Cloth, $67.00. Paper, $57.00. 375pp. .... Vendor G0259

347 BINFORD GENEALOGY SUPPLEMENT, by M.L. Bruner. 1934.
     Paper. $19.50. 126pp. .... Vendor G0259

348 BINGHAM FAMILY IN THE UNITED STATES: DESCENDANTS, THO-
     MAS BINGHAM OF CONNECTICUT, by Donna G. Bingham Munger. 1996.
     Indexed. Illus.
     Cloth. $50.00. 600pp. .... Vendor G0411

349 GENEALOGY OF THE BINGHAM FAMILY IN THE UNITED STATES
     ESPECIALLY OF THE STATE OF CONNECTICUT, compiled by Theodore

A. Bingham; edited by Gwen Campbell. 1988. Indexed. Query with SASE.
Paper. $30.00. 161pp. .... Vendor G0303

350 **GEN. OF THE BINGHAM FAM. IN THE U.S. ESP. OF CONN.**, by T.A. Bingham. 1898.
Cloth, $47.50. Paper, $37.50. 288pp. .... Vendor G0259

351 **THE BINGHAM FAM. IN THE U.S., ESP. OF THE STATE OF CONN., INCL. NOTES ON THE BINGHAMS OF PHILA. & OF IRISH DESC.: MEDIAEVAL RECORDS; ARM. BEARINGS, ETC.**, by T.A. Bingham. 3 vols. 1927–30.
Cloth, $79.00/vol. Paper, $69.00/vol. 473+434+447pp. ..... Vendor G0259

352 **GEN. OF THE BINNEY FAM. IN THE U.S.**, by C.J.F. Binney. 1886.
Cloth, $46.50. Paper, $36.50. 278pp. .... Vendor G0259

353 **BIRD FAMILY HISTORY**, by Booth, Maycock, and Poulson. 1961.
Cloth, $36.50. Paper, $26.50. 171pp. .... Vendor G0259

354 **[Bisbee]. FAM. RECORDS OF SOME OF THE DESC. OF THOMAS BESBEDGE (BISBEE) OF SCITUATE, MASS., 1634**, by W.B. Lapham. 1876.
Paper. $10.00. 48pp. .... Vendor G0259

355 **BISHOP FAMILIES IN AMER., BOOK III: RICHARD OF SALEM**, by I.E. Bishop. 1966.
Paper. $16.00. 80pp. .... Vendor G0259

356 **BISHOP FAMILIES OF AMERICA, BOOK VIII: EDWARD BISHOP OF SALEM**, by I.E. Bishop. 1967.
Cloth, $31.00. Paper, $21.00. 115pp. .... Vendor G0259

357 **FAM. HIST. OF JOHN BISHOP OF WHITBURN, SCOT. & SOME AMER. DESC.**, by Scott and Montgomery.
Cloth, $35.00. Paper, $25.00. 148pp. .... Vendor G0259

358 **RECORD OF DESC. OF JOHN BISHOP, ONE OF THE FOUNDERS OF GUILFORD, CT., IN 1639**, by W.W. Cone and G.A. Root. 1951.
Cloth, $52.50. Paper, $42.50. 277pp. .... Vendor G0259

359 **MEMORIAL CONCERNING THE FAMILY OF BISPHAM IN GREAT BRITAIN & THE U.S.**, by W. Bispham. 1890.
Cloth, $67.00. Paper, $57.00. 348pp. .... Vendor G0259

360 **BISSELL FAM. EXTR. FROM "HIST. OF WINDSOR, CONN."** 1892.
Paper. $7.00. 34pp. .... Vendor G0259

361 **GEN. RECORD & HIST. OF THE BITTNER–WERLEY FAMS.: DESC. OF MICHAEL BITTNER & SEBASTIAN WERLEY (1753–1930)**, by J.W Bittner. 1930.
Paper. $37.00. 239pp. .... Vendor G0259

362 **GEN. OF DESC. OF JOSEPH BIXBY, 1621–1701, OF IPSWICH & BOXFORD, MA., WHO SPELL THE NAME BIXBY, BIGSBY, BYXBEE, ETC., & OF THE BIX\BY FAM. IN ENG., DESC. OF WALTER BEKESBY (1427) OF THORPE MORIEUX, SUFFOLK**, by W.G. Bixby. Pts. I–III. 1914.
Cloth, $109.00. Paper, $99.00. 707pp. .... Vendor G0259

363   **BLACKBURN GENEALOGY, WITH NOTES ON THE WASHINGTON FAM. THROUGH INTERMARRIAGE, CONTAINING CERTAIN HIST. FACTS ON VA. LORE & MT. VERNON, INCL. RECORDS OF ALLIED FAMS.**, by Vinnetta W. Ranke. 1939.
Cloth, $36.00. Paper, $26.00. 158pp. .... Vendor G0259

364   **THE BLACKHALLS OF THAT ILK & BARRA: HEREDITARY CORONERS & FORESTERS OF THE BARLOCH**, by A. Morison. 1905 (Scotland).
Cloth, $38.00. Paper, $28.00. 180pp. .... Vendor G0259

365   **BLACKMAN & ALLIED FAM.**, by A.L. Holman. 1928.
Cloth, $49.00. Paper, $39.00. 258pp. .... Vendor G0259

366   **DESC. OF WM. BLACKSTONE**, by L. Sargent. 1857.
Paper. $8.50. 42pp. .... Vendor G0259

367   **BLACKWELL GENEALOGY: ANCESTORS, DESCENDANTS & CONNECTIONS OF MOORE CARTER & SARAH ALEXANDER (FOOTE) BLACKWELL (BOOK I, GENEALOGY ONLY)**, by E.M. Blackwell. 1948.
Cloth, $33.00. Paper, $23.00. 126pp. .... Vendor G0259

368   **DESCENDANTS OF JOSEPH BLACKWELL OF VIRGINIA**, by Carol A. Hauk. 1995. Indexed.
Paper. $35.00. 107pp. .... Vendor G0340

369   **ANCESTORS OF THE MEMBERS OF THE BLAIR SOCIETY FOR GENEALOGICAL RESEARCH**, by Kathleen B. Rheman. 1990. Indexed.
Paper. $11.50. 155pp. .... Vendor G0384

370   **BLAIR FAMILY BIBLE RECORDS**, by Mark Andrew Davis. 1994. Indexed.
Paper. $11.50. 58pp. .... Vendor G0384

371   **BLAIR FAMILY MARRIAGES, 1600–1900**, by Sue Blair Kimbrel. 1994. Indexed.
Paper. $17.25. 94pp. .... Vendor G0384

372   **BLAIR FAM. OF NEW ENGLAND**, by E.W. Leavitt. 1900.
Cloth, $44.50. Paper, $34.50. 197pp. .... Vendor G0259

373   **BLAIRS OF, IN AND THROUGH OHIO PRIOR TO 1900**, by Charlotte Blair Stewart. 1994.
Bound, $44.50. Unbound, $34.50. 364pp. .... Vendor G0384

374   **[Blair]. GENEALOGICAL FILE OF DR. ELEANOR M. HIESTAND-MOORE**, by Gerry Carlisle. 1990. Indexed.
Blair family correspondence, 1895 through 1923.
Paper. $23.00. 465pp. .... Vendor G0384

375   **PROCEEDINGS OF TENNESSEE BLAIR SEMINAR**, by Raymond R. Parker. 1995. Indexed.
Paper. $11.50. 37pp. .... Vendor G0384

376   **THE BLAIR FAMILY MAGAZINE**, by Nancy Knox Schaffer and Charlotte Blair Stewart, Editors.
Newsletter of the Blair Society for Genealogical Research, published quar-

terly, queries free to members, $3.00 for non-members. Indexes and back issues available.
Subscription. $15.00/year .... Vendor G0384

377 **ANCESTRY OF EDWARD WALES BLAKE & CLARISSA MATILDA GLIDDEN, WITH 90 ALLIED FAMILIES,** by Edith Bartlett Sumner. 1948.
Cloth, $59.50. Paper, $49.50. 322pp. .... Vendor G0259

378 **BLAKE FAM. A GEN. HIST. OF WILLIAM BLAKE OF DORCHESTER & HIS DESC.,** by S. Blake. 1857.
Cloth, $31.00. Paper, $21.00. 140pp. .... Vendor G0259

379 **DESCENDANTS OF JASPER BLAKE, EMIGRANT FROM ENGLAND TO HAMPTON NH, ca. 1643, 1649–1979,** by Carlton E. Blake. 1980.
Cloth, $89.50. Paper, $79.50. 553pp. .... Vendor G0259

380 **INCREASE BLAKE OF BOSTON, HIS ANC. & DESC.; WM. OF DORCHESTER & HIS FIVE CHILDREN,** by F. Blake. 1898.
Cloth, $34.00. Paper. $24.00. 147pp. .... Vendor G0259

381 **THE ANC. & ALLIED FAM. OF NATHAN BLAKE, 3RD, & SUSAN (TORREY) BLAKE OF EAST CORINTH, VT.,** by A.T.B. Fenno-Gendrot. 1916.
Cloth, $42.00. Paper, $32.00. 212pp. .... Vendor G0259

382 **ANC. OF BENJ. FERRIS BLAKENEY & HIS WIFE STELLA PERONNE SABIN,** by J.C. Frost. 1926.
Cloth, $58.00. Paper, $48.00. 309pp. .... Vendor G0259

383 **BLAKENEYS IN AMERICA, WITH REFERENCE TO ENGLISH–IRISH FAMILIES,** by J.O. Blakeney. 1928.
Paper. $19.50. 103pp. .... Vendor G0259

384 **GENEALOGY OF THE BLAKEY FAMILY & DESCENDANTS, WITH GEORGE, WHITSITT, HADEN, ANTHONY, STOCKTON, GIBSON & MANY OTHER RELATED ANTECEDENTS,** by L.A. Kress. 1942.
Paper. $19.00. 96pp. .... Vendor G0259

385 **BLANKENSHIP ANCESTORS,** by Gayle King Blankenship. 1995. Indexed. Illus.

BLAIR
Society for Genealogical Research

For more information, Write:
Edward P. Blair
20 W. College Ave. / Brownsburg, IN 46112-1253

Abbott, Agee, Ballow, Batte, Binion, Blankenship, Branch, Burford, Chastain, Cocke, Davis, Dunn, Gaulding, Goodwin, Hancock, Harris, Jackson, Johnston, Jones, LaFeit, Ligon, Lound, Mallory, Marcum, Moseley, Perdue, Stewart, Tanner, White, Worley. Referenced; 8¹/₂ x 11; 16.6 pitch.
Cloth. $46.00. 476pp. .... Vendor G0034

386 **BLATCHFORD MEMORIAL II: A GEN. REC. OF THE FAM. OF REV. SAMUEL BLATCHFORD, D.D., WITH SOME MENTION OF ALLIED FAMS.**, by E.W. Blatchford. 1912.
Cloth, $31.00. Paper, $21.00. 123pp. .... Vendor G0259

387 **BLAUVELT FAMILY GENEALOGY: A COMPREHENSIVE COMPILATION OF THE DESCENDANTS OF GERRIT HENDRICKSEN (BLAUVELT), 1620–1687, WHO CAME TO AMERICA IN 1638**, by Louis L. Blauvelt. 1957.
Cloth, $145.00. Paper, $135.00. 1,064pp. .... Vendor G0259

388 **BLAZER AND B-426 FAMILY ARCHIVES**, by John A. Blazer. 1993. Indexed. Illus.
Contains history, emigration, 9 family lines, 5,109 family members, 1,780 in-law family names, military service, family documents; 8¹/₂ x 11 format.
Cloth. $70.00. 743pp. .... Vendor G0209

389 **GEN. OF THE BLETHEN FAM.**, by A. Blethen. 1911.
Paper. $19.50. 108pp. .... Vendor G0259

390 **HISTORY OF THE BLICKENSDERFER FAMILY IN AMERICA**, by Jacob Blickensderfer. (1900?).
Paper. $11.00. 56pp. .... Vendor G0259

391 **BLISH FAMILY GEN., 1637–1905**, by J.K. Blish. 1905.
Cloth, $57.50. Paper, $47.50. 376pp. .... Vendor G0259

392 **BLISS & HOLMES DESCENDANTS: GENEALOGICAL DATA, BIOGR. SKETCHES OF THE DESC. OF EPHRAIM BLISS OF SAVOY, MA., & ISRAEL HOLMES OF WATERBURY, CT., & RELATED FAMILIES**, by E.B. & A.B. Dayton. 1961.
Cloth, $38.00. Paper, $28.00. 184pp. .... Vendor G0259

393 **GEN. OF THE BLISS FAM. IN AMERICA, FROM ABOUT 1550 TO 1880**, by J.H. Bliss. 1881.
Cloth, $109.00. Paper, $99.00. 811pp. .... Vendor G0259

394 **FIVE FAMILIES OF CHARLESTOWN, R.I.: BLIVEN, CRANDALL, MACOMBER, MONEY & TAYLOR, WITH APPENDIX**, by Earl P. Crandall. 1993.
Cloth, $39.00. Paper, $29.00. 165+120pp. .... Vendor G0259

395 **ASAHEL BLODGETT OF HUDSON & DORCHESTER, N.H., HIS AMER. ANC. & DESC.**, by I.D. Blodgett. 1906.
Cloth, $33.00. Paper, $23.00. 144pp. .... Vendor G0259

396 **DESC. OF RICHARD BLOOD OF BELLINGHAM & CHARLTON, MASS.**, by C.W. Barlow. 1952.
Paper. $7.50. 37pp. .... Vendor G0259

397 THE STORY OF THE BLOODS, INCL AN ACCT. OF THE EARLY GEN. OF THE FAM. IN AMER. IN GENEAL. LINES FROM ROBT. BLOOD OF CONCORD & RICHARD BLOOD OF GROTON [MASS.], by R.D. Harris. 1960.
Cloth, $42.50. Paper, $32.50. 201pp. .... Vendor G0259

398 BLOSS–PYLES–ROSS–SELLARDS—A GENEALOGICAL HISTORY, by Harry Leon Sellards, Jr. 1990. Indexed. Illus.
Related families: **Smith, Adkins, Scalf, Booth, Ferguson, Napier, Ballangee, Queen, Lewis.**
Cloth. $40.00. 512pp. .... Vendor G0445

399 BOARDMAN GENEALOGY, 1525–1895, by C. Goldthwaite. 1895.
Cloth, $109.50. Paper, $99.50. 791pp. .... Vendor G0259

400 THE ANC. OF WILLIAM FRANCIS JOSEPH BOARDMAN, HART-FORD, CONN., by W.F.J. Boardman. 1906.
Cloth, $76.00. Paper, $66.00. 419pp. .... Vendor G0259

401 THE DESCENDANTS OF FREDERICK AND MARIA (REICHARD) BOCK, compiled by Melvin L. Bock. 1991. Indexed. Illus.
Cloth. $25.00. 336pp. .... Vendor G0293

402 DEAR "COUSIN": A CHARTED GENEALOGY OF THE DESCEN-DANTS OF ANNEKE JANS BOGARDUS (1605–1663) TO THE 5TH GENERATION, by William Brower Bogardus. 1996. Indexed. Illus.
Includes all known vital data on descendants and spouses; identification of sources; most common errors and incorrect or unproven lines of descent; and more.
Cloth. $29.50 in US, $33.00 US in Canada. Approx. 195pp. . Vendor G0452

403 GEN. HIST. OF THE ANC. & DESC. OF GEN. ROBERT BOGARDUS, by M. Gray. 1927.
Cloth, $55.00. Paper, $45.00. 281pp. .... Vendor G0259

404 BOGART FAM., EXTR. FROM GEN. NOTES OF N.Y. & NEW ENG. FAMS., by S.V. Talcott. 1883.
Paper. $9.50. 47pp. .... Vendor G0259

405 THE BOGART FAM.: TUNIS GYSBERT BOGAERT & HIS DESC., by J.A. Bogart. 1959.
Cloth, $54.00. Paper, $44.00. 280pp. .... Vendor G0259

406 FIVE BOGERT FAMILIES: DESCENDANTS OF EVERT, JAN LAURENCZ, CORNELIS, GUYSBERT, AND HARMENSE MYNDERTSE BOGERT, by Herbert S. Ackerman. n.d.
Cloth, $88.00. Paper, $78.00. 488+40pp., typescript .... Vendor G0259

407 MORE BOGERT FAMILIES: DESCENDANTS OF CORNELISE JANSEN, GYSBERT UYTEN, AND HENRY BOGERT, WITH OTHER BOGERT FAMILIES, by Herbert S. Ackerman. n.d.
Cloth, $76.00. Paper, $66.00. 374+56pp., typescript .... Vendor G0259

408 BOGUE & ALLIED FAMS., by V.T. Bogue. 1947.
Cloth, $85.00. Paper, $75.50. 439+49pp. .... Vendor G0259

409 **BOHLANDER FAMILY & EARLY HIST. OF DUPAGE CO., ILL.**, by W.F. Bohlander. 1937.
Paper. $14.00. 72pp. .... Vendor G0259

410 **BOHRER–BORAH–BORER GEN.**, by Camden Borah Meyer. 1965.
Cloth, $89.50. Paper, $79.50. 519pp. .... Vendor G0259

411 **CHRONICLES OF THE BOIT FAM. & THEIR DESC., & OTHER ALLIED FAMS.**, by R.A. Boit. 1915.
Cloth, $49.00. Paper, $39.00. 260pp. .... Vendor G0259

412 **GEN. OF THE BOLLES FAM. IN AMER.**, by J. Bolles. 1865.
Paper. $14.00. 71pp. .... Vendor G0259

413 **DESCENDANTS OF ROBERT BOLLING OF VIRGINIA**, by Carol A. Hauk. 1995. Indexed.
Paper. $45.00. 290pp. .... Vendor G0340

414 **THE FAM. OF BOLTON IN ENG. & AMER., 1100–1894; A STUDY IN GEN.**, by H.C. and R.P. Bolton. 1895.
Cloth, $94.00. Paper, $84.00. 540pp. .... Vendor G0259

415 **BOLTON FAM. IN IRELAND WITH THEIR ENG. AND AMER. KINDRED**, by C.K. Bolton. 1937.
Paper. $18.50. 109pp. .... Vendor G0259

416 **THE BOLTONS OF OLD & NEW ENGLAND, WITH A GEN. OF THE DESC. OF WILLIAM BOLTON OF READING, MASS., 1720**, by C.K. Bolton. 1889.
Paper. $19.50. 98pp. .... Vendor G0259

417 **BOMBERGER: LANCASTER COUNTY ROOTS, 1722–1986**, by Lloyd Huber Bomberger; edited by Barbara Nissley Miller. 1986.
Paper. $21.00. 224pp. .... Vendor G0150

418 **AUTOBIOGR. REMINISCENCES OF REV. ALVAN BOND, D.D., 1793–1882; ANC. & DESC., PED. CHARTS OF ALVAN BOND & SARAH RICHARDSON, HIS WIFE; FACS. OF BOND GEN., 1826**, by H.R. Bond. 1896.
Cloth, $42.00. Paper, $32.00. 214pp. .... Vendor G0259

419 **[Bond]. CHICKAMAUGA AND THE UNDERGROUND RAILROAD**, by James O. Bond. 1993. Indexed. Illus.
Surnames: **Mills, Bond.**
Cloth. $10.00. 133pp. .... Vendor G0214

420 **BOND. (EXTR. "GEN. & HIST. OF WATERTOWN, MASS.").**
Paper. $9.00. 45pp. .... Vendor G0259

421 **[Bond]. FRIENDS FOR 340 YEARS**, by James O. Bond. 1995. Indexed. Illus.
Surnames: **Bond, Paradise, Beales, Harrold, Hockett, Hunt, Rogers.**
Cloth. $10.00. 158pp. .... Vendor G0214

422 **[Bond]. WALK CHEERFULLY OVER THE EARTH**, by James O. Bond. 1985. Illus.

Surnames: **Mills, Hunt, Williams, Mendenhall, Sell, Tatum.**
Cloth. $15.00. 336pp. .... Vendor G0214

423 **BONTECOU GENEALOGY: A RECORD OF THE DESCENDANTS OF PIERRE BONTECOU, HUGUENOT REFUGEE FROM FRANCE, IN THE LINES OF HIS SONS**, by John E. Morris. 1885.
Cloth, $53.00. Paper, $43.00. 271pp. .... Vendor G0259

424 **ANNALS OF THE BOODEYS IN NEW ENGLAND, WITH LESSONS FROM JOHN ELIOT**, by R.B. Caverly. 1880.
Cloth, $56.50. Paper, $46.50. 297pp. .... Vendor G0259

425 **BOONE FAMILY. GEN. HIST. OF DESC. OF GEORGE & MARY BOONE, WHO CAME TO AMERICA IN 1717**, by H. Spraker. 1922.
Cloth, $119.00. Paper, $109.00. 707pp. .... Vendor G0259

426 **THE BOONE FAMILY. A Genealogical History of the Descendants of George and Mary Boone Who Came to America in 1717**, by Hazel Atterbury Spraker. (1922) reprint 1993. Indexed. Illus.
Cloth. $40.00. 707pp. .... Vendor G0010

427 **BOOTH(E) FAMILY HISTORY—ONE LINEAGE FROM THOMAS, SR. (1705–1767) OF AMELIA CO., VA TO PRESENT**, by Timothy D. Booth. 1994. Indexed. Illus.
Nine generations with biographical chapters. Bibliography. Numbering system serves as index.
Paper. $30.00. 110pp. .... Vendor G0410

428 **ONE BRANCH OF BOOTH FAM., SHOWING CONNECTIONS WITH 100 MASS. BAY COL.**, by C.E. Booth. 1910.
Cloth, $41.00. Paper, $31.00. 237pp. .... Vendor G0259

429 **REPORT OF THE BOOTH ASSOCIATION OF THE U. S.**, by C. Smith. 1868.
Paper. $12.50. 64pp. .... Vendor G0259

430 **HIST. & GEN. RECORD OF THE DESC. OF RICHARD & JOAN BORDEN, WHO SETTLED IN PORTSMOUTH, R.I., MAY 1638**, by H.B. Weld. 1899.
Cloth, $55.00. Paper, $45.00. 348pp. .... Vendor G0259

431 **RICHARD BORDEN OF PORTSMOUTH, R. I. & DESC.**, edited by H.F. Johnston.
Paper. $11.00. 56pp. .... Vendor G0259

432 **THE BORDERS FAMILIES**, by William Steve Borders. 1989. Indexed. Illus.
The **Borders** in America from census reports, county records, and letters

from living Borders and their relatives. Research is continuing. The author welcomes letters of inquiry and additional input data.
Cloth. $25.00. 527pp. .... Vendor G0097

433 **DESCENT, NAME & ARMS OF BORLASE OF BORLASE, IN THE CO. OF CORNWALL,** by W. Borlase. 1888 (London).
Cloth, $46.00. Paper, $36.00. 207pp. .... Vendor G0259

434 **HIST. OF BORNEMAN FAM. IN AMERICA SINCE FIRST SETTLERS, 1721–1878,** by J.H. Borneman. 1881.
Cloth, $32.50. Paper, $22.50. 114pp. .... Vendor G0259

435 **BORTHWICK FAMILY: HISTORY & GENEALOGY OF THE FAMILY OF BORTHWICK, CHIEFLY IN SCOTLAND & AMERICA,** by H.M. Borthwick. 1903.
Paper. $19.50. 127pp. .... Vendor G0259

436 **GEN. OF THE BOSTWICK FAM. IN AMER. THE DESC. OF ARTHUR BOSTWICK OF STRATFORD, CONN.,** by H.A. Bostwick. 1901.
Cloth, $156.50. Paper, $146.50. 1,172pp. .... Vendor G0259

437 **GEN. REGISTER OF THE NAME OF BOSTWICK 1668–1850,** by E. Bostwick. 1851.
Paper. $10.00. 50pp. .... Vendor G0259

438 **BOSWORTH GENEALOGY: HISTORY OF THE DESCENDANTS OF EDWARD BOSWORTH WHO ARRIVED IN AMERICA IN 1634,** by M.B. Clarke. 1926.
Cloth, $33.00. Paper, $23.00. 122pp. .... Vendor G0259

439 **BOSWORTH, PTS. 1–4, HIST. OF THE DESC. OF EDWARD BOSWORTH, WHO ARRIVED IN AMER. IN 1634, WITH APPENDIX CONTAINING OTHER LINES OF AMER. BOSWORTHS,** by M.B. Clarke. 1926–31.
Cloth, $91.50. Paper, $81.50. 551pp. .... Vendor G0259

440 **BOSWORTH, PTS. 5–6, HIST. OF THE DESC. OF EDWARD BOSWORTH, WHO ARRIVED IN AMERICA IN 1634,** by M.B. Clarke. 1936–40.
Cloth, $79.50. Paper, $69.50. 464pp. .... Vendor G0259

441 **BOUCHER FAMILY (BOWSHER, BAUSCHER, BAUSHER, BOUSHER), COMPRISING A GEN. OF BRANCHES OF STRAWN, HARPSTER, TEDROW, CRYFER ET AL; DESC. OF DANIEL BOUCHER OF AL-BANY TWP., BERKS CO., PA., WITH NOTES OF OTHER BOUCHER FAMILIES,** by F.A. Burkhardt. 1917.
Cloth, $72.00. Paper, $62.00. 402pp. .... Vendor G0259

442 **BOUTON–BOUGHTON FAM., DESC. OF JOHN BOUTON OF FRANCE, WHO LANDED AT BOSTON, 1635, AND SETTLED AT NORWALK, CONN.,** by J. Boughton. 1890.
Cloth, $100.00. Paper, $90.00. 684pp. .... Vendor G0259

443 **MICHAEL BOWDEN & SOME DESC.,** by W. Bowden. 1960.
Paper. $11.00. 54pp. .... Vendor G0259

444 **BOWDITCH FAM. OF SALEM, MASS.; A GEN. SKETCH.** 1936.
Paper. $9.50. 50pp. .... Vendor G0259

445 **SOME ACCOUNT OF THE BOWDOIN FAM., WITH NOTES ON THE FAM. OF PORDAGE, LYNDE, NEWGATE, ERVING**, by T. Prime. 2nd. ed. 1894.
Paper. $10.00. 52pp. .... Vendor G0259

446 **FAM. OF GRIFFITH BOWEN, WELSH PURITAN IMGR., BOSTON, 1638–9, ESP. THE BRANCH OF SILAS BOWEN, BORN IN WOODSTOCK, CT., 1722**, by D. Bowen. 1893.
Cloth, $54.00. Paper, $44.00. 278pp. .... Vendor G0259

447 **LINEAGE OF THE BOWENS OF WOODSTOCK, CONN.**, by E.A. Bowen. 1897.
Cloth, $42.50. Paper, $32.50. 251pp. .... Vendor G0259

448 **MEM. OF THE BOWEN FAM.**, by E.C. Bowen. 1884.
Paper. $19.50. 102pp. .... Vendor G0259

449 **DESCENDANTS OF CONRAD BOWER, MARTIN EASTERDAY, SR., JOHN HOOVER, SR., AND GABRIEL SWINEHART, SR., FAMILIES FROM COLONIAL MARYLAND TO OHIO IN THE EARLY 1800'S**, by Arlene F. Mansfield. 1993. Indexed. Illus.
The book contains over 5,000 names. Some of the collateral lines include: **Dague, Friend, Grimm, Minnich, Neff, Swickard**, and **Tope**. The book includes 50 pages of references as well as early history of Frederick County, Maryland, and Jefferson and Harrison counties, Ohio.
Cloth. $32.50. 482pp. .... Vendor G0222

450 **DESCENDANTS OF JOHN BOWIE OF VIRGINIA**, by Carol A. Hauk. 1995. Indexed.
Paper. $30.00. 38pp. .... Vendor G0340

451 **THE BOWIES & THEIR KINDRED: A GEN. & BIOGR. HIST.**, by W.W. Bowie. 1899.
Cloth, $88.50. Paper, $78.50. 523pp. .... Vendor G0259

452 **BOWLBY FAMILIES IN ENGLAND AND AMERICA**, by Raymond E. Bowlby. 5 parts in 1. 1985–91.
Cloth, $89.50. Paper, $79.50. 534pp. .... Vendor G0259

453 **RECORD OF THE DESC. OF CHARLES BOWLER, ENGLAND—1740 —AMERICA, WHO SETTLED IN NEWPORT, R.I.**, by N.P. Bowler & C. B. Malone. 1905.
Cloth, $54.50. Paper, $44.50. 298pp. .... Vendor G0259

454 **THE BOWMANS, PIONEERING FAM. IN VA., KY. & THE NW TERRITORY**, by J.W. Wayland. 1943.
Cloth, $39.50. Paper, $29.50. 185pp. .... Vendor G0259

455 **WILLIAM BOWNE OF YORKSHIRE, ENGLAND & HIS DESCENDANTS**, by M.K. Reading. 1903.
Paper. $10.00. 47pp. .... Vendor G0259

456　**BOWSER FAMILY HISTORY,** by A.B. Bowser. 1922.
Cloth, $56.00. Paper, $46.00. 309pp. Vendor G0259

457　**THE DESCENDANTS OF CHENEY BOYCE, "ANCIENT PLANTER," AND RICHARD CRAVEN, INCLUDING THE FAMILIES OF CHAPPELL, COGGINS, GEE, POYTHRESS, RIVES, SCOTT, TATUM,** by John A. Brayton. 1996. Includes name, location, and slave index. The descendants for 7 generations of two Jamestown ancestors, throughout colonial Virginia, colonial North Carolina, and Tennessee, Arkansas, Alabama, Georgia, and South Carolina.
Cloth. $40 postpaid, NC residents add 6% sales tax.
Approx. 500+xxiv pp. . . . . Vendor G0302

458　**BOYD–PATTERSON ANCESTRY,** by H.M. Pitman and K.P.B. Hunt. 1967.
Cloth, $39.00. Paper, $29.00. 197pp. Vendor G0259

459　**HIST. OF THE BOYD FAM. & DESC., WITH HIST. SKETCHES OF THE FAM. IN SCOTLAND & IRELAND, WITH RECORDS OF THEIR DESC.,** by W.P. Boyd. 1912.
Cloth, $91.50. Paper, $81.50. 521pp. Vendor G0259

460　**HERE & THERE IN THE FAMILY TREE,** by A. Boyden. 1949.
Boyden family.
Cloth, $56.00. Paper, $46.00. 294pp. Vendor G0259

461　**THOMAS BOYDEN & DESC.,** by W. Boyden, etc. 1901.
Cloth, $50.00. Paper, $40.00. 267pp. Vendor G0259

462　**BOYDSTUN FAM.,** by G.C. Weaver. 1927.
Cloth, $34.00. Paper, $24.00. 147pp. Vendor G0259

463　**AMERICAN BOYERS,** by Charles C. Boyer; rev. by Melville J. Boyer. 1940.
Cloth, $109.50. Paper, $99.50. 663pp. Vendor G0259

464　**FRONTIER FARMER: AUTOBIOGRAPHY AND FAMILY HISTORY OF AARON A. BOYLAN 1827–1923,** by Aaron A. Boylan; edited by Katherine Lytle Sharp. 1993. Indexed. Illus.
Cloth. $25.00. 264pp. . . . . Vendor G0037

465　**BOYLE GENEALOGY. JOHN BOYLE OF VIRGINIA & KENTUCKY; NOTES ON LINES OF DESCENT WITH SOME COLLATERAL REFERENCES,** by John Boyle. 1909.
Cloth, $37.50. Paper, $27.50. 174pp. Vendor G0259

466　**AMER. BOYNTON DIRECTORY, WITH THE ADDRESS OF ALL KNOWN BOYNTONS, BOYINGTONS & BYINGTONS IN THE U.S. & BRIT. DOMINIONS,** by J. Boynton. 1884.
Cloth, $32.00. Paper, $22.00. 147pp. Vendor G0259

467　**A GEN. OF THE DESC. OF WM. & JOHN BOYNTON,** by J.F. and C.H. Boynton. 1897.
Cloth, $55.00. Paper, $45.00. 386pp. Vendor G0259

468　**REPRINT OF BETHAM'S HIST., GEN. & BARONETS OF THE BOYNTON FAM. IN ENG.,** by J. Boynton. 1884.
Paper. $7.50. 40pp. . . . . Vendor G0259

469 **SKETCHES OF THE BOZEMAN FAMILY**, by Joseph W. Bozeman. (1885) reprint 1981. Indexed.
Cloth. $22.00. 180pp. .... Vendor G0380

470 **BRACE LINEAGE**, by J.S. Brace. 1927.
Cloth, $50.00. Paper, $40.00. 224pp. .... Vendor G0259

471 **WM. BRACKEN OF NEW CASTLE CO., DELAWARE, & HIS DESCENDANTS**, by H.M. Bracken. 1901.
Paper. $16.00. 79pp. .... Vendor G0259

472 **BRACKENBURY OF LINCOLNSHIRE, VOL. I: WILLS, ETC.**, edited by K.F. Brackenbury. 1954.
Paper. $16.00. 68+15pp. .... Vendor G0259

473 **BENJAMIN BRACKETT OF THE CAROLINAS**, by Shirley B. Adair. 1993. Indexed. Illus.
Upton, Black, Boyd, Coe, Butler, Smith (related lines).
Paper. $25.00. 330pp. .... Vendor G0382

474 **DESC. OF ANTHONY BRACKETT OF PORTSMOUTH & CAPT. RICHARD BRACKETT OF BRAINTREE**, by H.I. Brackett. 1907.
Cloth, $103.50. Paper, $93.50. 624pp. .... Vendor G0259

475 **BRADBURY MEMORIAL. RECORDS OF SOME OF THE DESC. OF THOMAS BRADBURY OF AGAMENTICUS (YORK) IN 1634 AND OF SALISBURY, MA. IN 1638, WITH A BRIEF SKETCH OF THE BRADBURYS OF ENG.**, by W.B. Lapham. 1890.
Cloth, $51.00. Paper, $41.00. 320pp. .... Vendor G0259

476 **ANC. OF THE BRADFORDS OF AUSTERFIELD, CO. YORK.**, by W.B. Browne. (Repr. *NEHGR*) 1929.
Paper. $7.00. 38pp. .... Vendor G0259

477 **GOVERNOR WILLIAM BRADFORD & HIS SON MAJOR WILLIAM BRADFORD**, by J. Shepard. 1900.
Paper. $18.50. 103pp. .... Vendor G0259

478 **THE DESC. OF GOV. WM. BRADFORD THROUGH THE 1ST 7 GEN.**, by R.G. Hall. 1951.
Cloth, $106.50. Paper, $96.50. 645pp. .... Vendor G0259

479 **A BRADHAM FAMILY HISTORY AND GENEALOGY**, by Janet Bradham Brewster. 1986. Indexed. Illus.
This family history and genealogy is the first of its kind to be published on the **Bradham** surname. All official records, primary and secondary sources are documented. It documents earliest Bradham found in this country in 1665 and others who were here before the Revolution. Bradham families who settled in Virginia, South Carolina, North Carolina, Georgia, Florida, Texas, Illinois, and Indiana are emphasized. Chronologies of all Bradham families, as well as many descending allied families, have been brought forward to present-decade descendants.
Allied families through female lines include: **Allen, Benbow, Broadway, Brogdon, Brock, Burgess, Bryant, Coker, Corbett, Coskrey, Creecy, Gibson, Hodge, Holladay, Jayroe, Johnson, Jones, Kelly, Lanier, Lavender, Lewis,**

Mathis, McKnight, Pack, Player, Ragin, Rich, Ridgill, Rivers, Rodgers, Stukes, Tomlinson. Complete every name index—10,000+ names. Cloth. $35.00. 670pp. .... Vendor G0248

480   **MY FOREFATHERS: BRADHURST, BROADHURST, DE BRADEHURST,** by A.M. Bradhurst. 1910 (London). Cloth, $66.00. Paper, $56.00. 364pp. .... Vendor G0259

481   **HIST. OF THE BRADLEE FAM., WITH PARTICULAR REFERENCE TO THE DESC. OF NATHAN BRADLEY OF DORCHESTER, MASS.,** by S.B. Doggett. 1878. Paper, $9.00. 45pp. .... Vendor G0259

482   **ANCESTORS & DESC. OF MORRIS A. BRADLEY,** by Mrs. G. Rideout. 1948. Cloth, $38.00. Paper, $28.00. 176pp. .... Vendor G0259

483   **BRADLEY OF ESSEX COUNTY [MA.]: EARLY RECORDS, 1643–1746,** by E.B. Peters. 1915. Cloth, $45.00. Paper, $35.00. 221pp. .... Vendor G0259

484   **DESC. OF ISAAC BRADLEY OF CONN., 1650–1898; WITH A BRIEF HIST. OF THE BRADLEY FAMILIES IN NEW ENGLAND,** by L.A. Bradley. 1917. Cloth, $35.50. Paper, $25.50. 171pp. .... Vendor G0259

485   **GEN. FAM. OF AARON AND SARAH BRADLEY OF GUILFORD, CONN.,** by A.P. Lloyd. 1879. Paper. $9.00. 46pp. .... Vendor G0259

486   **NOTES RESPECTING THE BRADLEY FAM. OF FAIRFIELD, WITH NOTICES OF COLL. ANC. ON THE FEMALE SIDE,** by J.P. Bradley; edited by C. Bradley. 1894. Paper. $12.50. 69pp. .... Vendor G0259

487   **[Bradt]. A NORWEGIAN FAMILY IN COLONIAL AMERICA,** by Peter R. Christoph. 3rd ed. 1994. Cloth, $47.50. Paper, $37.50. 250pp. .... Vendor G0259

488   **DESCENDANTS OF ALBERT & ARENT ANDRIESSEN BRADT,** by Cynthia Brott Biasca. 1990. Cloth, $99.50. Paper, $89.50. 776pp. .... Vendor G0259

489   **ANCESTRY OF THOMAS CHALMERS BRAINERD,** compiled and edited by D.L. Jacobus. 1948. Cloth, $64.00. Paper, $54.00. 351pp. .... Vendor G0259

490   **GEN. OF THE BRAINERD FAM. IN THE U.S.; WITH SKETCHES OF INDIVIDUALS,** by D. Field. 1857. Cloth, $58.50. Paper, $48.50. 303pp. .... Vendor G0259

491   **BRALEY GENEALOGY: THE DESC. OF ROGER BRALEY, 1696–1913,** by G.L. Randall. 1913. Cloth, $71.00. Paper, $61.00. 393pp. .... Vendor G0259

492   **CASPER BRANNER OF VA. & DESC.,** by J. Branner. 1913. Cloth, $84.50. Paper, $74.50. 477pp. .... Vendor G0259

493 AN ACCT. OF SOME OF THE DESC. OF CAPT. THOMAS BRATTLE, by E.D. Harris. 1867.
Paper. $18.00. 90pp. .... Vendor G0259

494 [Brawley]. **THE BOLLING–GAY–GASTON–BRAWLEY PAPER TRAIL WITH ALLIED FAMILIES AND FRIENDS**, by Dorothy Perry Brawley and Frank L. Perry, Jr. 1995. Indexed. Illus.
Including families of **Adair, Brevard, Brumby, Carter, Davidson, Foote, Gage, Harris, Hemphill, Huggins, Knox, McFadden, McKnitt, Perry, Pocahontas, Rice, Robinson, Rolfe, Schneider, Trent,** and **Washington.**
Cloth. $80.00. 644pp. .... Vendor G0415

495 **SEVEN GENERATIONS OF BRAYS, OF MASS., ME., WISC. & MINN.,** by W.M. Bray. 1956.
Paper. $9.00. 43pp. .... Vendor G0259

496 **GEN. OF THE BRECK FAM., DESC. FROM EDWARD OF DORCHESTER & HIS BROTHERS IN AMER.,** by S. Breck. 1889.
Cloth, $50.00. Paper, $40.00. 281pp. .... Vendor G0259

497 **THE BREEDING/BREEDEN GENEALOGICAL EXCHANGE,** by Bruce A. Breeding, plus contributors. 1991–94 (7 issues). Indexed.
Send SASE for print-out of Tables of Contents.
Paper. $7.50/issue, incl. postage. 303 total pp. .... Vendor G0451

498 **BREESE FAM. OF ENGLAND & AMERICA, 1709–1875,** by E.E. Salisbury. 1885.
Paper. $12.00. 61pp. .... Vendor G0259

499 **PERSONAL REMINISC., WITH GEN. SKETCH OF AMER. BRANCH OF THE BREESE FAM.,** by J. Montgomery. 1884.
Paper. $15.00. 73pp. .... Vendor G0259

500 **THE BRELAND FAMILIES OF THE SOUTHERN STATES,** by Charles Gregory Breland. 1995. Indexed. Illus.
Other surnames included: **Bailey, Blades, Blount, Boyken, Cook, Copeland, Crain, Daniels, DeLoach, Easley, Fussell, Gantz, Grant, Johnson, Johnston, Kemp, Maner, Odom, Peirce, Smart, Stafford, Thornhill, Thurston, Varn, Wall, Williams, Wills.**
Cloth. $22.00. 101pp. .... Vendor G0398

501 **A HISTORY OF THE DESCENDANTS OF ABRAHAM BRENEMAN, LANCASTER COUNTY, PENNSYLVANIA,** by Charles D. Breneman. (1939) reprint 1988.
Cloth. $36.00. 566pp. .... Vendor G0150

502 **THE BRENNEMAN HISTORY,** by Albert H. Gerberich. 1938, 1988.
Basic genealogy of descendants of Melchior **Brenneman,** Lancaster Co. pioneer.
Cloth. $55.00. 1,217pp. .... Vendor G0150

503 **BRENNER–JAMES GENEALOGY,** by A.L. Brenner and B.A.B. Fleming. 1949.
Cloth, $57.50. Paper, $47.50. 304pp. .... Vendor G0259

504 DESCENDANTS OF COL. GILES BRENT, CAPT. GEORGE BRENT & ROBERT BRENT, IMMIGRANTS TO MARYLAND & VA., by C.H. Brent. 1946.
Cloth, $41.00. Paper, $31.00. 195pp. .... Vendor G0259

505 BRETT GEN., by L.B. Googenow. 1915.
Cloth, $94.00. Paper, $84.00. 545pp. .... Vendor G0259

506 GEN. OF LUDWIG BRETZ FAM. 1750–1890, by E. Parthemore. 1890.
Cloth, $40.00. Paper, $30.00. 149pp. .... Vendor G0259

507 HIST. OF THE BREWER FAM. OF N.C., TENN., IND., & ILL. 1936.
Paper. $15.00. 75pp. .... Vendor G0259

508 BREWSTER GENEALOGY, 1566–1907; DESC. OF WM. BREWSTER OF THE MAYFLOWER, by E. Jones. 2 vols. 1908.
Cloth, $197.50. Paper, $187.50. 1,493pp. .... Vendor G0259

509 MARK BREWSTER OF HULL, ENGLAND AND ALLIED FAMILIES IN AMERICA, by Marcus V. Brewster. 1991. Indexed. Illus.
This **Brewster** family history and genealogy starts with its first documented progenitor Jonathan Brewster b. ca. 1760 near Waltham Parish, Lincolnshire, Eng., a few miles from Immingham on River Humber where the Pilgrims with Elder Wm Brewster took ship for Holland in 1609. An in-depth biographical record of Jonathan's grandson, Mark Brewster of Hull, England, encompasses genealogical records of Mark's wife, Jane Ann **Atkey**, and her Atkey and **Yelf** antecedents from Isle of Wight. Treated likewise are ancestral lines of Atkey Brewster's wife, Mabel **Hiscock**, including surnames: **Dare, Fowler, Hewitt, Potter, Carpenter, Pierce,** and **Swingley.**
Appendix contains personal and official records. Throughout the book are 90 photographs, plus many maps and location illustrations. An every-name index totaling more than 1,100 makes for easy reference.
Cloth. $35.00. 352pp. .... Vendor G0249

510 AN ACCOUNT OF THE DESC. OF JOHN BRIDGE, CAMBRIDGE, 1632, by W.F. Bridge. 1884.
Paper. $19.50. 122pp. .... Vendor G0259

511 GEN. OF THE JOHN BRIDGE FAM. IN AMER., 1632–1924, rev. ed., by W.D. Bridge. 1924.
Cloth, $91.50. Paper, $81.50. 547pp. .... Vendor G0259

512 GENEALOGY OF SAMUEL WILLARD BRIDGES (1874–1943) & CAROLINE BRITTON BRIDGES (1873–1958), by R.E. Thomas. 1960.
Paper. $19.50. 129pp. .... Vendor G0259

513 BRIDGMAN FAMILY; DESCENDANTS OF JAMES BRIDGMAN, 1636–1894, by B.N. and J.C. Bridgman. 1894.
Cloth, $37.50. Paper, $27.50. 168pp. .... Vendor G0259

514 THE BRIGGS GEN. WITH ALLIED WHITE LINES, INCL. ANC. AND DESC. OF ICHABOD WHITE BRIGGS, 1609–1953.
Cloth, $31.00. Paper, $21.00. 116pp. .... Vendor G0259

515 WE & OUR KINFOLK: EPHRAIM & REBEKA WATERMAN BRIGGS, THEIR DESC. & ANC., edited by M.B. Briggs. 1887.
Cloth, $32.50. Paper, $22.50. 150pp. .... Vendor G0259

516 THE HIST. OF THE BRIGHAM FAM., A RECORD OF SEVERAL THOUSAND DESC. OF THOMAS BRIGHAM THE EMIGRANT, 1603– 1653, by W.I.T. Brigham; edited by E.E. Brigham. 1907.
Cloth, $90.00. Paper, $80.00. 636pp. .... Vendor G0259

517 THE HIST. OF THE BRIGHAM FAM., WITH ENG. ORIG. OF THOMAS BRIGHAM, THE EMIGRANT, 1603–35, VOL. II, by E.E. Brigham. 1927.
Cloth, $55.00. Paper, $45.00. 300pp. .... Vendor G0259

518 GEN. REGISTER OF SEVERAL ANCIENT PURITANS; VOL. II., THE BRIGHAM FAM., by A. Morse. 1859.
Cloth, $30.00. Paper, $20.00. 96pp. .... Vendor G0259

519 BRIGHT. EXTR. "GEN. & HIST. OF WATERTOWN, MASS."
Paper. $7.50. 36pp. .... Vendor G0259

520 THE BRIGHTS OF SUFFOLK, ENGLAND, & DESC. OF HENRY BRIGHT, JR., WHO CAME TO NEW ENGLAND IN 1630, & SETTLED IN WATERTOWN, MA., by J.B. Bright. 1858.
Cloth, $67.50. Paper, $57.50. 365pp. .... Vendor G0259

521 A PICTORIAL HIST. OF THE BRILLHARTS OF AMER., by J.A. Brillhart. 1926.
Cloth, $52.00. Paper, $42.00. 268pp. .... Vendor G0259

522 HISTORY OF THE BRINGHURST FAMILY WITH NOTES ON THE CLARKSON, DE PEYSTER & BOUDE FAMILIES, by J.G. Leach. 1901.
Cloth, $34.00. Paper, $24.00. 152pp. .... Vendor G0259

523 FAMILY OF JORIS DIRCKSEN BRINCKERHOFF, 1638 (WITH 1994 EVERY-NAME INDEX BY JERRI BURKET), by T. Van Wyck Brinkerhoff. 1887.
Cloth, $39.50. Paper, $29.50. 188pp. .... Vendor G0259

524 THE BRINKLEY AND ALLIED FAMILIES OF NANSEMOND CO., VIR-GINIA AND GATES CO., NORTH CAROLINA, by Freddie L. Brinkley. 1994. Indexed. Illus.
Cloth. $30.00. 243pp. .... Vendor G0434

525 DESC. OF OTTO HENRICH WILHELM BRINKMAN, by I.H. De Long. 1925.
Paper. $10.00. 55pp. .... Vendor G0259

526 BRISTOL GEN., by W.E. Bristol. 1967.
Cloth, $96.00. Paper, $86.00. 561pp. .... Vendor G0259

527 GENEALOGY BRITTON, by E.E. Britton. 1901.
Paper. $10.00. 50pp. .... Vendor G0259

528 JOHN TINNE BROCK OF CLARK COUNTY, KENTUCKY: ANCES-TORS AND DESCENDANTS, by James G. Faulconer. 1988. Indexed. Illus.
Paper. $12.00 incl. postage. 82pp. .... Vendor G0252

529 THE DESC. OF JOHN BROCKETT OF NEW HAVEN COLONY, by E.J. Brockett, et al. 1905.
Cloth, $50.00. Paper, $40.00. 266pp. .... Vendor G0259

530 **BROCKMAN SCRAPBOOK: BELL, BLEDSOE, BROCKMAN, BURRUS, DICKSON, JAMES, PEDAN, ET AL**, by W.E. Brockman. 1952. Cloth, $77.50. Paper, $67.50. 442pp. .... Vendor G0259

531 **RECORD OF THE BROCKMAN & DRAKE-BROCKMAN FAMILY**, by D.H. Drake-Brockman. 1936 (England). Cloth, $35.00. Paper, $25.00. 158pp. .... Vendor G0259

532 **BROCKWAY FAM., DESC. OF WOLSTON BROCKWAY**, by D.W. Patterson. 1890. Cloth, $33.50. Paper, $23.50. 167pp. .... Vendor G0259

533 **BRODNAX: THE BEGINNING. VOLUME 1**, by Mildred S. Ezell. 1995. Indexed. Illus.
  Brodnax from Godmersham, Kent, England (1400 AD) to Jamestown/ Williamsburg, VA (1700). Includes: **Brodnax, Travis, Champion, Johnson, Hall**. Volume II (***Brodnax: William Brodnax***) & Volume III (***Brodnax: Edward Brodnax***) in production.
  Soft cloth. $25.00. 250pp. .... Vendor G0323

534 **BROMLEY GEN., BEING A REC. OF THE DESC. OF LUKE WARWICK, R.I. & STONINGTON, CT.**, by V. Bromley. 1911. Cloth, $79.50. Paper, $69.50. 452pp. .... Vendor G0259

535 **BRONSDON & BOX FAMS PT. 1: ROBT. BRONSDON, MERCHANT, & HIS DESC. PT. 2: JOHN BOX, ROPEMAKER, & HIS DESC.**, by Marsh and Parker. Cloth, $63.00. Paper, $53.00. 332pp. .... Vendor G0259

536 **BROOKE FAM. OF WHITCHURCH, HAMPSHIRE, ENG.; ACCT. OF ACTING-GOV. ROBERT BROOKE MD. & COL. NINIAN BEALL OF MD. & DESC.**, by T.W. Balch. 1899. Paper. $12.50. 69pp. .... Vendor G0259

537 **THE BROOKFIELDS OF N. J., CONN., AND N. S.**, by H.M. Brookfield. Cloth, $32.00. Paper, $22.00. 159pp. .... Vendor G0259

538 **TWELVE GEN. IN AMER. LIN. OF W.L. BROOKFIELD, H.M. BROOKFIELD, & S.L. BROOKFIELD**, by H.M. Brookfield. 1937. Cloth, $59.00. Paper. $49.00. 310pp. .... Vendor G0259

539 **BROOKS & KINDRED FAMILIES**, by I.B. Kellam. 1950. Cloth, $69.50. Paper, $59.50. 392pp. .... Vendor G0259

540 **NATHANIEL BROOKS OF ASHFORD, CONNECTICUT, REVOLUTIONARY WAR PENSIONER—SOME OF HIS ANCESTORS AND DESCENDANTS, PLUS BRIEF GENEALOGIES OF FOUR ALLIED LINES: ALDRICH, BOOTHE, CORNWALL, KILLORAN-GURRY**, by Lela Brooks Fennell. 1989. Indexed. Illus. Documented. Maps. Three appendices.
  Henry **Brooks** is known to have been in Concord, Mass. in 1639 when he became a "Freeman." Although the first three generations of the Brooks Family are given in Appendix I, the main part of this family history starts with Henry's great-grandson, John, who moved from Woburn, Mass., to Ashford, Windham Co., Conn. about 1716. The story moves through John's grandson, Nathaniel, who served in the War of the Revolution, and through Nathaniel's sons, Jesse, John, and Theophilus who, in the early 1800s, were pioneers on the Holland

Purchase helping to push back the wilderness and settle western New York. It brings the account down to the present, including children in the thirteenth generation.

A few related surnames: **Aldrich, Allen, Alvord, Barnes, Boothe, Buck, Buffum, Cornwall, Davis, Doolittle, Druva, Farrell, Fennell, Gurry, Hall, Henderson, Herbold, Hilbert, Hubbard, Jackson, Johnson, Keenan, Killoran, Knowlton, McCormick, Moseley, Mousall, Orgek, Pearson, Pierce, Potter, Richards, Richardson, Sibley, Sinderson, Smith, Stripp, Taber, Utrich, Ward, Whiting, Woodward, Young.**
Cloth. $37.50. 225pp. .... Vendor G0396

541 **RIVER OF YEARS: A GENEALOGY AND NARRATIVE HISTORY OF THE BROOKS–CARTER FAMILY OF SOUTH CAROLINA,** by Glenna Whiteaker Wilding as told by Sister Mary Samuel Carter, OSU. 1995. Indexed. Illus.
Family history and anecdotal narrative spans four centuries of a family important in the growth of colonial Virginia and South Carolina.
Cloth. $31.70. 259pp. .... Vendor G0338

542 **TIMOTHY BROOKS OF MASS. & HIS DESC.,** by R.P. Brooks. 1927.
Paper. $8.00. 40pp. .... Vendor G0259

543 **GENEALOGY OF HENRY & MARY BROSIUS & THEIR DESCEN-DANTS; . . . ALSO SOME SHORT ACCOUNTS OF OTHER FAMILIES BEARING THE BROSIUS NAME,** by Lewis W. Brosius. 1928.
Cloth, $73.00. Paper, $63.00. 472pp. .... Vendor G0259

544 **RECORDS OF THE FAMILIES OF BROTHERS, SWAN, BONAR/ REEVES, BEARDSLEY,** by William P. Brothers. 1989. Indexed. Illus.
Paper. $16.50. 99pp. .... Vendor G0417

545 **BROUGHTON FAMILY OF MARCHWIEL, CONTRIBUTION TO THE HISTORY OF THE PARISH OF MARCHWIEL,** by Alfred N. Palmer. 1900 (England).
Paper. $9.00. 45pp. .... Vendor G0259

546 **BROUSSARD: DESCENDANTS OF FRANCOIS AND NICOLAS, VOL-UMES 1–4,** by Mitch Conover. Indexed.
Attempts to trace the descendancy of the two known lines of the **Broussard** Families of North America, and although there is the belief that the two families are parts of the same lineage, proof has yet to be established verifying this belief. This work does not include all the Broussards of North America, but rather, only those whose ties can be traced and verified. Contains 38,000 known Broussard related individuals.
Each of the 4 volumes numbers 500 or more pages and is hardbound with a burgundy cover with gold stamp lettering. Volumes 1, 2, and 3 contain the descendancy of Francois, with the index for these volumes being located in Volume 4. Volume 4 also contains the descendancy of Nicolas, with a separate index for Nicolas's descendants.
Hardbound. $135.00 for the set, plus s&h ($6.00 US, $12.00 CAN). 500+pp per volume .... Vendor G0114

547 **BROWN ANCESTRY, BEING ONE LINE OF DESCENT FROM GEORGE BROWN (1586–1611) OF SALISBURY, ENGLAND TO ROB-**

ERT C. BROWN (1913–1993) OF PARK RIDGE, ILLINOIS, by Patricia Brown Darling. (1993) reprint 1994. Indexed. Illus. Paper. $25.00+$2.90 p&h. 91pp. .... Vendor G0270

548 BROWN AND GLIDEWELL FAMILIES OF RANDOLPH COUNTY, ARKANSAS, by Shirley B. Adair. 1995. Indexed. Illus.
Hayley, Stokes, Bishop (Virginia connections).
Paper. $25.00. 315pp. .... Vendor G0382

549 BROWN DESC. OF IPSWICH, NEWBURY, SALISBURY, AND SALEM. (EXTR. FROM "ESSEX ANTIQUARIAN").
Paper. $9.00. 47pp. .... Vendor G0259

550 BROWN FAM. OF SCOTLAND & MD. (EXTR. VA. GEN.).
Paper. $11.50. 58pp. .... Vendor G0259

551 BROWN GENEALOGY; DESC. OF THOMAS, JOHN & ELEAZOR BROWN, SONS OF THOMAS & MARY (NEWHALL) BROWN OF LYNN, MA., 1629–1915, by C.H. Brown. 2 vols. 1907.
Cloth, $91.50/vol. Paper, $81.50/vol. 618+611pp. .... Vendor G0259

552 DESCENDANTS OF FRANCIS BROWN OF OLD RAPPAHANNOCK COUNTY, VIRGINIA, by Carol A. Hauk. 1995. Indexed.
Paper. $35.00. 225pp. .... Vendor G0340

553 GENEALOGICAL RECORD OF THE DESCENDANTS OF BROWN, RUNYAN, PETERS, NEEDHAM & ACKERMAN FAMILIES, WITH HIST. & BIOGR. SKETCHES, by D.E. Peters. n.d.
Cloth, $31.00. Paper, $21.00. 137pp. .... Vendor G0259

554 GENEALOGY OF THE BROWN FAM. OF PRINCE WILLIAM CO., VA., & ALLIED FAMILIES BLAND, BUCKNER, BYRNE, FAIRFAX, MORGAN, TEBBS, WATSON, ZIMMS & OTHERS, by J.E. Brown. 1930.
Cloth, $127.50. Paper, $117.50. 874pp. .... Vendor G0259

555 HANDBOOK OF OUR EXTENDED FAMILY: AN ACCOUNT OF SOME OF THE AMERICAN & EUROPEAN ANCESTORS OF JAMES M. BROWN & CHERLY (GUSTAFSON) BROWN & THE DESCENDANTS OF THOSE, by James M. Brown. 1992.
Cloth, $89.50. Paper, $79.50. 523pp. .... Vendor G0259

556 REP. TO THE BROWN ASSOC., U.S.A., by C. Smith. 1868.
Cloth, $32.00. Paper, $22.00. 126pp. .... Vendor G0259

557 REVOLUTIONARY SOLDIER SAMUEL BROWN AND SOME OF HIS FAMILY, by Faye M. (Brown) Lightburn. 1993. Indexed. Illus. 47-page supplement included.
   Twelve generations and history from Virginia, Kentucky, Missouri, and California. Over forty related families including Cooper, Hoy, Fugate, Boggs, Woods, and Tolson.
Cloth. $37.50. 466pp. .... Vendor G0311

558 THE NEW JERSEY BROWNS (AND ALLIED FAM.). 1931.
Cloth, $31.50. Paper, $21.50. 110pp. .... Vendor G0259

559 THE PHILIP BROWN FAMILY OF TULPEHOCKEN VALLEY, by Shirley M. Brown, Jeremy Lutz, and William Shuey. 1995.
Cloth. $50.00. 722pp. .... Vendor G0150

560 **WILLIAM BROWN, ENGLISH IMMIGRANT, OF HATFIELD AND LEICESTER, MASSACHUSETTS AND HIS DESCENDANTS c1669–1994**, by Carol Willits Brown. 1994. Indexed. Illus.
10 generations (encompassing every state), 4,600 every-name index, biographical sketches, photographs, DAR/SAR connections, Bible pages, Revolutionary/diary letters, anecdotes, etc. Extensive Athens and Washington counties, Ohio, **Browns** including **Cables**, **Glaziers**, and **Johnsons**. Publisher: Gateway Press, Baltimore.
Cloth. $39.00. 424pp. .... Vendor G0185

561 **CHAD BROWNE MEMORIAL, CONSISTING OF GEN. MEMOIRS OF A PORTION OF THE DESC. OF CHAD & ELIZABETH BROWNE, 1638– 1888**, by A.I. Bulkley. 1888.
Cloth, $33.50. Paper, $23.50. 173pp. .... Vendor G0259

562 **BROWNE. EXTR. "GEN. & HIST. OF WATERTOWN, MASS."**
Paper. $7.00. 34pp. .... Vendor G0259

563 **GEN. RECORD OF DESC. OF JOHN BROWNELL, 1773–1903**, by S. Brownell. 1903.
Paper. $11.00. 53pp. .... Vendor G0259

564 **GEN. OF THE BROWNINGS IN AMERICA FROM 1621 TO 1908**, by Edw. F. Browning. 1908.
Cloth, $149.50. Paper, $139.50. 982pp. .... Vendor G0259

565 **BRUBACHER GENEALOGY IN AMER.**, by J.N. Brubacher. 1882.
Cloth, $54.00. Paper, $44.00. 344pp. .... Vendor G0259

566 **HISTORY AND GENEALOGY OF THE BRUBAKER–BRUBACHER– BREWBAKER FAMILY IN AMERICA**, by Phares Brubaker Gibble. 1951, 1979.
Paper. $15.50. 93pp. .... Vendor G0150

567 **INDEX TO HISTORY AND GENEALOGY OF THE BRUBAKER– BRUBACHER–BREWBAKER FAMILY**, by Phares Brubaker Gibble. 1951.
Paper. $10.50. 22pp. .... Vendor G0150

568 **BOOK OF BRUCE. ANC. & DESC. OF KING ROBERT OF SCOTLAND**, by L.H. Weeks. 1907.
Cloth, $55.00. Paper, $45.00. 352pp. .... Vendor G0259

569 **[Bruce]. FAMILY HISTORY, 1788–1992**, by W.W. Denny and H.C. Bruce. 1992.
Paper. $19.00. 95pp. .... Vendor G0259

570 **FAMILY REC. OF THE BRUCES & THE CUMYNS, WITH AN HIST. INTRO. & APPENDIX**, by M.E.C. Bruce. 1870 (Scotland).
Cloth, $109.00. Paper, $99.00. 692pp. .... Vendor G0259

571 **GENEALOGY OF THE BRUMBACH FAM., INCL. THOSE USING . . . VARIATIONS OF THE ORIGINAL NAME & MANY OTHER CONNECTED FAMS.**, by G.M. Brumbaugh. 1915.
Cloth, $125.00. Paper, $115.00. 850pp. .... Vendor G0259

572 **DESCENDANTS OF THOMAS BRUMFIELD OF BERKS CO., PENN.:**

GENEALOGY & FAMILY HISTORY, 1720–1960, by Ray C. Brumfield
with Blackman O. Brumfield. 1962.
Cloth, $86.00. Paper, $76.00. 493pp. .... Vendor G0259

573   KNOWING THE BRUNERS, by Donald Lewis Osborn. 1968. Indexed. Illus.
Bruner/Brunner; Schifferstadt, Germany—1679–1729; Frederick County,
Maryland—1736–1821; other states through 1968. Ancestry chart insert. Illus-
trations (50). Names indexed.
Cloth. $55.00. 240pp. .... Vendor G0121

574   JOSEPH BRUNNER OF ROTHENSTEIN, SCHIFFERSTADT, AND
FREDERICK, by Donald Lewis Osborn. 1991. Indexed. Illus.
Ancestry (back to 1400s) and five descending generations of Frederick, Mary-
land immigrant Joseph Brunner, born 1678 (died 1753?), son of Heinrich and
Maria (Braun) Brunner of Rothenstein near Groenenbach, Germany. (Com-
panion volume to *Knowing the Bruners* [1968] with minimum repetition.)
Sources documented; abundant footnotes. Two marriages, descendants of Jacob
Sturm/Storm (1701–1757). Other families: Bruner, Gah, Saur, Strihl, Briggs,
Jeffries, Thomas, Sinn, Zimmerman, Ramsburg/Remsberg, Getzendanner.
Ancestry chart insert. Illustrations (57). Relics brought on ships. Gold Rush
and other letters. California minister's 1846–1872 journal. All names indexed.
Cloth. $155.00. 600pp. .... Vendor G0121

575   BRYANT FAMILY HISTORY, ANCESTRY & DESCENDANTS OF
DAVID BRYANT (1756) OF SPRINGFIELD, N.J., WASHINGTON CO.,
& WOLF LAKE, NOBLE CO., IND., by C.V. Braiden. 1913.
Cloth, $52.50. Paper, $42.50. 270pp. .... Vendor G0259

576   BUCHANAN ANCESTRY, by M.G. Buchanan. 1962.
Paper. $18.00. 93pp. .... Vendor G0259

577   FIRST GATHERING OF THE BUCHANAN CLAN, TROTTERS CREEK,
MIAMI CO., OHIO, WITH GEN. NOTES, 10/1/1892.
Paper. $10.00. 55pp. .... Vendor G0259

578   THE BUCHANAN BOOK, by A.W.P. Buchanan. 1911.
Cloth, $88.00. Paper, $78.00. 501pp. .... Vendor G0259

579   BUCK SURNAME BOOKLETS, by Paula Perkins Mortensen. 1988. Indexed.
Paper. $7.00. 30–40pp. .... Vendor G0228

580   JOHANNES BUCK, 1747–1790; CHRISTIAN & CATHERINE BUCK &
THEIR DESCENDANTS, 1754–1958, by Fisher, Ulrey, and Hetrick. 1958.
Cloth, $35.00. Paper, $25.00. xii+138pp. .... Vendor G0259

581   BUCKINGHAM FAMILY: THE DESC. OF THOMAS BUCKINGHAM
OF MILFORD, CT., by F.W. Chapman. 1872.
Cloth, $59.50. Paper, $49.50. 384pp. .... Vendor G0259

582   THE ANC. OF EBENEZER BUCKINGHAM, BORN IN 1748, & OF HIS
DESC., by J. Buckingham. 1892.
Cloth, $48.50. Paper, $38.50. 256pp. .... Vendor G0259

583   A BUCKNAM–BUCKMAN GENEALOGY, by Ann Theopold Chaplin. 1988.
Indexed.
Cloth. $40.00. 325pp. .... Vendor G0241

584 **GENEALOGICAL CHART OF THE BUDD FAMILY**, by S.H. Scheib. (1906) reprint 1992.
This elongated chart of Rev. Thomas **Budd**, who settled in New Jersey in the seventeenth century, is 36" x 72".
Paper. $20.00 .... Vendor G0069

585 **BUDD FAM., FIRST REUNION 8/14/1878, WITH BRIEF HIST. OF THE FAM., 1632–1881**, by E.G. Budd. 1881.
Paper. $13.50. 68pp. .... Vendor G0259

586 **HIST. OF THE BUELL FAM. IN ENG., FROM REMOTEST TIMES ... & IN AMER., FROM TOWN, PARISH, CHURCH & FAM. RECORDS**, by A. Welles. 1881.
Cloth, $71.50. Paper, $61.50. 384+xixpp. .... Vendor G0259

587 **DESCENDANTS OF RICHARD BUFORD OF VIRGINIA**, by Carol A. Hauk. 1995. Indexed.
Paper. $45.00. 211pp. .... Vendor G0340

588 **DESC. OF REV. PETER BULKELEY, WHO SETTLED AT CONCORD, MA. IN 1636**, by F.W. Chapman. 1875.
Cloth, $53.50. Paper, $43.50. 289pp. .... Vendor G0259

589 **REV. PETER BULKELEY; AN ACCT. OF HIS CAREER, HIS ANC. & ANC. OF HIS TWO WIVES, & HIS RELATIVES IN ENG. & NEW ENG., WITH A GEN. OF HIS DESC.**, by D.L. Jacobus. 1933.
Cloth, $149.00. Paper, $139.00. 1,073pp. .... Vendor G0259

590 **DESCENDANTS OF JOSIAH BULL JR. (1738–1813) OF DUTCHESS COUNTY, NY**, by Mary Lynch Young. 1992. Indexed. Illus.
Cloth. $40.00. 584pp. .... Vendor G0106

591 **RECORD OF THE DESC. OF JOHN & ELIZABETH BULL, EARLY SETTLERS IN PENN.**, by J.H. Bull. 1919.
Cloth, $70.00. Paper, $60.00. 387pp. .... Vendor G0259

592 **THE FAMILY OF STEPHEN BULL OF KINGHURST HALL, CO. WARWICK, ENGLAND & ASHLEY HALL, S. CARO., 1600–1960**, by H.D. Bull. 1961.
Cloth, $35.00. Paper, $25.00. 161pp. .... Vendor G0259

593 **BULLARD & ALLIED FAMS.; AMER. ANC. OF GEO. NEWTON BULLARD & MARY BULLARD**, by E. Bullard. 1930.
Cloth, $63.50. Paper, $53.50. 337pp. .... Vendor G0259

594 **SUPPLEMENT; OTHER BULLARDS, A GEN.** 1928.
Paper. $16.00. 86pp. .... Vendor G0259

595 **BULLEN. ANC. & DESC. OF PHILLIP OF JERSEY, ENG. & CHARLESTOWN, MASS.**, by M.L. and W.L. Holman. 1930.
Cloth, $35.00. Paper, $25.00. 170pp. .... Vendor G0259

596 **HIST. & GEN. OF THE FAMS. OF BULLOCH, STOBO & IRVINE OF CULTS**, by J.G.B. Bulloch. 1911.
Paper. $16.50. 102pp. .... Vendor G0259

597 **BUNKER FAMILY. BRANCHES EARLY IDENTIFIED WITH**

CHARLESTOWN & NANTUCKET, MASS., & DELAWARE & MARY-LAND, AS WELL AS EARLY BUNKERS & THOSE IN EUROPE, by C.W.O. Bunker. 1931.
Cloth, $125.00. Paper, $115.00. 797pp. .... Vendor G0259

598 BUNKER GENEALOGY. ANCESTRY & DESCENDANTS OF BEN-JAMIN[3] (JAMES[2], JAMES[1]) BUNKER, by E.C. Moran, Jr. 1942.
Cloth, $47.50. Paper, $37.50. 232pp. .... Vendor G0259

599 BUNKER GENEALOGY. DESC. OF JAMES BUNKER OF DOVER, N.H., by E.C. Moran, Jr. 1961.
Cloth, $73.50. Paper, $63.50. 405pp. .... Vendor G0259

600 BUNKER GENEALOGY. THE CHARLESTOWN & NANTUCKET, MASS., BRANCHES, & SOME UNCONNECTED GROUPS, by E.C. Moran, Jr. 1965.
Cloth, $56.50. Paper, $46.50. 302pp. .... Vendor G0259

601 BUNKER GENEALOGY, VOL. III, DOVER BRANCH, by Edward C. Moran, Jr., rev. by R.B. Christiansen, H.L. Bunker, and W. Bunker. 1982.
Cloth, $69.50. Paper, $59.50. 389pp. .... Vendor G0259

602 BUNTING FAMILY. OUR PEOPLE & OUR SELVES, by A.M. Bunting. 1909.
Cloth, $49.50. Paper, $39.50. 245pp. .... Vendor G0259

603 GEN. OF THE BURBANK FAM. & THE FAM. OF BRAN, WELLCOME, SEDGLEY & WELCH, by G. Sedgley. 1928.
Cloth, $97.00. Paper, $87.00. 586pp. .... Vendor G0259

604 ACCT. OF JOHN BURBEEN, WHO SETTLED AT WOBURN, MA., ABOUT 1660; & OF SUCH OF HIS DESC. AS HAVE BORNE THE SUR-NAME OF BURBEEN, by J. Walker. 1892.
Paper. $10.00. 52pp. .... Vendor G0259

605 DESC. OF ROBERT BURDICK OF RHODE ISL., by N.W. Johnson. 1937.
Cloth, $169.00. Paper, $159.00. 1,398pp. .... Vendor G0259

606 COLONISTS OF NEW ENG. & NOVA SCOTIA: BURGESS & HECKMAN FAMS., by K.F. Burgess. 1956.
Cloth, $34.00. Paper, $24.00. 134pp. .... Vendor G0259

607 MEMORIAL OF THE FAM. OF THOMAS & DOROTHY BURGESS WHO WERE SETTLED AT SANDWICH, PLYMOUTH COL., 1637, by E. Burgess. 1865.
Cloth, $36.50. Paper, $26.50. 212pp. .... Vendor G0259

608 THE BURGESS HISTORY TREE, by Paul F. Burgess. 1993. Indexed. Illus.
   Thomas **Burgess** and Dorothy (**Wayne** or **Phippen**) England to Sandwich, Mass; mostly New England, but has branches everywhere. **Littlefields**: England to Wells, Maine. Includes Thorton W. Burgess, author; Gelett Burgess, author; Burgess Battery Co.; 4 presidents; Mayflower connections; Adam & Eve connections; Royalty. All five children of Thomas and Dorothy are traced and many allied branches.
   Thousands of names including: **Nye, Worden, Perry, Freeman, Bassett, Gaunt, Bishop, Robinson**, and **Small**.
   Cloth. $44.00. 700pp. .... Vendor G0008

609 **HIST. & GEN. OF THE BURGNER FAM. IN THE U.S., AS DESC. FROM PETER BURGNER, A SWISS EMIGR. OF 1734**, by J. Burgner. 1890. Cloth, $33.00. Paper, $23.00. 171pp. .... Vendor G0259

610 **DESC. FROM THE FIRST ANC. IN AMER., JACOB BURHANS, 1660, & HIS SON, JAN BURHANS, 1663**, by S. Burhans, Jr. 1894. Cloth, $124.00. Paper, $114.00. 799+11pp. .... Vendor G0259

611 **BURKE & ALVORD MEM. A GEN. ACCT. OF THE DESC. OF RICHARD BURKE OF SUDBURY, MA.**, by J. Boutelle. 1864. Cloth, $45.50. Paper, $35.50. 239pp. .... Vendor G0259

612 **FAMILY HISTORY OF CHRISTIAN BURKHOLDER, 1746–1990**, by Paul Z. Burkholder. 1990. Cloth. $20.50. 537pp. .... Vendor G0150

613 **GEN. OF THE BURLEY OR BURLEIGH FAM. OF AMERICA**, by C. Burleigh. 1880. Cloth, $37.50. Paper, $27.50. 200pp. .... Vendor G0259

614 **BURNAP-BURNETT GEN.**, by H.W. Belknap. 1925. Cloth, $65.50. Paper, $55.50. 351pp. .... Vendor G0259

615 **BURNETT FAM. WITH COLL. BRANCHES**, by C. Burnett. 1950. Cloth, $58.00. Paper, $48.00. 316pp. .... Vendor G0259

616 **THE FAMILY OF BURNETT OF LEYS, WITH COLLATERAL BRANCHES**, compiled by G. Burnett; edited by J. Allardyce. 1901 (Scotland). Cloth, $71.00. Paper, $61.00. xxii+367pp. .... Vendor G0259

617 **BURNHAM FAM.; OR GEN. RECORDS OF THE DESC. OF THE FOUR EMIGR. OF THE NAME WHO WERE AMONG THE EARLY SETTLERS IN AMERICA**, by R.H. Burnham. 1869. Cloth, $94.00. Paper, $84.00. 546pp. .... Vendor G0259

618 **GEN. RECORDS OF THOMAS BURNHAM, THE EMIGR., WHO WAS AMONG THE EARLY SETTLERS AT HARTFORD, CT., & HIS DESC.**, by R.H. Burnham. 1884. Cloth, $48.50. Paper, $38.50. 292pp. .... Vendor G0259

619 **A GENERAL HIST. OF THE BURR FAM., 1193–1891**, by C.B. Todd. 2nd ed. 1891. Cloth, $88.50. Paper, $78.50. 572pp. .... Vendor G0259

620 **A GENERAL HIST. OF THE BURR FAM. WITH A GENL RECORD FROM 1193 TO 1902**, by C.B. Todd. 4th ed. 1902. Cloth, $86.00. Paper, $76.00. 600pp. .... Vendor G0259

621 **BURES OF SUFFOLK, ENG. & BURR OF MASS. BAY COLONY, NEW ENG.**, by C.R. Burr. 1926. Paper. $19.50. 131pp. .... Vendor G0259

622 **THE BURRAGE MEMORIAL. A GEN. HIST. OF THE DESC. OF JOHN BURRAGE, WHO SETTLED IN CHARLESTOWN, MASS., IN 1637**, by A.A. Burrage. 1877. Cloth, $49.50. Paper, $39.50. 265pp. .... Vendor G0259

623 **BURRILL FAM. OF LYNN DURING THE COL. & PROVINCIAL PERI-ODS, WITH SOME DESC.; A PAPER READ BEFORE THE LYNN HIST. SOCIETY,** by E.M. Burrill. 1907.
Paper. $10.00. 54pp. .... Vendor G0259

624 **EARLY DAYS IN NEW ENGLAND. LIFE & TIMES OF HENRY BURT OF SPRINGFIELD & SOME OF HIS DESC.,** by H.M. Burt & S.W. Burt. 1893.
Cloth, $88.50. Paper, $78.50. 620pp. .... Vendor G0259

625 **DESCENDANTS OF ABRAHAM & ELIZABETH ELECTA PAYNE BURTON OF SENECA CO., OH & KOSCUISKO/WABASH COS., IN,** by Conrad L. Burton. 1991. Indexed. Illus.
Paper. $10.00. 77pp. .... Vendor G0094

626 **DESC. OF JOSIAH BURTON OF MANCHESTER, VT.,** by W.L. Holman. 1926.
Cloth, $50.00. Paper, $49.00. 310pp. .... Vendor G0259

627 **DESCENDANTS OF LEWIS BURWELL OF VIRGINIA,** by Carol A. Hauk. 1995. Indexed.
Paper. $45.00. 367pp. .... Vendor G0340

628 **DESC. OF JOHN BUSH & JANE OSTERHOUDT OF KINGSTON, ULSTER CO., NY, 1791–1914,** by B. Bush. 1914.
Paper. $12.50. 63pp. .... Vendor G0259

629 **BUSHNELL 1580–1979,** by Patricia O'Boyle. 1979. Illus.
Paper. $25.00. 100pp. .... Vendor G0225

630 **BUSHNELL FAM. GEN.; ANC. & POSTERITY OF FRANCIS BUSHNELL (1580–1646) OF HORSHAM, ENGLAND, & GUILFORD, CONN., INCL. GEN. NOTES OF OTHER BUSHNELL FAM.** (print size in orig. book is quite small), by G.E. Bushnell. 1945.
Cloth, $51.50. Paper, $41.50. 276pp. .... Vendor G0259

631 **BOOK OF THE FAM. AND LINEAL DESC. OF MEDAD BUTLER,** by W.A. Butler. 1887.
Paper. $12.50. 61pp. .... Vendor G0259

632 **BUTLER FAMILY IN AMER.,** by W. Butler et al. 1909.
Cloth, $58.50. Paper, $48.50. 306pp. .... Vendor G0259

633 **BUTLER GEN. DEDICATION OF THE MONUMENT TO DEACON JOHN BUTLER, PELHAM, N.H., 1886.** 1887.
Paper. $8.00. 36pp. .... Vendor G0259

634 **BUTLERIANA, GENEALOGICA ET BIOGRAPHICA, OR GENEALOGICAL NOTES CONCERNING MARY BUTLER & HER DESCENDANTS, AS WELL AS THE BATES, HARRIS, SIGOURNEY & OTHER FAMILIES WITH WHICH THEY HAVE INTERMARRIED,** by J.D. Butler. 1888.
Cloth, $35.00. Paper, $25.00. 162pp. .... Vendor G0259

635 **BUTLERS & KINSFOLK: BUTLERS OF NEW ENGLAND & NOVA SCOTIA, & REL. FAMS. OF OTHER NAMES, INCL. DURKEES,** by E.E. Butler. 1944.
Cloth, $66.00. Paper, $56.00. 362pp. .... Vendor G0259

636 **TALES OF OUR KINSFOLK PAST & PRESENT. THE STORY OF OUR BUTLER ANC. FOR TEN GEN., FROM 1602 TO 1919**, by H.L. Butler. 1919.
Cloth, $94.50. Paper, $84.50. 552pp. .... Vendor G0259

637 **THOMAS BUTLER & HIS DESC., 1674–1886**, by G.H. Butler. 1886.
Cloth, $36.50. Paper, $26.50. 199pp. .... Vendor G0259

638 **THE GEN. REGISTRY OF THE BUTTERS FAM., DESC. OF WILLIAM BUTTER OF WOBURN, MASS., 1665, & OTHERS IN AMERICA**, by G. Butters. 1896.
Cloth, $84.00. Paper, $74.00. 476pp. .... Vendor G0259

639 **JOHN BUTTS: HIS ANCESTRY & SOME DESCENDANTS**, by A. Butts. 1898.
Cloth, $34.50. Paper, $24.50. 153pp. .... Vendor G0259

640 **HIST. OF THE BYE FAM. & SOME ALLIED FAMS.**, by A.E. Bye. 1956.
Cloth, $79.00. Paper, $69.00. 450pp. .... Vendor G0259

641 **THE BYERLY FAMILY IN THE VALLEY OF VIRGINIA**, by John F. Byerly, Jr. 1994. Indexed. Illus.
This seven-generation story of immigrant Joseph **Byerly** a.k.a. **Beyrer** includes travel, foods, recreation, education, and involvement in American life.
Cloth. $28.95. 244pp. .... Vendor G0409

642 **ABBY BYRAM & HER FATHER, THEIR ANC. & DESC.**, by J.M. McElroy. 1898.
Paper. $13.00. 65pp. .... Vendor G0259

643 **BYRD GEN. EXTR. FROM CAMPBELL GEN. (1927)**.
Paper. $24.00. 146pp. .... Vendor G0259

644 **DESCENDANTS OF WILLIAM BYRD OF VIRGINIA**, by Carol A. Hauk. 1995. Indexed.
Paper. $35.00. 218pp. .... Vendor G0340

645 **THE CABELLS & THEIR KIN: A MEMORIAL VOL. OF HISTORY, BIOGR. & GENEALOGY**, by A. Brown. 1939.
Cloth, $109.00. Paper, $99.00. 708pp. .... Vendor G0259

646 **HISTORY & GEN. OF THE CABOT FAM., 1475–1927**, by L. Vernon Briggs. 1927.
Cloth, $145.00. Paper, $135.00. 885pp. .... Vendor G0259

647 **DESC. OF NICHOLAS CADY, OF WATERTOWN, MASS., 1645–1910**, by O.P. Allen. 1910.
Cloth, $79.50. Paper, $69.50. 546pp. .... Vendor G0259

648 **HIST. OF THE CAHOON FAM.**, by I.M. Cahoon.
Paper. $10.00. 47pp. .... Vendor G0259

649 **CAIN**, by Mildred S. Ezell. 1988. Indexed. Illus.
Includes: **Cain, Seale, Wilkinson, Jagers, Gammill, Carraway, McGehee, Burris, Foreman, Blake, Braswell, Hardy, Hemby**.
Paper. $45.00. 604pp. .... Vendor G0323

650 **CALDWELL RECORDS. JOHN & SARAH (DILLINGHAM) CALDWELL, IPSWICH, MASS., & THEIR DESC.; FAM. CONNECTED WITH THEM BY MARRIAGE; OTHER CALDWELL FAM.**, by A. Caldwell. 1873.
Paper. $16.00. 82pp. .... Vendor G0259

651 **JOHN CALDWELL & SARAH DILLINGHAM CALDWELL, HIS WIFE, IPSWICH, MASS., 1654; GEN. RECORDS OF THEIR DESC., EIGHT GEN. 1654–1900**, by A. Caldwell and S. Kimball. 1904.
Cloth, $59.50. Paper, $49.50. 318pp. .... Vendor G0259

652 **[Caldwell]. WILLIAM COALDWELL, CALDWELL OR COLDWELL; & RECORD OF HIS DESC.**, by C.T. Caldwell. 1910.
Paper. $16.50. 82pp. .... Vendor G0259

653 **CHRISTOPHER CALE'S FAMILY OF PRESTON COUNTY, WEST VIRGINIA 1741–1973**, by Janice Cale Sisler. 1973. Indexed. Illus.
Cloth. $19.00+$2.50 postage. 754pp. .... Vendor G0438

654 **ROBERT CALEF OF BOSTON & ROXBURY & SOME OF HIS DESC.**, by W.W. Lunt. 1928.
Paper. $14.00. 68pp. .... Vendor G0259

655 **CALHOUN FAM. OF S. CARO.**, by A. Salley.
Paper. $8.50. 42pp. .... Vendor G0259

656 **THE STORY OF THE CALHOUNS OF JUDEA, CONN. (RENAMED WASHINGTON, 1779)**, by M.B. Calhoun. 1956.
Paper. $12.00. 57pp. .... Vendor G0259

657 **CALKINS MEM. MILITARY ROSTER**, by W.M. Calkins. 1903.
Cloth, $41.00. Paper, $31.00. 204pp. .... Vendor G0259

658 **GEN. OF THE CALL FAM. IN US**, by S. Call. 1908.
Paper. $11.00. 56pp. .... Vendor G0259

659 **NOTES ON THE CALTHORPE & CALTHROP IN THE COUNTIES OF NORFOLK & LINCOLNSHIRE & ELSEWHERE**, by C.W. Carr-Calthrop. 3rd ed. 1933.
Cloth, $34.00. Paper, $24.00. 129+22pp. .... Vendor G0259

660 **DESC. OF VA. CALVERTS**, by E.F. O'Gorman. 1947.
Cloth, $109.00. Paper, $99.00. 763pp. .... Vendor G0259

661 **CALVIN FAMILIES: ORIGIN & HIST. OF THE AMER. CALVINS WITH A PARTIAL GEN.**, by C.W. Calvin. 1945.
Cloth, $72.00. Paper, $62.00. 405pp. .... Vendor G0259

662 **FROM THE POTOMAC TO THE COLUMBIA—THE CAMBY OR CAMBE FAMILY**, by Patricia Hewitt Morrison. 1994. Indexed. Illus.
A pioneer history and migration of the **Camby/Cambe** family from Hampshire Co., VA (WV) to Athens Co., OH, 1804–1814. The book traces one branch to Clinton Co., IN, IL, WI, and the migration to Oregon Country 1845–1853. It details the hazards encountered on the Oregon Trail in 1845 and the family's role during the pioneer days in Tumwater, WA Territory.
Extensive research on seventeen family members who served in the Civil

War and their units. The family tree covers eight generations with 1,286 descendants where equal attention was given to both female and male lines. Photographs, every-name and location indexes are included. Fully documented.

Among the surnames included: **Black, Canby, Carpenter, Caudy, Collins, Condra, Courtney, Cumbe, Francis, Fuller, Glazier, Hesser, Hewett, Hewitt, Johnson, Love, Mace, McElfresh, Murphy, Ogden, Onstine, Packwood, Prather, Ramey, Stewart, Tucker, Wilds**, and **Young**.

Cloth. $35.00. 430pp. .... Vendor G0078

663 **THE JOHNSTON & BACON SCOTTISH CLAN HISTORIES: The Clan Cameron**, by Charles Ian Fraser. (1953) reprint 1993. Illus.
Paper. $8.95. 32pp. .... Vendor G0011

664 CAMPBELL CLAN IN VA., by L.L. Campbell. 1954.
Cloth, $37.00. Paper, $27.00. 154pp. .... Vendor G0259

665 CAMPBELL FAMILY HISTORY, by J. Montgomery Seaver. Illus.
Paper. $8.00. 72pp. .... Vendor G0011

666 CAMPBELL FAMILY HISTORY AND RELATED FAMILIES, by Gwen Campbell. 1988. Indexed.
Some descendants of James **Campbell** and Jane **Knox**. Query with SASE.
Paper. $27.00. 124pp. .... Vendor G0303

667 EARLIEST CAMPBELL FAMILIES IN MAINE, by Dr. L.A. Campbell. 1948.
Paper. $15.00. 77pp. typescript .... Vendor G0259

668 GEN. OF THE CAMPBELL, NOBLE, GORTON, SHELTON, GILMOUR & BYRD FAMS, & NUMEROUS OTHER FAMS. OF PROMINENCE IN AMER., WITH WHOM THEY HAVE INTERMARRIED, by M.C. Whitaker. 1927.
Cloth, $46.50. Paper, $36.50. 230pp. .... Vendor G0259

669 HIST. SKETCHES OF THE CAMPBELL, PILCHER & KINDRED FAMS., INCL. THE BOWEN, RUSSELL, OWEN, GRANT, GOODWIN, AMIS, CAROTHERS, HOPE, TALIAFERRO & POWELL FAMILIES, by M.C Pilcher. 1911.
Cloth, $78.50. Paper. $68.50. 444pp. .... Vendor G0259

670 TEXAS WAS THE MAGNET, ANCESTORS OF GWEN CAMPBELL— VOL I—FATHER'S LINES, by Gwen Campbell. 1995. Indexed. Illus.
Includes **Dorsett, Trammell, Haygood, Moore, Tubb, Watson**. Query with SASE.
Paper. $15.00. 78pp. .... Vendor G0303

671 TEXAS WAS THE MAGNET, ANCESTORS OF GWEN CAMPBELL— VOL II—MOTHER'S LINES, by Gwen Campbell. 1995. Indexed. Illus.
Includes **McGuffin, Davis, Shinault, Allsup, Wootan, Snowden**. Query with SASE.
Paper. $15.00. 102pp. .... Vendor G0303

672 THE JOHNSTON & BACON SCOTTISH CLAN HISTORIES: The Clan Campbell, by Andrew McKerral. 2nd ed. (1979) reprint 1993. Illus.
Paper. $8.95. 32pp. .... Vendor G0011

673 THE CANADAY/McCORMICK FAMILIES & THEIR ANCESTORS, by Lois (Canaday) Hupfer. 1993. Indexed. Illus.

Includes allied families of: **Bowyer, Bunds, Courtney, Davenport, Fiscus, Hauser, Kidd, Lauterbach, Logan, Lum, McWilliams, Newell, Ragland, Sapp, Spainhower** and others. Earliest Canaday ancestor is "John" of Revolutionary War. Spainhower family is taken back to "Arbogast Spainhower," born ca. 1578, Muttenz, Switzerland. **Ragland** line traced back to Charlemagne.
Cloth. $40.00. 780pp. .... Vendor G0018

674 CANDEE GEN., WITH NOTICES OF ALLIED FAM., by C. Baldwin. 1882.
Cloth, $42.00. Paper, $32.00. 240pp. .... Vendor G0259

675 A HIST. OF THOMAS & MATTHEW CANFIELD WITH A GEN. OF THEIR DESC. IN N.J., by F.A. Canfield. 1897.
Cloth, $44.00. Paper, $34.00. 228pp. .... Vendor G0259

676 ANDREW CANNON & HIS DESC., 1651–1912, by C.S. Williams. 1912.
Paper. $17.50. 54pp. .... Vendor G0259

677 [Canterbury]. GRANDMOTHER'S LETTER—A FAMILY GENEALOGY, by Marie Bowen Canterbury. 1992. Illus.

Family names: **Bowen/Boing, Canterbury, Chandler, Derien, Hjelm, Johnson, Kennedy, LoMonaco, Mariana, Matheny, McCown, Meadows, Morris, Myers, Perkio, Price, Rucker, Smith, Tobin, Waybright.**
Cloth. $40.00. 262pp. .... Vendor G0234

678 THE CANTINE FAMILY, DESCENDANTS OF MOSES CANTINE, by Alice Cantine Huntington. (1957) reprint 1982. Indexed.
Paper. $11.00. 82pp. .... Vendor G0450

679 CANTRELL FAM. A BIOGR. ALBUM & HIST. OF THE DESC. OF ZEBULON CANTRELL, THE IMMIGR., WITH DATA CONCERNING THE FAM. WHO ARE ALLIED BY MARRIAGE, 1700–1898, by C.G. Cantrell. 1898.
Cloth, $35.00. Paper, $25.00. 156pp. .... Vendor G0259

680 GEORGE WASHINGTON CANTRELL AND HIS WIFE, MARTHA ELIZABETH LEA CARVER OF WILSON COUNTY, TENNESSEE, by Mildred S. Wright. 1983. Indexed. Illus.
Curd, Logue, Price, Smith, Swingley, Wright, lineage charts.
Cloth, $35.00. Paper, $25.00. 80pp. .... Vendor G0145

681 CANTRILL–CANTRELL GEN. REC. OF THE DESC. OF RICHARD CANTRILL WHO WAS A RESIDENT OF PHILADELPHIA PRIOR TO 1689, & OF EARLIER CANTRILLS IN ENG. & AMER., by S.C. Christie. 1908.
Cloth, $45.00. Paper, $35.00. 271pp. .... Vendor G0259

682 CAPEN FAM.; DESC. OF BERNARD CAPEN OF DORCHESTER, MASS., by C. Hayden; rev. by J. Tuttle. 1929.
Cloth, $59.00. Paper, $49.00. 312pp. .... Vendor G0259

683 THE CAPLINGER–KEPLINGER FAMILY OF THE VALLEY OF VIRGINIA, by Lewis H. Yankey. 1990. Indexed.
Paper. $15.00. 108pp. .... Vendor G0365

684 **GEN. OF THE DESC. OF BANFIELD CAPRON FROM A.D. 1660–A.D. 1859**, by F.A. Holden. 1859.
Cloth, $49.00. Paper, $39.00. 263pp. .... Vendor G0259

685 **DESC. OF THOMAS CARHART**, by M. Dusenbury. 1880.
Cloth, $35.00. Paper, $25.00. 142pp. .... Vendor G0259

686 **GEN. OF THE CARNEY FAM., DESC. OF MARK CARNEY & SUZANN GOW, HIS WIFE, OF POWNALBORO, MAINE, 1751–1903**, by S.H. Carney, Jr. 1904.
Cloth, $39.50. Paper, $29.50. 227pp. .... Vendor G0259

687 **A GEN. HIST. OF THE REHOBOTH BRANCH OF THE CARPENTER FAM. IN AMER., BROUGHT DOWN FROM THEIR ENG. ANC. JOHN (1303)**, by A. Carpenter. 1898.
Cloth, $122.00. Paper, $112.00. 921pp. .... Vendor G0259

688 **CARPENTER–WIER FAMILY OF UPPER SO. CARO. & OTHER ANCESTORS, INCL. BENSON, BERRY, BLASSINGAME, CALDWELL, MAXWELL, RICHEY, SLOAN, STEWART, WILSON**, by H.B. McCoy. 1959.
Cloth, $61.00. Paper, $51.00. 326pp. .... Vendor G0259

689 **GEN. & HIST. RECORD OF THE CARPENTER FAM., WITH A BRIEF GEN. OF SOME DESC. OF WM. CARPENTER OF WEYMOUTH & REHOBOTH, MA., WM. OF PROVIDENCE, RI, SAMUEL OF PA. & EPHRAIM, TIMOTHY & JOSIAS OF LONG ISLAND**, by J. Usher. 1883.
Paper. $14.00. 70pp. .... Vendor G0259

690 **HIST. & GEN. OF THE CARPENTER FAM. IN AMER. FROM THE SETTLEMENT AT PROVIDENCE, R.I., 1637–1901**, by D.H. Carpenter. 1901.
Cloth, $65.25. Paper, $55.25. 375pp. .... Vendor G0259

691 **SAMUEL CARPENTER & HIS DESC.**, by E. and L.H. Carpenter. 1912.
Cloth, $59.50. Paper, $49.50. 320pp. .... Vendor G0259

692 **CARR FAM. RECORDS, EMBRACING THE REC. OF THE 1ST FAM.**

Mark Brewster of Hull, England
and Allied Families In America

Atkey, Carpenter, Dare, Fowler, Hiscock, Hewitt, Potter and Yelf

❧

6" x 9" 352 pp. Complete Name Index
Hard Cover—Cloth Bound Acid-free Paper $35.00 postpaid
Marcus V. Brewster, 316 Brockington St., Manning, SC 29102

WHO SETTLED IN AMER. & THEIR DESC., WITH BRANCHES WHO
CAME AT A LATER DATE, by E.C. Carr. 1894.
Cloth, $78.00. Paper, $68.00. 540pp. .... Vendor G0259

693 HOUSE OF CARR, A HIST. SKETCH OF THE CARR FAM. 1450–1926,
by W.L. Watson. 1926.
Paper. $12.00. 58pp. .... Vendor G0259

694 THE DESC. OF JAMES CARRELL & SARAH DUNGAN HIS WIFE, by
E.P. Carrell. 1928.
Cloth, $109.00. Paper, $99.00. 708pp. .... Vendor G0259

695 HIST. OF THE WM. CARROLL FAM. OF ALLEGHANY CO., N.Y., by
K. Stevenson. 1929.
Paper. $19.00. 100pp. .... Vendor G0259

696 DESCENDANTS OF GEORGE S. CARRIER AND MARIAH
FORESMAN, by Wilma May Myers. 1975. Indexed.
Cloth. $12.50. 130pp. .... Vendor G0260

697 GEN. OF A BRANCH OF THE CARRUTH FAM.; OR THE DESC. OF
JAMES CARRUTH OF PHILLIPSTON, by A. J. Carruth. 1926.
Paper. $12.50. 67pp. .... Vendor G0259

698 BI-CENTENARY MEM. OF JEREMIAH CARTER WHO CAME TO THE
PROV. OF PENN. IN 1682, A HIST. GEN. OF HIS DESC. DOWN TO
THE PRESENT, by T.M. Potts. 1883.
Cloth, $59.00. Paper, $49.00. 304pp. .... Vendor G0259

699 CARTER FAMILY HISTORY, by J. Montgomery Seaver. Illus.
Paper. $7.50. 54pp. .... Vendor G0011

700 DESCENDANTS OF JOHN CARTER OF VIRGINIA, by Carol A. Hauk.
1995. Indexed.
Paper. $60.00. 738pp. .... Vendor G0340

701 GEN. OF THE DESC. OF THOM. CARTER OF MASS. & CT.; ALSO
DESC. OF HIS BROTHERS, GRANDSON OF REV. THOM. CARTER,
WOBURN, MASS., 1642, by H.W. Carter. 1909.
Cloth, $64.00. Paper, $54.00. 341pp. .... Vendor G0259

702 THE CARTER TREE, TABULATED & INDEXED, by R.R. Carter and R.I.
Randolph. 1951.
Cloth, $48.00. Paper, $38.00. 241pp. .... Vendor G0259

703 THE DESC. OF CAPT. THOMAS CARTER OF "BARFORD,"
LANCASTER CO, VA., WITH ALLIED FAM., by J. Miller. 1912.
Cloth, $77.50. Paper, $67.50. 430pp. .... Vendor G0259

704 THE DESC. OF SAM'L & THOMAS, SONS OF REV. SAM'L CARTER,
1640–1886, by C. and S. Carter. 1886.
Cloth, $51.00. Paper, $41.00. 272pp. .... Vendor G0259

705 CARVER FAMILY OF NEW ENGLAND: ROBERT CARVER OF
MARSHFIELD & HIS DESC., by C.N. Carver. 1935.
Cloth, $41.00. Paper, $31.00. 204pp. .... Vendor G0259

706 **ROBERT CARVER OF MARSHFIELD, MA., & SOME DESC.**, by W. Jones. 1934.
Paper. $10.00. 49pp. .... Vendor G0259

707 **DESCENDANTS OF MILES CARY OF VIRGINIA**, by Carol A. Hauk. 1995. Indexed.
Paper. $45.00. 365pp. .... Vendor G0340

708 **CARY MEM.**, by S.F. Cary. 1874.
Cloth, $55.00. Paper, $45.00. 306pp. .... Vendor G0259

709 **JOHN CARY, PLYMOUTH PILGRIM**, by S. Cary. 1911.
Cloth, $51.00. Paper, $41.00. 274pp. .... Vendor G0259

710 **THE CARY FAM. IN AMERICA**, by H.G. Cary; appendix, **Jonathan Cary ye Third**, by I. H. Cary. 1907.
Paper. $17.00. 120pp. .... Vendor G0259

711 **THE CARY FAM. IN ENGLAND**, by H.G. Cary. 1906.
Paper. $16.00. 105pp. .... Vendor G0259

712 **THE VA. CARYS; ESSAY IN GEN.**, by F. Harrison. 1919.
Cloth, $43.00. Paper, $33.00. 223pp. .... Vendor G0259

713 **DESC. OF STEPHEN CASE OF MARLBORO NY, INCLUDING ALLIED FAMILIES**, by Lynn M. Case. 1971.
Paper. $17.00. 82pp. .... Vendor G0259

714 **JONATHAN CASE OF ONTARIO CO., NY**, by C. Case. 1915.
Cloth, $30.00. Paper, $20.00. 104pp. .... Vendor G0259

715 **EARLY FAM. OF CASEY IN RI**, by T. Casey. 1893.
Paper. $9.00. 45pp. .... Vendor G0259

716 **THE CASEYS OF THE STRAND: COUNTY WESTMEATH, IRELAND, CANADA, AND THE UNITED STATES, 1780 TO THE PRESENT**, by Cecelia E. Thomas. 1995. Indexed. Illus.
Cloth. $22.95 (includes postage & handling). 168pp. .... Vendor G0243

717 **GENEALOGICAL HISTORY OF THE CASSEL FAMILY IN AMERICA ... YELLES CASSEL ...**, by Daniel Kolb Cassel. (1896) reprint 1989.
Cloth. $33.00. 467pp. .... Vendor G0150

718 **GENEALOGICAL HISTORY OF THE CASSEL FAMILY IN AMERICA, BEING THE DESCENDANTS OF JULIUS KASSEL OR YELLES CASSEL, OF KRIESHEIM, BADEN, GERMANY**, by D.K. Cassel. 1896.
Cloth, $81.50. Paper, $71.50. 465pp. .... Vendor G0259

719 **EVERY-NAME INDEX TO THE GENEALOGICAL HISTORY OF THE CASSEL FAMILY**, by Albert Edwards. 1993.
Paper. $11.00. 55pp. .... Vendor G0150

720 **CASTOR FAMILY OF PENNSYLVANIA, AND THE CASTOR FAMILY OF NEW YORK**, by George C. Martin, Henry A.J. Castor, et al. 1910.
Cloth, $36.00. Paper, $26.00. 119+42pp. .... Vendor G0259

721 **CATE–CATES FAM. OF NEW ENG.**, by Cates and Sanborn. 1904.
Paper. $10.00. 52pp. .... Vendor G0259

722   **DESCENDANTS OF JOHN CATLETT OF VIRGINIA**, by Carol A. Hauk.
1995. Indexed.
Paper. $45.00. 300pp. .... Vendor G0340

723   **CATT & WILLETT FAMILIES OF SUSSEX, ENGLAND & BRITISH
COLUMBIA, CANADA, 1595–1993**, by Glenna Willett Metchette. 1993.
Cloth, $31.00. Paper, $21.00. 132pp. .... Vendor G0259

724   **SUPPLEMENT TO THE CATTELL FAMILY IN AMERICA**, by Donald
Heys Rogers. 1992. Indexed.
Paper. $11.50. 50pp. .... Vendor G0069

725   **CAVERLY FAM. GEN., 1116–1880**, by R.B. Caverly. 1880.
Cloth, $43.00. Paper, $33.00. 201pp. .... Vendor G0259

726   **HOUSE OF CESSNA**, by H. Cessna. 1903.
Cloth, $35.00. Paper, $25.00. 120pp. .... Vendor G0259

727   **HOUSE OF CESSNA, 2ND SERIES**, by H. Cessna. 1935.
Cloth, $41.00. Paper, $31.00. 199pp. .... Vendor G0259

728   **GEN. RECORD OF CHACE & HATHAWAY FAM., 1630–1900**, by C.V.
Case. 1900.
Paper. $8.00. 42pp. .... Vendor G0259

729   **CHADBOURNE–CHADBOURN GENEALOGY**, by W.M. Emery. 1904.
Paper. $13.00. 66pp. .... Vendor G0259

730   **NOTES ON DESCENDANTS OF JOHN & JOAN CHADWICK & RE-
LATED FAMS.**, by A.D. Kilham. 1966.
Paper. $19.50. 120pp. .... Vendor G0259

731   **CHAFEE & LE BOSQUET FAMS.: INFORMAL GEN. OF OLIVIA K.
CHAFFEE, HUSBAND MAURICE LEBOSQUET & THEIR CHILDREN**,
by O.K. LeBosquet. 1955.
Cloth, $33.00. Paper, $23.00. 228pp. .... Vendor G0259

732   **THE BERKSHIRE, VT., CHAFFEES & THEIR DESC., 1801–1911**, by
A.J. Elliot. 1911.
Cloth, $67.50. Paper, $57.50. 356pp. .... Vendor G0259

733   **THE CHAFFEE GEN.; DESC. OF THOMAS CHAFFEE OF HINGHAM,
HULL, REHOBOTH AND SWANSEA, MASS., 1635–1909**, by W.H. Chaffee.
1909.
Cloth, $93.00. Paper, $83.00. 663pp. .... Vendor G0259

734   **HIST. OF ROBT. CHAFFIN & HIS DESC. & OTHER CHAFFINS IN
AMER.**, by W.L. Chaffin. 1912.
Cloth, $64.00. Paper, $54.00. 337pp. .... Vendor G0259

735   **ANNUAL REPORT OF THE CHAMBERLAIN ASSOC. OF AMERICA,
1906–7, WITH FOUR GENERATIONS OF THE DESCENDANTS OF
HENRY CHAMBERLIN OF HINGHAM, ENG., & HINGHAM MA, &
OTHER PAPERS.** 1908.
Paper. $18.00. 90pp. .... Vendor G0259

736   **ANNUAL REPORT OF THE CHAMBERLAIN ASSOC. OF AMERICA,**

1908–10, WITH FOUR GENERATIONS OF THE DESCENDANTS OF WILLIAM CHAMBERLIN OF WOBURN & BILLERICA MA, & OTHER PAPERS. 1911.
Cloth, $36.00. Paper, $26.00. 159pp. .... Vendor G0259

737 **CHAMPION GEN.; HIST. OF THE DESC. OF HENRY CHAMPION OF SAYBROOK & LYME, CT., WITH SOME ACCT. OF OTHER FAM. OF THAT NAME**, by F. Trowbridge. 1891.
Cloth, $81.50. Paper, $71.50. 575pp. .... Vendor G0259

738 **CHANCELLOR FAMILY**, by J.C. Chancellor. 1963.
Paper. $13.50. 69pp. .... Vendor G0259

739 **A SKETCH OF THE CHANDLER FAM. IN WORCESTER, MASS.**, by E.O.P. Sturgis. 1903.
Paper. $7.00. 37pp. .... Vendor G0259

740 **CHANDLER FAM., DESC. OF WM. & ANNIS CHANDLER WHO SETTLED IN ROXBURY, MASS.**, 1637, by G. Chandler. 1883.
Cloth, $167.00. Paper, $157.00. 1,323pp. .... Vendor G0259

741 **DESC. OF ROGER CHANDLER OF CONCORD, MA, 1658**, by C.H. Chandler. 1949.
Cloth, $34.50. Paper, $24.50. 152pp. .... Vendor G0259

742 **CHAPIN BOOK OF GEN. DATA, WITH BRIEF BIOGR. SKETCHES OF THE DESC. OF DEA. SAMUEL CHAPIN**, Vol. I, by G.W. Chapin. 1924.
Cloth, $163.00. Paper, $153.00. 1,320pp. .... Vendor G0259

743 **CHAPIN BOOK, EIGHTH TO TWELFTH GENERATION**, Vol. II, by G.W. Chapin. 1924.
Cloth, $165.00. Paper, $155.00. 1,417pp. .... Vendor G0259

744 **CHAPIN GEN., CONTAINING A VERY LARGE PROPORTION OF THE DESC. OF DEA. SAM'L CHAPIN, WHO SETTLED IN SPRINGFIELD, MA.**, 1642, by O. Chapin. 1862.
Cloth, $68.50. Paper, $58.50. 376pp. .... Vendor G0259

745 **CHAPINS WHO SERVED IN THE FRENCH & INDIAN WARS 1754–1764; REV. WAR 1775–1783; WAR OF 1812–1815; & OTHERS**, by G.W. Chapin. 1895.
Paper. $10.00. 47pp. .... Vendor G0259

746 **PROCEEDINGS AT THE MTG. OF THE CHAPIN FAM. IN SPRING-FIELD, MA., SEPT. 17, 1862.** 1862.
Paper, $18.50. 97pp. .... Vendor G0259

747 **JOHN CHAPLIN (1758–1837) OF ROWLEY, MA. & BRIDGTON, ME., HIS ANC. & DESC.**, by M. and L. Ellis. 1949.
Cloth, $31.00. Paper, $21.00. 139pp. .... Vendor G0259

748 **A GEN.; EDWARD CHAPMAN OF IPSWICH, MASS., 1642–1678, & HIS DESC.**, by J. Chapman. 1893.
Cloth, $32.00. Paper, $22.00. 147pp. .... Vendor G0259

749 **CHAPMAN FAM., OR THE DESC. OF ROBERT CHAPMAN, ONE OF**

THE 1ST SETTLERS OF SAYBROOK CONN.; WITH GEN. NOTES OF WM. OF NEW LONDON; EDW. OF WINDSOR; JOHN OF STONINGTON & REV. BENJ. OF STONINGTON (ALL CONN.), by F.W. Chapman. 1854.
Cloth, $62.00. Paper, $52.00. 414pp. .... Vendor G0259

750 EDW. CHAPMAN OF IPSWICH, MASS., IN 1644, & SOME DESC., by Chapman and Lapham. 1878.
Paper. $7.00. 36pp. .... Vendor G0259

751 CHAPPELEAR FAMILY OF VIRGINIA & CONNECTING LINES, by G.W. Chappelear. 1932.
Cloth, $33.00. Paper, $23.00. 122pp. .... Vendor G0259

752 CHAPPELL, DICKIE, & OTHER KINDRED FAM. OF VA., 1635–1900, rev. ed. by P.E. Chappell. 1900.
Cloth, $69.00. Paper, $59.00. 384pp. .... Vendor G0259

753 CHASE FAMILY RECORDS, by J. Montgomery Seaver.
Paper. $17.00. 84pp. .... Vendor G0259

754 GEN. OF THE ANC. & DESC. OF JOSEPH CHASE WHO DIED IN SWANZEY, HIS WILL PROVED MARCH, 1725. 1874.
Paper. $17.00. 86pp. .... Vendor G0259

755 SEVEN GEN. OF THE DESC. OF AQUILA & THOMAS CHASE, by J. C. Chase and G.W. Chamberlain. 1928.
Cloth, $103.50. Paper, $93.50. 624pp. .... Vendor G0259

756 MEM. OF THE CHAUNCEYS, INCL. PRESIDENT CHAUNCEY, HIS ANC. & DESC., by W.C. Fowler. 1858.
Cloth, $68.50. Paper, $58.50. 377pp. .... Vendor G0259

757 THE GUARANTEE: P.W. CHAVERS, BANKER, ENTREPRENEUR, PHILANTHROPIST IN CHICAGO'S BLACK BELT OF THE TWEN-TIES, by Madrue Chavers-Wright. 2nd ed. 1985. Indexed. Illus.
The true story of **Chavers** adapting to Chicago, a city torn with race riots, after migrating from Columbus, Ohio. His trials in establishing a bank for the community, his crusading legislation to protect bank deposits and the impact on the family.
Cloth, $29.95. Paper, $18.95. 450pp. .... Vendor G0006

758 CHEEVER FAMILY, by J.T. Hassam. 1896.
Paper. $10.00. 54pp. .... Vendor G0259

759 JOHN CHENEY OF PLAISTOW, NH, ORANGE CO., VT., & MONROE CO., NY & HIS DESC., by E. Gundry. 1959.
Paper. $11.00. 55pp. .... Vendor G0259

760 THE CHENEY GEN., by C.H. Pope. 1897.
Cloth, $83.00. Paper, $73.00. 582pp. .... Vendor G0259

761 GEN. & CHART OF THE CHENOWETH & CROMWELL FAM. OF MARYLAND & VA., by A.C. Chenoweth. 1894.
Paper. $7.00. 35pp. .... Vendor G0259

762 **HISTORY OF THE CHENOWETH FAMILY, BEGINNING 449 A.D.,** by C.C. Hiatt. 1925.
Cloth, $47.50. Paper, $37.50. 240pp. .... Vendor G0259

763 **THE CHENOWETH FAMILY IN AMERICA**, by Richard C. and Shirley D. Harris. 1994. Indexed.
Cloth. $40.00. 706pp. .... Vendor G0357

764 **GEN. OF THE DESC. OF WILLIAM CHESEBROUGH OF BOSTON, REHOBETH, MA., THE FOUNDER & FIRST SETTLER OF STONINGTON, CT.**, by A.C. Wildey. 1903.
Cloth, $96.00. Paper, $86.00. 688pp. .... Vendor G0259

765 **GEN. OF THE CHILD, CHILDS, & CHILDE FAM., OF THE PAST & PRESENT IN THE U. S. & THE CANADAS, FROM 1630–1881**, by E. Child. 1881.
Cloth, $115.00. Paper, $105.00. 856pp. .... Vendor G0259

766 **A CHILDS FAMILY**, by Martha Childs and Virginia Westfall. 1992. Indexed. Illus. with clip art.
Meant to be a comprehensive listing of the descendants of Richard **Child(s)** of Barnstable, MA. However, this first edition is heavily weighted with the families of one of his descendants, originally of Erie Co., NY, who played a large part in the settlement of NE. Allied NE families are **Sybrants** and **Adamis**.
Paper. $10.00. 77pp. .... Vendor G0436

767 **CHIPMAN FAM. IN ME., A GEN.**, by A.L. Chipman. 1897.
Paper. $8.50. 44pp. .... Vendor G0259

768 **CHIPMANS OF AMERICA**, by A.L. Chipman. 1904.
Cloth, $44.50. Paper, $34.50. 232pp. .... Vendor G0259

769 **THE CHIPMAN LINEAGE, PARTICULARLY AS IN ESSEX CO., MASS.**, by R.M. Chipman. 1872.
Paper. $12.00. 59pp. .... Vendor G0259

770 **CHIPP FAMILY, IN ENG. & AMER., WITH GEN. TREE; ALSO, HIST. & GEN. NOTES ON ALLIED FAMS.**, by C.H. Burnett. 1933.
Cloth, $39.50. Paper, $29.50. 182pp. .... Vendor G0259

771 **CHISOLM GEN; BEING A RECORD OF THE NAME FROM 1254, WITH SKETCHES OF ALLIED FAM.**, by W. Chisolm. 1914.
Paper. $19.50. 101pp. .... Vendor G0259

772 **CHITTENDEN FAMILY. WILLIAM CHITTENDEN OF GUILFORD, CONN. & HIS DESC.**, by A. Talcott. 1882.
Cloth, $49.00. Paper, $39.00. 263pp. .... Vendor G0259

773 **[Chivington]. MY MOTHER'S PEOPLE—TO COLORADO THEY CAME**, by Patricia Kinney Kaufman. 1994. Illus.
A pioneer history—**Chivington, Rowlison, Runyan** plus.
Paper. $15.00. 109pp. .... Vendor G0315

774 **CHOATES IN AMER., 1643–1896, JOHN CHOATE & HIS DESC., CHEBACCO, IPSWICH, MA.**, by E. Jameson. 1896.
Cloth, $68.00. Paper, $58.00. 474pp. .... Vendor G0259

775 **[Chouteau]. CREOLES OF ST. LOUIS,** by P. Beckwith. 1893.
Cloth, $36.00. Paper, $26.00. 174pp. Vendor G0259

776 **CHRISTLIEB FAMILY,** by Benj. F. Christlieb. 1895.
Paper. $11.00. 52pp. . . . . Vendor G0259

777 **CHRISTOPHERS GENEALOGY. JEFFREY & CHRISTOPHER CHRISTOPHERS OF NEW LONDON, CT., & THEIR DESCENDANTS,** by J.R. Totten. 1921.
Cloth, $38.00. Paper, $28.00. 178pp. Vendor G0259

778 **CHRISTOPHERS GENEALOGY: JEFFREY AND CHRISTOPHER CHRISTOPHERS OF NEW LONDON, CONN.,** by John R. Totten. 1921.
Indexed. Illus.
Paper. $10.00. 178pp. . . . . Vendor G0182

779 **DESC. OF CAPT. SAMUEL CHURCH OF CHURCHVILLE,** by E.A. Emens. 1920.
Paper. $14.00. 80pp. . . . . Vendor G0259

780 **DESC. OF RICHARD CHURCH OF PLYMOUTH, MASS.,** by J.A. Church. 1913.
Cloth, $55.00. Paper, $45.00. 354pp. . . . . Vendor G0259

781 **SIMEON CHURCH OF CHESTER, CONN., 1708–1792, & HIS DESCENDANTS,** by Charles W. Church. 1914.
Cloth, $48.00. Paper, $38.00. 241pp. . . . . Vendor G0259

782 **THE HIST. OF THE CHURCH FAM.,** by Chase, French and Wade. 1887.
Cloth, $31.00. Paper, $21.00. 144pp. . . . . Vendor G0259

783 **DESCENDANTS OF WILLIAM CHURCHILL OF VIRGINIA,** by Carol A. Hauk. 1995. Indexed.
Paper. $45.00. 298pp. . . . . Vendor G0340

784 **THE CHURCHILL FAM. IN AMERICA,** by G.A. and N.W. Churchill. 1904.
Cloth, $99.50. Paper, $89.50. 722pp. . . . . Vendor G0259

785 **GEN. & HIST. OF THE CHUTE FAM. IN AMER., WITH SOME ACCT. OF THE FAM. IN GT. BRIT. & IRELAND, & AN ACCT. OF 40 ALLIED FAMS.,** by W.E. Chute. 1894.
Cloth, $73.00. Paper, $63.00. 493pp. . . . . Vendor G0259

786 **CILLEY FAM.; DESC. OF ROBERT SEELY,** by J.P. Cilley. 1878.
Paper, $10.00. 47pp. . . . . Vendor G0259

787 **GEN. OF THE CLAFLIN FAM., BEING A REC. OF ROBT. MACKCLOTHLAN, OF WENHAM, MA., & HIS DESC., 1661–1898,** by C.H. Wight. 1903.
Cloth, $70.00. Paper, $60.00. 473pp. . . . . Vendor G0259

788 **[Claghorn]. THE BARONY OF CLEGHORNE, A.D. 1203, LANARKSHORE, SCOTLAND, TO THE FAM. OF CLAGHORN, A.D. 1912, USA,** by W.C. Claghorn. 1912.
Cloth, $34.00. Paper, $24.00. 132pp. . . . . Vendor G0259

789 **CLAIBORNE OF VIRGINIA: DESCENDANTS OF COL. WILLIAM**

CLAIBORNE, by John Frederick Dorman, CG, FASG, in collaboration with Claiborne T. Smith, Jr., M.D. 1995. Indexed. Illus.
Also includes families of **Brereton, Thompson, Hoomes, Napier, Gregory, Lipscomb, Lawson, Jackson, Greenhill, Fox, Jones, Butts, Cocke, Willson, Trent,** and **Anderson.**
Cloth. $70.00. 856pp. .... Vendor G0435

790 CLAIBORNE PEDIGREE; A GEN. TABLE OF THE DESC. OF SECRE-TARY WM. CLAIBORNE OF THE JUNIOR BRANCH OF THE U.S., WITH SOME TRACINGS IN THE FEMALE LINE, by G.M. Claiborne. 1900.
Paper. $10.00. 51pp. .... Vendor G0259

791 CLAPP MEM. RECORD OF THE CLAPP FAM. CONTAINING SKETCHES OF THE ORIG. 6 EMIGR. & A GEN. OF THEIR DESC. BEARING THE NAME; WITH SUPPL. & THE PROCEEDINGS AT TWO FAM. MEETINGS, by E. Clapp. 1876.
Cloth, $87.00. Paper, $77.00. 536pp. .... Vendor G0259

792 A RECORD OF THE DESC. OF JOHN CLARK OF FARMINGTON, CONN., by J. Gay. 1882.
Paper. $18.50. 94pp. .... Vendor G0259

793 DEACON GEORGE CLARK(E), & SOME OF HIS DESC., by G.C. Bryant. 1949.
Cloth, $51.00. Paper, $41.00. 258pp. .... Vendor G0259

794 HISTORY OF THE DESCENDANTS OF CEPHAS CLARK, b. MEDFIELD, MASS., 1745, WITH SOME ACCT. OF HIS ANC. FROM THEIR ADVENT IN AMER., by C.W. Clark. 1926.
Paper, $19.00. 102pp. .... Vendor G0259

795 [Clark]. LOYALIST CLARKS, BADGLEYS & ALLIED FAM. PT. 1, ANC. & DESC. OF MATTHIAS & RACHEL ABBOTT BADGLEY; PT. 2, ROBT. & ISABEL KETCHUM CLARKE, UE LOYALISTS & THEIR DESC., by E. Watson. 1954.
Cloth, $64.00. Paper, $54.00. 338pp. .... Vendor G0259

796 RECORDS OF THE DESC. OF HUGH CLARK OF WATERTOWN, MASS., 1640–1866, by J. Clark. 1866.
Cloth, $49.00. Paper, $39.00. 261pp. .... Vendor G0259

797 THE CLARK GEN., SOME DESC. OF DANIEL CLARK OF WINDSOR, CONN., 1639–1913, by E.L. Walton. 1913.
Cloth, $52.00. Paper, $42.00. 278pp. .... Vendor G0259

798 THE EDWARD CLARK GENEALOGY 1676–1988, by Walter Burges Smith. 1988. Indexed. Illus. Book #1107.
Cloth. $49.00. 592pp. .... Vendor G0082

799 ANC. OF JEREMY CLARKE OF R.I., & DUNGAN GEN., by A.R. Justice. 1922.
Cloth, $90.50. Paper, $80.50. 538pp. .... Vendor G0259

800 CLARKE–CLARK GEN.; REC. OF THE DESC. OF THOMAS CLARKE (1623–1697) OF PLYMOUTH. 1884.
Cloth, $33.50. Paper, $23.50. 192pp. .... Vendor G0259

801   **CLARKE FAMS. OF R.I.**, by G.A. Morrison, Jr. 1902.
Cloth, $53.50. Paper, $43.50. 337pp. .... Vendor G0259

802   **CLARKE'S KINDRED GEN. A GEN. HIST. OF CERTAIN DESC. OF JOSEPH CLARKE, DORCHESTER, 1630. DENICE DARLING, EDWARD GRAY, & W. HORNE**, by A.P. Clarke. 1896.
Cloth, $36.50. Paper, $26.50. 185pp. .... Vendor G0259

803   **RECORDS OF SOME OF THE DESC. OF THOMAS CLARKE OF PLYMOUTH, 1623–1697**, by S.C. Clarke. 1869.
Paper. $8.50. 43pp. .... Vendor G0259

804   **RICHARD CLARKE OF ROWLEY, MASS., & HIS DESC. IN THE LINE OF TIMOTHY CLARK OF ROCKINGHAM, VT., 1638–1904**, by T.B. Peck. 1905.
Paper. $18.00. 93pp. .... Vendor G0259

805   **THE DESC. OF NATHANIEL CLARKE & HIS WIFE ELIZABETH SOMERBY OF NEWBURY, MASS. A HIST. OF TEN GEN., 1642–1902**, by G.K. Clarke. 1902.
Cloth, $65.00. Paper, $55.00. 468pp. .... Vendor G0259

806   **MEM. OF MATTHEW CLARKSON OF PHILA., 1735–1800**, by J. Hall; **& OF HIS BROTHER GERARDUS, 1737–1790**, by S. Clarkson. 1890.
Cloth, $49.00. Paper, $39.00. 259pp. .... Vendor G0259

807   **CLASON, CLAWSON, CLASSON, CLOSSON, CLAUSON; STEPHEN CLASON OF STAMFORD, CONN., IN 1654, & SOME OF HIS DESC., COMP. FROM DATA CHIEFLY COLLECTED BY OLIVER B. CLASON**, by W.B. Lapham. 1892.
Cloth, $34.00. Paper, $24.00. 160pp. .... Vendor G0259

808   **[Clawson]. "PRINCESS ELEANOR," BEING THE GENEALOGY (PATERNAL & MATERNAL) OF MARY ELEANOR CLAWSON KNAUS**, by Francis A. Knaus. 1991.
Cloth, $139.50. Paper, $129.50. 1,109pp. .... Vendor G0259

809   **GEN. & HIST. OF THE CLAY FAM.**, by H.H. Clay. 1916.
Cloth, $34.00. Paper, $24.00. 159pp. .... Vendor G0259

810   **CLEMENS FAM. CHRONOLOGY, BIRTHS, MARRIAGES, DEATHS**, by W.M. Clemens. 1914.
Paper, $12.50. 63pp. .... Vendor G0259

811   **ANC. & DESC. OF ROBERT CLEMENTS OF LEICESTERSHIRE AND WARWICKSHIRE, ENG.; FIRST SETTLER OF HAVERHILL, MASS.**, by P.W. Clement. 2 vols. 1927.
Cloth, $173.50. Paper, $163.50. 1,092pp. .... Vendor G0259

812   **GEN. OF BENJ. CLEVELAND, GR-GRANDSON OF MOSES CLEVELAND OF WOBURN, MA. NATIVE OF CANTERBURY, WINDHAM CO., CT.**, by H. Cleveland. 1879.
Cloth, $38.00. Paper, $28.00. 260pp. .... Vendor G0259

813   **GEN. OF THE CLEVELAND–CLEAVELAND FAMS., DESC. OF MOSES FROM WOBURN, MA. & ALEXANDER FROM VA.; & EDW. WINN**

FROM WOBURN, by E.J. and H.G. Cleveland. 3 vols. 1899. Cloth, $129.00/vol. Paper, $119.00/vol. 2,900pp. .... Vendor G0259

814 **CLINTON FAM. OF CONN.**, by E.J. Clinton. 1915. Paper. $8.00. 40pp. .... Vendor G0259

815 **THE GEN. & DESC. OF JOHN CLOUGH OF SALISBURY, MASS.**, edited by E.C. Speare; published by the John Clough Soc. 1952. Cloth, $85.00. Paper, $75.00. 511pp. .... Vendor G0259

816 **THE GEN. & DESC. OF JOHN CLOUGH OF SALISBURY, MASS. VOLUME II.** 1966. Cloth, $53.50. Paper, $43.50. 286pp. .... Vendor G0259

817 **GENEALOGY OF THE CLOYD, BASYE & TAPP FAMILIES IN AMERICA, WITH BRIEF SKETCHES REFERRING TO THE FAMILIES OF INGELS, JONES, MARSHALL & SMITH**, by A.D. Cloyd. 1912. Cloth, $56.50. Paper, $46.50. 297pp. .... Vendor G0259

818 **GEN. OF MOSES & SUSANNA COATES, WHO SETTLED IN PENN. IN 1717, & THEIR DESC.**, by T. Coates. 1906. Cloth, $54.00. Paper, $44.00. 319pp. .... Vendor G0259

819 **THOMAS COATES, ENG. TO PA., 1683, & THE COATES FAM. IN PHILA. CITY DIR., 1785–1901.** Paper. $8.50. 43pp. .... Vendor G0259

820 **HIST. OF THE COBB FAM., PT. 1–4**, by P. Cobb. 1907–1923. Cloth, $48.50. Paper, $38.50. 278pp. .... Vendor G0259

821 **THE COCHRANES OF RENFREWSHIRE, SCOTLAND. THE ANC. OF ALEXANDER COCHRANE OF BILLERICA & MALDEN, MA.**, by W.K. Watkins. 1904. Paper. $11.00. 53pp. .... Vendor G0259

822 **THE HOUSE OF COCKBURN OF THAT ILK & THE CADETS THEREOF**, by T.H. Cockburn-Hood. 1888. Cloth, $71.00. Paper, $61.00. 394pp. .... Vendor G0259

823 **COCKMAN FAMILY HISTORY**, by Margaret Cockman Kitchel and Dwain L. Kitchel. 1990. Indexed. Illus. Cloth. $60.00. 600pp. .... Vendor G0183

824 **THE CODMANS OF CHARLESTOWN & BOSTON, 1637–1929**, by C.C. Wolcott. 1930. Paper, $17.50. 89pp. .... Vendor G0259

825 **CODY FAMILY IN AMER., 1698: DESC. OF PHILIP & MARTHA OF MASS., BIOGR. & GEN.**, compiled by the Cody Fam. Assoc. 1954. Cloth, $51.00. Paper, $41.00. 257pp. .... Vendor G0259

826 **COE–WARD MEM'L, & IMMIGR. ANCESTORS**, by L.E. Coe. 1897. Cloth, $31.50. Paper, $21.50. 136pp. .... Vendor G0259

827 **ROBERT COE, PURITAN, HIS ANC. & DESC., 1340–1910, WITH NOTICES OF OTHER COE FAM.**, by J.G. Bartlett. 1911. Cloth, $95.00. Paper, $85.00. 664pp. .... Vendor G0259

828 **THOMAS COFFEY & DESC.**, by L.H. Coffey. 1931.
Paper, $19.50. 102pp. .... Vendor G0259

829 **EARLY WILLS ILLUS. THE ANC. OF HARRIOT COFFIN, WITH GEN.
& BIOGR. NOTES,** by W. Appleton. 1893.
Paper. $18.00. 89pp. .... Vendor G0259

830 **GATHERINGS TOWARD A GEN. OF THE COFFIN FAM.**, by W.
Appleton. 1896.
Paper. $10.00. 53pp. .... Vendor G0259

831 **[Coffin]. LIFE OF TRISTRAM COFFYN OF NANTUCKET, MA.;
REMINIS. OF DESC.; HIST. INFO. CONCERNING THE ANCIENT FAM.
OF COFFYN,** by A. Coffin. 1881.
Paper. $12.50. 64pp. .... Vendor G0259

832 **GENEALOGY OF THE COFFINBERRY FAMILY, DESC. OF GEORGE
LEWIS COFFINBERRY, 1760–1851, & HIS WIFE ELIZABETH
(LITTLE) COFFINBERRY, WITH RELATED FAMILIES COFFEN-
BERRY, GILKISON, KEASEY, PLATT,** compiled by B.B. Scott. 1927.
Paper. $13.00. 64pp. .... Vendor G0259

833 **THE COFFMAN–CALLAHAN CLAN OF WASHINGTON COUNTY,
OHIO,** by Hugh Coffman. 1993. Indexed. Illus.
Cloth. $30.00. 520pp. .... Vendor G0213

834 **COGGESHALLS IN AMER.; GEN. OF THE DESC. OF JOHN
COGGESHALL OF NEWPORT, WITH A BRIEF NOTICE OF THEIR
ENG. ANC.,** by C.P. and T.R. Coggeshall. 1930.
Cloth, $72.50. Paper, $62.50. 395pp. .... Vendor G0259

835 **THE COGSWELLS IN AMER.,** by E.O. Jameson. 1884.
Cloth, $98.00. Paper, $88.00. 707pp. .... Vendor G0259

836 **THE COIT FAM.: OR, THE DESC. OF JOHN COIT, AT SALEM, MASS.,
IN 1638, AT GLOUCESTER IN 1644, & AT NEW LONDON, CONN., IN
1650,** by F.W. Chapman. 1874.
Cloth, $64.00. Paper, $54.00. 341pp. .... Vendor G0259

837 **DESC. OF ISAAC COLBURN, JR. OF W. DEDHAM, MASS.,** by E.J. Cox.
Paper. $7.50. 28pp. .... Vendor G0259

838 **GEN. OF THE DESC. OF EDWARD COLBURN, COME FROM ENG.,
1635,** by G.A. Gordon and S.R. Coburn. 1913.
Cloth, $70.00. Paper, $60.00. 474pp. .... Vendor G0259

839 **A GEN. OF THE DESC. OF ABRAHAM COLBY & ELIZABETH
BLAISDELL, HIS WIFE, WHO SETTLED IN BOW IN 1768, BY ONE
OF THEM (H. COLBY).** 1895.
Cloth, $32.50. Paper, $22.50. 152pp. .... Vendor G0259

840 **COLBY FAM. OF AMESBURY & HAVERHILL, MASS. (EXTR. FROM
"THE OLD FAM. OF SALISBURY, MA." PART NINE).**
Paper. $10.00. 49pp. .... Vendor G0259

841 **DESC. OF EDWARD COLCORD OF N.H.,** by D.B. Colcord. 1908.
Cloth, $34.00. Paper, $24.00. 166pp. .... Vendor G0259

842 COLE FAMILY OF STARK, N.H. DESC. OF SOLOMON COLE OF BEVERLY, MASS., by H.W. Hardon. 1932.
Paper. $17.50. 90pp. .... Vendor G0259

843 ISAAC KOOL (COOL OR COLE) & CATHERINE SERVEN, MARRIED 1764 AT TAPPAN, N.Y.; THEIR DESC. COMPLETE TO 1876, ALSO THEIR AMER. ANC. FROM THE SETTLEMENT OF N.Y. CITY, by D. Cole. 1876.
Cloth, $50.00. Paper, $40.00. 269pp. .... Vendor G0259

844 THE DESCENDANTS OF ELISHA COLE, WHO CAME FROM CAPE COD TO WHAT IS NOW PUTNAM COUNTY, N.Y., ABOUT 1745, by Joseph O. Cole. (1909).
Cloth, $47.00. Paper, $37.00. 237pp. .... Vendor G0259

845 THE DESC. OF JAMES COLE OF PLYMOUTH, 1633, RECORD OF FAM. OF LT. THOMAS BURNHAM, IPSWICH, 1635; LT. EDWARD WINSHIP, CAMBRIDGE, 1634; SIMON HUNTINGTON; NORWICH, ENG., 1635, by E.B. Cole. 1908.
Cloth, $65.00. Paper, $55.00. 449pp. .... Vendor G0259

846 THE EARLY GEN. OF THE COLE FAM. IN AMER. (INCLUDING COLES AND COWLES), by F.T. Cole. 1887.
Cloth, $54.50. Paper, $44.50. 340pp. .... Vendor G0259

847 DESCENDANTS OF ROBERT COLEMAN OF VIRGINIA, by Carol A. Hauk. 1995. Indexed.
Paper. $45.00. 350pp. .... Vendor G0340

848 GEN. OF WILLIAM COLEMAN OF GLOUCESTER, by J.C. Coleman. 1906.
Cloth, $50.00. Paper, $40.00. 240pp. .... Vendor G0259

849 THE ROBERT COLEMAN FAM. FROM VA. TO TEXAS, 1652–1965, by J.P. Coleman. 1965.
Cloth, $79.50. Paper, $69.50. 451pp. .... Vendor G0259

850 COLES FAMILY OF VA.: ITS NUMEROUS CONNECTIONS, FROM EMIGR. TO AMERICA TO 1915, by W.B. Coles. 1931.
Cloth, $135.00. Paper, $125.00. 885pp. .... Vendor G0259

851 ROBERT COLGATE, THE IMMIGRANT: A GENEALOGY OF THE NEW YORK COLGATES & SOME ASSOCIATED LINES, by T. Abbe and H.A. Howson. 1941.
Cloth, $82.00. Paper, $72.00. 464pp. .... Vendor G0259

852 GEN. OF THE DESC. OF ANTHONY COLLAMER OF SCITUATE, MASS., by C. Hatch. 1915.
Cloth, $40.00. Paper, $30.00. 198pp. .... Vendor G0259

853 DESCENDANTS OF WILLIAM COLLIER OF VIRGINIA, by Carol A. Hauk. 1995. Indexed.
Paper. $30.00. 68pp. .... Vendor G0340

854 DESC. OF JOHN COLLIN: CYCLOPEDIA OF BIOGR., CONTAINING A HIST. OF THE FAM. & DESC. OF JOHN COLLIN, FORMER RESI-

DENT OF MILFORD, CT., TO WHICH IS APPENDED A NOTICE OF
THEIR KINDRED, by J.F. Collin. 1872.
Paper. $17.50. 124pp. .... Vendor G0259

855 REMINISC. OF ISAAC & RACHEL BUDD COLLINS, WITH ACCT. OF
SOME DESC. & HIST. OF A REUNION HELD AT PHILA., 1892, by J.
Collins etc. 1893.
Cloth, $34.50. Paper, $24.50. 164pp. .... Vendor G0259

856 THE COLLINS FAM.: A REC. OF THE DESC. OF WM. COLLINS &
ESTHER MORRIS FROM 1760 TO 1897, by W.H. Collins. 1897.
Cloth, $36.50. Paper, $26.50. 188pp. .... Vendor G0259

857 GENEALOGICAL MEMOIRS OF THE FAMILIES OF COLT &
COUTTS, by Charles Rogers. 1879 (London).
Paper. $12.00. 59pp. .... Vendor G0259

858 1644–1911; A GEN. RECORD OF THE DESC. OF QUARTERMASTER
GEORGE COLTON, by G.W. Colton. 1912.
Cloth, $99.00. Paper, $89.00. 598pp. .... Vendor G0259

859 DESCENDANTS OF DAVID COLTRANE & JAMES FRAZIER OF N.C.,
by Robert H. Frazier. 1961.
Paper. $19.50. 121pp. .... Vendor G0259

860 COLVER–CULVER FAMILY GENEALOGY, by Valerie Dyer Giorgi. 1984.
Indexed. Illus.
     Edward **Colver** of Groton, Connecticut through 13 generations of **Culver** in
America.
Cloth. $38.00. 692pp. .... Vendor G0090

861 COLVER–CULVER GEN., DESC. OF EDWARD COLVER OF BOSTON,
DEDHAM & ROXBURY, MASS., & NEW LONDON & MYSTIC, CONN.,
1635–1909, by F.L. Colver. 1910.
Cloth, $50.50. Paper, $40.50. 271pp. .... Vendor G0259

862 GENEALOGY OF JACOB COLVIN AND ALLIED FAMILIES, by Wanda
Williams Colvin. 1992. Indexed. Illus.
Cloth, $40.00. Paper, $25.00. 249pp. .... Vendor G0432

863 THE COMEY–COMEE FAM. IN AMER. DESC. OF DAVID COMEY OF
CONCORD, MASS. WITH NOTES ON THE MALTMAN FAM., by A.H.
Bent. 1896.
Paper. $10.00. 50pp. .... Vendor G0259

864 COMLY FAM. IN AMER.; DESC. OF HENRY & JOAN COMLY WHO
CAME TO AMER. IN 1682 FROM BEAMINSTER, SOMERSET, ENG.,
WITH SHORT ACCTS. OF THE ANC. OF CHAS. & DEBBY ANN
(NEWBOLD) COMLY, by G.N. Comly. 1939.
Cloth, $180.00. Paper, $170.00. 1,148pp. .... Vendor G0259

865 SUPPL. TO COMLY FAMILY IN AMERICA, BEING ADD. & CORR.,
by G.N. Comly. 1952.
Cloth, $32.00. Paper, $22.00. 142pp. .... Vendor G0259

866 COMSTOCK GENEALOGY: DESCENDANTS OF WILLIAM

COMSTOCK OF NEW LONDON, CT., WHO DIED AFTER 1662, TEN GENERATIONS, by Cyrus B. Comstock. 1907.
Cloth, $57.50. Paper, $47.50. 314pp. .... Vendor G0259

867 COMSTOCK–THOMAS ANC. OF RICHARD WILMOT COMSTOCK, by H.M. Pitman. 1964.
Cloth, $79.50. Paper, $69.50. 452pp. .... Vendor G0259

868 HISTORY & GEN. OF THE COMSTOCK FAM. IN AMERICA, by J.A. Comstock. 1949.
Cloth, $109.50. Paper, $99.50. 715pp. .... Vendor G0259

869 A HIST. & GEN. OF THE CONANT FAM. IN ENG. & AMER., 1520–1887, by F.O. Conant. 1887.
Cloth, $104.00. Paper, $94.00. 654pp. .... Vendor G0259

870 CONANT GEN., by F.O. Conant.
Paper. $9.00. 44pp. .... Vendor G0259

871 ROGER CONANT, A FOUNDER OF MASSACHUSETTS, by Clifford K. Shipton. 1944.
Cloth, $35.00. Paper, $25.00. 171pp. .... Vendor G0259

872 GEN. REC. OF THE CONDIT FAM., DESC. OF JOHN CUNDITT, A NATIVE OF GT. BRIT. WHO SETTLED IN NEWARK, NJ, 1678–1885, by J.H. and E. Condit. Rev. ed. 1916.
Cloth, $79.50. Paper, $69.50. 470pp. .... Vendor G0259

873 SOME ACCOUNT OF THE CONE FAMILY IN AMERICA, PRINCI-PALLY THE DESCENDANTS OF DANIEL CONE, WHO SETTLED IN HADDAM, CONN., IN 1662, by W.W. Cone. 1903.
Cloth, $94.00. Paper, $84.00. 546pp. .... Vendor G0259

874 CONGDON CHRONICLE, #1–18, by G.E. Congdon. 1921–1934.
Cloth, $46.00. Paper, $36.00. 240pp. .... Vendor G0259

875 [Congdon]. ONE HUNDRED THIRTY-EIGHT GEN. FROM ADAM; A PEDIGREE TRACED FROM ADAM TO THE PRESENT TIME, by G.E. Congdon. 1910.
Paper. $11.00. 55pp. .... Vendor G0259

876 A REC. OF BIRTHS, MARR. & DEATHS OF THE DESC. OF JOHN CONGER OF WOODBRIDGE, N.J., by C.G.B. Conger. 1903.
Cloth, $35.50. Paper, $25.50. 165pp. .... Vendor G0259

877 HIST. & GEN. OF AUTHOR'S BRANCH OF THE CONNET FAM., by A. Connet. 1905.
Paper. $10.00. 53pp. .... Vendor G0259

878 CONRAD CLAN. FAMILY OF JOHN STEPHEN CONRAD, SR. & AL-LIED LINES, by F.W. Coffman. 1939.
Cloth, $62.50. Paper, $52.50. 355pp. .... Vendor G0259

879 FAM. HIST. IN THE LINE OF JOS. CONVERSE OF BEDFORD, MASS., 1739–1828, by J.J. Putnum. 1897.
Paper. $15.00. 97pp. .... Vendor G0259

880   **FAM. RECORDS OF DEACONS J. W. CONVERSE & E. CONVERSE,**
      by W.G. Hill. 1887.
      Cloth, $47.00. Paper, $37.00. 246pp. .... Vendor G0259

881   **SOME ANC. & DESC. OF SAM'L CONVERSE, JR., MAJ. JAMES
      CONVERS, HON. HEMAN ALLEN, CAPT. JONATHAN BIXBY, SR.,** by
      C. Converse. 2 vols. 1905.
      Cloth, $142.00. Paper, $132.00. 989pp. .... Vendor G0259

882   **CONWAY FAM. OF LANCASTER CO., VA. (EXTR. VA. GEN.).**
      Paper. $14.50. 72pp. .... Vendor G0259

883   **DESCENDANTS OF EDWIN CONWAY OF VIRGINIA,** by Carol A. Hauk.
      1995. Indexed.
      Paper. $35.00. 224pp. .... Vendor G0340

884   **THE COOK GENEALOGY,** by J. Montgomery Seaver. Illus.
      Paper. $7.00. 32pp. .... Vendor G0011

885   **DESC. OF MORDECAI COOKE OF "MORDECAI'S MOUNT,"
      GLOUCESTER CO., VA., 1650, & THOMAS BOOTH OF WARE NECK,
      GLOUCESTER CO., VA., 1685,** by Dr. and Mrs W.C. Stubbs. 1923.
      Cloth, $59.50. Paper, $49.50. 286+35pp. .... Vendor G0259

886   **DESCENDANTS OF MORDECAI COOKE OF VIRGINIA,** by Carol A.
      Hauk. 1995. Indexed.
      Paper. $45.00. 382pp. .... Vendor G0340

887   **THE COOKE ANC.,** by Van Dycke and Cooke. 1960.
      Cloth, $37.50. Paper, $27.50. 162pp. .... Vendor G0259

888   **REC. OF DESC. OF WM. COOLBAUGH, 1765–1918.**
      Paper. $8.00. 40pp. .... Vendor G0259

889   **COOLEY GENEALOGY: DESC. OF ENSIGN BENJ. COOLEY, EARLY
      SETTLER OF SPRINGFIELD & LONGMEADOW, MA., & OTHER
      MEMBERS OF THE FAM. IN AMERICA,** by M.E. Cooley; compiled by
      V.B. Keatley. 1941.
      Cloth, $159.00. Paper, $149.00. 1,199pp. .... Vendor G0259

890   **DESCENDANTS OF DR ASAHEL & SALLY WILBUR COOLEY
      (SUPPL. TO "COOLEY GEN."),** by A.S. Cooley; edited by L.A.C. Cooley.
      1952.
      Cloth, $33.00. Paper, $23.00. 153pp. .... Vendor G0259

891   **THE DESCENDANTS OF ITHAMAR COOLEY AND SALLY WEBSTER
      SNOW OF GRAFTON COUNTY, NEW HAMPSHIRE AND DELAWARE
      COUNTY, IOWA, 1817–1995,** by Rick Crume. 1995. Indexed.
      Includes: **French, Muckler.**
      Paper. $6.00. 40pp. .... Vendor G0386

892   **DESC. OF JOHN & MARY COOLIDGE OF WATERTOWN, MASS., 1630,**
      by E.D. Coolidge. 1930.
      Cloth, $68.00. Paper, $58.00. 418pp. .... Vendor G0259

893   **ONE BRANCH OF THE COOLIDGE FAM., 1427–1963,** by F.C. Crawford.
      1964.
      Paper. $17.50. 91pp. .... Vendor G0259

894 THE STORY OF ANTHONY COOMBS & HIS DESC., by W.C. Coombs. 1913.
Cloth, $48.00. Paper, $38.00. 226pp. .... Vendor G0259

895 [Coons]. THE KOON–COONS FAMS. OF EASTERN N.Y.: HIST. OF THE DESC. OF MATTHAIES KUNTZ & SAMUEL KUHN (TWO DISTINCT FAMS.) WHICH CAME WITH THE PALATINE IMMIGR. & SETTLED IN THE HUDSON RIVER IN 1710, by W.S. Coons. 1937.
Cloth, $88.50. Paper, $78.50. 502pp. .... Vendor G0259

896 COOPER HIST. & GEN. 1681–1931, by M. Cooper. 1931.
Cloth, $32.50. Paper, $22.50. 116pp. .... Vendor G0259

897 COPELAND FAMILY: A COPELAND GEN., by W.T. Copeland. 1937.
Cloth, $124.50. Paper, $114.50. 821pp. .... Vendor G0259

898 COPPAGE–COPPEDGE FAMILY BULLETIN, VOL. I. 1950.
Paper. $11.00. 55pp. .... Vendor G0259

899 COPPAGE–COPPEDGE FAM. 1542–1955, By Monahan & Coppage. 1955.
Cloth, $35.00. Paper, $25.00. 126pp. .... Vendor G0259

900 GEN. OF THE CORBETT FAM., by E. Corbett. 1917.
Paper. $17.50. 85pp. .... Vendor G0259

901 DESCENDANTS OF HENRY CORBIN OF VIRGINIA, by Carol A. Hauk. 1995. Indexed.
Paper. $45.00. 335pp. .... Vendor G0340

902 HIST. & GEN. OF THE DESC. OF CLEMENT CORBIN OF MUDDY RIVER (BROOKLINE), MA. & WOODSTOCK, CT., WITH OTHER LINES OF CORBINS, by H. Lawson. 1905.
Cloth, $68.50. Paper, $58.50. 378pp. .... Vendor G0259

903 CORBOULD GENEALOGY [IN ENGLAND], by G.C.B. Poulter. 1935.
Cloth, $35.00. Paper, $25.00. 165pp. .... Vendor G0259

904 A GEN. RECORD OF THE CORLISS FAM. OF AMER., by A.W. Corliss (& others). 1st ed. 1875.
Cloth, $64.00. Paper, $54.00. 343pp. .... Vendor G0259

905 HISTORY OF THE CORNELIUS FAMILY IN AMERICA: HISTORI-CAL, GENEALOGICAL & BIOGRAPHICAL, by C.S. and S.F. Cornelius. 1926.
Cloth, $56.00. Paper, $46.00. 292pp. .... Vendor G0259

906 GEN. OF THE CORNELL FAM., BEING AN ACCT. OF THE DESC. OF THOMAS CORNELL OF PORTSMOUTH, R.I., by J. Cornell. 1902.
Cloth, $69.50. Paper, $59.50. 468pp. .... Vendor G0259

907 THE HOUSE OF CORNEWALL [FAMILY IN ENGLAND], by C. Reade. 1908 (England).
Cloth, $57.50. Paper, $47.50. 316pp. .... Vendor G0259

908 THE HIST. & GEN. OF THE CORNISH FAM. IN AMER., by J.E. Cornish. 1907.
Cloth, $55.00. Paper, $45.00. 353pp. .... Vendor G0259

909 **WM. CORNWALL & HIS DESC.; A GEN. HIST. OF THE FAM. OF WM. CORNWALL, WHO CAME TO AMER. IN 1633 & DIED IN MIDDLETON, CT, IN 1678,** by E. Cornwall. 1901. Cloth, $38.00. Paper, $28.00. 185pp. .... Vendor G0259

910 **HISTORY OF THE CORRY FAMILY OF CASTLECOOLE,** by the Earl of Belmore. 1891 (Dublin). Cloth, $56.50. Paper, $46.50. 296+13pp. .... Vendor G0259

911 **WILLIAM CORRY AND HIS DESCENDANTS,** by Mildred S. Ezell. 1990. Indexed. Illus.
Descendants of William **Corry,** Ulster, Ireland, immigrant to SC (1767 to present). Includes: **Corry; Caldwell/Calwell; Jefferies/Jeffries; McCombs; Monfort/Montfort; Patrick; Seawright; Stewart/Stuart.**
Hard cloth. $25.00. 560pp. .... Vendor G0323

912 **THREE HUNDRED YEARS WITH THE CORSON FAMS. IN AMER., INCL. STATEN ISL.–PENN. CORSONS; N.J. CORSONS; DUMFRIESSHIRE, SCOTLAND, CORSONS; NEW ENG. CORSONS; CANADIAN CORSONS,** by O. Corson. 2 vols. 1939. Cloth, $58.50/vol. Paper, $48.50/vol. 303+336pp. .... Vendor G0259

913 **THE CORWIN GEN. (CURWIN, CURWEN, CORWINE) IN THE U.S.,** by E.T. Corwin. 1872. Cloth, $57.50. Paper, $47.50. 318pp. .... Vendor G0259

914 **CORYS OF AMERICA ANCESTORS AND DESCENDANTS, 1ST EDITION,** by Al Bertus Cory. 1991. Indexed. Includes coat of arms. Cloth. $30.00. 903pp. .... Vendor G0298

915 **CORYS OF AMERICA ANCESTORS AND DESCENDANTS, 2ND EDITION VOL. I,** by Al Bertus Cory. 1994. Indexed. Cloth. $49.00. 920pp. .... Vendor G0298

916 **CORYS OF AMERICA ANCESTORS AND DESCENDANTS, 2ND EDITION VOL. II,** by Al Bertus Cory. 1994. Indexed. Cloth. $49.00. 803pp. .... Vendor G0298

917 **LINEAL ANC. OF RHODA AXTELL CORY, MOTHER OF CAPT. JAMES CORY: GEN., HIST., & BIOGR., PTS. 1 & 2,** by C.H. Cory, Jr. 1937. Cloth, $54.00. Paper, $44.00. 300pp. .... Vendor G0259

918 **[Cory]. LINEAL ANC. OF SUSAN KITCHELL MULFORD, MOTHER OF SUSAN MULFORD CORY: GEN., HIST. & BIOGR., PTS. 1 & 2,** by C.H. Cory, Jr. 1937. Cloth, $53.50. Paper, $43.50. 295pp. .... Vendor G0259

919 **LINEAL ANC. OF SUSAN MULFORD CORY, WIFE OF CAPT. JAMES CORY: GEN., HIST., & BIOGR., PTS. 1 & 2,** by C.H. Cory, Jr. 1937. Cloth, $74.00. Paper, $64.00. 437pp. .... Vendor G0259

920 **COTÉ GENEALOGY,** by Linda Dubé. 1992. Indexed. Illus. Five-volume set, with 1,200 photos. Paper. $85.00. 2,000pp. .... Vendor G0060

CORYS OF AMERICA

Ancestors and Descendants

SECOND EDITION

VOLUME I

Book I.. John CORY of Southold Long Island
NY. 875 pages, Indexed. 13,149 names , 4407
Marriages, 3,158 Locations, 14 Generations.
Covers New York, New Jersey, Ohio, Iowa,
Pennsylvania and more.

Book II. Willis, Witton, Downs, Cain, Philips
Kentucky and Virginia Locations. 503 names

VOLUME II

Book III..William CORY of Portsmouth RI.
603 pages, Indexed. 8,847 names 2,994 mar
2,252 Locations, 12 generations.
Book IV.. Thomas CORY of Chelmsford MA
91 pages, 478 mar, 484 places, 12 Generations
Book V..Progenitors who could not be linked
above. 109 pages 1,955 names 14 Gen.
Including Giles Cory the martyr, of Salem MA

Dates; John William Thomas and Giles from early 1600's to the present time

PRICE

Second Edition: Each Volume $49.00. Both Volumes $90.00 includes shipping

---

First Edition: Contains same progenitors less Information. $30.00 includes shipping

Please send check or Money order to
Al B. Cory 11056 Orange Cart Way Jacksonville, Florida 32223-7336   **(904) 886-9404**
AlBCory@aol.com

---

921 **ANCESTORS & DESCENDANTS OF SYLVANUS & ABIGAIL (SHERMAN) COTTLE**, by James B. Schwabe. (1977) rev. 1993. 2 pages of illustrations. Indexed.
Also 41 allied families.
Cloth. $45.00. 560pp. .... Vendor G0353

922 **A SHORT BIOGR. OF REV. JOHN COTTON OF BOSTON & GEN. OF HIS COTTON DESC.**, by L. Cooley. 1945.
Cloth, $34.00. Paper, $24.00. 125pp. .... Vendor G0259

923 **COURSENS FROM 1612 TO 1917, WITH THE STATEN ISLAND BRANCH**, by P.G. Ullman. 1917.
Paper. $18.00. 88pp. .... Vendor G0259

924 **BASSETT'S NOTES ON COVERT**, by L.A. Bryan. 1957.
Paper. $7.00. 32pp. .... Vendor G0259

925 **THE COVERT FAMILY: FOURTEEN GENERATIONS IN THE FINGER LAKES**, by Carl W. Fischer, William V. Covert, and Maurice L. Patterson. 1988. Indexed.
Cloth. $35.00. 682pp. .... Vendor G0093

926 **THE COVINGTONS: BEING A COLLECTION OF FAMILY INFO.**, by W.B. Covington. 1942.
Cloth, $42.00. Paper, $32.00. 201pp. .... Vendor G0259

927	ILLUSTRATED HIST. & BIOGR. SKETCH OF THE DESC. OF WIL-
LIAM COWDEN, WHO MIGRATED FROM IRELAND TO AMER.
ABOUT 1730, & OF JAMES GILLILAND, WHICH CAME FROM THE
SAME LAND & ABOUT THE SAME TIME (WITH CHARTS), by R.
Cowden. 1915.
Cloth, $37.50. Paper, $27.50. 179pp. .... Vendor G0259

928	COWDREY–COWDERY–COWDRAY GEN.; WM. COWDERY OF
LYNN, MASS., 1630 & HIS DESC., by M.B.A. Mehling. 1911.
Cloth, $79.50. Paper, $69.50. 451pp. .... Vendor G0259

929	GEN. OF THE COWLES FAMS. IN AMER., by C.D. Cowles. 2 vols. 1929.
Cloth, $208.00. Paper, $198.00. 1,510pp. .... Vendor G0259

930	COX FAMILY IN AMERICA: HISTORY & GENEALOGY OF THE
OLDER BRANCHES OF THE FAMILY FROM THE APPEARANCE OF
ITS FIRST REPRESENTATIVE IN THIS COUNTRY IN 1610, by H.M.
Cox. 1912.
Cloth, $61.00. Paper, $51.00. 325+11pp. .... Vendor G0259

931	COX FAMILIES OF HOLDERNESS, WITH PARTIAL GEN. OF THE
COX, RANDALL, NUTTER & PICKERING FAMS., & BIOGR.
SKETCHES OF FOUR BROTHERS, DESC. OF THESE FAMS., by L.S.
Cox. 1939.
Cloth, $47.00. Paper, $37.00. 235pp. .... Vendor G0259

932	ADDITIONS & CORRECTIONS FOR "THE COX FAMILIES OF
HOLDERNESS." 1949, 1957.
Cloth, $31.00. Paper, $21.00. 58+90pp. .... Vendor G0259

933	FROM THE BANKS OF THE DAN: A COX FAMILY GENEALOGY,
by Avis E. Cox and Marion R. Cox. 1994. Indexed. Illus. with photos and
documents.
Beginning in 1786 in Virginia and North Carolina through westward migration to present. End notes, footnotes, acid-free paper.
Cloth. $50.00. 477pp. .... Vendor G0427

934	[Cox]. HISTORY & GENEALOGY OF THE COCK–COCKS–COX FAM-
ILY, DESCENDED FROM JAMES & SARAH COCK OF
KILLINGWORTH UPON MATINECOCK, IN OYSTERBAY, L.I., N.Y.,
by G.W. Cocks and J. Cox, Jr. 1912.
Cloth, $61.50. Paper, $51.50. 345pp. .... Vendor G0259

935	COXE FAMILY, by F.W. Leach and A. duBin. 1938.
Paper. $12.00. 60pp. .... Vendor G0259

936	CRAFTS FAMILY. A GEN. & BIOGR. HIST. OF THE DESC. OF GRIF-
FIN & ALICE CRAFT OF ROXBURY, MASS, 1630–1890, by J.M. and
W.F. Crafts. 1893.
Cloth, $109.00. Paper, $99.00. 807pp. .... Vendor G0259

937	GEN. OF THE CRAGIN FAM., by C.H. Cragin. 1860.
Paper. $8.50. 42pp. .... Vendor G0259

938	CRAIG–LINKS, A QUARTERLY FOR ALL CRAIGS, edited by Ann
Burton.
Subscription. $15.50/year .... Vendor G0094

939 **CRAIGS & JAMESONS OF THE COLONIES**, by Edward Pete Craig, Jr. 1995. Indexed.
Compilation of all **Craig** and **Jameson** families from the early 1600s of Virginia and Pennsylvania and their descendants to 1800 and beyond, including movement west after the Revolution. Church, Court, and Revolutionary War records. Primary line of Thomas **Craig**, deceased 1798 in Albemarle County, Virginia, and John **Jameson**, his father-in-law.
Cloth. $42.95 .... Vendor G0146

940 **ANC. OF LEANDER HOWARD CRALL, MONOGRAPHS ON THE CRELL, HAFF, BEATTY & OTHERS**, by F. Allaben. 1908.
Cloth, $76.50. Paper, $66.50. 426pp. .... Vendor G0259

941 **ELDER JOHN CRANDALL OF RHODE ISLAND & HIS DESC.**, by J.C. Crandall. 1949.
Cloth, $119.00. Paper, $109.00. 797pp. .... Vendor G0259

942 **GEN. OF ELDER JOHN CRANDALL & HIS DESC.**, by A.P. Crandall. 1888.
Paper. $12.50. 62pp. .... Vendor G0259

943 **GEN. OF THE CRANE FAM., DESC. OF HENRY CRANE OF WETHERSFIELD & GUILFORD, CT.**, by E. Crane. 2 vols. 1900.
Cloth, $125.00. Paper, $115.00. 839pp. .... Vendor G0259

944 **[Crapo]. CERTAIN COMEOVERERS**, by H.H. Crapo. 2 vols. 1912.
Cloth, $149.00. Paper, $139.00. 1,044pp. .... Vendor G0259

945 **CRAWFORD EXCHANGE**, edited by Wilton M. Whisler. Indexed.
Back issues (15 volumes available). Information exchange among **Crawford** researchers, including variant spellings. Queries free to members.
$15/yr. membership includes set of 2 issues in U.S.; membership costs U.S. $20 elsewhere. 60+pp./yr. .... Vendor G0099

946 **A SELECTIVE HISTORY OF THE CREGO FAMILY**, by Roy Crego. 1993. Indexed.
Cloth. $29.95. 127pp. .... Vendor G0231

947 **CRENSHAW FAM. RECORD (IN VALENTINE PAPERS).**
Paper. $14.00. 70pp. .... Vendor G0259

948 **HIST. OF THE CRESAPS**, by J. and B. Cresap. 1937.
Cloth, $86.50. Paper, $76.50. 506pp. .... Vendor G0259

949 **STORY OF YOUR ANCESTORS: CRESSEY, 286 YEARS IN AMERICA**, by Ernest W. Cressey. 1935.
Cloth, $31.00. Paper, $21.00. 151pp. .... Vendor G0259

950 **CRESSWELL FAMILY AND THE AMERICAN CRISWELLS**, by Edgar Golden Criswell. (1931) reprint 1993. Illus.
Paper. $19.00. 157pp. .... Vendor G0126

951 **CRESWELL–CRISWELL GENEALOGICAL RECORDS**, by George Ely Russell. (1987) reprint 1994. Illus.
Paper. $20.00. 132pp. .... Vendor G0126

952 THE CRIDER FAMILY OF ROCKINGHAM COUNTY, VA, by Lewis H. Yankey. 1990. Indexed.
Paper. $13.00. 83pp. .... Vendor G0365

953 CRIPPEN–CRIPPIN FAMILY JOURNAL, by Donna Younkin Logan. 1993. Illus.
Surnames covered in publication include: **Crippen, Crippin, Grippen, Grippin**. This quarterly covers all **Crippen** et var families concentrating on records prior to 1900.
Subscription. $15/year. 80pp./yr. .... Vendor G0392B

954 DESCENDANTS OF ANTHONY CRISPELL, 1660–1950, PENNA. BRANCH, by E. Cobleigh. 1950.
Paper. $19.50. 102pp. .... Vendor G0259

955 CROCKER GENEALOGY [DESCENDANTS OF WM. CROCKER OF BARNSTABLE MA, 1612–1692], by J.R. Crocker, et al. 1962?
Cloth, $59.00. Paper, $49.00. 246+75pp. .... Vendor G0259

956 CROCKER. EXTR. FROM GEN. NOTES OF BARNSTABLE FAM.
Paper. $10.00. 51pp. .... Vendor G0259

957 CROCKETT FAMILY & CONNECTING LINES, BY FRENCH & ARMSTRONG. VOL. V, "NOTABLE SOUTHERN FAMS." 1928.
Cloth, $101.00. Paper, $91.00. 611pp. .... Vendor G0259

958 NOTABLE SOUTHERN FAMILIES, Volume V, by Zella Armstrong and Janie Preston Collup French. (1928) reprint 1993. Indexed.
The **Crockett** family and connecting lines.
Paper. $45.00. 611pp. .... Vendor G0011

959 CROCKETT FAM. OF NEW ENG., 1632–1943, by O. Crockett. 1943.
Paper. $8.00. 41pp. .... Vendor G0259

960 THE HOUSE OF CROMWELL. A GEN. HIST. OF THE FAM. & DESC. OF THE PROTECTOR (INCL. AMER. DESC.), by J. Waylen; rev. by J.G. Cromwell. 1897.
Cloth, $58.00. Paper, $48.00. 298pp. .... Vendor G0259

961 HISTORY OF THE CRONE, PENCE, SWITZER, WEAVER, HEATWOLE, STOUT, STEEL & FISSELL FAMILIES, FROM WHICH ARE DESCENDED JOHN S. CRONE & ELLA WEAVER CRONE, by F.L. Crone. 1916.
Paper. $10.00. 50pp. .... Vendor G0259

962 A CROSBY FAM. JOSIAH CROSBY, SARAH FITCH, & THEIR DESC., by N. Crosby. 1877.
Cloth, $33.00. Paper, $23.00. 143pp. .... Vendor G0259

963 CROSBY ANC., ROBERT, JONAH & JOEL CROSBY OF MAINE, by M.A. Crosby. 1939.
Paper. $12.50. 70pp. .... Vendor G0259

964 SIMON CROSBY, THE EMIGRANT; HIS ENG. ANC. & SOME OF HIS AMER. DESC., by E.D. Crosby. 1914.
Cloth, $36.50. Paper, $26.50. 183pp. .... Vendor G0259

965 **FAMILY OF EDWARD & ANN SNEAD CROSLAND, 1740–1957,** by Lulu C. Ricaud. 1958.
Cloth, $93.00. Paper, $83.00. 546pp. .... Vendor G0259

966 **MY CHILDREN'S ANC.; DATA CONCERNING NEW ENG. ANC. OF ROSELLE THEODORE CROSS & HIS WIFE, EMMA ASENATH (BRIDGMAN) CROSS,** by R.T. Cross. 1913.
Cloth, $41.50. Paper, $31.50. 212pp. .... Vendor G0259

967 **OUR JAMES CROW,** by E. Joyce Christiansen. 1970s. Illus.
Descendants of Virginia Revolutionary War veteran.
Paper. $18.95. 180pp. .... Vendor G0122

968 **JOHN CROWE & HIS DESC.,** by L. Crowell. 1903.
Paper. $19.00. 109pp. .... Vendor G0259

969 **CRUMB GENEALOGY: DESC. OF DANIEL CRUMB OF WESTERLY, R.I.,** by C.C. Fisk. 1956.
Cloth, $57.00. Paper, $47.00. 310pp. .... Vendor G0259

970 **THE CRUME FAMILY: DANIEL CRUME AND ELIZABETH BROOK(S) OF VIRGINIA, AND THEIR DESCENDANTS 1724–1994,** by Rick Crume. 1994. Indexed.
Includes: **Birkhead, Burkhead, Klinglesmith, Marks.**
Paper. $16.00. 188pp. .... Vendor G0386

971 **THE DESCENDANTS OF THE REV. MOSES CRUME AND SARAH MARKS OF BUTLER COUNTY, OHIO, 1766–1994,** by Rick Crume. 1994. Indexed.
Includes: **Deem, Kerchival.**
Paper. $8.00. 67pp. .... Vendor G0386

972 **CRUMMER FAMILIES IN THE UNITED STATES AND CANADA WHO CAME FROM IRELAND,** by Larry D. Crummer. 1994. Indexed. Illus.
Male and female lines traced to present. Vital statistics plus additional documents (census records, obituaries, probates, etc.).
Cloth. $58.00. 603pp. .... Vendor G0192

973 **GEN. OF THE CULBERTSON–CULBERSON FAM. WHO CAME TO AMER. BEFORE THE YEAR 1800, & SEVERAL FAM. THAT HAVE COME SINCE THEN,** by L. Culbertson. Rev. ed. 1923.
Cloth, $84.50. Paper, $74.50. 477pp. .... Vendor G0259

974 **CUMMINGS MEMORIAL; A GEN. HIST. OF THE DESC. OF ISAAC CUMMINGS, AN EARLY SETTLER OF TOPSFIELD, MASS.,** by G. Mooar. 1903.
Cloth, $77.50. Paper, $67.50. 535pp. .... Vendor G0259

975 **ISAAC CUMMINGS OF TOPSFIELD, MASS. & SOME OF HIS DESC.,** by M. Clark and others. 1899.
Paper. $7.50. 39pp. .... Vendor G0259

976 **ISAAC CUMMINGS, 1601–1677, OF IPSWICH IN 1638, & SOME OF HIS DESC.,** by A.O. Cummins. 1904.
Cloth, $109.00. Paper, $99.00. 661pp. .... Vendor G0259

977 **GEN. MEM. OF THE CUNNABELL, CONABLE OR CONNABLE FAM.**
1650–1886, by Connable and Newcomb. 1886.
Cloth, $44.50. Paper, $34.50. 187pp. .... Vendor G0259

978 **PICTORIAL GENEALOGY OF THE CUNNABELL, CONNABLE,**
CONABLE FAMILY, 1886–1935 (VOL. II OF 1886 BOOK, ABOVE), by
Ralph Connable. 1935.
Cloth, $39.50. Paper, $29.50. 190pp. .... Vendor G0259

979 **GEN. OF RICHARD CURRIER OF SALISBURY & AMESBURY, MASS.,**
& MANY OF HIS DESC., by H.L. Currier. **GEN. OF EZRA CURRIER OF**
BATH, N.H., & HIS DESC., by J. McN. Currier. 1910.
Cloth, $51.00. Paper, $41.00. 271pp. .... Vendor G0259

980 **[Curtin]. MEMORIES OF AN ILLINOIS FARM BOY**, by Paul J. Curtin.
1989. Illus.
With subtle sophistication and deceptively simple language, Paul Curtin
launches his readers on a journey back in time to a 160-acre farm in central
Illinois to discover the life he and his family led in the 1930s and 1940s—a life
dominated by work, family group activity, and cooperation. Includes 116 photos, illustrations, and maps as well as **Curtin, Colbrook**, and **Schauer** family
records.
Paper. $13.00. 216pp. .... Vendor G0327

981 **WEST LIMERICK ROOTS—THE LAURENCE CURTIN FAMILY OF**
KNOCKBRACK, COUNTY LIMERICK, IRELAND, by Paul J. Curtin.
1995. Indexed. Illus.
As a researcher pursuing his own Irish lineage, Paul Curtin has assembled a
vast amount of accumulated data on the family of his great-grandfather, Laurence
Curtin, and four neighboring Curtin families of west Limerick. Also included
are five disarmingly poignant letters written 1868–1889 by Laurence Curtin to
his two emigrant sons in America.
This book contains genealogical listings and histories of over 800 descendants of Curtin families, a succinct history of Ireland, origin of the Curtin
surname and coat of arms, information on Curtins around the world, plus 98
photos, maps, and illustrations.
Cloth. $28.00. 440pp. .... Vendor G0327

982 **GEN. OF THE CURTISS FAM.; RECORD OF THE DESC. OF WIDOW**
ELIZABETH CURTISS, WHO SETTLED IN STRATFORD, CONN.,
1639–40, by F. Curtiss. 1903.
Cloth, $52.00. Paper, $42.00. 283pp. .... Vendor G0259

983 **A GEN. OF THE CURTISS–CURTIS FAM. OF STRATFORD, CONN.; A**
SUPPL. TO THE 1903 ED., compiled by H.D. Curtis. 1953.
Cloth, $97.00. Paper, $87.00. 585pp. .... Vendor G0259

984 **A HIST. OF THE ANCIENT HOUSE OF CURWEN, OF WORKINGTON**
IN CUMBERLAND & ITS VARIOUS BRANCHES, BEING A COLLEC-
TION OF EXTRACTS FROM [MANY] AVAILABLE SOURCES, by J.F.
Curwen. 1928.
Cloth, $67.50. Paper, $57.50. 363pp. .... Vendor G0259

985 **GEN. OF THE CUSHING FAM.**, by L. Cushing. 1877.
Cloth, $33.50. Paper, $23.50. 117pp. .... Vendor G0259

986   THE GEN. OF THE CUSHING FAM.; ANC. & DESC. OF MATTHEW
       CUSHING WHO CAME TO AMER. IN 1638, by J.S. Cushing. 1905.
       Cloth, $94.00. Paper, $84.00. 668pp. .... Vendor G0259

987   A HIST. & BIOGR. GEN.; THE DESC. OF ROBERT CUSHMAN, PURI-
       TAN, 1617–1855, by H.W. Cushman. 1855.
       Cloth, $94.00. Paper, $84.00. 666pp. .... Vendor G0259

988   CUSHMAN GENEALOGY & GENERAL HIST., INCL. THE DESC. OF
       THE FAYETTE CO., PA. & MONONGALIA CO., VA, FAMILIES, by
       A.W. Burt 1942.
       Cloth, $77.00. Paper, $67.00. 432pp. .... Vendor G0259

989   THE PROCEEDINGS AT THE CUSHMAN CELEBRATION AT PLY-
       MOUTH, MASS., 1855, WITH AN ACCT. OF THE SERVICES AT THE
       GRAVE OF ELDER THOMAS CUSHMAN, by N.B. Shurtleff and H.W.
       Cushman. 1855.
       Paper. $17.00. 84pp. .... Vendor G0259

990   THE BERRYMAN CUSTER FAMILY, by Patricia Turner Ritchie. 1992. In-
       dexed. Illus.
       Paper. $15.00. 124pp. .... Vendor G0365

991   THE CUSTIS CHRONICLES: THE YEARS OF MIGRATION, by James
       B. Lynch, Jr. 1993. Indexed. Illus. Book #1170.
       Cloth. $36.50. 288pp. .... Vendor G0082

992   THE CUTHBERTS, BARONS OF CASTLE HILL, & THEIR DESC. IN
       S.C. & GA., by J. Bulloch. 1908.
       Paper. $19.00. 100pp. .... Vendor G0259

993   CUTHBERTSON FAMILIES OF MECKLENBERG AND UNION COUN-
       TIES OF NORTH CAROLINA 1911–1992, edited by Frances C. Vick from
       research by L.F. Cuthbertson, Jr. (deceased). 1993. Indexed.
       Cloth. $38.00. 390pp. .... Vendor G0161

994   A GEN. RECORD OF SEVERAL FAM. BEARING THE NAME OF CUT-
       LER IN THE U.S., by A. Morse. 1867.
       Paper. $16.00. 80pp. .... Vendor G0259

995   CUTLER MEMORIAL & GEN. HIST., by N.S. Cutler. 1889.
       Cloth, $109.50. Paper, $99.50. 665pp. .... Vendor G0259

996   A HIST. OF THE CUTTER FAM. OF NEW ENGLAND, by B. and R.W.
       Cutter. 1923.
       Cloth, $64.00. Paper, $54.00. 432pp. .... Vendor G0259

997   GEN. OF THE CUTTS FAM. IN AMER., by C. Howard. 1892.
       Cloth, $108.00. Paper, $98.00. 658pp. .... Vendor G0259

998   DESCENDANTS OF CORNELIUS DABNEY OF VIRGINIA, by Carol A.
       Hauk. 1995. Indexed.
       Paper. $30.00. 173pp. .... Vendor G0340

999   THE HISTORY & GENEALOGY OF THE DAGUE FAMILY, by Carrie
       M. Dague. 1938.
       Cloth, $49.00. Paper, $39.00. 253pp. .... Vendor G0259

1000 **DAILEY FAM.; BIOGR. HIST. & GEN. OF DESC. OF EBENEZER DAILEY OF COLUMBIA CO., NY,** by E. Fox. 1939.
Cloth, $40.00. Paper, $30.00. 186pp. Vendor G0259

1001 **DESC. OF THOMAS DAKIN OF CONCORD, MASS.,** by A.H. Dakin. 1938.
Cloth, $109.00. Paper, $99.00. 716pp. . . . . Vendor G0259

1002 **HISTORY OF THE FAMILY OF DALLAS & THEIR CONNECTIONS & DESC. FROM THE 12TH CENT.,** by J. Dallas. 1921.
Cloth, $99.00. Paper, $89.00. 611pp. Vendor G0259

1003 **DESCENDANTS OF NICOLA DALL'AVA INCLUDING RELATED FAMILIES, VIALE AND ROSSI OF VICENZA, ITALY AND BERK-SHIRE COUNTY, MASSACHUSETTS,** by Phyllis Walker Johnson. 1977.
Paper. $5.00. 60pp. . . . . Vendor G0178

1004 **THE DALLENBACK FAMILY IN AMERICA, 1710–1935,** by A.L Dillenbeck and K.M. Dallenbach. 1935.
Also **Dallenbach.**
Cloth, $77.50. Paper, $67.50. 439pp. Vendor G0259

1005 **THE NAME OF DALRYMPLE, WITH GEN. OF ONE BRANCH IN THE U. S.,** by W.H. Dalrymple. 1878.
Paper. $14.00. 68pp. . . . . Vendor G0259

1006 **BRAD DAMON MEMORIAL MICROFILM: 16MM,** by D. Bradford Damon, Richard A. Damon, and Warren L. Forsythe. (1935–1992) reprint 1994. Indexed.
Indexes almost 100,000 descendants of 8,000 surnames, especially New England area. Includes **Damon, Dunbar, Gardner, Jenkins, Perry, Tower, Woodworth**, and more.
$20.00 includes tax (only edition is 16mm microfilm).
3,000pp. . . . . Vendor G0401

1007 **DAMON MEMORIAL,** by B.M. Damon. 1897.
Paper. $12.00. 60pp. . . . . Vendor G0259

1008 **MEMORANDA OF SOME OF THE DESC. OF RICHARD DANA OF CAMBRIDGE,** by J. Dana. 1865.
Paper. $12.50. 64pp. . . . . Vendor G0259

1009 **THE DANA FAM. IN AMER.,** by E.E. Dana. 1956.
Cloth, $109.00. Paper, $99.00. 685pp. . . . . Vendor G0259

1010 **THE DANA SAGA: THREE CENTURIES OF THE DANA FAMILY IN CAMBRIDGE,** by Henry W.L. Dana. 1941.
Paper. $12.00. 61pp. . . . . Vendor G0259

1011 **DANCE FAMILY IN VIRGINIA,** by Leslie Lyle Campbell. 1951.
Cloth, $32.50. Paper, $22.50. 134pp. Vendor G0259

1012 **DANFORTH GEN.; NICHOLAS DANFORTH OF FRAMINGHAM, ENG. & CAMBRIDGE, MA. (1589–1638), & WM. OF NEWBURY, MA. (1640–1771) & DESC.,** by J. May. 1902.
Cloth, $72.00. Paper, $62.00. 492pp. Vendor G0259

1013 **DANIEL FAM. OF VA. & N.C. (EXTR. FROM "VA. GEN.").**
Paper. $8.50. 42pp. .... Vendor G0259

1014 **THE DANIELS FAMILY: A GENEALOGICAL HISTORY OF THE DE-SCENDANTS OF WILLIAM DANIELS OF DORCHESTER & MILTON, MASS., 1630–1951,** by J.H. Daniels, Jr. Vol. I. 1952.
Cloth, $51.50. Paper, $41.50. 264pp. .... Vendor G0259

1015 **THE DANIELS FAMILY, VOL. II, 1630–1957.** 1957.
Cloth, $83.00. Paper, $73.00. 484pp. .... Vendor G0259

1016 **DARBY GEN.; GEORGE DARBY (1726–1788) OF MONTGOMERY CO., MD.,** by R.C. Darby.
Cloth, $39.00. Paper, $29.00. 172pp. .... Vendor G0259

1017 **DARE FAMILY HISTORY,** by W.H. and N.L. Montgomery. 1939.
Cloth, $64.00. Paper, $54.00. 340pp. .... Vendor G0259

1018 **THE DESCENDANTS OF CAPTAIN WILLIAM DARE (VOL. 1) WIL-LIAM, HANNAH AND ROBERT,** by Robert Dallas Dare. 1993. Indexed.
First of several planned volumes on the descendants of William **Dare,** who died in 1720.
Paper. $36.00. 381pp. .... Vendor G0069

1019 **THE DESCENDANTS OF CAPTAIN WILLIAM DARE (VOL. 2) THE CHILDREN OF BENONI AND HANNAH DARE,** by Robert Dallas Dare. 1994. Indexed.
Children of Benoni are Elizabeth, Reuben, Eleanor, Elkanah, John, William, and Rachel. Volume 3 underway.
Paper. $36.00. 490pp. .... Vendor G0069

1020 **GATHERING OF CLAN DARLINGTON, WITH DESC. OF ABRAHAM DARLINGTON, ET AL.** 1853.
Paper. $10.00. 52pp. .... Vendor G0259

1021 **GEN. OF THE DARLINGTON FAM.: REC. OF THE DESC. OF ABRAHAM DARLINGTON OF BIRMINGHAM, CHESTER CO. PA., & OTHER FAMS. OF THE NAME,** by G. Cope. 1900.
Cloth, $97.00. Paper, $87.00. 693pp. .... Vendor G0259

1022 **DARNALL–DARNELL FAM., INCL. DARNEAL, DARNIELLE, DARNOLD, DURNELL, ET AL, WITH ALLIED FAMS.,** by Dr. H.C. Smith.
Cloth, $76.00. Paper, $66.00. 421pp. .... Vendor G0259

1023 **JOHN M. DARNELL OF MONROE COUNTY AND HARDIN COUNTY, KENTUCKY,** by Betty Rolwing Darnell. 1994. Indexed. Illus.
Paper. $15.00. 70pp. .... Vendor G0261

1024 **GEN. OF THE DART FAM. IN AMER.,** by T.L. Bolton. 1927.
Cloth, $45.00. Paper, $35.00. 235pp. .... Vendor G0259

1025 **A HIST. & GEN. OF THE DAVENPORT FAM. IN ENG. & AMER., 1086–1850,** by A.B. Davenport. 1851.
Cloth, $71.00. Paper, $61.00. 398pp. .... Vendor G0259

1026 **SUPPL. TO THE 1851 DAVENPORT GEN., CONTINUED TO 1876**, by A.B. Davenport. 1876.
Cloth, $78.00. Paper, $68.00. 437pp. .... Vendor G0259

1027 **ANCESTORS OF CURTIS TURNER DAVIDSON 1864–1924—MY WORKING NOTEBOOK**, by William Sheperd West.
Davidson family members include: Samuel, 1817–1870; James, 1784–1854; James, 1751–1819; William, –1779; James, –1744. Related families include **Coffin, Joseph, Wood, Hardy, Simonton, Claypole, Claypoole** primarily in Sussex County, Delaware and in nearby counties on Maryland's Eastern Shore. Interesting charts, photographs, etc. planned. Your information welcome.
Cloth. $30.00. Approx. 200pp. .... Vendor G0308

1028 **A BRIEF GENEALOGICAL HISTORY OF THE DAVIS FAMILY & ALLIED LINES**, by T.C. and W.C. Davis. 1934.
Paper. $8.00. 40pp. .... Vendor G0259

1029 **DAVIS FAMILY HISTORY**, by J. Montgomery Seaver. Illus
Paper. $8.50. 81pp. .... Vendor G0011

1030 **DAVIS FAMILY: HISTORY OF THE DESCENDANTS OF WILLIAM DAVIS & HIS WIFE MARY MEANS**, by T.K. Davis. 1912.
Cloth, $49.00. Paper, $39.00. 248pp. .... Vendor G0259

1031 **DAVIS FAM. OF EARLY ROXBURY & BOSTON**, by S.F. Rockwell. 1932.
Cloth, $59.00. Paper, $49.00. 326pp. .... Vendor G0259

1032 **DAVIS FAM. OF HAVERHILL & DOVER, MASS. (EXTR. FROM "OLD FAM. OF SALISBURY, MA." PART NINE & TEN)**.
Paper. $8.00. 40pp. .... Vendor G0259

1033 **DAVIS RECORDS (DEATHS, MARR., BIBLE), WASHINGON CO., OH.— EARLY GATEWAY TO THE WEST**, by H.C. Biedel. 1952.
Paper. $8.50. 43pp. .... Vendor G0259

1034 **DAVIS–WOODRUFF FAMILIES OF WESTERN KENTUCKY**, by Virginia Couchot. 1992.
Paper. $15.00. 74pp. .... Vendor G0259

1035 **DAYS OF OUR DAVIS**, by Louise (Moore) Burt. 1994. Indexed. Illus.
Histories of John **Davis** (1781–1856) from Hardy County, Virginia, son of James **Davis** and Nancy **Norton**, including four generations of his descendants. Lived Knox and Allen counties Ohio. Children: James, Matilda **Bishop**, Mary **Severe**, Nancy **Coleman**, Rebecca **Carter**, Rhoda **Meek**, John, Patsy **Cummings**, Sarah **Meek**, Ephraim, Leah **Clark**, Peter, Charles.
Cloth. $45.00. 300pp. .... Vendor G0286

1036 **DESCENDANTS OF SAMUEL DAVIS, I, OF ISLE OF WIGHT COUNTY, VIRGINIA**, by Richard R. Dietz. 1994. Indexed.
Thirteen generations are represented, from 1635 to the present; residing in North Carolina, Georgia, Louisiana, Florida, Texas, and California.
Paper, loose-leaf with holes for mounting in 3-ring binder.
$29.95. 292pp. .... Vendor G0023

1037 **DOLOR DAVIS, A SKETCH OF HIS LIFE, WITH RECORD OF HIS EARLIER DESC.**, by H. Davis. 1881.
Paper. $9.50. 46pp. .... Vendor G0259

1038 **GENEALOGIES OF THE DAVIS & GOSS FAMILIES, IN TWO PARTS,**
by H.W. CLark. 1905.
Cloth, $69.50. Paper, $59.50. 122+141pp. .... Vendor G0259

1039 **GEN. OF THE DESC. OF COL. JOHN DAVIS OF OXFORD, CT., WITH
PARTIAL GEN. OF HIS ANC.,** by G.T. Davis. 1910.
Cloth, $63.50. Paper, $53.50. 338pp. .... Vendor G0259

1040 **GENEALOGY OF THE CLINTON H. DAVIS FAMILY; SHORT SKETCH
OF THE LOST CREEK 7TH DAY BAPTIST CHURCH,** by W.M. Davis.
1935.
Paper. $19.00. 100pp. .... Vendor G0259

1041 **HIST. OF THE DESC. OF JOHN DAVIS, A NATIVE OF ENG., WHO
DIED IN E. HAMPTON, L.I., IN 1705. BROUGHT DOWN TO 1886–87,**
by A. Davis. 1888.
Cloth, $40.00. Paper, $30.00. 199pp. .... Vendor G0259

1042 **ONE LINE OF DESC. FROM DOLOR DAVIS & RICHARD EVERETT,**
by W.S. Crosby. 1911.
Paper. $12.50. 59pp. .... Vendor G0259

1043 **SAM'L DAVIS OF OXFORD, MA. & JOS. DAVIS OF DUDLEY, MASS.,
& THEIR DESC.,** by G. Davis. 1884.
Cloth, $87.00. Paper, $77.00. 618pp. .... Vendor G0259

1044 **THE DAVISES OF CARTERET COUNTY, NORTH CAROLINA,** by
Richard R. Dietz. 1995. Indexed.
From 1700 to 1920; 1,959 descendants and their spouses, of William Davis
of Pasquotank Co., NC, who resided in Carteret Co., NC.
Paper, loose-leaf with holes for mounting in 3-ring binder.
$24.95. 200pp. .... Vendor G0023

1045 **WALTER GOODWIN DAVIS,** by Danny D. Smith. 1985. Indexed. Illus. Book
#1114.
Paper. $14.00. 106pp. .... Vendor G0082

1046 **DAVISON FAM.,** by A.A. Davison. 1905.
Paper. $16.00. 78pp. .... Vendor G0259

1047 **GEN. RECORD OF THE DAVISON, DAVIDSON, DAVISSON FAM. OF
NEW. ENG.,** by H.R. Coles. 1899.
Cloth, $34.00. Paper, $24.00. 143pp. .... Vendor G0259

1048 **DAWES–GATES ANCESTRAL LINES: A MEM'L VOL. CONTAINING
THE AMER. ANCESTRY OF RUFUS R. DAWES. VOL. I: DAWES &
ALLIED FAMILIES,** by M.W. Ferris. 1943.
Cloth, $115.00. Paper, $105.00. 758pp. .... Vendor G0259

1049 **SOME DESCENDANTS OF FRANK DAWS OF CO. SUSSEX, EN-
GLAND, WITH INFORMATION ON ASSOC. KIPLINGER FAMILY,** by
Steve Roth. 1992.
Paper. $17.50. 89pp. .... Vendor G0259

1050 **A COLL. OF FAM. RECORDS WITH BIOGR. SKETCHES & OTHER**

MEM. OF THOSE BEARING THE NAME DAWSON, by C.C. Dawson. 1874.
Cloth, $97.00. Paper, $87.00. 572pp. .... Vendor G0259

1051 A RECORD OF THE DESC. OF ROBERT DAWSON, OF EAST HAVEN, CONN., INCL. BARNES, BATES & 31 OTHER FAM., by C.C. Davidson. 1874.
Cloth, $31.00. Paper, $21.00. 119pp. .... Vendor G0259

1052 A GEN. REG. OF THE DESC. IN MALE LINE OF ROBT. DAY OF HARTFORD, CT., WHO DIED IN 1648. 2nd ed. 1848.
Cloth, $32.00. Paper, $22.00. 129pp. .... Vendor G0259

1053 DAY GEN. A RECORD OF THE DESC. OF JACOB DAY & AN INCOMPLETE RECORD OF ANTHONY DAY, by the Gen. Comm. of the Day Assoc. 1916.
Cloth, $45.50. Paper, $35.50. 210pp. .... Vendor G0259

1054 SOME CHRONICLES OF THE DAY FAM., by E. Putnam. 1893.
Cloth, $35.50. Paper, $25.50. 159pp. .... Vendor G0259

1055 DAYTON GENEALOGY. STORY, DAYTON & TOMLINSON FAMILY, by L.D. Fessenden. 1902.
Cloth, $44.50. Paper, $34.50. 230pp. .... Vendor G0259

1056 DESC. OF THE DEACON FAM. OF ELSTOWE & LONDON, & SKETCHES OF ALLIED FAM., by E. Deacon. 1898.
Cloth, $76.00. Paper, $66.00. 420pp. .... Vendor G0259

1057 GEN. OF ISAAC DEAN OF GRAFTON, N.H., 4TH IN DESC. FROM JOHN OF TAUNTON, edited by J. Drummond. 1902.
Paper. $7.00. 35pp. .... Vendor G0259

1058 DESC. OF JOHN DEAN (1650–1727) OF DEDHAM, MASS., by M.D. Cooper. 1957.
Cloth, $43.00. Paper, $33.00. 217pp. .... Vendor G0259

1059 GEN. OF DEAN FAM., DESC. OF EZRA DEAN OF PLAINFIELD, CONN. & CRANSTON, RI, by A. Dean. 1903.
Cloth, $38.00. Paper, $28.00. 158pp. .... Vendor G0259

1060 HIST. OF WILLIAM DEAN FAM. OF CORNWALL, CONN., & CANFIELD, OHIO, by B.S. and J.E. Dean. 1903.
Paper. $14.00. 69pp. .... Vendor G0259

1061 WHERE WE CAME FROM, THE WILLIAM DEAN FAMILY AND THEIR ENVIRONS, by Howard J. Dean. 1993. Indexed. Illus.
Contains a history of Cahoonzie, N.Y. Contains data on the following surnames: **Birdsall, Bradford, Charney-Urso, Gimbel, Hardiman, Haviland, Higby, Hoffman, Lord, May, Niles, Schouppe, Steward, Terry, Thompson, Veitenheimer, Webster, Widmer,** and **Wood** families.
Cloth. $50.00. 704pp. .... Vendor G0267

1062 DEARING TRACKS THROUGHOUT AMERICA, by Betty V. Dearing. 1994. Indexed. Illus., over 100 pictures.
Descendants of Capt. John **Dearing,** born 1745 Virginia, through Tennessee,

Missouri, Texas. Some allied names: **Allen, Campster, Frazier, Hightower, Jett, Lankford, Lawrence, Livengood, Mooneyhan, Sinks, Trickey, Trolinder**. Plastic cover. $53.00. 430pp, including 39pp of index ...... Vendor G0266

1063 **DeARMOND FAMILIES OF AMERICA AND RELATED FAMILIES,** by Roscoe Carlise d'Armand. (1954) reprint 1986. A supplement and both indexes by Virginia Carlisle d'Armand.
Cloth. $59.00. 732pp. .... Vendor G0009

1064 **DeCAMP GEN., LAURENT DeCAMP OF NEW UTRECHT, N. Y., 1664 & HIS DESC.,** by G.A. Morrison. 1900.
Paper. $16.00. 77pp. .... Vendor G0259

1065 **RECORD OF THE DESC. OF EZEKIAL & MARY BAKER DeCAMP OF BUTLER CO., OHIO,** by J.M. DeCamp. 1896.
Cloth, $34.00. Paper, $24.00. 177pp. .... Vendor G0259

1066 **ALLIED ANCESTRY OF MARIA de CARPENTIER, WIFE OF JEAN PAUL JAQUET OF NEW NETHERLAND,** by E.J. Sellers. 1928.
Cloth, $47.50. Paper, $37.50. 236pp. .... Vendor G0259

1067 **GEN. OF THE DeCARPENTIER FAM. OF HOLLAND,** by E.J. Sellers. 1909.
Paper. $12.00. 59pp. .... Vendor G0259

1068 **GEN. OF THE DECKARD FAM. SHOWING ALSO THOSE DESC. FROM DECKER, DECKERT, DECHER, DECHERT, DECHERD, ETC.,** by P.E. Deckard. 1932.
Cloth, $143.00. Paper, $133.00. 893pp. .... Vendor G0259

1069 **GEN. OF THE de COU FAM., SHOWING THE DESC. FROM LEOREN des COU,** by S.E. and J.A. de Cou. 1910.
Cloth, $47.00. Paper, $37.00. 219pp. .... Vendor G0259

1070 **THE DEDMAN GENEALOGY WITH ALLIED FAMILIES ANTHONY, MASON, STEELMAN, WILLIAMS,** by Wanda Williams Colvin. 1983. Indexed. Illus.
Paper. $37.50. 303pp. .... Vendor G0432

1071 **[Deering–Dearing]. ABSTR. OF ENGLISH RECORDS, GATHERED PRINCIPALLY IN DEVONSHIRE & ESSEX IN A SEARCH FOR THE ANC. OF ROGER DEARING, 1624–76, & MATTHEW WHIPPLE, 1560– 1618,** edited by M.L. Holman and G.R. Marvin. 1929.
Cloth, $106.50. Paper, $96.50. 647pp. .... Vendor G0259

1072 **THE de FORESTS OF AVESNES (& OF NEW NETHERLAND). A HU-**

GUENOT THREAD IN AMER. COLONIAL HIST., 1494 TO 1900, by J.W. De Forest. 1900.
Cloth, $59.00. Paper, $49.00. 307pp. .... Vendor G0259

1073 **HISTORY OF THE DeGRAFFENRIED FAMILY, FROM 1191 TO 1925**, by T.P. DeGraffenried. 1925.
Cloth, $54.50. Paper, $44.50. 282pp. .... Vendor G0259

1074 **DeHAVEN NATIONAL FAMILY REGISTRY—NEWSLETTER**, by Dorothy W. Bertine and DeHaven Club. 1990/printed quarterly. Illus.
National DeHaven Family Registry—Descendants and allied families: **Levering, Op den Graeff, Pawling, Mybird, Rambo, Supplee, Wentz.** Club membership, newsletters, family histories, directory, reunions, etc.
Subscription. $10.00. av. 6 pp. .... Vendor G0407

1075 **HIST. OF THE DeHAVEN FAM.**, by H.D. Ross. 4th ed. 1929.
Paper. $9.50. 43pp. .... Vendor G0259

1076 **[De La Mater]. DESC. OF CLAUDE LE MAITRE WHO CAME FROM FRANCE & SETTLED AT NEW NETHERLANDS, NOW NY, IN 1652**, by L. De La Mater. 1882.
Cloth, $44.00. Paper, $34.00. 229pp. .... Vendor G0259

1077 **DELAND FAM. IN AMER.; A BIOGR. GEN.**, by F. Leete. 1943.
Cloth, $76.00. Paper, $66.00. 414pp. .... Vendor G0259

1078 **GEN., HIST. & ALLIANCES OF THE AMER. HOUSE OF DELANO, 1621–1899, WITH HIST. & HERALDRY OF MAISON DE FRANCHIMONT & DE LANNOY TO DELANO, 1096–1621**, by J.A. Deland and M.D. de Lannoy. 1899.
Cloth, $81.00. Paper, $71.00. 561pp. .... Vendor G0259

1079 **DeMARANVILLE GEN., DESC. OF LOUIS DeMARANVILLE**, by G.L. Randall. 1921.
Cloth, $38.00. Paper, $28.00. 152pp. .... Vendor G0259

1080 **[Demarest]. DAVID des MAREST OF THE FRENCH PATENT ON THE HACKENSACK & HIS DESC.**, by W. and M. Demarest. 1938.
Paper. $89.00. 576pp. .... Vendor G0259

1081 **GEN. OF DESC. OF JOHN DEMING OF WETHERSFIELD, CT. WITH HIST. NOTES**, by J. Deming. 1904.
Cloth, $97.00. Paper, $87.00. 702pp. .... Vendor G0259

1082 **GENEALOGY OF AARON DENIO OF DEERFIELD, MA., 1704–1925**, by F.B. and H.W. Denio. 1926.
Cloth, $63.00. Paper, $53.00. 345pp. .... Vendor G0259

DeHAVEN CLUB
National Family Registry
P.O. Box 2965
Denton, TX 76202

1083 **DENISON MEM., IPSWICH, MA., 1882. 200TH ANNIV. OF THE DEATH OF MAJ.-GEN. DANIEL DENISON. BIOGR. SKETCH OF D.D. SLADE; HIST. SKETCH, by** A. Caldwell. 1871.
Paper. $10.00. 52pp. .... Vendor G0259

1084 **A REC. OF THE DESC. OF CAPT. GEO. DENISON, OF STONINGTON, CT., by** Baldwin and Clift. 1881.
Cloth, $64.50. Paper, $54.50. 424pp. .... Vendor G0259

1085 **DENMAN FAM. HIST. FROM EARLIEST RECORDS TO THE PRESENT TIME, by** H.N. Harris. 1913.
Paper. $18.00. 88pp. .... Vendor G0259

1086 **[Denney]. DESCENDENTS OF ALLISON JAMES AND EMMA FROST DENNEY, by** Robert E. Pitts, et al. 1995. Illus.
Paper. Free. 36pp. .... Vendor G0383

1087 **DENNISON FAMILY OF N. YARMOUTH & FREEPORT, ME. ABNER DENNISON & DESC., by** G.M. Rogers; **DAVID DENNISON & DESC., by** A.L. Dennison. 1906.
Cloth, $34.00. Paper, $24.00. 148pp. .... Vendor G0259

1088 **DENNY FAM. IN ENG. & AMER. DESC. OF JOHN DENNY OF COMBS, SUFFOLK, ENG., 1439, by** C.C. Denny. 1886.
Cloth, $50.00. Paper, $40.00. 267pp. .... Vendor G0259

1089 **DERBY GEN., BEING A RECORD OF THE DESC. OF THOMAS DERBY OF STOW, MASS., by** V.A. Derby Bromley. 1905.
Cloth, $33.00. Paper, $23.00. 141pp. .... Vendor G0259

1090 **[De Rham]. "SMALLER NEW YORK" AND FAM. REMINISCENCES: De RHAM, SCHMIDT, BACHE, BARCLAY, PAUL RICHARD, by** "O.E.S." 1899.
Cloth, $26.00. Paper, $16.00. 78pp. .... Vendor G0259

1091 **GENEALOGY AND HISTORY OF THE DERTHICKS AND RELATED DERRICKS, by** Jack Taif Spencer and Robert Abraham Goodpasture. (1986) reprint 1995. Indexed. Illus.
Cloth, $89.50. Paper, $79.50. 585pp. .... Vendor G0259

1092 **GEN. OF THE DeVEAUX FAM., by** T.F. Devoe. 1885.
Cloth, $58.00. Paper, $48.00. 302pp. .... Vendor G0259

1093 **DEVENDORF FAMILY, by** O.W. Bell. 1932.
Paper. $19.50. 111pp. .... Vendor G0259

1094 **HISTORICAL & GENEALOGICAL RECORDS OF THE DEVENISH FAMILIES OF ENGLAND & IRELAND, by** R.J. Devenish and C.H. McLaughlin. 1948.
Cloth, $72.50. Paper, $62.50. 409pp. .... Vendor G0259

1095 **LIFE OF ADM. GEO. DEWEY, by** A.M. Dewey. **DEWEY FAM. HIST., by** L.M. Dewey, et al. 1898.
Cloth, $149.00. Paper, $139.00. 1,120pp. .... Vendor G0259

1096 **DESC. OF ANDREW DEWING OF DEDHAM, MA., WITH NOTES ON SOME ENG. FAM. OF THE NAME, by** B. Dewing. 1904.
Cloth, $35.00. Paper, $25.00. 173pp. .... Vendor G0259

1097 [DeWolf]. CHARLES D'WOLF OF GUADALUPE, HIS ANC. & DESC.; A COMPLETE GEN. OF THE "R.I. D'WOLF'S", THE DESC. OF SIMON, WITH THEIR COMMON DESC. FROM BALTHASAR OF LYME, CONN., **1668**, by C.B. Perry. 1902.
Cloth, $59.00. Paper, $49.00. 325pp. .... Vendor G0259

1098 DEXTER GEN.; BEING A RECORD OF THE FAM. DESC. FROM REV. GREGORY DEXTER, WITH NOTES & BIOGR. SKETCHES, by S.C. Newman. 1859.
Paper. $19.50. 108pp. .... Vendor G0259

1099 DEXTER GEN., 1642–1904, HIST. OF THE DESC. OF RICHARD DEXTER OF MALDEN, MA., by O.P. Dexter. 1904.
Cloth, $51.50. Paper, $41.50. 279pp. .... Vendor G0259

1100 GEN. OF THE DEXTER FAM. IN AMER., DESC. OF THOMAS DEXTER, TOGETHER WITH THE RECORD OF OTHER ALLIED FAM., by W.A. Warden and R.L. Dexter. 1905.
Cloth, $66.00. Paper. $56.00. 353pp. .... Vendor G0259

1101 DIBBLE FAM. OF CONN., by V. Lamb. 1949.
Cloth, $35.00. Paper, $25.00. 124pp. .... Vendor G0259

1102 DICKERMAN GEN.; DESC. OF THOMAS DICKERMAN, AN EARLY SETTLER OF DORCHESTER, MASS., with suppl. by E.D. and G.S. Dickerman. 1897 and 1922.
Cloth, $108.00. Paper, $98.00. 705pp. .... Vendor G0259

1103 GEN. HIST. OF THE DICKEY FAM., by R.S. Currier. 1935.
Cloth, $64.00. Paper, $54.00. 340pp. .... Vendor G0259

1104 GEN. OF THE DICKEY FAM., by J. Dickey. 1898.
Cloth, $59.50. Paper, $49.50. 322pp. .... Vendor G0259

1105 TO THE DESCENDANTS OF THOMAS DICKINSON, SON OF NATHANIEL & ANNA GULL DICKINSON, WETHERSFIELD, CT. & HADLEY, MA., by F. Dickinson. 1897.
Cloth, $32.00. Paper, $22.00. 144pp. .... Vendor G0259

1106 ANCESTORS AND DESCENDANTS OF JOHAN ADAM DIEHM THE IMMIGRANT OF 1754 AND EARLY SETTLER OF MONTGOMERY AND CHESTER COUNTIES, PENNSYLVANIA, by Patricia Shaffer Frappier. 1995. Indexed. Illus.
Cloth. $30.00. 419pp. .... Vendor G0389

1107 DILLE FAMILY. THREE HUNDRED YEARS IN AMER., by G.E., J.K. and E.K. Dille. 1965.
Cloth, $31.00. Paper, $21.00. 138pp. .... Vendor G0259

1108 GEN. OF THE DIMOND–DIMON FAM. OF FAIRFIELD, CT., WITH RECORDS OF THE DIMON–DYMONT FAM. OF E. HAMPTON, L.I. & NH, by E. Dimond. 1891.
Cloth, $38.50. Paper, $28.50. 179pp. .... Vendor G0259

1109 DINGS FAM. IN AMER. GEN., MEM. & COMMENTS, by M. Dings. 1927.
Cloth, $35.00. Paper, $25.00. 182pp. .... Vendor G0259

1110 **DINSMORE GEN. FROM 1620 TO 1925**, by M.H. Savage. 1927.
Cloth, $34.00. Paper, $24.00. 141pp. Vendor G0259

1111 **HIST. & GEN. OF THE DINSMOOR–DINSMORE FAM. OF SCOTLAND, IRELAND & AMER., 1600–1891, & FACTS RELATING TO THE FIRST SETTLERS OF LONDONDERRY, N.H.**, by L.M. Morrison. 1891.
Paper. $9.50. 48pp. . . . . Vendor G0259

1112 **DINWIDDIE FAMILY RECORDS, WITH ESPECIAL ATTENTION TO THE LINE OF WILLIAM WALTHALL DINWIDDIE, 1804–1882**, by E.D. Holladay. 1957.
Cloth, $39.50. Paper, $29.50. 191pp. Vendor G0259

1113 **KITH & KIN, GEN. DATA OF DIXON & COLLATERAL LINES**, by W. M. Dixon. 1922.
Cloth, $26.50. Paper, $16.50. 83pp. . . . . Vendor G0259

1114 **HIST. OF CHARLES DIXON, ONE OF THE EARLY ENG. SETTLERS OF SACKVILLE, N.B.**, by J.D. Dixon. 1891.
Cloth, $40.50. Paper, $30.50. 204pp. Vendor G0259

1115 **[Dixson]. THE BORDER OR RIDING CLANS FOLLOWED BY A HIST. OF THE CLAN DICKSON & A BRIEF ACCT. OF THE FAM. OF THE AUTHOR**, by B.H. Dixon. 1889.
Cloth, $39.50. Paper, $29.50. 223pp. Vendor G0259

1116 **DOAK FAM.**, by B.E. Hanes. 1931.
Paper. $19.50. 100pp. . . . . Vendor G0259

1117 **NOTABLE SOUTHERN FAMILIES, Volume VI**, by Zella Armstrong and Janie Preston Collup French. (1933) reprint 1993. Indexed.
The **Doak** family.
Paper. $12.50. 98pp. . . . . Vendor G0011

1118 **DOANE FAM.: I. DEACON JOHN DOANE, OF PLYMOUTH; II. DR. JOHN DONE, OF MD., & THEIR DESC., WITH NOTES ON ENG. FAM. OF THE NAME**, by A. Doane. 1902.
Cloth, $80.00. Paper, $70.00. 554pp. Vendor G0259

1119 **[Dodd]. GEN. & HIST. OF THE DANIEL DOD FAM. IN AMER., 1646–1940**, by A. Dodd and J.F. Folsom. 1940.
Cloth, $78.50. Paper, $68.50. 442pp. Vendor G0259

1120 **GEN. OF THE MALE DESC. OF DANIEL DODD, OF BRANFORD, CONN. & NATIVE OF ENG., 1646–1863**, by B. Dodd and J. Burnet. 1864.
Cloth, $43.00. Paper, $33.00. 221pp. Vendor G0259

1121 **GEN. & HIST. OF FAMS. OF FRANCIS DODDS & MARGARET CRAIG DODDS OF SPARTANBURG, S.C. & OF THE DODDS FAMS. OF BALTIMORE, INDIANA & ILLINOIS**, by L. Colby. 1929.
Cloth, $39.50. Paper, $29.50. 177pp. Vendor G0259

1122 **ANC. OF NATHAN DANE DODGE & HIS WIFE, SARAH SHEPARD DODGE, WITH NOTES**, by M. Parson. 1896.
Paper. $15.00. 76pp. . . . . Vendor G0259

1123 **DESC. OF TRISTRAM DODGE**, by T.R. Woodward. 1904.
Cloth, $42.00. Paper, $32.00. 241pp. .... Vendor G0259

1124 **GEN. OF THE DODGE FAM. OF ESSEX CO., MASS., 1629–1894**, by J.T. Dodge. 1894.
Cloth, $75.00. Paper, $65.00. 456pp. .... Vendor G0259

1125 **GEN. OF THE DODGE FAM. OF ESSEX CO., MASS., SECOND PART, 1629–1898**, by J.T. Dodge. 1898.
Cloth, $40.00. Paper, $30.00. 218pp. .... Vendor G0259

1126 **REPORT, FULL, AUTHENTIC, & COMPLETE, OF ALL THE ADDRESSES & PROCEEDINGS OF THE MEMORABLE FIRST REUNION OF THE DODGE FAM. IN AMER., AT SALEM, MASS., 1879**, by R. Dodge. 1879.
Paper. $10.00. 53pp. .... Vendor G0259

1127 **TRISTRAM DODGE & HIS DESC. IN AMER., WITH HIST. & ACCTS. OF BLOCK IS. & COW NECK, L.I., THEIR ORIG. SETTLEMENTS**, by R. Dodge. 1886.
Cloth, $47.00. Paper, $37.00. 248pp. .... Vendor G0259

1128 **DODSON–DOTSON, LUCAS, PYLES, ROCHESTER & ALLIED FAMILIES**, by S.E. Lucas, Jr. 1959.
Cloth, $47.50. Paper, $37.50. 239pp. .... Vendor G0259

1129 **THE DESC. OF NICHOLAS DOE**, by E. Doe. 1918.
Cloth, $59.00. Paper, $49.00. 375pp. .... Vendor G0259

1130 **A HIST. OF THE DOGGETT–DAGGETT FAM.**, by S.B. Doggett. 1894.
Cloth, $96.50. Paper, $86.50. 696pp. .... Vendor G0259

1131 **OUR COL. & CONTINENTAL ANC. ANC. OF MR. & MRS. LOUIS WM. DOMMERICH**, by I. de Forest. 1930.
Cloth, $59.25. Paper, $49.25. 328pp. .... Vendor G0259

1132 **DONALD FAM. WITH NOTES ON REL. FAM.**, by D. Gordon. 1906.
Paper. $16.00. 79pp. .... Vendor G0259

1133 **THE JOHNSTON & BACON SCOTTISH CLAN HISTORIES: The Clan Donald [Macdonalds, etc.]**, by I.F. Grant. (1952) reprint 1993. Illus.
Paper. $8.95. 32pp. .... Vendor G0011

1134 **GEN. REC. OF ONE BRANCH OF THE DONALDSON FAM. IN AMER.; DESC. OF MOSES DONALDSON, HUNTINGDON CO., PA., 1770**, by M. McKitrick. 1916.
Cloth, $64.00. Paper, $54.00. 332pp. .... Vendor G0259

1135 **THE DONNELLS & THEIR MACDONALD ANCESTORS: HISTORY & GEN., 157–1927, A.D.**, by E. and J. Donnell.
Cloth, $51.00. Paper, $41.00. 923pp. .... Vendor G0259

1136 **"TO AMERICA": THE STORY OF ALBERT AND HENRIETTA DONNER**, by Raymond K. Donner. 1994. Indexed. Illus.
Other surnames referenced are **Oehler, Ruehling, Kurz**, and **Wagenbreth**.
Paper. $10.00. 57pp. .... Vendor G0355

1137 **ABRAHAM DOOLITTLE & SOME OF HIS DESC.**, by O.P. Allen. 1893. Paper. $7.50. 38pp. .... Vendor G0259

1138 **THE DOOLITTLE FAM. IN AMERICA, PART VII, 1901–1908**, by W.F. Doolittle. 1908.
Cloth, $102.00. Paper, $92.00. 730pp. .... Vendor G0259

1139 **THE DOOLITTLE FAMILY IN AMERICA, PART VIII**, by L.S. Brown and M.R. Doolittle. 1967.
Cloth, $97.50. Paper, $87.50. 619pp. .... Vendor G0259

1140 **INDEX TO "THE DOOLITTLE FAMILY IN AMERICA,"** compiled by Victoria Reed. 1988.
Cloth, $40.00. Paper, $30.00. 247pp. .... Vendor G0259

1141 **RECORDS OF THE DORLAND FAM. IN AMER., INCL. PRINCIPAL BRANCHES DORLAND, DORLON-AN, DURLAND, DARLING IN THE US & CANADA**, by J. Cremer. 1898.
Cloth, $59.50. Paper, $49.50. 320pp. .... Vendor G0259

1142 **SOME DESCENDANTS OF JABEZ DORMAN OF ARUNDEL (1678–1765): TEN GENERATIONS OF DORMANS IN MAINE**, by Franklin A. Dorman. 1992.
Paper. $16.50. 112pp. .... Vendor G0259

1143 **DORSETTS IN AMERICA**, by Gwen Campbell. 1994. Indexed.
Listed alphabetically by first name and birthdate. Query with SASE.
Paper. $30.00. 315pp. .... Vendor G0303

1144 **DORSEY FAMILY. DESC. OF EDWARD DARCY–DORSEY OF VA. & MD. FOR FIVE GENERATIONS**, by Dorsey and Nimmo. 1947.
Cloth, $53.00. Paper, $43.00. 270pp. .... Vendor G0259

1145 **DOTY–DOTEN FAM. IN AMER. DESC. OF EDW. DOTY, AN EMIGRANT BY THE MAYFLOWER, 1620**, by E.A. Doty. 2 vols. 1897.
Cloth, $155.00. Paper, $145.00. 1,035pp. .... Vendor G0259

1146 **DOTY FAMILY HIST. & GEN.**, by E.E. VanSant. 1935.
Cloth, $30.00. Paper, $20.00. 104pp. .... Vendor G0259

1147 **[Doude–Dowd]. THE DESC. OF HENRY DOUDE WHO CAME FROM ENG. IN 1639**, by W.W. Dowd. 1885.
Cloth, $54.00. Paper, $44.00. 342pp. .... Vendor G0259

1148 **COLL. OF FAM. RECORDS, WITH BIOGR. SKETCHES & OTHER MEM. OF VARIOUS FAMS. & INDIVIDUALS OF THE NAME DOUGLAS**, by C. Douglas. 1879.
Cloth, $84.00. Paper, $74.00. 563pp. .... Vendor G0259

1149 **HISTORY OF THE HOUSE OF DOUGLAS, FROM THE EARLIEST TIMES TO THE LEGISLATIVE UNION OF ENGLAND & SCOTLAND**, by Sir H. Maxwell. 2 vols. in 1. 1902 (England).
Cloth, $109.50. Paper, $99.50. 324+318pp. .... Vendor G0259

1150 **LIFE & ANCESTRY OF FRANCIS DOUGLAS OF ABERDEEN & PAISLEY, SCOTLAND (WITH THE HISTORY OF THE HOUSE OF DOUGLAS)**, by W.K. Watkins. 1903.
Paper. $8.00. 37pp. .... Vendor G0259

1151 **THE DOVE FAMILY OF ROCKINGHAM COUNTY, VA**, by Lewis H. Yankey. 1991. Indexed.
Paper. $22.00. 146pp. .... Vendor G0365

1152 **JAMES DOWNEN OF CAMPBELL HILL, ILLINOIS**, by Robert L. Downen. 1992. Indexed.
Related lines: **Cully, Crocker, Twiss, Clope.**
Paper. $25.00. 90pp. .... Vendor G0408

1153 **THE DOWNERS OF AMERICA**, by D.R. Downer. 1900.
Cloth, $46.50. Paper, $36.50. 244pp. .... Vendor G0259

1154 **HISTORY OF THE PROTESTANT DOWNEYS OF THE COS. OF SLIGO, LEITRIM, FERMANAGH & DONEGAL & THEIR DESC.; ALSO THE HAWKSBY FAMILY OF COS. LEITRIM & SLIGO**, by C.C. Downey. 1931.
Cloth, $37.00. Paper, $27.00. 173pp. .... Vendor G0259

1155 **LAWRENCE DOWSE OF LEGBOURNE, ENG.; HIS ANC., DESC., & CONNECTIONS IN ENG., MASS. & IRELAND**, by W.B.H. Dowse. 1926.
Cloth, $66.50. Paper, $56.50. 359pp. .... Vendor G0259

1156 **DESC. OF JOHN DRAKE OF WINDSOR, CT.**, by F.B. Gay. 1933.
Cloth, $69.00. Paper, $59.00. 380pp. .... Vendor G0259

1157 **GEN. & BIOGR. ACCT. OF THE FAM. OF DRAKE IN AMERICA**, by S.G. Drake. 1845.
Paper. $10.00. 51pp. .... Vendor G0259

1158 **THE DRAKE FAM. IN ENG. & AMER. 1360–1895, & THE DESC. OF THOMAS DRAKE OF WEYMOUTH, MA., 1635–1691**, by L.S. Drake. 1896.
Cloth, $52.00. Paper, $42.00. 347pp. .... Vendor G0259

1159 **THE FAMILY OF NELSON DRAKE BACK TO 1630: N.Y. & MICHIGAN PIONEERS, WITH GENEALOGY SUPPLEMENT**, by F.N. Drake. 1963.
Cloth, $32.50. Paper, $22.50. 146pp. .... Vendor G0259

1160 **DRAPERS IN AMER., BEING A HIST. & GEN. OF THOSE OF THAT NAME & CONNECTION**, by T. Draper. 1892.
Cloth, $55.00. Paper, $45.00. 324pp. .... Vendor G0259

1161 **FAM. OF DRINKWATER OF CHESHIRE, LANCASHIRE, ETC. IN ENG.**, by Drinkwater and Fletcher. 1920.
Paper. $19.50. 112pp. .... Vendor G0259

1162 **DRIVER FAM.; A GEN. MEMOIR OF THE DESC. OF ROBERT AND PHEBE DRIVER OF LYNN, MASS.; WITH APPENDIX CONTAINING 23 ALLIED FAM.**, by H.R. Cooke. 1889.
Cloth, $95.00. Paper, $85.00. 556pp. .... Vendor G0259

1163 **DESCENDANTS OF SAMUEL AND HANNAH DRURY OF VERMONT, NEW YORK, AND KENTUCKY 1770 TO THE PRESENT**, by Linda Lightholder Kmiecik. 1991. Indexed. Illus.
Cloth. $43.00. 439pp. .... Vendor G0367

1164 **THE EARLY DRURY LINE OF NEW ENGLAND—SOME DESCEN-
DANTS TO 1850 OF HUGH[1] DRURY (c. 1617–1689)**, by Linda Lightholder
Kmiecik. 1990. Indexed.
Cloth. $32.00. 224pp. .... Vendor G0367

1165 **ANCESTRY OF RUFUS K. DRYER, WITH NOTES ON WILLIAM
DRYER OF REHOBETH & SOME OF HIS DESC.**, by J.F. Dryer. 1942.
Cloth, $53.50. Paper, $43.50. 280pp. .... Vendor G0259

1166 **DUDLEY. GEN. & FAM. RECORDS**, by D. Dudley. 1848.
Cloth, $34.50. Paper, $24.50. 150pp. .... Vendor G0259

1167 **HISTORY OF THE DUDLEY FAM., WITH GEN. TABLES, PEDIGREES,
ETC., NUMBER V**, by D. Dudley. 1891.
Paper. $18.50. 100pp. .... Vendor G0259

1168 **DUDLEY. NUMBER VII.** 1891.
Paper. $18.00. 100pp. .... Vendor G0259

1169 **HIST. OF THE DUDLEY FAM.**, by D. Dudley. 2 vols. 1894.
Cloth, $168.00. Paper, $158.00. 1,253pp. .... Vendor G0259

1170 **SUPPLEMENT TO 1894 "HIST. OF DUDLEY FAM."** 1898.
Paper. $18.00. 96pp. .... Vendor G0259

1171 **THE SUTTON–DUDLEYS OF ENG. & THE DUDLEYS OF MASS. IN
NEW ENG., FROM THE NORMAN CONQUEST TO THE PRESENT
TIME**, by G. Adlard. 1862.
Cloth, $37.50. Paper, $27.50. 186pp. .... Vendor G0259

1172 **YEARBOOK OF GOV. THOMAS DUDLEY FAM. ASSOC.** 1930–36.
Cloth, $48.00. Paper, $38.00. 252pp. .... Vendor G0259

1173 **THE DUFOUR SAGA: STORY OF 8 DUFOURS WHO CAME FROM
SWITZERLAND & FOUNDED VEVAY, SWITZERLAND CO., IND.**, by
J.L. Knox. 1942.
Cloth, $39.00. Paper, $29.00. 167pp. .... Vendor G0259

1174 **A GEN. OF THE DUKE–SHEPARD–VAN METRE FAM., FROM CIVIL,
MILITARY, CHURCH RECS. & DOCUMENTS**, by S.G. Smyth. 1902.
Cloth, $68.00. Paper, $58.00. 454pp. .... Vendor G0259

1175 **HENRY DUKE, COUNCILOR, & HIS DESCENDANTS & CONNEC-
TIONS, COMPRISING PARTIAL RECORDS OF MANY ALLIED FAMI-
LIES**, by Walter Garland Duke. 1949.
Cloth, $79.50. Paper, $69.50. 452pp. .... Vendor G0259

1176 **PRESTON AND SUSAN HUTSON DULANY 1800–1993 TENNESSEE,
ILLINOIS AND BEYOND**, by Ann Austin Hecathorn. 1993. Indexed. Illus.
Cloth. $32.00. 255pp. .... Vendor G0183

1177 **THE DUNAWAYS OF VA.**, by A.E. Clendening. 1959.
Cloth, $35.00. Paper, $25.00. 156pp. .... Vendor G0259

1178 **THE DESCENDANTS OF ROBERT DUNBAR OF HINGHAM, MASSA-
CHUSETTS**, by Ann Theopold Chaplin, C.G. 1992. Indexed.
Cloth. $43.00. 514pp. .... Vendor G0241

1179 **DESCENDANTS OF WILLIAM DUNCAN THE ELDER**, by N.R. Roy. 1959.
Cloth, $52.50. Paper, $42.50. 267pp. .... Vendor G0259

1180 **DUNCAN & GIBSON FAM.**, by H.W. Duncan. 1905.
Paper. $9.00. 44pp. .... Vendor G0259

1181 **THE STORY OF THOMAS DUNCAN & HIS SIX SONS**, by K.D. Smith. 1928.
Cloth, $39.00. Paper, $29.00. 174pp. .... Vendor G0259

1182 **SKETCH OF THE DUNCKLEE FAMILY & A HISTORY OF THE DESCENDANTS OF DAVID DUNCKLEE OF AMHERST NH, & HIS SISTER HANNAH DUNCKLEE HOWE OF MILFORD**, by A.M.L. Duncklee. 1908.
Cloth, $49.50. Paper, $39.50. 260pp. .... Vendor G0259

1183 **ANC. & DESC. OF RICHARD DUNHAM OF PENN. & HIS WIFE LAURA ALLEN**, by J. Crary. 1916.
Cloth, $30.00. Paper, $20.00. 102pp. .... Vendor G0259

1184 **GEN. OF DEA. JOHN DUNHAM OF PLYMOUTH, MASS., 1589–1669, & HIS DESC.**, by I.W. Dunham. 1907.
Cloth, $59.50. Paper, $49.50. 384pp. .... Vendor G0259

1185 **SUPPL. ENG. & AMER. BRANCHES OF THE DUNHAM FAM.**, by I. Dunham. 1907.
Paper. $11.00. 52pp. .... Vendor G0259

1186 **JACOB DUNHAM OF LEBANON, CONN., & MAYFIELD, N.Y., HIS ANC. & DESC.**, by S.D. Moore. 1933.
Paper. $10.00. 51pp. .... Vendor G0259

1187 **THE HOUSE OF DUNLAP**, by Rev. James Arthur McC. Hanna. 1956.
Cloth, $72.00. Paper, $62.00. 412pp. .... Vendor G0259

1188 **GENEALOGICAL HISTORY OF THE DUNLEVY FAMILY (DON LEVI, DUNLAVEY, ETC.)**, by G.D. Kelley. 1901.
Cloth, $69.50. Paper, $59.50. 373pp. .... Vendor G0259

1189 **GEN. OF THE DUNNELL–DWINELL FAM. OF NEW ENG.**, by H.G. Dunnel. 1862.
Paper. $17.00. 84pp. .... Vendor G0259

1190 **HENRY DUNSTER & HIS DESC.**, by S. Dunster. 1876.
Cloth, $54.00. Paper, $44.00. 343pp. .... Vendor G0259

1191 **GEN. OF THE DUNWOODY & HOOD FAMS. & COLL. BRANCHES; THEIR HIST. & BIOGR.**, by G. Cope. 1899.
Cloth, $36.00. Paper, $26.00. 172pp. .... Vendor G0259

1192 **A GEN. HIST. OF THE DUPUY FAM.**, by C.M. Dupuy, with add. by H. Dupuy. 1910.
Cloth, $40.00. Paper, $30.00. 175pp. .... Vendor G0259

1193 **THE HUGUENOT BARTHOLOMEW DUPUY & HIS DESC.**, by B.H. Dupuy. 1908.
Cloth, $68.00. Paper, $58.00. 455pp. .... Vendor G0259

1194 **DURAND FAMILY: DESCENDANTS OF DR JOHN DURAND, A HU-GUENOT, BORN 1664, LA ROCHELLE, FRANCE,** by S.R. Durand. 1965.
Cloth, $65.00. Paper, $55.00. 278pp. .... Vendor G0259

1195 **DURAND, WHALLEY, BARNES & YALE FAM.,** by F. Hewitt. 1912.
Cloth, $32.00. Paper, $22.00. 115pp. .... Vendor G0259

1196 **THE DESC. OF THOMAS DURFEE OF PORTSMOUTH, R.I.,** Vol. I, by W.F. Reed. 1902.
Cloth, $99.00. Paper, $89.00. 593pp. .... Vendor G0259

1197 **THE DESC. OF THOMAS DURFEE OF PORTSMOUTH, R.I.,** Vol. II. 1905
Cloth, $107.00. Paper, $97.00. 668pp. .... Vendor G0259

1198 **DUSENBURY FAMILY,** by B.A. Dusenbury. 1932.
Paper. $14.00. 69pp. .... Vendor G0259

1199 **DUSTON–DUSTIN FAM. GEN.,** by Kilgore and Curtis. 1937–1960.
Cloth, $49.00. Paper, $39.00. 247pp. .... Vendor G0259

1200 **DUSTON–DUSTIN FAM. GEN., 3RD & 4TH GEN.** 1948.
Paper. $9.50. 48pp. .... Vendor G0259

1201 **GEN. OF THE DUTTON FAM. OF PENN., WITH A HIST. OF THE FAM. IN ENG., & APPENDIX CONTAINING A SHORT ACCT. OF THE DUTTONS OF CONN.,** by G. Cope. 1871.
Paper. $17.00. 112pp. .... Vendor G0259

1202 **MEMORIALS OF THE DUTTONS OF DUTTON IN CHESHIRE, WITH NOTES REPECTING THE SHERBORNE BRANCH OF THE FAMILY,** n.a. 1901 (London).
Cloth, $57.50. Paper, $47.50. 296pp. .... Vendor G0259

1203 **DUVALS OF KENTUCKY, FROM VA., 1794–1935, DESCENDANTS & ALLIED FAMILIES,** by Margaret G. Buchanan. 1935.
Cloth, $51.00. Paper, $41.00. 265pp. .... Vendor G0259

1204 **DUYCKINCK & ALLIED FAMS.: RECORD OF THE DESC. OF EVERT DUYCKINCK WHO SETTLED IN NEW AMSTERDAM, NOW N.Y., IN 1638,** by Duyckinck and Cornell. 1908.
Cloth, $41.00. Paper, $31.00. 256pp. .... Vendor G0259

1205 **THE HIST. OF THE DESC. OF JOHN DWIGHT OF DEDHAM, MASS.,** by B.W. Dwight. 2 vols. 1874.
Cloth, $164.50. Paper, $154.50. 1,173pp. .... Vendor G0259

1206 **SOME RECORDS OF THE DYER FAM.,** by C. Joy-Dyer. 1884.
Paper. $19.50. 130pp. .... Vendor G0259

1207 **JOHANNES DYCKMAN OF FORT ORANGE AND HIS DESCENDANTS, VOL. I, THE FIRST FIVE GENERATIONS,** by Marjorie Dikeman Chamberlain. 1988. Indexed. Illus.
Cloth. $29.00. 147pp. .... Vendor G0194

1208 **JOHANNES DYCKMAN OF FORT ORANGE AND HIS DESCENDANTS,**

VOL. II, GENERATIONS SIX THROUGH TEN, by Marjorie Dikeman Chamberlain. 1994. Indexed. Illus.
Cloth. $49.00. 431pp. .... Vendor G0194

1209 3-D DATA, NEWSLETTER OF THE DYCKMAN/DIKEMAN/DYKEMAN FAMILY ASSOCIATION, by Marjorie Dikeman Chamberlain. 1985. Indexed. Subscription. $15/calendar year. Approx. 8pp/ issued quarterly ..... Vendor G0194A

1210 HEBRON DYER DESCENDANTS, PIONEER OF OHIO, by Leallah Franklin. 1991. Indexed. Illus.
Related families: **Blake, Bond, Briggs, Brown, Buroker, Caddy, Cain, Chamberlain, Cook, Cunningham, Davis, Dennis, Derr, Fogle, Haley, Keller, McKee, Milligan, Pickenpaugh, Predmore, Ralston, Reiley, Simons, Smith, Walters, Wheeler, Wiley, Woods.**
Cloth. $45.00. 406pp. .... Vendor G0304

1211 THE DYER SETTLEMENT. FT. SEYBERT, W.V. MASSACRE, WITH GEN. NOTES, by M. Talbot. 1937.
Paper. $12.00. 64pp. .... Vendor G0259

1212 HIST. OF THE EAGER FAM., FROM THE COMING OF THE 1ST IMMIGRANT, WILLIAM EAGER, IN 1630 TO 1952, by S.E. Trotter. 1952.
Cloth, $53.00. Paper, $43.00. 251pp. .... Vendor G0259

1213 ROBERT EAMES (AMES), 1640–1693, OF ANDOVER AND BOXFORD, MASS., by Wilmot S. Ames. 1943.
Cloth, $71.50. Paper, $61.50. 400pp. .... Vendor G0259

1214 EARLE FAMILY. RALPH EARLE & DESC., by P. Earle. 1888.
Cloth, $75.50. Paper, $65.50. 516pp. .... Vendor G0259

1215 HIST. & GEN. OF THE EARLES OF SECAUCUS, WITH AN ACCT. OF OTHER ENGLISH & AMER. BRANCHES, by I.N. Earle. 1924.
Cloth, $119.00. Paper, $109.00. 828pp. .... Vendor G0259

1216 DESCENDANTS OF JOHN EARLY OF VIRGINIA, by Carol A. Hauk. 1995. Indexed.
Paper. $45.00. 263pp. .... Vendor G0340

1217 HIST. OF THE EARLY FAM. IN AMER., by S.S. Early. 1896.
Paper. $10.50. 53pp. .... Vendor G0259

1218 THE FAM. OF EARLY WHICH SETTLED UPON THE EASTERN SHORE OF VA., by R.H. Early. 1920.
Cloth, $64.50. Paper, $54.50. 343pp. .... Vendor G0259

1219 A TENTATIVE OUTLINE OF U.S. EASLEY LINES, PRIMARILY TO THE YEAR 1800, by Virginia Easley De Marce. (1974) reprint 1985. Indexed.
Paper. $25.00. 317pp. .... Vendor G0324

1220 . . . NOW LIVING IN BOONE COUNTY, MISSOURI. OUR FAMILY GENEALOGIES. Volume I: The Family and Connections of Edward Everett Easley, by Virginia Easley De Marce. 1990. Indexed. Illus.
Focuses on the following Boone County pioneer families: **Easley, Fortney, Sutton,** and **Elgin.**
Cloth. $38.50. 679+pp. .... Vendor G0324

1221 **[Easley.]** . . . **NOW LIVING IN BOONE COUNTY, MISSOURI. OUR FAMILY GENEALOGIES. Volume II: The Family and Connections of Martha Catherine Cheavens**, by Virginia Easley De Marce. 1990. Focuses on the following Boone County pioneer families: **Cheavens, Self,** and **Black.**
Cloth. $38.50. 686+pp. .... Vendor G0324

1222 **EASTBURN FAMILY, BEING A GENEALOGICAL & HISTORICAL RECORD OF THE DESCENDANTS OF JOHN EASTBURN, WHO CAME TO AMERICA IN 1684, FROM BINGLEY, YORKSHIRE, & OF ROBERT EASTBURN, WHO . . . CAME TO AMERICA IN 1713 . . . AND SETTLED IN PHILADELPHIA, PA.**, by Hettie A. Walton and Eastburn Reeder. 1903.
Cloth, $41.00. Paper, $31.00. 206pp. .... Vendor G0259

1223 **MEMOIRS OF THE REV. JOSEPH EASTBURN, STATED PREACHER IN THE MARINER'S CHURCH, PHILADELPHIA, WHO DEPARTED THIS LIFE JAN. 30TH, 1828**, by Ashbel Green. 1828.
Cloth, $42.00. Paper, $32.00. 208pp. .... Vendor G0259

1224 **HIST. & GEN. OF THE EASTMAN FAM. OF AMERICA, CONT. BIOGR. SKETCHES & GEN. OF BOTH MALES & FEMALES**, by G.S. Rix. 1901.
Cloth, $149.00. Paper, $139.00. 1,000pp. .... Vendor G0259

1225 **DESC. OF JOSEPH EASTON, HARTFORD, CONN., 1636–1899**, by W.S. Easton. 1899.
Cloth, $48.50. Paper, $38.50. 257pp. .... Vendor G0259

1226 **EATON FAM. ASSOC. REPORT OF THE 6TH ANNUAL REUNION AT BOSTON, 1890.** 1891.
Paper. $7.00. 35pp. .... Vendor G0259

1227 **EATON FAM. OF NOVA SCOTIA, 1760–1929**, by A. Eaton. 1929.
Cloth, $48.00. Paper, $38.00. 253pp. .... Vendor G0259

1228 **HISTORY, GEN. & BIOGR., OF THE EATON FAMILY**, by N.Z.R. Molyneux. 1911.
Cloth, $109.00. Paper, $99.00. 782pp. .... Vendor G0259

1229 **HIST. OF THE EBERHARTS IN GERMANY & THE U.S., FROM 1265– 1890, WITH AN AUTOBIOGR. OF THE AUTHOR**, by Rev. U. Eberhart. 1891.
Cloth, $49.50. Paper, $39.50. 263pp. .... Vendor G0259

1230 **EBERWINE, DANIEL, MINER AND PLOUGH FAMILIES OF VINCENNES AND KNOX COUNTY, INDIANA, ANCESTRY AND DE-SCENDANTS OF JOHANN CHRISTOPH PHILLIP EBERWEIN FROM GOETTINGEN, GERMANY, ALLEN B. DANIEL FROM GALLATIN COUNTY, ILLINOIS, JACOB MINER FROM PLACE UNKNOWN, JACOB PLOUGH FROM SUSSEX COUNTY, NEW JERSEY**, by Esther Littleford Woodworth-Barnes. 1993. Indexed. Illus.
Cloth. $35.00. 103pp. .... Vendor G0054

1231 **A BIOGRAPHICAL HISTORY OF THE EBY FAMILY**, by Ezra E. Eby. (1889) 1979 revision.
Paper. $15.00. 160pp. .... Vendor G0150

1232 **DESCENDANTS OF ANDREW EBY–ABEY–ABEE IN THE CAROLI-NAS,** by Charles Moran Abee. 1983.
Cloth. $26.00. 214pp. .... Vendor G0150

1233 **FAMILY RECORD OF THE DESCENDANTS OF JACOB EBY, 1815–1896, AND MARY BINGEMAN,** by Wendell B. Eby. 1992.
Cloth. $28.00. 339pp. .... Vendor G0150

1234 **ZACHARIAS ECK FAM. RECORD,** by L.E. Cooper. 1959.
Paper. $19.50. 126pp. .... Vendor G0259

1235 **ANCESTORS & DESC. OF ZACHARIAH EDDY OF WARREN, PA.,** by B.B. Horton. 1930.
Cloth, $61.00. Paper, $51.00. 332pp. .... Vendor G0259

1236 **EDDY FAMILY IN AMERICA, 1940 SUPPL.,** by R.S. Eddy. 1940.
Cloth, $38.00. Paper, $28.00. 180pp. .... Vendor G0259

1237 **MEM. OF COL. JONATHAN EDDY OF EDDINGTON, ME., WITH SOME ACCT. OF THE EDDY FAM., & OF THE EARLY SETTLERS ON PENOBSCOT RIVER,** by J. Porter. 1877.
Paper. $14.00. 73pp. .... Vendor G0259

1238 **REC. OF THE EDGERLY FAM., DESC. OF THOMAS EDGERLY OF DURHAM, NH, 1630**, by E. Edgerly.
Paper. $9.00. 43pp. .... Vendor G0259

1239 **ZEPHANIAH EDMONDS AND ELISABETH HEMINGER—THEIR ANCESTORS AND DESCENDANTS**, by Kemble Stout. 1977. Indexed.
Paper. $15.00. 211pp. .... Vendor G0320B

1240 **EDSONS IN ENGLAND AND AMERICA, AND GENEALOGY OF THE EDSONS**, by Jarvis B. Edson. 1903.
Cloth, $101.50. Paper, $91.50. 630pp. .... Vendor G0259

1241 **GEN. ACCT. OF THE EDSONS OF BRIDGEWATER**, by T. Edson. 1864.
Paper. $12.00. 62pp. .... Vendor G0259

1242 **GEN. OF THE EDSONS**, by J.B. Edson. 1903.
Cloth, $40.00. Paper, $30.00. 184pp. .... Vendor G0259

1243 **NATHAN EDSON & HIS DESC.**, by G.T. Edson. 1926.
Paper. $10.00. 48pp. .... Vendor G0259

1244 **SEVERAL ANC. LINES OF JOSIAH EDSON & HIS WIFE, SARAH PINNEY. WITH A FULL GEN. HIST. OF THEIR DESC.**, by H.H. Wells and H.W. Van Dyke. 1901.
Paper. $19.00. 98pp. .... Vendor G0259

1245 **A GEN. REC. OF THE DESC. OF JOHN EDWARDS, 168(?)–1915**, by L.N. Edwards. 1916.
Cloth, $71.00. Paper, $61.00. 395pp. .... Vendor G0259

1246 **HISTORY OF THE EDWARDS–PERRY AND ALLIED FAMILIES**, by Carolyn Edwards Fleetwood and Joan Prevost Fortune. 1992. Indexed. Illus.
William Henry **Edwards** (1817–1883) was the son of Meredith **Edwards**. He married second Mary Elizabeth **Perry**, daughter of Micajah Perry of North Carolina. They had eleven children, all born in Warren County, Georgia. Each child has a chapter devoted to him/her and his/her descendants.
A second section is data on seven **Perry** brothers of Bute County, North Carolina and their descendants. Allied families include **Banks, Combs, Ferguson, Fields, George, Hamilton, Hawes, Jackson, Johnson, Lee, Love, Mayes, Moore, Stewart**, and **Ware**.
Cloth. $30.00. 254pp. .... Vendor G0317

1247 **RICHARD EDWARDS & HIS WIFE CATHERINE POND MAY; THEIR ANC., LIVES & DESC.**, by M. Edwards. 1931.
Cloth, $41.50. Paper, $31.50. 209pp. .... Vendor G0259

1248 **TIMOTHY & RHODA OGDEN EDWARDS OF STOCKBRIDGE, MA. & DESC.**, by W. Edwards. 1903.
Cloth, $36.00. Paper, $26.00. 172pp. .... Vendor G0259

1249 **EELS FAM. OF DORCHESTER, MA., IN THE LINE OF NATHANIEL EELS OF MIDDLETOWN, CT., 1633–1821, WITH NOTES ON THE LENTHALL FAM.**, by F. Star. 1903.
Cloth, $43.50. Paper, $33.50. 224pp. .... Vendor G0259

1250 **HISTORY & GENEALOGY OF THE EGE FAMILY IN THE U.S., 1738–1911**, by Thompson P. Ege. 1911.
Cloth, $64.00. Paper, $54.00. 281pp. .... Vendor G0259

1251 **"DOMINIE" JOHN JACOB EHLE & HIS DESCENDANTS,** by Boyd Ehle. 1930.
Paper. $11.00. 55pp. .... Vendor G0259

1252 **HISTORICAL SKETCH OF PHILIP FREDERICK EICHELBERGER, WHO CAME FROM ITTLINGER, GERMANY, IN 1728, & OF HIS DE-SCENDANTS, WITH A FAMILY REGISTER,** by A.W. Eichelberger. 1901.
Cloth, $48.00. Paper, $38.00. 160+79pp. .... Vendor G0259

1253 **EICHER NAME IN AMERICA,** by Von Gail Hamilton. (1974) reprint 1992. Indexed. Illus.
History & genealogy, including Pennsylvania families descended from early Swiss, French & German lineages (Amish & Mennonite). Includes photos.
Cloth. $58.50. 316pp. .... Vendor G0285

1254 **ANCESTRY OF THE JOHN FRANKLIN EISENHART FAMILY, WITH SUPPLEMENT,** by W.W. Eisenhart. 1951.
Cloth, $34.00. Paper, $24.00. 150+7pp. .... Vendor G0259

1255 **GEN. OF THE ELA FAM., DESC. OF ISRAEL ELA OF HAVERHILL, MASS.,** by D.H. Ela. 1896.
Paper. $9.00. 44pp. .... Vendor G0259

1256 **ELDER FAMILY NEWSLETTER,** by Donna Younkin Logan. 1992. Illus.
Publishes family research and records on all **Elder** families in the United States.
Subscription. $15.00/year. 80pp/yr .... Vendor G0392

1257 **GEN. OF DAVID ELDER & MARGERY STEWART,** by T.A. Elder. 1905.
Paper. $10.00. 52pp. .... Vendor G0259

1258 **ELDREDGE–STORY & ALLIED FAMILES, GEN. & BIOGR.** 1943.
Cloth, $33.00. Paper, $23.00. 130pp. .... Vendor G0259

1259 **A SKETCH OF THE ELIOT FAM.,** by W.G. Eliot. 1887.
Cloth, $35.00. Paper, $25.00. 177pp. .... Vendor G0259

1260 **GEN. OF THE DESC. OF JOHN ELIOT, "APOSTLE TO THE INDI-ANS," 1598–1905,** by W.H. Emerson. 1905.
Cloth, $63.60. Paper, $53.60. 356pp. .... Vendor G0259

1261 **GENEALOGY OF THE ELIOT FAMILY,** by Wm. H. Eliot; rev. by W.S. Porter. 1854.
Cloth, $39.50. Paper, $29.50. 184pp. .... Vendor G0259

1262 **THE FAM. OF WM. GREENLEAF ELIOT & ABBY ADAMS ELIOT OF ST. LOUIS, MO., 3RD ED., 1811–1943.** 1943.
Cloth, $34.00. Paper, $24.00. 157pp. .... Vendor G0259

1263 **THE ANC. & DESC. OF GEORGE ELKINTON OF BURLINGTON CO., N.J.,** by A. Adams. 1945.
Paper. $10.00. 48pp. .... Vendor G0259

1264 **GEORGE MICHAEL ELLER & HIS DESC. IN AMERICA, INCL. INFO. ON RELATED FAMS. OF VANNOY–VAN NOY, McNEIL, STOKER, WELKER & OTHERS,** by J.W. Hook. 1957.
Cloth, $85.00. Paper, $75.00. 485pp. .... Vendor G0259

1265 **THE JOHN ELLIOT FAM. OF BOSCAWEN, N. H.**, by H.A. Kimball. 1918.
Paper. $19.50. 132pp. .... Vendor G0259

1266 **THE JOHNSTON ELLIOTT FAMILY 1748—PA**, by Mrs. Jo Ann De Board Touchstone. 1991. Indexed. Illus.
Surnames: **Adams, Atkinson/Adkins, Bastin, Brown, Butt/Butts, Carman, Carr/Kerr, DeBoard/ DeBord, Duffield, Floyd, Godbey, Humphrey, McWhorter, Phelps, Smith, Taylor, Trowbridge, Wall, Wesley.**
Hardback. $40.00. 271pp. plus pictures .... Vendor G0236

1267 **BIOGR. SKETCHES OF RICHARD ELLIS, 1ST SETTLER OF ASHFIELD, MA. & HIS DESC.**, by E. Ellis. 1888.
Cloth, $71.50. Paper, $61.50. 483pp. .... Vendor G0259

1268 **[Ellis]. EARLY NEW ENGLAND PEOPLE: SOME ACCT. OF ELLIS, PEMBERTON, WILLARD, PRESCOTT, TITCOMB, SEWALL, LONGFELLOW & ALLIED FAMILIES**, by S.E. Titcomb. 1882.
Cloth, $55.00. Paper, $45.00. 293pp. .... Vendor G0259

1269 **HIST. OF THE ELLIS FAM., & DESC. OF WILLIAM ELLIS OF BIDEFORD, P.E.I.**, by P. Ellis. 1950.
Cloth, $68.50. Paper, $58.50. 368pp. .... Vendor G0259

1270 **THE ELLIS FAM.**, by K.S. Foos. 1900.
Paper. $19.00. 128pp. .... Vendor G0259

1271 **ELLSWORTH ANC.**, by G.E., M.S. and J.O. Ellsworth.
Cloth, $48.50. Paper, $38.50. 257pp. .... Vendor G0259

1272 **ELMER–ELMORE GEN.**, by W.W. Johnson. 1899.
Cloth, $30.00. Paper, $20.00. 96pp. .... Vendor G0259

1273 **FAM. MEMORIALS, HIST. & GEN. OF ELMORE FAM.**, by T.J. Elmore. 1880.
Paper. $8.00. 40pp. .... Vendor G0259

1274 **ELSTON FAMILY IN AMER.**, by J.S. Elston. 1942.
Cloth, $104.50. Paper, $94.50. 632pp. .... Vendor G0259

1275 **AN HIST. NARRATIVE OF THE ELY, REVELL & STACYE FAM., OF TRENTON & BURLINGTON, WEST JERSEY, 1678–1683, WITH GEN. OF THE ELY DESC. IN AMERICA**, by R.P. Ely et al. 1910.
Cloth, $66.50. Paper, $56.50. 445pp. .... Vendor G0259

1276 **HIST. OF THE ELY REUNION HELD AT LYME, CONN., JULY 10TH, 1878**, by M.E.D. Stuart. 1879.
Cloth, $33.50. Paper, $23.50. 158pp. .... Vendor G0259

1277 **THE ELY ANC.; LIN. OF RICHARD ELY OF PLYMOUTH, ENG., WHO CAME TO BOSTON ABOUT 1655 & SETTLED AT LYME, CONN., IN 1660**, by M.S. Beach, et al. 1902.
Cloth, $90.00. Paper, $80.00. 639pp. .... Vendor G0259

1278 **AN EMERSON–BENSON SAGA INCLUDING 194 ALLIED LINES**, by Edmund K. Swigart. 1994. Indexed. Illus.

Five or more generations: Massachusetts—**Emerson** (Ipswich), **Benson** (Hull), **Barrows** (Plymouth), **Besse** (Sandwich), **Blanchard** (Charlestown), **Bloss** (Watertown), **Booth** (Scituate), **Freeman** (Sudbury), **Hafford** (Braintree), **Hall** (Duxbury), **Lewis** (Cambridge), **Lord** (Ipswich), **Lyman** (Roxbury), **Merrill** (Newbury), **Moulton** (Salem), **Moulton** (Newbury), **Parry–Perry** (Watertown), **Rogers** (Plymouth), **Safford** (Ipswich), **Shaw** (Watertown), **Spear** (Braintree), **Stevens** (Taunton), **Sumner** (Dorchester), **Younglove** (Ipswich). Maine— **Moulton** (York). Connecticut—**Chittenden** (Guilford), **Lewis** (Hartford), **Lyman** (Hartford), **Stevens** (Stonington).
Cloth. $52.95. 718pp. .... Vendor G0100

1279 **THE ENG. EMERSONS: GEN. HISTORY OF THE FAM. FROM EAR-LIEST TIMES TO THE END OF THE 17TH CENT., INCL. MODERN PEDIGREES,** by P.H. Emerson. 1898.
Cloth, $51.00. Paper, $41.00. 320pp. .... Vendor G0259

1280 **THE HAVERHILL EMERSONS,** by C.H. Pope. Part 1. 1913.
Paper. $15.00. 106pp. .... Vendor G0259

1281 **THE HAVERHILL EMERSONS,** by C.H. Pope. Part 2. 1916.
Cloth, $47.00. Paper, $37.00. 248pp. .... Vendor G0259

1282 **THE IPSWICH EMERSONS, 1636–1900. A GEN. OF THE DESC. OF THOMAS EMERSON, WITH SOME ACCT. OF HIS ENG. ANC.,** by B.K. Emerson. 1900.
Cloth, $78.00. Paper, $68.00. 544pp. .... Vendor G0259

1283 **GEN. RECORDS OF DESC. OF JOHN & ANTHONY EMERY OF NEWBURY, MASS., 1690–1890,** by R. Emery. 1890.
Cloth, $103.00. Paper, $93.00. 621pp. .... Vendor G0259

1284 **MATERIALS TOWARD A GEN. OF THE EMMERTON FAM.,** by J.A. Emmerton. 1881.
Cloth, $47.00. Paper, $37.00. 248pp. .... Vendor G0259

1285 **EMMONS FAM. GEN. THOMAS EMMONS OF NEWPORT, R.I., WITH DESC. FROM 1639 TO 1905,** by E.N. Emmons. 1905.
Cloth, $53.00. Paper, $43.00. 287pp. .... Vendor G0259

1286 **HISTORY OF THE ENGLE FAMILY IN AMERICA, 1754–1927,** by Morris Engle. n.d.
Paper. $12.00. 161pp. .... Vendor G0150

1287 **ENO FAM. OF FRANCE & AMER. (EXTR. BASSETT GEN.).** 1926.
Paper. $7.00. 36pp. .... Vendor G0259

1288 **RECORD OF THE DESCENDANTS OF JAMES ENSIGN, THE PURI-TAN, 1634–1939,** by M.E. Ensign, et al. 1939.
Cloth, $63.00. Paper, $53.00. 340pp. .... Vendor G0259

1289 **HISTORY & GENEALOGY OF THE EPLER, OLDWILER, HUCKLE-BERRY, CARR & EWING FAMILIES,** E.E. Knudson. 1913.
Cloth, $34.50. Paper, $24.50. 137pp. .... Vendor G0259

1290 **DESCENDANTS OF DAVID ERB,** by Henry L. Erb. 1990.
Cloth. $25.00. 659pp. .... Vendor G0150

1291 **MY YESTERDAY PEOPLE—ERWIN, ROBERT, SMITH, THOMAS, TUCKER AND WITHERS FAMILIES,** by Ruth Erwin Moore. 1994. Indexed. Illus.
Cloth. $40.00. 376pp. .... Vendor G0379

1292 **ANCESTRY AND DESCENDANTS OF CONRAD ESSELTINE (ESSELSTYNE, ASSELSTINE), SOME ALLIED FAMILIES AND OTHER ASSELTYNES, WITH 1946 ADDENDUM,** by I.F. Johnson. 1943.
Paper. $16.00. 69+11pp. .... Vendor G0259

1293 **TWO HUNDRED YEARS OF THE ESSLINGER FAMILY,** by W.F. Esslinger. n.d.
Paper. $19.50. 116pp. .... Vendor G0259

1294 **GEN. OF THE ESTABROOK FAM., INCL. THE ESTERBROOKS & EASTERBROOKS IN THE U.S.,** by W.B. Estabrook. 1891.
Cloth, $56.00. Paper, $46.00. 359pp. .... Vendor G0259

1295 **ESTES GEN. 1097–1893,** by C. Estes. 1894.
Cloth, $75.00. Paper, $65.00. 417pp. .... Vendor G0259

1296 **OUR ETHEREDGE FAM. CIRCLES FROM 1753 TO 1953,** by H. Etheredge. 1953(?).
Paper. $14.50. 72pp. .... Vendor G0259

1297 **[Evans-Jackson]. THE JONES & EVANS FAM. OF PORTAGE & MAHONING COS., OHIO; & THE JACKSON & SOMERS FAM. OF PORTSMOUTH, N.H. & BUFFALO, N.Y.,** by O.O. and A.J. Evans. 1954.
Paper. $15.00. 74pp. .... Vendor G0259

1298 **THE EVELYNS IN AMERICA COMPILED FROM FAM. PAPERS & SOURCES, 1608–1805,** by G.D. Scull. 1881.
Cloth, $73.50. Paper, $63.50. 404pp. .... Vendor G0259

1299 **DESCENDANTS OF WALTER EVERENDEN, POWDERMAKER IN MASS., 1684,** by L.E. Wagstaff. 1966.
Paper. $19.00. 110pp. .... Vendor G0259

1300 **DESCENDANTS OF ANDREW EVEREST OF YORK, MAINE,** by W.L. Holman. 1955.
Cloth, $84.00. Paper, $74.00. 488pp. .... Vendor G0259

1301 **DESC. OF RICHARD EVERETT OF DEDHAM, MASS.,** by E.F. Everett. 1902.
Cloth, $71.50. Paper, $61.50. 389pp. .... Vendor G0259

1302 **REC. OF THE FAM. OF THOMAS EWING, WHO EMIGR. FROM IRELAND TO AMER. IN 1718,** by R.P. DuBois. 1858.
Paper. $7.50. 38pp. .... Vendor G0259

1303 **THE FAMILY OF PETER EVERLY (c. 1749–1819) OF PRESTON COUNTY WV WITH COLLATERAL BRANCHES,** by James H. Shaw. 1993. Indexed.
Paper. $50.00. 731pp. .... Vendor G0280

1304 **SUPPLEMENT TO THE FAMILY OF PETER EVERLY (c. 1749–1819),** by James H. Shaw. 1995. Indexed.
Paper. $15.00. 130pp. .... Vendor G0280

1305 **SKETCHES OF THE FAM. OF THOMAS, WILLIAM & JAMES EWING & THEIR DESC.**, by J.L. Ewing. 1910.
Cloth, $35.00. Paper, $25.00. 123pp. .... Vendor G0259

1306 **THE EWING GEN., WITH COGNATE BRANCHES**, by P.K. and M.E. Ewing. 1919.
Cloth, $46.50. Paper, $36.50. 244pp. .... Vendor G0259

1307 **THE ANC. OF MARGUERITE EYERMAN: A STUDY IN GEN. (OSTER, SCHAEFFER, ROESSEL, SCHNEIDER, BLACK, HELLER, WAGENER, KACHLEIN, BUTZ, SEWITS, BAHL, DETWILLER, ETC.)**, by J. Eyerman. 1898.
Paper. $10.00. 48pp. .... Vendor G0259

1308 **THE ANC. OF MARGUERITE & JOHN EYERMAN**, by J. Eyerman. Suppl. to 1898 ed. 1899.
Paper. $7.00. 35pp. .... Vendor G0259

1309 **FAHNESTOCK GENEALOGY. ANC. & DESC. OF JOHANN DIEDRICH FAHNESTOCK**, by H.M. Pinot. 1945.
Cloth, $77.50. Paper, $67.50. 442pp. .... Vendor G0259

1310 **FAM. MEM. OF THE FAHNESTOCKS IN THE U.S.**, by A.K. and W.F. Fahnestock. 1879.
Paper. $14.00. 69pp. .... Vendor G0259

1311 **GEN. OF THE FAIRBANKS FAM. IN AMERICA, 1633–1897**, by L.S. Fairbanks. 1897.
Cloth, $131.00. Paper, $121.00. 967pp. .... Vendor G0259

1312 **EARLY FAIRCHILDS IN AMERICA AND THEIR DESCENDANTS**, by Jean Fairchild Gilmore. (1991) reprint 1993. Indexed. Illus.
Cloth. $40.00. 659pp. .... Vendor G0292

1313 **THE FAIRFAXES OF ENG. & AMER. IN THE 17TH & 18TH CENT., INCL. LETTERS FROM & TO HON. WM. FAIRFAX OF VA. & HIS SONS**, by E.D. Neill. 1868.
Cloth, $44.50. Paper, $34.50. 234pp. .... Vendor G0259

1314 **DESC. OF JOHN FAIRFIELD OF WENHAM, VOL. I: FIRST FIVE GENERATIONS, WITH AN APPENDIX ON FAIRFIELD FAMS. IN ENG.**, by W.C. Fairfield. 1953.
Paper. $16.50. 82pp. .... Vendor G0259

1315 **DESC. OF JOHN FAIRMAN OF ENFIELD, CONN., 1638–1898**, by O.P. Allen. 1898.
Paper. $8.00. 38pp. .... Vendor G0259

1316 **THE FALES FAM. OF BRISTOL, R.I.; ANC. OF HALIBURTON FALES OF N.Y.**, by DeCoursey Fales. 1919.
Cloth, $63.00. Paper, $53.00. 332pp. . . . . Vendor G0259

1317 **FANCHER FAM.**, by W.H. Fancher. 1947.
Cloth, $34.00. Paper, $24.00. 144pp. . . . . Vendor G0259

1318 **HIST. OF THE FANNING FAM. A GEN. RECORD TO 1900 OF THE DESC. OF EDMUND FANNING, WHO SETTLED IN CONN. IN 1655,** by W.F. Brooks. 1905.
Cloth, $141.00. Paper, $131.00. 872pp. . . . . Vendor G0259

1319 **FANT FAMILY NOTEBOOK OF PRIMARY SOURCE RECORDS,** by Virginia Fant Bruce. 1990. Indexed.
Abstracts and copies of **Fant** records as found in census, cemetery, land, courthouse, Bible, and church records, etc.
Paper. $25.00. 60pp. . . . . Vendor G0191

1320 **12 GEN. OF FARLEYS,** by J. Farley, Jr. 1943.
Cloth, $49.00. Paper, $39.00. 260pp. . . . . Vendor G0259

1321 **VANOCATEN: A FARLEY–REID GENEALOGY,** by William S. Farley. 1993. Indexed. Illus.
Cloth. $48.75. 500pp. . . . . Vendor G0004

1322 **HIST. OF THOS. & ANNE (BILLOPP) FARMER & SOME OF THEIR DESC.,** by C.F. Billopp. 1907.
Cloth, $33.50. Paper, $23.50. 137pp. . . . . Vendor G0259

1323 **RALPH FARNHAM OF ANDOVER, MASS. & HIS DESC.,** by H.F. Johnston. 1950.
Paper. $15.00. 74pp. . . . . Vendor G0259

1324 **FARNSWORTH MEM. A REC. OF MATTHIAS FARNSWORTH & HIS DESC. IN AMER.,** by M.F. Farnsworth. 1897.
Cloth, $75.00. Paper, $65.00. 514pp. . . . . Vendor G0259

1325 **DESCENDANTS OF THOMAS FARR OF HARPSWELL, MAINE & NINETY ALLIED FAMILIES,** by E.B. Sumner. 1959.
Cloth, $69.50. Paper, $59.50. 390pp. . . . . Vendor G0259

1326 **FARREN–FERRIN. CAPT. JONATHAN FARREN OF AMESBURY, MASS. & SOME DESC.,** by Ferrin and Brennan. 1941.
Cloth, $47.00. Paper, $37.00. 222pp. . . . . Vendor G0259

1327 **FARWELL ANC. MEMORIAL. HENRY FARWELL OF CONCORD & CHELMSFORD, MASS.,** by D.P. and F.K. Holton. 1879.
Cloth, $53.00. Paper, $43.00. 258pp. . . . . Vendor G0259

1328 **FARWELL FAM. A HIST. OF HENRY FARWELL & HIS WIFE OLIVE (WELBY) FARWELL OF BOSTON, ENG., & CONCORD & CHELMSFORD, MA., 1605–1927, WITH 12 GEN. OF THEIR DESC. & LIN. OF MANY ALLIED FAM.,** by Farwell, Abbott and Wilson. 2 vols. 1929.
Cloth, $149.00. Paper, $139.00. 941pp. . . . . Vendor G0259

1329 **PIERRE FAUCONNIER & HIS DESCENDANTS, WITH SOME ACCT. OF ALLIED VALLEAUX,** by A.E. Helffenstein. 1911.
Cloth, $52.00. Paper, $42.00. 266pp. .... Vendor G0259

1330 **THOMAS FAULCONER AND HIS DESCENDANTS,** by James G. Faulconer. (1984) reprint 1995. Indexed.
Paper (unbound). $15.00 incl. postage. 200pp. .... Vendor G0252

1331 **THOMAS FAULCONER, DESCENDANTS AND RELATED TIDEWATER VIRGINIA FAMILIES,** by James G. Faulconer and Tommy L. West. 1994. Indexed.
Cloth. $25.00 incl. postage. 196pp. .... Vendor G0252

1332 **MY ANC. & THEIR DESC., THE FAULKNER FAM.,** by W.L. Brown.
Paper. $8.00. 38pp. .... Vendor G0259

1333 **DESCENDANTS OF MOORE FAUNTLEROY OF VIRGINIA,** by Carol A. Hauk. 1995. Indexed.
Paper. $30.00. 150pp. .... Vendor G0340

1334 **FAVILL FAMILY,** by S. Favill. 1899.
Paper. $9.00. 44pp. .... Vendor G0259

1335 **THE FAMILY OF JACOB FAWLEY (1802–1880) OF THE BROCKS GAP AREA, ROCKINGHAM CO., VA,** by Patricia Turner Ritchie. 1989. Indexed. Illus.
Cloth. $24.00. 464pp. .... Vendor G0365

1336 **THE HIST. OF THE FAXON FAM., CONTAINING A GEN. OF THE DESC. OF THOMAS FAXON OF BRAINTREE, MASS., & ALLIED FAM.,** by G. L. Faxon. 1880.
Cloth, $58.50. Paper, $48.50. 377pp. .... Vendor G0259

1337 **FAY GEN., JOHN FAY OF MARLBOROUGH & HIS DESC.,** by O.P. Fay. 1898.
Cloth, $64.00. Paper, $54.00. 420pp. .... Vendor G0259

1338 **ONE BRANCH OF THE FAY FAMILY TREE: AN ACCT. OF THE ANCESTORS & DESCENDANTS OF WILLIAM & ELIZABETH FAY OF WESTBORO MA & MARIETTA, OH,** by G. Johnson. 1913.
Cloth, $35.00. Paper, $25.00. 130pp. .... Vendor G0259

1339 **FEATHERSTONES & HALLS; GLEANINGS FROM OLD FAM. LETTERS & MSS.,** by M. Irwin. 1890.
Paper. $18.00. 99pp. .... Vendor G0259

1340 **MEMORIAL HIST. OF FELCH FAM. IN AMERICA & WALES,** by W.F. Felch. 1881.
Paper. $16.50. 98pp. .... Vendor G0259

1341 **100 YEARS OF FELDHAUSENS IN KANSAS,** by Feldhausen Family. Research by Pearl Anderson and Others. 1979. Illus.
Jacob and Theresa (**Dunks**) **Feldhausen** descendants from Ellenz Germany and Belgium to Green Bay Wisconsin to Kansas.
Cloth. $30.00. 221pp. .... Vendor G0063

1342 **GEN. OF THE FELL FAM. IN AMERICA DESC. FROM JOSEPH FELL WHO SETTLED IN BUCKS. CO., PENN., 1705**, by S.M. Fell. 1891. Cloth, $75.50. Paper, $65.50. 515pp. .... Vendor G0259

1343 **FELLOWS FAMILIES OF ONONDAGA COUNTY NEW YORK & THEIR ANCESTRY**, by Erwin W. Fellows. 1991. Indexed. Illus. Cloth. $26.50. 127pp. .... Vendor G0450

1344 **GEN. OF THE FELLOWS–CRAIG & ALLIED FAM. FROM 1619 TO 1919**, by F.H. Craig. 1919. Cloth, $32.50. Paper, $22.50. 151pp. .... Vendor G0259

1345 **JOSEPH & PHILENA (ELTON) FELLOWS: THEIR ANCESTORS & DESCENDANTS**, by M.M. Morris. 1940. Cloth, $71.00. Paper, $61.00. 404pp. .... Vendor G0259

1346 **THE DESCENDANTS & ANTECEDENTS OF ALFRED & CATHERINE (DAWLEY) FELLOWS**, by Charles Mathieson Otstot. 1987. Indexed. Illus. Paper. $20.00. 139pp. .... Vendor G0232

1347 **A REGISTER OF THE ANC. OF DORR E. FELT & AGNES McNULTY FELT**, by A.L. Holman. 1921. Cloth, $50.00. Paper, $40.00. 267pp. .... Vendor G0259

1348 **THE FELT GEN., A RECORD OF THE DESC. OF GEORGE FELT OF CASCO BAY**, by J.E. Morris. 1893. Cloth, $97.00. Paper, $87.00. 568pp. .... Vendor G0259

1349 **A GEN. HIST. OF THE FELTON FAM., DESC. OF LT. NATHANIEL FELTON WHO CAME TO SALEM, MASS., 1633**, by C. Felton. 1886. Cloth, $49.00. Paper, $39.00. 260pp. .... Vendor G0259

1350 **GEN. HIST. OF THE FELTON FAM.: ANC. & DESC. OF LT. NATHANIEL FELTON, WHO CAME TO SALEM, MASS. FROM GT. YARMOUTH, ENG., IN 1633, WITH BRIEF HIST. OF SOME FAMS. THAT INTERMARRIED WITH FELTONS DURING THE 1ST 150 YEARS**, by W.R. Felton. 1935. Cloth, $82.00. Paper, $72.00. 467pp. .... Vendor G0259

1351 **THE FELTON FAM.: DESC. OF LT. NATHANIEL FELTON, WHO CAME TO SALEM, MASS., IN 1633, (EXTENSION OF 1886 & 1935 BOOKS)**, by N.F. Koster. 1963. Cloth, $48.50. Paper, $38.50. 251pp. .... Vendor G0259

1352 **FENNER–BROUGHTON FAMILY HISTORY**, by Jim Fenner, Ph.D. 1995. Indexed. Illus.
    Descendants and ancestors of Capt. Arthur **Fenner** of R.I. and of George **Fenner** 1757–1827 of Herkimer Co., NY. Ancestors of Civil War soldier James Elory **Fenner** 1844–1912 and Hester Adamantha **Broughton** 1847–1922 of Crawford Co., PA to the colonies and England, and all descendants. Index of 1500+ names incl. **Bradford, Browne, Corey, Flower, Lyman, Pildner, Sanderson, Steele, Stellmach, Walker**, and **Williams**.
    Cloth. $38.00. 404pp. .... Vendor G0296

1353 **GEN. OF FENTON FAM., DESC. OF ROBERT FENTON OF WINDHAM, CONN.**, by W.L. Weaver. 1867. Paper. $7.00. 34pp. .... Vendor G0259

1354 **THE FENTON FAM. OF AMERICA & GREAT BRITAIN**, by T.A. Atkins. 1912.
Cloth, $33.00. Paper, $23.00. 154pp. Vendor G0259

1355 **DESCENDANTS OF JAMES AND ELIZABETH FLEMING FERGUSON, BEDFORD (NOW MARSHALL) COUNTY, TN,** by Herman W. Ferguson. 1988. Indexed.
Paper. $17.50. 135pp. . . . . Vendor G0056

1356 **GEN. OF DESC. OF JOHN FERGUSON OF SCOTLAND & U. S.,** by A.B. Ferguson. 1911.
Cloth, $32.50. Paper, $22.50. 112pp. Vendor G0259

1357 **THE DESCENDANTS OF DANIEL AND ELIZABETH FERGUSON OF SCOTLAND AND KORTRIGHT, DELAWARE COUNTY, NEW YORK, 1785–1995,** by Rick Crume. 1995. Indexed.
Includes: **Kelso, Robertson.**
Paper. $7.00. 61pp. . . . . Vendor G0386

1358 **THE FERGUSON FAM. IN SCOTLAND & AMER.,** by M.L. Ferguson. 1905.
Cloth, $35.50. Paper, $25.50. 142pp. Vendor G0259

1359 **RECORDS OF THE CLAN & NAME OF FERGUSSON, FERGUSON & FERGUS,** edited by J. and R.M. Fergusson. 1895 (Scotland).
Cloth, $104.00. Paper, $94.00. xxx+618pp. . . . . Vendor G0259

1360 **THE JOHNSTON & BACON SCOTTISH CLAN HISTORIES: The Fergussons,** by Sir James Fergusson. (1958) reprint 1993. Illus.
Paper. $8.95. 32pp. . . . . Vendor G0011

1361 **THOS. FERRIER & SOME DESC.,** by E.E. Lane. 1906.
Paper. $11.00. 56pp. . . . . Vendor G0259

1362 **PART. GEN. OF THE FERRIS FAM.,** by C. Crowell. 1899.
Paper. $12.00. 60pp. . . . . Vendor G0259

1363 **FIELD GENEALOGY, BEING THE RECORD OF ALL OF THE FIELD FAM. IN AMERICA WHOSE ANC. WERE IN THIS COUNTRY PRIOR TO 1700,** by F.C. Pierce. 2 vols. 1901.
Cloth, $169.00. Paper, $159.00. 1,196pp. . . . . Vendor G0259

1364 **FIELDS OF SOWERBY NEAR HALIFAX, ENG. & FLUSHING, N.Y., WITH SOME NOTICES OF THE FAMILIES OF UNDERHILL, BOWNE, BURLING, HAZARD & OSGOOD,** by O. Field. 1895.
Cloth, $31.00. Paper, $21.00. 138pp. Vendor G0259

1365 **GEN. OF THE FIELDS OF PROVIDENCE, R.I.,** by H.A. Brownell. 1878.
Paper. $13.00. 65pp. . . . . Vendor G0259

1366 **RECORD OF THE FAM. OF REV. DAVID D. FIELD, D.D., OF STOCKBRIDGE, MASS.,** by H.M. Field. 1880.
Cloth, $32.00. Paper, $22.00. 147pp. Vendor G0259

1367 **THE DESCENDANTS OF STEPHEN FIELD OF KING AND QUEEN COUNTY, VIRGINIA 1721,** by Alexander Lloyd Wiatt. 1992. Indexed. Illus.
The descendants of Stephen **Field** (d. 1721/2) of King and Queen County,

Virginia and his wife, Susannah Churchill **Jones**, are traced. The work includes a monograph about each member of the family through ten generations. There is also information on collateral families. These include: **Catesby, Cocke, Catlett, Jones, Lightfoot, Smith, Tabb, Taliaferro, Todd**, and **Wiatt**. Cloth. $12.50. 206pp. .... Vendor G0137

1368 **THE FIELDEN STREAM: A FAMILY HISTORY OF THE FIELDENS OF EAST TENNESSEE**, by Marvel Fielden. 1991. Indexed. Illus. Cloth. $75.00. 690pp. .... Vendor G0183

1369 **SO SOON FORGOTTEN. THREE THOUSAND FILLMORES: THE DESCENDANTS OF JOHN, THE MARINER, & HIS WIFE, ABIGAIL (TILTON) FILLMORE**, by Charles L. Fillmore; edited by Elizabeth F. Etter. 1984. Reprinted by permission. Cloth, $95.00. Paper, $85.00. 715pp. .... Vendor G0259

1370 **FILLOW, PHILO & PHILEO GEN.: A REC. OF THE DESC. OF JOHN FILLOW, HUGUENOT REFUGEE FROM FRANCE**, by D.H. Van Hoosear. 1888. Cloth, $53.50. Paper, $43.50. 274pp. .... Vendor G0259

1371 **MEMOIRS OF CLAN FINGON, WITH FAMILY TREE**, by Donald D. MacKinnon. 1909 (Scotland). Cloth, $49.00. Paper, $39.00. 246pp. .... Vendor G0259

1372 **FINNELL BIBLE RECORDS AND FINNELL CEMETERY TRAN-SCRIPTS**, by Arthur Louis Finnell. 1993. Indexed. Paper. $10.00. 56pp. .... Vendor G0256

1373 **JACOB FISCHER, THE IMMIGR. EARLY SETTLER IN THE PERKIOMAN VAL.**, by Dotterer and Strassburger. 1927. Paper. $8.00. 39pp. .... Vendor G0259

1374 **THE GEN. & DESC. OF LUKE FISH, SR., IN CHRONOLOGICAL OR-DER FROM 1760–1904**, by D. Fish. 1904. Paper. $16.00. 80pp. .... Vendor G0259

1375 **FISHBACK FAM. IN AMER. DESC. OF JOHN FISHBACK, THE EMIGR., WITH HIST. SKETCH OF HIS FAM. & THE COL. AT GERMANNA & GERMANTOWN, VA.**, by W.M. Kemper. 1914. Cloth, $66.50. Paper, $56.50. 356pp. .... Vendor G0259

1376 **DESCENDANTS AND HISTORY OF CHRISTIAN FISHER (1757–1838)**, by John M. Fisher; edited by Katie Beiler. 3rd ed. 1988. Cloth. $28.00. 568pp. .... Vendor G0150

1377 **GEN. OF JOSEPH FISHER & HIS DESC., & OF THE ALLIED FAM. OF FARLEY, FARLEE, FEHERMAN, PITNER, REEDER, & SHIPMAN**, by C.W. Fisher. 1890. Cloth, $46.50. Paper, $36.50. 243pp. .... Vendor G0259

1378 **LIFE OF GEORGE FISHER (1795–1873) & THE HIST. OF THE FISHER FAM. IN MISSISSIPPI**, by Parmenter, Fisher, and Mallette. 1959. Cloth, $57.00. Paper, $47.00. 299pp. .... Vendor G0259

1379 **THE FISHER GEN. RECORD OF THE DESC. OF JOSHUA, ANTHONY**

& CORNELIUS FISHER, OF DEDHAM, MASS. **1636–40**, by P.A. Fisher.
1898.
Cloth, $70.00. Paper, $60.00. 474pp. .... Vendor G0259

1380 **FISKE & FISH FAM.; THE DESC. OF SYMOND FISKE, LORD OF THE MANOR, STUDHAUGH, SUFFOLK CO., ENG., FROM THE TIME OF HENRY IV TO DATE, INCL. ALL AMER. MEMBERS OF THE FAM.**, by F.C. Pierce. 1896.
Cloth, $92.00. Paper, $82.00. 660pp. .... Vendor G0259

1381 **FISKE FAM. A HIST. OF THE FAM. (ANC. & DESC.) OF WM. FISKE, SEN., OF AMHERST, N.H., WITH BRIEF NOTICES OF OTHER BRANCHES**, by A.A. Fiske. 1867.
Cloth, $42.50. Paper, $32.50. 216pp. .... Vendor G0259

1382 **A FITCH FAMILY HISTORY**, by John Townsend Fitch. 1990. Indexed. Illus. Book #1175.
Cloth. $41.50. 288pp. .... Vendor G0082

1383 **GEN. OF THE FITCH FAM. IN NORTH AMERICA**, by J.G. Fitch. 1886.
Paper. $17.50. 116pp. .... Vendor G0259

1384 **HIST. OF THE FITCH FAM., 1400–1930**, by R.C. Fitch. 2 vols. 1930.
Cloth, $99.00. Paper, $89.00. 557pp. .... Vendor G0259

1385 **PURITAN IN THE WILDERNESS: A BIOGRAPHY OF THE REV. JAMES FITCH 1622–1702**, by John Townsend Fitch. 1993. Indexed. Illus. Book #1444.
Cloth. $43.50. 336pp. .... Vendor G0082

1386 **THE BIOGRAPHICAL & GENEALOGICAL RECORDS OF THE FITE FAMILIES IN THE U.S.**, by E.M.S. Fite. 1907.
Cloth, $38.00. Paper, $28.00. 175pp. .... Vendor G0259

1387 **GEN. OF THE FITTS OF FITZ FAM. IN AMER.**, by J.H. Fitts. 1869.
Paper. $18.00. 91pp. .... Vendor G0259

1388 **DESCENDANTS OF WILLIAM FITZHUGH OF VIRGINIA**, by Carol A. Hauk. 1995. Indexed.
Paper. $35.00. 145pp. .... Vendor G0340

1389 **FITZRANDOLPH FAMILY, FROM "FAMILY SKETCHES,"** by J.R. Wood. 1870.
Paper. $10.00. 49pp. .... Vendor G0259

1390 **FITZ RANDOLPH TRADITIONS: A STORY OF A THOUSAND YEARS**, by L.V.F. Randolph. 1907.
Cloth, $34.00. Paper, $24.00. 134pp. .... Vendor G0259

1391 **DESCENDANTS OF JOSIAH FLAGG OF BERKELEY CO. WV, WITH SKETCHES OF FLAGG, KEYES, FOSS, SHIVELEY, HUGHES, SLEMONS & CAMPBELL ANCESTRIES**, compiled by C.A. Flagg. 1920.
Paper. $18.00. 93pp. .... Vendor G0259

1392 **FAM. RECORDS OF THE DESC. OF GERSHOM FLAGG OF LANCASTER, MASS., WITH RECORDS OF THE FLAGG FAM. DESC.**

FROM THOMAS FLEGG OF WATERTOWN, MASS., by N.G. Flagg and L.C.S. Flagg. 1907.
Cloth, $36.00. Paper, $26.00. 173pp. Vendor G0259

1393 **[Flagg]. GEN. NOTES ON THE FOUNDING OF NEW ENG.; MY ANC. PART IN THAT UNDERTAKING**, by E. Flagg. 1926.
Cloth, $49.00. Paper, $39.00. 440pp. Vendor G0259

1394 **FLANDERS FAM. FROM EUROPE TO AMER.: BEING A HIST. OF THE FLANDERS FAM. IN AMER. & ITS PROBABLE ORIGIN IN EUROPE**, by E.F. Dunbar. 1935.
Cloth, $149.00. Paper, $139.00. 1,032pp. . . . . Vendor G0259

1395 **FLANINGAM FAMILY HISTORY**, by Ora L. Flaningam. 1991. Indexed. Illus.
This excellent genealogy contains all of the known descendants of Patrick **Flaningham**, who died in 1713.
Paper. $41.00. 740pp. . . . . Vendor G0069

1396 **GEORGE FLEEK & HIS DESC.: A HIST. OF THE FLEEKS & MALONEYS OF N.W. PA.**, by G. Southworth. 1958.
Cloth, $29.00. Paper, $19.00. 120pp. Vendor G0259

1397 **GEORGE FLEEK & HIS DESC.: HIST. OF THE FLEEKS & MALONEYS OF NW PENNA., WITH ADD. NOTES ON THE HIST. OF LITTLE COOLEY, PA.**, by G. Southworth. 1958.
Cloth, $31.00. Paper, $21.00. 120pp. Vendor G0259

1398 **FLEMING FAMILY & ALLIED LINES: BAIRD, BLAIR, BUTLER, COOK, CHILDS, CLARK, COLE, CRANE, ET AL**, by P.V. Lawson. 1903.
Cloth, $56.50. Paper, $46.50. 304pp. Vendor G0259

1399 **FLEMING FAMILY RECORDS**, by J.M. Seaver. 1929.
Paper. $8.00. 40pp. . . . . Vendor G0259

1400 **FLETCHER GEN.; AN ACCT. OF THE DESC. OF ROBERT FLETCHER OF CONCORD, MASS.**, by E.H. Fletcher. 1871.
Cloth, $46.50. Paper, $36.50. 279pp. Vendor G0259

1401 **GEN. IN PART OF THE FLETCHER–CROWDER–TUCKER FAM.**, by G.J. Anderson. 1909.
Paper. $15.00. 92pp. . . . . Vendor G0259

1402 **FLICKINGER FAM. HIST.**, by R.E. Flickinger. 1927.
Cloth, $119.00. Paper, $109.00. 820pp. . . . . Vendor G0259

1403 **A GEN. REGISTER OF THE DESC. OF THOMAS FLINT, OF SALEM**, by J. Flint and J.H. Stone. 1860.
Cloth, $31.50. Paper, $21.50. 150pp. Vendor G0259

1404 **THOMAS FLINT & WM. FLINT OF SALEM, MA. & THEIR DESC.; ALSO THE PROBABLY UNRELATED LINES OF LT. ROBT. FLINT OF SPROUTBROOK, MONTGOMERY CO., NY, & ROBT. FLINT OF VA. & TRENTON**, by A.M. Smith. 1931.
Cloth, $40.00. Paper, $30.00. 232pp. Vendor G0259

1405 **GENEALOGY OF THE FLORY–DINKEY FAMILY, WITH DIRECT AN-CESTORS INCL. BOYD, WALLACE, CARNAHAN, COBB, ET AL, & COLLATERAL LINES & ROYAL & MAGNA CARTA ANCESTRY,** by G.F. Dinkey. 1946.
Paper. $19.00. 98pp. .... Vendor G0259

1406 **BIOGR. GEN. OF THE VA.–KY. FLOYD FAM.,** by N.J. Floyd. 1912.
Cloth, $30.00. Paper, $20.00. 113pp. .... Vendor G0259

1407 **[Floyd-Jones]. THOMAS JONES, FT. NECK, QUEENS CO. LONG IS-LAND, 1695, & HIS DESC.: THE FLOYD-JONES FAM., WITH CONN. FROM THE YEAR 1066,** by T. Floyd-Jones. 1906.
Cloth, $39.50. Paper, $29.50. 183+11pp. .... Vendor G0259

1408 **A FAMILY HISTORY [FOGG, UPTON, MEAD, WARE & LOCKWOOD FAMILIES],** by F.F. McMaster. 1964.
Cloth, $36.00. Paper, $26.00. 158pp. .... Vendor G0259

1409 **FOGG FAM. OF AMER. REUNIONS OF THE FOGG FAM. (1ST TO 6TH) 1902–06,** by Fogg & Willis. 1907.
Cloth, $34.00. Paper, $24.00. 141pp. .... Vendor G0259

1410 **GEN. OF THE FOGG FAM. DESC. OF SAMUEL FOGGE,** by H. Fogg. 1903.
Paper. $9.50. 49pp. .... Vendor G0259

1411 **THE FOLEYS FROM COUNTY CLARE, IRELAND,** by Thomas R. and Harriet E. Foley. 1994. Indexed. Illus.
Cloth. $52.50. 317pp. .... Vendor G0335

1412 **THE FOLLETT–DEWEY, FASSETT–SAFFORD ANC. OF CAPT. MAR-TIN DEWEY FOLLETT (1765–1831) & HIS WIFE, PERSIS FASSETT (1767–1849),** by H.P. Ward. 1896.
Cloth, $47.00. Paper, $37.00. 249pp. .... Vendor G0259

1413 **A GEN. OF THE FOLSOM FAM. JOHN FOLSOM & HIS DESC. 1615–1882,** by J. Chapman. 1882.
Cloth, $49.00. Paper, $39.00. 297pp. .... Vendor G0259

1414 **GEN. OF THE FOLSOM FAM., 1638–1938. REV. & EXT. ED. INCL. ENG. RECORDS,** by E. Folsom. 2 vols. 1938.
Cloth, $169.00. Paper, $159.00. 1,135pp. .... Vendor G0259

1415 **[Fontaine]. MEMOIRS OF A HUGUENOT FAMILY and Other Family Manuscripts; Comprising an Original Journal of Travels in Virginia, New York, etc., in 1715 and 1716,** by Rev. James Fontaine; edited by Ann Maury. (1853) reprint 1994. Illus.
Drawn from authentic family papers of the famous Huguenot family of Jacques **Fontaine** and the families of Fontaine and **Maury**. Traces the history of the family of **De la Fontaine** in France, England, Ireland, and Virginia.
Paper. $37.00. 512pp. .... Vendor G0011

1416 **FOOTE FAMILY, COMPR. THE GEN. & HIST. OF NATHANIEL FOOTE, OF WETHERSFIELD, CT., & HIS DESC.,** by A.W. Foote. Vol. I. 1907.
Cloth, $99.00. Paper, $89.00. 607pp. .... Vendor G0259

1417 **FOOTE FAMILY.** Vol. II. 2nd ed. 1932.
Cloth, $109.00. Paper, $99.00. 723pp. . . . . Vendor G0259

1418 **FOOTE FAMILY, OR THE DESCENDANTS OF NATHANIEL FOOTE, ONE OF THE FIRST SETTLERS OF WETHERSFIELD, CT., WITH GENEALOGICAL NOTES OF PASCO FOOTE, WHO SETTLED IN SALEM, MA., & JOHN FOOTE & OTHERS WHO SETTLED MORE RECENTLY IN N.Y.**, by Nathaniel Goodwin. 1849.
Cloth, $62.00. Paper, $52.00. 360pp. Vendor G0259

1419 **FORBES & FORBUSH GEN.; THE DESC. OF DANIEL FORBUSH, WHO CAME FROM SCOTLAND ABOUT 1655 & SETTLED IN MARLBOROUGH, MASS. IN 1675**, by F.C. Pierce. 1892.
Cloth, $40.00. Paper, $30.00. 199pp. Vendor G0259

1420 **THE HOUSE OF FORBES**, ed. by A. and H. Tayler. 1937 (Scotland).
Cloth, $86.50. Paper, $76.50. 494pp. Vendor G0259

1421 **FORD FAMILY HISTORY**, by J.M. Seaver.
Paper. $7.00. 33pp. . . . . Vendor G0259

1422 **FORD FAMILY RECORDS**, by J. Montgomery Seaver. Illus.
Paper. $7.00. 33pp. . . . . Vendor G0011

1423 **FORD GEN.; AN ACCT. OF SOME OF THE FORDS WHO WERE EARLY SETTLERS IN NEW ENG., PARTICULARLY THE DESC. OF MARTIN–MATHEW FORD OF BRADFORD, ESSEX CO., MA.**, by E.R. Ford. 1916.
Cloth, $47.00. Paper, $37.00. 249pp. Vendor G0259

1424 **THE VALLEY OF THE SHADOW; A GEN. STUDY OF THE ANC. & DESC. OF CAPT. PAUL FORD OF LYMAN, MAINE, 1577–1952**, by P.G. Ford. 1953.
Paper. $11.50. 59pp. . . . . Vendor G0259

1425 **FOREMAN–FARMAN–FORMAN GEN. DESC. OF WM. FOREMAN, WHO CAME FROM LONDON, ENG., IN 1675 & SETTLED NEAR AN-NAPOLIS, MD.**, by E. Farman. 1911.
Cloth, $44.50. Paper, $34.50. 232pp. Vendor G0259

1426 **FORMAN GEN. DESC. OF ROBT. FORMAN OF KENT CO. MD., ROBT. FORMAN OF L.I., N.Y. & THE FORMAN FAM. OF MONMOUTH CO. N.J.**, by A.S. Dendridge. 1903.
Cloth, $33.00. Paper, $23.00. 151pp. Vendor G0259

1427 **A HIST. OF THE ANC. & DESC. OF WM. & DOROTHY WORTHEN FORREST OF CANTERBURY BOROUGH, N.H.**, by L.R.H. Cross. 1897.
Cloth, $32.00. Paper, $22.00. 145pp. Vendor G0259

1428 **FRANK FORST AND BERTHA GULATH OF ST. LOUIS, 1900**, by William L. Forst. 1995. Illus.
Includes the **Forst-Boul** ancestry (France) and the **Gulath-Schwarz** ancestry (Germany). Autobiographies of the eight children included. The Genealogy is indexed (not complete).
Cloth. $25.00. 200pp. . . . . Vendor G0207

1429 **THE FORSTHOFF FAMILIES AND THEIR CONNECTIONS**, by Lyle Brooks Watson. 1995. Indexed. Illus.
   This book traces several immigrant ancestors from their German origins to the present generations. An every-name index will assist you in tracing your own roots. **Forsthoff, Yaklin, Hartings, Rindler, Brooks, Kessen, Ashman, Vorsthoven, Wyant, Puthoff, Mader/Moeder, Goeke, Galland, Fullenkamp, Buschur, Bomholt, Lenzen, Rentz, Voskuhl**, and **Watson** are a few of the "connections."
   Cloth. $80.00. 285pp. .... Vendor G0366

1430 **MEMORIAL OF THE FAM. OF FORSYTH DE FRONSAC**, by F.G.F. de Fronsac. 1903.
   Paper. $18.50. 104pp. .... Vendor G0259

1431 **FORSYTHE, SCRIBNER, MOSELEY, ETC. FAMILY 16MM MICRO-FILM COMPILATIONS**, compiled by Warren Louis Forsythe. 1996. Indexed.
   Surnames covered on the various reels of microfilm include **Baird, Moses** (ca.1736–1782), 2,000 descendants originating in old PA/OH: computerized index to some descendancies by Stewart Baldwin.
   Forsyth: 1,000 families compiled by William H. Forsyth and Edward E. Forsyth. **Frame**: James (ca. 1729–1794), 1,000 descendants originating in old PA/OH. **Janes**: computerized index to the book by Reba **Neighbors Collins**. **Keith**: inferences from old Vermont vital records. **Kelker** and **Kolliker** of old PA and Switzerland: computerized index to the books. **Knowles**: 50 selected families of old NH/ME. **Lee** of old Nelson Co., KY, St. Mary's Co., MD. **Marshall** of old VA: 100 selected families. **Martin** of old VA/TN: 100 selected families. **Moseley** of old VA: 3,000 descendants. **Prince** of old MA: 300 people

in 2 separate lines. **Ramsay/Ramsey**: 500 people in 3 lines from old PA. **Rapier** of Old Nelson Co., KY, St. Mary's Co., MD. **Robe** of old PA/OH: computerized index to the 1,000 person descendancy by Margaret **Robe Summitt**. **Scribner**: 3,000 descendants originating from NH/CT: index to Raymond Scribner & Bourdon Scribner's work. **Stokely**: 500 descendants originating in old TN. **Tenley**: 1,000 descendants of old MD/KY etc. **Young**: 50 selected families of old NH/ME.
$20.00 per reel includes tax (16mm microfilm only).
Approx. 7,000pp. .... Vendor G0401

1432 **A FAMILY CALLED FORT: THE DESCENDANTS OF ELIAS FORT OF VIRGINIA**, by Homer T. Fort, Jr. and Drucilla Stovall Jones. 1970.
Cloth, $107.50. Paper, $97.50. 757pp. .... Vendor G0259

1433 **THE FORTINEUX FAMILY NEWS (THE FORTNEY, FORTNA, FORDNEY AND FURTNEY FAMILY NEWSLETTER)**. Issued quarterly.
Editor: Dean McKnight, 11409 Dewey Road, Silver Spring, MD 20906-4814.
E-mail: DeanM10529@aol.com
Researcher/Officer: Phillip G. Goff, 1097 Sanford's Walk, Tucker, GA 30084-1431. E-mail: GOFFPH@aol.com
Subscription. $10.00 for two years. 8 pp. .... Vendor G0416

1434 **THE FORTINEUX–FORTINET FAMILY (FORTNEY, FORTNA, FORDNEY, FURTNEY) IN AMERICA**, by Evajean Fortney McKnight. 1989.
20,000 every-name index. Illus.
Comprehensive genealogical history of the **Fortineux–Fortinet** family, from mid-1600s to present, relates their immigration to America from Otterberg, Germany during early 1700s. Earliest known ancestors Jonas **Fortineux** and Sara **Menton** were married ca. 1674 in the French Reformed Church built in Otterberg in 1154. As the family spread out in colonial America the name took on 39 various spellings. Included are biographies, maps, photographs, document reproductions.
Cloth. $45.00. 600pp. .... Vendor G0416

1435 **FOSDICK FAM., OYSTER BAY BRANCH 1583–1891, RECORD OF ANC. & DESC. OF SAMUEL FOSDICK OF OYSTER BAY**, by L.L. Fosdick. 1891.
Cloth, $36.50. Paper, $26.50. 137pp. .... Vendor G0259

1436 **ANNALS OF THE FOSDICK FAM.**, by R. Fosdick. 1953.
Cloth, $38.50. Paper, $28.50. 189pp. .... Vendor G0259

1437 **FOSSELMANN/FUSSELMAN AND ALLIED FAMILIES**, by Alice Ann Askew. (1982) second edition 1993. Indexed. Illus.
The **Fusselmans** and **Probsts** came from Minfeld and Kandel Germania to America in 1732. Many allied families including **Zeislof, Yerian, Barnes, Hess, Leibensperger, Weitzel, Minich**.
Paper. $16.00. 258pp. .... Vendor G0284

1438 **COL. JOSEPH FOSTER (1730–1804), HIS CHILDREN & GRANDCHILDREN, WITH SUPPLEMENTAL RECORDS, 1887–1947**, by J. Foster and E.A. Foster. 1947.
Cloth, $72.00. Paper, $62.00. 416pp. .... Vendor G0259

1439 **FOSTER GEN. A RECORD OF THE POSTERITY OF REGINALD FOS-**

TER, EARLY INHABITANT OF IPSWICH & ALL OTHER AMERICAN FOSTERS, by F.C. Pierce. 1899.
Cloth, $145.00. Paper, $135.00. 1,081pp. .... Vendor G0259

1440 PEDIGREE OF JESSE W. FOSTER: THE LINES OF FOSTER, COGGIN, FARLEY, PHELPS, BURRITT, CURTISS, LORD, SMITH, WEBSTER, & ALLIED FAMS., by G.E. Foster. 1897.
Cloth, $40.00. Paper, $30.00. 253pp. .... Vendor G0259

1441 THE FOSTER FAM. ONE LINE OF THE DESC. OF WILLIAM FOS-TER, SON OF REGINALD FOSTER OF IPSWICH, MASS., by P. Derby. 1872.
Paper. $7.00. 35pp. .... Vendor G0259

1442 GEN. OF THE DESC. OF THEOBALD FOUSE (FAUSS), INCL. MANY OTHER CONNECTED FAM., by G.M. Brumbaugh and J.G. Fouse. 1914.
Cloth, $58.00. Paper, $48.00. 302pp. .... Vendor G0259

1443 DESCENDANTS OF GEORGE FOWLE (1610/11?–1682) OF CHARLESTOWN, MASSACHUSETTS, by Eugene Chalmers Fowle. 1990. Indexed. Illus.
Cloth. $53.50. 316pp. .... Vendor G0406

1444 ANNALS OF THE FOWLER FAMILY, WITH BRANCHES IN VA., N.C., S.C., TENN., KY., ALABAMA, MISS., CALIF. & TEXAS, by G.D.F. Arthur. 1901.
Cloth, $61.00. Paper, $51.00. 327pp. .... Vendor G0259

1445 DESC. OF PHILIP & MARY FOWLER OF IPSWICH, MASS., 1590–1882, by M. Stickney. 1883.
Cloth, $50.00. Paper, $40.00. 269pp. .... Vendor G0259

1446 WILLIAM FOWLER, THE MAGISTRATE, & ONE LINE OF HIS DESC., by W.C. Fowler.
Paper. $7.50. 41pp. .... Vendor G0259

1447 FOX COUSINS BY THE DOZENS (INCLUDES ALLIED LINES ALDRIDGE, BALLARD, BERRYMAN, BROOKSHIRE, CONKWRIGHT, FISH, FRANKLIN, HAGGARD, HALEY, HUGHES, PARRISH, NOE, OLIVER, TODD, TUTTLE, VIVION), by Nellie Fox Adams and Bertha Fox Walton. 1976.
Cloth, $69.50. Paper, $59.50. 408pp. .... Vendor G0259

1448 FOX AND ADLER: A HISTORY OF TWO FAMILIES, by William Adler Fox. 1994. Indexed. Illus.
Ancestors and descendants of Simon **Fuchs** (1863–1930) and David **Adler** (1834–1886) and their German-Jewish families who emigrated to Cincinnati in the 1880s.
Cloth. $30.00. 144pp. .... Vendor G0162

1449 FOX FAM. MARRIAGES, by W.M. Clemens. 1916.
Paper. $9.00. 44pp. .... Vendor G0259

1450 HIST. OF THAT PT. OF THE FOX FAM. DESC. FROM THOMAS FOX OF CAMBRIDGE, MA., by N. Fox. 1899.
Cloth, $46.00. Paper, $36.00. 240pp. .... Vendor G0259

1451 **THE DESC. OF THOS. FOX OF CONCORD, MASS., THROUGH HIS SIXTH SON ISAAC, OF MEDFORD, MASS. & NEW LONDON, CONN.,** by G.H. Fox. 1931.
Paper. $10.00. 54pp. .... Vendor G0259

1452 **OUT OF THE HOUSE OF FRACHE: CHRISTOPHER & PETER & THEIR ASSOCIATED AMERICAN FAMILIES,** by Genevieve C. Kennedy. 1980.
Cloth, $57.50. Paper, $47.50. 311pp. .... Vendor G0259

1453 **DESC. OF ROBT FRANCIS OF WETHERSFIELD CT.; GEN. RECORDS OF VARIOUS BRANCHES OF THE FRANCIS FAM. OF CT. ORIGIN,** by C.E. Francis. 1906.
Cloth, $39.50. Paper, $29.50. 226pp. .... Vendor G0259

1454 **"TIME AND TIDE": A FRANCISCO FAMILY HISTORY,** by Virginia B. Fletcher. 1989. Indexed. Illus.
Surnames include: **Bowen, Francisco, Summerfield.**
Cloth. $38.00. 450pp. .... Vendor G0332

1455 **DESCENDANTS OF JAMES ISAIAH FRANKLIN (b. 1825, ST HELENA PARISH LA),** by Chaplain Dan Franklin. 1992.
Cloth, $51.50. Paper, $41.50. 257pp. .... Vendor G0259

1456 **DESCENDANTS OF SIMON FRASER OF LAGGAN, INVERNESS-SHIRE, SCOTLAND, & ALLIED FAMILIES IN SCOTLAND, CANADA & U.S.,** by M.I.F. Brewster. 1956.
Cloth, $44.00. Paper, $34.00. 219pp. .... Vendor G0259

1457 **HIST. OF THE FRASERS OF LOVAT, WITH GEN. OF THE PRINCIPAL FAMS. OF THE NAME; TO WHICH IS ADDED THOSE OF DUNBALLOCH & PHOPACHY,** by A. Mackenzie. 1906 (Scotland).
Cloth, $115.00. Paper, $105.00. 761pp. .... Vendor G0259

1458 **SOME FRASER PEDIGREES [OF INVERNESS-SHIRE, SCOTLAND],** by D. Warrand. 1934 (Scotland).
Cloth, $39.50. Paper, $29.50. 8+177pp. .... Vendor G0259

1459 **THE JOHNSTON & BACON SCOTTISH CLAN HISTORIES: The Clan Fraser of Lovat,** by Charles Ian Fraser. 2nd ed. (1966) reprint 1993. Illus.
Paper. $8.95. 32pp. .... Vendor G0011

1460 **FRASHER/FRAZIER FAMILY HISTORY—THEIR KINSMEN WEBB–THOMPSON–LOWE–WELLMAN–AKERS–ROBERTSON–HOOSER–BARTRAM,** by Harry Leon Sellards, Jr. 1991. Indexed. Illus.
Related families: **Maynard, Alley, Wilson, Adkins, Perry, Ferguson, Frasure, Smith, Napier, Carter.**
Cloth. $42.00. 568pp. .... Vendor G0445

1461 **FREEMAN GEN., PT. I: MEM. OF EDMUND OF SANDWICH & HIS DESC.; II: SAMUEL OF WATERTOWN & HIS DESC. & III: NOTES ON OTHER FREEMAN FAM.,** by F. Freeman. 2nd ed. 1875.
Cloth, $68.00. Paper, $58.00. 457pp. .... Vendor G0259

1462 **FREESE GEN.,** by C.N. Sinnett. 1929.
Paper. $14.00. 68pp. .... Vendor G0259

1463 A GEN. HIST. OF THE FRENCH & ALLIED FAMILIES, by M.Q. Beyer. 1912.
Cloth, $68.50. Paper, $58.50. 373pp. .... Vendor G0259

1464 AMER. ANC. OF CHARLES E. FRENCH & HIS WIFE ANNA RICH-
MOND WARNER, by A.R.W. French. 1894.
Cloth, $35.00. Paper, $25.00. 187pp. .... Vendor G0259

1465 CO. RECORDS OF THE SURNAMES FRANCUS, FRANCEIS, FRENCH
IN ENG., A.D. 1100–1350, by A.D.W. French. 1896.
Cloth, $86.50. Paper, $76.50. 602pp. .... Vendor G0259

1466 FRENCH FAMILY, 1555–1995: GENEALOGY OF THOMAS FRENCH
& SUSAN RIDDLESDALE (BOSTON, 1629), & THEIR NEW HAMP-
SHIRE & MAINE DESCENDANTS, by Eleanor M. Crouch. 1995.
Cloth, $39.50. Paper, $29.50. 170pp. .... Vendor G0259

1467 GEN. OF THE DESC. OF THOMAS FRENCH, WHO SETTLED IN
BERLINTON (BURLINGTON) WEST N.J., by H.B. French. Vol. I. 1909.
Cloth, $86.00. Paper, $76.00. 501pp. .... Vendor G0259

1468 GEN. OF THE DESC. OF THOMAS FRENCH. Vol. II. 1913.
Cloth, $115.00. Paper, $105.00. 743pp. .... Vendor G0259

1469 NOTES ON THE SURNAMES OF FRANCUS, FRANCEIS, FRENCH,
ETC., IN SCOTLAND, WITH AN ACCT. OF THE FRENCHES OF
THORNDYKES, by A.D.W. French. 1893.
Paper. $19.00. 109pp. .... Vendor G0259

1470 A BRIEF HIST. OF JOHN & CHRISTIAN FRETZ, & A COMPLETE
GEN. FAM. REG., by A. J. Fretz. 1890.
Cloth, $93.00. Paper, $83.00. 609pp. .... Vendor G0259

1471 FRISBEE–FRISBIE. EDWARD FRISBYE OF BRANFORD, CT., & HIS
DESC., WITH APPENDIX OF BRIEF LIN. OF FISKES, HASKELLS,
MABVIES, PARKES, by E. Frisbee. 1926.
Cloth, $119.00. Paper, $109.00. 778pp. .... Vendor G0259

1472 FROST FAM. IN ENG. & AMER., WITH SPECIAL REF. TO EDMUND
FROST & SOME DESC., by T. and E. Frost. 1909.
Cloth, $32.50. Paper, $22.50. 177pp. .... Vendor G0259

1473 FROST GENEALOGY; DESC. OF WM. FROST OF OYSTER BAY, NY,
SHOWING CONN. WITH THE WINTHROP, UNDERHILL, FEKE,
BROWN & WICKES FAMS., by J. Frost. 1912.
Cloth, $67.00. Paper, $57.00. 458pp. .... Vendor G0259

1474 SUPPLEMENT TO THE FROST GENEALOGY OF 1912, by Josephine C.
Frost. 1914. Indexed.
Paper. $5.75. 42pp. .... Vendor G0182

1475 FROST GENEALOGY IN FIVE FAM., by N.S. Frost. 1926.
Cloth, $74.00. Paper, $64.00. 410pp. .... Vendor G0259

1476 THE NICHOLAS FROST FAM., INCL. SUPPL., by J.E. Frost. 1943.
Cloth, $35.50. Paper, $25.50. 170pp. .... Vendor G0259

1477 **FROTHINGHAM GENEALOGY**, by Wyman and Frothingham. 1916.
Cloth, $35.50. Paper, $25.50. 170pp. Vendor G0259

1478 **MEMOIR OF COL. JOSHUA FRY OF VA., WITH GEN. OF HIS DESC.
& ALLIED LINES**, by F. Slaughter.
Cloth, $33.50. Paper, $23.50. 113pp. Vendor G0259

1479 **FRYE GEN. ADRIAN OF KITTERY, MAINE: JOHN OF ANDOVER,
MASS., JOSHUA OF VA., THOMAS OF R.I., N.Y.**, by E.F. Barker. 1920.
Cloth, $39.00. Paper, $29.00. 194pp. Vendor G0259

1480 **THE CHARLES AND SARAH CUSTER FULK FAMILY,** by Patricia Turner
Ritchie. 1993. Indexed. Illus.
Cloth. $24.00. 325pp. . . . . Vendor G0365

1481 **THE FULL FAMILY, SIX GENERATIONS,** by Frances Lane Harris. 1994.
Indexed. Illus.
Full, Toothaker, Tibbetts, Morgan, Lane, Shadinger.
Paper. $13.00. 64pp. . . . . Vendor G0289

1482 **A BRIEF SKETCH OF THOMAS FULLER & HIS DESC., WITH HIST.
NOTES**, by J.F. Fuller. 1896.
Paper. $9.50. 47pp. . . . . Vendor G0259

1483 **ALDEN–FULLER RECORD. A RECORD OF THE DESC. OF LEMUEL
FULLER, SR.**, by M. Percy Black. 1896.
Paper. $15.00. 76pp. . . . . Vendor G0259

1484 **FULLER GEN.; RECORD OF JOSEPH FULLER, DESC., OF THOMAS
FULLER OF WOBURN & MIDDLETON, MASS.**, by E. Abercrombie. 1897.
Paper. $18.50. 101pp. . . . . Vendor G0259

1485 **GEN. OF SOME DESC. OF CAPT. MATTHEW FULLER, JOHN OF
NEWTON, JOHN OF LYNN, JOHN OF IPSWICH, & ROBERT OF
DORCHESTER & DEDHAM, WITH SUPPL. TO VOLS. I & II**, by W.H.
Fuller. 1914.
Cloth, $59.00. Paper, $49.00. 325pp. Vendor G0259

1486 **GEN. OF SOME DESC. OF EDWARD FULLER OF THE MAYFLOWER**,
by W.H. Fuller. 1908.
Cloth, $50.00. Paper, $40.00. 306pp. Vendor G0259

1487 **GEN. OF SOME DESC. OF DR. SAMUEL FULLER OF THE MAY-
FLOWER**, by W.H. Fuller. 1910.
Also includes a supplement to the *Gen. of Some Desc. of Edward Fuller of
the Mayflower* (see above listing).
Cloth, $44.00. Paper, $34.00. 263pp. Vendor G0259

1488 **GENEALOGY OF SOME DESCENDANTS OF THOMAS FULLER OF
WOBURN, WITH SUPPL. TO VOLS. I, II, III**, by W.H. Fuller. 1919.
Cloth, $52.50. Paper, $42.50. 271pp. Vendor G0259

1489 **GEN. OF THE FULLER FAM. DESC. FROM ROBERT FULLER OF
SALEM & REHOBETH, MASS.**, by N. Fuller. 1898.
Paper. $10.00. 50pp. . . . . Vendor G0259

1490 **FULTON–HAYDEN–WARNER ANC. IN AMER.**, by C.E. Leonard. 1923.
Cloth, $104.50. Paper, $94.50. 629pp. . . . . Vendor G0259

1491 **GEN. OF THE FULTON FAM., BEING DESC. OF JOHN FULTON, BORN IN SCOTLAND 1713. EMIGRATED TO AMERICA IN 1753. SETTLED IN NOTTINGHAM, CHESTER CO., PENN., 1762**, by H.R. Fulton. 1900.
Cloth, $45.50. Paper, $35.50. 238pp. Vendor G0259

1492 **BRIEF HIST. OF BISHOP HENRY FUNCK & OTHER FUNK PIONEERS, & A COMPLETE GEN. FAM. HIST., WITH BIOGR. OF DESC. FROM EARLIEST AVAILABLE RECORDS TO PRESENT**, by A.J. Fretz. 1899.
Cloth, $131.00. Paper, $121.00. 874pp. . . . . Vendor G0259

1493 **GAGE FAM.: JOHN GAGE OF IPSWICH & THOMAS OF YARMOUTH; WILLIAM OF FREETOWN; ROBERT OF WESTON; WILLIAM OF CANADA; GAGE FAM. OF THE SOUTH & ROBERT IN IRELAND**, by Rev. W. Gage. 1922.
Paper. $13.00. 65pp. . . . . Vendor G0259

1494 **REC. OF PIERCE GAGE & HIS DESC.**, by G. Gage. 1894.
Paper. $12.50. 62pp. . . . . Vendor G0259

1495 **DESCENDANTS OF THOMAS GAINES OF VIRGINIA**, by Carol A. Hauk. 1995. Indexed.
Paper. $45.00. 305pp. . . . . Vendor G0340

1496 **GALE FAM. RECORDS IN ENG. & U.S., & THE TOTTINGHAM FAM. OF NEW ENG., SOME ACCTS. OF THE BOGARDUS, WALDON & YOUNG FAM. OF N.Y.**, by G. Gale. 1866.
Cloth, $43.00. Paper, $33.00. 254pp. Vendor G0259

1497 **GEN. OF THE DESC. OF DAVID GALE OF SUTTON, MASS.**, by L.A.E. Gale. 1909.
Paper. $11.50. 57pp. . . . . Vendor G0259

1498 **HISTORY OF THE GALLEY FAMILY, WITH LOCAL & OLD-TIME SKETCHES IN THE YOUGH REGION**, by H. Galley and J.O. Arnold. 1908.
Cloth, $63.00. Paper, $53.00. 271pp. Vendor G0259

1499 **THE GEN. HIST. OF THE GALLUP FAM. IN THE U.S. WITH BIOGR. SKETCHES**, by J.D. Gallup. 1893.
Cloth, $65.00. Paper, $55.00. 329pp. Vendor G0259

1500 **DESC. OF JOHN GAMAGE OF IPSWICH, MASS.**, by A.L.G. Morton. 1906.
Paper. $16.00. 83pp. . . . . Vendor G0259

1501 **THE MOUNT DESERT WIDOW: GENEALOGY OF THE MAINE GAMBLE FAMILY FROM THE FIRST LANDING ON THE COAST OF MT. DESERT DOWN TO THE PRESENT DAY**, by G. and J.P. Cilley. 1896.
Cloth, $40.00. Paper, $30.00. 196pp. Vendor G0259

1502 **DESCENDANTS OF CHRISTIAN . . . AND ANNA GARBER OF LANCASTER COUNTY, PENNSYLVANIA**, by Allan A. Garber. 1985.
Cloth. $22.95. 138pp. . . . . Vendor G0150

1503 **JOHN H. GARBER AND BARBARA MILLER FAMILY RECORD**, by Floyd R. Mason.
In process . . . . Vendor G0345

1504 **NICHOLAS AND ELIZABETH GARBER FAMILY RECORD**, by Floyd R. Mason.
In process . . . . Vendor G0345

1505 **1599–1890. LION GARDINER & HIS DESC.**, by C.C. Gardiner. 1890.
Cloth, $39.00. Paper, $29.00. 195pp. Vendor G0259

1506 **THE GARDINERS OF NARRAGANSETT, A GEN. OF THE DESC. OF GEO. GARDINER, COLONIST, 1638**, by C.E. Robinson. 1919.
Cloth, $59.50. Paper, $49.50. 320pp. Vendor G0259

1507 **ANCESTRY OF DANIEL GARDNER V AND MARY (HODGES) GARDNER OF CHAMPAIGN, ILL., WITH OTHER GARDNER & HODGES RECORDS & HIST. & BIOGRAPHICAL NOTES**, by D. Hodges Gardner. 1915.
Paper. $11.00. 56pp. . . . . Vendor G0259

1508 **GARDNER/BALLARD AND ALLIED FAMILIES**, by O.W. and Leroy W. Gardner. 1995. Indexed. Illus.
Cloth. $60.00. 450+pp. . . . . Vendor G0310

1509 **GARDNER, GARDINER, GARDENER, GARNER NEWSLETTER**, by Sue Ann Gardner Shreve. 1994.
Queries accepted. Back issues available.
Subscription. $16.00 per year, published June and December . Vendor G0221

1510 **GARDNER HIST. & GEN.**, by L.M. and C.M. Gardner. 1907.
Cloth, $62.50. Paper, $52.50. 407pp. Vendor G0259

1511 **GARDNER HIST. & GEN.; DESC. OF THOMAS GARDNER (EXTR. FROM HEADLEY GEN.).** by A.J. Fretz. 1905.
Paper. $10.00. 49pp. . . . . Vendor G0259

1512 **GARDNER MEM'L: BIOGR. & GEN. REC. OF THE DESC. OF THOM. GARDNER, PLANTER, OF CAPE ANN, 1624; SALEM, 1626–74, THROUGH HIS SON LIEUT. GEO. GARDNER**, by F.A. Gardner. 1933.
Cloth, $54.00. Paper, $44.00. 295pp. Vendor G0259

1513 **THOMAS GARDNER, CAPE ANN 1623–1626, SALEM 1626–1674, & SOME OF HIS DESC., ESSEX CO., MA. & NO. NEW ENG. TO THE 8TH GEN. & NANTUCKET LINES TO THE 4TH GEN.**, by F.A. Gardner. 1907.
Cloth, $59.50. Paper, $49.50. 347pp. Vendor G0259

1514 **THE DESC. OF PETER GARLAND, MARINER, OF CHARLESTOWN, MASS., 1637**, by J. Garland. 1897.
Cloth, $38.00. Paper, $28.00. 219pp. Vendor G0259

1515 **GARNER—ONE LINE IN TENNESSEE AND TEXAS**, by Judy Montgomery. 1995. Indexed. Illus.
Direct line Blount, Anderson, Benton counties, Tennessee and Lampasas County, Texas. Allied **Henry, Parker, Bevill, Byrn, Duke**.
Cloth. $35.00. 205pp. . . . . Vendor G0388

1516 **GENEALOGY & STORY OF THE FAMILY OF ROBERT KIRTLEY GARNETT**, by H.E. Hobble & C.H. Garnett. 1955.
Cloth, $33.00. Paper, $23.00. 124pp. .... Vendor G0259

1517 **[Garr]. GENEALOGY OF THE DESCENDANTS OF JOHN GAR, OR MORE PARTICULARLY HIS SON, ANDREAS GAAR, WHO EMIGRATED FROM BAVARIA TO AMERICA IN 1732**, by J.W. and J.C. Garr. 1894.
Cloth, $99.50. Paper, $89.50. 608pp. .... Vendor G0259

1518 **HIST. OF WELCOME GARRETT & HIS DESC.**, by S.B. Garrett. 1909.
Cloth, $34.50. Paper, $24.50. 141pp. .... Vendor G0259

1519 **OUR GARRIGUES ANCESTORS, FRENCH HUGUENOTS CONNECTED TO CHARLEMAGNE & EUROPEAN ROYALTY**, by Patricia Wright Strati. 1992. Indexed. Illus.
Cloth. $40.00. 192pp. .... Vendor G0419

1520 **OUR GARST FAMILY IN AMERICA**, by W.T. Garst; edited by C.C. Garst. 1950.
Cloth, $65.00. Paper, $55.00. 363pp. .... Vendor G0259

1521 **THE DESC. OF AUTHUR GARY OF ROXBURY, MASS., WITH AN ACCT. OF THE POSTERITY OF STEPHEN GARY OF CHARLESTOWN, MASS. & A SO. CAROLINA FAM. OF THE SAME NAME**, by L. Brainerd. 1918.
Cloth, $45.00. Paper, $35.00. 235pp. .... Vendor G0259

1522 **[Gates]. DAWES–GATES ANCESTRAL LINES: A MEM'L VOL. CONTAINING THE AMER. ANC. OF RUFUS R. DAWES. VOL. II: GATES & ALLIED FAMILIES**, by M.W. Ferris. 1931.
Cloth, $127.50. Paper, $117.50. 918pp. .... Vendor G0259

1523 **[Gates]. OUR AMER. ANC.**, by F.T. Gates. 1928.
Cloth, $43.00. Paper, $33.00. 289pp. .... Vendor G0259

1524 **SILAS GATES OF STOW, MASS. & THE DESC. OF HIS SON PAUL GATES OF ASHBY**, by J. and S. Gates. 1907.
Cloth, $32.00. Paper, $22.00. 147pp. .... Vendor G0259

1525 **STEPHEN GATES OF BINGHAM & LANCASTER, MASS., & HIS DESC.**, by C.O. Gates. 1898.
Cloth, $57.50. Paper, $47.50. 370pp. .... Vendor G0259

1526 **GEDNEY & CLARKE FAM. OF SALEM, MA.**, by H. Waters. 1880.
Paper. $10.00. 52pp. .... Vendor G0259

1527 **GEE FAMILY: DESC. OF CHARLES GEE (d. 1709) & HANNAH G. (d. 1928) OF VA., WITH A CHAPTER ON THE ENGLISH BACK-GROUND**, by W.J. Fletcher. 1937.
Cloth, $39.00. Paper, $29.00. 157pp. .... Vendor G0259

1528 **GEN. OF THE GEER FAM. IN AMER. FROM 1635–1914**, by W. Geer and F.E. Youngs. 1914.
Cloth, $48.00. Paper, $38.00. 256pp. .... Vendor G0259

1529 **THE GEIGERS OF SOUTH CAROLINA**, compiled by Percy L. Geiger. (1950?)
Cloth, $39.50. Paper, $29.50. 191pp. .... Vendor G0259

1530 **GEIST RELATION: TWO HUNDRED YEARS IN AMERICA [DESC. OF CHRISTOPHER GEIST]**, by A.F. Geist. 1940.
Cloth, $139.50. Paper, $129.50. 925pp. .... Vendor G0259

1531 **JOHANN GENNING (1818–1898) AND HIS DESCENDANTS: A TOLEDO FAMILY**, by William B. Saxbe, C.G. 1988. Indexed. Illus.
With notes on the families of **Rust, Gunn, Kleinhans, Bruning, Holtgrieve**, and **Nesper**. Winner of the 1991 NGS Award for Excellence in Family History.
Cloth. $37.00. 292pp. .... Vendor G0328

1532 **GENTRY FAM. IN AMER.; 1676 TO 1909 INCL. NOTES ON THE CLAIBOURNE, HARRIS, SHARP & 12 OTHER FAMS.**, by R. Gentry. 1909.
Cloth, $62.50. Paper, $52.50. 406pp. .... Vendor G0259

1533 **ANCESTORS AND DESCENDANTS OF WARREN CAPERS GERADE AND PEARL EVA GIBSON INCLUDING SOME RELATED FAMILIES**, by William Allen Gerade. 1993. Illus.
The book records twelve generations in New England back to early 1600s covering surnames of **Gerade, Gibson, Amazeen, Walford, Arms, Hawks, Brown, Clifford, Forrest, Marsh**, and **Trefethen.**.
Cloth. $25.00. 330pp. .... Vendor G0283

1534 **HEINRICH GERNHARDT & HIS DESC.**, by J.M.M. Gernerd. 1904.
Cloth, $59.50. Paper, $49.50. 315pp. .... Vendor G0259

1535 **GEN. OF THE FAM. OF GAMALIEL GEROULD, SON OF DR. JACQUES JERAULD, OF THE PROVINCE OF LANGUEDOC, FRANCE**, by S.L. Gerould. 1885.
Paper. $17.00. 85pp. .... Vendor G0259

1536 **THE DESCENDANTS OF HENRY GIBBEL**, by Ira W. Gibbel. 1995.
Cloth. $42.00. 596pp. .... Vendor G0150

1537 **A GOLDEN LEGACY TO THE GIBBS IN AMERICA**, by M.B. Gibbs. 1893.
Paper. $15.50. 77pp. .... Vendor G0259

1538 **THE GIBBS FAM. OF R.I.**, by G. Gibbs. 1933.
Cloth, $40.00. Paper, $30.00. 195pp. .... Vendor G0259

1539 **JOHN GIBSON OF CAMBRIDGE, MASS. & HIS DESC., 1634–1899**, by M.C.C. Wilson. 1900.
Cloth, $79.50. Paper, $69.50. 547pp. .... Vendor G0259

1540 **THE GIDDINGS FAM.; OR, THE DESC. OF GEORGE GIDDINGS WHO CAME FROM ST. ALBANS, ENG. TO IPSWICH, MASS. IN 1635**, by M.S. Giddings. 1882.
Cloth, $44.00. Paper, $34.00. 227pp. .... Vendor G0259

1541 **ANCESTRY OF ELIHU B. GIFFORD (1830–1898) AND CATHERINE SANDOW BARROWS (1835–1917) OF SARATOGA COUNTY, NEW YORK, BUFFALO COUNTY WISCONSIN, AND SPOKANE COUNTY, WASHINGTON**, by Raymond L. Olson. 1989. Indexed. Includes 5 pictures.
Cloth. $23.00. 419pp. .... Vendor G0291

1542 **GIFFORD GEN., 1626–1896; DESC. OF WM. GIFFORD OF SANDWICH, MA., 1650**, by H.E. Gifford. 1896.
Cloth, $29.00. Paper, $19.00. 101pp. .... Vendor G0259

1543 **GILDART–GELDART FAMILIES**, by C.R. Gildart. 1962.
Cloth, $25.50. Paper, $15.50. 78pp. .... Vendor G0259

1544 **GILDERSLEEVE PIONEERS**, by W.H. Gildersleeve. 1941.
Cloth, $64.00. Paper, $54.00. 337pp. .... Vendor G0259

1545 **GILES MEM. GEN. MEM'L OF THE FAM. BEARING THE NAMES GILES, GOULD, HOLMES & OTHERS**, by J.A. Vinton. 1864.
Cloth, $91.00. Paper, $81.00. 608pp. .... Vendor G0259

1546 **[Gill]. NOTES HIST. SUR L'ORIGINE DE LA FAM. GILL DE SAINT-FRANCOIS DU LAC & ST THOMAS DE PIERREVILLE; HIST. DE MA PROPRE FAM.**, by C. Gill. 1887.
Paper. $15.00. 96pp. .... Vendor G0259

1547 **HISTORY & DESCENDANTS OF JAMES GILLESPIE 1760–1990**, by La Roux Gillespie. 1990. Indexed. Illus.
Paper. $35.00. 261pp. .... Vendor G0238

1548 **THE GILLESPIE CLAN NEWSLETTER**, by La Roux Gillespie. Annual. Indexed. Illus.
Subscription. $12.00 per year. 32pp. .... Vendor G0238

1549 **SEARCHES INTO THE HIST. OF THE GILLMAN OR GILMAN FAM., INCL. VARIOUS BRANCHES IN ENG., IRE., AMER. & BELGIUM**, by A.W. Gillman. 1895.
Cloth, $67.00. Paper, $57.00. 360pp. .... Vendor G0259

1550 **GEN. OF THE GILLSON/JILLSON FAM.**, by D. Jillson. 1876.
Cloth, $50.00. Paper, $40.00. 266pp. .... Vendor G0259

1551 **GILMAN FAMILY. TRACED IN THE LINE OF HON. JOHN GILMAN OF EXETER, N.H., WITH ACCT. OF MANY OTHER GILMANS IN ENG. & AMER.**, by A. Gilman. 1869.
Cloth, $52.00. Paper, $42.00. 324pp. .... Vendor G0259

1552 **THE GILMERS IN AMER.**, by J.G. Speed. 1897.
Cloth, $41.00. Paper, $31.00. 208pp. .... Vendor G0259

1553 **WILLIAM GILMOR–SARAH HANNA, 1778; ARTHUR SCOTT, JR–ANN HAMILTON, 1788. THE UNION OF THE FOUR FAMILIES IN THE**

MARRIAGE OF WM. GILMOR & AGNES SCOTT, 1820, by E. Gilmor. 1932.
Cloth, $46.00. Paper, $36.00. 238pp. .... Vendor G0259

1554 **GIST FAM. OF SO. CAROLINA, & ITS MARYLAND ANC.**, by W. Gee. 1934.
Paper. $20.00. 101pp. .... Vendor G0259

1555 **GLADDING BOOK; HIST. RECORD & GEN. CHART OF THE GLADDING FAM. & ACCTS. OF REUNIONS OF 1890 & 1900 AT BRISTOL RI, THEIR ANC. HOME**, by H. Gladding. 1901.
Cloth, $38.00. Paper, $28.00. 189pp. .... Vendor G0259

1556 **VIRGINIA GENEALOGIES: GENEALOGY OF THE GLASSELL FAMILY OF SCOTLAND & VA.**, ALSO OF THE FAMILIES OF BALL, BROWN, CONWAY, DANIEL, EWELL, HOLLYDAY, LEWIS, LITTLEPAGE, & OTHERS OF VA. & MARYLAND, by H.E. Hayden. 1891.
Cloth, $59.50. Paper, $49.50. 777pp. .... Vendor G0259

1557 **GEN. OF THE DESC. OF THOMAS GLEASON OF WATERTOWN, MA., 1607–1909**, by L. Wilson. 1909.
Cloth, $94.00. Paper, $84.00. 672pp. .... Vendor G0259

1558 **HISTORY OF THE GLEN FAM. OF SO. C. & GEORGIA**, by J.G.B. Bulloch. 1923.
Cloth, $32.00. Paper, $22.00. 134pp. .... Vendor G0259

1559 **DESCENDANTS OF CHARLES GLIDDEN OF PORTSMOUTH & EXETER, N.H.**, by G.W. Chamberlain; edited by L.G. Strong. 1925.
Cloth, $75.00. Paper, $65.00. 420pp. .... Vendor G0259

1560 **GEN. OF THE GLOVER CLANS**, by C.M. Glover. 1938.
Paper. $10.00. 50pp. .... Vendor G0259

1561 **GLOVER MEM. & GEN.: AN ACCT. OF JOHN GLOVER OF DORCHESTER & DESC. WITH A SKETCH OF GLOVERS WHO FIRST SETTLED IN N.J., VA., & OTHER PLACES**, by A. Glover. 1867.
Cloth, $86.00. Paper, $76.00. 612pp. .... Vendor G0259

1562 **DESCENDANTS OF JOHANES GNAEGE AND JOHN KENEGE . . . AND RELATED FAMILIES**, by Eugene Ellis Kenaga. 1988.
Cloth. $46.00. 537pp. .... Vendor G0150

1563 **THE GOADS—A FRONTIER FAMILY**, by Kenneth F. Haas. (1984) reprint 1995.
Paper. $16.95. 152pp. .... Vendor G0359

1564 **GOBLE GENEALOGY AND FAMILY HISTORY; ROLVENDEN & ADJACENT PARISHES, KENT, ENGLAND**, compiled and edited by Terence T. Quirke, Jr., Ph.D., C.G. 1994.
Six generations, starting before 1638, including U.S., Canadian, and New Zealand descendants; 17 appendices, including 13 wills.
Paper. $25.00. 92pp. .... Vendor G0143

1565 **GENEALOGY OF THE DESC. OF EDWARD GODDARD**, by W.A. Goddard. 1833.
Paper. $19.00. 95pp. .... Vendor G0259

1566 **GEN. OF THE GODING FAM.**, by F.W. Goding. 1906.
Cloth, $34.50. Paper, $24.50. 176pp. .... Vendor G0259

1567 **GOFF–DAVIS ANCESTRAL LINES: THE ANCESTRY OF MOULTON BABCOCK GOFF AND HIS WIFE AGNES HOPKINS DAVIS,** by Lois B. Goff. 1993. Indexed.
171 ancestral lines, including New England settlers with concentrations of families in Hartford, Connecticut, and Springfield, Massachusetts, Dutch and French Huguenots in New Netherlands and the Raritan Valley of New Jersey, and Welsh immigrants to Wisconsin.
TAG says "this impressive volume . . . uses her sources cautiously and presents her conclusions judiciously." *NYG&BR* says, "All New York researchers are advised to check her list of families, as she may well have discovered a relevant published source which they have overlooked." *NGSQ* adds, "Researchers working on early New England, Dutch, Huguenot, and early New York families will want to include this book on their reading list."
Cloth. $38.00. 436pp. .... Vendor G0166

1568 **GEN. NOTES BEARING UPON THE NEW ENG. ANC. OF THE CHILDREN OF WILLIAM JOHNSON GOLDTHWAIT & MARY LYDIA PITMAN-GOLDTHWAIT OF MARBLEHEAD, MASS.**, by H. Tutt.
Paper. $8.00. 39pp. .... Vendor G0259

1569 **DESC. OF THOMAS GOLDTHWAITE OF SALEM, MASS., WITH SOME ACCT. OF THE GOLDTHWAITE FAM. IN ENG.**, by C. Goldthwaite. 1899.
Cloth, $74.00. Paper, $64.00. 418pp. .... Vendor G0259

1570 **VA. COUSINS. A STUDY OF THE ANC. & POSTERITY OF JOHN GOODE OF WHITBY, A VA. COLONIST OF THE 17TH CENT., W/ NOTES ON REL. FAM., KEY TO SO. GEN. & HIST. OF THE SURNAME FROM 1148–1887,** by G. Goode. 1887.
Cloth, $92.00. Paper, $82.00. 526pp. .... Vendor G0259

1571 **GOODELL MEM. TABLETS,** by I. Goodell. 1892.
Paper. $8.00. 38pp. .... Vendor G0259

1572 **GOODENOWS WHO ORIGINATED IN SUDBURY, MASSACHUSETTS 1638 A.D.,** by Theodore James Fleming Banvard. 1994. Indexed. Illus.
Goodenough, Goodnow, scores of allied lines.
Cloth. $78.50. 952pp. .... Vendor G0116

1573 **GOODFELLOW FAMILIES IN NYS BEFORE 1800**, by Erwin W. Fellows. 1987. Indexed.
Cloth, $25.50. 108pp. .... Vendor G0450

1574 **HIST. & GEN. OF THE GOODHUE FAM. IN ENG. & AMER. TO THE YEAR 1890**, by Rev. J.E. Goodhue. 1891.
Cloth, $72.50. Paper, $62.50. 398pp. .... Vendor G0259

1575 THE GOODRICH FAM. IN AMER. A GEN. OF THE DESC. OF JOHN
& WILLIAM GOODRICH OF WETHERSFIELD, CONN., RICHARD
OF GUILFORD, CONN., & WILLIAM OF WATERTOWN, MASS., ALSO
A SHORT ACCT. OF THE FAM. IN ENG., by L.W. Case. 1889.
Cloth, $63.50. Paper, $53.50. 423pp. .... Vendor G0259

1576 GOODRIDGE GENEALOGY. THE DESC. OF WILLIAM GOODRIDGE
WHO CAME TO WATERTOWN, MASS. FROM BURY ST. EDMUNDS,
ENG. IN 1636, by E.A. Goodridge. 1918.
Cloth, $59.50. Paper, $49.50. 313pp. .... Vendor G0259

1577 GOODRIDGE MEM. DESC. & ANC. OF MOSES GOODRIDGE OF
MARBLEHEAD, MASS., OCT. 9, 1764, & DIED AT CONSTANTINE,
MICH., AUG. 23, 1838, by S. Perley. 1884.
Paper. $17.00. 87pp. .... Vendor G0259

1578 [Goodwin]. ENGLISH FAMILY PAPERS. ENGLISH GOODWIN FAM.
PAPERS, BEING MATERIAL COLL. IN THE SEARCH FOR THE ANC.
OF WILLIAM & OZIAS GOODWIN, EMIGR. OF 1632 & RESIDENTS
OF HARTFORD, CT., VOLS. I & II. 1921.
Cloth, $154.50. Paper, $144.50. 1,196pp. .... Vendor G0259

1579 ENGLISH GOODWIN FAM. PAPERS, V. III, INDEX. 1921.
Cloth, $64.50. Paper, $54.50. 349pp. .... Vendor G0259

1580 GOODWIN FAMILY IN AMER., by J. Goodwin. 1897.
Cloth, $41.50. Paper, $31.50. 200pp. .... Vendor G0259

1581 GOODWIN FAMILY. VARIOUS ANCESTRAL LINES OF JAMES
GOODWIN & LUCY MORGAN GOODWIN OF HARTFORD, CT., by
F.F. Starr. Vol. I. 1915.
Cloth, $59.50. Paper, $49.50. 317pp. .... Vendor G0259

1582 GOODWIN FAMILY. VARIOUS ANCESTRAL LINES OF JAMES
GOODWIN & LUCY MORGAN GOODWIN OF HARTFORD, CT., by
F.F. Starr. Vol. II.
Cloth, $85.00. Paper, $75.00. 481pp. .... Vendor G0259

1583 THE GOODWINS OF E. ANGLIA, by A. Jessop. 1889.
Paper. $7.00. 37pp. .... Vendor G0259

1584 THE GOODWINS OF KITTERY, YORK CO., MAINE, by J.S. Goodwin.
1898.
Paper. $19.00. 125pp. .... Vendor G0259

1585 THE GOODWINS WITH HARTFORD, CONN. DESC. OF WM. & OZIAS
GOODWIN, by Goodwin and Starr. 1891.
Cloth, $109.00. Paper, $99.00. 809pp. .... Vendor G0259

1586 GEN. OF THE GOODYEAR FAM., by G. Kirkman. 1899.
Cloth, $47.50. Paper, $37.50. 250pp. .... Vendor G0259

1587 GOOKIN FAMILY OF ENG. & AMER., 1400–1831, by E.E. Salisbury. 1885.
Paper. $17.00. 84pp. .... Vendor G0259

1588 HISTORICAL & GENEALOGICAL SKETCH OF THE GOOKIN FAM-
ILY OF ENGLAND, IRELAND, AMERICA, by R.N. Gookin. 1952.
Cloth, $41.00. Paper, $31.00. 191pp. .... Vendor G0259

1589 **GORBY FAMILY ORIGIN, HISTORY & GENEALOGY; DESC. OF SAMUEL & MARY (MAY) GORBY**, by A. Gorby. 1936.
Cloth, $57.00. Paper, $47.00. 304pp. .... Vendor G0259

1590 **DESCENDANTS OF ALLEN T. GORDEY OF GEORGIA, ALABAMA AND OUACHITA COUNTY, ARKANSAS**, by Wanda Williams Colvin. 1995. Indexed. Illus.
Paper. $16.00. 70pp. .... Vendor G0432

1591 **ALLIED FAMILIES: GORDON–MACY & HIDDLESTON–CURTIS ET AL**, by M.G. Carman and J.G. Flack. 1967.
Cloth, $45.00. 293pp. .... Vendor G0259

1592 **GORDON FAMILY RECORDS**, by J.M. Seaver.
Paper. $10.00. 52pp. .... Vendor G0259

1593 **THE JOHNSTON & BACON SCOTTISH CLAN HISTORIES: The Clan Gordon**, by Jean Dunlop. (1955) reprint 1993. Illus.
Paper. $8.95. 32pp. .... Vendor G0011

1594 **GORHAM. EXTR. FROM "GEN. NOTES OF BARNSTABLE FAM."**
Paper. $7.50. 40pp. .... Vendor G0259

1595 **NEW ENG. GORHAMS: MISC. NOTES FROM NEHGR.** 1896–1915.
Paper. $8.00. 40pp. .... Vendor G0259

1596 **THE ANCESTORS AND DESCENDANTS OF MINNIE HALE GORTON**, by Carolyn C. Volpe. 1994. Indexed. Illus.
Three chapters of general history since more than 100 ancestors came before 1650 and were founders of early towns. Chapters on **Alcott, Barrett, Beckwith, Day, Gorton, Hale, Norton, Scott** lines. Collateral families include **Bliss, Chapin, Goodrich, Howland, Loomis, Minot, Mitchell, Morgan, Olmstead, Peabody, Rogers, Winslow.**
Hardback. $35.00. 343pp. .... Vendor G0216

1597 **THE LIFE & TIMES OF SAMUEL GORTON: THE FOUNDERS & FOUNDING OF THE REPUBLIC & A HIST. OF THE COL. OF PROVIDENCE & R.I., WITH A GEN. OF SAMUEL GORTON'S DESC.**, by A. Gorton. 1907.
Cloth, $131.50. Paper, $121.50. 966pp. .... Vendor G0259

1598 **GOSNOLD & BACON, THE ANC. OF BARTHOLOMEW GOSNOLD. A COLLECTION**, by J.H. Lea. 1904.
Paper. $7.00. 36pp. .... Vendor G0259

1599 **FAM. OF PHILIP GOSS OF LANCASTER, MASS., & WINCHESTER, N. H. (EXTR. LAWRENCE–GOSS–POMROY GEN.)**, by J. Lawrence. 1881.
Paper. $7.50. 37pp. .... Vendor G0259

1600 **THE FAMILY OF ROBERT & LYDIA (NICHOLS) GOTT**, by Steve Roth and Beverly Franks. 1992.
Cloth, $99.50. Paper, $89.50. 575+95pp. .... Vendor G0259

1601 **GEN. HIST. OF GOTTSHALL FAM., DESC. OF JACOB GOTTSHALL**, by N.B. Grubb. 1924.
Cloth, $32.50. Paper, $22.50. 112pp. .... Vendor G0259

1602 **GOULDS OF RHODE ISLAND**, by R.G. Mitchell. 1875.
Paper. $18.00. 99pp. .... Vendor G0259

1603 **LIFE AND TIMES OF JOSEPH GOULD: REMINISCENCES OF SIXTY YEARS OF ACTIVE POLITICAL AND MUNICIPAL LIFE**, by W.H. Higgins. 1887.
Cloth, $37.50. Paper, $27.50. 304pp. .... Vendor G0259

1604 **THE FAM. OF ZACCHEUS GOULD OF TOPSFIELD**, by B.A. Gould. 1895.
Cloth, $55.50. Paper, $45.50. 360pp. .... Vendor G0259

1605 **GOURDIN: A FRENCH–AFRICAN–AMERICAN FAMILY FROM SOUTH CAROLINA**, by J. Raymond Gourdin. 1995. Indexed. Illus.
Cloth. $29.00. 320pp. .... Vendor G0205

1606 **MEM. OF THE SCOTTISH HOUSE OF GOURLAY**, by C. Rogers. 1888.
Cloth, $52.75. Paper, $42.75. 285pp. .... Vendor G0259

1607 **GOVE BOOK: HIST. & GEN. OF THE AMER. FAM. OF GOVE & NOTES OF EUROPEAN GOVES**, by W.H. Gove. 1922.
Cloth, $109.00. Paper, $99.00. 692pp. .... Vendor G0259

1608 **[Gowdy]. FAMILY HIST. COMPRISING THE SURNAMES OF GADE, GAUDIE, GAWDY, GOWDY, GAUDERN & VARIANT FORMS, FROM A.D. 800-A.D. 1919**, by M.M. Gowdy and G.T. Ridlon. 2 vols. in 1. 1919.
Cloth, $99.50. Paper, $89.50. xx+628pp. .... Vendor G0259

1609 **GRACE GENEALOGY AND FAMILY HISTORY; EAST SUSSEX, ENGLAND. 3RD EDITION**, compiled and edited by Terence T. Quirke, Jr., Ph.D., C.G. 1993.
Six generations, starting 1649; 20 appendices, including 15 wills.
Paper. $25.00. 83pp. .... Vendor G0143

1610 **CHART: HANS GRAF, BORN IN SWITZERLAND A.D. 1661, SETTLED IN AMERICA A.D. 1695**, by G.F. Groff and Emerson Stauffer. (1932) reprint 1979.
Paper. $8.00 .... Vendor G0150

1611 **GRAFTON FAMILY OF SALEM**, by H.W. Belknap. 1928.
Paper. $19.50. 103pp. .... Vendor G0259

1612 **HISTORY OF THE GRAHAM FAMILY [OF VA.]**, by David Graham. 1899.
Cloth, $31.00. Paper, $21.00. 119pp. .... Vendor G0259

1613 **THE JOHNSTON & BACON SCOTTISH CLAN HISTORIES: The Grahams**, by John Stewart. (1958) reprint 1993. Illus.
Paper. $8.95. 32pp. .... Vendor G0011

1614 **THE REV. JOHN GRAHAM OF WOODBURY, CONN., & HIS DESC.**, by H.G. Carpenter. 1942.
Cloth, $94.50. Paper, $84.50. 550pp. .... Vendor G0259

1615 **GRANBERRY FAM. & ALLIED FAM., INCL. THE ANC. OF HELEN WOODWARD GRANBERRY**, by Waterman and Jacobus. 1945.
Cloth, $71.00. Paper, $61.00. 383pp. .... Vendor G0259

1616 **LAUNCELOT GRANGER OF NEWBURY, MASS. & SUFFIELD, CONN. A GEN. HIST.,** by J.N. Granger. 1893.
Cloth, $99.00. Paper, $89.00. 587pp. .... Vendor G0259

1617 **HIST. OF GRANNIS FAM. IN AMER. 1630–1901,** by S.S. Grannis. 1901.
Paper. $10.00. 49pp. .... Vendor G0259

1618 **THE DESC. OF EDWARD GRANNIS, WHO WAS IN NEW HAVEN, CONN., AS EARLY AS 1649 & DIED THERE DEC. 10, 1719,** by F.A. Strong. 1927.
Cloth, $53.00. Paper, $43.00. 288pp. .... Vendor G0259

1619 **GRANT FAM. A GEN. HIST. OF THE DESC. OF MATTHEW GRANT OF WINDSOR, CT., 1601–1898,** by A.H. Grant. 1898.
Cloth, $99.00. Paper, $89.00. 602pp. .... Vendor G0259

1620 **GRANT FAM. EXTR. FROM "HIST. OF WINDSOR, CONN."** 1892.
Paper. $9.00. 45pp. .... Vendor G0259

1621 **REPORT OF THE 1ST REUNION OF THE GRANT FAMILY ASSOC. AT WINDSOR & HARTFORD, CT., ON OCT. 27, 1899,** edited by A.H. Grant. 1899.
Paper. $12.00. 58pp. .... Vendor G0259

1622 **THE JOHNSTON & BACON SCOTTISH CLAN HISTORIES: The Clan Grant,** by I.F. Grant. (1955) reprint 1993. Illus.
Paper. $8.95. 32pp. .... Vendor G0011

1623 **THE ROBERT NOEL GRANT FAMILY TREE,** by Robert N. Grant. 1986. Indexed. Illus.
    Ancestral surnames include **Wright, Broadhurst, Nickels, Cluff, Carrington, Judkins, Yeoman, Holmes, Sumlar, Hillman, Parr, Mayse, Lindopp, Marshall, Pate, Cathcart, Goodwin, Covell, Manter, Pymme, Piggin, Cottle, Coleman, Whitten, Pymme, Darby, Folger, Daggett.**
Paper. $.08 per page ordered. 3,700pp. .... Vendor G0404

1624 **THE HISTORY OF THE GRANVILLE FAMILY, TRACED BACK TO ROLLO, FIRST DUKE OF NORMANDY, WITH PEDIGREES, ETC.,** by R. Granville. 1895 (England).
Cloth, $84.50. Paper, $74.50. 489pp. .... Vendor G0259

1625 **BRANCHING OUT FROM STEPHEN GRAVES (1759–1828),** by Jessie Graves. 1991. Indexed.
Cloth. $30.50. 200pp. .... Vendor G0183

1626 **DEACON GEORGE GRAVES OF HARTFORD, CT,** by Kenneth V. Graves. 1995. Indexed. Illus.
Cloth. $35.00. 450pp. .... Vendor G0196

1627 **GEN. OF THE GRAVES FAM. IN AMER. SKETCH OF THE FAM. IN ENG. & GEN. OF THE FAM. OF THOMAS GRAVES OF HATFIELD, MASS.,** by J.C. Graves. Vol. I. 1896.
Cloth, $92.00. Paper, $82.00. 546pp. .... Vendor G0259

1628 **GRAVES FAMILIES OF RANDOLPH CO., NC,** by Kenneth V. Graves. 1995. Indexed. Illus.
Cloth. $65.00. 800pp. .... Vendor G0196

1629 **GRAVES FAMILIES OF THE WORLD**, by Kenneth V. Graves. 1994. Indexed.
Contains summaries of 239 **Graves/Greaves** families.
Cloth. $41.00. 509pp. .... Vendor G0196

1630 **GRAVES FAMILY NEWSLETTER**. Kenneth V. Graves, Editor. 1976–present. Indexed. Illus.
Includes all **Graves/Greaves** families.
Subscription. $20/year. 144pp/year .... Vendor G0196

1631 **REAR ADMIRAL THOMAS GRAVES OF CHARLESTOWN, MA**, by Kenneth V. Graves. 1994. Indexed.
Cloth. $23.00. 267pp. .... Vendor G0196

1632 **ROBERT GRAVES OF ANSON CO., NC AND CHESTERFIELD CO., SC**, by Kenneth V. Graves. 1980. Indexed.
Sixth generation descendant of Capt. Thomas **Graves** of VA.
Cloth. $26.00. 408pp. .... Vendor G0196

1633 **SAMUEL GRAVES OF LYNN, MA**, by Kenneth V. Graves. 1985. Indexed.
Cloth. $36.00. 446pp. .... Vendor G0196

1634 **THOMAS GRAVES OF HARTFORD, CT AND HATFIELD, MA**, by Kenneth V. Graves. 1985. Indexed.
Includes everything in John Card **Graves'** 1896 book plus much more.
Cloth. $46.00. 710pp. .... Vendor G0196

1635 **GRAY FAMILY & ALLIED LINES . . . BOWMAN, LINDSAY, MILLIS, DISK, PEEBLES, WILEY, SHANNON, LAMAR, McGEE**, by Jo White Linn. 1976. Reprinted by permission.
Cloth, $85.00. Paper, $75.00. 607pp. .... Vendor G0259

1636 **GRAY GENEALOGY, BEING A GENEALOGICAL RECORD & HISTORY OF THE DESCENDANTS OF JOHN GRAY OF BEVERLY, MASS., AND INCLUDING SKETCHES OF OTHER GRAY FAMILIES**, by M.D. Raymond. 1887.
Cloth, $57.50. Paper, $47.50. 316pp. .... Vendor G0259

1637 **JOSHUA GRAY OF YARMOUTH, MASS., & HIS DESC.**, by J.E. Thacher. 1914.
Cloth, $30.00. Paper, $20.00. 136pp. .... Vendor G0259

1638 **WILLIAM GRAY OF LYNN, MASS., & SOME DESC. (REPR. ESSEX INST. HIST. COLL.)**, by E. Gray. 1916.
Paper. $7.00. 35pp. .... Vendor G0259

1639 **DESCENDANTS OF JOHN GRAYSON OF SPOTSYLVANIA COUNTY, VIRGINIA**, by Carol A. Hauk. 1995. Indexed.
Paper. $30.00. 67pp. .... Vendor G0340

1640 **GEN. OF THE GREELY–GREELEY FAM.**, by G.H. Greeley. 1905.
Cloth, $124.50. Paper, $114.50. 915pp. .... Vendor G0259

1641 **A GEN. SKETCH OF THE DESC. OF THOMAS GREEN OF MALDEN, MASS.**, by S. Green. 1858.
Paper. $16.00. 80pp. .... Vendor G0259

1642 **AN ACCT. OF PERCIVAL & ELLEN GREEN & SOME OF THEIR DESC.,** by S.A. Green. 1876.
Paper. $13.50. 67pp. .... Vendor G0259

1643 **DESCENDANTS OF WILLIAM GREEN OF VIRGINIA,** by Carol A. Hauk. 1995. Indexed.
Paper. $30.00. 100pp. .... Vendor G0340

1644 **GEN. OF THE FAM. OF TIMOTHY & EUNICE ELLSWORTH GREEN,** by J.M. Green. 1904.
Cloth, $44.50. Paper, $34.50. 227pp. .... Vendor G0259

1645 **A GEN. SKETCH OF THE DESC. OF ROBERT GREENE OF WALES, MASS.,** by R. Greene. 1885.
Paper. $12.50. 64pp. .... Vendor G0259

1646 **ANCESTORS AND DESCENDANTS OF WILLIAM BROWNING GREENE AND MARY HOXSIE LEWIS WITH ALLIED FAMILIES,** by Wm. E. Wright. 1993. Indexed. Illus.
Table of Contents lists 42 surnames of Allied Families, including 10 or more generations of descendants of Joseph **Cross**, John **Kenyon**, Edward **Perry**, John **Segar**.
Cloth. $49.00. 778pp. .... Vendor G0363

1647 **DESC. OF JOSEPH GREENE OF WESTERLY, R.I.; ALSO, OTHER BRANCHES OF THE GREENES OF R.I. & OTHER LINES OF GREENES IN AMER.,** by F.L. Greene. 1894.
Cloth, $88.00. Paper, $78.00. 500pp. .... Vendor G0259

1648 **GREENE FAMILY & ITS BRANCHES FROM 861 TO 1904, BY LORA S. LA MANCE, TOGETHER WITH POEMS, DESCRIPTIONS OF THE TEXT,** by A.A. Stowe. 1904.
Cloth, $59.00. Paper, $49.00. 305pp. .... Vendor G0259

1649 **GREENE FAM. IN ENG. & AMER., WITH PEDIGREE CHARTS.** 1901.
Cloth, $40.00. Paper, $30.00. 168pp. .... Vendor G0259

1650 **GREENE (GREEN) FAM. OF PLYMOUTH COLONY,** by R.H. Greene. 1909.
Cloth, $32.50. Paper, $22.50. 145pp. .... Vendor G0259

1651 **GREENE FAMILY OF R.I., WITH HIST. REC. OF ENG. ANC., 1534–1902,** by L.B. Clarke. 2 vols. in 1. 1903.
Cloth, $129.00. Paper, $119.00. 892pp. .... Vendor G0259

1652 **GREENES OF WARWICK IN COLONIAL HIST.,** by H. Turner. 1877.
Paper. $13.50. 68pp. .... Vendor G0259

1653 **GREENLAW FAM. OF DEER ISLE, ME.,** by C. Greenlaw. 1955.
Paper. $8.50. 5pp. + 21 charts .... Vendor G0259

1654 **GEN. OF THE GREENLEAF FAM.,** by J. Greenleaf. 1854.
Paper. $16.00. 116pp. .... Vendor G0259

1655 **GEN. OF THE GREENLEAF FAM.,** by J.E. Greenleaf. 1896.
Cloth, $96.50. Paper, $86.50. 564pp. .... Vendor G0259

1656 **THE ANC. OF JANE MARIA GREENLEAF, WIFE OF WM. F. BOARDMAN, HARTFORD**, by W. Boardman. 1906.
Cloth, $30.00. Paper, $20.00. 133pp. .... Vendor G0259

1657 **DESCENDANTS OF EDWARD GREENLEE OF W. VIRGINIA**, by W.C. Greenlee. 1956.
Cloth, $76.00. Paper, $66.00. 436pp. .... Vendor G0259

1658 **GENEALOGY OF THE GREENLEE FAMILIES IN AMERICA, SCOTLAND, IRELAND & ENGLAND, WITH ANCESTORS OF ELIZABETH BROOKS GREENLEE & EMILY BROOKS GREENLEE, & GENEALOGICAL DATA ON THE McDOWELLS OF VIRGINIA & KENTUCKY**, by R.S. and R.L. Greenlee. 1908.
Cloth, $115.00. Paper, $105.00. 744pp. .... Vendor G0259

1659 **NOTES ON THE ANC. OF EBENEZER GREENOUGH, 1783–1847, & HIS WIFE, ABIGAIL ISRAEL, 1791–1868, & A LIST OF THEIR DESC.**, by F. Platt. 1895.
Paper. $8.00. 38pp. .... Vendor G0259

1660 **GREENWOOD FAM. OF NORWICH, ENG. IN AMER.**, by H.M. Pitman and M.M. Greenwood. 1934.
Cloth, $71.00. Paper, $61.00. 396pp. .... Vendor G0259

1661 **GREENWOOD GEN., 1154–1914; THE ANC. & DESC. OF THOMAS OF NEWTON, MASS., NATHANIEL & SAMUEL OF BOSTON, JOHN OF VA. & MANY LATER ARRIVALS IN AMER. ALSO THE EARLY HIST. OF THE GREENWOODS IN ENG.**, by F. Greenwood. 1914.
Cloth, $94.50. Paper, $84.50. 548pp. .... Vendor G0259

1662 **GREER AND RELATED FAMILIES SANDERS, SIMS, GLENN, CHRISTMAS, SMITH, FERRIS AND CARVER OF THE CAROLINAS AND VA.**, by Brent H. Holcomb. 1987 (reprinted by permission).
Paper. $18.50. 109pp. .... Vendor G0259

1663 **ANC. & DESC. OF HENRY GREGORY**, by G. Gregory. 1938.
Cloth, $86.00. Paper, $76.00. 492pp. .... Vendor G0259

1664 **BIOGR. & HIST. SKETCHES OF GRESHAM OF AMER. & OVERSEAS**, by A. Strange. 1913.
Paper. $10.00. 53pp. .... Vendor G0259

1665 **GEN. OF THE DESC. OF JASPER GRIFFING**, by C.J. Stone. 1881.
Cloth, $40.00. Paper, $30.00. 194pp. .... Vendor G0259

1666 **STEPHEN GRIFFING [OF N.Y.], HIS ANC. & DESC.**, by E.W. West. 1911.
Cloth, $47.00. Paper, $37.00. 234pp. .... Vendor G0259

1667 **GEN. OF THE GRIGGS FAM.**, by W.S. Griggs. 1926.
Cloth, $32.50. Paper, $22.50. 116pp. .... Vendor G0259

1668 **GRIMES FAM.**, by E.B. Grimes. 1946.
Paper. $14.00. 70pp. .... Vendor G0259

1669 **GENEALOGY OF THE GRIMMETT FAMILY, CONCERNING THE LINEAGE OF MRS PAUL BROWN (ELOISE RENFRO)**, by Mrs P. Brown. 1985.
Paper. $13.00. 64pp., handwritten .... Vendor G0259

1670 **GRISWOLD FAMILY**, by E.E. Salisbury. 1884.
Paper. $16.50. 82pp. .... Vendor G0259

1671 **GRISWOLD FAMILY OF ENG. & AMER.: EDWARD OF WINDSOR, MATTHEW OF LYME, MICHAEL OF WETHERSFIELD (ALL CONN.)**, by G.E. Griswold. 1943.
Cloth, $71.00. Paper, $61.00. 391pp. .... Vendor G0259

1672 **THE GROFF BOOK. VOL. I**, by Clyde L. Groff, Walter B. Groff, and Jane E. Best. 1985.
Cloth. $69.00. 432pp. .... Vendor G0150

1673 **"A FAMILY AFFAIR" CONCERNING CERTAIN DESC. OF CAPT. JOHN GROUT, WHO CAME FROM ENG. TO NEW ENG. EARLY IN THE 17TH CENT.**, by H.S.B. Osgood. 1949–52.
Paper. $19.50. 116pp. .... Vendor G0259

1674 **CAPT. JOHN GROUT OF WATERTOWN & SUDBURY, MASS., & SOME OF HIS DESC.**, by E.E. Jones. 1922.
Paper. $18.50. 124pp. .... Vendor G0259

1675 **A HIST. & GEN. OF THE GROVES FAM. IN AMER., DESC. OF NICHO-LAS LA GROVES OF BEVERLY, MASS.**, by W.T. Groves. 1915.
Paper. $11.00. 56pp. .... Vendor G0259

1676 **JOHN GROW OF IPSWICH. JOHN GROO (GROW) OF OXFORD**, by G.W. Davis. 1913.
Cloth, $51.00. Paper, $41.00. 274pp. .... Vendor G0259

1677 **GROWDON FAMILY, FROM "FAM. SKETCHES"**, by J. Wood. 1870.
Paper. $7.50. 37pp. .... Vendor G0259

1678 **GENERAL HISTORY OF THE HOUSE OF GUELPH, OR ROYAL FAM-ILY OF GREAT BRITAIN, FROM THE EARLIEST PERIOD IN WHICH THE NAME APPEARS UPON RECORD**, by Andrew Halliday, M.D. 1821 (England).
Cloth, $85.00. Paper, $75.00. 472+29pp. .... Vendor G0259

1679 **ANCESTRY OF CALVIN GUILD, MARGARET TAFT, JAMES HUMPHREYS & REBECCA COVELL MARTIN, 1620–1890**, by Howard R. Guild. 1891.
Paper. $9.00. 42pp. .... Vendor G0259

1680 **GEN. OF THE DESC. OF JOHN GUILD, DEDHAM, MASS.**, by C. Guild. 1867.
Cloth, $30.00. Paper, $20.00. 132pp. .... Vendor G0259

1681 **THE GEN. & HIST. OF THE GUILD, GUILE & GILE FAM.**, by C. Burleigh. 1887.
Cloth, $59.00. Paper, $49.00. 381pp. .... Vendor G0259

1682 **THE ANCESTRY OF DR. J.P. GUILFORD, VOL. I, SEVENTEENTH CENTURY NEW ENGLAND COLONIALS**, by Joan S. Guilford, Ph.D. 1990. Indexed.
107 Immigrants to New England between 1620 and 1675, their known ances-tries, and at least three generations of their descendants with corrections and

supplements to hundreds of published accounts. Families: **Allen, Amidon/ Harwood, Atkinson, Bacon, Bascom, Blott, Bridgman/Lyman, Brooks, Brown, Burlingame, Burt/March, Butler, Carwithen, Caswell, Cheney, Colvin, Cotton, Crafts, Cross, Curtis, Dean, Dill, Dimmock, Downing, Edwards/Baldwin, Emerson, Fletcher, Flower, Gardner, Green, Griggs, Guilford, Hall, Hanford/Hatherly, Hawley, Haynes, Herrick, Hoar/Channon, Hoskins/Winthrop, Huit, Janes, Jordan, Kinney, Kirby, Knight, Knowles, Knowlton, Lakin, Lamb, Laskin, Learned, Lippitt, Lobdell, Loker, Long, Marshall, Millard, Newell, Parker, Perry, Pierce, Platt, Prescott/Gawkroger-Platts, Pullen, Ralph, Ransom, Richmond, Robbins, Rogers, Root, Sheldon, Shelley, Shepard, Smith, Stearns/Barker, Stoddard, Stow/Bigge, Taft, Tay, Thurston, Upson, Wade, Ward, Warham/Dabinott, Wilbore, Willis, Wilton, Woodbury/Patch, Woodford, Woodmansey, Wright.**
Cloth. $44.00. xxiv+995pp. .... Vendor G0220

1683 **A GEN. OF THE DESC. OF HUGH GUNNISON OF BOSTON, MASS., 1610–1876**, by G.W. Gunnison. 1880.
Cloth, $43.00. Paper, $33.00. 222pp. .... Vendor G0259

1684 **THE HIST. & GEN. OF THE GURLEY FAM.**, by A.E. Gurley. 1897.
Cloth, $52.50. Paper, $42.50. 285pp. .... Vendor G0259

1685 **ANCESTRY OF JOHN S. GUSTIN & HIS WIFE SUSAN McCOMB, IN-CLUDING AN ACCT. OF JOHN HUBBARD, 2ND HUSBAND OF ELINOR SHEPHERD**, by S.A. Dewick. 1900.
Cloth, $32.00. Paper, $22.00. 136pp. .... Vendor G0259

1686 **GUSTINE COMPENDIUM**, by G.C. Weaver. 1929.
Cloth, $64.00. Paper, $54.00. 339pp. .... Vendor G0259

1687 **BRIEF HIST. OF A BRANCH OF THE GUTHRIE FAM.**, by S. Guthrie. 1889.
Paper. $12.50. 62pp. .... Vendor G0259

1688 **REC. OF THE GUTHRIE FAM. OF PENN., CONN., & VA., WITH ANC. OF THOSE WHO HAVE INTERMARRIED WITH THE FAM.**, by H.A. and E.G. Dunn. 1898.
Cloth, $35.50. Paper, $25.50. 170pp. .... Vendor G0259

1689 **THE SURNAME IS GWYN, GWYNN, GWYNNE**, by Carl Gwynn. 1992. Indexed. Illus.
Descendants of James **Gwynne** of Radnorshire, Wales (1686–1755) and other branches of the family. Includes wills, pedigree charts, biographies, and many pictures.
Cloth. $49.00. 440pp. .... Vendor G0334

1690 **A HIST. & GEN. OF THE HABERSHAM FAM., ALSO CLAY, STILES, CUMMING, & OTHER FAM.**, by J.G.B. Bulloch. 1901.
Cloth, $47.50. Paper, $37.50. 228pp. .... Vendor G0259

1691 **GEN. RECORD OF THE DESC. OF MOSES HADLEY & REBECCA PAGE, OF HUDSON N.H., TOGETHER WITH SOME ACCT. OF GEO. HADLEY OF IPSWICH, MASS. & HIS DESC.**, by S.P. Hadley. 1887.
Paper. $15.00. 88pp. .... Vendor G0259

1692 **NOTES ON THE QUAKER FAM. OF HADLEY**, by C. Hadley. 1916.
Paper. $12.00. 59pp. .... Vendor G0259

1693 **GENEALOGY OF DELBERT JAMES HAFF AND WIFE GRACE ISABEL BARSE, WITH MONOGRAPHS RELATIVE TO THE CHAMPION, DEWOLF, GRIFFIN, PECK, BUSH, BARSE, COOK & NICHOLS FAMILIES**, by D.J. Haff. 1936.
Paper. $19.50. 109pp. .... Vendor G0259

1694 **HISTORY OF THE HAIN FAMILY: DESCENDANTS OF GEORGE & VERONICA HAIN [SETTLED IN BERKS & LEBANON CO. PA., 1723]**, n.a. 1941.
Paper. $17.00. 88pp. .... Vendor G0259

1695 **ANC. OF THE HAINES, SHARP, COLLINS & OTHER FAM.; COMP. FROM NOTES OF THE LATE GEO. HAINES, WITH SOME ADD.**, by R. Haines. 1902.
Cloth, $78.50. Paper, $68.50. 456pp. .... Vendor G0259

1696 **DEACON SAMUEL HAINES OF WESTBURY, WILTSHIRE, ENG., & HIS DESC. IN AMERICA, 1635–1901**, by A.M. and T.V. Haines. 1902.
Cloth, $61.50. Paper, $51.50. 429pp. .... Vendor G0259

1697 **JOSHUA B. AND MARTHA J. HAINES OF WABASHA, MINNESOTA**, by Charles F. Berg. 1990.
Martha J. **Roberts**, Deacon Samuel **Haines**.
Cloth. $15.00. 79pp. .... Vendor G0348

1698 **[Haines]. "THE CLOVERCROFT CHRONICLES", 1314–1893**, by M.R. Haines. 1893.
Cloth, $63.50. Paper, $53.50. 347pp. .... Vendor G0259

1699 **HAKES FAMILY**, by H. Hakes. 1886.
Paper. $17.50. 87pp. .... Vendor G0259

1700 **HAKES FAMILY**, by H. Hakes. 1889.
Cloth, $43.00. Paper, $33.00. 220pp. .... Vendor G0259

1701 **JOEL HALBERT & HIS DESCENDANTS, BEING A HISTORICAL & GENEALOGICAL ACCOUNT OF JOEL HALBERT, IMMIGRANT TO ESSEX CO., VA., ABOUT 1700–1710 A.D. & HIS MANY DESCENDANTS SCATTERED THROUGHOUT AMERICA**, by F.P. and K. Waddell. 1947.
Cloth, $39.50. Paper, $29.50. 150pp. .... Vendor G0259

1702 **DESC. OF MAJOR SAMUEL HALE**, by E.H. Smith. 1902.
Paper. $18.50. 123pp. .... Vendor G0259

1703 **GEN. OF DESC. OF THOMAS HALE OF WALTON, ENG., & OF NEWBURY, MASS.**, by R.S. Hale. 1889.
Cloth, $77.00. Paper, $67.00. 427pp. .... Vendor G0259

1704 **HALE FAMILY. (EXTR. "PIONEER SETTLERS OF GRAYSON CO., VA.")**, by B.F. Nuckolls. 1914.
Paper. $7.00. 36pp. .... Vendor G0259

1705 **HALE–HOUSE, HOUSE & REL. FAMILIES, MAINLY OF THE CONN. RIVER VALLEY**, by Jacobus and Waterman. 1952.
Cloth, $119.00. Paper, $109.00. 914pp. .... Vendor G0259

1706 **THE ANC. OF CHARITY HALEY, 1755–1800, WIFE OF MAJ. NICHO-LAS DAVIS OF LIMINGTON, MAINE,** by W.G. Davis, Jr. 1916.
Paper. $18.00. 91pp. .... Vendor G0259

1707 **THOM. HALEY OF WINTER HARBOR & HIS DESC.,** by W.G. Davis and A. Haley. 1930.
Paper. $11.00. 55pp. .... Vendor G0259

1708 **ANCESTRY OF A FEW OF THE DESCENDANTS OF EDWARD HALL OF REHOBETH, MASS., WITH INTERMARRIAGES.** n.d.
Paper. $11.00. 56pp. .... Vendor G0259

1709 **GENEALOGICAL NOTES RELATING TO THE FAMILIES OF HON. LYMAN HALL OF GEORGIA; HON. SAMUEL HOLDEN PARSONS HALL OF BINGHAMTON, NY; & HON. NATHAN KELSEY HALL OF BUFFALO, NY,** by Theo. Parson Hall. 1886.
Cloth, $39.00. Paper, $29.00. 192pp. .... Vendor G0259

1710 **HALL FAM. OF NEW ENG. GEN. & BIOGR.,** by D. Hall. 1883.
Cloth, $108.50. Paper, $98.50. 800pp. .... Vendor G0259

1711 **JOHN HALL OF WALLINGFORD, CONN. A MONOGRAPH (WITH GEN.),** by J. Shepard. 1902.
Paper. $12.00. 61pp. .... Vendor G0259

1712 **JOHN JAMES HALL, HIS DESCENDANTS, AND OTHER HALLS OF ALABAMA,** by Margarette Hall Wood. 1988. Indexed. Illus.
Includes information on **Beasley, Brooks, Ledlow, Parker, Robinson** families associated with John James **Hall** and his descendants (six generations) and approximately 1,000 other Halls and their kin.
Cloth. $46.00. 341pp. .... Vendor G0299

1713 **MEMORANDA REL. TO THE ANC. & FAM. OF SOPHIA FIDELIA HALL,** by S.F.H. Coe. 1902.
Cloth, $40.00. Paper, $30.00. 231pp. .... Vendor G0259

1714 **SERIES OF SKETCHES OF THE LIN. ANC. OF THE CHILDREN OF SAM'L HOLDEN PARSONS HALL & HIS WIFE EMELINE BULKELEY OF BINGHAMTON, NY,** by C. Hall. 1896.
Cloth, $91.00. Paper, $81.00. 517pp. .... Vendor G0259

1715 **THE PEDIGREE OF FLETCHER GARRISON HALL,** by Garrison Kent Hall. 1979. Indexed. Illus.
Cloth. $13.50. 475pp. .... Vendor G0406

1716 **HALLET. EXTR. FROM "GEN. NOTES OF BARNSTABLE FAM."**
Paper. $10.50. 51pp. .... Vendor G0259

1717 **1992 ADDENDUM TO A HALLOCK GENEALOGY OF 1928,** by The Hallock Family Association. 1992. Indexed.
Cloth. $35.00. 495pp. .... Vendor G0325

1718 **THE DESC. OF PETER HALLOCK, WHO LANDED AT SOUTHOLD, LI, 1640,** by L. Hallock. 1926.
Cloth, $119.00. Paper, $109.00. 749pp. .... Vendor G0259

1719 **HALLOWELL–PAUL FAMILY HISTORY, INCL. THE ANCESTRY OF**

RELATED FAMILIES OF WORTH, LUKEN, JARRETT, MORRIS, SCULL, STOKES, HEATH & OTHERS, by M.P.H. Hough and A.H. Penrose. 1924.
Cloth, $42.00. Paper, $32.00. 16+189pp. .... Vendor G0259

1720 **RECORD OF A BRANCH OF THE HALLOWELL FAM., INCL. THE LONGSTRETH, PENROSE & NORWOOD BRANCHES**, by W.P. Hallowell. 1893.
Cloth, $47.00. Paper, $37.00. 246pp. .... Vendor G0259

1721 **THOMAS HALSEY OF HERTS., ENG. & SOUTHAMPTON, LI, 1591–1679, WITH HIS ANC. TO 8TH & 9TH GEN.**, by J.L. and E.D. Halsey. 1895.
Cloth, $64.00. Paper, $54.00. 550pp. .... Vendor G0259

1722 **GENEALOGY OF THE HALSTEAD FAMILY**, by J.H. Halstead. 1963.
Paper. $14.00. 71pp. .... Vendor G0259

1723 **GENEALOGY OF THE HAM FAMILY & THE YOUNG FAMILY**, by T.C. Ham. 1949.
Paper. $15.00. 87pp. .... Vendor G0259

1724 **GEN. RECORD OF THE HAMBLETON FAM. DESC. OF JAMES HAMBLETON OF BUCKS CO., PENN., d. 1751. MENTION OF OTHER HAMBLETONS IN AMER. & ENG.**, by C.J. Hambleton. 1887.
Paper. $17.00. 108pp. .... Vendor G0259

1725 **THE GEN. OF THE HAMILTON FAM. FROM 1716–1894**, by S. Hamilton. 1894.
Cloth, $30.00. Paper, $20.00. 133pp. .... Vendor G0259

1726 **THE HAMILTONS OF WATERBOROUGH, YORK COUNTY, MAINE**, by Samuel King Hamilton. (1912) reprint 1986. Indexed. Illus. Book #1266.
Cloth. $59.00. 544pp. .... Vendor G0082

1727 **THE HAMILTONS OF WATERBOROUGH (YORK CO., MAINE) THEIR ANC. & DESC.**, by S.K. Hamilton. 1912.
Cloth, $76.50. Paper, $66.50. 423pp. .... Vendor G0259

1728 **A GEN. OF JAMES HAMLIN OF BARNSTABLE, MASS., ELDEST SON OF JAMES HAMLIN, THE IMMIGR., 1639–1902**, by H.A. Andrews. 1902.
Cloth, $208.50. Paper, $198.50. 1,411pp. .... Vendor G0259

1729 **HAMLIN FAM.; A GEN. OF CAPT. GILES HAMLIN OF MIDDLETOWN, CT., 1654–1900**, by H.F. Andrews. 1900.
Cloth, $71.00. Paper, $61.00. 479pp. .... Vendor G0259

1730 **HAMLINS OF NEW ENG., DESC. OF JAMES & ANNA HAMLIN**, by S.M. Hamlin. 1936.
Paper. $13.00. 65pp. .... Vendor G0259

1731 **HIST. OF THE HAMLIN FAM., WITH GEN. OF EARLY SETTLERS OF THE NAME IN AMER., 1629–1894**, by H.F. Andrews. 1894.
Cloth, $31.00. Paper, $21.00. 130pp. .... Vendor G0259

1732 **THE HAMMERS & ALLIED FAMILIES, WITH THEIR FAM. CIRCLES CENTERING IN PENDLETON CO., W.V.**, by E.B. Boggs. 1950.
Cloth, $38.00. Paper, $28.00. 176pp. .... Vendor G0259

1733 **A HIST. & GEN. OF THE DESC. OF WM. HAMMOND OF LONDON, ENG., & HIS WIFE, ELIZABETH PENN, THROUGH THEIR SON, BENJAMIN, OF SANDWICH & ROCHESTER, MASS.**, 1600–1894, by R. Hammond. 1894.
Cloth, $50.00. Paper, $40.00. 320pp. .... Vendor G0259

1734 **HIST. & GEN. OF THE HAMMOND FAM. IN AMER., WITH AN ACCT. OF THE EARLY HIST. OF THE FAM. IN NORMANDY & GR. BRIT., 1000–1902**, by F. Hammond. Vol. I. 1902.
Cloth, $108.00. Paper, $98.00. 674pp. .... Vendor G0259

1735 **HIST. & GEN. OF THE HAMMOND FAM. IN AMER., WITH AN ACCT. OF THE EARLY HIST. OF THE FAM. IN NORMANDY & GR. BRIT., 1000–1902** by F.S. Hammond. Vol. II. 1904.
Cloth, $129.00. Paper, $119.00. 881pp. .... Vendor G0259

1736 **JOSEPH HAMPTON & THE PENN. QUAKERS**, by V.B. Hampton. 1940.
Cloth, $32.50. Paper, $22.50. 116pp. .... Vendor G0259

1737 **FAM. RECORDS OF BRANCHES OF THE HANAFORD, THOMPSON, HUCKINS, PRESCOTT & ALLIED FAM.**, by M.E.N. Hanaford. 1915.
Cloth, $65.00. Paper, $55.00. 345pp. .... Vendor G0259

1738 **SOME DESCENDANTS OF JOHN HANCOCK (1733–1802) OF GOOCHLAND, FLUVANNA & PATRICK COS., VA.**, by R.R. and W. Hancock. 1938(?)
Paper. $19.00. 86pp. typescript .... Vendor G0259

1739 **A CONTRIBUTION TO THE GEN. OF THE HANDERSON FAM.**, by H.E. Handerson. 1885.
Paper. $14.00. 80pp. .... Vendor G0259

1740 **HANEY FAM.**, by J.L. Haney. 1930.
Paper. $9.00. 46pp. .... Vendor G0259

1741 **DESC. OF REV. THOMAS HANFORD OF CONN.**, by A.C. Golding. 1936.
Cloth, $37.50. Paper, $27.50. 153pp. .... Vendor G0259

1742 **GEN. OF THE HANNUM FAM. DESC. FROM JOHN & MARGERY HANNUM**, by Curtis H. Hannum. 1911.
Cloth, $109.00. Paper, $99.00. 702pp. .... Vendor G0259

1743 **WILLIAM HANNUM OF NEW ENGLAND, & SOME DESC.**, by W.H. Hannum. 1936.
Paper. $13.50. 67pp. .... Vendor G0259

1744 **HAPGOOD FAMILY: DESC. OF SHADRACH, 1656–1898**, by W. Hapgood. 1898.
Includes supplement.
Cloth, $84.50. Paper, $74.50. 590pp. .... Vendor G0259

1745 **HARBAUGH HISTORY. A DIRECTORY, GEN. & SOURCE BOOK OF FAM. RECORDS**, by C.B. and J.L. Cooprider. 1947.
Cloth, $78.50. Paper, $68.50. 441pp. .... Vendor G0259

1746 **ANNALS OF THE HARBOUGH FAM. IN AMER., 1736–1856**, by H. Harbough. 1856.
Cloth, $40.00. Paper, $30.00. 148pp. .... Vendor G0259

1747 **HARDENBERGH FAMILY: A GEN. COMP.**, by M. Miller. 1958.
Cloth, $89.50. Paper, $79.50. 520pp. .... Vendor G0259

1748 **A NARRATIVE HIST. OF THE HARDING FAM.**, by A.K. Holt. 1904.
Cloth, $31.00. Paper, $21.00. 142pp. .... Vendor G0259

1749 **THE HARDINGS IN AMER. A GEN. REGISTER OF THE DESC. OF JOHN HARDING OF ENG. BORN 1567**, by W.J. Harding. 1925.
Cloth, $38.00. Paper, $28.00. 209pp. .... Vendor G0259

1750 **HARDY & HARDIE, PAST & PRESENT**, by H.C. and E.N. Hardy. 1935.
Cloth, $189.00. Paper, $179.00. 1322pp. .... Vendor G0259

1751 **HIST. & GEN. OF THE HARLAN FAM., & PARTICULARLY OF THE DESC. OF GEORGE & MICHAEL HARLAN WHO SETTLED IN CHESTER CO., PENN., 1687**, by A.H. Harlan. 1914.
Cloth, $169.50. Paper, $159.50. 1,065pp. .... Vendor G0259

1752 **HARMAN GEN. (SO. BRANCH) WITH BIOGR. SKETCHES 1700–1924**, by J.N. Harman, Sr. 1925.
Cloth, $68.50. Paper, $58.50. 376pp. .... Vendor G0259

1753 **HARMAN–HARMON GEN. & BIOGR., WITH HIST. NOTES, 19 BC TO 1928 AD**, by J.W. Harman. 1928.
Cloth, $80.50. Paper, $70.50. 471pp. .... Vendor G0259

1754 **HARMON GENEALOGY, COMPRISING ALL BRANCHES IN NEW ENG.**, by A.C. Harmon. 1920.
Cloth, $69.50. Paper, $59.50. 383pp. .... Vendor G0259

1755 **KITH AND KIN, THE HARPERS FROM DREWRY, HEPSY AND PALMYRA**, by Joseph D. Harper. 1994. Indexed.
Paper. $30.00. 488pp. .... Vendor G0242

1756 **HARRINGTON FAMILY IN AMER.**, by E. Harrington. 1907.
Paper. $19.00. 127pp. .... Vendor G0259

1757 **MANUSCRIPT OF HARRINGTON FAMILY GAZETTEER**, by George H. Harrington. 1941.
Cloth, $135.00. Paper, $125.00. 878pp. typescript .... Vendor G0259

1758 **A HIST. OF JAMES HARRIS OF NEW LONDON, CT. & HIS DESC., 1640–1878**, by N.H. Morgan. 1878.
Cloth, $46.00. Paper, $36.00. 239pp. .... Vendor G0259

1759 **COLLATERAL ANCESTRY OF STEPHEN HARRIS (b. SEPT. 4, 1798) & MARIANNE SMITH (b. APRIL 2, 1805)**, by J.S Harris. 1908.
Cloth, $38.00. Paper, $28.00. 190pp. .... Vendor G0259

1760 **GEN. & BIOGR. SKETCHES OF THE N.J. BRANCH OF THE HARRIS FAM. IN THE U.S.**, by S. Keifer. 1888.
Cloth, $65.50. Paper, $55.50. 350pp. .... Vendor G0259

1761 **HARRIS FAMILY FROM A.D. 1630 IN TWO LINES**, by D.J. and N.D. Harris. 1909.
Cloth, $34.00. Paper, $24.00. 131pp. .... Vendor G0259

1762 **ROBERT HARRIS & DESC. WITH NOTICES OF MOREY & METCALF FAM.**, by L.M. Harris. 1861.
Paper. $11.00. 56pp. .... Vendor G0259

1763 **THE FIVE THOMAS HARRISES OF ISLE OF WIGHT CO., VA**, by John A. Brayton. 1995.
   Separates and untangles the various **Harris** families of seventeenth-century Isle of Wight Co., VA, and improves on previous Harris research.
Paper. $15.00 postpaid, NC residents add 6% sales tax. 190+xviii pp. Vendor G0302

1764 **ARIS SONIS FOCISQUE; A MEM. OF AN AMER. FAM., THE HARRISONS OF SKIMINO**, by F. Harrison. 1910.
Cloth, $76.00. Paper, $66.00. 437pp. .... Vendor G0259

1765 **BRIEF HIST. OF THE FIRST HARRISONS OF VA., DESC. OF CUTHBERT HARRISON (1600–1915)**, by H.T. Harrison. 1915.
Paper. $8.00. 40pp. .... Vendor G0259

1766 **DESCENDANTS OF BENJAMIN HARRISON OF VIRGINIA**, by Carol A. Hauk. 1995. Indexed.
Paper. $45.00. 394pp. .... Vendor G0340

1767 **PARTIAL HIST. OF THE HARRISON FAM.**, by W. Harrison.
Paper. $10.00. 53pp. .... Vendor G0259

1768 **SETTLERS BY THE LONG GREY TRAIL. Some Pioneers to Old Augusta County, Virginia, and Their Descendants, of the Family of Harrison and Allied Lines**, by J. Houston Harrison. (1935) reprint 1994. Indexed. Illus.
   Includes a detailed genealogy of the **Harrisons** of Augusta and their Harrison cousins. Other lines traced include: **Bear, Bowman, Brown, Burkholder, Byrd, Campbell, Chrisman, Conrad, Craven, Creed, Davis, Davison, Decker, Ewing, Gaines, Gordon, Hanna, Henkel, Henton, Herring, Hemphill, Hinkle, Hite, Hollingsworth, Hopper, Houston, Howard, Jordon, Keezells, Kennerly, Koontz, Lincoln, Logan, McWilliams, Martz, Mauzy, Monroe, Moore, Newman, Ott, Pickering, Price, Smith, Watson, Williams, Williamson, Woodley, and Yancey**.
Paper. $47.50. 665pp. .... Vendor G0011

1769 **SETTLERS BY THE LONG GREY TRAIL; SOME PIONEERS TO OLD AUGUSTA CO., VA. & THEIR DESCENDANTS, OF THE FAMILY OF HARRISON & ALLIED LINES**, by J. Houston Harrison. 1935.
Cloth, $109.00. Paper, $99.00. 666pp. .... Vendor G0259

1770 **THE HARRISONS FROM HOUSTON COUNTY, TEXAS 1835–1993**, by Hilde Shuptrine Farley. 1994. Indexed. Illus.
   Willliam D. **Harrison** and Jane Patton Harrison and their allied families: **Patton, Morgan, Shuptrine, Vickers, Julian**, and others.
Cloth. $28.00. 297pp. .... Vendor G0024

1771 **THE STORY OF THE "DINING FORK" [THE HISTORY OF THE HARRISONS OF HARRISON CO OH, FROM JOHN HARRISON, FOUNDER OF THE TOWN OF SCIO IN 1826]**, by Joseph T. Harrison. 1927.
Cloth, $39.50. Paper, $29.50. 370pp. .... Vendor G0259

1772 **EDWARD HART DESCENDANTS & ALLIED FAMILIES**, by Clara Hart
Kennedy. 1939.
Cloth, $48.00. Paper, $38.00. 239pp. .... Vendor G0259

1773 **GEN. HIST. OF DEACON STEPHEN HART & HIS DESC., 1632–1875**,
by A. Andrews. 1875.
Cloth, $101.00. Paper, $91.00. 606pp. .... Vendor G0259

1774 **JOSEPH HART & HIS DESC.**, by C.C. Hart. 1901.
Cloth, $32.50. Paper, $22.50. 124pp. .... Vendor G0259

1775 **REC. OF THE HART FAM. OF AMER., DESC. FROM DEA. STEPHEN
HART (EXTR. FROM BASSETT GEN.)**. 1926.
Paper. $8.00. 40pp. .... Vendor G0259

1776 **THE DESC. OF LEWIS HART & ANNE ELLIOTT WITH ADD. GEN. &
HIST. DATA ON THE FAMS. OF HART, WARNER, CURTISS,
McCOLLEY, THOMPSON, TORRANCE & VOSBURGH**, by J.S.
Torrance. 1923.
Cloth, $69.50. Paper, $59.50. 380pp. .... Vendor G0259

1777 **THE HARTMAN FAMILY OF MEDINA COUNTY, OHIO**, by Elissa
Scalise Powell. (1992) reprint 1993. Indexed. Illus.
Including **Hummel, Heller**.
Paper. $11.50. 60pp. .... Vendor G0098

1778 **CLEMENS GEORG AND SOPHIA THERESA STRIEBER HARTMANN:
ANCESTORS AND DESCENDANTS**, by Marianne Elizabeth Hall Little.
1993. Indexed. Illus.
Limited Edition; DeWitt County, Texas. **Hartman, Hartmann, Strieber,
Woods**.
Cloth, $65.00. Paper, $45.00. 100pp. .... Vendor G0264

1779 **CLEMENS GEORG AND SOPHIA THERESA STRIEBER HARTMANN:
ANCESTORS AND DESCENDANTS, VOLUME 2**, by Marianne Elizabeth
Hall Little. 1995. Indexed. Illus.
Limited Edition; DeWitt County, Texas. **Hartman, Hartmann, Strieber,
Woods**.
Cloth, $70.00. Paper, $50.00. 125pp. .... Vendor G0264

1780 **GEN. HIST. OF SAMUELL HARTT FROM LONDON, ENG. TO LYNN,
MASS., 1640, & DESC. TO 1903, NICHOLAS, ISAAC & OTHERS**, by
J.H. Hart. 1903.
Cloth, $105.00. Paper, $95.00. 631pp. .... Vendor G0259

1781 **HARTWELL FAM. ACCT. OF THE DESC. OF WM. HARTWELL OF
CONCORD, MA., 1636–1895**, by L. Densmore. 1895.
Cloth, $36.50. Paper, $26.50. 176pp. .... Vendor G0259

1782 **JOHN HARVARD & HIS ANC.**, by H.F. Waters. 1885.
Paper. $9.00. 46pp. .... Vendor G0259

1783 **ANC. OF COL. JOHN HARVEY OF NORTHWOOD, N.H.**, by J. Treat.
1907.
Paper. $10.00. 47pp. .... Vendor G0259

1784 **THE DESC. OF ELISHA HARVEY FROM 1719 TO 1914,** by J.W. Knappenberger. 1914.
Paper. $9.00. 44pp. .... Vendor G0259

1785 **THE HARVEY BOOK, GIVING THE GEN. OF CERTAIN BRANCHES OF THE AMER. FAMS. OF HARVEY, NESBITT, DIXON & JAMESON,** by O.J. Harvey. 1899.
Cloth, $149.50. Paper, $139.50. 1,057pp. .... Vendor G0259

1786 **THE HARVEY NAME BOOK,** by Lois G. Harvey. (1983) reprint 1995. Indexed.
Paper. $12.00. 144pp. .... Vendor G0260

1787 **A GEN. HIST. OF THE HARWOOD FAM., DESC. FROM ANDREW HARWOOD, WHOSE ENG. HOME WAS IN DARTMOUTH, DEVENSHIRE, & WHO EMIGR. TO AMER. & RESIDED IN BOSTON, MA.,** by W.H. Harwood. 3rd ed. 1911.
Cloth, $31.00. Paper, $21.00. 155pp. .... Vendor G0259

1788 **A GEN. HIST. OF THE SALEM HARWOODS, DESC. OF HENRY & ELIZABETH HARWOOD WHO CAME FROM ENG. WITH GOV. WINTHROP & SETTLED IN CHARLESTOWN, MA.,** by W.H. Harwood. Vol. II. 1912.
Paper. $15.00. 75pp. .... Vendor G0259

1789 **A GEN. HIST. OF THE CONCORD HARWOODS, DESC. OF NATHANIEL HARWOOD, SON OF JOHN HARWOOD OF LONDON, ENGLAND, WHO SETTLED WITH ELIZABETH HIS WIFE, IN CONCORD, MASS., ABOUT 1665,** by W.H. Harwood. Vol. III. 1912.
Paper. $19.50. 129pp. .... Vendor G0259

1790 **HASBROUCK FAMILY IN AMERICA, WITH EUROPEAN BACKGROUND,** by Kenneth E. Hasbrouck. 2 vols. 1961.
Cloth, $125.00. Paper, $115.00. 837pp. .... Vendor G0259

1791 **LINEAGE OF THE HASBROUCK FAMILY (HUGUENOT ABRAHAM), EXTR. "OLDE ULSTER,"** by A.L. Snyder.
Paper. $12.00. 61pp. .... Vendor G0259

1792 **A SHORT ACCT. OF THE DESC. OF WILLIAM HASKELL OF GLOUCESTER, MASS. (REPR. "ESSEX INST. HIST. COLL."),** by U.G. Haskell. 1896.
Paper. $12.50. 62pp. .... Vendor G0259

1793 **CHRON. OF THE HASKELL FAM.,** by I. Haskell. 1943.
Cloth, $54.00. Paper, $44.00. 294pp. .... Vendor G0259

1794 **A BRIEF HIST. OF ELKANAH HASKIN & DESC. OF HIS SON ENOCH, 1700–1890,** by D.C. Haskin. 1890.
Paper. $10.00. 53pp. .... Vendor G0259

1795 **HASKINS GENEALOGY: THE DESCENDANTS OF JONAS HASKINS (1788–1837) OF DUTCHESS CO., NEW YORK, AND UHRICHSVILLE, OHIO,** by James W. Lowry. 1992. Indexed. Illus.
Includes **Arnold, Barry, Beck, Bovey, Brown, Caves, Clark, Davis, Dittoe,**

Ferguson, Finch, Fowler, Gallagher, Hard, Hickok, LaRue, McCullough, McGee, McGuire, Meek, Meredith, Miller, Milone, Noble, Orr, Pennock, Smith, Thompson, Umpleby, Van Blarcum.
Cloth. $29.95. 350pp. .... Vendor G0035

1796 **HASTINGS MEMORIAL. A GEN. ACCT. OF THE DESC. OF THOMAS HASTINGS OF WATERTOWN, MA., FROM 1634 TO 1864,** by L.N.H. Buckminster. 1866.
Cloth, $35.50. Paper, $25.50. 183pp. .... Vendor G0259

1797 **MAJOR TIMOTHY HATCH OF HARTFORD & HIS DESC.,** by E.H. Fletcher. 1879.
Paper. $7.50. 36pp. .... Vendor G0259

1798 **PHILIP HATCH OF YORK CO., MAINE & SOME OF HIS DESC.,** by H.I. Hiday. 1949.
Paper. $7.00. 34pp. .... Vendor G0259

1799 **THOMAS HATCH OF BARNSTABLE & SOME OF HIS DESC. (SOC. OF COL. WARS IN N.J.),** by C. Pack. 1930.
Cloth, $67.50. Paper, $57.50. 363pp. .... Vendor G0259

1800 **HATFIELD AND PHILLIPS FAMILIES OF EASTERN KENTUCKY AND SOUTHWESTERN WEST VIRGINIA,** by Harry Leon Sellards, Jr. 1993. Indexed. Illus.
Related families: **McCoy, Ball, Bevins, Coleman, Smith, Blackburn, Blankenship, Chapman, Charles, Deskins, Ratliff, Reynolds, Varney, Dotson, Justice, Musick, Runyon, Scott, Lowe, Williamson.**
Cloth. $40.00. 478pp. .... Vendor G0445

1801 **HATFIELD FAMILY HISTORY,** by Harry Leon Sellards, Jr. 1995. Indexed. Illus.
Hatfield families of George Goff (1715), John (1717), Joseph (1739–1832), Captain Andrew (1737–1813), John (1773–1836), Edward (1770) and related.
Cloth. $62.00. 960pp. .... Vendor G0445

1802 **THE HATFIELDS OF WESTCHESTER: A GEN. OF THE DESC. OF THOMAS HATFIELD, OF NEW AMSTERDAM & MAMARONECK, WHOSE SONS SETTLED IN WHITE PLAINS, WESTCHESTER CO., N.Y.,** by A. Hatfield. 1935.
Cloth, $44.50. Paper, $34.50. 222pp. .... Vendor G0259

1803 **DESC. OF SIMEON HATHAWAY, ALSO CONTAINING SOME LIN. OF BRECKENRIDGE, BINGHAM, CASS, HINSDILL, LYMAN, MARTIN, McCOY, SMITH, SHEPARD, & WARNER,** by E.H. Parks. 1957.
Paper. $13.50. 68pp. .... Vendor G0259

1804 **ANTECEDENTS OF KELLY, KEVIN AND BRIAN HAUGHTON, VOL. II, DAVENPORT AND RELATED FAMILIES,** by Beverly and Ken Haughton. 1987. Indexed. Illus.
Ancestry in America and England through one grandmother. Surnames include: **Davenport, Goble, Slingsby, Rushton, Graves, Haner, Ferrill, Reed, Challenor, Clemens, Cook, Arnold, Finney, Baughman,** and others.
Cloth. $15.00. Paper, $10.00. 243pp. .... Vendor G0200

1805 **ANTECEDENTS OF KELLY, KEVIN AND BRIAN HAUGHTON, VOL. III, BACON AND RELATED FAMILIES**, by Beverly and Ken Haughton. 1992. Indexed. Illus. Ancestry in America and England through one grandfather. Surnames include: **Bacon, Shepley, Swett, Field, Walkerley, Bashforth, Loring, Jones, Selby, Marshall, Wilder, Hibbard, Wilkinson, Kenworthy**, and others. Cloth. $20.00. 482pp. .... Vendor G0200

1806 **GEN. OF DESC. OF RICHARD HAVEN OF LYNN, ETC.**, by J. Adams. Rev. ed. 1849. Paper. $19.00. 104pp. .... Vendor G0259

1807 **SGT. RICHARD HAVEN OF LYNN & ONE LINE OF HIS DESC., WITH SOME COLL. BRANCHES**, by W. Haven. 1927. Paper. $18.50. 104pp. .... Vendor G0259

1808 **THE HAVENS FAMILY IN NEW JERSEY, WITH ADDITIONAL NOTES ON THE TILTON, FIELDER, HANCE, OSBORN, DAVISON, COX & GIFFORD FAMILIES, CONNECTED BY MARRIAGE**, by Henry C. Havens. 1933. Cloth, $32.50. Paper, $22.50. 103+30pp. .... Vendor G0259

1809 **HAVILAND–LOUNSBURY–MOULINIER GENEALOGY & MEMOIRS**, by M.B. Moulinier. n.d. Cloth, $35.00. Paper, $25.00. 169pp. .... Vendor G0259

1810 **EDMOND HAWES OF YARMOUTH, MASS., AN EMIGRANT TO AMER. IN 1635, HIS ANC., & SOME OF HIS DESC.**, by J.W. Hawes. 1914. Cloth, $44.50. Paper, $34.50. 231pp. .... Vendor G0259

1811 **RICHARD HAWES OF DORCHESTER, MASS., & SOME OF HIS DESC.**, by F.M. Hawes. 1932. Cloth, $49.50. Paper, $39.50. 263pp. .... Vendor G0259

1812 **THE HAWKER, PETTIT AND McCLINTOCK FAMILIES OF ALDEN, FREEBORN COUNTY, MINNESOTA**, by Mary Hawker Bakeman. 1990. Indexed. Illus. Paper. $10.00. 74pp. .... Vendor G0246

1813 **[Hawkins]. ANCESTRAL LINES OF JENNIS COWEN (HAWKINS) ROBINSON, THROUGH HAWKINS, SATTERLY, MILLS, ET AL**, by M. Francis. 1935. Paper. $19.50. 117pp. .... Vendor G0259

1814 **HAWLEY & NASON ANC.**, by E.H. Everett. 1929. Paper. $12.50. 78pp. .... Vendor G0259

1815 **A HIST. OF THE PROGENITORS & SOME SO. CAROLINA DESC. OF COL. ANN HAWKES HAY, WITH COLLATERAL GEN., 500–1908**, by C.J. Colcock. 1908. Cloth, $46.00. Paper, $36.00. 216pp. .... Vendor G0259

1816 **HAYDEN FAM. MAGAZINE, VOL. III, INCL. HIST., BIOGR., & FAM. RECORDS.** 1931. Cloth, $40.00. Paper, $30.00. 202pp. .... Vendor G0259

1817 **HAYDEN FAM. MAGAZINE, VOL. IV.** 1932.
Cloth, $41.00. Paper, $31.00. 206pp. Vendor G0259

1818 **HAYDEN FAM. MAGAZINE, VOL V.** 1933.
Cloth, $30.00. Paper, $20.00. 133pp. Vendor G0259

1819 **RECORDS OF THE CONN. LINE OF THE HAYDEN FAMILY,** by J.H.
Hayden. 1888.
Cloth, $61.00. Paper, $51.00. 329pp. Vendor G0259

1820 **THOMAS HAYDON—ENGLAND TO VIRGINIA—1657,** by Robert
Haydon. 1995. Indexed. Illus.
The life and times of Thomas **Haydon** circa 1640 to 1717.
Cloth. $39.00. 100pp. . . . . Vendor G0372

1821 **BICENTENNIAL GATHERING OF DESC. OF HENRY HAYES AT
UNIONVILLE, PENN., WITH GEN. DATA.** 1906.
Paper. $14.00. 89pp. . . . . Vendor G0259

1822 **DESCENDANTS OF RICHARD HAYES OF LYME, CT., THROUGH HIS
SON, TITUS HAYES,** by H.M. Weeks, edited by R.H. Cooke. 1904.
Cloth, $40.00. Paper, $30.00. 192pp. Vendor G0259

1823 **GEORGE HAYES OF WINDSOR & HIS DESC.,** by C.W. Hayes. 1883.
Cloth, $55.00. Paper, $45.00. 354pp. Vendor G0259

1824 **HAYES FAMILY: ORIGIN, HISTORY, GENEALOGY,** by R.S. Hayes. 1928.
Cloth, $79.50. Paper, $69.50. 464pp. Vendor G0259

1825 **HAYES, JOHNSON AND ALLIED FAMILIES GENEALOGICAL FAM-
ILY HISTORY,** by Charles Clifton Hayes. 1994. Indexed. Illus.
Cloth. $70.00. 520pp. . . . . Vendor G0183

1826 **JOHN HAYES OF DOVER, N.H.: A BOOK OF HIS FAMILY,** by K.F.
Richmond. 2 vols. 1936.
Cloth, $139.50. Paper, $129.50. 911pp. . . . . Vendor G0259

1827 **[Hayes]. JOHN HENRY HEES (HASE, HAISE, HAYES) & HIS DESCEN-
DANTS, 1750–1982,** by Mrs Mary Wilder Hayes & David W. Hayes. 1982.
Cloth, $74.00. Paper, $64.00. 422pp. Vendor G0259

1828 **HIST. OF THE HAYFORD FAM., 1100–1900, ITS CONNECTIONS BY
THE BONNEY, FULLER & PHINNEY FAM. WITH THE MAYFLOWER
1620 CHICKERING FAM., 1356–1900,** by O. Hayford. 1901.
Cloth, $51.00. Paper, $41.00. 253pp. Vendor G0259

1829 **ANC. & DESC. OF JOHN RUSSELL HAYNES (INCL. HAINES, COT-
TON, BRADSTREET, DUDLEY, HUBBARD, & BRAINERD FAM.),** by
G.W. Burch. 1924.
Cloth, $38.50. Paper, $28.50. 151pp. Vendor G0259

1830 **WALTER HAYNES OF SUTTON MANDEVILLE, WILTSHIRE, ENG.,
& SUDBURY, MASS., & HIS DESC., 1583–1928,** by F. Haynes. 1929.
Cloth, $45.00. Paper, $35.00. 235pp. Vendor G0259

1831 **HAYNIE FAM. OF NORTHUMBERLAND CO., VA.,** by G. Torrence. 1949.
Paper. $8.00. 41pp. . . . . Vendor G0259

1832 **GEORGE W. AND THOMAS HAYS OF WILCOX COUNTY, ALABAMA AND OUACHITA COUNTY, ARKANSAS,** by Wanda Williams Colvin. 1995. Indexed. Illus.
Paper. $16.00. 71pp. .... Vendor G0432

1833 **JAMES HAYWARD, b. APR. 4, 1750, KILLED IN THE BATTLE OF LEXINGTON, APR. 19, 1775, WITH GEN. NOTES REL. TO THE HAYWARDS,** by W.F. Adams. 1911.
Paper. $11.00. 58pp. .... Vendor G0259

1834 **HAZARD FAM. OF R.I., 1635–1894. BEING A GEN. & HIST. OF THE DESC. OF THOMAS HAZARD,** by C.E. Robinson. 1895.
Cloth, $49.50. Paper, $39.50. 298pp. .... Vendor G0259

1835 **GEN. SKETCHES OF ROBT & JOHN HAZELTON & SOME DESC. WITH BRIEF NOTICES OF OTHER NEW ENG. FAM. BEARING THIS NAME,** by W. Lapham. 1892.
Cloth, $56.00. Paper, $46.00. 368pp. .... Vendor G0259

1836 **HAZEN FAMILY IN AMERICA; A GENEALOGY,** by T.E. Hazen. 1947.
Cloth, $159.00. Paper, $149.00. 1,175pp. .... Vendor G0259

1837 **BRIEF HIST. & GEN. OF THE HEARNE FAM., 1066 TO 1907,** by W.T. Hearne. 1907.
Cloth, $105.00. Paper, $95.00. 755pp. .... Vendor G0259

HAZARD GENEALOGY

Title: *The Ancestry and Posterity of Harry Williams Hazard III (1918–1989)*
Compiled by Harry W. Hazard III; edited & published by Mary J. Hazard
Publ. 1993, cloth, 9x11.5 in., 624 pp.
Indexed (more than 5400 names)
71 6-gen. pedigree charts, 12 pp. pictures, 358 pp. family histories, 28 pp. references
Maps: CT, DE, MD, MA, NJ, NY, PA, RI, VA/WV, with dates of county org.
Tables & lists: occupations, education, immigrant arrivals, marriage data, geographical locations of families
Primary ancestral lines: Hazard, Willson, Williams, Low (31 gen., to 1040), Reeves
Includes: Ayer, Babbidge, Ballard, Bateman, Bereman, Bowen, Buttolph, Clap, Clarkson, Clement, Cogswell, Davis, Dawson, dePeyster, Evans, Ford, Fullerton, Gardner, Hall, Hallett, Harris, Herrick, Joslin, Lowe, Manning, Marston, Osgood, Pike, Riley, Sayre, Shepard, Stone, Sumner, Thompson, Walling, Warner, Woodbury, many others
Cost: $35 (incl. shipping) from: Mary J. Hazard, 600 Seneca Pkwy., Rochester, NY 14613. (Phone: 716-254-9133)

1838 **BARTHOLOMEW HEATH OF HAVERHILL, MASSACHUSETTS AND SOME OF HIS DESCENDANTS**, by Valerie Dyer Giorgi. 1994. Indexed. Cloth. $43.00. 567pp. .... Vendor G0090

1839 **GEN. RECORD OF ONE BRANCH OF HEATH, CLARK & CONE FAM.**, by D. Stilwell. 1905. Paper. $8.00. 42pp. .... Vendor G0259

1840 **WILLIAM HEATH OF ROXBURY, MASSACHUSETTS AND SOME OF HIS DESCENDANTS**, by Valerie Dyer Giorgi. 1993. Indexed. Illus. Cloth. $38.00. 441pp. .... Vendor G0090

1841 **DAVID HEATWOLE AND HIS DESCENDANTS**, by Harry Anthony Brunk. 1987. Cloth. $44.00. 1,121pp. .... Vendor G0150

1842 **THE GENEALOGY OF ADAM HEINECKE & HENRY VANDERSAAL, FROM 1747–1881**, by S. Heinecke. 1881. Paper. $16.00. 81pp. .... Vendor G0259

1843 **GENEALOGY OF ADAM HEINECKE & HENRY VANDERSAAL, 1747 TO 1881, WITH A BRIEF ACCT. OF THE AUTHOR'S TRAVELS IN ABOUT 16 YEARS AS AN EVANGELIST**, by Rev. Samuel Heinecke. 2nd ed. 1881. Cloth, $55.00. Paper, $45.00. 302pp. .... Vendor G0259

1844 **HELMER FAMILY. PHILIP HELMER, THE PIONEER, & HIS DESC.**, by P.W. Williams. 1931–2. Cloth, $37.50. Paper, $27.50. 183pp. .... Vendor G0259

1845 **[Helwig]. THIS IS MY LINE**, by Bette Jean K. Helwig. 1979. Cloth, $41.00. Paper, $31.00. 214pp. .... Vendor G0259

1846 **HEMBY**, by Mildred S. Ezell. 1987. Indexed. Illus. Includes: **Hemby, Godley, Hammond**. Paper. $15.00. 92pp. .... Vendor G0323

1847 **GEN. RECORD OF ONE BRANCH OF THE HEMENWAY FAM. 1634–1880**, by A. Hemenway. 1880. Paper. $18.00. 92pp. .... Vendor G0259

1848 **THE MASS. HEMENWAY FAM., DESC. OF RALPH HEMENWAY OF ROXBURY 1634**, by M. and C. Newton. 1912. Paper. $11.00. 56pp. .... Vendor G0259

1849 **RALPH HEMENWAY OF ROXBURY, MASS., 1634, & HIS DESC., WITH DIETZ GEN.**, by C.A. Newton. Vol. II. 1943. Cloth, $38.50. Paper, $28.50. 152pp. .... Vendor G0259

1850 **DIARY OF JOSHUA HEMPSTEAD, 1711–1758, WITH AN ACCT. OF A JOURNEY MADE FROM NEW LONDON TO MARYLAND**. 1901. Cloth, $122.50. Paper, $112.50. 750pp. .... Vendor G0259

1851 **RECORDS OF THE ANNUAL HENCH & DROMGOLD REUNIONS, HELD IN PERRY CO., PENN., 1897–1912**, by L.D. Emig. 1913. Cloth, $38.50. Paper, $28.50. 191pp. .... Vendor G0259

1852 **THE PASTORAL YEARS OF REV. ANTHONY HENCKEL 1692–1717**, by Ann Hinkle Gable. 1991. Illus. Book #1189.
Cloth. $23.50. 127pp. .... Vendor G0082

1853 **GENEALOGY OF THE HENDERSHOT FAMILY IN AMERICA**, by A.E. Hendershot. 1961.
Cloth, $43.00. Paper, $33.00. 213pp. .... Vendor G0259

1854 **ANC. & DESC. OF LT. JOHN HENDERSON OF GREENBRIAR CO., VA., 1650–1900**, by J.L. Miller. 1902.
Paper. $8.00. 37pp. .... Vendor G0259

1855 **HENDERSON CHRONICLES, DESC. OF ALEXANDER HENDERSON OF SCOTLAND**, by J.N. McCue. 1915.
Cloth, $32.50. Paper, $22.50. 113pp. .... Vendor G0259

1856 **HENDERSONS OF EARLY NORTH CAROLINA PT 3 (1850–70). A Beginning Survey of the People Using the Henderson Name from the NC Census and Other Records**, by Robert H. Henderson. 1995. Indexed.
Paper. $17.00. 150pp+index .... Vendor G0442

1857 **HENDERSONS OF EARLY SOUTH CAROLINA PT 3 (1850–70). A Beginning Survey of the People Using the Henderson Name from the SC Census and Other Records**, by Robert H. Henderson. 1994.
Paper. $20.00. 186pp. .... Vendor G0442

1858 **OUR HOUSE OF HENDERSON. A Documented History of One Henderson Lineage from the Time of Colonial America to 1991**, by Robert H. Henderson. 1991.
Cloth. $32.95. 278pp. .... Vendor G0442

1859 **HENDRICK GENEALOGY: DANIELD HENDRICK OF HAVERHILL, MA, & HIS DESCENDANTS, WITH AN APPENDIX CONTAINING BRIEF ACCTS. OF SEVERAL OTHER HENDRICK FAMILIES**, by Chas. T. Hendrick. 1923.
Cloth, $109.50. Paper, $99.50. 699pp. .... Vendor G0259

1860 **HENDRICKSON. NOTES ON THE MESSENGER & HENDRICKSON FAM. & DESC.**, by M.P. Ferris. 1916.
Paper. $16.00. 79pp. .... Vendor G0259

1861 **HENKEL MEMORIAL; 1ST SERIES, #4, & 2ND SERIES, #1–3**, by A. Stapleton.
Cloth, $38.00. Paper, $28.00. 155pp. .... Vendor G0259

1862 **MEMORIES REVISITED. THE LIFE AND FAMILY OF W.W. "BILL" HENLEY 1905–1982 AND REBA ELIZABETH MIARS HENLEY 1905–1994: THEIR LIVES, DESCENDANTS AND ANCESTORS**, by Betty Ann Henley Vollenweider. 1995. Indexed. Illus.
Additional surnames: **Thompson, Jefferis, Smith, King, Sowell, Moore, Stratton**. Over 2,900 names indexed; over 1,400 photographs.
Cloth. $50.00. 680pp. .... Vendor G0443

1863 **DESCENDANTS OF PHILIP HENRY**, rev. ed. by James E. Jones. (1844) reprint 1925.
Paper. $14.00. 68pp. .... Vendor G0259

1864 **GENEALOGY OF THE HENRY FAM.**, by D.F. Henry. 1919.
Paper. $13.00. 67pp. .... Vendor G0259

1865 **HENRY FAMILY HISTORY: DESCENDANTS OF JAMES HENRY SR. OF CONNECTICUT**, by Alan D. Henry. 1993.
Cloth, $39.50. Paper, $29.50. 193pp. .... Vendor G0259

1866 **HENRY FAMILY RECORDS**, by J. Montgomery Seaver.
Paper. $7.00. 32pp. .... Vendor G0259

1867 **HIST. OF THE HENRY FAM (KY.)**, by J. Henry. 1900.
Cloth, $30.00. Paper, $20.00. 125pp. .... Vendor G0259

1868 **REC. OF DESC. OF SIMON HENRY (1766–1854) & RHODA PARSONS (1774–1847), HIS WIFE, WITH APP. CONTAINING SOME ACCT. OF THEIR ANC. & OF COLL. LINES**, by F.A. Henry. 1905.
Paper. $13.00. 65pp. .... Vendor G0259

1869 **THE DESC. OF SAMUEL HENRY OF HADLEY & AMHERST, MASS., 1734–1790, & LURANA CADY, HIS WIFE**, by W.H. Eldridge. 1915.
Cloth, $46.00. Paper, $36.00. 240pp. .... Vendor G0259

1870 **GEN. & HIST. OF THE HEPBURN FAM. OF THE SUSQUEHANNA VALLEY, WITH REF. TO OTHER FAM. OF THE SAME NAME**, by J.P. Meginness. 1894.
Cloth, $38.00. Paper, $28.00. 185pp. .... Vendor G0259

1871 **THE HERKIMERS & SCHUYLERS, AN HIST. SKETCH OF THE TWO FAM., WITH GEN. OF THE DESC. OF GEORGE HERKIMER, WHO SETTLED IN THE MOHAWK VALLEY, N. Y., IN 1721**, by P.S. Cowen. 1903.
Cloth, $32.00. Paper, $22.00. 147pp. .... Vendor G0259

1872 **THE HERNDON FAMILY OF VIRGINIA, Volume One: The First Three Generations**, by Dr. John Goodwin Herndon, Ph.D. (1947) reprint 1995. Indexed. One illustration.
This outstanding genealogy of the **Herndon** family is a must for anyone with a Herndon ancestor. Includes biographic sketches, including additions and corrections, and a full-name index.
Cloth. $26.00. 77pp. .... Vendor G0425

1873 **THE HERNDONS OF THE AMERICAN REVOLUTION. Part I: John Herndon [ca. 1700–1786], of Charlotte County, Virginia, and His Known Descendants Through the Seventh Generation of the Family in America**, by Dr. John Goodwin Herndon, Ph.D. 1950. Indexed.
Cloth. $15.00. 77pp. .... Vendor G0425

1874 **THE HERNDONS OF THE AMERICAN REVOLUTION. Part II: Edward Herndon [ca. 1702–1759], of Spotsylvania County, Virginia, and His Known Descendants Through the Seventh Generation of the Family in America**, by John Goodwin Herndon, Ph.D. 1951. Indexed.
Cloth. $15.00. 90pp. .... Vendor G0425

1875 **THE HERNDONS OF THE AMERICAN REVOLUTION. Part III: William Herndon [ca. 1706–ca. 1773], of Orange County, Virginia, and His**

Known Descendants Through the Seventh Generation of the Family in America, by John Goodwin Herndon, Ph.D. 1952. Indexed.
Cloth. $15.00. 106pp. .... Vendor G0425

1876 **THE HERNDONS OF THE AMERICAN REVOLUTION. Part IV: Richard Herndon [prob. b. ca. 1708–d. post 1754], of Caroline County, Virginia, and His Known Descendants Through the Seventh Generation of the Family in America**, by John Goodwin Herndon, Ph.D. 1952. Indexed.
Cloth. $15.00. 119pp. .... Vendor G0425

1877 **THE HERNDONS OF THE AMERICAN REVOLUTION. Part VI: #82 William Herndon [b. ca. 1737–d. ca. 1796], of Prince William County, Virginia, and His Known Descendants of the Family in America**, by Dudley L. Herndon, Jr. 1992. Indexed. Two illustrations.
All known descendants.
Cloth. 6" x 9". $45.00. 560pp. .... Vendor G0425

1878 **THE HERNDONS OF THE AMERICAN REVOLUTION. Part VII: #84 John Herndon [b. ca. 1741–d. ca. 1805], of Fauquier County, Virginia, and His Known Descendants of the Family in America**, by Dudley L. Herndon, Jr. 1993. Indexed. Two illustrations.
All known descendants.
Cloth. 6" x 9". $33.00. 310pp. .... Vendor G0425

1879 **THE HERNDONS OF THE AMERICAN REVOLUTION. Part VIII: #57 Lewis Herndon [b. ca. 1738–d. ca. 1796], of Goochland County, Virginia, and His Known Descendants of the Family in America**, by Dudley L. Herndon, Jr. 1994. Indexed. Two illustrations.
All known descendants.
Cloth. 6" x 9". $37.00. 460pp. .... Vendor G0425

1880 **GENEALOGICAL RECORD OF REV. HANS HERR & HIS DIRECT LINEAL DESCENDANTS, FROM HIS BIRTH A.D. 1639 TO THE PRESENT, CONTAINING THE NAMES, ETC., OF 13,223 PERSONS**, by T.W. Herr. 1908.
Cloth, $125.00. Paper, $115.00. 785pp. .... Vendor G0259

1881 **GENEALOGICAL RECORD OF REVEREND HANS HERR AND HIS DIRECT LINEAL DESCENDANTS**, by Theodore W. Herr. 3rd ed. (1908) Reprint and revision, 1994.
Cloth. $43.00. 800pp. .... Vendor G0150

1882 **A GEN. REGISTER OF THE NAME & FAM. OF HERRICK, FROM THE SETTLEMENT OF HENERIE HERICKE IN SALEM, MASS., 1629 TO 1846**, by J. Herrick. 1846.
Paper. $12.00. 60pp. .... Vendor G0259

1883 **HERRICK GEN. A GEN. REGISTER OF THE NAME & FAM. OF HERRICK, FROM THE SETTLEMENT OF HENERIE HERICKE IN SALEM, MASS., 1629 TO 1846**, by J. Herrick. Revised, augmented, and brought down to 1885 by L.C. Herrick. 1885.
Cloth, $75.50. Paper, $65.50. 527pp. .... Vendor G0259

1884 **HERRICK GENEALOGY. ONE LINE OF DESC. FROM JAMES HERRICK, WHO SETTLES AT SOUTHAMPTON, L.I., ABOUT 1653;**

WITH PARTICULAR ATTENTION TO DESC. OF REV. CLAUDIUS HERRICK (YALE, 1798) & HIS WIFE HANNAH PIERPONT, by H.C. Brown. 1950.
Paper. $18.50. 95pp. .... Vendor G0259

1885 LINEAGE & TRADITION OF THE HERRING, CONYERS, HENDRICK, BODDIE, PERRY, CRUDUP, DENSON & HILLIARD FAMILIES, by R.H. Hendrick. 1916.
Cloth, $37.00. Paper, $27.00. 172pp. .... Vendor G0259

1886 HERSHEY FAMILY HISTORY, by Henry Hershey. 1929.
Cloth, $55.00. Paper, $45.00. 291pp. .... Vendor G0259

1887 HERSHEY FAMILY HISTORY, by Henry Hershey. (1929) reprint 1989.
Cloth. $25.00. 291pp. .... Vendor G0150

1888 HERSHEY FAMILY OF LANCASTER AND CUMBERLAND COUNTIES, PENNSYLVANIA AND LINCOLN COUNTY, ONTARIO: A CHRONOLOGICAL STUDY OF DEED ABSTRACTS, by Gary Marks. 1995. Indexed.
Benjamin **Hershey** (b. 1741), wife Catharine **Landis**, migrated to Lincoln County, Ontario.
Paper. $8.00. 31pp. .... Vendor G0413

1889 BRIEF BIOGRAPHICAL MEMORIAL OF JACOB HERTZLER, & A COMPLETE GENEALOGICAL FAMILY REGISTER, 1730 TO 1883, by J. Hertzler, Sr. 1885.
Cloth, $69.50. Paper, $59.50. 384pp. .... Vendor G0259

1890 THE HERTZLER–HARTZLER FAMILY HISTORY, by Silas Hertzler. (1952) reprint 1989.
Cloth. $46.00. 773pp. .... Vendor G0150

1891 THE OTHER HERTZLER–HARTZLERS, by Emanuel C. Hertzler. 1995.
Cloth. $28.50. 590pp. .... Vendor G0150

1892 FAM. RECORD OF THE HESS FAM. FROM THE FIRST IMMIGRANT, by J.H. Hess. 1880.
Paper. $15.00. 73pp. .... Vendor G0259

1893 HISTORY & GENEALOGY OF THE DESCENDANTS OF JOHN LAWRENCE HESTER & GODFREY STOUGH, 1752–1905 (WITH ADDENDUM TO 1908), by M.M. Hester. 1905–8.
Cloth, $68.00. Paper, $58.00. 323+43pp. .... Vendor G0259

1894 THE HESTER NEWSLETTER (QUARTERLY), by Lucile Novak. 1980– .
Subscription. $6.00/year. 12pp./issue .... Vendor G0125

1895 THE JOHN AND MILLEY HESTER FAMILY, by Lucile Kaufmann Novak and Gladis M. Kaufmann. 1977. Indexed. Illus.
Hester: Granville, Stokes County, North Carolina—1770s–present; Shelby County, Indiana—1820s. Related families: **Carrell, Crews, Crim, Fair, Fulp, Linville, Rigsbee, Starbuck, Wicker, Workman**.
Cloth. $17.00. 339pp. .... Vendor G0125

1896 **A HIST. OF THE HEVERLY FAM., INCL. OTHER SPELLINGS**, by H.F. Mears. 1945.
Cloth, $51.00. Paper, $41.00. 340pp. .... Vendor G0259

1897 **LT. JOSHUA HEWES, A NEW ENG. PIONEER, & SOME OF HIS DESC.**, by E. Putnam. 1913.
Cloth, $109.00. Paper, $99.00. 673pp. .... Vendor G0259

1898 **THE HEWITTS OF ATHENS COUNTY, OHIO**, by Susan L. Mitchell. 1989. Indexed. Illus.
Received Ohio Association of Historical Societies & Museums' Outstanding Achievement Award, 1990; Council of Ohio Genealogists' William H. & Benjamin Harrison Award, 1991.
Cloth. $42.50. 455pp. .... Vendor G0068

1899 **HEYDONS IN ENG. & AMER., A FRAGMENT OF FAM. HIST.**, by W.B. Hayden. 1877.
Paper. $9.00. 46pp. .... Vendor G0259

1900 **GEN. OF THE HIBBARD FAM.; DESC. OF ROBT. HIBBARD OF SALEM, MA.**, by A.G. Hibbard. 1901.
Cloth, $77.00. Paper, $67.00. 428pp. .... Vendor G0259

1901 **SUPPLEMENTS TO THE 1901 "GENEALOGY OF THE HIBBARD FAMILY,"** by Frederick A. Hibbard and Robert E. Patterson. 1991.
Cloth, $41.00. Paper, $31.00. 209pp. .... Vendor G0259

1902 **GENEALOGY OF THE HIBBARD FAMILY, WHO ARE DESCENDANTS OF ROBERT HIBBARD OF SALEM, MASS.: UPDATE OF 1901 ED.**, by Frederic A. Hibbard. 1992.
Cloth, $49.50. Paper, $39.50. 268pp. .... Vendor G0259

1903 **HICKOK GENEALOGY. DESCENDANTS OF WILLIAM HICKOKS OF FARMINGTON, CT., WITH ANCESTRY OF CHARLES NELSON HICKOK.** 1938.
Cloth, $82.00. Paper, $72.00. 469pp. .... Vendor G0259

1904 **HICKS FAM. MEM.; HICKS & ALLIED FAM.**, by E.H. Johnson. 1894.
Paper. $11.00. 56pp. .... Vendor G0259

1905 **THE ANDREW HICKS AND CHARLES STONE FAMILIES**, by Lucile Kaufmann Novak. 1977. Indexed. Illus.
Hicks: Cornwall County, England, to Knox County, Ohio, 1835. **Stone**: England to Ohio, 1820s; Richland County, Ohio, 1853. Related families: **Baker, Congdon, Ford, Hobbs, McCullough, McFarland, McMillan, Scoggan, White**.
Cloth. $12.50. 129pp. .... Vendor G0125

1906 **GEN. OF HIESTER FAM.**, by V.E.C. Hill. 1903.
Paper. $12.50. 64pp. .... Vendor G0259

1907 **EDWARD HIGBY & HIS DESC.**, by C.D. Higby. 1927.
Cloth, $79.75. Paper, $69.75. 467pp. .... Vendor G0259

1908 **JESSE HIGGINS & DAVID HIGGINS, COLONIAL RESIDENTS AT EASTHAM, MASS. & PIONEER SETTLERS AT WEST EDEN, ME.:**

THEIR ANCESTORS IN AMER. & THEIR DESC. ON MT. DESERT ISLAND, compiled by Harvard DeLorraine Higgins. 1990.
Cloth, $39.50. Paper, $29.50. 200pp. .... Vendor G0259

1909 **RICHARD HIGGINS, A RESIDENT & PIONEER SETTLER AT PLY-MOUTH & EASTHAM, MASS., & AT PISCATAWAY, N.J., & HIS DESC.**, by K.C. Higgins. 1918.
Cloth, $109.00. Paper, $99.00. 799pp. .... Vendor G0259

1910 **HIGGINS. SUPPL. TO ABOVE LISTING.** 1924.
Cloth, $42.00. Paper, $32.00. 216pp. .... Vendor G0259

1911 **DESC. OF THE REV. FRANCIS HIGGINSON**, by T.W. Higginson. 1910.
Paper. $12.50. 84pp. .... Vendor G0259

1912 **THE HIGLEYS & THEIR ANC.**, by M.C. Johnson. 1896.
Cloth, $103.00. Paper, $93.00. 748pp. .... Vendor G0259

1913 **HILDEBRAND FAMILY DATA**, by A.B. Sartori.
Paper. $12.00. 37pp. .... Vendor G0259

1914 **GEN. & BIOGR. SKETCHES OF THE HILDRETH FAM., 1652–1840**, by S.P. Hildreth. 1840.
Cloth, $64.00. Paper, $54.00. 339pp. .... Vendor G0259

1915 **ORIGIN & GEN. OF THE HILDRETH FAM. OF LOWELL, MASS.**, by P. Reade. 1892.
Paper. $14.00. 71pp. .... Vendor G0259

1916 **EBENEZER HILL, THE LITTLE MINISTER OF MASON, NH: A SKETCH & A GENEALOGY**, by C.E. and J.B. HIll. 1923.
Paper. $16.50. 82pp. .... Vendor G0259

1917 **GEN. OF THE HILL, DEAN, PINCKNEY, AUSTIN, BARKER, ANDER-SON, RHOADES & FINCH FAMS.**, by F. Couch. 1907.
Cloth, $32.00. Paper, $22.00. 124pp. .... Vendor G0259

1918 **HILL FAMILY GENEALOGY, EXTENDING A LINE OF JOHN HILL OF DORCHESTER, MASS., 1633 TO 1993, INCLUDING ALLIED FAMI-LIES STARK, MONROE, GRIFFITH, JAYCOCKS, McCALLUM, LOCKE, CHASE & PHELIX**, by Lauralee (Hill) Clayton & Mary Jean (Stark) Farnham. 1993.
Cloth, $69.50. Paper, $59.50. 395pp. .... Vendor G0259

1919 **JOHN HILL OF DORCHESTER, MA., 1663, & 5 GEN. OF HIS DESC. ALSO AN ACCT. OF THE HILL FAM. OF POUNDSFORD, ENG.**, by J.G. Bartlett. 1904.
Paper. $15.00. 103pp. .... Vendor G0259

1920 **HIST. & GEN. COLL. REL. TO THE DESC. OF REV. JAMES HILLHOUSE**, by M.P. Hillhouse. 1924.
Cloth, $109.00. Paper, $99.00. 694pp. .... Vendor G0259

1921 **ANC. CHRONOLOGICAL RECORD OF THE HILLMAN FAM., 1550–1905**, by H.W. Hillman. 1905.
Cloth, $37.00. Paper, $27.00. 203pp. .... Vendor G0259

1922 **GEN. DATA, ANC. & DESC. OF WILLIAM HILLS, ENG. EMIGRANT TO NEW ENG. IN 1632, & OF JOSEPH HILLS IN 1638**, by W. and T. Hills. 1902.
Cloth, $34.00. Paper, $24.00. 148pp. .... Vendor G0259

1923 **THE HILLS FAM. IN AMER.; THE ANC. & DESC. OF WILLIAM HILLS, 1632, JOSEPH HILLS, 1638, & THE GREAT-GRANDSONS OF ROBERT HILLS, 1794–1806, (WITH 1908 SUPPLEMENTARY RECORD)**, by W.S. Hills, edited by T. Hills. 1906.
Cloth, $120.00. Paper, $110.00. 734+36pp. .... Vendor G0259

1924 **HINCKLEYS OF MAINE**, by Marlene Hinckley Groves. 1993. Indexed. Illus. Book #1450.
Cloth. $33.95. 384pp. .... Vendor G0082

1925 **HIST. & GEN. OF THE HINDS FAM.**, by A. Hinds. 1899.
Cloth, $71.00. Paper, $61.00. 394pp. .... Vendor G0259

1926 **[Hiner]. HERITAGE HISTORY**, by Vallie Jo Whitfield. Indexed. Illus. **Hiner** and **Heiner** families.
Cloth. $25.00. 265pp. .... Vendor G0253

1927 **FAM. REC. OF THE DESC. OF SGT. EDW. HINMAN OF STRATFORD, CT., 1650**, by R. Hinman. 1856.
Paper. $16.00. 80pp. .... Vendor G0259

1928 **HIST. OF THE HINMANS, WITH RECORD OF KINDRED FAM.**, by A. V. Hinman. 1907.
Paper. $15.00. 75pp. .... Vendor G0259

1929 **HINSDALE GEN.: DESC. OF ROBT. HINSDALE OF DEDHAM, MEDFIELD, HADLEY & DEERFIELD MA, WITH ACCT. OF THE FRENCH FAM. OF DE HINNIDAL**, by H. Andrews. 1906.
Cloth, $86.50. Paper, $76.50. 508pp. .... Vendor G0259

1930 **HINSHAW–HENSHAW FAM.**, by W. Hinshaw and M. Custer. 1911.
Paper. $13.00. 66pp. .... Vendor G0259

1931 **THOMAS HINSHAW & OTHERS**, by J.E. Hinshaw. 1911.
Paper. $10.00. 49pp. .... Vendor G0259

1932 **THE GEN. OF THE HITCHCOCK FAM., WHO ARE DESC. FROM MATTHIAS HITCHCOCK OF EAST HAVEN, CONN., & LUKE HITCHCOCK OF WETHERSFIELD, CONN.**, by E. Hitchcock, Sr., edited by D. Marsh. 1894.
Cloth, $76.50. Paper, $86.50. 563pp. .... Vendor G0259

1933 **DESCENDANTS OF YOST HITE OF VIRGINIA**, by Carol A. Hauk. 1995. Indexed.
Paper. $35.00. 171pp. .... Vendor G0340

1934 **HOADLEY GEN. A HIST. OF THE DESC. OF WM. HOADLEY OF BRANFORD, CONN., TOGETHER WITH SOME ACCT. OF OTHER FAM. OF THE NAME**, by F.B. Trowbridge. 1894.
Cloth, $54.00. Paper, $44.00. 295pp. .... Vendor G0259

1935 **THE DESCENDANTS OF EZEKIEL J. HOAG AND ALVIRA HOOPER OF CHENANGO COUNTY, NEW YORK AND McKEAN COUNTY, PENNSYLVANIA, 1800–1995,** by Rick Crume. 1995. Indexed.
Paper. $8.00. 71pp. .... Vendor G0386

1936 **HIST. & GEN. OF THE HOAGLAND FAM. IN AMER., 1638–1891,** by D.H. Carpenter. 1891.
Cloth, $52.00. Paper, $42.00. 276pp. .... Vendor G0259

1937 **HOAR FAM. IN AMER. & ITS ENG. ANC.; A COMPILATION FROM COLLECTIONS MADE BY GEORGE FRISBIE HOAR, (REPR. *NEHGR*),** by H.S. Nourse. 1899.
Paper. $7.50. 37pp. .... Vendor G0259

1938 **WM. HOBART, HIS ANC. & DESC.,** by L. Hobart. 1886.
Cloth, $39.50. Paper, $29.50. 193pp. .... Vendor G0259

1939 **HOBSON FAMILY LINEAGE, DESCENDANTS OF GEORGE AND ELIZABETH HOBSON,** by Jay Hobson. 1994. Indexed. Illus.
Complete 12,000 name index. Includes the following families: **Allen, Brown, Clark, Cook, Cox, Davis, Hadley, Hinshaw, Johnson, Jones, Marshall, Matthews, Phillips, Reece, Russell, Shore, Smith, Taylor, Thompson, Vestal, Williams.**
Cloth. $45.00. 772pp. .... Vendor G0352

1940 **DESCENDANTS OF BARBARA HOCHSTEDLER AND CHRISTIAN STUTZMAN,** by Harvey Hostetler. 1938.
Cloth. $38.00. 1,391pp. .... Vendor G0150

1941 **DESCENDANTS OF JACOB HOCHSTETLER, THE IMMIGRANT OF 1736,** by Harvey Hostetler. 1912.
Cloth. $30.00. 1,191pp. .... Vendor G0150

1942 **DESCENDANTS OF JACOB HOCHSTETLER, IMMIGR. OF 1736,** by H. Hochstetler. 1912.
Cloth, $169.00. Paper, $159.00. 1,191pp. .... Vendor G0259

1943 **HODGE GEN. FROM THE 1ST OF THE NAME IN U.S., WITH A NUMBER OF ALLIED FAM.,** by O.J. Hodge. 1900.
Cloth, $80.00. Paper, $70.00. 455pp. .... Vendor G0259

1944 **GEN. RECORD OF THE HODGES FAM. IN NEW ENG., 1633–1853,** by A.D. Hodges. 1853.
Paper. $13.50. 71pp. .... Vendor G0259

1945 **GENEALOGICAL RECORDS OF THE HODGES FAM. OF NEW ENG., TO DEC. 31, 1894**, by A.D. Hodges, Jr. 1896.
Cloth, $96.50. Paper, $86.50. 566pp. Vendor G0259

1946 **GEN. OF THE HODGKINS FAM. OF MAINE**, by E.B. Hodgkins. 1927.
Paper. $19.50. 98pp. . . . . Vendor G0259

1947 **GEN. OF DESC. OF NICHOLAS HODSDON (HODGDON) 1635–1904**, by A.L. White. 1904.
Cloth, $38.00. Paper, $28.00. 164pp. . . . . Vendor G0259

1948 **HOFFELBAUER GENEALOGY 1585–1993**, by Lewis Bunker Rohrbach. 1993. Indexed. Illus. Book #1112.
Cloth. $63.50. 672pp. . . . . Vendor G0082

1949 **GEN. OF THE HOFFMAN FAM.; DESC. OF MARTIN HOFFMAN, WITH BIOGR. NOTES**, compiled by E.A. Hoffman. 1899.
Cloth, $80.00. Paper, $70.00. 545pp. . . . . Vendor G0259

1950 **HOLCOMB(E) GENEALOGY. A GEN., HIST. & DIRECTORY OF THE HOLCOMB(E)S OF THE WORLD, INCL. THE ANCIENT & MODERN ENG. BRANCH, THE AMER. BRANCHES & OTHERS**, by J. Seaver. 1925.
Cloth, $52.00. Paper, $42.00. 283pp. typescript . . . . Vendor G0259

1951 **MEMORIES OF WALTER HOLCOMB OF TORRINGTON, CONN., WITH A FEW DEPARTURES IN GEN., PUBLIC RECORDS, ETC.**, by W. Holcomb. 1935.
Paper. $7.50. 47pp. . . . . Vendor G0259

1952 **THE HOLCOMBS, SOME ACCT. OF THEIR ORIGIN, SETTLEMENT & SCATTERMENT, ETC., INCL. 1ST & 2ND HOLCOMB REUNIONS, 1879 & 1886**. 1887.
Paper. $7.00. 33pp. . . . . Vendor G0259

1953 **THE HOLCOMBES: NATION BUILDERS**, by E.W. McPherson. 1947.
Cloth, $152.50. Paper, $142.50. 1,346pp. typescript . . . . Vendor G0259

1954 **HOLDEMAN DESCENDANTS: A COMPILATION OF GENEALOGI-**

HOGLE FAMILY

Family Branch 'M'
One of 6 Branches
Years 1700 - 1995
Bound Book with Pictures
Documents & Family Data Sheets
Fully Indexed
Price per book $50.00
+ $3.00 U.S. postage
Francis M. Hogle, Jr.
P. O. Box 887
Daytona Beach FL 32115

CAL & BIOGR. RECORD OF THE DESCENDANTS OF CHRISTIAN HOLDEMAN, 1788–1846, by Edwin L. Weavern. 1937.
Cloth, $97.00. Paper, $87.00. 574pp. Vendor G0259

1955 **HOLDEN GEN.; ANC. & DESC. OF RICHARD & JUSTINIAN HOLDEN, & OF RANDALL HOLDEN,** by E. Putnam. Vols I & II. 1923–26.
Cloth, $147.00. Paper, $137.00. 985pp. . . . . Vendor G0259

1956 **THE HOLDERS OF HOLDERNESS. A HIST. & GEN. OF THE HOLDER FAM. WITH ESPECIAL REFERENCE TO CHRISTOPHER HOLDER, PIONEER QUAKER MINISTER IN NEW ENG. (1656),** by C.F. Holder. 1902.
Cloth, $67.00. Paper, $57.00. 358pp. Vendor G0259

1957 **DESCENDANTS OF JOHN HOLLADAY OF VIRGINIA,** by Carol A. Hauk. 1995. Indexed.
Paper. $30.00. 60pp. . . . . Vendor G0340

1958 **ANCESTORS & DESCENDANTS 1600–1994 JOHN GOODMAN HOLLAND,** by J.C. Holland, II. 1994. Indexed.
Paper. $25.00. 135pp. . . . . Vendor G0309

1959 **THE LANCASHIRE [ENGLAND] HOLLANDS,** by Bernard Holland. 1917 (London).
Cloth, $67.00. Paper, $57.00. 16+357pp. . . . . Vendor G0259

1960 **DESC. OF VALENTINE HOLLINGSWORTH, SR.,** by J.A. Stewart. 1925.
Cloth, $42.00. Paper, $32.00. 214pp. . . . . Vendor G0259

1961 **HOLLINGSWORTH GEN. MEMORANDA IN THE U.S., FROM 1682 TO 1884,** by W.B. Hollingsworth. 1884.
Cloth, $31.50. Paper, $21.50. 144pp. . . . . Vendor G0259

1962 **HOLLISTER FAM. OF AMER.; LT. JOHN HOLLISTER OF WETHERSFIELD, CONN., & HIS DESC.,** by L.W. Case. 1886.
Cloth, $111.50. Paper, $101.50. 805pp. . . . . Vendor G0259

1963 **GEN. OF HOLLON & REL. FAM., EARLY SETTLERS OF E. KY. & THEIR DESC.,** by C. Hollon. 1958.
Paper. $18.00. 108pp. . . . . Vendor G0259

1964 **COLONIAL COUSINS [THE HOLLOWAY FAMILY OF YORK CO., VA.],** by G.E. Hopkins. 1940.
Paper. $18.00. 89pp. . . . . Vendor G0259

1965 **HOLLOWAY–AMISS–LEAVELL FAMILY,** edited by L.C. Morrell. 1952.
Paper. $13.00. 62pp. . . . . Vendor G0259

1966 **WILLIAM HOLLOWAY OF TAUNTON, MASS., IN 1637, & HIS DESCENDANTS, 1586–1949,** by E.H. Pendleton. 1950.
Cloth, $65.00. Paper, $55.00. 356pp. . . . . Vendor G0259

1967 **HOLLYMAN FAM., A GEN. & HIST. REC. OF THE DESC. OF CHRISTOPHER HOLLYMAN OF ISLE OF WIGHT CO., VA. & REL. FAM.,** by G. Holleman. 1953?
Cloth, $51.00. Paper, $41.00. 275pp. . . . . Vendor G0259

1968 **THE HOLMANS IN AMERICA, CONCERNING THE DESC. OF SOLAMAN HOLMAN WHO SETTLED IN W. NEWBURY, MASS., IN 1692–3, ONE OF WHOM IS WM. HOWARD TAFT,** by D.E. Holman. 1909. Cloth, $64.50. Paper, $54.50. 45+295pp. .... Vendor G0259

1969 **THE DESC. OF GEORGE HOLMES OF ROXBURY, 1594–1908, TO WHICH IS ADDED THE DESC. OF JOHN HOLMES OF WOODSTOCK, CONN.,** by G.A. Gray. 1908. Cloth, $78.00. Paper, $68.00. 432pp. .... Vendor G0259

1970 **THE DESCENDANTS OF WILLIAM AND HONOR (WELLS) HOLMES, MARRIED 1740 BALTIMORE, MD, VOLUME III, THROUGH SON JAMES,** by Fern Maynard. 1992. Indexed. Paper. $6.00. 86pp. .... Vendor G0226

1971 **THE DESCENDANTS OF WILLIAM AND HONOR (WELLS) HOLMES, MARRIED 1740 BALTIMORE, MD, VOLUME IV, THROUGH DAUGH-TER SARAH AND HUSBAND ALEXANDER McCLEAN,** by Fern Maynard. 1993. Indexed. Paper. $5.00. 47pp. .... Vendor G0226

1972 **THE DESCENDANTS OF WILLIAM AND HONOR (WELLS) HOLMES, MARRIED 1740 BALTIMORE, MD, VOLUME V, THROUGH DAUGH-TER ELIZABETH AND HUSBAND GEORGE WELLS,** by Fern Maynard. 1995. Indexed. Paper. $12.50. 232pp. .... Vendor G0226

1973 **GEN. HIST. OF THE HOLT FAM. IN THE US; PARTICULARLY THE DESC. OF NICHOLAS HOLT OF NEWBURY & ANDOVER, MA., 1634–1644, & OF WM. HOLT OF NEW HAVEN, CT.,** by D.S. Durrie. 1864. Cloth, $57.50. Paper, $47.50. 367pp. .... Vendor G0259

1974 **THE FIRST 3 GEN. OF THE HOLT FAM. IN AMER.,** by the Holt Assoc. of Amer. 1930. Cloth, $68.50. Paper, $58.50. 370pp. .... Vendor G0259

1975 **HOLTZCLAW FAMILY, 1540–1935,** by B.C. Holtzclaw. 1936. Cloth, $49.50. Paper, $39.50. 249pp. .... Vendor G0259

1976 **HOLWAY–RICH HERITAGE: HISTORY & GENEALOGY OF TWO CAPE COD FAMILIES,** by Richard Thomas Holway. 2 vols. 1992. Indexed. Illus. Book #1389. Cloth. $41.00. 640pp. .... Vendor G0082

1977 **HISTORICAL REPORT OF THE HONAKER FAMILY IN AMERICA, 2ND ED.,** by Fred W. Goshorn. (1954) updated and reprinted in 1994. Illus. Paper. $7.50. 29pp. .... Vendor G0268

1978 **HONAKER FAMILY HISTORY BOOK—THE AMERICAN DESCENDANCY,** edited by Frieda Patrick Davison. 1996. Indexed. Illus. Identifies 14,000 descendants of Hans Jacob **Honaker**, who arrived in Phila-delphia from Switzerland in 1749. Cloth. $60.00. 800pp. .... Vendor G0268

1979 **HONAKER FAMILY NEWSLETTER** (quarterly). Original year of publica-tion, 1992.

Family history; current birth, death, marriage listings; humor; features; queries.

Subscription. $15/year. 12pp. .... Vendor G0268

1980 **HONEYMAN FAM. (HONYMAN, HUNNEMAN, ETC.) IN SCOTLAND & AMERICA, 1548–1908,** by A.V.D. Honeyman. 1909.
Cloth, $65.00. Paper, $55.00. 345pp. .... Vendor G0259

1981 **HONEYWELL HERITAGE.** Newsletter, published 4x/year.
Dues $20.00 .... Vendor G0356

1982 **THE AMERICAN DESCENDANTS OF SAMUEL HONEYWELL OF BIDEFORD, DEVONSHIRE, ENGLAND,** by Samuel Willet Honeywell. 1971. Indexed. Illus.
Cloth. $35.00. 202pp. .... Vendor G0356

1983 **THE DESCENDANTS OF ROGER AND AMBROSE HUNNEWELL (HONEYWELL),** by Samuel Willet Honeywell. 1972. Indexed.
Cloth. $35.00. 275pp. .... Vendor G0356

1984 **JOHN HOOD OF LYNN, MASS. & SOME OF HIS DESC. (REPR. ESSEX INST. HIST. COLL.),** by J.H. Bosson. 1909.
Paper. $10.00. 46pp. .... Vendor G0259

1985 **THE TUNIS HOOD FAMILY: ITS LINEAGES & TRADITIONS,** by D.O. Hood. 1960.
Cloth, $97.50. Paper, $87.50. 602pp. .... Vendor G0259

1986 **DESCENDANTS OF RICE HOOE OF VIRGINIA,** by Carol A. Hauk. 1995. Indexed.
Paper. $30.00. 116pp. .... Vendor G0340

1987 **JAMES HOOK & VIRGINIA ELLER; FAMILY HIST. & GEN.,** by J.W. Hook. 1925.
Cloth, $39.00. Paper, $29.00. 171pp. .... Vendor G0259

1988 **HUMPHREY HOOKE OF BRISTOL, & HIS FAMILY & DESCENDANTS IN ENGLAND & AMERICA DURING THE 17TH CENT.,** by F. Todd. 1938.
Cloth, $41.00. Paper, $31.00. 201pp. .... Vendor G0259

1989 **THE DESC. OF REV. THOMAS HOOKER, HARTFORD, CONN., 1586–1908,** by E. Hooker. 1909.
Cloth, $92.00. Paper, $82.00. 558pp. .... Vendor G0259

1990 **A BIOGR. SKETCH OF EIGHT GEN. OF HOOPERS IN AMER.; WILLIAM HOOPER, 1635, TO IDOLENE SNOW (HOOPER) CROSBY, 1883,** by W.S. Crosby. 1906.
Paper. $9.00. 42pp. .... Vendor G0259

1991 **HOOPER GEN.,** by C.H. Pope and T. Hooper. 1908.
Cloth, $59.50. Paper, $49.50. 321pp. .... Vendor G0259

1992 **A CHAPTER OF HOPKINS GEN., 1735–1905,** by E. Harrison. 1905.
Cloth, $61.50. Paper, $51.50. 396pp. .... Vendor G0259

1993 **HOPKINS FAM. MARRIAGES,** by W.M. Clemens. 1916.
Paper. $10.00. 48pp. .... Vendor G0259

1994 **HOPKINS OF VIRGINIA & RELATED FAMILIES,** by Walter Lee Hopkins. 1931.
Cloth, $71.50. Paper, $61.50. 405pp. .... Vendor G0259

1995 **[STEPHEN] HOPKINS OF THE MAYFLOWER: PORTRAIT OF A DISSENTER,** by Margaret Hodges. 1972.
Cloth, $41.00. Paper, $31.00. 274pp. .... Vendor G0259

1996 **GEN. OF THE HORD FAM.,** by A.H. Hord. 1898.
Cloth, $43.00. Paper, $33.00. 199pp. .... Vendor G0259

1997 **ANCESTORS AND DESCENDANTS OF MOSES MUSSER HORNING AND LAVINIA MUSSER GEHMAN,** by Lester G. Weber. 1988.
Cloth. $21.95. 607pp. .... Vendor G0150

1998 **HORSFORD–HOSFORD. YE HORSEFORDE BOOKE; THE HORSFORD–HOSFORD FAM. IN THE U.S.A.,** by H.H. Hosford. 1936.
Cloth, $48.50. Paper, $38.50. 256pp. .... Vendor G0259

1999 **ANC. & DESC. OF ISAAC HORTON OF LIBERTY, N.Y.,** by B.B. Horton. 1912.
Paper. $11.00. 52pp. .... Vendor G0259

2000 **[Horton]. ANC. OF HORACE EBENEZER & EMMA (BABCOCK) HORTON,** by H.E. Horton. 1920.
Cloth, $31.00. Paper, $21.00. 117pp. .... Vendor G0259

2001 **DESCENDANTS OF THOMAS HORTON,** by A.J. Horton. 1912.
Cloth, $32.00. Paper, $22.00. 131pp. .... Vendor G0259

2002 **HORTON GEN. & HIST., DESC. OF RICHARD & NATHANIEL HORTON OF PA.,** by G.W. Alloway. 1929.
Cloth, $35.00. Paper, $25.00. 141pp. .... Vendor G0259

2003 **HORTON GENEALOGY. CHRONICLES OF THE DESCENDANTS OF BARNABAS HORTON OF SOUTHOLD, LONG ISLAND, WITH APPENDIX AND 1879 ADDENDA,** by George F. Horton. 1876.
Cloth, $62.50. Paper, $52.50. 252+83pp. .... Vendor G0259

2004 **THE HORTONS IN AMER.; CORRECTED REPR. OF 1876 WORK BY G.F. HORTON,** by A.H. Horton. 1929.
Cloth, $97.50. Paper, $87.50. 650pp. .... Vendor G0259

2005 **THE HOSFORD GENEALOGY—A HISTORY OF THE DESCENDANTS OF WILLIAM HOSFORD SOMETIME RESIDENT OF BEAMINSTER, DORSETSHIRE; DORCHESTER, MASSACHUSETTS; WINDSOR, CONNECTICUT; AND CALVERLEIGH, DEVONSHIRE,** by Norman F. Hosford and David H. Hosford. 1993. Indexed. Illus.
Cloth. $59.00. xviii+662pp. .... Vendor G0171

2006 **THE FAMILY AND DESCENDANTS OF HENRY HOSHAL 1650–1980,** by Glenn Kilmer. 1980. Indexed. Illus.
Cloth. $36.75. 296pp. .... Vendor G0329

2007 **HOSKINS FAMILIES OF SEVENTEENTH-CENTURY AMERICA**, by George Ely Russell. (1964) reprint 1991. Indexed.
Paper. $5.00. 21pp. .... Vendor G0126

2008 **HOSMER GENEALOGY. THE DESC. OF JAMES HOSMER WHO EMIGRATED TO AMER. IN 1635 & SETTLED IN CONCORD, MASS.**, by G.L. Hosmer. 1928.
Cloth, $52.00. Paper, $42.00. 271pp. .... Vendor G0259

2009 **THE HOSMER HERITAGE: ANCESTORS AND DESCENDANTS OF THE EMIGRANT THOMAS HOSMER (1603–1687). VOL. I**, by Ronald L. Roberts. 1984. Indexed. Illus.
Descendants of Thomas **Hosmer** of Hartford, Conn. Period covered: 1580–1775. Footnoted. Maps, photographs, facsimile documents, transcriptions, bibliography. Size: 8½" x 11".
Cloth. $47.50. 509pp. .... Vendor G0400

2010 **THE HOSMER HERITAGE: ANCESTORS AND DESCENDANTS OF THE EMIGRANT THOMAS HOSMER (1603–1687). VOL. II**, by Ronald L. Roberts. 1987. Indexed. Illus.
Period covered: 1775–1880.
Cloth. $49.50. 661pp. .... Vendor G0400

2011 **THE HOSMER HERITAGE: ANCESTORS AND DESCENDANTS OF THE EMIGRANT THOMAS HOSMER (1603–1687). VOL. III**, by Ronald L. Roberts. 1991. Indexed. Illus.
Period covered: 1880–1950.
Cloth. $50.00. 685pp. .... Vendor G0400

2012 **HIST. OF THE DESC. OF JOHN HOTTEL (IMMIGR. FROM SWITZERLAND) & AN AUTHENTIC GEN. FAM. REG. OF TEN GEN. FROM 1732 TO 1929**, by W.D. and L.M. Huddle. 1930.
Cloth, $175.00. Paper, $165.00. 1,182pp. .... Vendor G0259

2013 **THE HOTTINGER–YANKEY FAMILIES INCLUDING NESSELRODT/ NAZELROD, RATCLIFF, HALTERMAN, DELAWDER, DOVE, WRATCHFORD, FEEZLE, AND OTHERS**, by Lewis H. Yankey. 1991. Indexed.
Paper. $33.00. 364pp. .... Vendor G0365

2014 **HOUGH AND HUFF FAMILIES OF THE UNITED STATES, VOL. VI— THE WEST, 1850–1900**, by Granville W. Hough. 1977.
Census and family data through 1900, plains, mountain, and western states.
Paper. $21.25. 175pp. .... Vendor G0119

2015 **HOUGH AND HUFF FAMILIES OF THE UNITED STATES, 1620–1900, HOUGH FAMILIES OF THE SOUTH—PART A**, by Granville W. Hough. 1978.
Census and family data through 1900, Maryland through South Carolina.
Paper. $21.25. 251pp. .... Vendor G0119

2016 **[Hough]. TALES OF OUR PEOPLE**, by Granville W. Hough. 1989.
Stories of the **Hough** and **Huff** families as they moved across the nation.
Paper. $21.25. 359pp. .... Vendor G0119

2017 **A HOUGHTON FAMILY FROM RALPH HOUGHTON OF LANCASTER, MA. 1652 TO ROSAMOND HOUGHTON VAN NOY OF CONOVER, WI. 1992 AND HER BROTHERS, NIECES & NEPHEWS, COUSINS BENNETT, HAIGHT AND HOUGHTON**, by Rosamond Houghton Van Noy. 1992. Indexed. Illus.
Paper. $32.00. 170pp. .... Vendor G0245

2018 **HIST. & GEN. OF THE HOUGHTON FAM. 1896.**
Paper. $18.00. 100pp. .... Vendor G0259

2019 **REPORT TO THE HOUGHTON ASSOC., U.S.A., MADE BY COLUMBUS SMITH, 1869, ALSO SEVERAL GEN. OF DIFFERENT BRANCHES OF THE FAM. 1869.**
Paper. $12.50. 60pp. .... Vendor G0259

2020 **THE HOUGHTON GEN.; THE DESC. OF RALPH & JOHN HOUGHTON OF LANCASTER, MA.**, by J. Houghton. 1912.
Cloth, $83.00. Paper, $73.00. 608pp. .... Vendor G0259

2021 **FREDERICK WILLIAM HOLZHAUSEN-HOUSE AND SARAH POWELL HOUSE: ANCESTORS AND DESCENDANTS**, by Marianne Elizabeth Hall Little. 1993. Indexed. Illus.
Limited Edition; DeWitt County, Texas.
Cloth, $65.00. Paper, $45.00. 100pp. .... Vendor G0264

2022 **HOUSE–BROWN GENEALOGY: SOME DESCENDANTS OF WM. HOUSE (c.1642–1703/4) & GEORGE BROWN (c. 1714–1770) & RELATED FAMILIES**, by Charles Staver House. 1984.
Cloth, $99.00. Paper, $89.00. 681pp. .... Vendor G0259

2023 **GENEALOGY OF THE HOUSER, RHORER, DILLMAN, HOOVER FAMILIES**, by W.W. Houser, et al. 1910.
Cloth, $47.50. Paper, $37.50. 239pp. .... Vendor G0259

2024 **BRIEF BIOGRAPHICAL ACCOUNTS OF MANY MEMBERS OF THE HOUSTON FAMILY, WITH GENEALOGICAL TABLE**, by S.R. Houston. 1882.
Cloth, $75.50. Paper, $65.50. 420pp. .... Vendor G0259

2025 **HOUSTON FAMILY IN VA.**, by L.L. Campbell. 1956.
Paper. $16.00. 77pp. .... Vendor G0259

2026 **THE HOVEY BOOK, DESCRIBING ENG. ANC. & AMER. DESC. OF DANIEL HOVEY OF IPSWICH, MA.**, compiled by the Daniel Hovey Assoc. 1914.
Cloth, $84.50. Paper, $74.50. 487pp. .... Vendor G0259

2027 **ABRAHAM HOWARD OF MARBLEHEAD, MA., & HIS DESC.**, by Howard, Holden, and Howard. 1897.
Paper. $14.00. 71pp. .... Vendor G0259

2028 **DESCENDANTS OF CLAIBORNE HOWARD, SOLDIER OF THE AMERICAN REVOLUTION, INCLUDING BARNARD, BRINDLE, CAMPBELL, CLEMONS, COOK, DENNY, ETC.**, by G.W. Cook. 1960.
Cloth, $39.50. Paper, $29.50. 186pp. .... Vendor G0259

2029 **DESC. OF JOHN HOWARD OF BRIDGEWATER, MASS., 1643–1903**, by H. Howard. 1903.
Cloth, $62.50. Paper, $52.50. 330pp. .... Vendor G0259

2030 **HIST. OF ISAAC HOWARD OF FOSTER, R.I., & HIS DESC.**, by D. Howard. 1901.
Cloth, $35.00. Paper, $25.00. 168pp. .... Vendor G0259

2031 **HOWARD GEN. A GEN. REC. EMBRACING ALL KNOWN DESC. IN THIS COUNTRY OF THOMAS & SUSANNA HOWARD**, by J.C. Howard. 1884.
Cloth, $41.50. Paper, $31.50. 238pp. .... Vendor G0259

2032 **HOWARD LIN. ANC. OF IDA BOYDSTUN WELCH THROUGH HER MOTHER EOLINE F. HOWARD BOYDSTUN**, by G. Weaver. 1929.
Cloth, $44.50. Paper, $34.50. 230pp. .... Vendor G0259

2033 **"THE LION & THE ROSE," THE GREAT HOWARD STORY: NOR-FOLK LINE, 957–1646; SUFFOLK LINE, 1603–1917**, by Ethel Richardson. 2 vols. in 1. 1922 (England).
Cloth, $85.00. Paper, $75.00. 615pp. .... Vendor G0259

2034 **HOWE FAMILY GATHERING, HARMONY GROVE, S. FRAMINGHAM MA, 1871**, by E. Nason. 1871.
Paper. $9.00. 46pp. .... Vendor G0259

2035 **[Howe]. GEN. OF ABRAHAM OF ROXBURY, JAMES OF IPSWICH, ABRAHAM OF MARLBOROUGH & EDWARD OF LYNN, MA., WITH APPENDIX**, by D.W. and G.B. Howe. 1929.
Cloth, $107.50. Paper, $97.50. 655pp. .... Vendor G0259

2036 **GEN. OF JOHN HOWE OF SUDBURY & MARLBOROUGH, MA**, by D. Howe; rev. by G.B. Howe. 1929.
Cloth, $83.50. Paper, $73.50. 564pp. .... Vendor G0259

2037 **DESC. OF JOHN & MARY HOWES OF MONTGOMERY CO., MD.**, by J.J.W. Howes. 1946.
Paper. $10.50. 53pp. .... Vendor G0259

2038 **GEN. OF THE HOWES FAM. IN AMER. DESC. OF THOMAS HOWES, YARMOUTH, MASS., 1637–1892**, by J.C. Howes. 1892.
Cloth, $41.00. Paper, $31.00. 209pp. .... Vendor G0259

2039 **BRIEF GEN. & BIOGR. HIST. OF ARTHUR, HENRY & JOHN HOWLAND & THEIR DESC.**, by F. Howland. 1885.
Cloth, $69.00. Paper, $59.00. 463pp. .... Vendor G0259

2040 **JOHN HOWLAND OF THE MAYFLOWER, VOL. I, DESIRE[2] HOWLAND DESCENDANTS**, by Elizabeth Pearson White. 1990. Indexed. Illus. Book #1131.
Cloth. $63.50. 736pp. .... Vendor G0082

2041 **JOHN HOWLAND OF THE MAYFLOWER, VOL. 2, JOHN[2] HOWLAND DESCENDANTS**, by Elizabeth Pearson White. 1993. Indexed. Illus. Book #1314.
Cloth. $53.50. 512pp. .... Vendor G0082

2042 **THE HOWLAND HEIRS; BEING THE STORY OF A FAM. & A FOR-TUNE**, by W.M. Emery. 1919.
Cloth, $86.50. Paper, $76.50. 492pp. .... Vendor G0259

2043 **[Hoyle]. GEN. OF PEITER HEYL (HOYLE) & HIS DESC., 1100–1936, WITH INTERMARRIED FAMILIES OF ARNOLD, BESS, BYRD, CANSLER, ET AL**, by E.H. Rucker. 1938.
Cloth, $208.00. Paper, $198.00. 1,539pp. .... Vendor G0259

2044 **A GENEALOGICAL HISTORY OF THE HOYT, HAIGHT, AND HIGHT FAMILIES**, by David W. Hoyt. (1857) reprint 1993. Indexed. Illus. Book #1264.
Cloth. $59.00. 736pp. .... Vendor G0082

2045 **A GEN. HIST. OF THE HOYT, HAIGHT & HIGHT FAM., WITH A LIST OF THE FIRST SETTLERS OF SALISBURY & AMESBURY, MASS.**, by D.W. Hoyt. 1871.
Cloth, $114.00. Paper, $104.50. 698pp. .... Vendor G0259

2046 **GENEALOGICAL HISTORY OF THE HOYT, HAIGHT, AND HIGHT FAMILIES... AMESBURY, MA AND CT LINES**, by David W. Hoyt. (1871) reprint 1993. Indexed. Illus.
Cloth. $58.50. 708pp. .... Vendor G0077

2047 **HOYT, HAIGHT & HIGHT FAMILIES (SUPPLEMENTAL FEMALE NAME INDEX, FOR 1871 HHH)**, by Roy F. Olson, Jr. 1993. Indexed.
Paper. $7.00. 62pp. .... Vendor G0077

2048 **HOYT FAM., A GEN. HIST. OF JOHN OF SALISBURY & DAVID OF DEERFIELD, & THEIR DESC.**, by D.W. Hoyt. 1857.
Cloth, $35.00. Paper, $25.00. 144pp. .... Vendor G0259

2049 **HOYT'S ISSUE**, by Roy F. Olson, Jr. 1983. Indexed. Illus.
Write for information. 40pp. twice a year .... Vendor G0077

2050 **RECORD OF THE HOYT FAM. MEETING, 1866**, by D.W. Hoyt. 1866.
Paper. $12.50. 64pp. .... Vendor G0259

2051 **ONE THOUSAND YEARS OF HUBBARD HIST., 866 TO 1895**, by E.W. Day. 1895.
Cloth, $75.50. Paper, $65.50. 512pp. .... Vendor G0259

2052 **THE HUBBARD–THOMPSON MEM'L; GEN. RECORD & HIST. ACCT. OF THE ANC. & DESC. OF EBENEZER HUBBARD & MARY THOMP-SON, HIS WIFE**, by L.K. Stewart. 1914.
Cloth, $76.50. Paper. $66.50. 423pp. .... Vendor G0259

2053 **HIST. OF THE HUBBELL FAM., CONTAINING A GEN. REC.**, by W. Hubbell. 1881.
Cloth, $84.50. Paper, $74.50. 478pp. .... Vendor G0259

2054 **HISTORY OF THE HUBBELL FAMILY, CONTAINING GENEALOGI-CAL RECORDS OF THE ANCESTORS AND DESCENDANTS OF RICHARD HUBBELL, 1086 TO 1915**, by Walter Hubbell. 1915.
Cloth, $72.00. Paper, $62.00. 406pp. .... Vendor G0259

2055 **HUBER–HOOVER FAMILY HISTORY: BIOGRAPHICAL & GENEA-LOGICAL HISTORY OF THE DESCENDANTS OF HANS HUBER**

FROM THE TIME OF HIS ARRIVAL IN PA. TO THE 11TH GENERA-
TION, by Harry M. Hoover. 1928.
Cloth, $59.00. Paper, $49.00. 335pp. .... Vendor G0259

2056 **HUBER–HOOVER FAMILY HISTORY: BIOGRAPHICAL AND GENEA-
LOGICAL HISTORY . . . TO THE ELEVENTH GENERATION**, by Harry
M. Hoover. (1928) reprint 1992.
Cloth. $15.00. 335pp. .... Vendor G0150

2057 **THE HUBER–HOOVER FAMILY HISTORY INDEX**, compiled by Jerri
Lynn Burkett. 1993.
Cloth. $12.95. 96pp. .... Vendor G0150

2058 **HUCKINS FAMILY. ROBERT HUCKINS OF THE DOVER COMBINA-
TION & SOME OF HIS DESC.**, by H.W. Hardon. 1916.
Cloth, $42.00. Paper, $32.00. 195pp. .... Vendor G0259

2059 **HUFFORD FAMILY HISTORY, 1729–1909**, by F.P. Hoffert. 1909.
Cloth, $51.00. Paper, $41.00. 269pp. .... Vendor G0259

2060 **HUGHES & ALLIED FAM.**, by D.D. and W.H. Hughes. 1879.
Cloth, $51.00. Paper, $41.00. 253pp. .... Vendor G0259

2061 **HUGHES FAMILY RECORDS**, by J.M. Seaver.
Paper. $8.00. 39pp. .... Vendor G0259

2062 **HUGHES OF N.C. ANCESTRAL JOURNAL OF THE HUGHES FAMI-
LIES & THEIR INTERLINKS**, by Thelma R. Johnson Nelson. 1994.
Cloth, $67.00. Paper, $57.00. 380pp. .... Vendor G0259

2063 **JAMES HUGHES 1843–1921: BIOGRAPHY OF A WESTERN PIONEER**,
by La Roux Gillespie and Helen Gillespie. 1983. Indexed. Illus.
Paper. $35.00. 243pp. .... Vendor G0238

2064 **AMERICAN ANCESTRY OF FRDERIC LOUIS HUIDEKOPER &
REGINALD SHIPPEN HUIDEKOPER OF WASHINGTON DC**, by F.L.
Huidekoper. 1931.
Paper. $13.00. 62pp. .... Vendor G0259

2065 **HULING GENEALOGY, DESCENDANTS OF JAMES AND MARGA-
RET HULING OF NEWPORT, RHODE ISLAND, AND LEWES, DELA-
WARE**, by Esther Littleford Woodworth-Barnes; Jane Fletcher Fiske, Editor.
1984. Indexed. Illus.
Cloth. $39.00. 706pp. .... Vendor G0054

2066 **A RECORD OF THE DESC. OF RICHARD HULL OF NEW HAVEN,
260 YEARS IN AMERICA**, by P.F. Mason. 1894.
Paper. $15.50. 78pp. .... Vendor G0259

2067 **HULL FAMILY IN AMER.**, by C.H. Weygant. 1913.
Cloth, $91.00. Paper, $81.00. 647pp. .... Vendor G0259

2068 **REV. JOSEPH HULL & SOME DESC.**, by A. Hull. 1904.
Paper. $12.50. 64pp. .... Vendor G0259

2069 **EARLY AMER. HIST. HUME & ALLIED FAM.**, by W.E. Brockman. 1926.
Cloth, $47.00. Paper, $37.00. 217pp. .... Vendor G0259

2070 **ABSTR. OF WILLS & MEM. CONCERNING ENGLISH HUMPHREYS, COLL. FROM THE . . . RECORD OFFICES OF GT. BRITAIN (ADD. TO "HUMPHREYS GEN.").** 1887.
Paper. $18.00. 106pp. .... Vendor G0259

2071 **HUMPHREYS FAM. IN AMER.**, by F. Humphreys. et al.
Vol. I. 1883. Cloth, $61.50. Paper, $51.50. 398pp. .... Vendor G0259

2072 **HUMPHREYS FAMILIES IN AMERICA.** Vol. II. 1884.
Cloth, $78.00. Paper, $68.00. 437pp. .... Vendor G0259

2073 **HUMPHREYS FAMILIES IN AMERICA (DORCHESTER & WEYMOUTH FAMILIES)**, by Gilbert Nash. 1883.
Cloth, $49.00. Paper, $39.00. 275pp. .... Vendor G0259

2074 **DESC. OF CHARLES HUMPHRIES OF VA., NATHANIEL POPE OF VA., REUBEN BROCK I OF IRELAND, & AARON PARKER OF VA.**, by J.D. Humphries. 1938.
Paper. $12.50. 63pp. .... Vendor G0259

2075 **THOMAS HUNGERFORD OF HARTFORD & NEW LONDON, CONN., & SOME OF HIS DESC., WITH THEIR ENG. ANC.**, by F.P. Leach. 1924.
Paper. $7.00. 34pp. .... Vendor G0259

2076 **HUNGERFORD. ADD. & CORR. FOR ABOVE**, by F.P. Leach. 1932.
Paper. $12.00. 60pp. .... Vendor G0259

2077 **GEN. HIST. OF THE HUNSICKER FAMILY,** by H.A. Hunsicker. 1911.
Cloth, $66.50. Paper, $56.50. 358pp. .... Vendor G0259

2078 **A GEN. HIST. OF THE ROBERT & ABIGAIL PANCOAST HUNT FAMS.,** by C.C. Hunt. 1906.
Cloth, $37.00. Paper, $27.00. 202pp. .... Vendor G0259

2079 **GEN. OF THE NAME & FAM. OF HUNT,** by T. Wyman. 1862–3.
Cloth, $65.50. Paper, $55.50. 430pp. .... Vendor G0259

2080 **HUNT FAMILY RECORDS,** by J.M. Seaver.
Paper. $7.50. 38pp. .... Vendor G0259

2081 **JOSEPH HUNTER & RELATED FAMILIES BECKWITH, BIRD, MEDLEY, PHILLIPS, RILEY & SIKES OF S.E. MISSOURI,** by S.B. and M.A.M. Hunter; edited by F.E. Snider. 1959.
Cloth, $68.50. Paper, $58.50. 374pp. .... Vendor G0259

2082 **HUNTING OR HUNTTING FAM. IN AMER.,** by T. Huntting. 1888.
Paper. $16.50. 83pp. .... Vendor G0259

2083 **A GEN. MEMOIR OF THE HUNTINGTON FAM. IN THIS COUNTRY, DESC. OF SIMON & MARGARET HUNTINGTON,** by E.B. Huntington. 1863.
Cloth, $77.00. Paper, $67.00. 428pp. .... Vendor G0259

2084 **HUNTINGTON FAM. IN AMER.; A GEN. MEMOIR OF THE KNOWN DESC. OF SIMON HUNTINGTON, 1613–1915.** 1915.
Cloth, $169.00. Paper, $159.00. 1,205pp. .... Vendor G0259

2085 **JOHN HUNTLEY OF LYME, CONN. & HIS DESC.,** by H.F. Johnston. 1949.
Paper. $15.00. 72pp. .... Vendor G0259

2086 **ANCESTORS & DESCENDANTS OF THE IOWA HUNTOONS,** by Joe Crockett Huntoon, Jr. 1971.
Paper. $19.50. 169pp. .... Vendor G0259

2087 **[Huntoon]. PHILIP HUNTON & HIS DESC.,** by D. Huntoon. 1881.
Paper. $17.00. 113pp. .... Vendor G0259

2088 **[Huntoon–Hunton]. THE HUNTTONS OF COLONIAL KINGSTON, N.H.,** by Robert Jay Evans. 1984.
Cloth, $49.50. Paper, $39.50. 306pp. .... Vendor G0259

2089 **HIST. & GEN. OF THE FAM. OF HURD IN THE U.S.; ALSO A PARTIAL HIST. OF THE NEW ENG. FAMS. OF HEARD & HORD,** by D.D. Hurd. 1910.
Cloth, $54.00. Paper, $44.00. 339pp. .... Vendor G0259

2090 **HURLBUT GEN.; A RECORD OF THE DESC. OF THOMAS HURLBUT OF SAYBROOK & WETHERSFIELD, CONN.,** by H.H. Hurlbut. 1888.
Cloth, $79.00. Paper, $69.00. 545pp. .... Vendor G0259

2091 **VIRGINIA ORIGINS OF THE HURSTS OF SHENANDOAH,** by Bruce A. Breeding. 1996.
Send SASE for information .... Vendor G0451

2092 **THE DESC. OF ABEL HUSE OF NEWBURY (1602–1690)**, by H.P. Huse. 1935.
Cloth, $78.50. Paper, $68.50. 438pp. . . . . Vendor G0259

2093 **THE HISTORY OF JOHN HUSON, FROM NORTH CAROLINA TO ALABAMA, HIS HUSON/HUSTON/HOUSTON DESCENDANTS, AND THE ALLIED PIONEER FAMILIES OF CLEPPER, ROBINSON, DEEN, AND GILMORE**, by Margarette Hall Wood. 1990. Indexed. Illus.
Nine proven generations plus three more in Virginia based on circumstantial evidence and proven after publication.
Cloth. $46.00. 335pp. . . . . Vendor G0299

2094 **HUGH HUTCHINS OF OLD ENGLAND. A HISTORY OF THE HUTCHINS FAMILIES OF OLD ENGLAND AND THEIR FIRST SETTLEMENTS IN THE WESTERN WORLD**, by Jack Randolph Hutchins and Richard Jasper Hutchings. 1984. Indexed.
Including genealogies of **Thomas Hutchins of Salem** (Second Edition), **Elias Hutchings of Nauvoo**, and **Enoch Hutchings of Kittery**.
Cloth. $40.00. 904pp. . . . . Vendor G0029

2095 **JACOB HUTCHINS OF ATHOL: REVOLUTIONARY SOLDIER. RECORDS OF ALL HUTCHINS, HUTCHINGS, HUTCHENS, HUTCHIN DURING THE REVOLUTIONARY WAR PERIOD**, by Jack Randolph Hutchins. 1976. Indexed.
Including reprints of: *Strangeman Hutchins of Virginia* by Mr. & Mrs. Crider (1936) and *David Hutchins of Attleboro* by Charles Hutchins (1878).
Cloth. $25.00. 383pp. . . . . Vendor G0029

2096 **JOHN HUTCHINS OF HAVERHILL. A GENEALOGY OF THE OLDEST NEW ENGLAND HUTCHINS FAMILY, BASED ON RESEARCH BY DR. EDWIN COLBY BYAM**, by Jack Randolph Hutchins. 1975. Indexed.
Cloth. $80.00. 545pp. . . . . Vendor G0029

2097 **NICHOLAS HUTCHINS OF LYNN AND GROTON, MASSACHUSETTS, AND HIS DESCENDANTS**, by Marvin Clayton Hutchins. 1989. Indexed. Illus.
Cloth. $23.00. xviii+398pp. . . . . Vendor G0198

2098 **ROBERT HUTCHINS OF COLONIAL AMERICA. THE HISTORICAL HUTCHINS FAMILY RECORDS**, by Jack Randolph Hutchins. 1992. Indexed.
Compendium of **Hutchins–Hutchings–Hutchens** records before the mid-1800s.
Cloth. $45.00. 1,355pp. . . . . Vendor G0029

2099 **THOMAS HUTCHINS OF SALEM. A GENEALOGY OF THIS LARGE HUTCHINS FAMILY OF NEW ENGLAND, NEW YORK, ONTARIO AND THE WEST**, by Jack Randolph Hutchins. 1972. Indexed.
Cloth. $40.00. 801pp. . . . . Vendor G0029

2100 **WILLIAM HUTCHINS OF CAROLINA. THE HISTORICAL RECORDS OF THE CAROLINA HUTCHINS, HUTCHINGS, HUTCHENS, WITH**

A SUPPLEMENT TO THE BOOK "ROBERT HUTCHINS OF COLO-
NIAL AMERICA," by Jack Randolph Hutchins. 1995. Indexed. Illus.
Includes an all-name index.
Cloth. $45.00. 752pp. .... Vendor G0029

2101 A BRIEF GEN. OF THE DESC. OF WILLIAM HUTCHINSON & THO-
MAS OLIVER, by W.H. Whitmore. 1865.
Paper. $7.50. 38pp. .... Vendor G0259

2102 A GEN. OF THE HUTCHINSON FAM. OF YORKSHIRE, & OF THE
AMER. BRANCH OF THE FAM. DESC. FROM RICHARD
HUTCHINSON OF SALEM, MASS. (REPR. *NEHGR*), by J.L. Chester.
1868.
Paper. $7.00. 33pp. .... Vendor G0259

2103 NOTES UPON THE ANC. OF WILLIAM HUTCHINSON & ANNE
MARBURY, by J.L. Chester. 1866.
Paper. $10.00. 48pp. .... Vendor G0259

2104 THE BOOK OF BROTHERS; THE HIST. OF THE HUTCHINSON FAM.
1852.
Paper. $9.50. 48pp. .... Vendor G0259

2105 THE HUTCHINSON FAM.; OR, THE DESC. OF BERNARD
HUTCHINSON OF COWLAM, ENG., by P. Derby. 1870.
Paper. $15.00. 107pp. .... Vendor G0259

2106 THE HYDE GEN.; DESC. FROM WILLIAM HYDE OF NORWICH, by
R.H. Walworth. 2 vols. 1864.
Cloth, $193.00. Paper, $183.00. 1,446pp. .... Vendor G0259

2107 OUR HERITAGE: REC. OF INFO. ABOUT THE HYNES, WAIT, POW-
ERS, CHENAULT, MAXET, BREWSTER, STARR & McINTOSH FAMI-
LIES, by L.P. Hynes. 1957.
Paper. $18.00. 93pp. .... Vendor G0259

2108 OUR PIONEER ANCESTORS; RECORD OF AVAILABLE INFO. AS TO
THE HYNES, CHENAULT, DUNN, McKEE, ANDERSON, TAYLOR,
FINLEY, LETCHER & HOUSTON FAMS. IN THE DIRECT LINE OF
ANC. OF SAMUEL B. & ELLEN M. ANDERSON HYNES, by Riggs and
Riggs. 1941.
Cloth, $42.00. Paper, $32.00. 207pp. .... Vendor G0259

2109 SIMON IDE, WITH A GEN. OF THE IDE FAM., by Flanders et al. 1931.
Cloth, $65.00. Paper, $55.00. 347pp. .... Vendor G0259

2110 GENEALOGY OF THE IMBRIE FAMILY OF WESTERN PA.: DESCEN-
DANTS OF JAMES IMBRIE, PIONEER SETTLER, & HIS WIFE
EUPHAMIA SMART, by A.M. Imbrie et al. 1953.
Cloth, $41.00. Paper, $31.00. 194pp. .... Vendor G0259

2111 THE GEN. & HIST. OF THE INGALLS FAM. IN AMER., GIVING THE
DESC. OF EDMUND INGALLS, WHO SETTLED AT LYNN, MASS., IN
1629, by C. Burleigh. 1903.
Cloth, $58.50. Paper, $48.50. 324pp. .... Vendor G0259

2112 **THE INGALLS FAM. IN ENG. & AMER., IN COMM. OF THE 300TH ANNIVERSARY OF THE SETTLEMENT OF LYNN, MASS.**, by E. and F. Ingalls. 1930.
Paper. $16.50. 84pp. .... Vendor G0259

2113 **A GEN. OF THE INGERSOLL FAM. IN AMER., 1629–1925**, by L.D. Avery. 1926.
Cloth, $99.00. Paper, $89.00. 596pp. .... Vendor G0259

2114 **THE INGERSOLLS OF HAMPSHIRE. A GEN. HIST. OF THE FAM. FROM THEIR SETTLEMENT IN AMER., IN THE LINE OF JOHN INGERSOLL OF WESTFIELD, MASS.**, by C.S. Ripley. 1893.
Paper. $18.00. 107pp. .... Vendor G0259

2115 **INGHAM FAMILY: OR JOSEPH INGHAM & HIS DESC., 1639–1871.** 1871.
Paper. $12.00. 59pp. .... Vendor G0259

2116 **AN ANCIENT FAMILY: A GENEALOGICAL STUDY SHOWING THE SAXON ORIGIN OF THE FAMILY OF INGPEN**, by A.R. Ingpen. 1916 (England).
Cloth, $43.50. Paper, $33.50. 208pp. .... Vendor G0259

2117 **TO THE DESCENDANTS OF TIMOTHY INGRAHAM: INFORMATION RESPECTING THE GREAT INGRAHAM ESTATE, IN GREAT BRITAIN**, by G.R. Gladding. 1859.
Paper. $16.00. 80pp. .... Vendor G0259

2118 **INGRAM, DESCENDANTS OF WINIFRED NELMS & JOSEPH INGRAM [OF VA. & N.C.]**, by M.K.L. Davis. 1950.
Paper. $8.00. 39pp. typescript .... Vendor G0259

2119 **AN ACCT. OF THE FAMILY OF INNES**, compiled by Duncan Forbes of Culloden (1698), with an appendix of Charters & Notes, edited by C. Innes. 1864.
Cloth, $55.00. Paper, $45.00. 286pp. .... Vendor G0259

2120 **SKETCH OF THE IRELAND FAM.**, by J. Ireland. 1907.
Paper. $8.00. 41pp. .... Vendor G0259

2121 **SOME ACCT. OF THE IRELAND FAM. OF LONG ISLAND 1644–1880**, by J.N. Ireland. 1880.
Paper. $10.00. 51pp. .... Vendor G0259

2122 **THE IRETON NEWSLETTER**, by La Roux Gillespie. Annual. Indexed. Illus.
Subscription. $12 per year. 32pp. .... Vendor G0238

2123 **THE IRETONS OF CANADA, VOL. 1**, by La Roux Gillespie. 1993. Indexed. Illus.
Paper. $45.00. 300pp. .... Vendor G0238

2124 **THE IRETONS OF IRELAND, VOL. 1**, by La Roux Gillespie. 1989.
Paper. $45.00. 357pp. .... Vendor G0238

2125 **DESC. OF JAMES IRISH, 1710–1940, & ALLIED FAM.**, by J.J.W. Howes. 1941.
Cloth, $53.00. Paper, $43.00. 261pp. .... Vendor G0259

2126 **DESC. OF JOHN IRISH THE IMMIGRANT, 1629–1963, & ALLIED FAMS.**, by W.L. and S.B. Irish. 1964.
Cloth, $105.00. Paper, $95.00. 662pp. . . . . Vendor G0259

2127 **SKETCH OF GEN. JAS. IRISH OF GORHAM, MAINE, WITH FAM. RECORDS,** by L. Oak. 1898.
Paper. $14.00. 70pp. . . . . Vendor G0259

2128 **THE IRVINES & THEIR KIN: A HISTORY OF THE IRVINE FAMILY & THEIR DESCENDANTS,** by L. Boyd. 1898.
Paper. $18.00. 115pp. . . . . Vendor G0259

2129 **THE IRVINES & THEIR KIN. HISTORY OF THE IRVINE FAM. & THEIR DESCENDANTS; ALSO, SKETCHES OF THEIR KINDRED,** by L. Boyd. 1908.
Cloth, $77.50. Paper, $67.50. 432pp. Vendor G0259

2130 **GEN. OF THAT BRANCH OF THE IRWIN FAM. IN N.Y., FOUNDED IN THE HUDSON RIVER VALLEY BY WM. IRWIN, 1700–1787,** by R.S. Hosmer and M.T. Fielder. 1938.
Cloth, $49.50. Paper, $39.50. 258pp. Vendor G0259

2131 **ANCESTRY OF MARY ISAAC, c. 1549–1613, WIFE OF THOMAS APPLETON OF LITTLE WALDINFIELD, CO. SUFFOLK, & MOTHER OF SAMUEL APPLETON OF IPSWICH, MASS.,** by W.G. Davis. 1955.
Cloth, $71.00. Paper, $61.00. 400pp. . . . . Vendor G0259

2132 **GEN. OF THE ISBELL FAM.,** by M.I. Scott. 1929.
Cloth, $48.50. Paper, $38.50. 256pp. Vendor G0259

2133 **ISHAM GENEALOGY: BRIEF HIST. OF JIRAH ISHAM OF NEW LONDON, CT., & HIS DESC., FROM 1670 TO 1940,** by M.A. Phinney. 1940.
Cloth, $37.00. Paper, $27.00. 179pp. Vendor G0259

2134 **THE ISHAMS IN ENGLAND & AMER.: 850 YEARS OF HIST. & GEN.,** by H.W. Brainard. 1938.
Cloth, $108.50. Paper, $98.50. 672pp. Vendor G0259

2135 **GEN. OF THE IVES FAM., INCL. A HIST. OF THE EARLY SETTLE-MENTS,** by A.C. Ives. 1932.
Cloth, $58.50. Paper, $48.50. 321pp. Vendor G0259

2136 **A BRANCH OF THE JACKSON CORRELATED FAM., 1730–1911,** by S. Jackson. 1911.
Paper. $12.50. 60pp. . . . . Vendor G0259

2137 **A JACKSON FAMILY HISTORY: PUTNAM CO, TN AND BEYOND,** by Michael Stephen Jackson. 1993. Indexed. Illus. 90+ photos.
Descendants of James **Jackson**, Esq., and Sarah/Sally **Cox** of Putnam Co., Tennessee, are listed as well as related and unrelated Jacksons. James had five children: Rebecca, who married Spencer **Phillips**; Nancy Jane, who married John Washington **Hicks**; William, who married Rebecca **Dickson**; John, aka "Sheepeye," who married Mahala **Austin**, Catherine **Ford**, and Hannah **Henry**; and Luvisa, who married James M. **Burnett**. (A major portion of the book is dedicated to John "Sheepeye" **Jackson** and his descendants.)
Cloth. $60.00. 835pp. . . . . Vendor G0224

2138 **HIST. OF EPHRAIM JACKSON, 1ST ANC. TO COME TO AMER., & HIS DESC., 1684–1960**, by J. Cross. 1961.
Cloth, $72.50. Paper, $62.50. 398pp. .... Vendor G0259

2139 **HON. JONATHAN JACKSON & HANNAH TRACY JACKSON: THEIR ANCESTORS & DESCENDANTS**, by E.C. and J.J. Putnam. 1907.
Paper. $14.00. 70pp. .... Vendor G0259

2140 **PROCEEDINGS OF THE SESQUI–CENT. GATHERING OF THE DESC. OF ISAAC & ANN JACKSON AT HARMONY GROVE, CHESTER CO., PA. (AUG., 1875)**, with the fam. gen. comp. by the Publ. Comm. 1878.
Cloth, $68.50. Paper, $58.50. 372pp. .... Vendor G0259

2141 **THEIR LIFE IN THE LAND. A FAMILY HISTORY OF JACKSON, THOMPSON, LETT, COPLEY, WILSON, WILLIAMSON**, by Harry Leon Sellards, Jr. 1985. Indexed. Illus.
Related families: **Webb, Adkins, Ferguson, Crabtree, Smith, Wellman, Osborn, Booth, Bartram**.
Cloth. $40.00. 401pp. .... Vendor G0445

2142 **JACOBY FAM. GEN.; REC. OF THE DESC. OF THE PIONEER PETER JACOBY OF BUCKS CO., PA.**, by H.S. Jacoby. 1930.
Cloth, $108.00. Paper, $98.00. 680pp. .... Vendor G0259

2143 **A VIRGINIA GENEALOGY: THOMAS JAMES (CLERK OF KINGSTON PARISH, 1783–1796), ANCESTRY & DECENDANTS, 1653–1961**, by E.H. Ironmonger. 1961.
Cloth, $69.50. Paper, $59.50. 374+28pp. .... Vendor G0259

2144 **HOLLIS JAMES DESCENDANTS, PIONEER OF OHIO**, by Leallah Franklin. 1994. Indexed. Illus.
Related families: **Anderson, Bailey, Baker, Balis, Cain, Chamberlain, Dennis, Derr, Dyer, Fogle, Harmon, Heifner, Hensel, McKee, Mellon, Musgrave, Pfieffer, Pickenpaugh, Predmore, Ralph, Ralston, Ramge, Richards, Sanders, Steward, Stoneking, Stout, Walters, Wheeler, Wiley, Wollam**.
Cloth. $45.00. 337pp. .... Vendor G0304

2145 **WILLIAM JAMES (1771–1832) OF ALBANY NY & HIS DESCENDANTS, WITH NOTES ON COLLATERAL LINES**, by K.B. Hastings. 1924.
Paper. $11.00. 53pp. .... Vendor G0259

2146 **THE JAMESONS IN AMERICA, 1647–1900. GEN. RECORDS & MEMO-RANDA**, by E.O. Jameson. 1901.
Cloth, $85.00. Paper, $75.00. 615pp. .... Vendor G0259

2147 **JANES FAM. A GEN. & BRIEF HIST. OF THE DESC. OF WM. JANES, THE EMIG. ANC. OF 1637**, by F. Janes. 1868.
Cloth, $76.00. Paper, $66.00. 419pp. .... Vendor G0259

2148 **GEN. OF THE JAQUETT FAM.**, by E.J. Sellers. 1907.
Cloth, $44.00. Paper, $34.00. 226pp. .... Vendor G0259

2149 **THE JAQUITH FAMILY IN AMERICA**, by George Oakes Jaquith and Georgetta Jaquith Walker. 1982. Indexed. Illus.
Cloth. $78.50. 817pp. .... Vendor G0406

2150 **JARVIS FAMILY, OR, THE DESC. OF THE 1ST SETTLERS OF THE NAME IN MASS. & LONG ISLAND & THOSE WHO HAVE RECENTLY SETTLED IN OTHER PARTS OF THE U.S. & BRIT. AMER.,** by Jarvis, Jarvis, and Wetmore. 1879.
Cloth, $66.50. Paper, $56.50. 347pp. .... Vendor G0259

2151 **JAY FAMILY OF LAROCHELLE & N.Y. PROVINCE & STATE,** by L.J. Wells. 1938.
Paper. $12.50. 64pp. .... Vendor G0259

2152 **THE ENGLISH ANCESTRY OF THOMAS JEFFERSON,** by Dabney N. McLean. 1996. Illus.
Begins with the ancestry of Henry **Soane**, Jefferson's great-great-grandfather, and his wife and follows the **Field** and **Jefferson** lines of descent to Thomas Jefferson.
Paper. $12.50. 84pp. .... Vendor G0011

2153 **JELKE & FRAZIER & ALLIED FAM.,** by L.E. DeForest. 1931.
Paper. $18.50. 64pp. .... Vendor G0259

2154 **JENKINS FAMILY BOOK,** by R.E. Jenkins. 1904.
Cloth, $42.50. Paper, $32.50. 244pp. .... Vendor G0259

2155 **JENKS FAM. OF AMER.,** by W.B. Browne. 1952.
Cloth, $120.00. Paper, $110.00. 739pp. .... Vendor G0259

2156 **A GEN. HIST. OF THE JENNINGS FAM. IN ENG. & AMER. VOL II, THE AMER. FAM.,** by W.H. Jennings. (Vol. I not publ.) 1899.
Cloth, $109.00. Paper, $99.00. 828pp. .... Vendor G0259

2157 **A JENNINGS FAMILY GENEALOGY AS DESCENDED FROM CHARLES LAWSON JININGS OF MARYLAND AND NORTH CAROLINA, TO THE SEVENTH GENERATION OF SAMUEL B. JININGS IN AMERICA 1774–1985,** by Shirley Jennings Weber. 1988. Indexed. Illus.
Book contains history **Jennings** estate, copies of family Bibles, wills. Surnames: **Allen, Bonafield, Hays, McCord, McMurtrey, Mabery, Robeson, Wriston, Long, Richardson**.
Cloth. $26.00. 602pp. .... Vendor G0235

2158 **JENNINGS, DAVIDSON & ALLIED FAMILIES: GENEALOGICAL LIST & HIST. OF THE DESCENDANTS OF THE IMMIGRANTS JOHN JENNINGS, SOUTHAMPTON NY, & JOHN DAVISON, AUGUSTA CO. VA,** by Lillie P. White. 1944.
Cloth, $52.50. Paper, $42.50. 269pp. .... Vendor G0259

2159 **WILLIAM MORGAN JESSE AND HIS DESCENDANTS,** by Bev Jesse Shuptrine and Harry Shuptrine. 1995. Indexed. Illus.
Cloth. $40.00. 730pp. .... Vendor G0326

2160 **EDW. JESSUP OF W. FARMS, WESTCHESTER CO. NY, & HIS DESC., WITH AN APP. OF RECORDS OF OTHER AMER. FAM. OF THE NAME,** by H. Jesup. 1887.
Cloth, $66.00. Paper, $56.00. 465pp. .... Vendor G0259

2161 **JEWELL REGISTER, DESC. OF THOMAS JEWELL OF BRAINTREE,** by P. and J. Jewell. 1860.
Paper. $17.50. 104pp. .... Vendor G0259

A Quarterly Publication

TIDEWATER VIRGINIA FAMILIES:
A Magazine of History & Genealogy

Presenting research in the Virginia counties of Caroline, Charles City, Elizabeth City, Essex, Gloucester, Hanover, Henrico, James City, King George, King & Queen, King William, Lancaster, Mathews, Middlesex, New Kent, Northumberland, Richmond, Warwick, Westmoreland and York.

Editor: Virginia Lee Hutcheson Davis

Subscription Volume 5: $22.00/year US ($25.00 Canada/overseas). All subscriptions begin with the May issue and include four issues. Subscriptions to Volumes 1 thru 4 (4 issues each) $25.00 per volume, $30.00 Canada/overseas.

Tidewater Virginia Families

316 Littletown Quarter   Williamsburg, VA 23185-5519

2162 **HIST. & GEN. OF THE JEWETTS OF AMER.; REC. OF EDWARD JEWETT OF BRADFORD, ENG., & OF HIS SONS, SETTLERS OF ROWLEY, MASS., IN 1639,** by F. Jewett. 2 vols. 1908.
Cloth, $169.00. Paper, $159.00. 1,216pp. .... Vendor G0259

2163 **JOCELYN–JOSLIN–JOSLYN–JOSSELYN FAMILY,** by Edith S. Wessler. 1962.
Cloth, $57.50. Paper, $47.50. 310pp. .... Vendor G0259

2164 **THE JOHNES FAM. OF SOUTHAMPTON, LONG ISLAND, 1629–1886,** by E.R. Johnes. 1886.
Paper. $9.50. 46pp. .... Vendor G0259

2165 **ANC. OF SARAH JOHNSON, WIFE OF JOSEPH NEAL, OF LITCHFIELD, MAINE,** by W.G. Davis. 1960.
Paper. $17.50. 104pp. .... Vendor G0259

2166 **FENTON WESLEY JOHNSON AND HIS WIFE FLORENCE GENEVIEVE BAILEY,** by Phyllis Walker Johnson. 1991. Indexed. Illus.
Cloth. $20.00. 105pp. .... Vendor G0178

2167 **GEN. OF CAPT. JOHN JOHNSON OF ROXBURY, MASS., GENERATIONS I TO XIV,** by F.L. Johnson; edited by P.F. Johnson and A.J. Modern. 1951.
Cloth, $86.50. Paper, $76.50. 499pp. .... Vendor G0259

2168 **HIST. & GEN. OF ONE LINE OF DESC. FROM CAPT. EDWARD JOHNSON, TOGETHER WITH HIS ENG. ANC., 1500–1914,** by A. Johnson. 1914.
Cloth, $48.00. Paper, $38.00. 232pp. .... Vendor G0259

2169 **JACOB JOHNSON OF HARPSWELL, MAINE & HIS DESC.,** by C.N. Sinnett. 1907.
Cloth, $36.00. Paper, $26.00. 132pp. .... Vendor G0259

2170 **JOHNSON & ALLIED FAM. OF LINCS., ENG., BEING THE ANC. & POSTERITY OF LAWRENCE JOHNSON OF PHILA., PENN.,** by R.W. Johnson, Sr., and L.J. Morris. 1934.
Cloth, $80.50. Paper, $70.50. 478pp. .... Vendor G0259

2171 **JOHNSON GEN. RECORDS OF THE DESC. OF JOHN JOHNSON OF IPSWICH & ANDOVER, MASS., 1635–1892; WITH AN APPENDIX CONTAINING RECORDS OF TIMOTHY JOHNSON OF ANDOVER,** by W.W. Johnson. 1892.
Cloth, $41.50. Paper, $31.50. 200pp. .... Vendor G0259

2172 **JOHNSON–STEBBINS. ONE LINE OF DESC. FROM JOHN JOHNSON OF ROXBURY, MASS. TO LYDIA STEBBINS,** by F.Z. Rossiter. 1907.
Paper. $15.00. 75pp. manuscript .... Vendor G0259

2173 **THE GEORGIA RECORDS OF CALEB JOHNSON/JOHNSTON,** by Mildred S. Ezell. 1984. Indexed. Illus.
Includes: **Johnson/Johnston, Waggonman.**
Paper. $7.50. 47pp. .... Vendor G0323

2174 **THE JOHNSONS & THEIR KIN, OF RANDOLPH, N.C.,** by J.O. Shaw. 1955.
Cloth, $43.50. Paper, $33.50. 214pp. .... Vendor G0259

2175 **GEN. RECORD OF PETER JOHNSTON, WITH HIST. OF CLAN,** by C.E. Johnston. 1900.
Cloth, $32.50. Paper, $22.50. 118pp. .... Vendor G0259

2176 **THE JOHNSTONS OF SALISBURY, WITH A BRIEF SUPPL. CONCERNING THE HANCOCK, STROTHER, & PRESTON FAM.,** by W.P. Johnston. 1897.
Cloth, $39.50. Paper, $29.50. 216pp. .... Vendor G0259

2177 **HIST., GEN. & BIOGR. ACCT. OF THE JOLLIFFE FAM. OF VA., 1652–1893. ALSO SKETCHES OF COGNATE FAM.,** by W. Jolliffe. 1893.
Cloth, $48.00. Paper, $38.00. 245pp. .... Vendor G0259

2178 **A GEN. OF THE FAM. OF CERENO UPHAM JONES OF WEYMOUTH, NOVA SCOTIA (A DESC. OF LEWIS JONES OF ROXBURY, MASS., 1640),** by M.E.R. Jones. 1905.
Paper. $8.00. 38pp. .... Vendor G0259

2179 **CAPT. ROGER JONES OF LONDON & VA. SOME ANC. & DESC. WITH NOTICE OF OTHER FAM.,** by L. Jones. 1891.
Cloth, $54.00. Paper, $44.00. 296pp. .... Vendor G0259

2180 **DESC. OF JOEL JONES, OF MASS. & PA., 1764–1845. ALSO AN ACCT.**

OF HIS ANC. BACK TO LEWIS & ANN OF WATERTOWN, MA. ALSO DESC. OF LEMUEL SMITH OF MA. & PA., 1770–1817, by E. Smith. 1925.
Cloth, $75.00. Paper, $65.00. 414pp. .... Vendor G0259

2181 DESCENDANTS OF JOSHUA JONES OF ALABAMA AND SOLOMON KING OF NORTH CAROLINA 1771–1994, by Nadine Young Billingsley. 1994. Indexed.
Documented from wills, census, legal, church, newspapers, letters, and interviews. Over 8,000 names. Extended families include: **Handley, Boggs, Allred, Bicknell.**
Cloth. $55.00. 620pp. .... Vendor G0306

2182 DESCENDANTS OF ROGER JONES OF VIRGINIA, by Carol A. Hauk. 1995. Indexed.
Paper. $30.00. 48pp. .... Vendor G0340

2183 FAMILY RECORD OF THE JONES FAMILY, OF MILFORD MA & PROVIDENCE RI, WITH CONNECTIONS & DESCENDANTS, WITH ANCESTRY & FAMILY OF LORANIA CARRINGTON JONES, by G.F. Jones. 1884.
Cloth, $38.00. Paper, $28.00. 182pp. .... Vendor G0259

2184 GEN. OF DAVID JONES, by E.M. Beales. 1903.
Cloth, $35.00. Paper, $25.00. 184pp. .... Vendor G0259

2185 HIST. & GEN. OF THE ANC. & DESC. OF CAPT. ISRAEL JONES WHO REMOVED FROM ENFIELD TO BARKHAMSTED, CONN., IN 1759. 1629–30–1902, by L.N. Parker. 1902.
Cloth, $49.50. Paper, $39.50. 303pp. .... Vendor G0259

2186 JONES & RELATED FAMILIES: A GEN. COMP. & HISTORY, INCL. STUBBS, GIFFORD, JOHNSON, HAWKINS, SMALL, HOBSON, GREEN & OTHERS, by C.B. Jones. 1951.
Cloth, $77.50. Paper, $67.50. 436pp. .... Vendor G0259

2187 JONES FAM. OF LONG ISLAND, DESC. OF MAJ. THOMAS JONES (1665–1726) & ALLIED FAM., by J.H. Jones. 1907.
Cloth, $78.00. Paper, $68.00. 435pp. .... Vendor G0259

2188 LEAVES FROM A FAMILY TREE, BEING RANDOM RECORDS, LETTERS & TRADITIONS OF THE JONES, STIMSON & CLARKE FAMILIES OF HOPKINTON, MEDFIELD, NORTON & BOSTON, MASS., & PROVIDENCE, R.I., by L. Diman. 1941.
Paper. $19.00. 121pp. .... Vendor G0259

2189 PETER & RICHARD JONES GENEALOGIES, by A.B. Fothergill. 1924.
Cloth, $67.00. Paper, $57.00. 363pp. .... Vendor G0259

2190 SOME OF THE DESC. OF LEWIS & ANN JONES OF ROXBURY, MASS., THROUGH THEIR SON JOSIAH, & GRANDSON JAMES, by W.B. Trask. 1878.
Paper. $14.00. 83pp. .... Vendor G0259

2191 THE DESCENDANTS OF ANN (POWELL) JONES OF PHILADELPHIA,

WIDOW OF SAMUEL JONES OF LLANIGON, BRECONSHIRE, WALES; 1765–1995, by Rick Crume. 1995. Indexed.
Includes: **Bellingham, Morgan, Parry.**
Paper. $16.00. 174pp. .... Vendor G0386

2192 **THE HENRY AND MARY STEEVES JONES FAMILY OF NEW BRUNSWICK, OHIO, IOWA, AND PART II: OTHER ANCESTRIES OF JOHN AND VIOLA ELLIS JONES,** by Marvin T. Jones. 1993. Indexed. Illus.
The lives and times of nine generations of this family are told through records, family stories, and photographs. The second portion gives brief summaries of Makepeace Crary **Gallop, Simmons, Tisdale, Rogers, Osgood, Ellis, Tull, Roach,** and other lines.
Cloth. $30.00. 150pp. .... Vendor G0420

2193 **JORDAN MEMORIAL. FAM. RECORDS OF THE REV. ROBERT JORDAN & HIS DESC. IN AMER.,** by T.F. Jordan. 1882.
Cloth, $87.00. Paper, $77.00. 495pp. .... Vendor G0259

2194 **A BRIEF HIST. OF THE JOY FAM.,** by One of Them (C.C. Joy Dyer). 1876.
Paper. $7.50. 37pp. .... Vendor G0259

2195 **THOMAS JOY & HIS DESC.,** by J.R. Joy. 1900.
Cloth, $40.00. Paper, $30.00. 225pp. .... Vendor G0259

2196 **THOS. JUDD & HIS DESC.,** by S. Judd. 1856.
Cloth, $33.00. Paper, $23.00. 112pp. .... Vendor G0259

2197 **THE DESC. OF ROBERT JUNKINS OF YORK CO., MAINE,** by H.A. Davis. 1938.
Cloth, $40.00. Paper, $30.00. 197pp. .... Vendor G0259

2198 **[Justus]. FAMILY HISTORY OF WESTERN NORTH CAROLINA,** by Joyce J. Parris. 1994. Indexed.
Paper. $21.50. 218pp. .... Vendor G0295

2199 **JUSTIS, JUSTUS, JUSTICE FOR ALL; A COMPILATION OF EARLY AMERICAN FAMILY RECORDS,** by Joyce Justus Parris. 1993. Indexed. Illus.
Paper. $23.00. 223pp. .... Vendor G0295

2200 **A HIST. OF THE KAGY REL. IN AMER., FROM 1715 TO 1900,** by F. Keagy. 1899.
Cloth, $95.50. Paper, $85.50. 675pp. .... Vendor G0259

2201 **GENEALOGY OF THE DESCENDANTS OF PETER & ELIZABETH DRUSHEL KANDEL, 1783–1942,** by W.E. Kandel. 1942.
Cloth, $31.00. Paper, $21.00. 120pp. .... Vendor G0259

2202 **THE BAVARIAN CONNECTION: THE GEORGE AND WALBURGA KARCH FAMILY AND THEIR DESCENDANTS,** by Allen W. Bernard. 1994. Indexed. Illus.
Foreword by Don Heinrich Tolzman, Director of German-American Studies, University of Cincinnati.

Documents the historic and sociological background of George and Walburga (**Riedl**) **Karch** and 324 descendants, including the **Heffner** and **Bernard** families. Immigrants from the Oberpfalz Region of Bavaria, they arrived in 1852. By 1868 they moved to Mercer County, Ohio where they purchased land and gained prominence. Chronicles four generations: 116 family descriptions, essays, and numerous illustrations, maps, photographs, pedigree and generational charts. Register System format. Fine quality acid-free paper. Cloth. $39.00. 274+xivpp. .... Vendor G0431

2203 **HIST. OF CAPT. JOHN KATHAN OF DUMMERSTON, VT.**, by D.L. Mansfield. 1902.
Cloth, $38.50. Paper, $28.50. 147pp. .... Vendor G0259

2204 **KAUFMAN–KAUFFMAN: THE HOUSE OF MAIDENCREEK**, by Frank Llewellyn Kaufman and Odette J. Mordant Kaufman. 1992. Indexed. Illus.
Cloth. $47.00. 572pp. .... Vendor G0414

2205 **KAUFMAN–KAUFFMAN: THE HOUSE OF OLEY**, by Frank Llewellyn Kaufman and Odette J. Mordant Kaufman. 1994. Indexed. Illus.
Cloth. $88.00. 1,204pp. .... Vendor G0414

2206 **KAUFMANN FAMILIES FROM GRINDELWALD, SWITZERLAND: CHRISTIAN AND ULRICH OF HOLMES COUNTY, OHIO; RUDOLPH OF TETON COUNTY, WYOMING; PETER OF KNOX COUNTY, OHIO**, by Lucile Kaufmann Novak and Gladis M. Kaufmann. 1982. Indexed. Illus.
Kaufman(n): Grindelwald records 1508–1950; Christian to United States—1880; Urlich—ca. 1862; Rudolph—1900; Peter—1885. Related families: **Bohren, Durtschi, Inaebnit, Bergundthal**.
Cloth. $25.00. 282pp. .... Vendor G0125

2207 **FAMILY HISTORY & A LIST OF THE DESCENDANTS OF JOHN KEARNS & HIS WIFE MARGARET GROUGHBROUGH**, by R. Kearns. 1909.
Paper. $12.00. 66pp. .... Vendor G0259

2208 **"DOWN IN THE BARNS": THE KECKS OF CLAIBORNE CO., TN**, by Virginia B. Fletcher. 1983. Indexed. Illus.
Surnames include: **Keck, Ousley, Yadon**.
Cloth. $30.00. 440pp. .... Vendor G0332

2209 **MORE KECKS OF CLAIBORNE CO., TN**, by Virginia B. Fletcher. 1992. Indexed. Illus.
Surnames include: **Keck, Sowder**.
Cloth. $32.00. 318pp. .... Vendor G0332

2210 **GEN. REC. OF THE KECK FAM.**, by Keck and Grasselli. 1905.
Paper. $12.50. 66pp. .... Vendor G0259

2211 **[Keen–Kyn]. DESCENDANTS OF JORAM KYN OF NEW SWEDEN**, by G.B. Keen. 1913.
Cloth, $58.00. Paper, $48.00. 318pp. .... Vendor G0259

2212 **GEN. OF THE KEEN FAM. OF WAYNE CO., ILL.**, by H.T. Keen. 1965.
Paper. $19.00. 132pp. .... Vendor G0259

2213 **KEEN KIN—THE KEEN FAMILY OF ARKANSAS & OKLAHOMA**, by
Roy B. Young. 1990. Illus.
Reid—Prince—Eubanks—Brock—Stillwell.
Cloth. $38.95. 200pp. .... Vendor G0405

2214 **[Keen–Kyn]. THE DESC. OF JORAM KYN, FOUNDER OF "UPLAND-
NEW SWEDEN" (NOW CHESTER, PA.) & WHOSE DESC. WERE
SOME OF THE EARLIEST SETTLERS OF WABASH CO., IL (FROM
"PA. MAG. HIST. & BIOGR.).** 1878–82.
Cloth, $49.50. Paper, $39.50. 243pp. .... Vendor G0259

2215 **KEENE FAM. HIST. & GEN.**, by E. Jones. 1923.
Cloth, $64.50. Paper, $54.50. 343pp. .... Vendor G0259

2216 **JOHN KEEP OF LONGMEADOW, MASS., 1660–1676, & HIS DESC.**, by
F.E. Best. 1899.
Cloth, $44.50. Paper. $34.50. 263pp. .... Vendor G0259

2217 **KEESE FAM. HIST. & GEN. 1690–1911**, by W.T. Keese. 1911.
Paper. $10.00. 48pp. .... Vendor G0259

2218 **A GEN. OF THE DESC. OF BENJ. KEITH THROUGH TIMOTHY, SON
OF REV. JAMES KEITH**, by Z. Keith. 1889.
Paper. $18.50. 114pp. .... Vendor G0259

2219 **[Kelker]. GENEALOGICAL RECORD OF THE FAMILY OF
KOELLIKER OF HERRLIBURG, DISTRICT MEILEN, CANTON
ZURICH, SWITZERLAND, WITH RECORD OF THE FAMILY OF
KELKER SINCE THEIR ARRIVAL IN THIS COUNTRY IN 1743**, by J.J.
Hess and R.F. Kelker. 1883.
Cloth, $34.00. Paper, $24.00. 132pp. .... Vendor G0259

2220 **DESCENDANTS OF HENRY KELLER OF YORK CO., PA, &
FAIRFIELD CO., OH**, by E. Shumaker, et al. 1924.
Cloth, $99.50. Paper, $89.50. 594pp. .... Vendor G0259

2221 **HISTORY OF THE KELLER FAM.**, by E. Keller. 1905.
Cloth, $39.50. Paper, $29.50. 192pp. .... Vendor G0259

2222 **GENEALOGICAL HISTORY OF THE KELLEY FAMILY, DESC. FROM
JOSEPH KELLEY OF NORWICH, CT., WITH MUCH BIOGR. MAT-
TER CONCERNING THE FIRST FOUR GENERATIONS AND NOTES
OF INFLOWING FEMALE LINES**, by Hermon A. Kelley. 1897.
Cloth, $31.00. Paper, $21.00. 122+15pp. .... Vendor G0259

2223 **THE KELLOGGS IN THE OLD WORLD & THE NEW**, by T. Hopkins. 3
vols. 1903.
Cloth, $265.00/set. Paper, $255.00/set. 897+848+321pp. .... Vendor G0259

2224 **A GENEALOGICAL ACCOUNT OF THE DESCENDANTS OF JOHN
KELLY OF NEWBURY, MASS.**, by G.M. Kelly. 1886.
Cloth, $38.50. Paper, $28.50. 178pp. .... Vendor G0259

2225 **THE ANC. & DESC. OF SETH KELLY, 1762–1850, OF BLACKSTONE,
MASS.**, by W.P. Kelly. 1937.
Paper. $14.00. 71pp. .... Vendor G0259

2226 **GENEALOGY OF THE DESC. OF WM. KELSEY, WHO SETTLED AT CAMBRIDGE, MA., IN 1632; AT HARTFORD, CT. IN 1636; & AT KILLINGSWORTH, CT., IN 1663**, Vol. I., by Claypool, Clizbee, and Kelsey. 1928.
Cloth, $57.00. Paper, $47.00. 295pp. .... Vendor G0259

2227 **GENEALOGY OF THE DESC. OF WM. KELSEY, WHO SETTLED AT CAMBRIDGE, MA., IN 1632; AT HARTFORD, CT. IN 1636; & AT KILLINGSWORTH, CT., IN 1663**, Vol. II., by Claypool, Clizbee, and Kelsey. 1929.
Cloth, $76.50. Paper, $66.50. 424pp. .... Vendor G0259

2228 **GENEALOGY OF THE DESC. OF WM. KELSEY, WHO SETTLED AT CAMBRIDGE, MA., IN 1632; AT HARTFORD, CT. IN 1636; & AT KILLINGSWORTH, CT., IN 1663**, Vol. III., by Claypool, Clizbee, and Kelsey. 1947
Cloth, $149.00. Paper, $139.00. 1,018pp. .... Vendor G0259

2229 **GENEALOGY OF THE KEMBLE (KIMBLE) FAMILY IN AMERICA**, by Kemble Stout. 1992. Indexed.
Cloth. $65.00. 653pp. .... Vendor G0320B

2230 **TWO CENTURIES OF KEMMERER FAM. HIST., 1730–1929**, W.A. Backenstoe. 1929.
Cloth, $37.00. Paper, $27.00. 152pp. .... Vendor G0259

2231 **THE NEW ENGLAND KEMPS,** by A.J. Weise. 1904.
Cloth, $41.00. Paper, $31.00. 193pp. .... Vendor G0259

2232 **KENDALL–GELETTE–ELLIS FAMILY HISTORY (W. CENTRAL MINN. 1860),** by Willis W. Denny. 1994.
Cloth, $32.00. Paper, $22.00. 111pp. .... Vendor G0259

2233 **MEMORIAL OF JOSIAH KENDALL, ONE OF THE FIRST SETTLERS OF STERLING, MASS., & SOME OF HIS ANC. & OF HIS DESC.,** by O. Kendall. 1884.
Cloth, $33.00. Paper, $23.00. 153pp. .... Vendor G0259

2234 **KENFIELD HISTORY: SOME LINES OF DESCENT FROM WILLIAM CANFIELD OF NORTHAMPTON, MASS.,** by Earl P. Crandall. 1993.
Paper. $19.50. 125pp. .... Vendor G0259

2235 **GEN. OF THE KENNAN FAM.,** by T.L. Kennan. 1907.
Cloth, $30.00. Paper, $20.00. 134pp. .... Vendor G0259

2236 **EARLY AMER. HIST.; KENNEDY & ALLIED FAM.,** by W.E. Brockman. 1926.
Paper. $14.00. 71pp. .... Vendor G0259

2237 **HIST. & GEN. ACCT. OF THE PRINCIPAL FAMS. OF THE NAME OF KENNEDY, WITH NOTES & ILLUS.,** by R. Pitcairn. 1830 (Scotland).
Cloth, $44.50. Paper, $34.50. 218pp. .... Vendor G0259

2238 **KENNEDY FAMILY RECORDS,** by J. Montgomery Seaver. 1929.
Paper. $7.00. 34pp. .... Vendor G0259

2239 **KENNEDY FAMILY RECORDS,** by J. Montgomery Seaver.
Paper. $7.00. 33pp. .... Vendor G0011

2240 **SOME DESCENDANTS OF ANDREW KENNEDY & MARGARET (PEGGY) HATFIELD, 1824–1989,** by Genevieve Curran Kennedy. 1989.
Cloth, $59.50. Paper, $49.50. 302pp. .... Vendor G0259

2241 **THE JOHNSTON & BACON SCOTTISH CLAN HISTORIES: The Kennedys,** by Sir James Fergusson. (1958) reprint 1993. Illus.
Paper. $8.95. 32pp. .... Vendor G0011

2242 **DESC. OF ABSALOM KENT OF ENG. & VA.,** by A.S. Kent. 1933.
Paper. $19.00. 101pp. .... Vendor G0259

2243 **GEN. OF THE DIFFERENT FAM. BEARING THE NAME OF KENT IN THE U.S., THEIR POSSIBLE ENG. ANC., 1295–1898,** by L.V. Briggs. 1898.
Cloth, $54.00. Paper, $44.00. 346pp. .... Vendor G0259

2244 **LETTERS & OTHER PAPERS OF DANIEL KENT, EMIGRANT & REDEMPTIONER, TO WHICH HAVE BEEN ADDED A FEW INTERESTING HAWLEY & SPACKMAN PAPERS,** by E.L. Barnard. 1904.
Cloth, $35.00. Paper, $25.00. 135pp. .... Vendor G0259

2245 **THOMAS KENT (1748–1835) AND HIS DESCENDANTS,** by Doris Bankes Kent. 1995. Indexed. Illus.
      Allied families: **Eagon, Fry, Hinegardner, Hoge, Hook, Johnson, Odenbaugh, Ralston, Reed, Smith, White.**
Cloth. $47.00. 441pp. .... Vendor G0201

2246 **AMERICAN KENYONS: HIST. OF KENYONS & ENGLISH CONNEC-
TIONS OF AMERICAN KENYONS; GEN. OF THE AMERICAN
KENYONS OF RHODE ISL.; MISC. KENYON MATERIAL**, by H.N.
Kenyon. 1935.
Cloth, $54.50. Paper, $44.50. 285pp. .... Vendor G0259

2247 **KERFOOT–KEARFOTT & ALLIED FAMILIES IN AMERICA**, by R.R.
Kearfott. 1948.
Cloth, $38.00. Paper, $28.00. 170pp. .... Vendor G0259

2248 **KERLEY & ALLIED FAM. OF THE SOUTH**, by W.C. Carley. 1945.
Cloth, $35.00. Paper, $25.00. 128pp. .... Vendor G0259

2249 **KETTERMAN FAMILY HIST.**, by L.C. Ketterman. 1985.
Cloth, $69.00. Paper, $59.00. 380pp. .... Vendor G0259

2250 **KEY & ALLIED FAMILIES**, by J.C. Lane. 1931.
Cloth, $84.25. Paper, $74.25. 495pp. .... Vendor G0259

2251 **GEN. ROBERT KEYES OF WATERTOWN, MASS., 1633, SOLOMON
KEYES OF NEWBURY & CHELMSFORD, MASS., 1653, & THEIR
DESC.**, by A. Keyes. 1880.
Cloth, $51.50. Paper, $41.50. 326pp. .... Vendor G0259

2252 **THE COMING TOGETHER OF THE KEYES AND GAGE FAMILIES**,
by William M. Gage. 1986. Indexed. Illus., 31 photos, 20 maps and drawings.
Connects the history of certain families descending from Robert **Keyes**
(Watertown, N.Y., 1633) and James **Gage** (New Windsor, N.Y., 1777) to the
history of America from 1630 to 1910.
Cloth. $30.00. 404pp. .... Vendor G0247

2253 **KICKERS OF THE SOUTH**, by Ann K. Blomquist. 1987. Indexed. Illus.
Cloth. $35.00. 220pp. .... Vendor G0374

2254 **A GEN. OF THE KIDDER FAM., COMPRISING THE DESC. IN THE
MALE LINE OF ENSIGN JAMES KIDDER, 1626–1676, OF CAM-
BRIDGE & BILLERICA, MA.**, by M.H. Stafford. 1941.
Cloth, $119.00. Paper, $109.00. 750pp. .... Vendor G0259

2255 **HIST. OF THE KIDDER FAM., 1320–1676, INCL. THE BIOGR. OF OUR
EMIGR. ANC. JAMES KIDDER & A GEN. OF HIS DESC. THROUGH
HIS SON, JOHN, WHO SETTLED IN CHELMSFORD, MA., 1681**, by F.
Kidder. 1886.
Cloth, $36.50. Paper, $26.50. 174pp. .... Vendor G0259

2256 **THE KIGH, MANN, REAGIN, AND SYKES FAMILIES**, by Marion Mann,
M.D. 1995. Indexed. Illus.
Including the **Branch, Brown, Dean, Fort, Gerran, Leake, Marquis, Moses,
Oakes, Powell, Reid, Trammell, Walk, Wilkey, Wingfield**, and **Woods**
families.
Cloth. $38.00. 218pp. .... Vendor G0316

2257 **HIST. & ANTIQ. OF THE NAME & FAM. OF KILBOURN (IN VAR.
ORTHOGRAPHY)**, by P. Kilbourne. 1856.
Cloth, $67.50. Paper, $57.50. 444pp. .... Vendor G0259

2258 **HIST. OF THE KILMER FAM. IN AMER.**, by C.H. Kilmer. 1897.
Cloth, $38.00. Paper, $28.00. 214pp. Vendor G0259

2259 **HIST. OF THE KIMBALL FAM. IN AMER., 1634–1897; ALSO ANC. OF THE KEMBALLS OR KEMBOLDES OF ENG., WITH ACCT. OF THE KEMBLES OF BOSTON,** by L.A. Morrison and S.P. Sharples. 1897.
Cloth, $161.00. Paper, $151.00. 1,278pp. . . . . Vendor G0259

2260 **THE HISTORY OF THE KIMBALL FAMILY IN AMERICA, REVISED EDITION, VOLUME I,** by Leonard A. Morrison and Stephen P. Sharples. (1897) rev. ed. vol. I, 1990. Indexed.
Containing Richard **Kimball**, the emigrant ancestor, and the first six generations of his descendants; with additional information on allied families. New and corrected information added to original publication.
Cloth. $35.00. 498pp. . . . . Vendor G0043

2261 **REC. OF THE FAM. OF LEVI KIMBALL & SOME OF HIS DESC.,** by L. Darbee. 1861, rev. 1913.
Cloth, $35.75. Paper, $25.75. 173pp. Vendor G0259

2262 **THE JOSEPH KIMBALL FAMILY: GENEALOGICAL MEMOIR OF THE ASCENDANTS & DESCENDANTS OF JOSEPH KIMBALL OF CANTERBURY, NH; TEN GENERATIONS, 1634–1885,** by J. Kimball. 1885.
Paper. $18.00. 103pp. . . . . Vendor G0259

2263 **THE LT. MOSES & JEMIMA CLEMENT KIMBALL FAM.,** by P.K. Skinner. 1941.
Cloth, $30.50. Paper, $20.50. 138pp. Vendor G0259

2264 **DESC. OF RICHARD KIMBER: GEN. HIST. OF THE DESC. OF RICHARD KIMBER OF GROVE, BERKS., ENG., CONTAINING THE FAMS. IN THE U.S. FROM SETTLEMENTS IN PA. & NY, FAMS. IN ENG. & DESC. IN AUSTRALIA,** by S.A. Kimber. 1894.
Paper. $17.50. 91pp. . . . . Vendor G0259

2265 **GENEALOGY OF THE KIMBERLY FAMILY,** by D.L. Jacobus. 1950.
Cloth, $36.50. Paper, $26.50. 176pp. Vendor G0259

2266 **CLEMENT KING OF MARSHFIELD, MA., 1668, & HIS DESCENDANTS,** by G.A. Morrison, Jr. 1898.
Paper. $13.00. 65pp. . . . . Vendor G0259

2267 **KING FAMILY HISTORY. VOLS. I–II,** by H. Harold Hartzler. 1984.
Cloth. $40.00. 997pp+449-p. index . . . . Vendor G0150

2268 **KING FAM. OF SUFFIELD, CT., ITS ENG. ANC., 1389–1662, & AMER. DESC., 1662–1908,** by C. King. 1908.
Cloth, $73.50. Paper, $63.50. 655pp. Vendor G0259

2269 **KING GENEALOGY & ITS BRANCHES MOULTONS, SEDGWICKS & SHAWS, & THEIR DESCENDANTS BEARING OTHER NAMES: RECORD OF THE DESCENDANTS OF WM. KING OF MONSON, MASS., 1770 (BOTH MALE & FEMALE LINES TO 1897) & COMPLETE RECORD OF THE ANCESTRY OF WM. KING & HIS WIFE HELEN**

LAMPHEAR KING FROM THE 16TH CENTURY, WITH APPENDIX, by Harvey B. King. 1897.
Cloth, $34.00. Paper, $24.00. 142pp. .... Vendor G0259

2270 THE KING FAMILY HERALDRY, by George A. Morrison. 1910. Illus.
Paper. $5.00. 35pp. .... Vendor G0182

2271 DESC. OF HENRY KINGMAN. SOME EARLY GEN. OF THE KINGMAN FAM., by B. Kingman. 1912.
Paper. $15.00. 102pp. .... Vendor G0259

2272 GEN. REC. OF THE EARLY ENG. ANC. TO AMER., & LINES OF DESC. TO NATHANIEL KINGSBURY OF KEENE, N.H. & DESC. OF THREE DAUGHTERS: ABIGAIL KINGSBURY WHITE, HANNAH KINGSBURY WHITE, CLOE KINGSBURY SUMNER, by F.B. Kingsbury. 1904.
Paper. $12.50. 63pp. .... Vendor G0259

2273 GEN. OF THE DESC. OF HENRY KINGSBURY OF IPSWICH & HAVERHILL, MASS., by F.J. Kingsbury and M.K. Talcott. 1905.
Cloth, $102.00. Paper, $92.00. 732pp. .... Vendor G0259

2274 LES ANCÊTRES PATERNELS DE WILFRID KINGSLEY (1885–1948) ET DE BLANCHE GOYETTE (1886–1975), by Robert Serré. 1995. Indexed. Illus.
Paper. CAN $10.00. 40pp. .... Vendor G0111

2275 THE KINNEARS & THEIR KIN. A MEM. VOL. OF HIST., BIOGR. & GEN., by White & Maltby. 1916.
Cloth, $99.00. Paper, $89.00. 596pp. .... Vendor G0259

2276 [Kinsey]. A FAMILY HISTORY, by G.S. Kinsey.
Paper. $7.00. 35pp. .... Vendor G0259

2277 A HISTORY OF JACOB KINSEY (KINTZY) & HIS DESCENDANTS, by Wm. Kinsey. 1934.
Cloth, $43.50. Paper, $33.50. 202pp. .... Vendor G0259

2278 GEN. RECORD OF THE DESC. OF ROBT. KINSMAN OF IPSWICH, MASS, 1624–1875, by L.W. Stickney. 1876.
Cloth, $49.50. Paper, $39.50. 258pp. .... Vendor G0259

2279 HIST. NOTES OF FAM. OF KIP OF KIPSBURG & KIPS BAY, N.Y., by W.I. Kip. 1871.
Paper. $10.00. 49pp. .... Vendor G0259

2280 HIST. OF THE KIP FAM. IN AMER., by Kip and Hawley. 1928.
Cloth, $81.00. Paper, $71.00. 462pp. .... Vendor G0259

2281 THE KIRBYS OF NEW ENG. A HIST. OF THE DESC. OF JOHN KIRBY OF MIDDLETOWN, CONN., & OF JOSEPH KIRBY OF HARTFORD, CONN., & OF RICHARD KIRBY OF SANDWICH, MASS., by M.E. Dwight. 1898.
Cloth, $67.00. Paper, $57.00. 455pp. .... Vendor G0259

2282 GEN. OF THE DESC. OF JOHN KIRK, 1660–1705, by M.S. Roberts; edited by G. Cope. 1912–1913.
Cloth, $109.50. Paper, $99.50. 729pp. .... Vendor G0259

2283 **HIST. GEN. OF THE KIRK FAM., AS ESTABLISHED BY ROGER KIRK, WHO SETTLED AT NOTTINGHAM, CHESTER CO., PENN., c. 1714,** by C.H. Stubbs. 1872.
Cloth, $41.00. Paper, $31.00. 252pp. .... Vendor G0259

2284 **BRIEF HIST. OF KIRKBRIDE FAM., WITH SPECIFIC REFERENCE TO DESC. OF DAVID KIRKBRIDE 1775–1830,** by S.A. Kirkbride. 1913.
Paper. $12.50. 64pp. .... Vendor G0259

2285 **KISTLER FAM., DESC. FROM GEORGE KISTLER, JR. OF BERKS CO., PENN.,** by F.K. Sprague. 1944.
Paper. $10.00. 47pp. .... Vendor G0259

2286 **KITE FAM.,** by V.A. Kite.
Cloth, $33.50. Paper, $23.50. 122pp. .... Vendor G0259

2287 **KITTREDGE FAMILY IN AMERICA,** by M.T. Kittredge. 1936.
Cloth, $42.50. Paper, $32.50. 215pp. .... Vendor G0259

2288 **THE KLINGERS FROM THE ODENWALD, HESSE, GERMANY ca. 1610–1989,** by Mary Klinger. 1989. Indexed.
Cloth. $52.00. 680pp. .... Vendor G0447

2289 **KNAPP FAM. IN AMER. A GEN. OF THE DESC. OF WM. KNAPP, WHO SETTLED IN WATERTOWN MASS., IN 1630, INCL. A PEDIGREE OF HIRAM KNAPP,** by A. Knapp. 1909.
Paper. $15.00. 76pp. .... Vendor G0259

2290 **NICHOLAS KNAPP GENEALOGY,** by Alfred A. Knapp. 1953.
Cloth, $129.50. Paper, $119.50. 900pp. .... Vendor G0259

2291 **SEVEN CENTURIES IN THE KNEELAND FAM.,** by S.F. Kneeland. 1897.
Cloth, $84.00. Paper, $74.00. 583pp. .... Vendor G0259

2292 **KNEISLY GEN.,** by H. Kneisly. 1932.
Paper. $9.00. 46pp. .... Vendor G0259

2293 **GEN. OF KNEPPER FAM. OF U.S. 1681–1911,** by M. Knepper. 1911.
Cloth, $32.50. Paper, $22.50. 132pp. .... Vendor G0259

2294 **KNICKERBACKER–VIELE. SKETCHES OF ALLIED FAMILIES, TO WHICH IS ADDED AN APPENDIX CONTAINING FAM. DATA,** by K.K. Viele. 1916.
Cloth, $32.50. Paper, $22.50. 134pp. .... Vendor G0259

2295 **ABEL KNIGHT OF GUILFORD COUNTY, NORTH CAROLINA, HIS ANCESTORS, HIS DESCENDANTS AND SUMMARIES OF KNIGHT FAMILIES WHO RESIDED NEAR THEM,** by Jane Kyhl Beekman. 1992. Indexed.
    Knight families 1600s England, PA, NC, OH, TN, IN, etc. Connecting families: **Boren, Cain, Chew, Hunt, Lee, Lomax, Meredith, Stanley, Thomas,** etc. Extensive references.
Cloth, $32.00. Paper, $25.00. 284pp. .... Vendor G0073

2296 **RESEARCH NOTES ON KNIGHT AND LOMAX ALLIED FAMILIES, PART I,** by Jane Kyhl Beekman. 1993.

Baldwin, Bates, Bennett, Bogue, Boren, Bottorff, Boyd, Brasher, Brown, Cain, Calhoun, Carey, Chew, Clark, Coffin, Cook, Cox, Davis, Dilworth, Ditto, Dwiggins, Farrington, Hare, Haughey, Hiatt, Hill, Hinkson, Hunt, Jessop, Kersey, Ladd, Lee, Martin, Maudlin, Mendenhall, Meredith, Mills, Moorman, Morris, Moseley, Nagle, Newby, Nicks, Osborn, Pitts, Plumley, Puckett, Radcliffe, Ralston, Rayl, Reiff, Ruberson, Scott, Shelly, Short, Shugart, Stanley, Starbuck, Study, Sweet, Thomas, Vickers, Way, Willcutts, Winslow. Extensive References. Individual families may be purchased separately. Enclose SASE for information.
Paper. $20.00. 150pp. . . . . Vendor G0073

2297 **RESEARCH NOTES ON KNIGHT AND LOMAX ALLIED FAMILIES, PART II**, by Jane Kyhl Beekman. 1996.

Adams, Bachiler, Battin, Boyd[2], Brown[2], Bryant, Cockey, Coxe[2], Davenport, Davis[1], Davis[3], Dillinger, Dixon, Dungan, Few, Freeborn, Greenberry, Hammond, Hill[2], Hobbs, Holbrook, Hopwood, Howard, Large, Latham, Lomax, Lowe, Mayall, Maynard, Moone, Reiff/Rieff[2], Stanfield, Swift, Thornbrough, Weaver, Welschans, White, Wing. Extensive References. Families available separately. Enclose SASE for information.
Prices and number of pages vary depending on family . . . . . . Vendor G0073

2298 **KNISELY–WOLF & NORRIS–McCOY FAMILIES**, by J.C. Knisely. 1923.
Paper. $16.00. 81pp. . . . . Vendor G0259

2299 **READING BACKWARDS ON MY KNOTT HERITAGE**, by Mrs. Barbara Knott Horsman. 1994. Indexed. Illus.

Information on the 17th-century **Knott** families of Virginia, Granville Co., NC and Maryland. All known information compiled and presented on **James Knott** of Accomack Co., VA who arrived in 1617 and possible connection to the author's family. Many family lines are traced from the 17th century to present-day families. Migration of the **Knott** families from Virginia to Maryland, North Carolina, Georgia, Tennessee, and California. Also connection to the **Knott**'s Berry Farm in Buena Park, CA. Allied families are traced from the 17th century on: **Stegall, Wells, Tuck, Hester, Wilson**, and **Green**.
Cloth. $30.00. 432pp. . . . . Vendor G0115

2300 **KNOWLES FAM. OF EASTHAM, MASS.**, by C.T. Libby.
Paper. $14.00. 72pp. . . . . Vendor G0259

2301 **THE HIST. & GEN. OF THE KNOWLTONS OF ENG. & AMER.**, by C.H.W. Stocking. 1897.
Cloth, $87.50. Paper, $77.50. 610pp. . . . . Vendor G0259

2302 **KNOWLTON. ERRATA & ADDENDA; WITH A COMPLETE INDEX TO BOTH BOOKS**, by G.H. Knowlton. 1903.
Cloth, $46.00. Paper, $36.00. 239pp. . . . . Vendor G0259

2303 **GENEALOGICAL MEMOIRS OF JOHN KNOX, & OF THE FAMILY OF KNOX**, by Charles Rogers. 1879.
Cloth, $38.00. Paper, $28.00. 184pp. . . . . Vendor G0259

2304 **KNOX FAM.; GEN. & BIOGR. SKETCH OF THE DESC. OF JOHN KNOX OF ROWAN CO., N.C. & OTHERS**, by H. Goodman. 1905.
Cloth, $45.00. Paper, $35.00. 266pp. . . . . Vendor G0259

2305 **WILLIAM KNOX OF BLANDFORD, MA.; A RECORD OF THE BIRTHS, MARRIAGES & DEATHS OF SOME OF HIS DESC.**, by N. Foote. 1926.
Cloth, $58.50. Paper, $48.50. 302pp. .... Vendor G0259

2306 **THIRTY ANCESTORS OF RICHARD HENRY KOCH (KOCH, NEUFANG, BOCK, BOLICH, BECK, ET AL)**, by R.H. Koch. 1939.
Cloth, $59.50. Paper, $49.50. 327pp. .... Vendor G0259

2307 **THE KOHLHAGEN FAMILY GENEALOGY**, by Sue Ann Gardner Shreve. 1994. Indexed. Illus.
Eleven generations, includes—**Gardner, Becker, Hendrickson, Nusberger, Barkley, Hormel, Hoehn, Shreve, Bettenhausen, Koppelmann, Seemann, Burmeister, Danckwart, Helmboldt, Horn, Schliemann, Schumacher, Bockenhauers, Wichert, Rantzen, Bohnsack, Westphal.** Includes 1995 supplement.
Paper. $60.00. 216pp. .... Vendor G0221

2308 **[Koiner].** **HISTORICAL SKETCH OF MICHAEL KEINADT & MARGARET DILLER, HIS WIFE, THE HISTORY & GENEALOGY OF THEIR NUMEROUS POSTERITY IN THE AMERICAN STATES UP TO THE YEARS 1893**, by A.K., A.T., and E.T. Koiner. 1893.
Cloth, $37.50. Paper, $27.50. 171pp. .... Vendor G0259

2309 **KOINER. SUPPLEMENT ONLY.** 1941.
Paper. $7.00. 34pp. .... Vendor G0259

2310 **DIELMAN KOLB & HIS DESC., 1648–1880, (IN CUSTER GEN.)**, by A.W. Storer.
Paper. $12.00. 60pp. .... Vendor G0259

2311 **GENEALOGICAL HISTORY OF THE KOLB, KULP OR CULP FAMILY AND ITS BRANCHES**, by Daniel Kolb Cassel. (1895) reprint 1990.
Cloth. $33.00. 584pp. .... Vendor G0150

2312 **KOLB–KULP–CULP FAMILY**, compiled by the History Committee. 1936.
Cloth, $32.00. Paper, $22.00. 110pp. .... Vendor G0259

2313 **GEN. OF THE KOOLOCK FAM. OF SUSSEX CO., DELAWARE, 1657–1897**, by E.J. Sellers. 1897.
Paper. $15.00. 76pp. .... Vendor G0259

2314 **BIOGRAPHICAL & OTHER MATERIAL RELATED TO THE KOTHE FAMILY, 1748–1891**, by W. Kothe; edited by H.W. Kothe. 1961.
Paper. $15.00. 74pp. .... Vendor G0259

2315 **TRAILS AND TALES—KRAMER–THOMAS AND CONNECTING FAMILIES**, by Rhoda Joy Morley. 1994. Indexed. Illus.
Genealogies of John **Cramer/Kramer** 1800 in Montgomery Co., PA; Daniel M. **Barnes** b. 1809 NC; Woodson A. **Thomas** b. 1808 VA; John **Hodges** b. TN 1802–3; Simon **Bozarth** residing in VA ca. 1700; Henry **Burton** d. White Co., TN 1853; Daniel **Pitchford** residing in VA 1761.
Cloth. $30.00. 119pp. .... Vendor G0322

2316 **A BRIEF HIST. OF JOHN VALENTINE KRATZ, & A COMPLETE GEN. FAM. REGISTER**, by A.J. Fretz. 1892.
Cloth, $51.50. Paper, $41.50. 315pp. .... Vendor G0259

2317 **THE NAME KREIDER [FIRST REPORT, COMMITTEE ON KREIDER–GREIDER GENEALOGY]**, by Amos K. Stauffer. 1929.
Paper. $9.50. 4pp. . . . . Vendor G0150

2318 **SECOND ANNUAL REPORT OF THE COMMITTEE ON KREIDER–GREIDER GENEALOGY . . . 1930**, by Kreider–Grieder Reunion. 1930.
Paper. $9.50. 4pp. . . . . Vendor G0150

2319 **THIRD REPORT OF THE COMMITTEE ON KREIDER–GREIDER GENEALOGY . . . 1933**, by Amos K. Stauffer, Wilmer A. Kreider, and Reuben K. Light. 1933.
Paper. $9.50. 4pp. . . . . Vendor G0150

2320 **FOURTH REPORT OF THE COMMITTEE ON KREIDER–GREIDER GENEALOGY . . . 1934**, by Amos K. Stauffer, Wilmer A. Kreider, and Reuben K. Light. 1934.
Paper. $9.50. 4pp. . . . . Vendor G0150

2321 **KREKLER AND RELATED FAMILIES**, by Bessie K. Schafer. 1963.
Paper. $7.00. 35pp. . . . . Vendor G0259

2322 **JOHN KUECHMANN AND MARGARET KREHE OF MUSCATINE, IOWA: THEIR ANCESTORS IN GERMANY AND THEIR DESCENDANTS IN AMERICA**, by Gene Swain Kuechmann. 1990. Indexed. Illus.
Cloth. $25.00. 151pp. . . . . Vendor G0101

2323 **SOME SCRAPS OF HISTORY REGARDING THOMAS KUNDERS & HIS CHILDREN; ALSO, A LIST OF THE DESCENDANTS FOR SIX GENERATIONS OF HIS YOUNGEST SON, HENRY CUNREDS OF "WHITPAIN," 1683–1891**, by H. Conrad. 1891.
Cloth, $31.00. Paper, $21.00. 128pp. Vendor G0259

2324 **OUR DANISH ANCESTORS—THE KYHL AND HANSEN FAMILIES OF IOWA**, by Jane Kyhl Beekman. 1995. Indexed.
Enclose SASE for information.
Approx. 200pp. . . . . Vendor G0073

2325 **PARTIAL HIST. OF KYLE, KILE, COYLE FAM. IN AMER.**, by O.M. Kile. 1958.
Cloth, $45.00. Paper, $35.00. 186pp. Vendor G0259

2326 **THE ROLL OF THE HOUSE OF LACY. PEDIGREES, MIL. MEMOIRS & SYNOPTICAL HIST. OF THE ANCIENT & ILLUSTRIOUS FAM. OF DELACY, FROM THE EARLIEST TIMES, IN ALL ITS BRANCHES, TO THE PRESENT DAY. FULL NOTICES ON ALLIED FAM. & A MEM. OF THE BROWNES (CANADA)**, by deLacy-Bellingari. 1928.
Cloth, $75.00. Paper, $65.00. 417pp. Vendor G0259

2327 **LADD FAM. THE DESC. OF DANIEL OF HAVERHILL, MASS., JO-SEPH OF PORTSMOUTH, N.H., JOHN OF BURLINGTON, N.J., JOHN OF CHARLES CITY CO., VA.,** by W. Ladd. 1890.
Cloth, $77.00. Paper, $67.00. 425pp. .... Vendor G0259

2328 **A GEN. OF THE LAKE FAM. OF GREAT EGG HARBOR, N.J., DESC. FROM JOHN LAKE OF GRAVESEND, L.I. WITH NOTES ON THE GRAVESEND & STATEN ISLAND BRANCHES,** by A. Adams and S. Risley. 1915.
Cloth, $70.00. Paper, $60.00. 386pp. .... Vendor G0259

2329 **A HISTORY OF MY PEOPLE AND YOURS: INCLUDING THE FAMILIES OF NICHOLAS LAKE, AND OTHERS,** by Claud Nelson McMillan. 1956. Indexed. Illus.
Includes also: the **McMillan** family; **Woods** family; **Congdon** family; **Temple** family; **Cramton** family—and notes on the **Allen** family. Documents, portraits, colonial coat-of-arms.
Cloth. $30.00. 822pp. .... Vendor G0186

2330 **LAMB FAM. MARRIAGES,** by W.M. Clemens. 1916.
Paper. $8.00. 40pp. .... Vendor G0259

2331 **NATHAN LAMB OF LEICESTER, MASS., HIS ANC. & DESC.,** by C.F. Lamb. 1930.
Paper. $19.00. 96pp. .... Vendor G0259

2332 **SAMUEL LAMB OF PENNSYLVANIA AND SOME OF HIS DESCEN-DANTS,** by Alan J. Lamb. 1993. Indexed. Illus.
Paper. $25.00. 260pp. .... Vendor G0265

2333 **ROGER LAMBERT & HIS DESC.,** by I. Lambert. 1933.
Paper. $12.50. 61pp. .... Vendor G0259

2334 **THE LAMBERT FAM. OF SALEM, MASS., & THE WIFE OF THOMAS LORD OF HARTFORD, CONN., (REPR. ESSEX INST. HIST. COLL.),** by H.W. Belknap. 1918.
Paper. $10.00. 48pp. .... Vendor G0259

2335 **GEN. OF THE LAMBORN FAM., WITH EXTR. FROM HIST., BIOGR., ANECDOTES, ETC.,** by S. Lamborn. 1894.
Cloth, $72.00. Paper, $62.00. 487pp. .... Vendor G0259

2336 **LAMONT–ELDREDGE FAM. REC.,** by B.E. Lamont. 1948.
Cloth, $63.00. Paper, $53.00. 334pp. .... Vendor G0259

2337 **SKETCH OF THE LAMPTON FAM. IN AMER., 1740–1914,** by C. Keith. 1914.
Paper. $12.00. 59pp. .... Vendor G0259

2338 **DESC. OF WILLIAM LAMSON OF IPSWICH, MASS., 1634–1917,** by W. Lamson. 1917.
Cloth, $75.00. Paper, $65.00. 414pp. .... Vendor G0259

2339 **MEM. OF ELDER EBENEZER LAMSON OF CONCORD, MA.; HIS ANC. & DESC., 1635–1908,** by O. and F. Lamson. 1908.
Paper. $19.00. 125pp. .... Vendor G0259

2340 **JOSEPH LANCASTER OF AMESBURY & SOME OF HIS DESC.**, by J.S. Ware. 1933.
Cloth, $30.00. Paper, $20.00. 125pp. Vendor G0259

2341 **LANCASTER FAMILY OF MARYLAND & KENTUCKY: HIST. OF ENGLISH ANCESTRY, EMIGR. TO THE COL. OF MD., PIONEERS OF KY.**, by Samuel Lancaster. n.d.
Cloth, $42.50. Paper, $32.50. 200pp. Vendor G0259

2342 **LANCASTER FAM. THOMAS & PHEBE LANCASTER OF BUCKS CO. PA. & THEIR DESC., 1711–1902**, by H.L. Lancaster. 1902.
Cloth, $49.50. Paper, $39.50. 302pp. Vendor G0259

2343 **LANDIS FAM. OF LANCASTER CO.**, by D.B. Landis. 1888.
Paper. $17.50. 90pp. . . . . Vendor G0259

2344 **LANDON GEN.: THE FRENCH & ENG. HOME & ANC., WITH SOME ACCT. OF THE DESC. OF JAMES & MARY VAILL LANDON IN AMER,; ALSO, SOME BOARDMAN GEN**, by J.O. Landon. 1928.
Cloth, $72.50. Paper, $62.50. 402pp. Vendor G0259

2345 **AND A CAST OF THOUSANDS: HIST. OF THE LANE FAMILY OF CANADA & THE US, FROM THEIR ARRIVAL IN 1819 TO THE PRESENT**, by James K. Raywalt. 1989.
Cloth, $99.50. Paper, $89.50. 751pp. Vendor G0259

2346 **ELURA MORGAN FULL LANE, HER DESCENDANTS AND ANCES-TORS**, by Frances Lane Harris. 1986. Indexed. Illus.
Surnames: **Lane, Full, Morgan, Chaffee, Tibbetts, Withee**.
Paper. $18.00. 111pp. . . . . Vendor G0289

2347 **LANE GEN.**, by Chapman and Fitts. 3 vols. 1891–1902.
Cloth, $115.00. Paper, $105.00. 1,034pp. . . . . Vendor G0259

2348 **LAYNE–LAIN–LANE GENEALOGY, BEING A COMPILATION OF NAMES & HISTORICAL INFORMATION OF MALE DESCENDANTS OF 16 BRANCHES OF THE LAYNE–LAIN–LANE FAMILY IN THE U.S.**, by F.B. Layne. 1962.
Cloth, $62.00. Paper, $52.00. 336pp. Vendor G0259

2349 **[Lane]. ONTARIO CANADA ANCESTORS**, by Frances Lane Harris. (1987) reprint 1988. Indexed. Illus.
Lane, Youmans, Maybee, Henley, Hancock, Taylor.
Paper. $13.00. 143pp. . . . . Vendor G0289

2350 **LANSING FAM., EXTR. FROM GEN. NOTES OF N. Y. & NEW ENG. FAM.**, by S.V. Talcott. 1883.
Paper. $11.50. 53pp. . . . . Vendor G0259

2351 **LANTZ FAMILY RECORD, BEING A BRIEF ACCT. OF THE LANTZ FAM. IN THE U.S.**, by Jacob W. Lantz. 1931.
Cloth, $51.50. Paper, $41.50. 265pp. Vendor G0259

2352 **THE LANTZ FAMILY OF ROCKINGHAM COUNTY, VA**, by Lewis H. Yankey. 1990. Indexed.
Paper. $20.00. 174pp. . . . . Vendor G0365

2353 **CONCERNING JOHN LAPHAM & SOME OF HIS DESCENDANTS,** by M.W. Perkins. 1948?
Paper. $13.50. 67pp. .... Vendor G0259

2354 **LAPHAM FAMILY IN AMERICA: 13,000 DESCENDANTS, INCL. DESC. OF JOHN (DEVONSHIRE, ENG. TO PROVIDENCE, RI, 1673), & THOMAS (KENT, ENG. TO SCITUATE, MASS., 1634), ALSO GENEALOGICAL NOTES OF OTHER LAPHAM FAMS,** by B.B.B. Aldridge. 1953.
Cloth, $95.00. Paper, $85.00. 552pp. .... Vendor G0259

2355 **LARIMER, McMASTERS & ALLIED FAMS.,** by R. Mellon. 1903.
Cloth, $36.50. Paper, $26.50. 196pp. .... Vendor G0259

2356 **LASHER GEN.,** by C. Rich. 1904.
Cloth, $50.00. Paper, $40.00. 270pp. .... Vendor G0259

2357 **LASHER LINEAGE AND SUPPLEMENT,** by Eileen Lasher Powers. (1982) reprint 1994. Indexed.
Cloth. $76.50. 487+58pp. .... Vendor G0450

2358 **GEN. OF LATHAM–HILL–MONTFORT–LITTLEJOHN–MCCULLOCH–CAMPBELL–BROWNRIGG FAM.,** by W. Bailey. 1899.
Paper. $12.50. 66pp. .... Vendor G0259

2359 **ANCESTORS & DESCENDANTS OF FRANCIS LATHROP, 1545–1992,** by Lois Roberta Cook White. 1992.
Paper. $16.50. 82pp. .... Vendor G0259

2360 **GEN. MEMOIR OF THE LO-LATHROP FAM. THE DESC. OF REV. JOHN LATHROP OF SCITUATE & BARNSTABLE, MASS., & MARK LATHROP OF SALEM & BRIDGEWATER, MASS.,** by E.B. Huntington. 1884.
Cloth, $68.00. Paper, $58.00. 464pp. .... Vendor G0259

2361 **NOTES ON HIST. REFERENCES TO THE SCOTTISH FAM. OF LAUDER,** by J. Young. 1884.
Cloth, $31.00. Paper, $21.00. 154pp. .... Vendor G0259

2362 **A GEN. CHART OF THE DESC. OF CHRISTIAN LAUFFER, THE PIONEER,** by J.A. Lauffer. 1906.
Cloth, $45.00. Paper, $35.00. 188pp. .... Vendor G0259

2363 **LAUGHLIN HIST., 1807–1907,** by J.W. Laughlin. 1907.
Paper. $12.50. 64pp. .... Vendor G0259

2364 **DESC. OF MAJ. SAM'L LAWRENCE OF GROTON, MA., WITH SOME MENTION OF ALLIED FAM.,** by R. Lawrence. 1904.
Cloth, $54.00. Paper, $44.00. 355pp. .... Vendor G0259

2365 **FAM. OF LAWRENCE–GOSS–POMROY,** by J. Lawrence. 1881.
Paper. $17.50. 92pp. .... Vendor G0259

2366 **GEN. OF THE FAM. OF JOHN LAWRENCE OF WISSET, SUFFOLK, ENG. & OF WATERTOWN & GROTON, MA.,** by J. Lawrence. 1869.
Cloth, $53.00. Paper, $43.00. 332pp. .... Vendor G0259

2367 **HIST. GEN. OF THE LAWRENCE FAM., 1635–1858,** by T. Lawrence. 1858.
Cloth, $42.00. Paper, $32.00. 240pp. .... Vendor G0259

2368 HIST. SKETCHES OF SOME MEMBERS OF THE LAWRENCE FAM., by R.M. Lawrence. 1888.
Cloth, $42.00. Paper, $32.00. 215pp. .... Vendor G0259

2369 LAWRENCE–ROBERTS–HEETER–BEGGS–HARDY, by Gayle King Blankenship. 1990. Indexed. Illus.
MD-VA: **Roberts.** PA: **Beggs, Furhman, Hardy, Heeter, Robson.** TN: **Shipp.** VA: **Doan, Hayton, Lawrence, Puckett, Trent, Whitely, Womack.** VA-NC: **Lawrence.** WV: **Beggs, Lawrence.** England: **Hardy, MacKay, Stephenson.** Referenced; 8¹/₂ x 11.
Cloth. $36.00. 231pp. .... Vendor G0034

2370 MEM. OF ROBT. LAWRENCE, ROBT. BARTLETT, & THEIR DESC., by H.B. Lawrence. 1888.
Cloth, $39.00. Paper, $29.00. 223pp. .... Vendor G0259

2371 LAWSON–CHESTER GENEALOGY, compiled by Altshuler Gen. Svc. 1946.
Paper. $10.00. 50pp. .... Vendor G0259

2372 LAYNE GENEALOGY, by F.B. Layne. 1953.
Cloth, $49.00. Paper, $39.00. 251pp. .... Vendor G0259

2373 JOHN LAZELL OF HINGHAM, MASS., & SOME DESC. (REPR. *NEHGR*), by T.S. Lazell.
Paper. $18.00. 107pp. .... Vendor G0259

2374 THE ANC. & POSTERITY OF JOHN LEA OF CHRISTIAN MALFORD, WILTS., ENG., & PENN., 1503–1906, by J.H. and G.H. Lea. 1906.
Cloth, $101.50. Paper, $91.50. 611pp. .... Vendor G0259

2375 LAWRENCE LEACH OF SALEM, MA., & SOME OF HIS DESC., by L.P. Leach. 1924–6.
Cloth, $65.00. Paper, $55.00. 344pp. .... Vendor G0259

2376 LEADBETTER RECORDS, by J.E. Ames. 1917.
Cloth, $59.50. Paper, $49.50. 317pp. .... Vendor G0259

2377 LEARNED FAM. (LEARNED, LARNED, LEARNARD, LANNARD, & LERNED), BEING DESC. OF WM. LEARNED WHO WAS OF CHARLESTOWN, MASS., IN 1632, by W.L. Learned. 2nd ed. 1898.
Cloth, $88.00. Paper, $78.00. 510pp. .... Vendor G0259

2378 LEAVENS NAME, INCL. LEVINGS, 1632–1903, by P. Leavens. 1903.
Cloth, $38.00. Paper, $28.00. 152pp. .... Vendor G0259

2379 A GEN. OF THE LEAVENWORTH FAM. IN THE U.S., by E.W. Leavenworth. 1873.
Cloth, $68.50. Paper, $58.50. 376pp. .... Vendor G0259

2380 LEAVITT–JENNINGS ROOTS AND BRANCHES, by Edna Jennings Zeavin. 1993. Indexed. Illus.
Paper. $35.00. 253pp. .... Vendor G0183

2381 THE LEAVITTS OF AMER.: A COMP. OF FIVE BRANCHES & GLEANINGS FROM NEW ENG. TO CALIF. & CANADA, by C.G. Steer. 1924.
Cloth, $49.50. Paper, $39.50. 254pp. .... Vendor G0259

2382 **DESC. OF FRANCIS Le BARON OF PLYMOUTH, MASS.**, by M. Le Baron Stockwell. 1904.
Cloth, $91.50. Paper, $81.50. 521pp. . . . . Vendor G0259

2383 **HANLEY CASTLE & THE HOUSE OF LECHMERE.** 1881 (England).
Paper. $16.00. 79pp. . . . . Vendor G0259

2384 **LeCONTE HISTORY & GENEALOGY, WITH PARTICULAR REFERENCE TO GUILLAUME LeCONTE OF NEW ROCHELLE & NEW YORK, & HIS DESCENDANTS,** by Richard LeConte Anderson. 2 vols. 1981.
Cloth, $169.00. Paper, $159.00. 1,350pp. . . . . Vendor G0259

2385 **DESCENDANTS OF RICHARD LEE OF VIRGINIA,** by Carol A. Hauk. 1995. Indexed.
Paper. $45.00. 247pp. . . . . Vendor G0340

2386 **GATHERING OF THE DESC. & KINSMEN OF JOHN LEE, ONE OF THE EARLY SETTLERS OF FARMINGTON, CONN., HELD IN HARTFORD, CONN., 1884,** by W.W. Lee. 1885.
Paper. $19.50. 128pp. . . . . Vendor G0259

2387 **JOHN LEE OF AGAWAM (IPSWICH), MA., 1634–1671, & HIS DESC. OF THE NAME OF LEE,** by W. Lee. 1888.
Cloth, $88.00. Paper, $78.00. 506pp. . . . . Vendor G0259

2388 **JOHN LEE OF FARMINGTON, HARTFORD CO., CONN., & HIS DESC.,** by S.M. Lee. 1878.
Cloth, $37.00. Paper, $27.00. 182pp. . . . . Vendor G0259

2389 **JOHN LEE OF FARMINGTON, HARTFORD CO. CT, & HIS DESCENDANTS, 1634–1897,** by L. and S.F. Lee. 2nd ed. 1897.
Cloth, $97.00. Paper, $87.00. 572pp. . . . . Vendor G0259

2390 **LEE FAM. OF HOUNSFIELD, N.Y. & RELATED FAM.,** by W.J. Coates. 1941.
Paper. $19.00. 102pp. . . . . Vendor G0259

2391 **LEE OF VIRGINIA, 1642–1892; BIOGR. & GEN. SKETCHES OF THE DESC. OF COL. RICHARD LEE, WITH BRIEF NOTICES OF REL. FAMS. OF ALLERTON, ARMISTEAD, ETC.,** by E.J. Lee. 1895.
Cloth, $84.00. Paper, $74.00. 586pp. . . . . Vendor G0259

2392 **THE LEE FAM. OF MARBLEHEAD (REPR. ESSEX INST. HIST. COLL.),** by T.A. Lee. 1916.
Cloth, $32.50. Paper, $22.50. 152pp. . . . . Vendor G0259

2393 **THE LEE GENEALOGY,** by J. Montgomery Seaver.
Paper. $7.50. 61pp. . . . . Vendor G0011

2394 **THE LAWRENCE LEESE FAMILY: TWO CENTURIES IN AMERICA (1741–1941),** by Charles Leese. 1941.
Cloth, $44.00. Paper, $34.00. 214pp. . . . . Vendor G0259

2395 **THE FAM. OF WILLIAM LEETE, ONE OF THE FIRST SETTLERS OF GUILFORD, CT. & GOV. OF THE NEW HAVEN & CONN. COLONIES,** by E. Leete. 1884.
Cloth, $36.00. Paper, $26.00. 168pp. . . . . Vendor G0259

2396 **DESC. OF WILLIAM LEETE, ONE OF THE FOUNDERS OF GUILFORD, CT., PRES. OF THE FED. OF COLONIES, & GOV. OF NEW HAVEN & CONN. COLONIES,** by E. Leete. 2nd ed. 1934.
Cloth, $73.50. Paper, $63.50. 408pp. .... Vendor G0259

2397 **PENNSYLVANIA LeFEVRES,** by George Newton LeFevre and Franklin D. LeFevre. 1979.
Cloth. $13.00. 256pp. .... Vendor G0150

2398 **GEN. OF THE LEFFERTS FAM., 1650–1878,** by T.G. Bergen. 1878.
Cloth, $36.50. Paper, $26.50. 172pp. .... Vendor G0259

2399 **1637–1897. THE LEFFINGWELL REC. A GEN. OF DESC. OF LT. THOMAS LEFFINGWELL, A FOUNDER OF NORWICH, CT.,** by A. and C. Leffingwell. 1897.
Cloth, $49.00. Paper, $39.00. 263pp. .... Vendor G0259

2400 **LEFTWICH–TURNER FAMILIES OF VA. & THEIR CONNECTIONS,** by W.L. Hopkins. 1931.
Cloth, $68.50. Paper, $58.50. 368pp. .... Vendor G0259

2401 **BIOGR. SKETCHES OF HUGUENOT SOLOMON LEGARE; ALSO HIS FAM. EXTENDING TO THE 4TH GEN. OF HIS DESC.,** by E.C.K. Fludd. 1886.
Cloth, $31.50. Paper, $21.50. 144pp. .... Vendor G0259

2402 **LEGH FAMILY OF ENGLAND: THE HOUSE OF LYME, FROM ITS FOUNDATION TO THE END OF THE 18TH CENTURY,** by Lady Newton. 1917.
Cloth, $74.00. Paper, $64.00. 423pp. .... Vendor G0259

2403 **PIERRE LeGRAND IN VIRGINIA—1700,** by Louis Everett LeGrand. 1995. Indexed.
Cloth. $38.00. 360pp. .... Vendor G0346

2404 **DESCENDANTS OF DANIEL LEHMAN . . . (1776–1847) . . . LANCASTER COUNTY . . . FRANKLIN COUNTY, PENNSYLVANIA,** by Daniel R. Lehman. 1983.
Cloth. $26.00. 429pp. .... Vendor G0150

2405 **A LEIGHTON GENEALOGY: DESCENDANTS OF THOMAS LEIGHTON OF DOVER, NEW HAMPSHIRE,** by Perley M. Leighton. 2 vols. 1989. Indexed. Illus.
Cloth. $64.50. 1,154pp. .... Vendor G0406

2406 **LEIGHTON GEN. AN ACCT. OF THE DESC. OF CAPT. WM. LEIGHTON OF KITTERY, ME.; WITH COLLATERAL NOTES REL. TO OTHER FAM. OF YORK CO. & ITS VICINITY,** by T.F. Jordan. 1885.
Paper. $19.00. 136pp. .... Vendor G0259

2407 **MEMORIALS OF THE LEIGHTONS OF ULISHAVEN, FORFARSHIRE, & OTHER SCOTTISH FAMILIES OF THE NAME, A.D. 1260–1518 (WITH ADDED PEDIGREES THROUGH 1920'S),** by Clarance F. Leighton. 1912.
Cloth, $37.00. Paper, $27.00. 126+56pp. .... Vendor G0259

2408 **LELAND MAGAZINE; OR, A GEN. RECORD OF HENRY LELAND &
HIS DESC., 1653–1850,** by S. Leland. 1859.
Cloth, $46.00. Paper, $36.00. 279pp. .... Vendor G0259

2409 **HIST. OF THE LENT (van LENT) FAM. IN THE U.S., GEN. & BIOGR.,
1638–1902,** by N.B. Lent. 1903.
Cloth, $33.50. Paper, $23.50. 171pp. .... Vendor G0259

2410 **LENZ FAMILY. HISTORY OF THE AMERICAN BRANCH ESTAB-
LISHED AT STONE ARABIA, N.Y., IN 1854, BY FRIEDRICH KONRAD
LENZ OF WERDORF, GERMANY,** by E.E. Lenz. 1937.
Cloth, $41.00. Paper, $31.00. 187pp. .... Vendor G0259

2411 **ANNALS OF THE LEONARD FAM.,** by F. Koster. 1911.
Cloth, $44.00. Paper, $34.00. 226pp. .... Vendor G0259

2412 **LEONARD MEM.: GEN., HIST., & BIOGR. OF SOLOMON LEONARD,
1637, OF DUXBURY & BRIDGEWATER, MASS. & SOME OF HIS
DESC.,** by M. Leonard. 1896.
Cloth, $80.00. Paper, $70.00. 454pp. .... Vendor G0259

2413 **MEM. OF THE LEONARD, THOMPSON & HASKELL FAMS., WITH
COLL. FAMS.,** by C. Goodenough. 1928.
Cloth, $64.50. Paper, $54.50. 344pp. .... Vendor G0259

2414 **STEPHEN BANKS LEONARD OF OWEGO, TIOGA CO., N.Y.,** by W.A.
Leonard. 1909.
Cloth, $64.50. Paper, $54.50. 342pp. .... Vendor G0259

2415 **HISTORICAL RECORDS OF THE FAMILY OF LESLIE, FROM 1067
TO 1869, COLLECTED FROM PUBLIC RECORDS & AUTHENTIC
PRIVATE SOURCES,** by Col. Leslie, K.H. 3 vols. in 2. 1869 (Scotland).
Cloth, $144.50. Paper, $134.50. 430+681pp. .... Vendor G0259

2416 **THE LESLIES OF TARBERT, CO. KERRY, & THEIR FOREBEARS,**
by P.L. Pielou. 1935.
Cloth, $43.50. Paper, $33.50. 224pp. .... Vendor G0259

2417 **LeSTRANGE RECORDS. A CHRONICLE OF THE EARLY
LeSTRANGES OF NORFOLK [ENGLAND] & THE MARCH OF WALES,
1100–1310,** by H. LeStrange. 1916 (London).
Cloth, $71.00. Paper, $61.00. 407pp. .... Vendor G0259

2418 **A MEMOIR, BIOGR. & GEN., OF SIR JOHN LEVERETT, GOVER-
NOR OF MASS., 1673–9, & ONE OF THE FAM. GENERALLY,** by C.E.
Leverett. 1856.
Cloth, $40.50. Paper, $30.50. 203pp. .... Vendor G0259

2419 **LEVERING FAMILY HIST. & GEN.,** by J. Levering. 1897.
Cloth, $145.00. Paper, $135.00. 975pp. .... Vendor G0259

2420 **LEVERING FAMILY, OR A GEN. ACCT. OF WIGARD & GERHARD
LEVERING, TWO OF THE PIONEER SETTLERS OF ROXBOROUGH
TWP., PHILA. CO. (PA.) & THEIR DESC.,** by H. Jones. 1858.
Cloth, $41.00. Paper, $31.00. 203pp. .... Vendor G0259

2421 **DESCENDANTS OF ZACHARY AND HENRY LEWIS OF SPOT-SYLVANIA COUNTY, VIRGINIA,** by Carol A. Hauk. 1995. Indexed. Paper. $35.00. 176pp. .... Vendor G0340

2422 **EDMUND LEWIS OF LYNN, MASS., & SOME OF HIS DESC.,** by G.H. Lewis. 1908. Cloth, $37.00. Paper, $27.00. 181pp. .... Vendor G0259

2423 **GEN. OF THE LEWIS & KINDRED FAM.,** by J.M. McAllister and L.B. Tandy. 1906. Cloth, $75.00. Paper, $65.00. 416pp. .... Vendor G0259

2424 **GEN. OF THE LEWIS FAM. IN AMER. [PRIMARILY VA.],** by W.T. Lewis. 1893. Cloth, $68.00. Paper, $58.00. 458pp. .... Vendor G0259

2425 **LEWISES, MERIWETHERS AND THEIR KIN,** by Sarah Travers Lewis (Scott) Anderson. (1938) reprint 1995. Indexed. Illus. Features six pre–1740 **Lewis** families and their multiple connections. Cloth. $40.00. 652pp. .... Vendor G0010

2426 **LEWIS FAM. OF WALES & AMER. (EXTR. BASSETT GEN.).** 1926. Paper. $8.00. 42pp. .... Vendor G0259

2427 **LEWIS OF WARNER HALL, The History of a Family,** by Merrow E. Sorley. (1935) reprint 1991. Indexed. Illus. Cloth. $45.00. 887pp. .... Vendor G0010

2428 **LEWIS OF WARNER HALL: THE HIST. OF A FAM. INCL. THE GEN. OF THE MALE & FEMALE LINES, BIOGR. SKETCHES OF ITS MEMBERS, & THEIR DESC. FROM OTHER EARLY VA. FAM.,** by M.E. Sorley. 1935. Cloth, $142.50. Paper, $132.50. 887pp. .... Vendor G0259

2429 **RANDALL LEWIS OF HOPKINTON, RI, & DELAWARE CO., NY & SOME DESC.,** by F. and E. Lewis. 1929. Cloth, $43.00. Paper, $33.00. 200pp. .... Vendor G0259

2430 **THE WELSH LINEAGE OF JOHN LEWIS (1592–1657), EMIGRANT TO GLOUCESTER, VIRGINIA. Revised Edition,** by Grace McLean Moses. (1984, 1992) reprint 1995. Paper. $10.00. 68pp. .... Vendor G0011

2431 **WM. LEWIS OF STOKE–BY–NAYLAND, ENG., & SOME OF HIS ANC. & DESC.,** by I. Lewis. 1932. Cloth, $30.00. Paper, $20.00. 106pp. .... Vendor G0259

2432 **L'HOMMEDIEU GENEALOGY,** by Wm. A. and P.H. L'Hommedieu. 2 vols. 1951(?) Cloth, $69.50/vol. Paper, $59.50/vol. 930pp. .... Vendor G0259

2433 **LIBBY FAM. IN AMER., 1602–1881,** by C.T. Libby. 1882. Cloth, $89.50. Paper, $79.50. 628pp. .... Vendor G0259

2434 **DESCENDANTS OF JOHN AND PHILIP LIGHTFOOT OF VIRGINIA,** by Carol A. Hauk. 1995. Indexed. Paper. $30.00. 94pp. .... Vendor G0340

2435 **LIGON FAM. & CONNECTIONS**, Vol. I, by W.D. Ligon, Jr. 1947.
Cloth, $144.50. Paper, $134.50. 943pp. .... Vendor G0259

2436 **LIGON FAM. & CONNECTIONS**, Vol. II., by W.D. Ligon, Jr. 1957.
Cloth, $45.00. Paper, $35.00. 232pp. .... Vendor G0259

2437 **MAJOR JOHN LILLIE, 1755–1801. THE LILLIE FAM. OF BOSTON,
1663–1896**, by E.L. Pierce. Rev. ed. 1896.
Paper. $18.00. 122pp. .... Vendor G0259

2438 **HIST. OF THE LINCOLN FAM.; AN ACCT. OF THE DESC. OF SAMUEL
LINCOLN OF HINGHAM, MASS., 1637–1920**, by W. Lincoln. 1923.
Cloth, $100.00. Paper, $90.00. 728pp. .... Vendor G0259

2439 **SOME DESCENDANTS OF STEPHEN LINCOLN OF WYMONDHAM,
ENG.; EDMUND LARKIN OF ENG.; THOMAS OLIVER OF BRISTOL,
ENG.; ETC.**, by W.E. Lincoln. 1930.
Cloth, $59.50. Paper, $49.50. 322pp. .... Vendor G0259

2440 **STEPHEN LINCOLN OF OAKHAM, MASS., HIS ANC. & DESC.**, by
J.E. Morris. 1895.
Paper. $18.00. 109pp. .... Vendor G0259

2441 **THE ANCESTRY OF ABRAHAM LINCOLN**, by J.H. Lea and J.R.
Hutchinson. 1909.
Cloth, $50.00. Paper, $40.00. 310pp. .... Vendor G0259

2442 **THE LINDSAYS OF AMER. A GEN. NARRATIVE & FAM. RECORD**,
by M.I. Lindsay. 1889.
Cloth, $46.00. Paper, $36.00. 293pp. .... Vendor G0259

2443 **GENEALOGICAL HISTORY OF THE FAMILY OF WM. LINN, WHO
CAME FROM BELFAST, IRELAND, IN 1771**, by Margarett V. Hull. 1932.
Cloth, $35.00. Paper, $25.00. 146pp. .... Vendor G0259

2444 **[Linzee]. THE LINDESEIE & LIMESI FAM. OF GR. BRITAIN, INCL.
THE PROBATES AT SOMERSET HOUSE, LONDON, FROM 1300–1800,
& THE LINZEE FAM. OF GR. BRITAIN & THE U.S.**, by J.W. Linzee. 2
vols. 1917.
Cloth, $145.00. Paper, $135.00. 931pp. .... Vendor G0259

2445 **LIPPINCOTT—FIVE GENERATIONS OF THE DESCENDANTS OF
RICHARD AND ABIGAIL LIPPINCOTT**, by Judith M. Olsen. 1982. In-
dexed.
Includes related families of **Allen, Andrews, Atkinson, Budd, Coles, Corlies,
Cowperthwaite, Curtis, Gaskill, Elkinton, Roberts, Shinn, Shattuck, Stokes,**
and **Woolley**. (Sixth generation available 1996.)
Paper. $20.50. 471pp. .... Vendor G0069

2446 **THE LIPPINCOTTS IN ENGLAND & AMERICA**, edited from the papers
of J.S. Lippincott. n.d.
Paper. $8.50. 43pp. .... Vendor G0259

2447 **THE LITCHFIELD FAM. IN AMER., PART 1**, nos. 1–5 in one vol., by W.J.
Litchfield. 1901–06.
Cloth, $69.00. Paper, $59.00. 384pp. .... Vendor G0259

2448 **[Littell]. KIN OF MY GRANDCHILDREN, VOLUME I, STORM/ ARNOLD**, by Judge Noble K. Littell. 1990. Indexed. Illus.
Sturm in Germany became **Storm** in the colonies. Traced through Pennsylvania, Kentucky, Indiana, and westward. Allied families: **Arnold, McHargue, Hood, Land, Lindsay, Moore, Nichols, Taylor, Whitaker**.
Cloth. $30.00. viii+382pp. .... Vendor G0133

2449 **[Littell]. KIN OF MY GRANDCHILDREN, VOLUME II, McCARTY/ CURRY**, by Judge Noble K. Littell. 1991. Indexed. Illus.
Nicholas **McCarty**, Kentucky pioneer, died St. Clair's Defeat, 1791, daughter married Thomas **Curry**. Separate chapters on **Asher, Seaton, Thompson, Gregson, Brasier, Farr**. Allied families include **Chenoweth, McGinnis, Ratts, Stierwalt, Shumaker, Whitaker**.
Cloth. $38.50. vi+634pp. .... Vendor G0133

2450 **[Littell]. KIN OF MY GRANDCHILDREN, VOLUME III, SHIELDS WITH WHEELER & WHARTON, TONEY, RICHIE/RITCHEY/ RITCHIE, ELSWICK, HYATT**, by Judge Noble K. Littell. 1992. Indexed. Illus.
The interconnecting families of **Shields**, Ireland; **Wheeler, Wharton**, Kentucky; **Toney**, Accomac, Virginia; **Richie**, from England, 1768; **Elswick**, Kentucky and West Virginia; and **Hyatt**, Maryland.
Cloth. $37.50. vi+488pp. .... Vendor G0133

2451 **LITTELL FAMILIES HISTORY & GENEALOGY**, by Judge Noble K. Littell. 1994. Indexed. Illus.
After 30 years research and contributions from 500+ Littell Family Association members this publication, in 2 volumes, is a reality. The several **Littell/ Little/Lytle** lines are set forth in detail.
Cloth. $80.00. vi+1,464pp. .... Vendor G0133

2452 **DESCENDANTS OF PETER LITTIG, GODFREY ROGGE & OTHERS**, by M.D. Littig et al. 1944.
Paper. $8.00. 40pp. .... Vendor G0259

2453 **GENEALOGY OF THE LITTLE FAMILY. DESCENDANTS OF GEORGE LITTLE, WHO CAME TO NEWBURY, MA, IN 1640**, by G.T. Little. 1877.
Paper. $16.50. 82pp. .... Vendor G0259

2454 **THE DESC. OF GEORGE LITTLE WHO CAME TO NEWBURY, MASS., IN 1640**, by G.T. Little. 1882.
Cloth, $90.00. Paper, $80.00. 638pp. .... Vendor G0259

2455 **MEM. REL. TO THE LITTLEFIELDS, ESP. TO THE DESC. OF EDMUND WHO FOUNDED THE MASS. BRANCH OF THE FAM. IN 1690 AT BRAINTREE**, by G. Littlefield. 1897.
Paper. $16.00. 80pp. .... Vendor G0259

2456 **THE LITTLEFORD FAMILY OF DOWNERS GROVE TOWNSHIP, DUPAGE COUNTY, ILLINOIS, THE ANCESTORS AND DESCENDANTS OF GEORGE WELLINGTON LITTLEFORD, 1825–1910, BORN BUCKINGHAMSHIRE, ENGLAND, AND HIS WIFE ANN JONES, 1830–1891, BORN MONMOUTHSHIRE, WALES**, by Esther Littleford Woodworth-Barnes. 1990. Indexed. Illus.
Cloth. $35.00. 123pp. .... Vendor G0054

2457 **LIVERMORE FAM. OF AMER.**, by W.E. Thwing. 1902.
Cloth, $85.00. Paper, $75.00. 479pp. .... Vendor G0259

2458 **LIVEZEY FAMILY: A GENEALOGICAL & HISTORICAL RECORD**, by C.H. Smith. 1934.
Cloth, $78.00. Paper, $68.00. 440pp. .... Vendor G0259

2459 **LIVEZEY SUPPLEMENT, 1954–1964**, by C.A. Livezey. 1964.
Paper. $17.00. 85pp. .... Vendor G0259

2460 **A LIVINGSTON GENEALOGICAL REGISTER**, by Howland Davis and Arthur Kelly. 1995. Indexed.
Cloth. $56.50. 713pp. .... Vendor G0450

2461 **LIVINGSTON FAMILY IN AMERICA & ITS SCOTTISH ORIGINS**, by Florence van Rensselaer, edited by William Laimbeer. 1949.
Cloth, $73.00. Paper, $63.00. 413pp. .... Vendor G0259

2462 **THE LIVINGSTONS OF LIVINGSTON MANOR; THE HIST. OF THE BRANCH WHICH SETTLED IN N.Y. WITH AN ACCT. OF ROBERT LIVINGSTON OF ALBANY & HIS PRINCIPLE DESC.**, by E.B. Livingston. 1910.
Cloth, $85.50. Paper, $75.50. 623pp. .... Vendor G0259

2463 **THE LLIFF GENEALOGIST: SOURCE RECORDS**, by George Ely Russell. 1987. Illus.
Paper. $12.00. 90pp. .... Vendor G0126

2464 **A REC. OF THE DESC. OF ROBERT LLOYD, WHO CAME FROM WALES & SETTLED IN THE WELSH TRACT AT MERION, PA., ABOUT 1684**, by R.L. Lloyd. 1947.
Paper. $18.00. 119pp. .... Vendor G0259

2465 **GENEALOGICAL NOTES RELATING TO THE FAMILIES OF LLOYD, PEMBERTON, HUTCHINSON, HUDSON & PARKE**, by J.P. Parke and T. Ward; edited by T.A. Glenn. 1898.
Paper. $18.00. 89pp. .... Vendor G0259

2466 **LLOYD MANUSCRIPTS. WELSH RECORDS FROM THE COLLECTION OF THE LATE HOWARD WILLIAMS LLOYD. GEN. OF THE FAMS. OF AWBREY–VAUGHAN, BLUNSTON, BURBECK, GARRET, ETC.** 1912.
Cloth, $78.00. Paper, $68.00. 437pp. .... Vendor G0259

2467 **LOAR GENEALOGY, WITH COGNATE BRANCHES, 1774–1947**, by Emma Loar Gaddis. 1947.
Cloth, $69.50. Paper, $59.50. 387pp. .... Vendor G0259

2468 **SIMON LOBDELL—1646 OF MILFORD, CONN., & HIS DESC.; NICHOLAS LOBDEN (LOBDELL)—1635 OF HINGHAM, MA., & SOME DESC.**, by J. Lobdell. 1907.
Cloth, $76.50. Paper, $66.50. 425pp. .... Vendor G0259

2469 **BOOK OF THE LOCKES: A GEN. & HIST. RECORD OF DESC. OF WM. LOCKE OF WOBURN, WITH APPENDIX CONTAINING A HIST. OF THE LOCKES IN ENG.; ALSO INCL. FAM. OF JOHN LOCKE OF**

HAMPTON, NH & KINDRED FAMS. & INDIVIDUALS, by J.G. Locke. 1853.
Cloth, $62.00. Paper, $52.00. 406pp. Vendor G0259

2470 HIST. & GEN. OF CAPT. JOHN LOCKE, 1627–96, OF PORTSMOUTH & RYE, NH, & HIS DESC.; ALSO OF NATHANIEL LOCKE OF PORTS-MOUTH, & A SHORT ACCT. OF THE HIST. OF THE LOCKES IN ENG., by A.H. Locke. 1916.
Cloth, $119.50. Paper, $109.50. 730pp. . . . . Vendor G0259

2471 DESC. OF ROBERT LOCKWOOD, COLONIAL & REV. HIST. OF THE LOCKWOOD FAM. IN AMER. FROM A.D. 1630, by F.A. Holden and E.D. Lockwood. 1889.
Cloth, $144.00. Paper, $134.00. 909pp. . . . . Vendor G0259

2472 DESC. OF BALTHASER & SUSANNA LOESCH, by W. Lesh. 1914.
Paper. $13.50. 68pp. . . . . Vendor G0259

2473 LOGAN FAM. OF KENTUCKY. EXTR. FROM "HIST. FAMS. OF KY.," by T.M. Green.
Paper. $19.00. 115pp. . . . . Vendor G0259

2474 GENEALOGIES OF THE LOMEN (RINGSTAD), BRANDT & JOYS FAMILIES, by G.J. Lomen. 1929.
Cloth, $65.50. Paper, $55.50. 361pp. Vendor G0259

2475 TWO HUNDRED YEARS OF THE LONDON FAMILY IN AMERICA, by O.L. Cox. 1976.
Cloth, $69.50. Paper, $59.50. 400pp. Vendor G0259

2476 HISTORY OF THE LONG FAMILY OF PENNSYLVANIA, by W.G. Long. 1930.
Cloth, $66.00. Paper, $56.00. 365pp. Vendor G0259

2477 ISAAC AND MAGDALENE LONG FAMILY RECORD, by Floyd R. Mason.
In process . . . . Vendor G0345

2478 HIST. OF THE LONGACRE–LANGAKER–LONGENECKER FAM. Publ. for the committee. 1902.
Cloth, $50.00. Paper, $40.00. 310pp. Vendor G0259

2479 THE DESCENDANTS OF JACOB LONGYEAR OF ULSTER CO., NEW YORK, by Edmund J. Longyear. 1942.
Cloth, $99.00. Paper, $89.00. 622pp. Vendor G0259

2480 DESC. (BY FEMALE BRANCHES) OF JOSEPH LOOMIS, WHO CAME

+---+
| **Descendants of** |
| James L. Logan (1798–1881) |
| Elizabeth M. Logan (1804–1880) |
| Miriam Bales |
| (317) 284-0470 |
+---+

FROM BRAINTREE, ENG., IN 1638 & SETTLED IN WINDSOR, CT., IN 1639, by E. Loomis. 2 vols. 1880.
Cloth, $159.00. Paper, $149.00. 1,132pp. .... Vendor G0259

2481 DESC. OF JOSEPH LOOMIS IN AMER. & HIS ANTECEDENTS IN THE OLD WORLD, by E.S. Loomis. Rev. ed. 1908.
Cloth, $145.00. Paper, $135.00. 859pp. .... Vendor G0259

2482 LOOS FAM. GENEALOGY, 1535–1958, by S.L. Bast. 1959.
Cloth, $47.00. Paper, $37.00. 245pp. .... Vendor G0259

2483 ANC. & DESC. OF LT. TOBIAS LORD, by C. Lord. 1913.
Cloth, $52.00. Paper, $42.00. 263pp. .... Vendor G0259

2484 HISTORY OF THE DESCENDANTS OF NATHAN LORD OF ANCIENT KITTERY, ME., by C.C. Lord; edited by G.E. Lord. 1912.
Cloth, $43.00. Paper, $33.00. 218pp. .... Vendor G0259

2485 LORING GEN., by C.H. Pope, with K.P. Loring. 1917.
Cloth, $78.50. Paper, $68.50. 443pp. .... Vendor G0259

2486 ANC. & DESC. OF DANIEL LOTHROP, SR., 1545–1901, by G.D.R. Hubbard. 1901.
Paper. $7.50. 37pp. .... Vendor G0259

2487 LIFE ON THE OHIO FRONTIER; A COLLECTION OF LETTERS FROM MARY LOTT TO DEACON JOHN PHILLIPS; 1826–1846, by Jacqueline Miller Bachar. 1994. Indexed. Illus.
Surnames include **Lott, Miller, Phillips, Williams, Clark, Wells, Trumbull, Rosenkranz, Tripp, Bates, Hewitt, Russell**, etc.
Cloth. $33.00. 152pp. .... Vendor G0102

2488 LOTT FAM. IN AMER., INCL. ALLIED FAM. CASSELL, DAVIS, GRAYBEAL, HARING, HEGEMAN, HOGG, KERLEY, PHILLIPS, THOMPSON & OTHERS, by A. Phillips. 1942.
Cloth, $39.00. Paper, $29.00. 179pp. .... Vendor G0259

2489 GENEALOGY OF THE LOUCKS FAMILY, BEGINNING WITH JOHANN DIETRICH LOUCKS & HIS DESCENDANTS IN DIRECT LINE TO JOSEPH LOUCK, & ALL HIS KNOWN & TRACEABLE DESC. TO DATE, by E.M. McBrier. 1940.
Cloth, $58.50. Paper, $48.50. 22+295pp. .... Vendor G0259

2490 GEN. REC. OF THE DESC. OF CALEB LOUD, CHILD OF FRANCIS LOUD & ONNER PRINCE LOUD, by W. Loud. 1889.
Paper. $14.50. 83pp. .... Vendor G0259

2491 BRIEF GENEALOGY OF THE LOUGHRY FAMILY OF PA., by J.A. Jewett. 1923.
Paper. $17.00. 85pp. .... Vendor G0259

2492 GEN. OF THOMAS LOVE OF NO. CAROLINA & TENN. & HIS BROTHERS, ROBERT & JAMES, by R.A. Love. 1955.
Paper. $10.00. 47pp. .... Vendor G0259

2493 LOVE LETTERS, by Pat Love Stubblefield and Researchers. 1984. Indexed.

A newsletter for everyone with the **Love** surname—base file of over 6,000. Subscription. $13.50, tax incl. 62+pp. .... Vendor G0385

2494 **LOVE–LOOMIS FAM. HIST.**, by B.W. Loomis. 1963.
Cloth, $30.00. Paper, $20.00. 127pp. .... Vendor G0259

2495 **LOVEJOY GEN., WITH BIOGR. & HIST., 1460–1930**, by C.E. Lovejoy. 1930.
Cloth, $80.50. Paper, $70.50. 470pp. .... Vendor G0259

2496 **GEN. OF THE LOVELAND FAM. IN THE U.S., 1635 TO 1892, CONTAINING THE DESC. OF THOMAS LOVELAND OF WETHERSFIELD, NOW GLASTONBURY, CONN.**, by J.B. and G. Loveland. 3 vols. 1892.
Cloth, $135.50. Paper, $125.50. 838pp. .... Vendor G0259

2497 **THE EXPEDITIONS OF CAPT. JOHN LOVEWELL & HIS ENCOUNTERS WITH THE INDIANS, WITH A BIOGRAPHICAL SKETCH OF CAPT. LOVEWELL**, by Frederic Kidder. 1865.
Paper. $19.00. 123pp. .... Vendor G0259

2498 **THE ANC. OF THE JOHN LOWE FAM. CIRCLE & THEIR DESC.**, by E.M. Merriam. 1901.
Cloth, $35.00. Paper, $25.00. 189pp. .... Vendor G0259

2499 **THE HIST. GEN. OF THE LOWELLS OF AMER. FROM 1639–1899**, by D.R. Lowell. 1899.
Cloth, $140.50. Paper, $130.50. 878pp. .... Vendor G0259

2500 **SOME ACCT. OF THE LOWER FAMILY IN AMERICA, PRINCIPALLY OF THE DESCENDANTS OF ADAM LOWER, WHO SETTLED IN WILLIAMSPORT PA IN 1779**, by J.L. Lower. 1913.
Cloth, $35.00. Paper, $25.00. 144pp. .... Vendor G0259

2501 **LOWNDES FAM. OF SO. CAROLINA**, by G.B. Chase. 1876.
Paper. $7.50. 38pp. .... Vendor G0259

2502 **THE LOWRYS; ROBERT & MARY LOWRY & CHILDREN (6 GEN.)**, by L. and H. Lowry. 1921.
Cloth, $30.00. Paper, $20.00. 118pp. .... Vendor G0259

2503 **LUCAS GENEALOGY**, by A. Kemp. 1964.
Cloth, $85.50. Paper, $75.50. 495pp. .... Vendor G0259

2504 **LUDWIG GEN. SKETCH OF JOS. LUDWIG, b. IN GERMANY IN 1699, & HIS WIFE & FAM., WHO SETTLED AT "BROAD BAY," WALDOBORO, 1753**, by M.R. Ludwig. 1866.
Cloth, $39.50. Paper, $29.50. 223pp. .... Vendor G0259

2505 **[Lukin]. GEN. NOTES & PEDIGREES OF THE LOVEKYN–LUCKYN–LUKIN FAM. IN ENG.**, by A.T. Tudor-Craig. 1932.
Paper. $11.50. 58pp. .... Vendor G0259

2506 **GENEALOGY OF THE LUM FAMILY**, by Edward H. Lum. 1927.
Cloth, $52.50. Paper, $42.50. 270pp. .... Vendor G0259

2507 **EDW. LUMAS OF IPSWICH, MA. & SOME DESC.**, by G. Lewis, E. Loomis, and C. Lummus. 1917.
Paper. $9.50. 43pp. .... Vendor G0259

2508 **LUNDY FAMILY & THEIR DESC. OF WHATSOEVER SURNAME, WITH BIOGR. SKETCH OF BENJ. LUNDY,** by W.C. Armstrong. 1902. Cloth, $72.00. Paper, $62.00. 485pp. . . . . Vendor G0259

2509 **ANCESTRY OF ABEL LUNT, 1769–1806, OF NEWBURY, MA.,** by W.G. Davis. 1963. Cloth, $52.00. Paper, $42.00. 269pp. Vendor G0259

2510 **HIST. OF THE LUNT FAM. IN AMER.,** by T. Lunt. 1913. Cloth, $59.00. Paper, $49.00. 306pp. Vendor G0259

2511 **COTTONWOOD ROOTS,** by Kem Luther. 1993. Illus.
Account of the author's journey from his birthplace in Broken Bow, Nebraska, eastward across the Midwest to New York State and back into time as **Luther** carries out genealogical research on his family.
Cloth. $23.50. xii+152pp. . . . . Vendor G0050

2512 **HISTORY OF THE LYBARGER FAMILY,** by D.F. Lybarger. 1921.
Paper. $19.00. 101pp. . . . . Vendor G0259

2513 **FRANCES LYFORD OF BOSTON & EXETER, & SOME DESC.,** by W.L. Welch. 1902.
Paper. $17.50. 88pp. . . . . Vendor G0259

2514 **LYLE FAMILY: ANCESTRY & POSTERITY OF MATTHEW, JOHN, DANIEL & SAMUEL LYLE, PIONEER SETTLERS IN VA.,** by O.K. Lyle. 1912.
Cloth, $65.00. Paper, $55.00. 361pp. Vendor G0259

2515 **THE LYLES OF PENNSYLVANIA, BEING AN ACCT. OF THE ORIGIN, MIGRATIONS & GENERATIONS OF THE FAMILY,** by Alvin Dinsmore White. 1963.
Cloth, $63.00. Paper, $53.00. 343pp. Vendor G0259

2516 **GEN. OF THE LYMAN FAM. IN GR. BRITAIN & AMER.; THE ANC. & DESC. OF RICHARD LYMAN, FROM HIGH ONGAR IN ENG., 1631,** by L. Coleman. 1872.
Cloth, $77.50. Paper, $67.50. 549pp. Vendor G0259

2517 **PROCEEDINGS AT THE REUNION OF THE LYMAN FAM. HELD AT MT. TOM & SPRINGFIELD, MASS., 1871.** 1871.
Paper. $12.50. 60pp. . . . . Vendor G0259

2518 **LYNCH FAMILIES OF THE SOUTHERN STATES: LINEAGES & COURT RECORDS,** by L.D. Hines; edited by D.F. Wulfeck. 1966.
Cloth, $69.50. Paper, $58.50. 373pp. Vendor G0259

2519 **LYNCH RECORD, CONTAINING BIOGRAPHICAL SKETCHES OF MEN OF THE NAME LYNCH, 16TH TO 20TH CENTURY, TOGETHER WITH INFORMATION REGARDING THE ORIGIN OF THE NAME,** by E.C. Lynch. 1925.
Cloth, $35.00. Paper, $25.00. 154pp. Vendor G0259

2520 **THE DIARIES OF BENJ. LUNDE & OF BENJ. LYNDE, JR.,** with an appendix, edited by F. Oliver. 1880.
Cloth, $50.00. Paper, $40.00. 267pp. Vendor G0259

2521 **LYON (CONN. & N.J.) MEM.: FAMS. OF CONN. & N.J., INCL. RECS. OF THE IMMIGR. RICHARD LYON OF FAIRFIELD, HENRY LYON OF FAIRFIELD**, by Lyon, Johnson, and Lyons. 1907.
Cloth, $68.00. Paper, $58.00. 453pp. .... Vendor G0259

2522 **LYON MEM.; N.Y. FAM., DESC. FROM THE IMMIGR. THOMAS LYON, OF RYE**, edited by Miller and Lyons. 1907.
Cloth, $94.00. Paper, $84.00. 539pp. .... Vendor G0259

2523 **LYON (OF MASS.), MEM., MASS. FAM., INCL. DESC. OF THE IMMIGR. WM. LYON OF ROXBURY, PETER & GEO. OF DORCHESTER, WITH INTRO. ON THE ENG. ANC. OF THE AMER. FAM.**, by Lyon, Lyon, and McPike. 1905.
Cloth, $72.50. Paper, $62.50. 491pp. .... Vendor G0259

2524 **MacDONALD–McDONALD FAMILY RECORDS**, by J. Montgomery Seaver. Illus.
Paper. $7.50. 54pp. .... Vendor G0011

2525 **MacDONALD–McDONALD FAMILY RECORDS**, by J. Montgomery Seaver.
Paper. $11.00. 54pp. .... Vendor G0259

2526 **THE JOHNSTON & BACON SCOTTISH CLAN HISTORIES: The Clan MacGregor**, by W.R. Kermack. (1953) reprint 1993. Illus. Paper. $8.95. 32pp. .... Vendor G0011

2527 **GEN. RECORDS OF THE DESC. OF DAVID MACK TO 1879**, by S. Smith and C.S. Smith. 1879. Paper. $15.00. 81pp. .... Vendor G0259

2528 **MACK GEN.; THE DESC. OF JOHN MACK OF LYME, CONN., WITH APPENDIX CONTAINING GEN. OF ALLIED FAM., ETC.**, by S. Martin. 1903. Cloth, $229.00. Paper, $219.00. 1,788pp. .... Vendor G0259

2529 **THE JOHNSTON & BACON SCOTTISH CLAN HISTORIES: The Clan Mackay**, by Margaret O. MacDougall. (1953) reprint 1993. Illus. Paper. $8.95. 32pp. .... Vendor G0011

2530 **HIST. OF THE MacKENZIES, WITH GEN. OF THE PRINCIPAL FAMS. OF THE NAME**, by A. MacKenzie. Rev. ed. 1904. Cloth, $93.00. Paper, $83.00. 663pp. .... Vendor G0259

2531 **THE JOHNSTON & BACON SCOTTISH CLAN HISTORIES: The Clan Mackenzie**, by Jean Dunlop. (1953) reprint 1993. Illus. Paper. $8.95. 32pp. .... Vendor G0011

2532 **THE JOHNSTON & BACON SCOTTISH CLAN HISTORIES: The Clan Mackintosh**, by Jean Dunlop. (1960) reprint 1993. Illus. Paper. $8.95. 32pp. .... Vendor G0011

2533 **MACLAY MEMORIAL, SKETCHING THE LIN., LIFE & OBSEQUIES OF HON. WM. B. MACLAY**, by O.B. Judd. 1884. Cloth, $38.75. Paper, $28.75. 192pp. .... Vendor G0259

2534 **THE JOHNSTON & BACON SCOTTISH CLAN HISTORIES: The Clan Maclean**, by John Mackechnie. (1954) reprint 1993. Illus. Paper. $8.95. 32pp. .... Vendor G0011

2535 **MacLEOD. A SHORT SKETCH OF THEIR CLAN, HISTORY, FOLK-LORE, TALES & BIOGR. NOTICES OF SOME EMINENT CLANSMEN**, by R.C. MacLeod. 1906 (Scotland). Paper. $19.50. 118pp. .... Vendor G0259

2536 **MacLEOD HIST., WITH THE GEN. OF THE PRINCIPAL FAM. OF THE NAME [IN SCOTLAND]**, by A. MacKenzie. 1889. Cloth, $81.00. Paper, $71.00. 463pp. .... Vendor G0259

2537 **THE JOHNSTON & BACON SCOTTISH CLAN HISTORIES: The Clan MacLeod**, by I.F. Grant. (1953) reprint 1993. Illus. Paper. $8.95. 32pp. .... Vendor G0011

2538 **THE MacMILLANS & THEIR SEPTS**, by S. MacMillan. 1952 (Scotland). Cloth, $31.00. Paper, $21.00. 126pp. .... Vendor G0259

2539 **THE CLAN MacNEIL (CLANN NIALL) OF SCOTLAND**, by the MacNeil of Barra. 1923 (London). Cloth, $44.00. Paper, $34.00. 227pp. .... Vendor G0259

2540 **MACOMB FAM. RECORD, BEING AN ACCT. OF THE FAM. SINCE THE SETTLEMENT IN AMERICA**, by H. Macomb, rev. by P. McComb. 1917.
Cloth, $42.00. Paper, $32.00. 206pp. .... Vendor G0259

2541 **THE MACOMBER GEN.**, by E.S. Stackpole.
Cloth, $48.00. Paper, $38.00. 252pp. .... Vendor G0259

2542 **THE MacQUEENS, BEING A BRIEF HIST. OF THE ORIGIN OF THE MacQUEEN FAM.**, by J.A. Nydegger. 1928.
Paper. $18.50. 111pp. .... Vendor G0259

2543 **HISTORY OF THE CLAN MACRAE, WITH GENEALOGIES**, by A. Macrae. 1899 (Scotland).
Cloth, $81.00. Paper, $71.00. 22+442pp. .... Vendor G0259

2544 **GEN. OF THE MACY FAM., 1635–1868**, by S. Macy. 1868.
Cloth, $68.00. Paper, $58.00. 457pp. .... Vendor G0259

2545 **US MADDYS: AN ACCOUNT OF THE FAMILY IN ENGLAND & THE DESCENDANTS OF WILLIAM MADDY OF FAIRFAX OF FAIRFAX CO., VA., & JAMES MADDY OF FAIRFAX & ORANGE CO.**, by Olive Maddy. 1950.
Cloth, $54.00. Paper, $44.00. 280pp. .... Vendor G0259

2546 **[Maese]. FOLLOWING IN THE FOOTSTEPS OF OUR ANCESTORS FROM SANTA FE TO MAES CREEK**, by Arthur F. Maes. 1995. Illus.
The history of the **Maese** family starting in Santa Fe with their journey and settlement of Maes Creek in Huerfano County, Colorado spanning over two hundred years. Included are the Hispanic families: **Maes(e), Torres, Vigil, Martín(ez), Lujan, Sanches, Arellano**, and **Red Track** and **Good Cow** of the Oglala Sioux.
Paper. $27.95. 160pp. .... Vendor G0341

2547 **MAGILL–McGILL GENEALOGY, FROM THE 1700'S**, by Eunice Parr McGill. 1963.
Paper. $11.50. 57pp. .... Vendor G0259

2548 **MAIN–MAINE FAM. OF STONINGTON, CONN.**, by A. Aspinall. 1911.
Paper. $12.00. 57pp. .... Vendor G0259

2549 **THE GEN. OF THE MAKEPEACE FAMS. IN THE U.S., 1637–1857**, by W. Makepeace. 1858.
Paper. $15.00. 107pp. .... Vendor G0259

2550 **JOHN MALLET, THE HUGUENOT, & HIS DESC., 1694–1894**, by A.S. Mallett. 1895.
Cloth, $53.00. Paper, $43.00. 342pp. .... Vendor G0259

2551 **GENEALOGY OF THE MALLORYS OF VA.**, by H.R. Mallory. 1954.
Paper. $13.00. 65pp. .... Vendor G0259

2552 **JEREMIAH DUMAS MALONE, A GENEALOGICAL OUTLINE**, by E.E. Malone. 1949.
Cloth, $35.00. Paper, $25.00. 159pp. .... Vendor G0259

2553 **MALTBY–MALTBIE FAM. HIST.**, by D.M. Verril. 1916.
Cloth, $78.00. Paper, $68.00. 435pp. Vendor G0259

2554 **MALTBY–MOREHOUSE FAMILY: A LIST OF PEDIGREES WITH GE-NEALOGICAL NOTES**, edited by G.L. Morehouse. 1895.
Cloth, $35.00. Paper, $25.00. 157pp. Vendor G0259

2555 **MANLY FAMILY: ACCOUNT OF THE DESCENDANTS OF CAPT. BASIL MANLY OF THE REVOLUTION, & RELATED FAMILIES**, by Louise Manly. 1930.
Cloth, $64.50. Paper, $54.50. 351pp. Vendor G0259

2556 **REC. OF THE MANN FAM. GEN. OF THE DESC. OF RICHARD MANN OF SCITUATE, MA.**, by G. Mann. 1884.
Cloth, $47.50. Paper, $37.50. 251pp. Vendor G0259

2557 **MIND YOUR MANNERS. LIFE & ANCESTORS OF RICHARD HERBERT MANNER**, by Marcella Stephenson and Clarence Stephenson. 1989. Illus.
Ancestral lines: **Manner, Titterington, Armstrong, Clark, Walker, Hindman, Todd, Rambo, Abraham, Wynne.**
Paper. $24.50. 140pp. . . . . Vendor G0041

2558 **NOTES ON THE MANNING FAM. OF CO. KENT, ENG. WITH ADD. NOTES ON THE WATERS, PROCTOR & WHITFIELD FAM. (Repr. *NEHGR*)**, by H.F. Water. 1897.
Paper. $7.00. 35pp. . . . . Vendor G0259

2559 **THE GEN. & BIOGR. HIST. OF THE MANNING FAM. OF NEW ENG. & DESC. FROM SETTLEMENT IN AMER. TO PRESENT TIME**, by W.H. Manning. 1902.
Cloth, $140.00. Paper, $130.00. 865pp. . . . . Vendor G0259

2560 **THE DESC. OF RICHARD & GILLIAN MANSFIELD, WHO SETTLED IN NEW HAVEN, 1639, WITH SKETCHES OF SOME OF THE MOST DISTINGUISHED & CONNECTIONS OF OTHER NAMES**, by H. Mansfield. 1885.
Cloth, $38.00. Paper, $28.00. 198pp. Vendor G0259

2561 **MARGESON AND RELATED FAMS.**, by H.M. Spinney.
Paper. $18.00. 95pp. . . . . Vendor G0259

2562 **MARIS FAM. IN THE U.S. REC. OF THE DESC. OF GEO. & ALICE MARIS, 1683–1885**, by G. and A.M. Maris. 1885.
Cloth, $46.00. Paper, $36.00. 279+33pp. . . . . Vendor G0259

2563 **WARREN AND ETHEL (GARLAND) MARKWITH, THEIR ANCES-TORS, DESCENDANTS AND RELATED FAMILIES**, by Joseph H. Vance. 1982. Indexed. Illus.
Big page size: 8¹/₂ x 11 inches. Extensive historical background, biographical sketches, records, maps, illustrations, photographs. Every-name index has over 11,500 entries. Every **Markwith** descendant should have this book! Virtually every **Markwith** descendant in America can be traced to one family living in Essex County, New Jersey in the late 18th century. There were three sons: (1) John C., born 25 Nov 1774; married Elizabeth **Muckridge** in New Jersey; died

30 Nov 1836, Darke County, Ohio. (2) Daniel, born about 1779; married —; died June 1830, Essex County, New Jersey. (3) Richard J., born 1789; married three times, lastly to Rachel **Brown** in New Jersey; died June 1871, Delaware County, Ohio. Chapters devoted to related families: **Nealeigh, Brown, Langston, Sliger, Shields, Garland, Ferguson, Albright, Davis, Burk, Clapp.** Write or call author for free brochure.
Paper. $22.00. 270pp. .... Vendor G0239

2564 **GEN. OF THE FAM. OF GEO. MARSH, WHO CAME FROM ENG. IN 1635 & SETTLED IN HINGHAM, MA.**, by E.J. Marsh. 1887.
Cloth, $40.00. Paper, $30.00. 229pp. .... Vendor G0259

2565 **GEN. OF THE JOHN MARSH OF SALEM, & HIS DESC., 1633–1888**, by L. Marsh; rev. by D. Marsh. 1888.
Cloth, $46.00. Paper, $36.00. 283pp. .... Vendor G0259

2566 **GEN. OF THE MARSH FAM. OUTLINE FOR FIVE GEN., WITH ACCTS. OF THE 3RD FAM. REUNION AT LAKE PLEASANT IN 1886**, edited by D.W. Marsh. 1886.
Paper. $12.00. 60pp. .... Vendor G0259

2567 **MARSH GEN., GIVING SEVERAL THOUSAND DESC. OF JOHN MARSH OF HARTFORD, CT., 1636–1895**, by D. Marsh. 1895.
Cloth, $75.50. Paper, $65.50. 585pp. .... Vendor G0259

2568 **DESCENDANTS OF JOHN MARSHALL OF VIRGINIA**, by Carol A. Hauk. 1995. Indexed.
Paper. $35.00. 141pp. .... Vendor G0340

2569 **MARSHALL FAMILY, OR A GEN. CHART OF THE DESC. OF JOHN MARSHALL & ELIZABETH MARKHAM, HIS WIFE**, by W.M. Paxton. 1885.
Cloth, $63.00. Paper, $53.00. 415pp. .... Vendor G0259

2570 **MARSHALL FAM. RECORD, WITH HASKELL, BOUTWELL, BARRETT, & ALLIED FAM.**, by F.B. Kingsbury. 1913.
Paper. $15.00. 103pp. .... Vendor G0259

2571 **MARSTON ENG. ANC. WITH SOME ACCT. OF THE AMER. IMMIGRANTS OF THE NAME**, by M.L. Holman. 1929.
Paper. $8.00. 41pp. .... Vendor G0259

2572 **MARSTON GEN., IN TWO PARTS**, by N.W. Marston. 1888.
Cloth, $101.00. Paper, $91.00. 607pp. .... Vendor G0259

2573 **MEMOIRS OF THE MARSTONS OF SALEM, WITH A BRIEF GEN. OF SOME OF THEIR DESC. (Repr. *NEHGR*)**, by J.L. Watson. 1873.
Paper. $9.50. 48pp. .... Vendor G0259

2574 **ADAM MARTIN (1755–1835) AND THOMAS ROY MUSICK (1757–1842)—ST. LOUIS COUNTY, MISSOURI PIONEERS—THEIR ANCESTORS, DESCENDANTS, AND RELATED FAMILIES, HILDEBRAND, PEIRA, ROY, AND NEVILLE**, by Michal Martin Farmer. 1989. Indexed. Illus.
Cloth. $45.00. 678pp. .... Vendor G0312

2575 A MARTIN FAMILY SAGA, by Reta M. Evans. 1992. Indexed. Illus.
Allied families: **Burnett, Dodson, Killingsworth, Lewis, Manire, Scoggin, Shipley, Stanley** and **Woodlee.**
Cloth. $42.00. 448pp. .... Vendor G0012

2576 DESCENDANTS OF JOHN MARTIN OF BRUNSWICK AND OLD BRISTOL, MAINE, by Kenneth Alton Clark. 1993.
Paper. $16.00. 81pp. .... Vendor G0259

2577 GEN. NOTICES & HIST. OF THE MARTIN FAM. OF NEW ENG., WHO SETTLED AT WEYMOUTH & HINGHAM IN 1635, WITH ACCT. OF THEIR DESC., by H. Martin. 1880.
Cloth, $66.50. Paper, $56.50. 358pp. .... Vendor G0259

2578 GEN. OF THE MARTIN FAM., by C.W. Francis. 1918.
Cloth, $56.60. Paper, $46.50. 319pp. .... Vendor G0259

2579 MARTIN FAMILY [OF IRELAND, U.S. & CANADA], by G.C. Martin. 1914.
Cloth, $35.00. Paper, $25.00. 144pp. .... Vendor G0259

2580 MARTIN FAMILY QUARTERLY, by Michal Martin Farmer. 1975–87. Indexed. Illus.
Send for brochure .... Vendor G0312

2581 MARTIN GENEALOGY. DESC. OF LT. SAMUEL MARTIN OF WETHERSFIELD, CT., SHOWING DESC. FROM ROYALTY; ALSO GIVING BRIEF HIST. OF, & DESC. FROM, RELATED COL. FAMS., by T.A. Hay. Vol. I. of 1. 1911.
Cloth, $56.50. Paper, $46.50. 291pp. .... Vendor G0259

2582 [Martin]. THE GENEALOGY OF THE WEBSTER, MARTIN, DOZIER, STAPLES, & STARKE FAMILIES OF WILKES COUNTY, GEORGIA— THEIR ANCESTORS, DESCENDANTS, & KIN—BRASWELL, WYATT, & MARTIN, by Michal Martin Farmer. 1994. Indexed. Illus.
Cloth. $65.00. 848pp. .... Vendor G0312

2583 THE MARTIN GENEALOGY, by J. Montgomery Seaver. Illus.
Paper. $7.50. 60pp. .... Vendor G0011

2584 DESC. OF REINOLD & MATTHEW MARVIN OF HARTFORD, CT, 1638 & 1635, SONS OF EDW. MARVIN OF GT. BENTLEY, ENG., by G. and W. Marvin. 1904.
Cloth, $99.50. Paper, $89.50. 659pp. .... Vendor G0259

2585 ENG. ANC. OF REINOLD & MATTHEW MARVIN OF HARTFORD, CONN., 1638, by W.T.R. Marvin. 1900.
Cloth, $37.50. Paper, $27.50. 184pp. .... Vendor G0259

2586 GEN. SKETCH OF THE DESC. OF REINOLD & MATTHEW MARVIN, WHO CAME TO NEW ENG. IN 1635, by T.R. Marvin. 1848.
Paper. $11.00. 56pp. .... Vendor G0259

2587 MARVIN AND DOLAN DESCENDANTS, by Harry T. Dolan, Jr. 1992. Indexed. Illus.

Three appendices include records of the **Willcox** family of Chenango County, NY and the **Sinnott** and **Denis** families of Broome County, NY.
Cloth. $28.00. 266pp. .... Vendor G0351

2588 **A RECORD OF THE DESC. OF ROBERT MASON, OF ROXBURY, MASS.**, by W.L. Mason. 1891.
Paper. $7.50. 39pp. .... Vendor G0259

2589 **CAPT. JOHN MASON, FOUNDER OF NEW HAMPSHIRE ... WITH LETTERS & OTHER HIST. DOCUMENTS, WITH A MEMOIR BY C.W. TUTTLE**, edited by J.W. Dean. 1887.
Cloth, $84.50. Paper, $74.50. 491pp. .... Vendor G0259

2590 **DESC. OF CAPT. HUGH MASON IN AMERICA**, by E.W. Mason. 1937.
Cloth, $119.00. Paper, $109.00. 867pp. .... Vendor G0259

2591 **DESCENDANTS OF GEORGE MASON OF VIRGINIA**, by Carol A. Hauk. 1995. Indexed.
Paper. $30.00. 72pp. .... Vendor G0340

2592 **ENOCH & ELIZABETH MASON, THEIR ANCESTRY & DESCENDANTS**, by S.S. Mason. 1911.
Paper. $18.00. 91pp. .... Vendor G0259

2593 **GEN. OF THE SAMPSON MASON FAM.**, by A.H. Mason. 1902.
Cloth, $47.00. Paper, $37.00. 288pp. .... Vendor G0259

2594 **JOHN MASON AND MARY ANN MILLER**, by Floyd R. Mason. 1986. Indexed. Illus.
William **Mason** and Barbara **Cline** of VA and nine children. John **Mason** family is carried thru nine generations.
Cloth. $33.00. 367pp. .... Vendor G0345

2595 **MASON FAMILY NEWSLETTER**, by Paula Perkins Mortensen. 1987. Indexed.
Subscription. $10.00/year. 12pp. .... Vendor G0228

2596 **[Massey]. UPCOUNTRY REFLECTIONS—1900–1903 AND 1906**, by Sara Hunter Kellar. 1993. Indexed. Illus.
Personal diaries of Jane Duncan Todd **Massey**, Oconee County, South Carolina. Helpful for those searching in that area and/or for **Duncan, Todd, Massey, Hunter, Cowan, Lee, Rankin, Trotter, Glazener** names!
Paper. $15.00. 295pp. .... Vendor G0212

2597 **BRIEF HISTORY OF BISHOP JACOB MAST AND OTHER MAST PIONEERS**, by C.Z. Mast. (1911) reprint 1989.
Cloth. $39.00. 822pp. .... Vendor G0150

2598 **LIN. OF REV. RICHARD MATHER**, by H. Mather. 1890.
Cloth, $78.00. Paper, $68.00. 540pp. . . . . Vendor G0259

2599 **HIST. OF THE MATHESONS, WITH GEN. OF THE VAR. BRANCHES [IN SCOTLAND]**, by A. MacKenzie. 1882.
Paper. $15.00. 72pp. . . . . Vendor G0259

2600 **MATHEWS FAMILY HISTORY; DESCENDANTS OF JOHN LAUGHLIN MATHEWS, SR.** (1828–1895), by Nathan Mathews. 1990. Indexed. Illus.
Other major family groups: **Conley, Fiveash, Galbreath, Johnson, McDilda, Sherouse**, and **Spivey**.
Cloth. $37.50. 145pp. . . . . Vendor G0399

2601 **COL. TIMOTHY MATLACK, PATRIOT & SOLDIER, HADDONFIELD NJ**, by Dr A.M. Stackhouse. 1910.
Paper. $19.00. 105pp. . . . . Vendor G0259

2602 **MATTESONS IN AMER.: ORIG. RECORDS OF EARLY MATTESON PIONEERS**, by P. Matteson. 1960.
Paper. $8.50. 42pp. . . . . Vendor G0259

2603 **MATTHEWS, PAGE, WILSON, DEAN, BARTLETT & RELATED FAMILIES**, by Kermit Dean Matthews. 1993.
Cloth, $55.00. Paper, $45.00. 290pp. . . . . Vendor G0259

2604 **JOHN MAULL (1714–1753) OF LEWES, DELA.: A GEN. OF HIS DESC. IN ALL BRANCHES**, by B. Maull, edited by R.F. Bailey. 1941.
Cloth, $53.50. Paper, $43.50. 241+39pp. . . . . Vendor G0259

2605 **GEN. OF THE MAULSBY FAM. FOR FIVE GENERATIONS, 1699–1902**, by C.M. Payne. 1902.
Cloth, $30.00. Paper, $20.00. 147pp. . . . . Vendor G0259

2606 **MEMORIALS OF THE MAURAN FAMILY**, by J.E. Mauran and J.C. Stockbridge. 1893.
Cloth, $39.50. Paper, $29.50. 171pp. . . . . Vendor G0259

2607 **MAXSON FAM. OF R.I.**, by Johnston and Jones.
Paper. $13.50. 68pp. . . . . Vendor G0259

2608 **MAXWELL HISTORY AND GENEALOGIES**, by Fay Maxwell. 1977. Indexed. Illus. ISBN 1-885463-17-0.
Begins with Sir Robert **Maxwell** of 12th century and moves through migratory sojourn to Ulster Ireland and on to America to become Revolutionary War soldiers with General Washington. Includes many states. Related names include: **Alexander, Anderson, Beasley, Carson, Hussey, Houston, Marshall, McCullough, Ogilvee–Ogilvie–Ogilvy–Ogilbay, Roberts, Snively, Stingley, Williams**.
Paper. $34.75. 165pp. . . . . Vendor G0135

2609 **MAXWELL HISTORY & GENEALOGY, INCLUDING ALLIED FAMILIES**, by Houston, Blaine, and Mellette. 1916.
Cloth, $106.50. Paper, $96.50. 642pp. Vendor G0259

2610 **CHARLES MAY & HIS DESCENDANTS, WHO SETTLED AT MAYS**

CROSS ROADS IN OLD EDGEFIELD CO., S.C., edited by H. Woodson. 1956.
Cloth, $53.00. Paper, $43.00. 287pp. .... Vendor G0259

2611 **GEN. OF DESC. OF JOHN MAY WHO CAME FROM ENG. TO ROXBURY IN AMER., 1640,** by S. May, et al. 1878.
Cloth, $41.50. Paper, $31.50. 212pp. .... Vendor G0259

2612 **[Maydew]. A KANSAS FARM FAMILY,** by Randall C. Maydew, Editor & Publisher. 1993. Illus.
Cloth. $25.00. 313pp. .... Vendor G0007

2613 **MEMOIR & GEN. OF THE MARYLAND & PENN. FAM. OF MAYER,** by B. Mayer.
Cloth, $37.00. Paper, $27.00. 179pp. .... Vendor G0259

2614 **MAYHAM FAMILY, 1795–1950: FAMILY OF HENRY MAHAM OF BLENHEIM HILL, SCHOHARIE CO., NY,** by G. Raymond. 1950.
Paper. $12.50. 63pp. .... Vendor G0259

2615 **MAYHUGH OF VA. & KY., & ALLIED FAM.,** by M. Thompson. 1957.
Paper. $19.50. 100pp. .... Vendor G0259

2616 **BRIEF MEMOIR OF MAYNARD FAM., ETC.,** by C.P. Stevens. 1916.
Paper. $13.00. 64pp. .... Vendor G0259

2617 **JOHN MAYNARD OF SUDBURY, MASS. & DESC.,** by W.E. Gould. 1914.
Paper. $8.00. 38pp. .... Vendor G0259

2618 **McALLISTER FAMILY RECORDS, COMP. FOR THE DESCENDANTS OF ABRAHAM ADDAMS McALLISTER & HIS WIFE JULIA ELLEN (STRATTON) McALLISTER OF COVINGTON, VA.,** by J. Gray McAllister. 1912.
Paper. $17.50. 88pp. .... Vendor G0259

2619 **THE DESCENDANTS OF JAMES McCABE AND ANN PETTIGREW,** by Allan E. Marble. 1986. Indexed. Illus.
Cloth. $33.50. 252pp. .... Vendor G0406

2620 **CAPTAIN JOHN McCALL, 1726–1812: HIS ANCESTORS AND DESCENDANTS,** by Clare M. McCall. 1985. Indexed. Illus.
Cloth. $45.50. 213pp. .... Vendor G0406

2621 **McCALL–TIDWELL & ALLIED FAM.,** by E.T. McCall. 1931.
Cloth, $109.00. Paper, $99.00. 672pp. .... Vendor G0259

2622 **DAVID McCALLUM & ISABEL SELLARS: THEIR ANTECEDENTS, DESCENDANTS & COLLATERAL RELATIVES,** by L. Farrell and F.J.H. Hooker. 1949.
Cloth, $47.50. Paper, $37.50. 234pp. .... Vendor G0259

2623 **McCALLUM FAMILY & DESCENDANTS OF DUNCAN McCALLUM; COLONIAL ANCESTORS OF THE JOHN McCALLUM BRANCH, & OTHER ALLIED LINES,** by I.F. Johnson. 1957.
Paper. $15.00. 77pp. .... Vendor G0259

2624 **DESCENDANTS OF DENNIS McCARTY OF VIRGINIA**, by Carol A. Hauk. 1995. Indexed.
Paper. $30.00. 64pp. .... Vendor G0340

2625 **THOMAS McCARTY OF NORTHAMPTON CO., PA. & SOME DESC. (IN LANCASTER FAM.)**, by H. Lancaster. 1902.
Paper. $12.50. 63pp. .... Vendor G0259

2626 **McCLANAHAN FAMILY, DESC. OF ROBERT OF IRELAND & VA.**, by H. White. 1894.
Paper. $9.00. 43pp. .... Vendor G0259

2627 **FOUR GEN. OF THE McCLARY FAM. FROM ANDREW McCLARY OF ULSTER, 1726**, by H.P. McClary. 1896.
Paper. $10.00. 52pp. .... Vendor G0259

2628 **[McClaughry]. GEN. OF THE MacCLAUGHRY FAMILY: A SCOTO-IRISH FAMILY FROM GALLOWAY, SCOTLAND, APPEARING IN IRELAND ABOUT 1600, & EMIGR. TO N.Y. IN 1765**, by C.C. McClaughry. 1913.
Cloth, $81.00. Paper, $71.00. 459pp. .... Vendor G0259

2629 **THE JOHN McCLENAHAN FOLK: BIOGRAPHY & GENEALOGY**, by J.M. Henderson. 1911.
Paper. $19.00. 125pp. .... Vendor G0259

2630 **THE McCLENDON PAPERS OF LEONARDO ANDREA**, transcribed by Richard R. Dietz. 1995.
All data gathered on the surname **McLendon/McClendon** by the professional genealogist.
Paper, loose-leaf with holes for mounting in 3-ring binder.
$39.95. 450pp. .... Vendor G0023

2631 **McCLUNG GEN.; A GEN. & BIOGR. RECORD OF THE McCLUNG FAM. FROM THE TIME OF THEIR EMIGRATION TO THE YEAR 1904**, by W. McClung. 1904.
Cloth, $54.00. Paper, $44.00. 296pp. .... Vendor G0259

2632 **McCLURE FAM. GEN.**, by J.A. McClure. 1914.
Cloth, $45.00. Paper, $35.00. 232pp. .... Vendor G0259

2633 **McCONNELL MARRIAGES & GEN. ANC., DESC. & MARR. OF A VA. FAM.**, by H. and M. Addington. 1929.
Paper. $7.50. 36pp. .... Vendor G0259

2634 **McCORMICK FAM. RECORD & BIOGR.**, by L.J. McCormick. 1896.
Cloth, $86.50. Paper, $76.50. 490pp. .... Vendor G0259

2635 **WM. McCOY & HIS DESC. ALSO A HIST. OF THE FAM. OF ALEXANDER McCOY**, by L. McCoy. 1904.
Cloth, $41.50. Paper, $31.50. 204pp. .... Vendor G0259

2636 **ANCESTORS AND DESCENDANTS OF LORENZO PORTER McCRAY**, by Patricia (Wright) Morrison. 1988. Indexed. Illus.
A genealogy of the **McCray, Lilley, Blakeslee**, and related families of Western New York and vicinity.
Cloth. $25.00. 87pp. .... Vendor G0112

2637 **GEN. OF THE McCULLOUGH FAM. & OTHER SKETCHES**, by J. McCullough. 1912.
Paper. $18.50. 100pp. .... Vendor G0259

2638 **McCUTCHEN**, by McCutchen Trace Association.
Historical and genealogical newsletter for any spelling of McCutcheon or for anyone with McCutcheon ancestors, including **McCutcheon, McCutchen, McCutchan, McCutchin, MacCutcheon.** Two newsletters per year when you join the McCutchen Trace Association.
Membership fee. $7.50/year .... Vendor G0104

2639 **McCUTCHEON (CUTCHEON) FAM. RECORDS. ALLIED FAM. OF McCLARY, TRIPP, BROWN, AND CRITCHETT**, by F. McKee. 1931.
Cloth, $65.00. Paper, $55.00. 352pp. .... Vendor G0259

2640 **McDANIEL FAM. RECORD**, by C.G. Harris. 1929.
Cloth, $38.50. Paper, $28.50. 161pp. .... Vendor G0259

2641 **McDONOUGH–HACKSTAFF ANCESTRY**, by R. Macdonough. 1901.
Cloth, $89.00. Paper, $79.00. 538pp. .... Vendor G0259

2642 **McDOWELL FAM. OF KENTUCKY. EXTR. FROM "HIST. FAMS. OF KY.,"** by T.M. Green.
Paper. $19.00. 117pp. .... Vendor G0259

2643 **SCOTCH-IRISH McELROYS IN AMERICA, A.D. 1717– A.D. 1900**, by J.M. McElroy. 1901.
Cloth, $38.00. Paper, $28.00. 183pp. .... Vendor G0259

2644 **[McFarlan]. OUR KINDRED: MacFARLAN & STERN FAMS. OF CHESTER CO., PA. & NEW CASTLE CO., DELAWARE**, by C. Stern. 1885.
Cloth, $34.00. Paper, $24.00. 179pp. .... Vendor G0259

2645 **GEN. OF THE McFARLAND FAM. OF HANCOCK CO., MAINE**, by D.Y. McFarland. 1910.
Paper. $12.00. 58pp. .... Vendor G0259

2646 **[McFarlane]. HIST. OF CLAN MacFARLANE, MacFARLAN, MacFARLAND, MacFARLIN**, by C.M. Little. 1893.
Cloth, $48.00. Paper, $38.00. 254pp. .... Vendor G0259

2647 **GEN. HIST. OF THE McGAFFEY FAM., INCL. ALSO THE FELLOWS, ETHRIDGE & SHERMAN FAMILIES**, by G.W. McGaffey. 1904.
Cloth, $33.50. Paper, $23.50. 145pp. .... Vendor G0259

2648 **McGAVOCK FAMILY: GEN. HIST. OF JAMES McGAVOCK & HIS DESCENDANTS, FROM 1760 TO 1903**, by Robert Gray. 1903.
Cloth, $38.00. Paper, $28.00. 175pp. .... Vendor G0259

2649 **McGILL FAM.: CELTICS, ULSTERMEN & AMER. PIONEERS: HIST., HERALDRY, & TRAD.,** by A. McGill. 1910.
Cloth, $54.00. Paper, $44.00. 345pp. .... Vendor G0259

2650 **McGUFFINS IN NORTH AMERICA**, by Gwen Campbell. 1993. Indexed.
Listed alphabetically by first name and birthdate, includes **Magoffin, McGaffin, McGiffin, McGoffin.**
Query with SASE.
Paper. $30.00. 287pp. .... Vendor G0303

2651 **McGUIRE FAM. IN VA. (IRISH ANC.)**, by W.G. Stannard. 1926.
Cloth, $35.00. Paper, $25.00. 126pp. .... Vendor G0259

2652 **ALEXANDER FOSTER McILRAITH (1858–1945) GENEALOGY IN-CLUDING THE FOSTER, CHARLAND, GAVIN AND LOVE LINES: ONTARIO, NORTH DAKOTA, WASHINGTON, QUEBEC, MANITOBA, AND ALBERTA**, compiled and edited by Terence T. Quirke, Jr., Ph.D., C.G. 1987. Indexed. Illus.
Eight generations, starting 1789; 105 photos, four maps, seven charts.
Paper. $25.00. 257pp. .... Vendor G0143

2653 **DESC. OF MICUM McINTIRE, A SCOT. HIGHLANDER DEPORTED BY CROMWELL & SETTLED AT YORK, ME. ABOUT 1668**, by R.H. McIntire. 1940.
Cloth, $33.50. Paper, $23.50. 158pp. .... Vendor G0259

2654 **DESC. OF PHILIP McINTIRE, A SCOT. HIGHLANDER DEPORTED BY CROMWELL & SETTLED AT READING, MA., ABOUT 1660**, by R. McIntire. 1941.
Cloth, $42.50. Paper, $32.50. 218pp. .... Vendor G0259

2655 **THE McINTIRE FAM., DESC. OF MICUM MECANTIRE OF YORK CO., MAINE**, by H.A. Davis. 1939.
Cloth, $49.50. Paper, $39.50. 251pp. typescript .... Vendor G0259

2656 **GEN. OF HUGH McKAY & HIS DESC.**, by W. Kean. 1895.
Paper. $15.00. 76pp. .... Vendor G0259

2657 **GEN. OF THE McKEAN FAM. OF PA., WITH BIOGR. OF THE HON. THOMAS McKEAN**, by R. Buchanan. 1890.
Cloth, $47.00. Paper, $37.00. 288pp. .... Vendor G0259

2658 **HIST. OF DESC. OF DAVID McKEE**, by J. McKee. 1892.
Cloth, $32.50. Paper, $22.50. 112pp. .... Vendor G0259

2659 **STORY OF THE McKELVEYS IN AMERICA, INCLUDING HIST. & BIOGR. SKETCHES IN GENEALOGICAL ARRANGEMENT**, by E.J. McK. Mabon. 1928.
Paper. $18.00. 88pp. .... Vendor G0259

2660 **THE SCOTCH ANC. OF WILLIAM McKINLEY, PRESIDENT OF THE U.S.**, by E.A. Claypool. 1897.
Paper. $10.00. 46pp. .... Vendor G0259

2661 **GEN. OF THE McKINSTRY FAM., WITH ESSAY ON THE SCOT-IRISH IMMIGR. TO AMER.**, by W. Willis. 1866.
Paper. $10.00. 46pp. .... Vendor G0259

2662 **THE McLENDONS OF CARROLL COUNTY, GEORGIA AND RE-LATED FAMILIES**, by Lois Clouse McLendon. 1989. Indexed. Illus.
Stories in three parts.
Part I—Isaac Newton **McLendon**, his Ancestors and Descendants.
Part II—Other **McLendon**s in Carroll County.
Part III—Related Families: **Rowe, Beavers, Denney, Laminack, Lovvorn, Martin, Moore**, and **Stipe**.
Cloth. $30.00. 296pp. .... Vendor G0059

2663 **COLLECTIONS FOR A HISTORY OF THE ANCIENT FAMILY OF McMATH**, by F.M. McMath. 1937.
Cloth, $53.00. Paper, $43.00. 272pp. .... Vendor G0259

2664 **THE DESCENDANTS OF ARMSTRONG McMORRIS AND MARY McCRAY OF LISBURN, IRELAND, AND HARPERSFIELD, DELAWARE COUNTY, NEW YORK, 1738–1995**, by Rick Crume. 1995. Indexed.
Includes: **Olmsted**.
Paper. $11.00. 120pp. .... Vendor G0386

2665 **McNAIR–McNEAR & McNEIR GEN.**, by J.B. McNair. 1923.
Cloth, $58.50. Paper, $48.50. 322pp. .... Vendor G0259

2666 **McNAIR SUPPLEMENT TO ABOVE**, by J.B. McNair. 1928.
Cloth, $62.25. Paper, $52.25. 349pp. .... Vendor G0259

2667 **McNAIR–McNEAR & McNEIR GEN.**, by J.B. McNair. 1955.
Cloth, $81.00. Paper, $71.00. 457pp. .... Vendor G0259

2668 **McNAIR SUPPLEMENT TO ABOVE**, by J.B. McNair. 1960.
Cloth, $56.60. Paper, $46.50. 314pp. .... Vendor G0259

2669 **McNARY FAMILY, WITH FAM. TREES & HIST.** 1907.
Cloth, $41.00. Paper, $31.00. 236pp. .... Vendor G0259

2670 **THE WILLIAM McNEAR FAMILY, 1770–1990**, by John David McNair. 1990.
Paper. $13.00. 63pp. .... Vendor G0259

2671 **BEGINNING IN BELFAST: DESCENDANTS OF SAMPSON STUART McNEILL**, by Carolyn Chapman. 1994.
Paper. $19.50. 82pp. .... Vendor G0259

2672 **TALES OF OUR FOREFATHERS, & BIOGR. ANNALS OF FAM. ALLIED TO THOSE OF McPIKE, GUEST & DUMONT**, by E.F. McPike. 1898.
Cloth, $37.00. Paper, $27.00. 181pp. .... Vendor G0259

2673 **McQUEEN: SOME DESCENDANTS OF ALEXANDER McQUEEN OF GIRVAN, SCOTLAND**, by Jeanne Waters Strong. 1995. Indexed. Illus.
Cloth. $20.00. 50pp. .... Vendor G0086

2674 **McQUISTON–McCUISTON–McQUESTEN FAMILIES, 1620–1937**, by L.B. McQuiston. 1937.
Cloth, $119.00. Paper, $109.00. 750pp. .... Vendor G0259

2675 **McWILLIE & CUNNINGHAM FAMILIES**, by R.B. Johnson. 1914.
Cloth, $43.50. Paper, $33.50. 219pp. .... Vendor G0259

2676 **HIST. & GEN. OF THE MEAD FAM., OF FAIRFIELD CO., CONN., EASTERN N.Y., WESTERN VT. & WESTERN PENN., FROM 1180–1900**, by S.P. Mead. 1901.
Cloth, $85.00. Paper, $75.00. 480pp. .... Vendor G0259

2677 **MEAD. INDEX TO ABOVE.** 1907. (May be ordered bound with above.)
Paper. $12.00. 73pp. .... Vendor G0259

2678 **DESCENDANTS OF ANDREW MEADE OF VIRGINIA**, by Carol A. Hauk. 1995. Indexed.
Paper. $30.00. 98pp. .... Vendor G0340

2679 **SOME DESC. OF JOHN & LUCY (ROCKWELL) MEARS OF WINDSOR, CONN.**, by H. Healy. 1960.
Cloth, $32.50. Paper, $22.50. 116pp. .... Vendor G0259

2680 **MEEK GEN., WITH SKETCHES OF ADAM MEEK & HIS DESC., 1640–1902**, by H. Meek. 1902.
Paper. $10.00. 54pp. .... Vendor G0259

2681 **RECORD OF THE DESC. OF VINCENT MEIGS, WHO CAME FROM DORSETSHIRE, ENG., TO AMER. ABOUT 1635**, by R.J. Meigs. 2nd ed. 1934.
Cloth, $44.50. Paper, $34.50. 230pp. .... Vendor G0259

2682 **[Mellick]. MOELICH–MALICK–MELLICK GEN., EXTR. FROM "STORY OF AN OLD FARM,"** by A.D. Mellick. 1889.
Paper. $17.00. 85pp. .... Vendor G0259

2683 **DIE FAMILIE MENDELSSOHN, 1729–1847. VOL. II, 1836–1847 (LETTERS OF FELIX & FANNY MENDELSOHN, IN GERMAN)**, by S. Hensel. 1898 (Berlin).
Cloth, $71.00. Paper, $61.00. 400pp. .... Vendor G0259

2684 **THREE HUNDRED YEARS IN AMERICA WITH THE MERCERS**, by Dolores Graham Doyle. 1991. Indexed. Illus.
Cecil, Dickerson, Dunlap, Eastlick, Matson, McCallister, Peringer, Prentice, Russell, Stetzel, VanBlaricom, Webb/Boone, Witten, and more.
Cloth. $25.00. 200pp. .... Vendor G0255

2685 **SOME MERIAMS & THEIR CONNECTION WITH OTHER FAM.**, by R.N. Meriam. 1888.
Paper. $10.00. 52pp. .... Vendor G0259

2686 **MERIVALE FAMILY MEMORIALS**, by A.W. Merivale. 1884.
Cloth, $62.00. Paper, $52.00. 404pp. .... Vendor G0259

2687 **THE MERIWETHERS & THEIR CONNECTIONS. A FAM. RECORD GIVING THE GEN. OF THE MERIWETHERS IN AMERICA**, by L.H.A. Minor. 1892.
Cloth, $34.00. Paper, $24.00. 180pp. .... Vendor G0259

2688 **MERRIAM GEN. IN ENG. & AMER.**, by C. Pope. 1906.
Cloth, $89.50. Paper, $79.50. 515pp. .... Vendor G0259

2689 **GEN. OF THE MERRICK–MERICK–MYRICK FAM. OF MASS., 1636–1902**, by G. B. Merrick. 1902.
Cloth, $73.00. Paper, $63.00. 502pp. .... Vendor G0259

2690 **[Merrill]. GEN. PUBL. IN 1864, AS APPENDIX TO HIS BOOK "MY WIFE & MY MOTHER; ANC. OF FRANCES E. MERRILL & NAOMI HUMPHREY,"** by H. Barbour. 1885.
Paper. $16.00. 84pp. .... Vendor G0259

2691 **REUNION OF DESCENDANTS OF NATHANIEL MERRIMAN AT**

WALLINGFORD, CT., 1913, WITH A MERRIMAN GENEALOGY FOR FIVE GENERATIONS, by Donald L. Jacobus. 1914.
Cloth, $39.50. Paper, $29.50. 186pp. Vendor G0259

2692 [Merritt]. GENEALOGY OF THE SOMERSETSHIRE FAMILY OF MERIET [MERRITT], TRACED IN AN UNBROKEN LINE FROM THE REIGN OF THE CONFESSOR TO ITS EXTINCTION IN THE REIGN OF HENRY V, by B.W. Greenfield; rev. by D. Merritt. 1914.
Cloth, $34.00. Paper, $24.00. 131pp. Vendor G0259

2693 REVISED MERRITT REC., by D. Merritt. 1916.
Cloth, $43.50. Paper, $33.50. 204pp. Vendor G0259

2694 HENRY MERROW OF READING, MASS. & HIS DESC. NAMED MERROW, MARROW & MERRY, by O.E. Merrow. 1954.
Cloth, $108.00. Paper, $98.00. 659pp. . . . . Vendor G0259

2695 WALTER MERRYMAN OF HARPSWELL, MAINE, & HIS DESC., by C.N. Sinnett. 1905.
Paper. $17.50. 123pp. . . . . Vendor G0259

2696 MILES MERWIN, 1623–1697, & ONE BRANCH OF HIS DESC., by C.G. Newton. 1909.
Paper. $19.00. 105pp. . . . . Vendor G0259

2697 MILES MERWIN, 1772–1859; HIS ANC. & DESC., by C.G. Newton. 1903.
Paper. $17.50. 87pp. . . . . Vendor G0259

2698 MESICK GEN., by J.F. Mesick.
Paper. $10.00. 46pp. . . . . Vendor G0259

2699 GEN. OF THE DESC. OF CHRISTIAN & HANS MEYER (MOYER) & OTHER PIONEERS, by A.J. Fretz. 1896.
Cloth, $115.00. Paper, $105.00. 739pp. . . . . Vendor G0259

2700 GEN. OF THE MEYER FAM., by H. Meyer. 1890.
Paper. $19.50. 131pp. . . . . Vendor G0259

2701 LINEAGE OF THE CHRISTIAN MEYER FAMILY (NY, 1710), EXTR. "OLDE ULSTER," by T.B. Meyers.
Paper. $18.00. 94pp. . . . . Vendor G0259

2702 GEN. OF THE MICKLEY FAMILY OF AMER., WITH BRIEF GEN. REC. OF THE MICHELET FAM. OF METZ & SOME INTERESTING & VALUABLE CORRESPONDENCE, BIOGR. SKETCHES, OBITS. & HIST. MEM., by M. Mickley. 1893.
Cloth, $37.50. Paper, $27.50. 182pp. Vendor G0259

2703 REGISTER OF THE MIDDLEBROOK FAM., DESC. OF JOSEPH MIDDLEBROOK OF FAIRFIELD, CONN., by L.F. Middlebrook. 1909.
Cloth, $62.00. Paper, $52.00. 411pp. Vendor G0259

2704 MIEDEMA, HET MIEDEMA-BOEK ("THE MIEDEMA BOOK"); GENEALOGISH OVERZICHT VAN ALLE FRIESE GESLCHTEN MIEDEMA, DEEL I, by W.T. Vleer. IN FRISIAN. 1955.
Paper. $15.00. 96pp. . . . . Vendor G0259

2705 **ANNALS OF MILES ANC. IN PA. & STORY OF A FORGED WILL**, by C.H. Banes. 1895.
Cloth, $35.00. Paper, $25.00. 182pp. .... Vendor G0259

2706 **JOHN MILES OF CONCORD, MASS., & HIS DESC.**, by J.M. Miles. 1920.
Paper. $10.00. 48pp. .... Vendor G0259

2707 **HISTORY & GENEALOGY OF THE MILK–MILKS FAMILY**, by Grace Croft, et al. 1952.
Cloth, $57.00. Paper, $47.00. 308pp. .... Vendor G0259

2708 **THE DESCENDANTS OF AARON MILLEMAN OF KINGSTON, RHODE ISLAND**, by Carol R. Austin. 1994. Indexed. Illus.
Also includes **Milliman, Millemon, Millerman, Millermon, Ashworth, Bass, Bentley, Brown, Browning, Burnett, Clifford, Cobb, Harlan, Fidler, Geiger, Handley, Harlan, Jackson, Johnson, Kelly, Koontz, Lambert, Lyon, Mason, Matteson, McIntyre, Neilson, Owen, Saxon, Shockey, Shuck, Thomas, Williams**, and **Wright**.
Cloth. $60.00. 715pp. .... Vendor G0294

2709 **ADAM MILLER AND ANNA BARBARA KOGER FAMILY RECORD**, by Floyd R. Mason.
In process .... Vendor G0345

2710 **ALEXANDER MILLER AND JANE EVANS FAMILY RECORD**, by Floyd R. Mason.
In process .... Vendor G0345

2711 **ANC. OF SARAH MILLER OF ME.**, by W. Davis. 1939.
Paper. $17.50. 93pp. .... Vendor G0259

2712 **DESC. OF CAPT. JOSEPH MILLER OF WEST SPRINGFIELD, MASS., 1698–1908**, by C.S. Williams. 1908.
Paper. $8.00. 39pp. .... Vendor G0259

2713 **HIST. & GEN. OF THE FAM. OF MILLER, WOODS, HARRIS, WALLACE, MAUPIN, OLDHAM, KAVANAUGH & BROWN, & OTHERS**, by W.H. Miller. 1906.
Cloth, $128.00. Paper, $118.00. 855pp. .... Vendor G0259

2714 **JOHN CLARENCE CALHOUN MILLER FAMILY, AN APPENDIX TO SKETCH OF MILLER & CALHOUN–MILLER FAMILIES (1927)**, by M. Miller Hayes. 1961.
Paper. $11.00. 56pp. .... Vendor G0259

2715 **MATTHIAS MILLER AND HIS 17 CHILDREN**, by Floyd R. Mason.
In process .... Vendor G0345

2716 **MICHAEL MILLER FAMILY RECORD**, by Floyd R. Mason. 1993. Indexed. Illus.
Immigrant Michael **Miller** and Susanna **Bechtol** of PA & MD, and their 10 children are carried through 11 generations.
Cloth. $49.50. 1,003pp. .... Vendor G0345

2717 **MICHAEL MILLER OF 1692**, by Floyd R. Mason. 1986. Indexed.
Paper. $4.00. 25pp. .... Vendor G0345

2718 **MILLER FAMILY: AN ADDRESS DELIVERED BEFORE THE MILLER REUNION AT NO. WALDOBORO, MAINE, SEPT. 7, 1904, WITH GENEALOGY**, by Frank B. Miller. 1909.
Paper. $10.00. 47pp. .... Vendor G0259

2719 **MILLER FAMILY: DESC. OF FRANK MILLER, WHO SETTLED IN WALDOBOROUGH, MA (NOW ME.) IN 1753**, by F.B. Miller. 1934.
Cloth, $47.00. Paper, $37.00. 174pp. .... Vendor G0259

2720 **THE DAVID AND ANNA MILLER STORY**, by Arlene Huss, Winifred Paul, Florence Stauffer, et al. 1979.
Cloth. $12.00. 430pp. .... Vendor G0150

2721 **THE DIARIES OF JOHN M. MILLER OF WESTWOOD/CINCINNATI, OHIO: EXCERPTS FROM 1869–1870 AND 1881–1894**, compiled by Susan R. Alexander. 1993. Indexed. Illus.
John M. **Miller** (1822–1894) was the son of Mary (**Ludlow**) and George Carter **Miller**. His wife was the former Huldah Woodhull **Nicholas**, daughter of Sarah (**Woodhull**) and Elias **Nicholas**. Huldah and John Miller had 13 children. John Miller's diaries reflect his busy life as a devoted family man, staunch Presbyterian, carriage-manufacturing company president, and involved citizen. His first-person account vividly evokes the horse-and-buggy days of late 19th-century Westwood (where he lived) and Cincinnati (where he worked).
Other frequently mentioned surnames include **Applegate, Bruce, Burnham, Davis, Drake, Ernst, Gamble, Gibson, Glasby, Hazen, Hedges, Hinsch, Kugler, Lawrence, Logan, McMicken, Moore, Mussey, Oehlman, Peterson, Powell, Ricketts, Rowland, Sanders, Sayre, Walker, Ward, Williams, Wilson**, and **Wise**.
Besides the 34-page name index, supplementary material consists of pictures of people, carriages, and buildings; maps; family notes and charts; and a table of notable events and items.
Cloth. $54.95. 634pp. .... Vendor G0028

2722 **THE MILLERS OF MILLERBURG & THEIR DESC.**, by J.B. Nicklin Jr. 1923.
Cloth, $89.50. Paper, $79.50. 514pp. .... Vendor G0259

2723 **[Milliken]. HIST. OF THE FAMS. MILLINGAS & MILLANGES OF SAXONY & NORMANDY, GEN. & BIOGR. OF THEIR POSTERITY SURNAMED MILLIKEN, MILLIKIN, ETC., 800–1907**, by G.T. Ridlon. 1907.
Cloth, $116.00. Paper, $106.00. 882pp. .... Vendor G0259

2724 **THE DESCENDANTS OF JOHN MILLIMAN OF KINGSTON, RHODE ISLAND**, by Carol R. Austin. 1994. Indexed. Illus.
Other families included: **Baker, Barlow, Brookhiser, Burdue, Carlton, Coburn, DeForest, Dobbin, Ellis, Fox, Goodell, Hart, Heath, Kellogg, Mansfield, Owen, Smith, Strong**, and **Whaley**. Also includes some unconnected **Milliman** families and families of later Milliman immigrants.
Cloth. $55.00. 723pp. .... Vendor G0294

2725 **MILLIS & ALLIED FAM.**, by F. Millis. 1944.
Paper. $12.50. 64pp. .... Vendor G0259

2726 **ANDREW MILLS & HIS DESCENDANTS, WITH GENEALOGIES OF RELATED FAMILIES,** by E.M.L. Taylor. 1944.
Cloth, $33.00. Paper, $23.00. 150pp. .... Vendor G0259

2727 **FAM. OF CAPT. JOHN MILLS OF MEDWAY & SHERBURN, MA., & AMHERST, N.H.,** by W.C. Hill. 1942.
Cloth, $31.00. Paper, $21.00. 136pp. .... Vendor G0259

2728 **MILLS FAM. MARRIAGES,** by W.M. Clemens. 1916.
Paper. $10.00. 52pp. .... Vendor G0259

2729 **THE MILLS, COPE & RELATED FAMILIES OF GA.,** by T.H. and J.H. Goddard, Sr. 1962.
Cloth, $61.00. Paper, $51.00. 326pp. .... Vendor G0259

2730 **DESCENDANTS OF JOHN MINEAR (1732?–1781),** by C.J. Maxwell. 1948.
Cloth, $46.50. Paper, $36.50. 232pp. .... Vendor G0259

2731 **ONE BRANCH OF THE MINER FAM., WITH EXTENSIVE NOTES ON THE WOOD, LOUNSBERRY, ROGERS & 50 OTHER ALLIED FAM. OF CONN. & L.I.,** by L.M. Selleck. 1928.
Cloth, $51.00. Paper, $41.00. 275pp. .... Vendor G0259

2732 **DESCENDANTS OF DOODES MINOR OF VIRGINIA,** by Carol A. Hauk. 1995. Indexed.
Paper. $30.00. 126pp. .... Vendor G0340

2733 **A GEN. RECORD OF THE MINOT FAM. IN AMER. & ENG.,** by J.G. Minot. 1897.
Paper. $10.50. 55pp. .... Vendor G0259

2734 **DESCENDANTS OF JOHN MITCHELL OF DRUMORE TOWNSHIP, LANCASTER COUNTY, PENNSYLVANIA, 2 VOLS.,** by Warren A. Brannon. 1991. Indexed.
Make checks payable to John Mitchell Family Assoc.
Surnames: **Alexander, Clark, Finney, Henderson, Jordan, McCullough, Mitchell, Pickens, Porter, Theaker, Shoff.**
Cloth. $45.00. 1,247pp. .... Vendor G0321

2735 **MITCHELL FAMILY RECORDS,** by J.M. Seaver.
Paper. $8.00. 41pp. .... Vendor G0259

2736 **THE MITCHELL RECORD,** by C.B. Mitchell. 1925.
Cloth, $37.00. Paper, $27.00. 183pp. .... Vendor G0259

2737 **MOFFATANA BULLETIN, GEN. NOTES ON MOFFAT.** 1907–15.
Paper. $9.00. 44pp. .... Vendor G0259

2738 **LUDWIG MOHLER & HIS DESC. 1696–1921,** by C.G. Dunning. 1921.
Paper. $12.50. 63pp. .... Vendor G0259

2739 **HIST., GEN., & BIOGR. OF THE MOLYNEUX FAM.,** by N.Z. Molyneux. 1904.
Cloth, $68.00. Paper, $58.00. 370pp. .... Vendor G0259

2740 **MONCURE. EXTR. FROM "VA. GENS."**
Paper. $8.00. 40pp. .... Vendor G0259

2741 **NOTES ON THE MONGOLD FAMILY OF ROCKINGHAM COUNTY, VA AND HARDY COUNTY, WV**, by Lewis H. Yankey. 1995. Indexed. Paper. $14.00. 84pp. .... Vendor G0365

2742 **MONNET FAM. GEN., AN EMPHASIS OF A NOBLE HUGUENOT HERITAGE, SOMEWHAT OF THE FIRST IMMIG., ISAAC & PIERRE MONNET**, by O.E. Monnette. 1911.
Cloth, $179.00. Paper, $169.00. 1,245pp. .... Vendor G0259

2743 **THE MONROE BOOK. The History of the Munro Clan from its Origins in Scotland to Settlement in New England and Migration to the West 1652–1850 and Beyond**, by Joan S. Guilford, Ph.D. 1993. Indexed.
Cloth. $44.00. xvii+877pp. .... Vendor G0223

2744 **THE PORTSMOUTH, N.H. RACE OF MONSONS, MUNSONS, MANSONS; RICHARD MONSON & DESC.**, by M.A. Munson. 1910.
Paper. $18.50. 89pp. .... Vendor G0259

2745 **HIST. & GEN. OF PETER MONTAGUE, OF NANSEMOND & LANCASTER COS., VA., & HIS DESC., 1621–1894**, by G.W. Montague. 1894.
Cloth, $87.00. Paper, $77.00. 494pp. .... Vendor G0259

2746 **HIST. & GEN. OF THE MONTAGUE FAM. OF AMER., DESC. FROM RICHARD MONTAGUE OF HADLEY, MASS., & PETER OF LANCASTER CO., VA., WITH GEN. NOTES OF OTHER FAMS. BY NAME OF MONTAGUE**, compiled by G.W. and W.L. Montague. 1886.
Cloth, $127.50. Paper, $117.50. 785pp. .... Vendor G0259

2747 **MEETING OF THE MONTAGUE FAM. AT HADLEY, MASS., 1882**, edited by R. Montague. 1882.
Paper. $19.00. 107pp. .... Vendor G0259

2748 **A GEN. HISTORY OF THE MONTGOMERYS & THEIR DESCEN-DANTS**, by D.B. Montgomery. 1903.
Cloth, $77.50. Paper, $67.50. 436pp. .... Vendor G0259

2749 **GEN. HIST. OF THE FAM. OF MONTGOMERY, INCL. THE PEDI-GREE CHART**, by T.H. Montgomery. 1863.
Cloth, $45.00. Paper, $35.00. 170pp. .... Vendor G0259

2750 **ORIGIN & HIST. OF THE MONTGOMERYS: COMTES DE MONT-GOMERY, PONTHIEU, ALENCON & LAMARCHE; EARLS OF ARUNDEL, CHICHESTER, SHREWSBURY, ET AL. [ABOUT FAM. IN EUROPE]**, By B.G. de Montgomery.
Cloth, $57.50. Paper, $47.50. 303pp. .... Vendor G0259

2751 **THE MONTGOMERY GEN. (DESC. OF ELIAS)**, by C.G. Hurlburt. 1926.
Paper. $13.50. 66pp. .... Vendor G0259

2752 **MOOAR (MOORS) GEN. ABRAHAM MOOAR OF ANDOVER & HIS DESC.**, by G. Mooar. 1901.
Paper. $19.00. 97pp. .... Vendor G0259

2753 **FAMILY ALBUM: AN ACCT. OF THE MOODS OF CHARLESTON, S.C. & CONNECTED FAMILIES**, by T.McA. Stubbs. 1943.
Cloth, $49.50. Paper, $39.50. 246pp. .... Vendor G0259

2754 **DESCENDANTS OF LEVI MOODY & REBECCA WAGES (b. 1801, DARLINGTON CO. SC & b. 1811, SC),** by Chaplain Dan Franklin. 1993. Cloth, $51.00. Paper, $41.00. 247pp. Vendor G0259

2755 **DESCENDANTS OF ENSIGN JOHN MOOR OF CANTERBURY, N.H., b. 1696–d. 1786,** by H.P. Moore. 1918. Cloth, $67.00. Paper, $57.00. 370pp. Vendor G0259

2756 **ANCESTORS & DESCENDANTS OF ANDREW MOORE, 1612–1897,** by J.A.M. Passmore. 2 vols. 1897. Cloth, $189.00. Paper, $179.00. 1,599pp. . . . . Vendor G0259

2757 **ANCESTRY OF SHARPLESS & RACHEL (ROBERTS) MOORE, WITH THEIR DIRECT ANC., TO & INCL. 36 FIRST OR IMMIGRANT ANC., WITH SOME OLD WORLD PEDIGREES & ORIGINS & DIRECT DESC.,** by B.M. Haines. 1937. Cloth, $43.50. Paper, $33.50. 214pp. Vendor G0259

2758 **MEMORIAL OF RANSOM BALDWIN MOORE & ALLIED FAMS.,** by W.B. Towne. 1920. Cloth, $32.50. Paper, $22.50. 138pp. Vendor G0259

2759 **MOORE AND ALLIED FAMS.: ANC. OF WM. HENRY MOORE,** by L.E. and A.L. de Forst. 1938. Cloth, $103.00. Paper, $93.00. 744pp. Vendor G0259

2760 **MOORE FAMILY HISTORY, 1599–1962,** by A.L. Moore. 1962. Paper. $8.50. 42pp. . . . . Vendor G0259

2761 **MOORE FAMILY RECORDS,** by J.M. Seaver. Paper. $17.50. 89pp. . . . . Vendor G0259

2762 **REV. JOHN MOORE OF NEWTOWN, L.I., & SOME OF HIS DESC.,** by J.W. Moore. 1903. Cloth, $78.00. Paper, $68.00. 541pp. Vendor G0259

2763 **MORAGNES IN AMERICA AND RELATED FAMILIES,** by Nell H. Howard and Bessie W. Quinn. 1973. Indexed.
A detailed history of the Moragne families descended from Pierre **Moragne** and Cecile **Bayle** who came from France to the Abbeville District, South Carolina prior to the Revolution. Surviving part of Pierre's diary included. Related families are: **Williams**—England to Rappahannock County, Virginia 1650; **Quarles**—King William County, Virginia 1695; **Read**—Virginia 1704; **Whorton**—Hall County, Georgia ca. 1800 (Mike Whorton, Attalla, Alabama has traced this line to the first Lord **Wharton**, England); **Fulgham**—Virginia; **Wilson**—Etowah County, Alabama; **Young**—Lincolnton County, North Carolina 1777; **Sutherlin**—South Carolina 1787; **Forney**—Alsace, France 1721; Pennsylvania and North Carolina 1754; **Abernathy**—Abernathy, Scotland 13th century, Charles City County, Virginia 1655; **Hughes**—North Carolina 1840; **Thayer**—Gloucestershire, England 13th century, Boston 1640; **Fortune**—Kentucky 1798; **Hodges**—Essex County, Virginia 1756, South Carolina 1763; **Howard**—North Carolina 1730, New Jersey 1777; **Yeilding**—North Carolina 1705, Blount County, Alabama 1800s; **Hillsman**—Amelia County, Virginia 1760; **Mynatt**—England 1727, Fauquier County, Virginia 1771; **Burns**—North Carolina 1780; **Dobbins**—Granville County, North Carolina 1740, South Carolina York District 1785.

Most of these families have been followed as they scattered over the 50 states. 62 pages of index.
Cloth. $20.00. 566pp. .... Vendor G0168

2764 **DESCENDANTS OF FRANKLIN PEIRCE MORAN & MARY ADELAIDE SNYDER MORAN, WITH FAMILY TREE OF EARLY MORAN ANCESTORS (FROM HEZEKIA OF MONTGOMERY CO. MD.)**, by Evelyn Brown, Opal Sikes, and Max Moran. 1991.
Cloth, $69.00. Paper, $59.00. 373pp. .... Vendor G0259

2765 **MORAN FAMILY: 200 YEARS IN DETROIT**, by J.B. Moran. 1949.
Cloth, $38.00. Paper, $28.00. 152+32pp. .... Vendor G0259

2766 **CHRONICLES OF THE MORE FAMILY**, edited by Grace Van Dyke More. 1955.
Cloth, $73.50. Paper, $63.50. 424pp. .... Vendor G0259

2767 **HISTORY OF THE MORE FAMILY, & AN ACCOUNT OF THEIR RE-UNION IN 1890, WITH A GENEALOGICAL RECORD**, by David Fellows More. 1893.
Cloth, $73.00. Paper, $63.00. 409pp. .... Vendor G0259

2768 **ANC. & DESC. OF GERSHOM MOREHOUSE, JR., OF REDDING, CONN., A CAPT. IN THE AMER. REV.**, by C. Morehouse.
Paper. $8.00. 40pp. .... Vendor G0259

2769 **MOREHEAD FAMILY OF N. CARO. & VA.**, by J. Morehead. 1921.
Cloth, $34.00. Paper, $24.00. 147pp. .... Vendor G0259

2770 **GEN. OF ONE BRANCH OF MOREY FAM. 1631–1890**, by E.W. Leavitt. 1890.
Paper. $7.50. 36pp. .... Vendor G0259

2771 **A HIST. OF THAT BRANCH OF THE MORGAN FAM. BEGINNING WITH JAMES OF NEW LONDON, THROUGH LINE OF COL. SAM'L & SYBIL HUNTINGTON MORGAN OF WEATHERSFIELD, VT. TO 1911**, by C.W. Morgan. 1911.
Paper. $15.00. 93+7pp. .... Vendor G0259

2772 **A HISTORY OF THE DESCENDANTS OF HENRY OSCAR MORGAN & ELLEN JANE MANDIGO**, by James K. Raywalt. 1991.
Cloth, $39.00. Paper, $29.00. 203pp. .... Vendor G0259

2773 **FAM. OF MORGAN, STANLEY & BLATCHLEY**, by A.S. Blatchley. 1929.
Paper. $8.50. 43pp. .... Vendor G0259

2774 **"LIMBUS PATRUM MORGANIAE AT GLAMORGANIAE": GEN. OF THE OLDER FAMS. OF LORDSHIPS MORGAN & GLARMORGAN**, by G.T. Clark. 1886.
Cloth, $89.00. Paper, $79.00. 620pp. .... Vendor G0259

2775 **MORGAN GEN. A HIST. OF JAMES MORGAN OF NEW LONDON, CONN., & HIS DESC., 1607–1869. WITH AN APPENDIX CONTAINING THE HIST. OF MILES OF SPRINGFIELD, MA., & SOME OF HIS DESC.**, by N.H. Morgan. 1869.
Cloth, $52.00. Paper, $42.00. 281pp. .... Vendor G0259

2776 **THE ANC. OF DANIEL MORRELL OF HARTFORD, WITH HIS DESC. & SOME CONTEMPORARY FAM.**, by F.V. Morrell. 1916.
Cloth, $31.00. Paper, $21.00. 132pp. .... Vendor G0259

2777 **MORRILL KINDRED IN AMER. AN ACCT. OF THE DESC. OF ABRAHAM MORRILL OF SALISBURY, MASS., 1632–1662**, by A.M. Smith. 2 vols. 1914–1931.
Cloth, $99.00. Paper, $89.00. 132pp. .... Vendor G0259

2778 **A GEN. & HIST. REG. OF THE DESC. OF EDW. MORRIS OF ROXBURY, MASS., AND WOODSTOCK, CONN.**, by J.F. Morris. 1887.
Cloth, $76.50. Paper, $66.50. 423pp. .... Vendor G0259

2779 **EPHRAIM & PAMELA (CONVERSE) MORRIS, THEIR ANC. & DESC.**, by T.S. Morris. 1894.
Cloth, $41.00. Paper, $31.00. 207pp. .... Vendor G0259

2780 **MEM. OF THE DESC. OF AMOS MORRIS OF EAST HAVEN, CONN.**, by E. Hart and O. Street. 1853.
Paper. $19.00. 103pp. .... Vendor G0259

2781 **MORRIS FAM. OF PHILA.; DESC. OF ANTHONY MORRIS, 1654–1721**, by R.C. Moon. 3 vols. 1898.
Cloth, $71.00/vol. Paper, $61.00/vol. 1,257pp. .... Vendor G0259

2782 **MORRIS FAM. OF PHILA. (1ST SUPPL.). Vol. IV.** 1908.
Cloth, $48.00. Paper, $38.00. 210pp. .... Vendor G0259

2783 **MORRIS FAM. OF PHILA. (2ND SUPPL.). Vol. V.** 1909.
Cloth, $59.00. Paper, $49.00. 295pp. .... Vendor G0259

2784 **MORRIS GENEALOGY**, by J.M. Seaver.
Paper. $10.00. 51pp. .... Vendor G0259

2785 **[Morrison]. HIST. OF THE MORISON OR MORRISON FAM.; A COMPLETE HIST. OF MOST SETTLERS OF LONDONDERRY, NH, OF 1719 & THEIR DESC., WITH GEN. SKETCHES, [ALSO OTHER N.H. MORISONS], & BRANCHES OF MORISONS OF DEL., PA., VA. & NOVA SCOTIA**, by L.A. Morrison. 1880.
Cloth, $69.50. Paper, $59.50. 468pp. .... Vendor G0259

2786 **THE JOHNSTON & BACON SCOTTISH CLAN HISTORIES: The Clan Morrison**, by Alick Morrison. (1956) reprint 1993. Illus.
Paper. $8.95. 32pp. .... Vendor G0011

2787 **THE MORRISONS—THEY CAME TO THE LAND THAT HUDGIN DRAINS**, by Glenn Hamilton Morrison. 1994. Indexed. Illus.
Georgia, Arkansas **Morrisons. Harper's, Dabney's, McClatchy's**. 16 pages old Morrison clan stories from Scotland.
Paper. $22.00. 200pp. .... Vendor G0381

2788 **ALEXANDER MORROW (1745–1817) OF BROOKE COUNTY (W)VIRGINIA AND HIS DESCENDANTS**, by Anne Morrow Nees. 1993. Indexed. Illus.
Allied names: **Morehead, Aten, Armstrong, Cameron, Elliott, Forsha, Karr, Lindbergh, Lockard, Owings, Swearingen**. Left northern Ireland with wife and seven children in 1793 and settled in northern Virginia Panhandle. Ten generations: maps, charts, documents, photos.
Cloth. $37.00. 475pp. .... Vendor G0025

2789 **THE PIONEER WRITINGS OF JOSIAH MORROW**, by Josiah Morrow; compiled & edited by Dallas R. Bogan. 1993. Indexed.
Paper. $17.90. 275pp. .... Vendor G0335

2790 **MEMORIAL OF THE FAM. OF MORSE**, by H.D. Lord. 1896.
Cloth, $97.00. Paper, $87.00. 556pp. .... Vendor G0259

2791 **MORSE GEN.; REV. OF THE MEM. OF THE MORSE FAM., BY ABNER MORSE, 1850**, by Morse and Leavitt. 2 vols. 1903–1905.
Cloth, $100.00. Paper, $90.00. 596pp. .... Vendor G0259

2792 **GENEALOGY OF THE MORTON FAMILY, WITH RELATED GENE-ALOGIES**, by W.M. Morton. 1930.
Paper. $9.00. 47pp. .... Vendor G0259

2793 **GEORGE MORTON OF PLYMOUTH COL. & SOME OF HIS DESC.**, by J.K. Allen. 1908.
Paper. $10.00. 46pp. .... Vendor G0259

2794 **MEM. RELATING TO THE ANC. & FAM. OF HON. LEVI PARSONS MORTON, V.P. OF THE U.S. (1889–1893)**, by J.G. Leach. 1894.
Cloth, $41.50. Paper, $31.50. 198pp. .... Vendor G0259

2795 **MORTON FAM. RECORD FROM 1668–1881 (SETTLED HATFIELD, MASS.)**, by C. Morton. 1881.
Paper. $10.00. 48pp. .... Vendor G0259

2796 **THE MORTONS & THEIR KIN: A GENEALOGY AND A SOURCE BOOK**, by D. Morton. 1920.
Cloth, $129.00. Paper, $119.00. 899pp. .... Vendor G0259

2797 **THE STEM OF MORTON: COLLECTION OF GENEALOGICAL NOTES RESPECTING THE FAMILY OF MORTON, CHIEFLY SEATED IN THE WAPENTAKE OF STRAFFORD-CUM-TICKHILL, S. YORK-SHIRE**, by W. Morton. 1895 (London).
Cloth, $57.50. Paper, $47.50. 311pp. .... Vendor G0259

2798　**GEN. OF MOSELEY FAM., SKETCH OF ONE BRANCH**, by E.S. Moseley. 1878.
Paper. $11.50. 56pp. .... Vendor G0259

2799　**HIST. SKETCHES OF JOHN MOSES OF PLYMOUTH, PORTSMOUTH, WINDSOR & SIMSBURY**, by Z. Moses. 1890.
Cloth, $33.50. Paper, $23.50. 138pp. .... Vendor G0259

2800　**HIST. SKETCHES OF JOHN MOSES OF PLYMOUTH, JOHN MOSES OF WINDSOR, & SIMSBURY, & JOHN MOSES OF PORTSMOUTH, ALSO A GEN. RECORD OF SOME OF THEIR DESC.**, by Z. Moses. 1890–1907.
Cloth, $54.50. Paper, $44.50. 298pp. .... Vendor G0259

2801　**ORIG. & HIST. OF MOSHER FAM., & GEN. OF ONE BRANCH OF THE FAM., 1660–1898**, by W. Mosher. 1898.
Paper. $10.00. 44pp. .... Vendor G0259

2802　**ANC. & DESC. OF ADAM & ANNE MOTT**, by T. Cornell. 1890.
Cloth, $49.00. Paper, $39.00. 419pp. .... Vendor G0259

2803　**JAMES MOTT OF DUTCHESS CO., N.Y., & HIS DESC.**, by E.D. Harris. 1911.
Paper. $12.50. 62pp. .... Vendor G0259

2804　**A GEN. REGISTER OF SOME OF THE DESC. OF JOHN MOULTON OF HAMPTON, & OF JOSEPH OF PORTSMOUTH**, by T. Moulton. 1873.
Paper. $9.00. 44pp. .... Vendor G0259

2805　**HIST. OF THE MOULTON FAM. REC. OF THE DESC. OF JAMES MOULTON OF SALEM & WENHAM, MA., 1629 TO 1905**, by E. and H. Moulton. 1905.
Paper. $11.00. 56pp. .... Vendor G0259

2806　**MOULTON ANNALS**, by H.W. Moulton, edited by C. Moulton. 1906.
Cloth, $80.00. Paper, $70.00. 454pp. .... Vendor G0259

2807　**SOME DESC. OF JOHN & WILLIAM MOULTON OF HAMPTON, N.H., 1592–1892**, by A.F. Moulton. 1892.
Paper. $19.00. 99pp. .... Vendor G0259

2808　**HISTORY & GEN. RECORD OF THE MOUNT & FLIPPIN FAMS.**, by J.A. Mount. 1954.
Cloth, $31.00. Paper, $21.00. 120pp. .... Vendor G0259

2809　**MOWER FAM. HIST.; A GEN. REC. OF THE MAINE BRANCH OF THIS FAM.**, by W.L. Mower. 1923.
Cloth, $47.50. Paper, $37.50. 251pp. .... Vendor G0259

2810　**A FAM. HIST. RICHARD MOWRY OF UXBRIDGE, MASS.; HIS ANC. & HIS DESC.**, by W.A. Mowry. 1878.
Cloth, $46.00. Paper, $36.00. 239pp. .... Vendor G0259

2811　**DESC. OF JOHN MOWRY OF RI**, by W.A. Mowry. 1909.
Cloth, $54.00. Paper, $44.00. 292pp. .... Vendor G0259

2812 **DESC. OF NATHANIEL MOWRY OF RI**, by W. Mowry. 1878.
Cloth, $64.50. Paper, $54.50. 343pp. .... Vendor G0259

2813 **DESC. OF NATHANIEL MOWRY OF R.I.; SUPPL.** 1900.
Paper. $19.00. 95pp. .... Vendor G0259

2814 **MUDGE MEM.: BEING A GEN., BIOGR. & HIST. ACCT. OF THE NAME OF MUDGE IN AMER., 1638 TO 1868**, by A. Mudge. 1868.
Cloth, $66.00. Paper, $56.00. 457pp. .... Vendor G0259

2815 **THE MUELLER–MENKEL FAMILY GENEALOGY**, by Carl W. Troyer. 1994.
Major families: **Mueller, Schulte, Troyer, Bargman, Hagen, Zeller, Peterson, Yoder, Martin**.
Hardbound. $25.00. 127pp. .... Vendor G0378

2816 **DESCENDANTS OF NOAH & MARGARET CROSBY MULLIN: A SCRAPBOOK FAMILY HISTORY**, by Ann Mullin Burton. 1994. Indexed. Illus.
Paper. $17.00. 205pp. .... Vendor G0094

2817 **MUMFORD MEM.: BEING THE STORY OF THE NEW ENG. MUMFORDS FROM THE YEAR 1655 TO THE PRESENT TIME**, by J.G. Mumford. 1900.
Cloth, $52.00. Paper, $42.00. 279pp. .... Vendor G0259

2818 **DESCENDANTS OF FRANCIS MUNCY I, WITH GENEALOGY OF ALLIED FAMILIES**, by M.E. Shaw. Rev. ed. 1956.
Cloth, $59.50. Paper, $49.50. 357pp. .... Vendor G0259

2819 **NICHOLAS MUNDY & DESC. WHO SETTLED IN N.J. IN 1665**, by E.F. Mundy. 1907.
Cloth, $34.50. Paper, $24.50. 160pp. .... Vendor G0259

2820 **MUNGER BOOK; SOMETHING OF MUNGERS, 1639–1914, INCL. SOME WHO MISTAKENLY WRITE THE NAME MONGER & MONGOR**, by J.B. Munger. 1915.
Cloth, $106.00. Paper, $96.00. 634pp. .... Vendor G0259

2821 **HISTORY OF THE MUNROS OF FOWLIS, WITH GEN. OF THE PRINCIPAL FAMS. OF THE NAME, TO WHICH ARE ADDED THOSE OF LEXINGTON (MASS.) & NEW ENG.**, by A. MacKenzie. 1908 (Scotland).
Cloth, $105.00. Paper, $95.00. 632pp. .... Vendor G0259

2822 **SKETCH OF THE MUNRO CLAN; ALSO OF WILLIAM MUNRO WHO, DEPORTED FROM SCOTLAND, SETTLED IN LEXINGTON, MASS., & SOME OF HIS POSTERITY**, by J.P. Munroe. 1900.
Paper. $16.00. 80pp. .... Vendor G0259

2823 **THE JOHNSTON & BACON SCOTTISH CLAN HISTORIES: The Clan Munro**, by Charles Ian Fraser. (1954) reprint 1993. Illus.
Paper. $8.95. 32pp. .... Vendor G0011

2824 **A GEN. OF THE MUNSELL FAM. (MUNSILL, MONSELL, MAUNSELL) IN AMERICA**, by F. Munsell. 1884.
Cloth, $31.50. Paper, $21.50. 130pp. .... Vendor G0259

2825 **[Munsell]. AN HIST. & GEN. ACCT. OF THE ANCIENT FAM. OF MAUNSELL–MANSELL–MANSEL**, by W.W. Mansell. 1850 (London). Paper. $17.50. 88pp. .... Vendor G0259

2826 **MUNSEY–HOPKINS GEN., BEING THE ANC. OF ANDREW CHAUNCEY MUNSEY & MARY JANE MERRILL HOPKINS**, by D.O.S. Lowell. 1920. Cloth, $46.00. Paper, $36.00. 233pp. .... Vendor G0259

2827 **MUNSON RECORD, 1637–1887. GEN. & BIOGR. ACCT. OF CAPT. THOMAS MUNSON (PIONEER OF HARTFORD & NEW HAVEN) & HIS DESC.**, by M. Munson. 2 vols. 1895. Cloth, $179.00. Paper, $169.00. 1,263pp. .... Vendor G0259

2828 **MURDOCK GENEALOGY. ROBERT MURDOCK OF ROXBURY, MASS., & SOME OF HIS DESCENDANTS, WITH NOTES ON THE DESCENDANTS OF JOHN MUNRO OF PLYMOUTH; GEO. MURDOCK OF PLAINFIELD, CT.; PETER MURDOCK OF SAYBROOK, CT.; WM. MURDOCK OF PHILADELPHIA, & OTHERS**, by Jos. B. Murdock. 1925. Cloth, $54.00. Paper, $44.00. 274pp. .... Vendor G0259

2829 **MURPHY FAM.; GEN., HIST., & BIOGR., WITH OFFICIAL STATS. OF THE PART PLAYED BY MEMBERS OF THIS NUMEROUS FAM. IN THE MAKING & MAINTENANCE OF THIS GREAT AMER. RE-PUBLIC**, by M.W. Downes. 1909. Cloth, $67.50. Paper, $57.50. 363pp. .... Vendor G0259

2830 **MURRAY–CONWELL GENEALOGY & ALLIED FAMILIES**, by M.L. Lawrence and G.L. Lombard. 1938. Paper. $19.50. 115pp. .... Vendor G0259

2831 **THE DESC. OF JONATHAN MURRAY OF E. GUILFORD, CONN.**, by W.B. Murray. 1956. Cloth, $71.50. Paper, $61.50. 385pp. .... Vendor G0259

2832 **NOTES ON THE ANCIENT FAMILY OF MUSGRAVE OF MUSGRAVE, WESTMORLAND [ENGLAND], & ITS VARIOUS BRANCHES IN CUMBERLAND, YORKSHIRE, NORTHUMBERLAND, ETC.**, by Percy Musgrave. 1911 (England). Cloth, $59.50. Paper, $49.50. 351pp. .... Vendor G0259

2833 **GENEALOGY OF JOHN AND SUSANNA (WEBER) MUSSER FAMILY**, by Elmer L. Musser. 1980. Cloth. $19.00. 496pp. .... Vendor G0150

2834 **MYERS FAMILY HISTORY, 1717–1989**, by Clara W. Martin and Clara M. Martin. 1989. Cloth. $10.50. 89pp. .... Vendor G0150

2835 **MYERS HISTORY: SOME DESCENDANTS OF HANS MEIER OF PEQUEA, LANCASTER COUNTY, PENNSYLVANIA**, by Dorothy M.K. Adams. 1987. Cloth. $30.50. 222pp. .... Vendor G0150

2836 **HIST. NOTICE OF JOSEPH MYGATT OF CAMBRIDGE, WITH A RECORD OF HIS DESC.**, by F.T. Mygatt. 1853.
Cloth, $30.00. Paper, $20.00. 116pp. .... Vendor G0259

2837 **MYLIN [FAMILY HISTORY]**, by Doris E. Mylin Biechler. 1988.
Paper. $21.00. 95pp. .... Vendor G0150

2838 **JOACHIM NAGEL AND HIS DESCENDANTS**, by Marion Nagle Rhoads and Janet Snyder Welsh. 1990. Indexed. Illus.
This history begins before 1627 in Isenburg, Germany and traces the family from 1749 in Pennsylvania to the present. Other names include **Boyer, Buehler, Coleman, Dreisbach, McCardell, Old, Webb, Withington, Youngman**.
Cloth. $30.00. 295pp. .... Vendor G0251

2839 **[Nash]. FIFTY PURITAN ANC., 1628–1660; GEN. NOTES, 1560–1900**, by E.T. Nash. 1902.
Cloth, $33.00. Paper, $23.00. 194pp. .... Vendor G0259

2840 **NASH FAM., OR RECORDS OF THE DESC. OF THOMAS NASH OF NEW HAVEN, CT., 1640**, by S. Nash. 1853.
Cloth, $58.50. Paper, $48.50. 304pp. .... Vendor G0259

2841 **NAVARRE. OR, RESEARCHES AFTER THE DESC. OF ROBERT NAVARRE, WHOSE ANC. ARE THE NOBLE BOURBONS OF FRANCE, & SOME HIST. NOTES ON FAMS. INTERMARRIED WITH NAVARRES**, by C. Denissen. 1897.
Cloth, $76.00. Paper, $66.00. 418pp. .... Vendor G0259

2842 **ANC. OF JOSEPH NEAL, 1769–C.1835, OF LITCHFIELD, ME., INCL. HALL, WHITE, ROGERS, TILDEN, TWISDEN, CLAPP, WRIGHT, FORD, HATCH & HOLBROOK LINES FROM MASS.**, by W.G. Davis. 1945.
Cloth, $33.50. Paper, $23.50. 145pp. .... Vendor G0259

2843 **THE NEAL NAME BOOK—NAIL, NAILLE . . . NIEL, NULL**, by Lois G. Harvey. (1985) reprint 1995. Indexed.
Paper. $10.00. 89pp. .... Vendor G0260

2844 **CHARTER & RECORDS OF NEALES OF BERKLEY, YATE & CORSHAM [ENGLAND]**, by John A. Neale. 1906 (England).
Cloth, $51.00. Paper, $41.00. 263pp. .... Vendor G0259

2845 **SOME NEBLETTS IN AMERICA**, by Dorothy Neblett Perkins. 1994. Indexed. Illus.
Allied lines: **Bon Durant, Barbee, Hurd, Heard, Hightower, Harrison**, and **Wyatt**.
Cloth. $43.00. 787pp. .... Vendor G0375

Dr. Frank L. & Odette J. Kaufman
2794 Hyannis Way
Sacramento CA 95827
Northern California

2846 **NEEDHAMS OF WALES, MASS., & STAFFORD, CONN.**, by G.O. Chapman. 1942.
Cloth, $30.00. Paper, $20.00. 93pp. .... Vendor G0259

2847 **[Neff]. A CHRONICLE, TOGETHER WITH A LITTLE ROMANCE, REGARDING RUDOLF & JACOB NAF, OF FRANKFORD, PENN., & THEIR DESC., INCL. AN ACCT. OF THE NEFFS IN SWITZERLAND & AMERICA**, by E.C. Neff. 1886.
Cloth, $65.50. Paper, $55.50. 352pp. .... Vendor G0259

2848 **NEFF ADDENDA.** 1899.
Paper. $7.00. 35pp. .... Vendor G0259

2849 **THE NEFF–NAEF FAMILY: A HISTORY OF THE DESCENDANTS OF HENRY NEFF**, by William A. Neff. 1991.
Cloth. $41.00. 467pp. .... Vendor G0150

2850 **NELL FAM. IN THE U. S.**, by R. B. Nell. 1929.
Paper. $19.00. 104pp. .... Vendor G0259

2851 **ANTHONY NELSON, 17TH CENT. PENNA. & N.J., & SOME OF HIS DESC.**, by E.G. Van Name. 1962.
Paper. $11.00. 53pp. .... Vendor G0259

2852 **DESC. OF JOHN NELSON & HIS CHILDREN, & NOTES ON THE FAM. OF TAILER & STOUGHTON**, by T. Prime. 2nd ed. 1894.
Paper. $12.00. 61pp. .... Vendor G0259

2853 **DESCENDANTS OF JOHN NELSON, SR.—MARY TOBY, STAFFORD CO., VA., 1740–1959, WITH RELATED FAMILIES**, by Olive N. Gibson. 1959.
Cloth, $64.00. Paper, $54.00. 350pp. .... Vendor G0259

2854 **DESCENDANTS OF THOMAS NELSON OF VIRGINIA**, by Carol A. Hauk. 1995. Indexed.
Paper. $35.00. 216pp. .... Vendor G0340

2855 **A GEN. OF THE NESBIT, ROSS, PORTER, TAGGART FAM. OF PENN.**, by B.T. Hartman. 1929.
Cloth, $46.00. Paper, $36.00. 242pp. .... Vendor G0259

2856 **NEVILLE FAMILY OF ENG. & THE U.S.**, by W.E.N. Wilson. 1964.
Paper. $19.00. 115pp. .... Vendor G0259

2857 **NEVIN GENEALOGICA (SOME DESC. OF DANIEL NEVIN, CUMBERLAND VALLEY, PA., 1770)**, by John D. Nevin. 2 vols. in 1. 1919–29.
Cloth, $75.00. Paper, $65.00. 435pp. .... Vendor G0259

2858 **JOANNES NEVIUS, SCHEPEN & 3RD SECRETARY OF NEW AMSTERDAM, & HIS DESC., 1627–1900**, by A. Van Doren Honeyman. 1900.
Cloth, $109.00. Paper, $99.00. 732pp. .... Vendor G0259

2859 **GENEALOGICAL RECORD OF THE DESCENDANTS OF ANDREW NEWBAKER OF HARDWICK TWP., WARREN CO., NJ, WITH HIST. & BIOGR. SKETCHES**, by A.J. Fretz. 1908.
Paper. $8.50. 42pp. .... Vendor G0259

2860 **THE NEWBERRY FAM. OF WINDSOR, CONN., IN THE LINE OF CLARINDA (NEWBERRY) GOODWIN OF HARTFORD, CONN., 1634–1866**, by F.F. Starr. 1898.
Paper. $13.50. 70pp. .... Vendor G0259

2861 **ANDR EW NEWCOMB, 1618–1686, & HIS DESC.: A REV. ED. OF "GEN. MEM." OF THE NEWCOMB FAM. (1874)**, by B.M. Newcomb. 1923.
Cloth, $154.50. Paper, $144.50. 1,021pp. .... Vendor G0259

2862 **GEN. MEMOIR OF THE NEWCOMB FAM. CONTAINING RECORDS OF NEARLY EVERY PERSON OF THE NAME IN AMERICA FROM 1635–1874**, by J.B. Newcomb. 1874.
Cloth, $86.00. Paper, $76.00. 600pp. .... Vendor G0259

2863 **THOMAS NEWELL, WHO SETTLED IN FARMINGTON, CONN., 1632, & HIS DESC.**, by M.A. Hall. 1878.
Cloth, $50.00. Paper, $40.00. 268pp. .... Vendor G0259

2864 **[Newhall]. THE RECORD OF MY ANC.**, by C.L. Newhall. 1899.
Cloth, $43.00. Paper, $33.00. 222pp. .... Vendor G0259

2865 **GEN. NOTES ON DESC. OF THOMAS NEWTON OF FAIRFIELD, CT.**, by N. Lull; **& HENRY WALLBRIDGE OF PRESTON, CT.**, by W. Wallbridge. 1896.
Paper. $8.00. 39pp. .... Vendor G0259

2866 **GENEALOGY, BIOGR., HIST.; BEING A RECORD OF THE DESC. OFRICHARD NEWTON OF SUDBURY & MARLBOROUGH, MASS., 1638, WITH GEN. OF FAMILIES DESC. FROM THE IMMIGRANTS**, by E.N. Leonard. 1915.
Cloth, $119.00. Paper, $109.00. 880pp. .... Vendor G0259

2867 **HIST. OF THE NEWTON FAM. OF COL. AMER., WITH AMER. HIST. OF FAM. INTEREST NOT OBTAINABLE ELSEWHERE**, Vol. I., by C.A. Newton. 1927.
Paper. $16.00. 96pp. .... Vendor G0259

2868 **REV. ROGER NEWTON, DECEASED 1683, AND ONE LINE OF HIS DESCENDANTS, AND ABNER NEWTON, 1764–1852, HIS ANCESTORS AND DESCENDANTS**, by Caroline G. Newton. 1912.
Cloth, $54.00. Paper, $44.00. 280pp. .... Vendor G0259

2869 **NICE FAMILY HISTORY: THE ANCESTORS AND DESCENDANTS OF JOSEPH NICE (1791–1874) AND HIS WIFE MARY CLEMMER (1794–1882)**, by Hazel N. Hassan. 1993. Indexed. Illus.
Paper. $19.00. 400pp. .... Vendor G0263

2870 **DESCENDANTS OF GEORGE NICHOLAS OF VIRGINIA**, by Carol A. Hauk. 1995. Indexed.
Paper. $35.00. 156pp. .... Vendor G0340

2871 **SERGEANT FRANCIS NICHOLLS OF STRATFORD, CONN., 1639, & THE DESC. OF HIS SON CALEB NICHOLLS**, by W. Nicholls. 1909.
Paper. $16.00. 101pp. .... Vendor G0259

2872 **ANC. OF WILLARD ATHERTON NICHOLS, WHO PARTICIPATED IN THE CIVIL & MILITARY AFFAIRS OF THE AMERICAN COLONIES**, by W.A. Nichols. 1911.
Paper. $15.00. 77pp. .... Vendor G0259

2873 **HISTORICAL DATA OF THE NICHOLSON ADAMS & ALLIED FAMILIES**, by Mrs J.L. Mims. 1944.
Paper. $14.00. 68pp. .... Vendor G0259

2874 **DESC. OF JULES AUGUSTE NICOLET (1834–1912) OF NEUCHATEL, SWITZERLAND, WHO SETTLED IN ALTON, ILLINOIS**, by H.F. Kershner. 1969.
Paper. $11.00. 50pp. .... Vendor G0259

2875 **OUR SOLOMON NIDIFFER CLAN**, compiled by Mary Smith Witcher; edited by Fay Louise Smith Arellano. 1992. Indexed. Illus.
Includes affiliated lines of: **Arthur, Blevins, Carey, Lunday, Ward, Nix.**
Soft binding. $30.00. 283pp. .... Vendor G0393

2876 **THE FAMILY OF NIVEN, WITH BIOGRAPHICAL SKETCHES [AND THE VOYAGES, LETTERS & DIARIES OF CAPT. JOHN NIVEN]**, by John Niven. 1960.
Cloth, $47.00. Paper, $37.00. 252pp. .... Vendor G0259

2877 **CHRISTOPHER NOBLE OF PORTSMOUTH, N. H., & SOME OF HIS DESC.**, by F.A. Davis.
Paper. $9.00. 45pp. .... Vendor G0259

2878 **HIST. & GEN. OF THE FAM. OF THOMAS NOBLE, OF WESTFIELD, MASS., WITH GEN. NOTES OF OTHER FAM. BY THE NAME OF NOBLE**, by L.M. Boltwood. 1878.
Cloth, $118.00. Paper, $108.50. 870pp. .... Vendor G0259

2879 **JONATHAN & TAMESIN NORRIS OF MAINE, THEIR ANC. & DESC.**, by H.M. Norris. 1906.
Paper. $12.00. 60pp. .... Vendor G0259

2880 **LIN. & BIOGR. OF THE NORRIS FAM. IN AMER., FROM 1640 TO 1892**, by L.A. Morrison. 1892.
Cloth, $41.00. Paper, $31.00. 207pp. .... Vendor G0259

2881 **NORRIS FAM. OF MD.**, by T.M. Myers. 1916.
Cloth, $32.50. Paper, $22.50. 119pp. .... Vendor G0259

2882 **AN ACCT. OF THE CELEBRATION OF THE DIAMOND WEDDING OF FREDERICK & HARRIET NORTH, WITH GEN.**, by F.A. North. 1890.
Paper. $16.00. 80pp. .... Vendor G0259

2883 **JOHN NORTH OF FARMINGTON, CT., & HIS DESC., WITH AN ACCT. OF OTHER NORTH FAMS.**, by D. North. 1921.
Cloth, $63.00. Paper, $53.00. 334pp. .... Vendor G0259

2884 **NORTHRUP–NORTHROP GEN.; REC. OF THE KNOWN DESC. OF JOSEPH NORTHRUP, AN ORIG. SETTLER OF MILFORD, CONN., IN 1639**, by A.J. Northrup. 1908.
Cloth, $84.00. Paper, $74.00. 473pp. .... Vendor G0259

2885 **FIRST NOTHSTEIN FAMILY HISTORY, 1750–1950 [DESC. OF PETER NOTHSTEIN OF PA.]**. n.a. 1950.
Cloth, $32.50. Paper, $22.50. 119+26pp. .... Vendor G0259

2886 **JAMES NOURSE & HIS DESC.**, by M.C.N. Lyle. 1897.
Cloth, $32.50. Paper, $22.50. 167pp. .... Vendor G0259

2887 **NOWLIN-STONE–STONE GENEALOGY: RECORD OF THE DESCEN-DANTS OF JAMES NOWLIN, WHO CAME TO PITTSYLVANIA CO., VA., FROM IRELANDABOUT 1700; ALSO A RECORD OF THE DE-SCENDANTS OF GEORGE STONE AND OF JAMES HOSKIN STONE WHO WAS b. PITTSYLVANIA CO. IN 1778**, by James E. Nowlin. 1916.
Cloth, $92.00. Paper, $82.00. 548pp. .... Vendor G0259

2888 **DESC. OF REV. WM. NOYES, b. ENG. 1568, IN DIRECT LINE TO LAVERNE NOYES GIFFEM & FRANCES NOYES GIFFEN, INCL. AL-LIED FAMS. STANTON, SANFORD, THOMPSON, HOLDREDGE, ETC.** 1900.
Paper. $16.50. 115pp. .... Vendor G0259

2889 **GEN. RECORD OF SOME OF THE NOYES DESC. OF JAMES, NICHO-LAS & PETER NOYES**, Vol. I., by H. and H. Noyes. 1904.
Cloth, $99.00. Paper, $89.00. 575pp. .... Vendor G0259

2890 **GEN. RECORD OF SOME OF THE NOYES DESC. OF JAMES, NICHO-LAS & PETER NOYES**, Vol. II., by H. and H. Noyes. 1904.
Cloth, $75.50. Paper, $65.50. 437pp. .... Vendor G0259

2891 **NOYES GILMAN ANCESTRY; BEING A SERIES OF SKETCHES, WITH A CHART OF THE ANC. OF CHARLES PHELPS NOYES & EMILY H. (GILMAN) NOYES, HIS WIFE**, by C.P. Noyes. 1907.
Cloth, $85.00. Paper, $75.00. 478pp. .... Vendor G0259

2892 **SKETCH OF JOHN MILTON NUNN & SALLY HEISTON NUNN, THEIR ANC. & DESC.**, by C. and H. Nunn. 1939.
Paper. $13.00. 64pp. .... Vendor G0259

2893 **NUTTING GEN. A RECORD OF SOME OF THE DESC. OF JOHN NUT-TING OF GROTON, MA.**, by J.K. Nutting. 1908.
Cloth, $46.50. Paper, $36.50. 278pp. .... Vendor G0259

2894 **GEN. OF THE NYE FAM.**, by G. Nye and F. Best, edited by D.F. Nye. 1907.
Cloth, $99.00. Paper, $89.00. 704pp. .... Vendor G0259

2895 **OAKS–OAKES FAM. REG., NATHANIEL OAK OF MARLBORO, MASS., & 3 GEN. OF HIS DESC.**, by H.L. Oak. 1906.
Paper. $18.50. 90pp. .... Vendor G0259

2896 **GEN. REC. OF THE DESC. OF MARTON OBERHOLTZER, WITH HIST. & BIOGR.**, by A.J. Fretz. 1903.
Cloth, $43.00. Paper, $33.00. 254pp. .... Vendor G0259

2897 **THE OBERHOLTZER BOOK**, by Barbara B. Ford. 1995. Indexed. Illus.
A foundation book of **Oberholtzer** immigrants and unestablished lines.
Cloth. $33.00. 424pp. .... Vendor G0368

2898 **THE O'BRIENS OF MACHIAS, MAINE. PATRIOTS OF THE AMERI-CAN REVOLUTION, TOGETHER WITH A SKETCH OF THE CLAN O'BRIEN,** by Sherman and Murray. 1904.
Paper. $16.50. 87pp. .... Vendor G0259

2899 **ODELL GENEALOGY IN THE US & CANADA (1635–1935); TEN GEN. IN AMER. IN DIRECT LINE,** by M.A.L. Pool. 1935.
Cloth, $31.00. Paper, $21.00. 123pp. .... Vendor G0259

2900 **GEN. OF THE ODIORNE FAM., WITH NOTICES OF OTHER FAM. CONNECTED THEREWITH,** by J.C. Odiorne. 1875.
Cloth, $43.00. Paper, $33.00. 232pp. .... Vendor G0259

2901 **OGDEN FAM. HIST. IN THE LINE OF LT. BENJAMIN OGDEN OF NEW YORK (1735–1780) & HIS WIFE, RACHEL WESTERVELT,** by A. Vermilve. 1906.
Paper. $18.00. 119pp. .... Vendor G0259

2902 **OGDENS OF SO. JERSEY. THE DESC. OF JOHN OGDEN OF FAIRFIELD, CONN. & NEW FAIRFIELD, N.J., b. 1673; d. 1745,** by W.O. Sheeler and E.D. Halsey. 1894.
Paper. $7.00. 36pp. .... Vendor G0259

2903 **QUAKER OGDENS IN AMER. DAVID OGDEN OF YE GOODE SHIP "WELCOME" & HIS DESC., 1682–1897,** by C. Ogden. 1898.
Cloth, $42.00. Paper, $32.00. 245pp. .... Vendor G0259

2904 **THE OGDEN FAM. IN AMER. (ELIZABETHTOWN BRANCH) & THEIR ENG. ANC. JOHN OGDEN, THE PILGRIM, & HIS DESC., 1640–1906; THEIR HIST., BIOGR. & GEN.,** by W.O. Wheeler. 1907.
Cloth, $89.50. Paper, $79.50. 526pp. .... Vendor G0259

2905 **[Ogle-Bertram]. OGLE & BOTHAL: HISTORY OF THE BARONIES OFOGLE, BOTHAL & HEPPLE, & OF THE FAMILIES OF OGLE & BERTRAM WHO HELD POSSESSION OF THOSE BARONIES IN NORTHUMBERLAND, TO WHICH IS ADDED ACCTS. OF SEVERAL BRANCHES . . . BEARING THE NAME OF OGLE,** by Sir Henry Ogle. 1902 (England).
Cloth, $85.00. Paper, $75.00. 426+70pp. .... Vendor G0259

2906 **THE ENGLISH ORIGIN OF JOHN OGLE, FIRST OF THE NAME IN DELAWARE,** by F.H. Hibbard and S. Parks. 1967.
Paper. $9.50. 47pp. .... Vendor G0259

2907 **OLCOTT FAM. OF HARTFORD, CONN., IN THE LINE OF EUNICE OLCOTT GOODWIN, 1639–1807,** by F. Starr. 1899.
Paper. $16.50. 84pp. .... Vendor G0259

2908 **THE DESC. OF THOMAS OLCOTT, ONE OF THE FIRST SETTLERS OF HARTFORD, CONN.,** by N. Goodwin; rev. by H. Olcott. 1874.
Paper. $18.50. 124pp. .... Vendor G0259

2909 **A COMPLETE RECORD OF THE JOHN OLIN FAM., 1678–1893,** by C.C. Olin. 1893.
Cloth, $40.00. Paper, $30.00. 234pp. .... Vendor G0259

2910 **BIOGR. SKETCHES & RECORDS OF THE EZRA OLIN FAM.**, by G.S. Nye. 1892.
Cloth, $78.50. Paper, $68.50. 441pp. Vendor G0259

2911 **A GEN. OF THE DESC. OF THOMAS OLNEY, AN ORIGINAL PRO- PRIETOR OF PROVIDENCE, R.I.**, WHO CAME FROM ENG. IN 1635, by J.H. Olney. 1889.
Cloth, $54.50. Paper, $44.50. 298pp. Vendor G0259

2912 **GEN. OF THE OLMSTED FAM. IN AMER. THE DESC. OF JAMES & RICHARD OLMSTED, 1632–1912**, by H.K. Olmsted; rev. by G.K. Ward. 1912.
Cloth, $92.00. Paper, $82.00. 539pp. Vendor G0259

2913 **THE OLMSTED FAMILY IN AMERICA**, by Henry King Olmsted and George Ward. (1912) reprint 1994.
Includes the supplements of 1914, 1920, 1923, and 1928 plus the separate 158-page index listed below.
Cloth. $60.00. 704pp. . . . . Vendor G0093

2914 **ALL-NAME INDEX TO THE 1912 OLMSTED FAMILY IN AMERICA**, by Walter Steesy. 1989.
32,065 entries; includes supplements for 1914, 1920, 1923, and 1928.
Paper. $10.00. 158pp. . . . . Vendor G0093

2915 **ANCESTRY AND DESCENDANTS OF EDWARD OLSON (BORN OLAUS EDWARD THALLAUG) (1862–1946) AND URSULA (ANNIE) KLEINHANS (1866–1949)**, by Raymond L. Olson. 1992. Indexed. Includes 5 pictures.
Cloth. $32.00. 200pp. . . . . Vendor G0291

2916 **SOME HIST. NOTICES OF THE O'MEAGHERS OF IBERRIN**, by J.C. O'Meagher. 1890.
Cloth, $42.00. Paper, $32.00. 216pp. Vendor G0259

2917 **GEN. OF THE ONDERDONK FAM. IN AMER.**, by E. and A. Onderdonk. 1910.
Cloth, $68.50. Paper, $58.50. 374pp. Vendor G0259

2918 **OPDYKE GENEALOGY, CONTAINING THE OPDYCK–OPDYCKE– UPDIKE AMER. DESCENDANTS OF THE WESEL & HOLLAND FAMS.**, by C.W. Opdyke. 1889. (Does not include illustrations published with some original copies.)
Cloth, $87.50. Paper, $77.50. 499pp. Vendor G0259

2919 **THE ANCESTRY OF SAMUEL BLANCHARD ORDWAY, 1844–1916**, by Dean Crawford Smith; edited by Melinde Lutz Sanborn. 1990. Indexed. Illus.
Cloth. $38.50. 395pp. . . . . Vendor G0406

2920 **SHORT ACCT. OF FAM. OF ORMSBY OF PITTSBURGH, PENN.**, by O.O. Page. 1892.
Paper. $10.00. 48pp. . . . . Vendor G0259

2921 **AN ACCT. OF THE DESC. OF THOMAS ORTON OF WINDSOR, CONN., 1641**, by E. Orton. 1896.
Cloth, $39.50. Paper, $29.50. 220pp. Vendor G0259

2922 **A HIST. OF THE ORVIS FAM. IN AMER.**, by F.W. Orvis. 1922.
Cloth, $40.00. Paper, $30.00. 203pp. .... Vendor G0259

2923 **GENEALOGY OF EDWARD AND SARAH (BURCHETT) OSBORN OF FLOYD COUNTY, KENTUCKY,** by Donald Lewis Osborn. 1970.
Edward killed two men, 1813.
Paper. $5.00. 12pp. .... Vendor G0121

2924 **THOMAS OSBORNE OF ASHFORD, KENT, ENGLAND & SOME OF HIS AMERICAN DESCENDANTS,** by Daniel J. Weeks. Rev. ed. 1994.
Paper. $7.00. 32pp. .... Vendor G0259

2925 **A GEN. OF THE DESC. OF JOHN, CHRISTOPHER & WILLIAM OSGOOD WHO SETTLED IN NEW ENG. EARLY IN THE 17TH CENTURY,** by I. Osgood. 1894.
Cloth, $72.00. Paper, $62.00. 491pp. .... Vendor G0259

2926 **A GEN. MEMOIR OF THE FAM. OF RICHARD OTIS, & COLLATERALLY OF THE FAM. OF BAKER, VARNEY, WALDRON (& OTHERS),** by H.N. Otis. 1851.
Paper. $10.00. 50pp. .... Vendor G0259

2927 **A GEN. & HIST. MEMOIR OF THE OTIS FAM. IN AMER.**, by W.A. Otis. 1924.
Cloth, $119.00. Paper, $109.00. 729pp. .... Vendor G0259

2928 **SOME OF THE DESC. OF EPHRAIM OTIS & RACHEL (HERSEY) OTIS OF SCITUATE, MASS.**, by R.L. Weis. 1943.
Paper. $15.00. 74pp. .... Vendor G0259

2929 **A HISTORY OF THE OTSTOT(T) FAMILY IN AMERICA—SUPPLEMENT,** by Charles Mathieson Otstot. 1988. Indexed. Illus.
Paper. $20.00. 517pp. .... Vendor G0232

2930 **HE WORE A PINK CARNATION: A BIOGRAPHY OF DR. M.C. OVERTON,** by Nan Overton West. 1992. Indexed. Illus.
Pioneer doctor and builder of Lubbock, Texas.
Paper. $12.95. 175pp. .... Vendor G0244

2931 **THE OVERTON FAMILY: 700 YEARS—FROM ENGLAND TO VIRGINIA, KENTUCKY AND TEXAS—ANCESTORS, SOME DESCENDANTS AND ALLIED LINES,** by Nan Overton West. 1995. Indexed. Illus.
Allies include: **Booker, Clough, Garland, Garnett, Gerard, Grundy, Harris, Jennings, Lawson, Poindexter, Robertson, Shipp, Slye, Whitworth.**
Cloth. $55.00. 600+pp. .... Vendor G0244

2932 **DESC. OF JOHN OWEN OF WINDSOR, CONN. (1622–1699),** by R.D. Owen. 1941.
Cloth, $93.00. Paper, $83.00. 535pp. .... Vendor G0259

2933 **[Owen]. GENEALOGY OF SEVERAL ALLIED FAMILIES: FRAZER, OWEN, BESSELLIEU, CARTER, SHAW, ET AL,** by Charles Owen Johnson. 1961.
Cloth, $93.50. Paper, $83.50. 543pp. .... Vendor G0259

2934 **OWEN FAMILY RECORDS,** by J. Montgomery Seaver. 1929.
Paper. $7.00. 34pp. .... Vendor G0259

2935 **OYER AND ALLIED FAMILIES—THEIR HISTORY AND GENEAL-OGY**, by Phyllis Smith Oyer. 1988. Indexed. Illus.
Supplement I to this book is also available (see next listing). You can order the original book and the supplement as a set for $37.50.
Supplement I of the 1988 book documents that Oyers and the many families who traveled to America with them originated in Switzerland and Germany. Extensive historical, religious, and genealogical details are given with sources. Illustrations include documents. Families: **Bargy, Becker, Breitenbecker, Clemens, Dillenbach, Gardinier, Finster, Folts, Hochstatter, Lentz, Muller, Rima, Rinkle, Schenk, Widrig**, of the very early families; dozens of later surnames. Every-name indexes. **Eyer/Ayer** are variant spellings.
Cloth. $33.50. 380pp. .... Vendor G0354

2936 **OYER AND ALLIED FAMILIES—SUPPLEMENT I**, by Phyllis Smith Oyer. 1994. Indexed. Illus.
See above listing for *Oyer and Allied Families—Their History and Genealogy.*
Paper. $12.50. 94pp. .... Vendor G0354

2937 **THE PACAS OF MARYLAND AND THEIR RELATIVES**, by E.C. Paca. 1994. Indexed. Illus.
Paper. $22.00. 167pp. .... Vendor G0403

2938 **CELEBRATION OF THE 250TH ANNIVERSARY OF THE LANDING OF SAMUEL PACKARD IN THIS COUNTRY, AUG. 10, 1638, HELD AT BROCKTON, MASS., AUG. 10, 1888**, issued by Packard Mem. Assoc. 1888.
Paper. $14.00. 72pp. .... Vendor G0259

2939 **DESCENDANTS OF JOHN PAGE OF VIRGINIA**, by Carol A. Hauk. 1995. Indexed.
Paper. $45.00. 220pp. .... Vendor G0340

2940 **GENEALOGICAL REGISTERS OF ANCESTORS & DESC. OF . . . LEMUEL PAGE & POLLY PAIGE, PETER JOSLIN & SARAH KIDDER, WITH BRIEF ACCTS. OF THEM & THEIR ANCESTORS**, by Luke J. Page. 1887.
Cloth, $35.00. Paper, $25.00. 155pp. .... Vendor G0259

2941 **GEN. OF THE PAGE FAM. IN VA.; ALSO A CONDENSED ACCT. OF THE NELSON, WALKER, PENDLETON & RANDOLPH FAMS., WITH REF. TO . . . OTHER DISTINGUISHED FAMS. IN VA.**, by R.C.M. Page. 1872.
Cloth, $46.00. Paper, $36.00. 275pp. .... Vendor G0259

2942 **GENEALOGY OF THE PAGE FAMILY IN VA., ALSO A CONDENSED ACCT. OF THE NELSON, WALKER, PENDLETON & RANDOLPH FAMILIES WITH REFERENCES TO OTHER DISTINQUISHED FAMILIES IN VA.**, by R.C.M. Page. 2nd ed. 1893.
Cloth, $55.00. Paper, $45.00. 275pp. .... Vendor G0259

2943 **HIST. & GEN. OF THE PAGE FAM. FROM 1257 TO THE PRESENT, WITH A BRIEF HIST. & GEN. OF THE ALLIED FAMS. NASH & PECK**, by C.N. Page. 1911.
Cloth, $31.00. Paper, $21.00. 143pp. .... Vendor G0259

2944 **STORY OF OUR FOREBEARS: PAGE, BRADBURY, FESSENDEN & PERLEY FAMS.**, by R.P. Reed. 1903.
Cloth, $30.00. Paper, $20.00. 154pp. .... Vendor G0259

2945 **THE FAMILY OF JOHN PAGE OF HAVERHILL, MASS.: A COMPREHENSIVE GEN. FROM 1614 TO 1977**, by Lynn Case and Page Sanderson. 1978.
Cloth, $47.50. Paper, $37.50. 250pp. .... Vendor G0259

2946 **WISCONSIN PAGE PIONEERS & KINFOLD**, by Turner, Turner, & Sayre. 1953.
Cloth, $84.50. Paper, $74.50. 485pp. .... Vendor G0259

2947 **ANCESTORS & DESCENDANTS OF DAVID PAINE & ABIGAIL SHEPARD OF LUDLOW, MA., 1463–1913**, compiled by C.P. Ohler. 1913.
Cloth, $49.50. Paper, $39.50. 252pp. .... Vendor G0259

2948 **FAM. OF ROBERT TREAT PAINE, SIGNER OF THE DECLARATION OF INDEPENDENCE, INCL. MATERNAL LINES**, by S.C. Paine and C.H. Pope. 1912.
Cloth, $63.50. Paper, $53.50. 336pp. .... Vendor G0259

2949 **HIST. OF SAMUEL PAINE, JR, 1778–1861, & HIS WIFE PAMELA CHASE PAINE, 1780–1856, RANDOLPH, VT., & THEIR ANC. & DESC.**, by A. Paine. 1923.
Cloth, $45.00. Paper, $35.00. 218pp. .... Vendor G0259

2950 **PAINE FAM.**, by N.E. Paine. 1928.
Cloth, $37.50. Paper, $27.50. 184pp. .... Vendor G0259

2951 **PAINE FAM. RECORDS. A JOURNAL OF GEN. & BIOGR. INFO. RESPECTING THE AMER. FAM. OF PAYNE, PAINE, PAYN, ETC.**, by H.D. Paine. 2 vols. in 1. 1880–3.
Cloth, $72.50. Paper, $62.50. 522pp. .... Vendor G0259

2952 **PAINE GEN., IPSWICH BRANCH**, by A.W. Paine. 1881.
Cloth, $37.50. Paper, $27.50. 184pp. .... Vendor G0259

2953 **[Paine]. THE DISCOVERY OF A GRANDMOTHER. GLIMPSES INTO THE HOMES & LIVES OF EIGHT GEN. OF AN IPSWICH–PAINE FAM.**, by H.H. Carter. 1920.
Cloth, $64.00. Paper, $54.00. 343pp. .... Vendor G0259

2954 **PALGRAVE FAM. MEMORIALS**, by C. and S. Parker. 1878.
Cloth, $41.00. Paper, $31.00. 208pp. .... Vendor G0259

2955 A GEN. REC. OF THE DESC. OF JOHN & MARY PALMER OF CON-
CORD, CHESTER (NOW DELAWARE) CO., PA., ESP. THROUGH
THEIR SON, JOHN JR. & SONS-IN-LAW, WM. & JAMES TRIMBLE,
by L. Palmer. 1875.
Cloth, $84.00. Paper, $74.00. 474pp. .... Vendor G0259

2956 BRIEF GEN. HIST. OF THE ANC. & DESC. OF DEA. STEPHEN
PALMER OF CANDIA, NH, WITH SOME ACCT. OF OTHER LINES
OF DESC. FROM THOMAS PALMER, A FOUNDER OF ROWLEY, MA.,
1635, by F. Palmer. 1886.
Cloth, $30.00. Paper, $20.00. 106pp. .... Vendor G0259

2957 PALMER–BURLINGHAM GENEALOGY. DESCENDANTS OF CALEB
PALMER (1775–1854) AND ELIPHALET BURLINGHAM (c.1785–
c.1840). [Including the 1982 28-page supplement with corrections and additions, and the ancestry and life of John Carpenter (1775–1859) and his
descendants.], by Dale C. Kellogg. 1974. Indexed. Illus.
Cloth. $17.00. 190pp. .... Vendor G0051

2958 THE PANCOAST FAMILY IN AMERICA, by Bennett S. Pancoast. 1981.
Indexed.
A classic work on the **Pancoast** family.
Paper. $20.50. 490pp. .... Vendor G0069

2959 THE PANCOAST FAMILY IN AMERICA, VOL. 2, by Bennett S. Pancoast;
edited by Mrs. Barbara Price. 1994. Indexed.
Families in this second volume include the eighth, ninth, and tenth
generations.
Paper. $30.00. 572pp. .... Vendor G0069

2960 THE PARDEE GEN., by D.L. Jacobus. 1927.
Cloth, $115.00. Paper, $105.00. 701pp. .... Vendor G0259

2961 BIOGR. SKETCH OF THE PARK FAM. OF WASHINGTON CO., PENN.,
by W.J. Park. 1880.
Cloth, $34.00. Paper, $24.00. 121pp. .... Vendor G0259

2962 THE PARK FAMILY OF PENNSYLVANIA. TWO HUNDRED YEARS
1793–1993, by Clarence D. Stephenson. 1993. Illus.
Ancestral lines: **Park, Lang, Bailey, Cochran, Linton, Agnew, Hjelm
(Helm), Craig, Sutor, Brady, Martin, Barbor (Barbour)**.
3-ring binder. $35.00. Pennsylvania residents add 6% tax (less $2.50 postage). 367pp + index .... Vendor G0041

2963 GEN. OF THE PARKE FAMS. OF MASS.; INCL. RICHARD OF CAM-
BRIDGE, WM. OF GROTON, & OTHERS, by F.S. Parks. 1909.
Cloth, $53.00. Paper, $43.00. 263pp. .... Vendor G0259

2964 PARKE OF CONN., GEN. OF THE PARKE FAM. OF CONN., INCL.
ROBERT PARKE OF NEW LONDON, EDWARD PARKS OF
GUILFORD, & OTHERS, by F.S. Parks. 1906.
Cloth, $53.00. Paper, $43.00. 333pp. .... Vendor G0259

2965 SUPPL. TO THE PARKE FAM. OF CONN., by F.S. Parks. 1934.
Paper. $19.00. 97pp. .... Vendor G0259

2966 **FAM. RECORDS. PARKER–POND–PECK, 1636–1892,** by E.P. Parker. 1892. Paper. $10.00. 51pp. .... Vendor G0259

2967 **GEN. & BIOGR. NOTES OF JOHN PARKER OF LEXINGTON & HIS DESC., SHOWING HIS EARLIER ANC. IN AMER. FROM DEA. THO- MAS OARKER OF READING, MA., FROM 1635 TO 1893,** by T. Parker. 1893.
Cloth, $78.00. Paper, $68.00. 528pp. .... Vendor G0259

2968 **GLEANINGS FROM COL. & AMERICAN RECORDS OF PARKER & MORSE FAMILIES, 1585–1915,** by Wm. T. Parker. 1915.
Paper. $13.00. 62pp. .... Vendor G0259

2969 **GLEANINGS FROM PARKER RECORDS, 1271 TO 1893,** by W.T. Parker. 1894.
Paper. $10.00. 51pp. .... Vendor G0259

2970 **HISTORY OF PETER PARKER & SARAH RUGGLES OF ROXBURY, MASS., & THEIR ANC. & DESC.,** by J.W. Linzee. 1913.
Cloth, $99.50. Paper, $89.50. 609pp. .... Vendor G0259

2971 **LINEAGE OF MALCOLM METZGER PARKER FROM JOHANNES DELANG,** by Dr I.H. DeLong. 1926.
Paper. $13.00. 62pp. .... Vendor G0259

2972 **PARKER IN AMER., 1630–1910, GEN., BIOGR., & HIST.,** by A. Parker. 1911.
Cloth, $91.00. Paper, $81.00. 608pp. .... Vendor G0259

2973 **INDEX TO ALL PARKER NAMES IN "PARKER IN AMER.,"** by A.G. Parker (1910); comp. by R. Lee. 1970.
Paper. $10.00. 51pp. .... Vendor G0259

2974 **JOHN PARKHURST, HIS ANC. & DESC.,** by G.H. Parkhurst. 1897.
Paper. $10.00. 51pp. .... Vendor G0259

2975 **PARLEE & RELATED FAMILIES,** by Helen Spinney. n.d.
Paper. $15.00. 69+34pp. .... Vendor G0259

2976 **THE PARLIN GEN., THE DESC. OF NICHOLAS OF CAMBRIDGE, MASS.,** by F.E. Parlin. 1913.
Cloth, $53.00. Paper, $43.00. 289pp. .... Vendor G0259

2977 **PARR CONNECTIONS (IN RECORD OF WM. WEAVER),** by R.I. Weaver. 1925.
Paper. $7.00. 36pp. .... Vendor G0259

2978 **A COMP. OF THE AVAILABLE RECORDS COVERING DIRECT DESC. OF HENRY, JOEL, ANSEL & ABSOLOM, SONS OF HENRY PARRISH (1740) & GRANDSONS OF JOEL PARRISH (1700); ALSO DESC. OF HENRY JACKSON PARRISH,** by J.T. Parrish. 1948.
Cloth, $74.00. Paper, $64.00. 410pp. .... Vendor G0259

2979 **PARRISH FAMILY, INCL. THE ALLIED FAMILIES OF BELT, BOYD, COLE–MALONE, CLOKEY, GARRETT, MERRYMAN, PARSONS, PRICE & TIPTON,** by Boyd and Gottschalk. 1935.
Cloth, $73.00. Paper, $63.00. 413pp. .... Vendor G0259

2980 **PARRISH FAM. (PHILA.) INCL. THE RELATED FAMS. OF COX, DILLINGER, ROBERTS, CHANDLER, MITCHELL, PAINTER & PUSEY**, by Wharton and Parrish. 1925.
Cloth, $63.50. Paper, $53.50. 336pp. .... Vendor G0259

2981 **HIST. OF THE PARSHALL FAM., 1066 TO THE CLOSE OF THE 19TH CENT.**, by J.C. Parshall. 1903.
Cloth, $51.00. Paper, $41.00. 309pp. .... Vendor G0259

2982 **JAMES PARSHALL & DESC.**, by J. Parshall. 1900.
Paper, $8.00. 42pp. .... Vendor G0259

2983 **GEN. RECORD OF THE FAM. OF PARSONS & LEONARD OF W. SPRINGFIELD, MA.**, by S. Parsons. 1867.
Paper. $7.00. 36pp. .... Vendor G0259

2984 **PARSONS FAM.; DESC. OF CORNET JOSEPH PARSONS, SPRING-FIELD 1636–NORTHAMPTON 1655**, by H. Parsons. 2 vols. 1912–20.
Cloth, $179.00. Paper, $169.00. 1,223pp. .... Vendor G0259

2985 **GEN. OF THE PARTHEMORE FAM., 1744–1885**, by E.W.S. Parthemore. 1885.
Cloth, $47.50. Paper, $37.50. 250pp. .... Vendor G0259

2986 **DESC. OF GEORGE PARTRIDGE OF DUXBURY, MASS.**, by G.H. Partridge. 1915.
Paper. $9.50. 46pp. .... Vendor G0259

2987 **DESC. OF JOHN PARTRIDGE OF MEDFIELD, MASS.**, by G.H. Partridge. 1904.
Paper. $10.00. 46pp. .... Vendor G0259

2988 **ANC. OF JAMES PATTEN OF KENNEBUNKPORT, MAINE**, by W.G. Davis. 1941.
Cloth, $32.50. Paper, $22.50. 113pp. .... Vendor G0259

2989 **GEN. WILLIAM PATTEN OF CAMBRIDGE, 1635, & HIS DESC.**, by T.W. Baldwin. 1908.
Cloth, $48.50. Paper, $38.50. 300pp. .... Vendor G0259

2990 **GEN. OF THE PATTERSON, WHEAT & HEARN FAMS.**, by R.E.H. Randle. 1926.
Cloth, $51.00. Paper, $41.00. 261pp. .... Vendor G0259

2991 **JAMES PATTERSON OF CONESTOGA MANOR, & HIS DESCEN-DANTS**, by Edmund H. Bell and Mary H. Colwell. 1925.
Cloth, $58.50. Paper, $48.50. 313pp. .... Vendor G0259

2992 **[Patterson]. WEST SAXONY 452—AMERICA 1992**, by Richard E. Patterson. 1992. Indexed.
Cloth. $65.00. 560pp. .... Vendor G0183

2993 **ANC. OF KATHARINE CHOATE PAUL**, by E.J. Paul. 1914.
Cloth, $70.00. Paper, $60.00. 386pp. .... Vendor G0259

2994 **PHILIP PAUL OF STOCKLINCH SOMERSET, ENGLAND AND SOME**

OF HIS DESCENDANTS IN OLD GLOUCESTER COUNTY, NEW JER-
SEY AND ELSEWHERE, by Gordon W. Paul. 1983. Indexed. Illus.
Cloth. $19.50. 228pp. .... Vendor G0069

2995 JOSEPH PAULL OF ILMINSTER, SOMERSET, ENG. & SOME DE-
SCENDANTS WHO HAVE RESIDED IN PHILADELPHIA, by H.N. Paul.
1933.
Cloth, $34.00. Paper, $24.00. 157pp. .... Vendor G0259

2996 PAULL–IRWIN: A FAMILY SKETCH, by E.M. Paul. 1915.
Cloth, $42.50. Paper, $32.50. viii+198pp. .... Vendor G0259

2997 THE PAXTONS: THEIR ORIGIN IN SCOTLAND & MIGR. THROUGH
ENG. & IRELAND TO THE COL. OF PA., WHENCE THEY MOVED
SOUTH & WEST, by W. Paxton. 1903.
Cloth, $86.50. Paper, $76.50. 485pp. .... Vendor G0259

2998 THE PAYNES OF HAMILTON: A GEN. & BIOGR. RECORD, by A.F.P.
White. 1912.
Cloth, $49.50. Paper, $39.50. 245pp. .... Vendor G0259

2999 THOMAS PAYNE OF SALEM & HIS DESC., THE SALEM BRANCH
OF THE PAINE FAM., by N.E. Paine. 1928.
Cloth, $37.50. Paper, $27.50. 184pp. .... Vendor G0259

3000 A GEN. OF THE DESC. OF MOSES & HANNAH (FOSTER) PEABODY,
by M.E. Perley. 1904.
Paper. $10.00. 47pp. .... Vendor G0259

3001 A GEN. OF THE PEABODY FAM., WITH A PARTIAL RECORD OF
THE R.I. BRANCH, by C.M. Endicott. 1867.
Paper. $13.00. 65pp. .... Vendor G0259

3002 PEABODY (PAYBODY, PABODY, PABODIE) GEN., by S. Peabody. 1909.
Cloth, $102.00. Paper, $92.00. 614pp. .... Vendor G0259

3003 THE PEAK–PEAKE FAMILY HISTORY, by Cyrus H. Peake and Carol J.
Snow. 1975, 1977. Indexed. Illus.
    Covers: General History (family origins and growth, notable members);
Branches in Great Britain; Branches in United States (Christopher of Massa-
chusetts, William of Massachusetts and Vermont, John of Maryland); Branches
in Australia and New Zealand.
Paper. $39.00. 554pp. .... Vendor G0158

3004 PEARCE GEN.; BEING THE RECORD OF THE POSTERITY OF RI-
CHARD PEARCE, AN EARLY INHABITANT OF PORTSMOUTH, R.I.,
by F.C. Pierce. 1888.
Cloth, $32.50. Paper, $22.50. 150pp. .... Vendor G0259

3005 SOME OF JOHN PEARL'S DESC., by A.H. Dow.
Paper. $7.00. 33pp. .... Vendor G0259

3006 HIST. & GEN. OF THE PEARSALL FAM. IN ENG. & AMER., by C.E.
Pearsall. 3 vols. 1928.
Cloth, $99.00/vol. Paper, $89.00/vol. 1,806pp. .... Vendor G0259

3007 **CRISPIN PEARSON OF BUCKS, CO., PA., 1748–1806**, by A.P. Darrow; edited by W.C. Armstrong. 1932.
Cloth, $35.00. Paper, $25.00. 166pp. .... Vendor G0259

3008 **PEARSON, PLACES & THINGS, A QUARTERLY VOL. IV**, by Bettina P.H. Burns. 1992.
Index to this volume appears in Vol. V.
Paper. $12.00. 124pp. .... Vendor G0254

3009 **PEARSON, PLACES & THINGS, A QUARTERLY VOL. V**, by Bettina P.H. Burns. 1993.
Index to this volume appears in Vol. VI.
Paper. $12.00. 162pp. .... Vendor G0254

3010 **SEEK & YE SHALL FIND: PEARSON (ALL SPELLINGS)**, by Bettina (Pearson) Higdon Burns. 3 vols. Indexed. Illus.
Volume I: 1979. $40.00. 345pp.
Volume II: 1985. $50.00. pp.349–838.
Volume III: 1990. $60.00. pp.839–1263.
The set is available for $130.00.
Each Section II concerns compiler's Jeremiah **Pierson** first found in White Oak Company, Onslow County, NC, in 1754. Vol. I begins with Deacon John **Pearson** in Rowley, MA before 1643; Vol. II begins with Rev. Abraham **Pierson** in Boston, MA by 1639; Vol. III begins with Henry **Pierson** in Lynn, MA in 1635.
Cloth .... Vendor G0254

3011 **GEN.-HIST. REC. OF DESC. OF JOHN PEASE, SR., LAST OF ENFIELD, CT.**, by Fiske and Pease. 1869.
Cloth, $72.50. Paper, $62.50. 401pp. .... Vendor G0259

3012 **NEW HAMPSHIRE BRANCH OF THE PEASE FAMILY, BEING THE RESULTS OF A SEARCH FOR THE ANCESTORS OF PATTY PEASE WHO MARRIED JOHN PICKERING OF BARNSTEAD, N.H.**, by L.S. Cox. 1946.
Paper. $13.00. 64pp. .... Vendor G0259

3013 **PEASE FAM. OF ENG. & NEW ENG.**, by F. Pease. 1849.
Paper. $7.00. 34pp. .... Vendor G0259

3014 **THE EARLY HIST. OF THE PEASE FAM. IN AMER.**, by A.S. Pease. 1869.
Paper. $18.50. 96pp. .... Vendor G0259

3015 **THE PEASLEES & OTHERS OF HAVERHILL, MA., & VICINITY**, by E.A. Kimball. 1899.
Paper. $15.00. 72pp. .... Vendor G0259

3016 **A GEN. ACCT. OF THE DESC. IN THE MALE LINE OF WM. PECK, ONE OF THE FOUNDERS IN 1638 OF THE COL. OF NEW HAVEN, CONN.**, by D. Peck. 1877.
Cloth, $48.00. Paper, $38.00. 253pp. .... Vendor G0259

3017 **A GEN. HIST. OF THE DESC. OF JOSEPH PECK, WHO EMIGR. IN 1638. ALSO AN APPENDIX WITH AN ACCT. OF THE BOSTON &**

HINGHAM PECKS, THE DESC. OF JOHN OF MENDON, MASS. (OTH-
ERS OF HARTFORD, NEW HAVEN & MILFORD, CONN.), by I. Peck.
1868.
Cloth, $66.50. Paper, $56.50. 443pp. .... Vendor G0259

3018 PECKHAM GENEALOGY. ENG. ANC. & AMER. DESC. OF JOHN
PECKHAM OF NEWPORT, RI, 1630, by S. Peckham. 1922(?).
Cloth, $101.00. Paper, $91.00. 602pp. .... Vendor G0259

3019 PEFFLEY–PEFFLY–PEFLEY FAMILIES IN AMERICA, & ALLIED
FAMILIES, 1729-1938, by M.M. and E.C. Frost. 1938.
Cloth, $53.50. Paper, $43.50. 245+30pp. .... Vendor G0259

3020 PEIRCE FAMILY OF THE OLD COLONY; OR THE LIN. DESC. OF
ABRAHAM PEIRCE, WHO CAME TO AMER. AS EARLY AS 1623, by
E.W. Peirce. 1870.
Cloth, $75.00. Paper, $65.00. 510pp. .... Vendor G0259

3021 PEIRCE FAM. REC., 1687–1893. NEW ED. REV. WITH NOTICES OF
RELATED FAM. HARDY, GRAFTON, GARDENER, DAWES, LATHROP,
CORDIS, RUSSELL, HASWELL, GRAY, CHIPMAN, BLANCHARD,
HOLLAND, MAY, WEST, ETC., by E.W. West. 1894.
Paper. $19.50. 101pp. .... Vendor G0259

3022 SOLOMON PEIRCE FAM. GEN., WITH A REC. OF HIS DESC., ALSO
AN APP. WITH THE ANC. OF SOLOMON & HIS WIFE AMITY
FESSENDEN, by M. Bailey. 1912.
Cloth, $38.50. Paper, $28.50. 190pp. .... Vendor G0259

3023 A GENEALOGICAL HISTORY OF THE PELT FAMILY BRANCH OF
THE VAN PELT FAMILY TREE, by Chester H. Pelt, Sr. 1992.
Cloth, $32.00. Paper, $22.00. 140pp. .... Vendor G0259

3024 GEN. OF THE PELTON FAM. IN AMER., BEING A RECORD OF THE
DESC. OF JOHN PELTON, WHO SETTLED IN BOSTON ABOUT 1630–
1632, by J.M. Pelton. 1892.
Cloth, $101.00. Paper, $91.00. 722pp. .... Vendor G0259

3025 JOHN PEMBER: THE HISTORY OF THE PEMBER FAMILY IN
AMERICA, by C.P. Hazen. 1939.
Cloth, $62.00. Paper, $52.00. 342pp. .... Vendor G0259

3026 HIST. OF JUDGE JOHN PENCE & DESC., by K. Pence. 1912.
Cloth, $35.00. Paper, $25.00. 126pp. .... Vendor G0259

3027 BRIAN PENDLETON & HIS DESC., 1599–1910, WITH SOME ACCT.
OF THE PEMBLETON FAMS. & NOTICES OF OTHER PENDLETONS,
by E.H. Pendleton. 1910.
Cloth, $117.50. Paper, $107.50. 871pp. .... Vendor G0259

3028 DESCENDANTS OF PHILIP PENDLETON OF VIRGINIA, by Carol A.
Hauk. 1995. Indexed.
Paper. $45.00. 260pp. .... Vendor G0340

3029 GENEALOGY OF THE DESCENDANTS OF SAMUEL PENFIELD,
WITH A SUPPLEMENT OF DR LEVI BUCKINGHAM LINE AND THE

GRIDLEY, DWIGHT, BURLINGHAM, DEWEY & PYNCHEON COLLATERAL LINES, by Florence B. Penfield. 1963.
Cloth, $59.50. Paper, $49.50. 320pp. .... Vendor G0259

3030 **A GEN. RECORD OF THE DESC. OF MOSES PENGRY OF IPSWICH, MASS.,** by W.M. Pingry. 1881.
Cloth, $38.00. Paper, $28.00. 186pp. .... Vendor G0259

3031 **GEN. GLEANINGS CONTRIBUTORY TO A HIST. OF THE FAM. OF PENN (REPR. PENN. MAG.),** by J.H. Lea. 1890.
Paper. $10.00. 51pp. .... Vendor G0259

3032 **PENN IN HAND,** edited by Jane Adams Clarke.
4-page newsletter plus 2-page "Research Tip," published quarterly.
Free with membership to The Genealogical Society of Pennsylvania
(GSP) .... Vendor G0202

3033 **THE FAM. OF WM. PENN, FOUNDER OF PA., ANC. & DESC.,** by H.M. Jenkins. 1899.
Cloth, $44.00. Paper, $34.00. 270pp. .... Vendor G0259

3034 **A GEN. RECORD OF THE DESC. OF THOMAS PENNEY OF NEW GLOUCESTER, ME.,** by J.W. Penney. 1897.
Cloth, $35.00. Paper, $25.00. 167pp. .... Vendor G0259

3035 **SOME DESCENDANTS OF EPHRAIM PENNINGTON OF ROWAN CO. NC, INCLUDING THOSE OF PENNINGTON'S POINT, McDONOUGH COUNTY, ILLINOIS,** by Marvin T. Jones. 1994. Indexed. Illus.
This book documents the relationship of Richard and Timothy to Ephraim **Pennington**. It notes Richard's marriage to Hannah Boone **Stewart** and their moves to Montgomery Co, VA, Wilkes Co, NC, and Monroe Co, KY. **Boone, Smithers, Houser, Farrington, Osborn, Hammer, Herndon, Pile.**
Cloth. $32.50. 200pp. .... Vendor G0420

3036 **THE DESCENDANTS OF JAMES PENNINGTON AND MARY PRICE OF QUEENSBURY PARISH, YORK COUNTY, NEW BRUNSWICK, CANADA, 1758–1994,** by Rick Crume. 1994. Indexed
Includes: Grant, Hovey, McKeen.
Paper. $16.00. 182pp. .... Vendor G0386

3037 **THE PENNOCKS OF PRIMITIVE HALL,** by George Valentine Massey II. 1951.
Cloth, $32.50. Paper, $22.50. 139pp. .... Vendor G0259

3038 **PENNYPACKER REUNION, OCTOBER 4, 1877,** by S.W. Pennypacker. 1878.
Paper. $10.50. 55pp. .... Vendor G0259

3039 **PEPPERRELL IN AMER.,** by C.H.C. Howard. 1906.
Cloth, $30.50. Paper, $20.50. 110pp. .... Vendor G0259

3040 **HISTORY OF UFTON COURT & THE PARISH OF UFTON (CO. OF BERKS [ENG.]) & OF THE PERKINS FAMILY,** by A. Mary Sharp. 1892 (London).
Cloth, $53.50. Paper, $43.50. 276pp. .... Vendor G0259

3041 **PERKINS FAM. IN OLDEN TIMES. CONTENTS OF A SERIES OF LETTERS, BY M. PARKYNS**, edited by D. Perkins. 1916.
Paper. $18.00. 88pp. .... Vendor G0259

3042 **PERKINS FAM. IN THE U.S. IN 1790**, by D.W. Perkins. 1911.
Paper. $10.00. 48pp. .... Vendor G0259

3043 **PERKINS FAMILY NEWSLETTER**, by Paula Perkins Mortensen. 1986. Indexed.
Subscription. $10.00/year. 12pp. .... Vendor G0228

3044 **THE DESC. OF EDWARD PERKINS OF NEW HAVEN, CONN.**, by C.E. Perkins. 1914.
Cloth, $31.00. Paper, $21.00. 135pp. .... Vendor G0259

3045 **THE FAM. OF JOHN PERKINS OF IPSWICH, MASS.**, by G.A. Perkins. 1889.
Cloth, $60.00. Paper, $50.00. 499pp. .... Vendor G0259

3046 **HIST. & GEN. OF THE PERLEY FAM.**, by M.V.B. Perley. 1906.
Cloth, $125.50. Paper, $115.50. 770pp. .... Vendor G0259

3047 **PERONI ROOTS AND PERONEY–PERNEY BRANCHES**, by Warren W. and Jean (Wilson) Perney. 1994. Indexed. Illus.
Vinyl. $25.00. 179pp. .... Vendor G0422

3048 **DANIEL PERRIN, "THE HUGUENOT," & HIS DESC. IN AMERICA OF THE SURNAMES PERRINE, PERINE, & PRINE, 1665–1910**, by H.D. Perrine. 1910.
Cloth, $79.00. Paper, $69.00. 553pp. .... Vendor G0259

3049 **GEN. OF THE PERRIN FAM.**, by G. Perrin. 1885.
Cloth, $44.00. Paper, $34.00. 224pp. .... Vendor G0259

3050 **INCOMPLETE HIST. OF THE DESC. OF JOHN PERRY OF LONDON, 1604–1955**, by Bertram Adams. 1955.
Cloth, $115.00. Paper, $105.00. 738pp. .... Vendor G0259

3051 **OUR PERRY FAM. IN MAINE; ITS ANC. & DESC.**, by C.N. Sinnett. 1911.
Paper. $19.00. 127pp. .... Vendor G0259

3052 **PERRYS OF R.I. & TALES OF SIVER CREEK, THE BOSWORTH–PERRY HOMESTEAD**, by C.B. Perry. 1913.
Cloth, $33.00. Paper, $23.00. 115pp. .... Vendor G0259

3053 **THE PERSHING FAM. IN AMER. A COLLECTION OF HIST. & GEN. DATA**, by E. Pershing. 1924.
Cloth, $78.00. Paper, $68.00. 434pp. .... Vendor G0259

3054 **CONRAD PETERS & WIFE CLARA SNIDOW: THEIR DESCENDANTS & ANCESTRY**, by O.E. Peters. n.d.
Cloth, $45.00. Paper, $35.00. 229pp. .... Vendor G0259

3055 **PETERS LINEAGE. FIVE GEN. OF THE DESC. OF DR. CHARLES PETERS OF HEMPSTEAD**, by M. Flint. 1896.
Cloth, $36.00. Paper, $26.00. 175pp. .... Vendor G0259

3056 **PETERS OF NEW ENG. A GEN. & FAM. HIST.**, by E. and E. Peters. 1903. Cloth, $69.00. Paper, $59.00. 470pp. .... Vendor G0259

3057 **GEORGE PETERSHEIM FAMILY**, by Petersheim Descendants. 1979. Indexed.
Over 5,200 families listed, includes: **Beachy, Beiler, Bender, Blank, Bontrager, Brenneman, Byler, Esh, Fisher, Gascho, Gingerich, Glick, Hershberger, Kauffman, King, Lapp, Mast, Miller, Riehl, Schrock, Smucker, Stoltzfus, Swartzentruber, Umble, Yoder, Zehr, Zook.**
Cloth. $11.50. 616pp. .... Vendor G0053

3058 **HIST. & GEN. ACCT. OF THE PETERSON FAM.: GEN. REC. & SKETCHES OF THE DESC. OF LAWRENS PETERSON & NANCY JONES-PETERSON, WHO PLANTED THE FAM. TREE IN AMER. BEFORE THE REV. WAR,** by W.H., S.J., and C.E. Peterson. 1926. Cloth, $69.00. Paper, $59.00. 372pp. .... Vendor G0259

3059 **PETTINGELL GEN.**, by J.M. Pettengell and C. Pope. 1906. Cloth, $99.00. Paper, $89.00. 596pp. .... Vendor G0259

3060 **PEYTON FAM. OF CAMBRIDGESHIRE, ENG. & GLOUCESTER & WESTMORELAND CO., VA. (EXTR. FROM "VA. GENS.").** Paper. $19.50. 110pp. .... Vendor G0259

3061 **GEN. OF DR. FRANCIS J. PFEIFFER, PHILA., PA. & HIS DESC., 1734–1899,** by E. Sellers. 1899. Paper. $14.00. 67pp. .... Vendor G0259

3062 **PHELPS FAM. EXTR. FROM "HIST. OF WINDSOR, CONN."** 1892. Paper. $10.00. 51pp. .... Vendor G0259

3063 **PHELPS FAM. OF AMER. & THEIR ENG. ANC.**, by Phelps and Servin. 2 vols. 1899. Cloth, $245.00. Paper, $235.00. 1,865pp. .... Vendor G0259

3064 **A GEN. OF THE PHILBRICK & PHILBROOK FAM., DESC. FROM THE EMIGRANT, THOMAS PHILBRICK, 1583–1667,** by J. Chapman. 1886. Cloth, $40.00. Paper, $30.00. 202pp. .... Vendor G0259

3065 **BRIEF HISTORY OF THE PHILLIPS FAMILY, BEGINNING WITH THE EMIGRATION FROM WALES AND A DETAILED GENEALOGY OF THE DESCENDANTS OF JOHN AND BENJAMIN PHILIPS, PIONEER CITIZENS OF WILSON CO., TENN.,** by Harry Phillips. 1935. Cloth, $52.00. Paper, $42.00. 261pp. .... Vendor G0259

3066 **DESC. OF HIRAM & MARY PHILLIPS, WITH ANC. OF JOHN SOLOMON GINTHER [& REL. STOCKER, HASS & HELLER FAMS.]**, by E.M. Firestone and J.E. Stewart. n.d.
Paper. $9.00. 44pp. .... Vendor G0259

3067 **FAM. OF JOHN PHILLIPS, SR. OF DUXBURY & MARSHFIELD**, by A. Ames. 1903.
Paper. $9.00. 43pp. .... Vendor G0259

3068 **PHILLIPS FAM. OF ENG. & NEW ENG., 1593–1877**, by E. Salisbury. 1885.
Paper. $8.50. 43pp. .... Vendor G0259

3069 **PHILLIPS GEN. INCL. THE FAM. OF GEO. PHILLIPS, FIRST MINISTER OF WATERTOWN, MA., 1630 TO PRESENT. ALSO PHILLIPS FAM. IN DUXBURY, SOUTHBORO, MARSHFIELD & IPSWICH, MA.**, by A. Phillips. 1885.
Cloth, $41.50. Paper, $31.50. 245pp. .... Vendor G0259

3070 **SOME OF THE DESCENDANTS OF ASAPH PHILLIPS AND ESTHER WHIPPLE OF FOSTER, RHODE ISLAND**, by Kenneth W. Faig, Jr. 1993.
Indexed. Illus.
Paper. $35.00. 375pp. .... Vendor G0211

3071 **PHINNEY GEN.; BRIEF HIST. OF EBENEZER PHINNEY OF CAPE COD & HIS DESC., 1637–1947**, by M.A. Phinney. 1948.
Cloth, $32.00. Paper, $22.00. 146pp. .... Vendor G0259

3072 **THE DESC. OF JOHN PHOENIX, AN EARLY SETTLER IN KITTERY, MAINE**, by S.W. Phoenix. 1867.
Paper. $12.00. 59pp. .... Vendor G0259

3073 **ANC. & DESC. OF SHERWOOD & PICKEL FAM., U.E. LOYALISTS, IN CANADA**, by W.U. Pickel. 1948.
Paper. $12.50. 62pp. .... Vendor G0259

3074 **GEN. DATA RESPECTING JOHN PICKERING OF PORTSMOUTH, N. H., & HIS DESC.**, by R.H. Eddy. 1884.
Paper. $7.00. 36pp. .... Vendor G0259

3075 **PICKERING GEN.; ACCT. OF THE 1ST THREE GENERATIONS OF THE PICKERING FAM. OF SALEM, MA., & THE DESC. OF JOHN & SARAH (BURRILL) PICKERING OF THE 3RD GEN.**, by Ellery and Bowditch. 3 vols. 1897.
Cloth, $186.00. Paper, $176.00. 1,284pp. .... Vendor G0259

3076 **PIERCE GEN.; THE REC. OF THE POSTERITY OF THOMAS PIERCE, EARLY INHABITANT OF OF CHARLESTOWN**, by F.B. Pierce, edited by F.C. Pierce. 1882.
Cloth, $57.00. Paper, $47.00. 369pp. .... Vendor G0259

3077 **PIERCE GEN., #IV; RECORD OF THE POSTERITY OF CAPT. MICHAEL, JOHN, & CAPT. WM. PIERCE, WHO CAME TO THIS COUNTRY FROM ENG.**, by F.C. Pierce. 1889.
Cloth, $78.50. Paper, $68.50. 441pp. .... Vendor G0259

3078 SEVEN PIERCE FAMILIES: RECORD OF BIRTHS, DEATHS & MAR-
RIAGES OF THE FIRST SEVEN GENERATIONS OF PIERCES IN
AMERICA, INCLUDING DESCENDANTS OF ABIAL PEIRCE, by H.C.
Pierce. 1936.
Cloth, $67.50. Paper, $57.50. 48+324pp. .... Vendor G0259

3079 [Pierce]. THE RECORD OF JOHN PERS OF WATERTOWN, MASS.,
WHO CAME FROM NORWICH, ENG., WITH NOTES ON THE HIST.
OF OTHER FAM. OF PEIRCE, PIERCE, PEARSE, ETC., by F.C. Peirce.
1880.
Cloth, $52.00. Paper, $42.00. 283pp. .... Vendor G0259

3080 PIERPONT GEN. & CONNECTING LINES. PARTICULARLY REV.
JOHN PIERPONT OF HOLLIS ST. CHURCH, BOSTON, by M.P. Barnum
and A.E. Boardman. 1928.
Paper. $8.50. 42pp. .... Vendor G0259

3081 PIERREPONT GENS. ESP. THE LINE FROM HEZEKIAH PIERPONT,
SON OF REV. JAMES PERPONT OF NEW HAVEN, by H.M. Pierpont.
1913.
Cloth, $42.00. Paper, $32.00. 211pp. .... Vendor G0259

3082 DESC. OF STEPHEN PIERSON OF SUFFOLK CO., ENG. & NEW
HAVEN & DERBY, CT., by F. Pierson. 1895.
Paper. $7.00. 33pp. .... Vendor G0259

3083 PIERSON GEN. RECORD, by L.B. Pierson. 1878.
Paper. $19.00. 106pp. .... Vendor G0259

3084 PARTIAL HISTORY OF JAMES DUNCAN PIETY, HIS FOREBEARS
& DESCENDANTS, 1796–1948, by W.P. Morgan. 1948.
Cloth, $33.00. Paper, $23.00. 150pp. .... Vendor G0259

3085 ANC. OF CHAS. STINSON PILLSBURY & JOHN SARGENT
PILLSBURY, by M.L. Holman. 2 Vols. 1938.
Cloth, $192.00. Paper, $182.00. 1,212pp. .... Vendor G0259

3086 PILLSBURY FAMILY; BEING A HIST. OF WILLIAM & DOROTHY
PILLSBURY (OR PILSBERY) OF NEWBURY IN NEW ENG., & THEIR
DESC. TO THE 11TH GEN., by D.B. Pilsbury & E.A. Getchell. 1898.
Cloth, $50.25. Paper, $40.25. 336pp. .... Vendor G0259

3087 RICHARD PINKHAM OF OLD DOVER, N.H., & HIS DESC., by C.N.
Sinnett. 1908.
Cloth, $58.50. Paper, $48.50. 308pp. .... Vendor G0259

3088 GEN. OF ELISHA PIPER, OF PARSONFIELD, ME., & HIS DESC., INCL.
PORTIONS OF OTHER REL. FAM., & AN APPENDIX CONT. THE GEN.
OF ASA PIPER OF BOSTON, STEPHEN PIPER OF NEWFIELD, ME.
& THEIR IMMEDIATE DESC., FROM 1630 TO 1889, by H. Piper. 1889.
Paper. $17.50. 121pp. .... Vendor G0259

3089 DESC. OF JOHN PITMAN, FIRST OF THE NAME IN R.I., by C.M.
Thurston. 1868.
Paper. $10.00. 48pp. .... Vendor G0259

3090 **HISTORY & PEDIGREE OF THE FAMILY PITMAN OF DUNCHI-
DEOCK, EXETER, & COLLATERALS, & OF THE PITMANS OF
ALPHINGTON, NORFOLK & EDINBURGH,** by C.E. Pitman. 1920 (London).
Cloth, $37.50. Paper, $27.50. 181pp. .... Vendor G0259

3091 **FOREBEARS & DESCENDENTS OF STERLING CHAMBERS PITTS,**
by Robert E. Pitts, et al. 1994. Illus.
Paper. Free. 34pp. .... Vendor G0383

3092 **MEM. OF THE LIVES & SERVICES OF JAMES PITTS & SONS JOHN,
SAMUEL & LENDALL DURING THE AMER. REV., 1760–1780. WITH
GEN. & HIST. APPENDIX,** by D. Goodwin, Jr. 1882.
Paper. $13.00. 69pp. .... Vendor G0259

3093 **LT. ROGER PLAISTED OF KITTERY, MAINE, & SOME OF HIS DESC.,**
by M.F. King. 1904.
Paper. $13.00. 66pp. .... Vendor G0259

3094 **THE HOUSE OF PLANT OF MACON, GA., WITH GENEALOGIES &
HIST. NOTES,** by G.S. Dickerman. 1900.
Cloth, $43.50. Paper, $33.50. 259pp. .... Vendor G0259

3095 **PLANTAGENET DESCENT: 31 GENERATIONS FROM WILLIAM THE
CONQUEROR TO TODAY,** by Thomas R. Moore. 1995. Indexed. Illus.
Thomas R. Moore's book brings to life the 31 generations from **William the
Conqueror** and his **Queen Matilda** (both descendants of the Emperor
Charlemagne), through English royalty to Princess Elizabeth **Plantagenet,** then
through the nobility and gentry of England, the glittering Elizabethan Age, high
offices in Ireland, to William **Moore** who came to Canada in 1817, then down
one line of his estimated 55,000 descendants alive today (with many surnames)
to contemporary joyous professional and personal lives in Manhattan. Mr. Moore,
the distinguished New York lawyer, author, and connoisseur, received his B.A.
magna cum laude from Yale University and his J.D. from Harvard Law School.
Cloth. $49.50. 242+xviii pp. .... Vendor G0318

3096 **PLATT GENEALOGY IN AMERICA, FROM THE ARRIVAL OF RICH-
ARD PLATT IN NEW HAVEN, CONN., IN 1638,** by Charles Platt, Jr. 1963.
Cloth, $81.00. Paper, $71.00. 453pp. .... Vendor G0259

3097 **PLATT LIN. A GEN. RESEARCH & RECORD,** by G. Platt. 1891.
Cloth, $61.50. Paper, $51.50. 398pp. .... Vendor G0259

3098 **A GEN. & HIST. NOTICES OF THE FAM. OF PLIMPTON OR
PLYMPTON IN AMER., & OF PLUMPTON IN ENG.,** by L.B. Chase.
1884.
Cloth, $42.00. Paper, $32.00. 240pp. .... Vendor G0259

3099 **REGISTER OF PLOWMANS IN AMER. . . . & EXTR. FROM ENG. &
AMER. RECORDS,** by B.H.F. Plowman. 1901.
Paper. $17.50. 90pp. .... Vendor G0259

3100 **THE PLUMBS, 1635–1800,** by H.B. Plumb. 2nd ed. 1893.
Paper. $19.00. 102pp. .... Vendor G0259

3101 **PLUMER GEN. FRANCIS PLUMER, WHO SETTLED AT NEWBURY, MASS., & SOME DESC.**, by S. Perley. 1917.
Cloth, $49.00. Paper, $39.00. 259pp. .... Vendor G0259

3102 **PLUMMER SYSTEM OF GEN. ENUMERATION. LIN. OF FRANCIS PLUMER, NEWBURY MA, 1635**, by A. Plummer. 1904.
Paper. $12.50. 64pp. .... Vendor G0259

3103 **TEN THOUSAND PLUNKETTS: PARTIALLY DOC. REC. OF THE FAMS. OF CHARLES PLUNKETT OF NEWBERRY CO., SC; HIS BROTHER PETER PLUNKETT OF OLD BARNWELL DIST., SC; & REL. FAMS.**, by E.P. Ivy. 1969.
Cloth, $85.00. Paper, $75.00. 528pp. .... Vendor G0259

3104 **POCAHONTAS, ALIAS MATOAKA, & HER DESCENDANTS THROUGH HER MARRIAGE AT JAMESTOWN, VA., WITH JOHN ROLFE, GENTLEMAN**, by W. Robertson. 1887.
Paper. $10.00. 84pp. .... Vendor G0259

3105 **POCAHONTAS, ALIAS MATOAKA, and Her Descendants Through Her Marriage at Jamestown, Virginia in April, 1614, With John Rolfe, Gentleman**, by Wyndham Robertson and Robert A. Brock. (1887) reprint 1993.
Cloth. $10.00. 84pp. .... Vendor G0010

3106 **ORIGIN OF THE EARLY HIST. OF THE FAMS. OF POE, WITH FULL PEDIGREES OF THE IRISH BRANCH OF THE FAMS. & A DISCUSSION OF THE TRUE ANC. OF EDGAR ALLEN POE**, by E.T. Bewley. 1906.
Paper. $16.00. 102pp. .... Vendor G0259

3107 **POETKER FAMILIES IN NORTH AMERICA**, by Nannie Ellis Houser and Elmer Andrew Houser, Jr. 1993. Indexed. Illus.
The definitive genealogy of the **Poetker** family in North America with fully indexed data on over 4,000 families in the four major branches in Ohio, Indiana, and Canada and their origins in Germany and Russia. Historical and Lutheran and Mennonite backgrounds and migration routes are detailed. Surname spellings include **Petker, Poetker, Poettcker, Potker**, and **Pottker**. Collateral families include: **Bartelt, Bussman, Dever, Dyck, Ellis, Fast, Katterhenry, Martens, Meyer, Moore, Reese, Ring, Thiesen**, and **Wiens**.
Paper. $32.00. 232pp. .... Vendor G0052

3108 **POGUE/POLLOCK/POLK GENEALOGY AS MIRRORED IN HISTORY, From Scotland to Northern Ireland/Ulster, Ohio, and Westward**, by L. Welch Pogue; John Marshall Pogue, M.D., Editor and Research Scholar. 1990. Indexed. 50pp. of illustrations.
The book has extensive citations of authorities, over 200 photos of members of Clan families, maps, charts, appendices, a large bibliography, and a 50-page person/subject index. The book is enlivened by the recounting of historical items, scientific discoveries, inventions, and events occurring as Clan members came along. It is sewn through the fold, glued, and the grain direction is parallel with the spine, thus complying with the highest binding standards. In the interests of long preservation, the dust jacket, the caseboards (heavy and covered with Library Buckram F group), and the text are all on alkaline paper which meets the current ANSI standard for permanence, being acid-free, lignin-free, sulphur-free, and buffered with high alkaline reserve.

The book has, thus far, won six Awards (four from genealogical societies and two from historical societies). One of the six was the National Genealogical Society's "Award for Excellence: Genealogy and Family History."

Allied surnames—the following are a few descendants who have entries in the book: **Albright, Atherton, Barnes, Brook, Chambers, Curtis, Douglas, French, Hutchison, Macklin, Miller, Scott, Stewart, Taylor, Timberman, Yost.**

Cloth. $35.00. Approx. 800pp. .... Vendor G0444

3109 **POLK FAMILY AND KINSMEN**, by Wm. Harrison Polk. 1912.
Cloth, $115.00. Paper, $105.00. 742pp. .... Vendor G0259

3110 **BIOGRAPHICAL SKETCH OF OLIVER POLLOCK, ESQ., OF CARLISLE, PA., U.S. COMMERCIAL AGENT, 1776–1884, WITH GENEALOGICAL NOTES OF HIS DESCENDANTS**, by Horace E. Hayden. 1883.
Paper. $12.00. 59pp. .... Vendor G0259

3111 **ROMANCE & HISTORY OF ELTWEED POMEROY'S ANCESTORS IN NORMANDY & ENGLAND**, by A.A. Pomeroy. 1909.
Paper. $16.00. 81pp. .... Vendor G0259

3112 **HISTORY & GENEALOGY OF THE POMEROY FAMILY: COLLATERAL LINES IN FAMILY GROUPS, NORMANDY, GREAT BRITAIN & AMERICA, COMPRISING THE ANCESTORS & DESCENDANTS OF ELTWEED POMEROY, FROM BEAMINSTER, CO. DORSET, ENGLAND, 1630**, by Albert A. Pomeroy. 1912.
Cloth, $149.50. Paper, $139.50. 962pp. .... Vendor G0259

3113 **POMEROY, PART III**, by A.A. Pomeroy. 1922.
Cloth, $63.00. Paper, $53.00. 342pp. .... Vendor G0259

3114 **A GEN. RECORD OF DANIEL POND & HIS DESC.**, by E.D. Harris. 1873.
Cloth, $41.50. Paper, $31.50. 210pp. .... Vendor G0259

3115 **GEN. RECORDS OF SAMUEL POND & HIS DESC.**, by D.S. Pond. 1875.
Cloth, $35.00. Paper, $25.00. 126pp. .... Vendor G0259

3116 **THE HIST. OF EDWARD POOLE OF WEYMOUTH, MASS. (1635) & HIS DESC.**, by M.E. Poole. 1893.
Cloth, $35.50. Paper, $25.50. 164pp. .... Vendor G0259

3117 **A MEM. & GEN. OF JOHN POORE: TEN GENERATIONS, 1615–1880**, by A. Poore. 1881.
Cloth, $53.00. Paper, $43.00. 332pp. .... Vendor G0259

3118 **FAM. OF BERNARD POORMAN OF PENN. & OHIO (IN SNYDER GEN.)**, by A.B. Grove. 1892.
Paper. $7.50. 31pp. .... Vendor G0259

3119 **A HIST. OF THE DORCHESTER POPE FAM., 1634–1888. WITH SKETCHES OF OTHER POPES IN ENG. & AMER.**, by C.H. Pope. 1888.
Cloth, $54.00. Paper, $44.00. 340pp. .... Vendor G0259

3120 **GENEALOGY OF THOMAS POPE (1608–1683) & HIS DESCENDANTS**, by Worden, Langworthy and Burch. 1917.
Cloth, $34.00. Paper, $24.00. 143pp. .... Vendor G0259

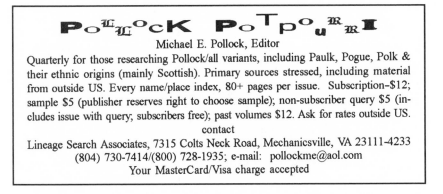

Pᴏᴸᴸ**ᴏᴄK Pᴏ**ᵀ**pᴏ**ᵤ**ᴿ**ᴿ**I**

Michael E. Pollock, Editor

Quarterly for those researching Pollock/all variants, including Paulk, Pogue, Polk & their ethnic origins (mainly Scottish). Primary sources stressed, including material from outside US. Every name/place index, 80+ pages per issue. Subscription–$12; sample $5 (publisher reserves right to choose sample); non-subscriber query $5 (includes issue with query; subscribers free); past volumes $12. Ask for rates outside US.

contact

Lineage Search Associates, 7315 Colts Neck Road, Mechanicsville, VA 23111-4233
(804) 730-7414/(800) 728-1935; e-mail: pollockme@aol.com
Your MasterCard/Visa charge accepted

3121 **A GEN. OF THE DESC. OF RICHARD PORTER, WHO SETTLED AT WEYMOUTH, MASS., 1635, & ALLIED FAM.; ALSO SOME ACCT. OF THE DESC. OF JOHN PORTER, WHO SETTLED AT HINGHAM, MASS., 1635, & SALEM (DANVERS), MASS., 1644**, by J.W. Porter. 1878.
Cloth, $64.50. Paper, $54.50. 344pp. Vendor G0259

3122 **A PORTER PEDIGREE, BEING AN ACCT. OF THE ANC. & DESC. OF SAMUEL & MARTHA (PERLEY) PORTER OF CHESTER, N.H.**, by J. Porter. 1907.
Cloth, $34.00. Paper, $24.00. 161pp. Vendor G0259

3123 **DESC. OF JOHN PORTER OF WINDSOR, CT., 1635–9**, by H.P. Andrews. 2 vols. 1893.
Cloth, $66.00/vol. Paper, $56.00/vol. 436+451pp. . . . . Vendor G0259

3124 **THE DESC. OF MOSES & SARAH KILHAM PORTER OF PAWLET, VT., WITH SOME NOTICE OF THEIR ANC.**, by J.S. Lawrence. 1910.
Cloth, $36.50. Paper, $26.50. 203pp. Vendor G0259

3125 **THE PORTER FAM. PROCEEDINGS AT THE REUNION OF THE DESC. OF JOHN PORTER, OF DANVERS, HELD AT DANVERS, MASS., JULY 17TH, 1895**. 1897.
Paper. $14.00. 72pp. . . . . Vendor G0259

3126 **THE PORTERFIELDS**, by Frank B. Porterfield. 1948.
Cloth, $64.00. Paper, $54.00. 345pp. Vendor G0259

3127 **POST FAMILY**, by M.C. de T. Post. 1905.
Cloth, $66.00. Paper, $56.00. 352pp. Vendor G0259

3128 **GEN. OF THE POTTER FAMS. & THEIR DESC. IN AMER., WITH HIST. & BIOGR. SKETCHES**, by C.W. Potter. 1888.
Cloth, $48.00. Paper, $38.00. 300pp. Vendor G0259

3129 **HIST. COLL. RELATING TO THE POTTS FAM. IN GT. BRIT. & AMER., WITH AN HIST-GEN. OF THE DESC. OF DAVID POTTS, AN EARLY ANGLO-WELSH SETTLER OF PA.**, by T.M. Potts. 1901.
Cloth, $104.50. Paper, $94.50. 735pp. . . . . Vendor G0259

3130 **MEM. OF THOMAS POTTS, JR., WHO SETTLED IN PENN., WITH AN HIST.-GEN. ACCT. OF HIS DESC. TO THE 8TH GEN.**, by T.P. James. 1874.
Cloth, $77.50. Paper, $67.50. 430pp. Vendor G0259

3131 **[Potts]. OUR FAM. RECORD**, by T.M. Potts. 1895.
Cloth, $64.00. Paper, $54.00. 434pp. Vendor G0259

3132 **POUND & KESTER FAM. AN ACCT. OF THE ANC. OF JOHN POUND (b. 1735) & WM. KESTER (b. 1733) & A GEN. RECORD OF ALL THEIR DESC.**, by J.E. Hunt. 1904.
Cloth, $104.00. Paper, $94.00. 628pp. Vendor G0259

3133 **AUTHENTIC GEN. MEM'L HIST. OF PHILIP POWELL OF MIFFLIN CO., PA. & HIS DESC. & OTHERS**, by J. Powell. 1880.
Cloth, $67.00. Paper, $57.00. 447pp. Vendor G0259

3134 **FAMILY RECORDS OF THE POWELL & GRIFFITHS (WITH POETRY OF JOHN POWELL)**, by Rachel Powell. 1866.
Paper. $19.50. 119pp. . . . . Vendor G0259

3135 **POWELL FAMILY OF ALLEGANY COUNTY, MARYLAND—DESCEN-DANTS OF WILLIAM POWELL**, by George Ely Russell. 1990. Indexed. Illus.
Paper. $16.00. 117pp. . . . . Vendor G0126

3136 **POWERS FAM., GEN. & HIST. RECORD OF WALTER POWER & SOME DESC. TO THE 9TH GEN.**, by A.H. Powers. 1884.
Cloth, $38.00. Paper, $28.00. 199pp. Vendor G0259

3137 **POWERS–BANKS ANC. CHARLES POWERS, 1819–1871, & HIS WIFE LYDIA ANN BANKS, 1829–1919**, by W. Powers. 1921.
Cloth, $58.75. Paper, $48.75. 325pp. Vendor G0259

3138 **A COLL. OF SOME FACTS ABOUT SOME OF THE DESC. OF JOHN PRATT OF DORCHESTER, MA.** n.d.
Paper. $7.50. 37pp. typescript . . . . Vendor G0259

3139 **1538–1900. THE ANC. & THE DESC. OF JOHN PRATT OF HARTFORD, CONN.**, by C.B. Whittelsey. 1900.
Cloth, $40.50. Paper, $30.50. 204pp. Vendor G0259

3140 **PHINEAS PRATT & SOME OF HIS DESC. A MONOGRAPH**, by E.F. Pratt. 1897.
Cloth, $34.50. Paper, $24.50. 164pp. Vendor G0259

3141 **PRATT FAM. A GEN. REC. OF MATHEW PRATT OF WEYMOUTH, MASS. & HIS AMER. DESC., 1623–1889**, by F.G. Pratt, Jr. 1890.
Cloth, $44.00. Paper, $34.00. 226pp. Vendor G0259

3142 **PRATT FAM.; OR, THE DESC. OF LT. WM. PRATT, ONE OF THE 1ST SETTLERS OF HARTFORD & SAYBROOK; WITH GEN. NOTES OF JOHN OF HARTFORD, PETER OF LYME, JOHN PRATT TAYLOR OF SAYBROOK**, by F. Chapman. 1864.
Cloth, $64.50. Paper, $54.50. 421pp. Vendor G0259

3143 SKETCH OF THE LIFE OF SAMUEL F. PRATT, WITH SOME ACCT. OF THE EARLY HIST. OF THE PRATT FAM. A PAPER READ BEFORE THE BUFFALO HIST. SOC., MARCH 10TH, 1873, by W.P. Letchworth. 1874.
Cloth, $41.50. Paper, $31.50. 211pp. .... Vendor G0259

3144 GEN. SKETCH OF THE 1ST THREE GEN. OF PREBLES IN AMER.; WITH AN ACCT. OF ABRAHAM PREBLE THE EMIGRANT, & OF BRIG. GEN. JEDEDIAH PREBLE & HIS DESC., by G.H. Preble. 1868.
Cloth, $64.00. Paper, $54.00. 340pp. .... Vendor G0259

3145 [Prehn]. JOURNAL OF A GENEALOGIST, WITH ANCESTRAL WILLS, (INCLUDES ANDERSON, BASS, ELDER, GADDY, GRIGGS, INGERSOLL, KELSEY, LEWIS, WEST(F)ALL, WRIGHT FAMILIES), by Alyene E. Westall Prehn. 1980.
Cloth, $125.00. Paper, $115.00. 864pp. .... Vendor G0259

3146 HIST. & GEN. OF THE PRENTICE–PRENTISS FAMS. IN NEW ENG., 1631–1883, by C.J.F. Binney. 2nd ed. 1883.
Cloth, $67.50. Paper, $57.50. 453pp. .... Vendor G0259

3147 WARREN PRENTICE, 1827–1916—SAILOR, SOLDIER, EARLY SETTLER, by Willard J. Prentice. (1986), reprint 1994 includes supplement. Indexed. Illus.
Descendants of Thomas **Prentice**.
Paper. $15.00. 210pp. .... Vendor G0331

3148 WM. PRESBREY OF LONDON, ENG., & TAUNTON, MASS., & HIS DESC., 1690–1918, by J.W. Presby. 1918.
Cloth, $32.50. Paper, $22.50. 151pp. .... Vendor G0259

3149 PRESCOTTS UNLIMITED [Newsletter]. Doris Cline Ward, Editor. 1980.
English Research project—regarding ancestry of John of Massachusetts, James of New Hampshire, and John of Virginia.
Subscription. $10.50 per year. 14pp quarterly .... Vendor G0044

3150 THE PRESCOTT MEM. A GEN. MEMOIR OF THE PRESCOTT FAM. IN AMER., by W. Prescott. 1870.
Cloth, $110.00. Paper, $100.00. 667pp. .... Vendor G0259

3151 DESCENDANTS OF ROGER PRESTON OF IPSWICH & SALEM VILLAGE, by C.H. Preston. 1931.
Cloth, $66.00. Paper, $56.00. 355pp. .... Vendor G0259

3152 PRESTON GEN.; TRACING THE HIST. OF THE FAM. FROM ABOUT 1040, edited by L.A. Wilson and W.B. Preston. 1900.
Cloth, $68.50. Paper, $58.50. 376pp. .... Vendor G0259

3153 A GEN. OF THE DESC. OF REV. JACOB PRICE, EVANGELIST-PIONEER, by G.F.P. Wanger. 1926.
Cloth, $134.50. Paper, $124.50. 832pp. .... Vendor G0259

3154 PRICE FAMILY HISTORY, by J. Montgomery Seaver.
Paper. $8.00. 41pp. .... Vendor G0259

3155 **THE FAMILY OF JOHN PRICE & NANCY AGNES MOORE**, by Elberta Price Griffiths. 1982. Indexed. Illus.
John **Price** born 1763, PA, died 1831, Morgan Co., OH. Nancy **Moore** born 1767, DE, died 1856, Morgan Co. Eight children traced; descendants in AZ, CA, FL, MD, MI, MO, OH, OR, TX. **Bailey** history included and Civil War diary of John Laughlin **Price**.
Cloth. $16.95. 136pp. .... Vendor G0282

3156 **THE PRICE, BLAKEMORE, HAMBLEN, SKIPWITH AND ALLIED LINES**, by Mayor Jay Price. 1992. Indexed. Illus.
Cloth. $85.00. 930pp. .... Vendor G0183

3157 **DESC. OF WM. PRICHARD**, by A.M. Prichard. 1912.
Paper. $12.00. 61pp. .... Vendor G0259

3158 **PRIEST FAMILY. COLLECTION OF DATA . . . CONCERNING VARIOUS BRANCHES OF THE PRIEST FAM.**, by G.E. Foster. 1900.
Cloth, $79.00. Paper, $69.00. 549pp. .... Vendor G0259

3159 **NOTES—GENEALOGICAL, BIOGRAPHICAL & BIBLIOGRAPHICAL—OF THE PRIME FAMILY**, by E.D.G. Prime. 1888.
Paper. $19.50. 118pp. .... Vendor G0259

3160 **SOME ACCT. OF THE PRIME FAM. OF ROWLEY, MASS., WITH NOTES ON THE FAMS. OF PLATTS, JEWETT, & HAMMOND**, by T. Prime. 1887.
Paper. $8.00. 40pp. .... Vendor G0259

3161 **[Prime]. THE AUTOBIOGRAPHY OF AN OCTOGENARIAN, WITH THE GENEALOGY OF HIS ANCESTORS & SKETCHES OF THEIR HISTORY**, by Daniel N. Prime. 1873.
Cloth, $54.00. Paper, $44.00. 293pp. .... Vendor G0259

3162 **THE GEN. OF THE PRINCE FAM. FROM 1660 TO 1899**, by F.A. Prince. 1899.
Cloth, $33.00. Paper, $23.00. 153pp. .... Vendor G0259

3163 **PRINDLE GEN., EMBRACING THE DESC. OF WM. PRINGLE, THE 1ST SETTLER, & ALSO THE ANC. & DESC. OF ZALMON PRINDLE, 1654–1906**, by F.C. Prindle. 1906.
Cloth, $56.50. Paper, $46.50. 352pp. .... Vendor G0259

3164 **THE PRINTUP FAMILY IN AMERICA, 1695–1988**, by Stephen L. Lawton and Robert A. Printup. 1989. Indexed. Illus.
Traces male and female descendants of William **Printup**. Son, William, Jr. (fluent in Mohawk dialect), served as interpreter for Sir William Johnson during 1750–1764. Thirteen generations; biographical sketches; wills; gravestone inscriptions; correspondence during 1846–1889. Partial list of allied names: **Adams, Allen, Anthony, Armstrong, Barrow, Blissit, Branham, Breymann, Brown, Bunker, Card, Cass, Clarke, Cody, Connelly, Cooper, Davis, Dickson, Dockstader, Emmons, Fish, Fowler, Frank, Freeman, Gibbs, Girvan, Glann, Griffith, Grover, Hall, Hamilton, Harris, Hart, Henderson, Huxley, Johnson, Jones, Kerr, Lathrop, Laugharn, Leaphart, Leidy, Lingenfelter, Martin, McKisson, McLendon, Meyer, Mills, Mitchell, Morgan, Newsom, Nichols, Oetjen, Ouderkerk, Owens, Parkes, Philipse, Phillips, Porter, Putman,**

Quinn, Robertson, Robinson, Rogers, Schermerhorn, Scott, Seagraves, Shields, Shults, Smith, Sternbergh, Sternburgh, Sterns, Usry, Van Wie, Van Wormer, Verdery, Walker, Watson, Wessel[s], Williams, Wilson, Wright, **Zielley**. 6" x 9" format. LC 89-83643.
Cloth. $27.50. 739pp. .... Vendor G0045

3165 **A LITTLE INFO. ON THE PRIOR–PRYOR FAM.**, by H.E. Pryor.
Paper. $12.50. 58pp. .... Vendor G0259

3166 **A GEN. OF THE DESC. OF ROBERT PROCTOR OF CONCORD & CHELMSFORD, MA., WITH NOTES OF SOME CONNECTED FAM.**, by Mr. and Mrs. W.L. Proctor. 1898.
Cloth, $56.50. Paper, $46.50. 315pp. .... Vendor G0259

3167 **PROCTOR GATHERING IN COMM. OF THE 100TH WEDDING ANNIVERSARY OF THEIR PROGENITORS JOSEPH PROCTOR & ELIZABETH EPES, WITH THE GEN. OF THE FAM.** 1868.
Paper. $10.00. 46pp. .... Vendor G0259

3168 **DESCENDANTS OF JOHANN JOST PROPPER/PROPER 1710 GERMAN PALATINE IMMIGRANT**, by Lewis G. Proper. 1996. Indexed, 23,000 entries. Documented.
Includes 70 illustrations, 50 biographies; war records—Revolutionary, War 1812, Spanish-American, Mexican, Civil War; partial genealogies. **Keller, Houghtaling, Ostrander, Rice, Allen.**
Hardcover. Contact author for price. Approx. 800pp. .... Vendor G0439

3169 **PROUTY (PROUTE) GEN.**, by C.H. Pope. 1910.
Cloth, $42.00. Paper, $32.00. 247pp. .... Vendor G0259

3170 **BIOGR. & GEN. NOTES OF THE PROVOST FAM. FROM 1545–1895**, by A.J. Provost. 1895.
Cloth, $30.00. Paper, $20.00. 147pp. .... Vendor G0259

3171 **PETER PRUDDEN: A STORY OF HIS LIFE AT NEW HAVEN & MILFORD, CONN., WITH THE GEN. OF SOME OF HIS DESC.**, by L.E. Prudden. 1901.
Cloth, $35.00. Paper, $25.00. 169pp. .... Vendor G0259

3172 **PUCKETT POINTS: FAM. OF RICHARD PUCKETT OF LUNENBURG CO., VA.**, by J.D. Gallaway. 1931.
Paper. $8.00. 39pp. .... Vendor G0259

3173 **DESC. OF GEO. PUFFER OF BRAINTREE, MASS., 1639–1915**, by C. Nutt. 1915.
Cloth, $58.50. Paper, $48.50. 376pp. .... Vendor G0259

3174 **[Pugh]. CAPON VALLEY. Its Pioneers and Their Descendants, 1698 to 1940**, by Maud Pugh. (1948) reprint 1995. Illus.
Consists primarily of genealogical essays and Bible records referring to the pioneering **Pugh** family and allied family lines.
Paper. $28.50. 350pp. .... Vendor G0011

3175 **ANC. & DESC. OF JONATHAN PULFISER OF POLAND & SUMNER, MAINE**, by W.E. Pulfiser. 1928.
Paper. $14.00. 71pp. .... Vendor G0259

3176 **A TRIBUTE TO THE MEM. OF JOHN PUNCHARD; A SERMON PREACHED AT HIS FUNERAL, FEB. 16, 1857, & AN APPENDIX CONTAINING THE GEN. OF THE PUNCHARD FAM.**, by S.M. Worcester. 1857.
Paper. $14.00. 69pp. .... Vendor G0259

3177 **ALLIED FAMS. OF PURDY, FAUCONNIER [FALCONER], ARCHER & PERRIN**, by A.F. Perrin and M.F.P. Meeker. 1911.
Paper. $16.50. 114pp. .... Vendor G0259

3178 **HIST. OF THE PUTNAM FAM. IN ENG. & AMER. (INCL. "PUTNAM LEAFLETS")**, by E. Putnam. 2 vols. 1891–1908.
Cloth, $109.00. Paper, $99.00. 720pp. .... Vendor G0259

3179 **PUTNAM LINEAGE: HIST.-GEN. NOTES CONCERNING THE PUTTENHAM FAM. IN ENGLAND, WITH LINES OF ROYAL DESC., & THE ANC. OF JOHN PUTNAM OF SALEM & DESC. THROUGH FIVE GEN., WITH SOME ACCT. OF OTHER PUTNAM FAMS. & THE PUTNAMS OF THE MOHAWK VAL.**, by E. Putnam. 1907.
Cloth, $61.00. Paper, $51.00. 400pp. .... Vendor G0259

3180 **THE HON. SAMUEL PUTNAM & SARAH (GOOLL) PUTNAM, WITH A GEN. RECORD OF THEIR DESC. (REPR. DANVERS HIST. COLL.)**, by E.C. Putnam and H. Tapley. 1922.
Paper. $8.00. 42pp. .... Vendor G0259

3181 **PYLDREN–DUMMER FAM., 1100–1884**, by E. Salisbury. 1885.
Paper. $14.00. 70pp. .... Vendor G0259

3182 **QUATTLEBAUM FAMILY HISTORY**, by M.M. Quattlebaum. 1950.
Cloth, $58.50. Paper, $48.50. 280pp. .... Vendor G0259

3183 **GEN. OF THE QUICK FAM. IN AMERICA (1625–1942)**, by A.C. Quick. 1942.
Cloth, $87.50. Paper, $77.50. 507pp. .... Vendor G0259

3184 **GEN. HIST. OF THE QUINBY (QUIMBY) FAM. IN ENG. & AMER.**, by H.C. Quimby. 1915.
Cloth, $104.00. Paper, $94.00. 604pp. .... Vendor G0259

3185 **THE QUINBY–QUIMBY FAM. OF SANDWICH, N.H.**, by H.C. Quinby. Vol. 2 of above. 1923.
Cloth, $92.00. Paper, $82.00. 533pp. .... Vendor G0259

3186 **QUINCY FAM. IN ENG. & AMER., 1559–1877**, by E. Salisbury. 1885.
Paper. $16.00. 81pp. .... Vendor G0259

3187 **GEN. OF THE RAGLAND FAM. & NUMEROUS OTHER FAM. OF PROMINENCE IN AMER. WITH WHOM THEY HAVE INTERMARRIED**, by M. Strong. 1928.
Cloth, $31.00. Paper, $21.00. 129pp. .... Vendor G0259

3188 **THE RAINIER REPORT**, The Rainier Society of France and America, by Dr. Lawrence Kent, Editor.
Concerned with the genealogy of the **Rainier** family of France and America. Direct inquiries require a SASE .... Vendor G0448

3189 **RAKESTRAWS OF THE COLONIES**, by Edward Pete Craig, Jr. 1995. Indexed.

Compilation of all **Rakestraw** families from the late 1600s of Pennsylvania and Virginia and their descendants to 1800 and beyond, including movement west to Ohio and south to the Carolinas and Georgia after the Revolution. Church, Court, and Revolutionary War records.

Cloth. $42.95 .... Vendor G0146A

3190 **RAMSDELL FAMILY. WILLIAM RAMSDELL GENEALOGY**, by William Ramsdell. 1991.

Paper. $12.00. 60pp. .... Vendor G0259

3191 **RAMSEYS OF YORK COUNTY, PA; FRANKLIN COUNTY, OH; TAZEWELL, WOODFORD, LIVINGSTON, & McLEAN COUNTIES, IL; LIVINGSTON, DE KALB, BATES, & VERNON COUNTIES, MO; WELD COUNTY, CO; LASSEN, MODOC, & MERCED COUNTIES, CA**, by Lynn Marks. 1992. Indexed.

Fiche only. $6.00. 318pp. .... Vendor G0413

3192 **GEN. OF THE RAND FAM. IN THE US**, by F. Rand. 1898.

Cloth, $45.00. Paper, $35.00. 269pp. .... Vendor G0259

3193 **A BIOGR. HIST. OF ROBERT RANDALL & HIS DESC., 1608–1909**, by W.L. Chaffin. 1909.

Cloth, $50.00. Paper, $40.00. 267pp. .... Vendor G0259

3194 **GEN. OF A BRANCH OF THE RANDALL FAM., 1666 TO 1879**, by P.K. Randall.

Cloth, $53.00. Paper, $43.00. 389pp. .... Vendor G0259

3195 **GENEALOGY OF THE DESC. OF STEPHEN RANDALL & ELIZABETH SWAZEY: 1624–1668. LONDON, ENG.; 1668–1738, R.I. & CONN.; 1738–1906, LONG ISL., N.Y.**, by S.M. Randall. 1906.

Paper. $13.00. 64pp. .... Vendor G0259

3196 **RANDALL & ALLIED FAMILIES: WILLIAM RANDALL (1609–1693) OF SCITUATE & HIS DESCENDANTS WITH ANCESTRAL FAMILIES**, by F.A. Randall. 1943.

Cloth, $99.00. Paper, $89.00. 596pp. .... Vendor G0259

3197 **DESCENDANTS OF WILLIAM RANDOLPH OF VIRGINIA**, by Carol A. Hauk. 1995. Indexed.

Paper. $45.00. 350pp. .... Vendor G0340

3198 **THE RANDOLPHS OF VA. A COMP. OF THE DESC. OF WM. RANDOLPH OF TURKEY ISL. & HIS WIFE MARY ISHAM OF BERMUDA HUNDRED**, by R.I. Randolph.

Cloth, $72.50. Paper, $62.50. 404pp. .... Vendor G0259

3199 **THE RANKIN & WHARTON FAM. & THEIR GEN.**, by S.M. Rankin. 1931.

Cloth, $54.00. Paper, $44.00. 295pp. .... Vendor G0259

3200 **HISTORICAL OUTLINE OF THE RANSOM FAMILY OF AMERICA, AND GENEALOGICAL RECORDS OF THE COLCHESTER, CT., BRANCH**, by Wyllys C. Ransom. 1903.

Cloth, $72.00. Paper, $62.00. 408pp. .... Vendor G0259

3201 **RATHBONE FAM., EXTR. FROM GEN. NOTES OF N.Y. & NEW ENG. FAM.**, by S.V. Talcott. 1883.
Paper. $8.00. 40pp. .... Vendor G0259

3202 **RATHBONE GEN. A COMPLETE HIST. OF THE RATHBONE FAM., FROM 1574 TO DATE**, by J.C. Cooley. 1898.
Cloth, $114.00. Paper, $104.00. 827pp. .... Vendor G0259

3203 **INDEX TO RATHBONE GEN.**, compiled by M. Dale. 1966.
Cloth, $36.00. Paper, $26.00. 253pp. .... Vendor G0259

3204 **RAUENZABNER TO ROUTSON: A FAMILY ON THE MOVE**, by John P. Dern and M. Marjorie Waidner. 1993. Indexed. Illus. Book #1453.
Cloth. $63.95. 779pp. .... Vendor G0082

3205 **RAVENEL RECORDS. HIST. & GEN. OF THE HUGUENOT FAM. OF RAVENEL, OF S.C.; WITH SOME INCIDENTAL ACCT. OF THE PARISH OF ST JOHNS BERKELEY, THEIR PRINCIPAL LOCATION**, by H.E. Ravenel. 1898.
Cloth, $46.00. Paper, $36.00. 279pp. .... Vendor G0259

3206 **RECORDS OF THE RAWLE FAM., COLL. FROM THE NAT'L ARCHIVES, PARISH REG. & OTHER SOURCES**, by E.J. Rawle. 1898.
Cloth, $53.00. Paper, $43.00. 336pp. .... Vendor G0259

3207 **NOTES RELATING TO RAWLINS, OR ROLLINS, WITH NOTICES OF EARLY SETTLERS OF THE NAME IN AMERICA & FAM. RECORDS OF THOMAS, OF BOSTON; NICHOLAS, OF NEWBURY; WILLIAM OF GLOUCESTER**, by J.R. Rollins. 1870.
Paper. $16.50. 84pp. .... Vendor G0259

3208 **ANC. OF EDWARD RAWSON**, by E.B. Crane. 1887.
Paper. $10.00. 54pp. .... Vendor G0259

3209 **MEMOIR OF EDWARD RAWSON, WITH GEN. NOTICES OF HIS DESC.**, by S.S. Rawson. 1849.
Cloth, $40.00. Paper, $30.00. 148pp. .... Vendor G0259

3210 **RAWSON FAMILY. A REV. MEM. OF EDWARD RAWSON, SEC. OF THE COL. OF MASS. BAY, 1650 TO 1686**, by E.B. Crane. 1875.
Cloth, $65.00. Paper, $55.00. 350pp. .... Vendor G0259

3211 **DESC. OF RICHARD RAYMOND. VOL. I, PT. I.**, by S.E. Raymond and Louvera H. Raymond. 1969.
Cloth, $44.50. Paper, $34.50. 227pp. .... Vendor G0259

3212 **DESC. OF RICHARD RAYMOND. PT. II.**, by S.E. Raymond and Louvera H. Raymond. 1970.
Cloth, $64.00. Paper, $54.00. 340pp. .... Vendor G0259

3213 **DESC. OF RICHARD RAYMOND. PT. III.**, by S.E. Raymond and Louvera H. Raymond 1971.
Cloth, $92.00. Paper, $82.00. 534pp. .... Vendor G0259

3214 **DESC. OF RICHARD RAYMOND. PT. IV.**, by S.E. Raymond and Louvera H. Raymond. 1972.
Cloth, $86.00. Paper, $76.00. 510pp. .... Vendor G0259

Winner

National Genealogical Society's
1993 Book Award for Excellence in
Genealogical Methods and Sources

Genealogical Resources
in English Repositories

by Joy Wade Moulton

1992 Supplement
**updating access information for 226 English repositories
plus 1996 Update**

$39.00 book and supplement $5.75 supplement only

**Hampton House, P.O. Box 21534
Columbus, Ohio 43221-1534**

Ohio residents add 5.75% sales tax

3215 **GEN. OF THE RAYMOND FAM. OF NEW ENG. 1630 TO 1886, WITH A HIST. SKETCH OF SOME OF THE RAYMONDS OF EARLY TIMES,** by S. Raymond. 1886.
Cloth, $49.00. Paper, $39.00. 304pp. Vendor G0259

3216 **RAYMOND GEN. DESC. OF JOHN & WM. RAYMOND,** by S.E. Raymond and L.H. Raymond. 1972.
Cloth, $139.00. Paper, $129.00. 886pp. . . . . Vendor G0259

3217 **ALLIED FAMILIES OF READ, CORBIN, LUTTRELL, & BYWATERS OF CULPEPER CO., VA.,** by A.M. Prichard. 1930.
Cloth, $56.00. Paper, $46.00. 292pp. Vendor G0259

3218 **GEN. OF THE BROTHERS & SISTERS & FAM. & DESC. OF ISRAEL, ABNER, JOHN, POLLY, WILLIAM, WOLCOTT, LEWIS & NATHANIEL READ,** by H.M. Dodd. 1912.
Cloth, $58.00. Paper, $48.00. 301pp. Vendor G0259

3219 **THE READS & THEIR RELATIVES, BEING AN ACCOUNT OF COL. CLEMENS & MADAM READ OF BUSHY FOREST, LUNENBURG CO. VA., THEIR EIGHT CHILDREN, THEIR DESCENDANTS, & ALLIED FAMILIES,** by Alice Read. 1930.
Cloth, $109.50. Paper, $99.50. 688pp. . . . . Vendor G0259

3220 **DESCENDANTS OF GEORGE READE OF VIRGINIA,** by Carol A. Hauk. 1995. Indexed.
Paper. $60.00. 617pp. . . . . Vendor G0340

3221 **RECORD OF THE READES OF BARTON COURT, BERKSHIRE, WITH A SHORT PRECIS OF OTHER LINES OF THE NAME,** by C. Reade. 1899.
Cloth, $33.50. Paper, $23.50. 148pp. Vendor G0259

3222 **GEN. & BIOGR. MEMOIRS OF THE READING, HOWELL, YERKES, WATTS, LATHAM, & ELKINS FAMILIES,** by J. Leach. 1898.
Cloth, $59.00. Paper, $49.00. 296pp. Vendor G0259

3223 **HISTORY OF THE REDFEARN FAMILY,** by D.H. Redfearn. Rev. ed. 1954.
Cloth, $67.50. Paper, $57.50. 376pp. Vendor G0259

3224 **GEN. HIST. OF THE REDFIELD FAM. IN THE U.S.; A REV. & EXTENSION OF THE GEN. TABLES COMP. IN 1839,** by W.C. Redfield. 1860.
Cloth, $65.00. Paper, $55.00. 345pp. Vendor G0259

3225 **JOHN REDINGTON OF TOPSFIELD, MASS. & SOME OF HIS DESCENDANTS, WITH NOTES ON THE WALES FAMILY,** by C.M.R. Carter, edited by J.G. Leach. 1909.
Paper. $17.00. 86pp. . . . . Vendor G0259

3226 **DESCENDANTS OF READE OR REED: WILLIAM READE & MABEL (KENDALL), HIS WIFE; SUPPLY REED & SUSANNAH (BYAM), HIS WIFE; JOHN REED & REBECCA (BEARCE), HIS WIFE,** by F.L.S. Meadows, with J.M. Ames. 1937.
Cloth, $54.00. Paper, $44.00. 285pp. Vendor G0259

3227 HIST. & GEN. OF THE REED FAM.: JOHANN PHILIB RIED, RIETH, RITT, RUDT, ETC., IN EUROPE & AMERICA, AN EARLY SETTLER OF SALFORD TWP., (NEW GOSHENHOPPEN, PHILA. CO, PA.), by W.H. Reed. 1929.
Cloth, $91.50. Paper, $81.50. 529pp. .... Vendor G0259

3228 HIST. OF THE REED FAM. IN EUROPE & AMERICA, by J.W. Reed. 1861.
Cloth, $99.00. Paper, $89.00. 596pp. .... Vendor G0259

3229 REED DESC. 13 GEN., INCL. THE ANC. & DESC. OF PAUL REED, 1605–1955. ALSO OTHER DESC. OF HIS IMMIG. ANC. WM. READE, b. 1609, ENG., by B.B. Aldridge. 1955.
Cloth, $33.50. Paper, $23.50. 139pp. .... Vendor G0259

3230 REED FAMILY HISTORY, by J.M. Seaver.
Paper. $13.00. 62pp. .... Vendor G0259

3231 REED GENEALOGY, DESC. OF WM. READE OF WEYMOUTH, MASS., FROM 1635–1902, by J.L. Reed. 1901.
Cloth, $105.00. Paper, $95.00. 786pp. .... Vendor G0259

3232 REED–READ LIN. CAPT. JOHN REED OF PROVIDENCE, RI & NORWALK, CT., & HIS DESC. THROUGH HIS SONS JOHN & THO-MAS, 1660–1909, by E. Reed-Wright. 1909.
Cloth, $119.00. Paper, $109.00. 796pp. .... Vendor G0259

3233 REED/READ/REID ROOTS, VOLUME 1, by Rose Caudle Terry. 1994. Indexed. Illus.
Queries published free.
Paper. $10.45. 34pp. .... Vendor G0061

3234 REED/READ/REID ROOTS, VOLUME 2, by Rose Caudle Terry. 1995. Indexed. Illus.
Queries published free. Future volumes expected or may already be completed.
Paper. $10.45. 32pp. .... Vendor G0061

3235 REID RELATIONS—THE ASA REID FAMILY OF ARKANSAS, by Roy B. Young and Billy Reid. 1991. Illus.
Gaston—Simonton—Castleberry—Prince—Keen.
Cloth. $38.95. 200pp. .... Vendor G0405

3236 DESCENDANTS OF JOHN GEORGE REIFF: REIFF, REIF, RIEFF, RIEF, RIFFE, RIFE, by Fred J. Riffe. 1995. Indexed. Illus.
Cloth. $54.00. 848pp. .... Vendor G0277

3237 FAMILY HISTORY & RECORD BOOK OF THE DESCENDANTS OF JOHAN FRIEDRICH REITZ, THE PIONEER, WHO LANDED AT PHILADELPHIA, PA., SEPT. 7, 1748, by J.J. Reitz. 1930.
Cloth, $54.50. Paper, $44.50. 289pp. .... Vendor G0259

3238 REMICK GEN., COMP. FROM THE MSS. OF LT. OLIVER PHILBRICK REMICK FOR THE MAINE HIST. SOC., by W.L. Holman. 1933.
Cloth, $44.50. Paper, $34.50. 211pp. .... Vendor G0259

3239 **THE FAM. OF REQUA, 1678–1898,** by A.C. Requa. 1898.
Paper. $15.00. 102pp. .... Vendor G0259

3240 **RESSEGUIE FAMILY. A HIST. & GEN. REC. OF ALEXANDER RESSEGUIE OF NORWALK, CT., & FOUR GEN. OF HIS DESC.,** by J.E. Morris. 1888.
Paper. $19.50. 99pp. .... Vendor G0259

3241 **GEORGE REX GEN. ANC. & DESC. OF GEORGE REX, FIRST OF ENG. TO PENNA. IN 1771,** by L.F. Rex. 1933.
Cloth, $41.50. Paper, $31.50. 192pp. .... Vendor G0259

3242 **GEN. HIST. & PATERNAL LINE OF DESC. FROM ARTHUR REXFORD OF ENG. & CONN.,** by J.D. Rexford. 1891.
Paper. $16.00. 77pp. .... Vendor G0259

3243 **ANC. & DESC. OF WM. & ELIZ. REYNOLDS OF NORTH KINGSTOWN, R.I.,** by T.A. Reynolds. 1903.
Paper. $8.00. 42pp. .... Vendor G0259

3244 **HISTORY & ONE LINE OF DESCENDANTS OF ROBERT & MARY REYNOLDS (1630?–1928) OF BOSTON, WITH THE HYATT FAMILY OF PRINCETON, NJ,** by M.H. Reynolds. 1928.
Paper. $18.00. 92pp. .... Vendor G0259

3245 **HISTORY & SOME OF THE DESCENDANTS OF ROBERT & MARY REYNOLDS (1630?–1931) OF BOSTON, MASS.,** compiled by M.H. Reynolds. 1931.
Cloth, $47.50. Paper, $37.50. 236pp. .... Vendor G0259

3246 **REPORTS OF REYNOLDS FAM. ASSOC., INCL. GEN. NOTES.** 1923, 1929.
Paper. $16.00. 117pp. .... Vendor G0259

3247 **REYNOLDS FAMILY ASSOC. 16TH ANNUAL REPORT.** 1907.
Paper. $11.00. 53pp. .... Vendor G0259

3248 **REYNOLDS FAMILY ASSOC. 31ST ANNUAL REPORT, WITH HIST. COLLECTION,** compiled by A. Rippier. 1922.
Cloth, $52.00. Paper, $42.00. 280pp. .... Vendor G0259

3249 **REYNOLDS FAMILY ASSOC. 33RD & 34TH ANNUAL REPORT, WITH GEN. & HIST. COLLECTION,** compiled by A. Rippier. 1925.
Cloth, $37.50. Paper, $27.50. 171pp. .... Vendor G0259

3250 **REYNOLDS FAMILY ASSOC. 37TH ANNUAL REPORT, WITH GEN. & HIST. COLLECTION,** compiled by A. Rippier. 1928.
Paper. $13.50. 67pp. .... Vendor G0259

3251 **REYNOLDS FAMILY ASSOC. 39TH & 40TH ANNUAL REPORT, WITH GEN. & HIST. COLLECTION,** comp. by A. Rippier. 1931.
Cloth, $32.50. Paper, $22.50. 139pp. .... Vendor G0259

3252 **REYNOLDS FAMILY ASSOC. 44TH–46TH ANNUAL REPORT, WITH GEN. & HIST. COLLECTION,** compiled by A. Rippier. 1937.
Paper. $19.00. 94pp. .... Vendor G0259

3253 **REYNOLDS FAMILY RECORDS**, by J.M. Seaver.
Paper. $7.50. 37pp. .... Vendor G0259

3254 **REYNOLDS–RENNOLDS FAM. OF ENG. & VIRGINIA, 1530–1948, BEING THE HIST. OF CHRISTOPHER REYNOLDS OF CO. KENT, ENG. & HIS DESC. IN VA., ETC.**, by S.F. Tillman. 1948.
Cloth, $49.50. Paper, $39.50. 255pp. .... Vendor G0259

3255 **THE HIST. & DESC. OF JOHN & SARAH REYNOLDS (1630?–1923), OF WATERTOWN, MASS. & WETHERSFIELD, STAMFORD & GREENWICH, CONN.**, by M.H. Reynolds. 1924.
Cloth, $89.50. Paper, $79.50. 509pp. .... Vendor G0259

3256 **RHODES FAMILY IN AMERICA: A GENEALOGY & HISTORY, FROM 1497 TO THE PRESENT DAY**, by Howard J. Rhodes. 1959.
Cloth, $89.00. Paper, $79.00. 525pp. .... Vendor G0259

3257 **BY THE NAME OF RICE. AN HIST. SKETCH OF DEA. EDMUND RICE, THE PILGRIM (1594–1663), & OF HIS DESC.**, by C.E. Rice. 1911.
Paper. $15.00. 99pp. .... Vendor G0259

3258 **GEN. HIST. OF THE RICE FAM. & DESC. OF DEA. EDM. RICE, WHO CAME FROM BERKHAMSTEAD, ENG., & SETTLED AT SUDBURY, MA., IN 1638**, by A.H. Ward. 1858.
Cloth, $62.00. Paper, $52.00. 387pp. .... Vendor G0259

3259 **"WE SOUGHT THE WILDERNESS" (MEMOIR OF SOME DESC. OF DEA. EDMUND RICE)**, by C.S. Rice. 1949.
Cloth, $49.50. Paper, $39.50. 257pp. .... Vendor G0259

3260 **EARLY RICH HIST. & ANC. OF JONATHAN RICH, JR., FT. COVINGTON, N.Y.**, by G. Rich. 1922.
Paper. $9.00. 48pp. .... Vendor G0259

3261 **GEN. DESC. OF JONATHAN RICH**, by G. Rich. 1892.
Paper. $8.00. 39pp. .... Vendor G0259

3262 **JOEL RICH ANCESTORS & DESCENDANTS, FROM DOVER NH, CAPE COD & GORHAM ME TO JACKSON PLANTATION, WALDO CO. (1677–1993)**, by Frances Morton-Rich DeMars. 1993.
Cloth, $39.50. Paper, $29.50. 175pp. .... Vendor G0259

3263 **RICHARD RICH OF EASTHAM ON CAPE COD & SOME DESC. (REPR. *NEHGR*)**, by E. Rich.
Paper. $18.00. 94pp. .... Vendor G0259

3264 **DESC. OF THOMAS RICHARDS OF DORCHESTER, MASS., b. ca. 1590. V. III OF "GEN. REG. OF SEVERAL ANCIENT PURITANS,"** by A. Morse. 1861.
Cloth, $48.50. Paper, $38.50. 243pp. .... Vendor G0259

3265 **THE DESCENDANTS OF URIAH AND ELIZABETH (ELLIS) RICHARDS—SOMERSETSHIRE, ENGLAND & LAKE COUNTY, IL-LINOIS**, by Marlys Lowham. 1996. Indexed. Illus.
Allied families: **Champion, Hawkins, Van Patten**.
Paper. $13.95 .... Vendor G0390

3266 **RICHARDSON–DEPRIEST FAM.**, by R. Roller. 1905.
Paper. $10.00. 50pp. .... Vendor G0259

3267 **RICHARDSON MEM., COMPRISING A FULL HIST. & GEN. OF THE POSTERITY OF THE THREE BROTHERS, EZEKIEL, SAMUEL & THOMAS RICHARDSON**, by J.A. Vinton. 1876.
Cloth, $119.00. Paper, $109.00. 959pp. .... Vendor G0259

3268 **RICHARDSON MEM. SUPPL.**, by I. and F. Richardson. 1898.
Paper. $7.00. 34pp. .... Vendor G0259

3269 **THOMAS RICHARDSON OF S. SHIELDS, DURHAM CO., ENG. & DESC. IN THE USA**, by M. Seaman. 1929.
Cloth, $46.00. Paper, $36.00. 241pp. .... Vendor G0259

3270 **RICHEY DESCENDANTS**, by C. Edelbute. n.d.
Paper. $18.00. 93pp., typescript .... Vendor G0259

3271 **RICHMOND FAMILY RECORDS, VOL. I, MARYLAND, VA., NEW ENG., IRELAND & SOMERSET**, by H.I. Richmond. 1933 (London).
Cloth, $47.00. Paper, $37.00. 232pp. .... Vendor G0259

3272 **RICHMOND FAMILY RECORDS, VOL. II: THE RICHMONDS ALIAS WEBB, OF WILTSHIRE [ENGLAND]**. 1935 (London).
Cloth, $52.00. Paper, $42.00. 265pp. .... Vendor G0259

3273 **RICHMOND FAMILY RECORDS, VOL. III: THE RICHMONDS OF WILTSHIRE [ENGLAND]**. 1938 (London).
Cloth, $59.50. Paper, $49.50. 327pp. .... Vendor G0259

3274 **THE RICHMOND FAM., 1594–1896, & PRE-AMER. ANC., 1040–1594**, by J.B. Richmond. 1897.
Cloth, $105.00. Paper, $95.00. 633pp. .... Vendor G0259

3275 **WILLIAM RICKETSON, WILLIAM RICKETSON, JR., & THEIR DESC.**, by G.W. Edes. 1917.
Paper. $19.00. 127pp. .... Vendor G0259

3276 **WILLIAM RICKETSON & HIS DESC., VOL. 2**, by G.W. Edes. 1932.
Cloth, $107.50. Paper, $97.50. 658pp. .... Vendor G0259

3277 **GEN. OF THE RICKS FAM. OF AMER.**, by G. Rix. 1908.
Cloth, $35.00. Paper, $25.00. 184pp. .... Vendor G0259

3278 **HISTORY & GENEALOGY OF THE RICKS FAMILY OF AMERICA (Rev. ed. of the Ricks Family of America, 1908). DESCENDANTS OF ISAAC RICKS (BORN IN ENGLAND, 1638) & HIS WIFE KATHREN, & ALLIED FAMILIES**, compiled by Howard Ricks, et al. 1957.
Cloth, $119.00. Paper, $109.00. 767pp. .... Vendor G0259

3279 **HIST. OF THE ANCIENT RYEDALES & THEIR DESC. IN NORMANDY, GT. BRIT., IRELAND & AMER., 860–1914, COMPRISING THE FAM. OF RIDDELL, RIDDLE, RIDLON, RIDLEY, ETC.**, by G.T. Ridlon. 1884.
Cloth, $108.00. Paper, $98.00. 796pp. .... Vendor G0259

3280 **THE DESCENDANTS OF EDWARD RIDDLE (1758–1826) & MARGA-RET McMILLAN (c.1769–c.1825)**, by Joan Riddle Giles. 1992.
Cloth, $59.50. Paper, $49.50. 438pp. .... Vendor G0259

3281 **DESC. OF RIDGWAY–RIDGEWAY FAM. IN ENG. & AMER.**, by G. Ridgway. 1926.
Cloth, $37.50. Paper, $27.50. 130pp. .... Vendor G0259

3282 **THE RIGGLEMAN FAMILY OF VIRGINIA & WEST VIRGINIA**, by Lewis H. Yankey. 1992. Indexed.
Paper. $26.00. 240pp. .... Vendor G0365

3283 **GEN. OF THE RIGGS FAM.; DESC. OF EDW. RIGGS OF ENG. & ROXBURY MA (b. 1590)**, by J. Wallace. 1901.
Cloth, $31.00. Paper, $21.00. 147pp. .... Vendor G0259

3284 **OUR PIONEER ANCESTORS, BEING A RECORD OF AVAILABLE INFORMATION AS TO THE RIGGS, BALDRIDGE, AGNEW, EARLE, KIRKPATRICK, VREELAND & ALLIED FAMILIES IN THE ANCESTRY OF SAM'L AGNEW RIGGS & CATHERINE DOANE EARLE RIGGS**, by H.E. Riggs. 1942.
Cloth, $47.00. Paper, $37.00. 230pp. .... Vendor G0259

3285 **RIGGS FAMILY OF MARYLAND; A GENEALOGICAL & HISTORICAL RECORD INCLUDING SEVERAL OF THE FAMILIES IN ENGLAND**, by J.B. Riggs. 1929.
Cloth, $91.00. Paper, $81.00. 534pp. .... Vendor G0259

3286 **THREE HUNDRED YEARS OF A FAMILY LIVING, BEING A HISTORY OF THE RILANDS OF SUTTON COLDFIELD [ENGLAND]**, by the Rev. W.K.R. Bedford. 1889 (England).
Cloth, $38.00. Paper, $28.00. 175pp. .... Vendor G0259

3287 **THE OLD HOME [ONE LINE OF DESCENT FROM ABRAHAM RINEHART & CATHERINE BROWER]**, by C. White. n.d.
Paper. $15.00. 72pp. .... Vendor G0259

3288 **THE GEN. OF THE DESC. OF JERE FOSTER RING & PHEBE ELLIS OF WELD, MAINE**, by H.P. Ring. 1931.
Paper. $8.50. 43pp. .... Vendor G0259

3289 **GEN. OF PART OF THE RIPLEY FAM.**, by H. Ripley. 1867.
Paper. $9.00. 48pp. .... Vendor G0259

3290 **RISLEY FAM. HIST., INCL. RECORDS OF SOME OF THE EARLY ENG. RISLEYS; A GEN. OF THE DESC. OF RICHARD RISLEY (1633) & (1636)**, by E.H. Risley. 1909.
Cloth, $50.00. Paper, $40.00. 318pp. .... Vendor G0259

3291 **RELIQUES OF THE RIVES (RYVES), BEING HIST. & GEN. NOTES OF THE ANCIENT FAM. OF RYVES OF CO. DORSET & THE RIVES OF VA.**, by J.R. Childs. 1929.
Cloth, $119.00. Paper, $109.00. 780pp. .... Vendor G0259

3292 **HIST.-GEN. OF THE RIX FAM. OF AMER.**, by G. Rix. 1906.
Cloth, $48.00. Paper, $38.00. 253pp. .... Vendor G0259

3293 **RIXEY GEN., WITH REF. TO THE MOREHEAD, HUNTON, GIBBS, HALL, THOMAS, JONES, LEWIS, CHANCELLOR, PENDLETON & OTHER ALLIED FAM.**, by R. Rixey. 1933.
Cloth, $78.00. Paper, $68.00. 436pp. .... Vendor G0259

3294 **ROACH, ROBERTS, RIDGEWAY & ALLIED FAMS.**, by M. Fair. 1951(?). Cloth, $51.50. Paper, $41.50. 258pp. .... Vendor G0259

3295 **ROARKS OF IRELAND & PEDIGREE OF NATHAN ROARK FAM. IN U.S.**, by M.I. Roark. 1950. Paper. $13.00. 64pp. .... Vendor G0259

3296 **HIST. OF THE ROBARDS FAM.**, by B. Farrior. 1959. Paper. $15.00. 74pp. .... Vendor G0259

3297 **HIST. OF THE ROBBINS FAM. OF WALPOLE, MASS.: DESC. OF WIL- LIAM & PRISCILLA ROBBINS**, by D.W. Robbins. 1949. Cloth, $53.50. Paper, $43.50. 60+221pp. .... Vendor G0259

3298 **ROBBINS FAM. EXTR. "HIST. OF WETHERSFIELD, CT."** 1904. Paper. $7.00. 36pp. .... Vendor G0259

3299 **ROBBINS, ROBINS, ROBIN: A FAMILY HISTORY**, by George S. Robbins. 1993. Indexed. Illus. Hardbound. $15.00. 254pp. .... Vendor G0364

3300 **GEN. OF THE ROBERDEAU FAM., INCL. A BIOGR. OF GEN. DANIEL ROBERDEAU OF THE REV. ARMY**, by R. Buchanan. 1876. Cloth, $39.00. Paper, $29.00. 196pp. .... Vendor G0259

3301 **DESCENDANTS OF GILES ROBERTS OF SCARBOROUGH, MAINE**, by Joann H. Nichols. 1994. Indexed. Cloth. $35.00. 210pp. .... Vendor G0300

3302 **ROBERTS FAMILY RECORDS**, by J. Montgomery Seaver. Paper. $9.00. 45pp. .... Vendor G0259

3303 **ROBERTS FAM. OF SIMSBURY, CONN., IN THE LINE OF CAPT. SAMUEL ROBERTS, 1742–1789**, by F. Starr. 1896. Paper. $10.00. 54pp. .... Vendor G0259

3304 **THE ROBERTS LEGACY: DESCENDANTS OF RUFUS ROBERTS (1782–1863) OF NIAGARA COUNTY, NEW YORK**, by Ronald L. Roberts. 1994. Indexed. Illus.
       Five appendices. Traces 31 New England and New York families which merged into **Roberts** line. Royal lineages. Footnoted. Size: 8½" x 11".
       Cloth. $50.00. 705pp. .... Vendor G0400

3305 **THE ROBERTS–ORME ANCESTRY, VOLUME I. Roberts, Muir, and Allied Families**, by John F. Vallentine et al. 1994. Includes 89-page index.
       Studies especially **Roberts, Baker, van Cleve, Brent(s), Garvin, Brawner, Muir, Boone, Tarleton, Cox, Stone** families in eastern U.S., Kentucky, and elsewhere.
       Cloth. U.S. $40 to U.S. postpaid. 346+xipp. .... Vendor G0275

3306 **THE ROBERTS–ORME ANCESTRY, VOLUME II. Orme, Wood, and Allied Families**, by John F. Vallentine et al. Includes 102-page annotated index.
       Studies especially **Orme, Selby, Miller, Woods, Morris, Wood, Farrington, Monk, Gray, Robertson, Sledge** families in eastern and southern U.S. and elsewhere.
       Cloth. U.S. $50 to U.S. postpaid. 443+xipp. .... Vendor G0275

3307 **THOMAS ROBERTS FAM. OF MARATHON, IOWA.** c.1960.
Cloth, $35.00. Paper, $25.00. 110pp. .... Vendor G0259

3308 **GEN. OF THE ROBERTSON, SMALL & RELATED FAM.**, by A.R. Small.
1907.
Cloth, $49.00. Paper, $39.00. 258pp. .... Vendor G0259

3309 **ROBERTSON FAMILY RECORDS,** by J.M. Seaver. 1928.
Paper. $19.50. 126pp. .... Vendor G0259

3310 **ROBERTSON, PURCELL, & RELATED FAMILIES,** by Laura P. Robertson.
1926.
Cloth, $48.00. Paper, $38.00. 242pp. .... Vendor G0259

3311 **THE DESCENDANTS OF EDWARD ROBERTSON AND MARY
McGREGOR OF BENDOCHY, PERTHSHIRE, SCOTLAND, AND
MIDDLEBURGH, SCHOHARIE COUNTY, NEW YORK, 1780–1995,** by
Rick Crume. 1995. Indexed.
Paper. $7.00. 56pp. .... Vendor G0386

3312 **THE JOHNSTON & BACON SCOTTISH CLAN HISTORIES: The
Robertsons,** by Iain Moncreiffe. 3rd ed. (1979) reprint 1993. Illus.
Paper. $8.95. 32pp. .... Vendor G0011

3313 **A HIST. & GEN. ACCT. OF ANDREW ROBESON OF SCOTLAND, N.J.
& PENN., & OF HIS DESC., 1653–1916,** by Robeson, Stroud, and Osborne.
1916.
Cloth, $119.00. Paper, $109.00. 776pp. .... Vendor G0259

3314 **DESCENDANTS OF REV. WILLIAM ROBINSON,** by B.E. Taylor. 1936.
Paper. $14.00. 71pp. .... Vendor G0259

3315 **MEMOIR OF THE REV. WILLIAM ROBINSON OF SOUTHINGTON,
CONN., WITH SOME ACCT. OF HIS ANC. IN THIS COUNTRY,** by E.
Robinson. 1859.
Cloth, $44.00. Paper, $34.00. 226pp. .... Vendor G0259

3316 **RECOLLECTIONS OF OLDER TIMES; ROWLAND ROBINSON OF
NARRAGANSETT & HIS UNFORTUNATE DAUGHTER, WITH GEN.
OF THE ROBINSON & HAZARD FAM. OF R.I. ALSO, GEN. SKETCH
OF THE HAZARDS OF THE MIDDLE STATES,** by T. Hazard. 1879.
Cloth, $50.00. Paper, $40.00. 264pp. .... Vendor G0259

3317 **ROBINSON FAM. GEN. & HIST. ASSOC. (THE ROBINSONS & THEIR
KIN FOLK, 1ST SERIES) OFFICERS, CONSTITUTION & BY-LAWS,
HIST. SKETCHES OF EARLY ROBINSON EMIGR. TO AMER.** 1902.
Paper. $19.50. 104pp. .... Vendor G0259

3318 **ROBINSON FAM. GEN. & HIST. ASSOC., 2ND SERIES.** 1904.
Paper. $16.00. 80pp. .... Vendor G0259

3319 **ROBINSON FAMILY JOURNAL,** by Helen N. Battleson, Editor. 1991.
Subscription. $24.00/year. About 48pp. per issue .... Vendor G0237

3320 **ROBINSON FAMILY JOURNAL, VOL. 1, NO. 1—ISSUE #1,** by Helen N.
Battleson, Editor. Nov. 1991.
    Two issues per year.
$7.50 for Back Issues post-paid. 34pp. .... Vendor G0237

3321 **ROBINSON FAMILY JOURNAL, VOL. 1, NO. 2—ISSUE #2,** by Helen N.
Battleson, Editor. May/Jun 1992.
Two issues per year.
$7.50 for Back Issues post-paid. 38pp. . . . . Vendor G0237

3322 **ROBINSON FAMILY JOURNAL, VOL 2, NO. 1—ISSUE #3,** by Helen N.
Battleson, Editor. Nov. 1992.
Two issues per year.
$7.50 for Back Issues post-paid. 40pp. . . . . Vendor G0237

3323 **ROBINSON FAMILY JOURNAL, VOL. 2, NO. 2—ISSUE #4,** by Helen N.
Battleson, Editor. May 1993.
Two issues per year.
$7.50 for Back Issues post-paid. 40pp. . . . . Vendor G0237

3324 **ROBINSON FAMILY JOURNAL, VOL. 3, NO. 1—ISSUE #5,** by Helen N.
Battleson, Editor. Nov. 1993
Two issues per year.
$7.50 for Back Issues post-paid. 44pp. . . . . Vendor G0237

3325 **ROBINSON FAMILY JOURNAL, VOL. 3, NO. 2—ISSUE #6,** by Helen N.
Battleson, Editor. May 1994
Two issues per year.
$7.50 for Back Issues post-paid. 48pp. . . . . Vendor G0237

3326 **ROBINSON FAMILY JOURNAL, VOL. 4, NO. 1—ISSUE #7,** by Helen N.
Battleson, Editor. Nov. 1994.
Two issues per year.
$7.50 for Back Issues post-paid. 48pp. . . . . Vendor G0237

3327 **ROBINSON FAMILY JOURNAL, VOL. 4, NO. 2—ISSUE #8,** by Helen N.
Battleson, Editor. May 1995.
Two issues per year.
$7.50 for Back Issues post-paid. 48pp. . . . . Vendor G0237

3328 **ROBINSON GEN. DESC. OF THE REV. JOHN ROBINSON, PASTOR
OF THE PILGRIMS,** Vol. I., by C.E. Robinson. 1928.
Cloth, $74.00. Paper, $64.00. 410pp. . . . . Vendor G0259

3329 **PEDIGREE OF ROBY OF CASTLE DONINGTON, COUNTY LEICES-
TER,** by H.J. Roby. 2nd ed. 1907 (England).
Paper. $14.00. 69pp. . . . . Vendor G0259

3330 **TRANSACTIONS OF THE ROCKEFELLER FAM. ASSOC., WITH GE-
NEALOGY, 1905–9,** edited by H.O. Rockefeller, et al. 1910.
Cloth, $69.00. Paper, $59.00. 382pp. . . . . Vendor G0259

3331 **TRANSACTIONS OF THE ROCKEFELLER FAM. ASSOC. FOR 1910–
1914, WITH GEN.,** edited by H.O. Rockefeller. 1915.
Cloth, $45.50. Paper, $46.50. 338pp. . . . . Vendor G0259

3332 **TRANSACTIONS OF THE ROCKEFELLER FAM. ASSOC., WITH GE-
NEALOGY, 1915–25,** edited by H.O. Rockefeller. 1926.
Cloth, $56.00. Paper, $46.00. 294pp. . . . . Vendor G0259

3333 **GEN. OF THE FAMS. OF JOHN ROCKWELL OF STAMFORD, CT., 1641, & RALPH KEELER OF HARTFORD, 1639,** by J. Boughton. 1903. Cloth, $87.00. Paper, $77.00. 615pp. .... Vendor G0259

3334 **ROCKWELL FAMILY IN AMER.: GEN. REC., FROM 1630 TO 1873,** by H.E. Rockwell. 1873. Cloth, $40.00. Paper, $30.00. 224pp. .... Vendor G0259

3335 **ROCKWELL FAM. IN ONE LINE OF DESC.,** by F. Rockwell. 1924. Cloth, $46.00. Paper, $36.00. 241pp. .... Vendor G0259

3336 **HIST. & GEN. RECORD OF THE DESC. OF TIMOTHY ROCKWOOD, 1727–1806,** by E.L. Rockwood. 1856. Cloth, $34.50. Paper, $24.50. 152pp. .... Vendor G0259

3337 **RODMAN FAM. GEN., 1620–1886,** by C.H. Jones. 1886. Cloth, $48.00. Paper, $38.00. 291pp. .... Vendor G0259

3338 **GEN. MEMOIR OF THE FAM. OF REV. NATHANIEL ROGERS OF IPSWICH, ESSEX CO., MASS., (Repr.** *NEHGR***),** by A.D. Rogers. 1851. Paper. $10.00. 48pp. .... Vendor G0259

3339 **JOHN ROGERS OF MARSHFIELD (MA) & SOME OF HIS DESC.,** by J.H. Drummond. 1898. Cloth, $39.50. Paper, $29.50. 221pp. .... Vendor G0259

3340 **JAMES ROGERS OF NEW LONDON, CONN., & HIS DESC.,** by J.S. Rogers. 1902. Cloth, $75.50. Paper, $65.50. 514pp. .... Vendor G0259

3341 **ROGERS–TURFLER FAMILY: A SEARCH FOR ANC.,** by I.N. Williams. 1946. Paper. $19.00. 120pp. .... Vendor G0259

3342 **THE ANC. & DESC. OF LUKE ROGERS & SARAH WRIGHT BROWN,** by E.B. Leatherbee. 1907. Paper. $14.00. 71pp. .... Vendor G0259

3343 **ROHRBACH GENEALOGY VOLUME III,** by Lewis Bunker Rohrbach. 1982. Indexed. Book #1111. Cloth. $49.00. 376pp. .... Vendor G0082

3344 **ROHRBOUGH FAMILY,** by F.W. Rohrbough. 1962. Cloth, $36.00. Paper, $26.00. 130pp. .... Vendor G0259

3345 **RECORD OF FAM. OF THE NAME OF RAWLINS OR ROLLINS IN THE U.S.,** by J.R. Rollins. 1874. Cloth, $56.00. Paper, $46.00. 362pp. .... Vendor G0259

3346 **FROM HENGELER TO TEXAS BEND, A ROLWING FAMILY HIS-TORY,** by Betty Rolwing Darnell. 1981. Indexed. Cloth. $12.00. 280pp. .... Vendor G0261

3347 **HIST. SKETCHES OF THE ROMER, VAN TASSEL, & ALLIED FAM.,** by J.L. Romer. 1917. Cloth, $34.00. Paper, $24.00. 159pp. .... Vendor G0259

3348 **DESC. OF PETER WILLEMSE ROOME**, by P. Warner. 1883.
Cloth, $74.00. Paper, $64.00. 410pp. Vendor G0259

3349 **ROOSEVELT GENEALOGY, 1649–1902**, by C.B. Whittlesey. 1902.
Paper. $18.00. 121pp. . . . . Vendor G0259

3350 **ROOT GEN. RECORDS, 1600–1870, COMPRISING THE HIST. OF THE
ROOT & ROOTS FAM. IN AMER.**, by J.P. Root. 1870.
Cloth, $78.00. Paper, $68.00. 533pp. Vendor G0259

3351 **ROPER FAM. OF STERLING & RUTLAND**, by E. Roper. 1904.
Cloth, $84.00. Paper, $74.00. 473pp. Vendor G0259

3352 **ROSE GENEALOGY, INCLUDING DESCENDANTS OF ISRAEL ROSE,
PIONEER OF WASHINGTON & OREGON, WITH ADD. & CORR.**, by
J.A. Nunamaker. 1963.
Paper. $16.00. 71+9pp. . . . . Vendor G0259

3353 **ROSEBOOM. 1630–1897. A BRIEF HIST. OF THE ANC. & DESC. OF
JOHN ROSEBOOM (1739–1832) & OF JESSE JOHNSON (1745–1832)**,
by C. and J. Roseboom, et al. 1897(?)
Cloth, $32.50. Paper, $22.50. 140pp. Vendor G0259

3354 **ROSENKRANS FAM. IN EUROPE & AMER.**, by A. Rosenkrans. 1900.
Cloth, $53.50. Paper, $43.50. 332pp. Vendor G0259

3355 **BETSY ROSS, THE GRISCOM LEGACY**, by Dr. William D. Timmins and
Robert W. Yarrington, Jr. 1983. Indexed.
Betsy's story, with much on the **Griscom(b)** family.
Cloth. $19.50. 310pp. . . . . Vendor G0069

3356 **THE JOHNSTON & BACON SCOTTISH CLAN HISTORIES: The Clan
Ross**, by Donald Mackinnon. (1957) reprint 1993. Illus.
Paper. $8.95. 32pp. . . . . Vendor G0011

3357 **THE ROSS FAMILY AND ALLIED LINES**, by Wanda Williams Colvin.
1994. Indexed. Illus.
Cloth, $49.00. Paper, $41.00. 337pp. Vendor G0432

3358 **THE ROTCHES [BIOGRAPHY & GENEALOGY OF THE ROTCH FAM-
ILY OF NANTUCKET & NEW BEDFORD, MASS.]**, by J.M. Bullard. 1947.
Cloth, $99.00. Paper, $89.00. 583pp. Vendor G0259

3359 **THE FAMILY OF NICHOLAS ROTH, AMER. SETTLERS FROM GER-
MANY, WITH INFORMATION ON ASSOC. FAMILIES OF WINTERS,
DARNOLD & KEPPLER**, by Steve Roth. 1992.
Cloth, $39.50. Paper, $29.50. 197pp. Vendor G0259

3360 **THE SWISS FAMILY ROTHENBERGER: Pioneer Farmers of Wiscon-
sin. Seven Generations in America and Related Families—Borchert,
Breseman, Bushman, Dix, Ingli, Thornton, etc.**, by Dean H. Roe. 1994. In-
dexed. Illus.
Book traces ancestors' and descendants' lives, also tells of life in America,
Switzerland, and Germany around time of immigration in 1847.
Cloth. $24.50. 306pp. . . . . Vendor G0349

3361 **ROUND–ROUNDS GEN. DESC. OF JOHN ROUND OF SWANSEA, MASS., WHO DIES 1716, AND ROUNDS FAMS. OF UNDETERMINED RELATIONSHIP**, by N.R. Nichols. 1928(?)
Cloth, $49.00. Paper, $39.00. 259pp. .... Vendor G0259

3362 **ROUSE, ZIMMERMAN, TANNER, HENDERSON, McCLURE, PORTER & ALLIED FAM.**, by E. R. Lloyd. 1932.
Cloth, $40.00. Paper, $30.00. 228pp. .... Vendor G0259

3363 **BIOGR. SKETCH OF SAMUEL ROWELL & NOTICES OF SOME OF HIS DESC., WITH A GEN. FOR SEVEN GEN., 1754–1898**, by R. Rowell. 1898.
Cloth, $42.50. Paper, $32.50. 216pp. .... Vendor G0259

3364 **LT. HERMAN ROWLEE (1746–1818), & HIS DESC.**, by W. Rowlee. 1907.
Cloth, $31.00. Paper, $21.00. 138pp. .... Vendor G0259

3365 **DESC. OF MOSES ROWLEY OF CAPE COD (c. 1715)**, by H.S. Russell. 1908.
Paper. $7.50. 33pp. .... Vendor G0259

3366 **THE ROY FAM. OF VA. & KY.**, by N.R. Roy. 1935.
Cloth, $38.50. Paper, $28.50. 190pp. .... Vendor G0259

3367 **HIST. OF CHRISTOPHER ROYER & HIS POSTERITY, (IN GIFT, KERN, ROYER GEN.)**, by A.K. Gift. 1909.
Paper. $8.50. 40pp. .... Vendor G0259

3368 **THE RUCKER FAM. GEN., WITH ANC., DESC., & CONNECTIONS**, by S.R. Wood. 1932.
Cloth, $97.50. Paper, $87.50. 585pp. .... Vendor G0259

3369 **AN IRISH RUDD FAMILY 1760–1988: RUDD ORIGINS AND OTHER IRISH RUDDS**, by Norman N. Rudd, Founder and Mari A. Rudd, Co-Founder & Editor. 1992. Indexed. Illus. Includes 1,100 pictures.
Focus on descendants of Gordon Arthur **Rudd** and Alicia **Wellwood**.
Cloth. $28.30 US, $30 CAN. 488pp. .... Vendor G0290

3370 **THE DESC. OF JOHN RUGG**, by E.R. Rugg. 1911(?)
Cloth, $99.00. Paper, $89.00. 580pp. .... Vendor G0259

3371 **THE GEN. OF THOMAS RUGGLES OF ROXBURY, 1637, TO THOMAS RUGGLES OF POMFRET, CONN. & RUTLAND, VT. THE GEN. OF ALITHEAH SMITH, OF HAMPTON, CONN., WIFE OF THOMAS RUGGLES, & THE PARTIAL GEN. OF THE DESC. OF SAML. LADD OF HAVERHILL, MASS.**, by F.L. Bailey. 1896.
Paper. $9.50. 44pp. .... Vendor G0259

3372 **GEN. OF THE RULISON, RULIFSON & ALLIED FAMS. IN AMER., 1689–1918**, by H.F. Rulison. 1919.
Cloth, $44.50. Paper, $34.50. 216pp. .... Vendor G0259

3373 **THE FAMILY OF ABRAHAM FRANKLIN RUNION & (1) SUSAN ELIZABETH RITCHIE (2) EDITH JANE DAVIS**, by Shirley C. Miller. 1994. Indexed.
Paper. $12.00. 53pp. .... Vendor G0365

3374 **RUNKLE FAM., BEING AN ACCT. OF THE RUNKLES IN EUROPE & THEIR DESC. IN AMER.**, by B. Fisher. 1899.
Cloth, $68.00. Paper, $58.00. 366pp. .... Vendor G0259

3375 **A GEN. OF THE RUNNELS & REYNOLDS FAM. IN AMER.**, by M. T. Runnels. 1873.
Cloth, $68.00. Paper, $58.50. 371pp. .... Vendor G0259

3376 **UP THE RUNYON/RUNION/RUNYAN TREE AND SUPPLEMENT TO TRACKING BAREFOOT RUNYAN**, by Marie Runyan Wright. 1993. Indexed. Illus.
This is a two-part format which is a well-documented family history of **Vincent Rongnion**, 1645–1713, a Huguenot, who came from France to America and married 1668, Ann Martha **Boutcher** in NJ. This 490-page text takes into account some of Vincent and Ann's children and discusses in detail many of their descendants throughout this book. Surnames, **Dafford, Garner, Kennedy, Lambert, Lindley, Massey, Tackett, Thompson, Triplett**, and others.
Cloth. $43.00. 490pp. .... Vendor G0091

3377 **RUSLING FAMILY**, by J.F. Rusling. 1907.
Cloth, $34.00. Paper, $24.00. 160pp. .... Vendor G0259

3378 **ACCT. OF SOME DESC. OF JOHN RUSSELL, WHO CAME TO BOSTON,1635; WITH SOME SKETCHES OF THE ALLIED FAM. OF WADSWORTH, TUTTLE & BERESFORD**, by G.W. Russell, edited by E.S. Welles. 1910.
Cloth, $57.50. Paper, $47.50. 318pp. .... Vendor G0259

3379 **ANCESTORS & DESCENDANTS OF ABEL RUSSELL, REV. SOLDIER FROM WESTFORD, MA. & FAYETTER (STARLING PLANTATION), ME., COMPRISING ONE OF THE LINES OF DESCENT FROM WM. & MARTHA RUSSELL OF CAMBRIDGE, MA., WHO CAME TO AMERICA FROM ENGLAND ABOUT 1640**, by A.J. Russell and S.R. Child. 1922.
Paper. $8.50. 40pp. .... Vendor G0259

3380 **DESC. OF JOHN RUSSELL OF WOBURN, MASS.**, by J.R. Bartlett. 1879.
Cloth, $45.00. Paper, $35.00. 212pp. .... Vendor G0259

3381 **DESC. OF WM. RUSSELL, CAMBRIDGE, MA., abt. 1640**, by H.S. Russell. 1900.
Paper. $10.00. 52pp. .... Vendor G0259

3382 **DESCENDANTS OF WILLIAM RUSSELL OF SALEM, MASS., 1674**, by George Ely Russell. 1989. Indexed. Illus.
Paper. $25.00. 272pp. .... Vendor G0126

3383 **GEN. REG. OF THE DESC. OF ROBERT & AGNES (LEITCH) RUSSELL, EMIGR. TO BENTON CO., MINN., & PIONEER EXPERIENCES**, by N. and R. Flint. 1923.
Paper. $9.50. 44pp. .... Vendor G0259

3384 **WILLIAM RUSSELL & DESCENDANTS, & THE RUSSELL FAMILY OF VA.**, by A.R. and L. des Cognets. 1960.
Cloth, $56.50. Paper, $46.50. 319pp. .... Vendor G0259

3385 **RECORD OF THE RUST FAM., EMBRACING THE DESC. OF HENRY RUST, WHO CAME FROM ENG. & SETTLED IN HINGHAM, MASS., 1634–1635**, by A.D. Rust. 1891.
Cloth, $94.00. Paper, $84.00. 544pp. .... Vendor G0259

3386 **RUST OF VIRGINIA, GEN. & BIOGRAPHICAL SKETCHES OF THE DESCENDANTS OF WILLIAM RUST, 1654–1940**, by E.M Rust. 1940.
Cloth, $83.00. Paper, $73.00. 42+462pp. .... Vendor G0259

3387 **DESCENDENTS OF JOHN GEORGE RUTH & ALLIED FAMILIES**, by Ruth Bailey Allen. 1993. 46-page index. 30 pages of illustrations.
John George **Ruth** landed in Philadelphia, 23 September 1741. He settled in Bucks County, PA where many of his descendents still reside. They married into many prominent German & Irish families in the area. Descendents in almost every state in United States. Allied families: **Bailey, Boehm, Canning, Deschler, Eckert, Fluck, Frank, Kunstman**, and **March**.
Cloth. $35.00 plus $4.00 p&h. 370pp. .... Vendor G0279

3388 **RUTLEDGE FAM. OF THE SOUTH**, by J.T. Cupit. 1954.
Paper. $9.00. 45pp. .... Vendor G0259

3389 **MORE RYAN ROOTS—DESCENDANTS OF WILLIAM AND D. RYAN OF VIRGINIA THROUGH THEIR SONS: WILLIAM, JOHN, PHILIP, JOSEPH, THOMAS WHO LIVED IN KENTUCKY, TENNESSEE, AND ALABAMA**, by Mildred B. Stout. 1994. Indexed. Illus.
Allied families include: **Koger, Neal, Parmley, Shepherd, Stephens, Trammell**.
Cloth. $45.00. 532pp. .... Vendor G0320A

3390 **THE LIFE OF AZUBAH FREEMAN RYDER, & A LIST OF HER IMMEDIATE ANC. & DESC.**, by J. Ryder. 1888.
Paper. $9.00. 45pp. .... Vendor G0259

3391 **THE PORT RYERSE JOURNAL**, edited by Phyllis A. Ryerse; research by Thomas A. Ryerson. 1994. Indexed. Illus.
This is the **Ryerse–Ryerson** family newsletter, which is published about three times a year. The newsletter corrects any errors in the family history book, plus includes lots of additions and articles—a must for those who want to stay up to date!
Subscription. $12.00 per year. 8–12pp. .... Vendor G0391

3392 **THE RYERSE–RYERSON FAMILY HISTORY 1574–1994**, by Thomas A. Ryerson and Phyllis A. Ryerse. 1994, second printing 1996. Indexed. Illus.
Book traces the **Ryerse–Ryerson** family in the Netherlands to America, then concentrates on the families of the brothers Samuel **Ryerse** and Joseph **Ryerson**,

```
Family Reports, with index:
Watts, Cowan, Olson, Cates, Mears,
Sawyer, Lindsey, Gibbs, Hereford,
Rutledge, Plantner, Haynes, Rust,
Corder, Flippo, Boggess, Robert.
Paper/comb bound. $20-40 ea. ppd
Fred Rutledge, 1208 Argonne Dr.
Baltimore MD 21218, 410 889 0035
Family members sought.
```

pioneers of Norfolk Co., Ontario, Canada. Early surnames include **Liger, Kniffen, Birdsell, Fick, Bostwick, Mitchell**, and **Williams**. Book has received excellent reviews in Canada and the U.S.
Cloth. $42.00. 427pp. .... Vendor G0391

3393 **GEN. & HIST. OF THE KNICKERBOCKER FAM. OF RYERSON, RYERSE, RYERSS; ALSO MARTENSE FAM.; ALL DESC. OF MARTIN & ADRISEN REYERSZ(EN), OF HOLLAND,** by A. Ryerson, edited by A. Holman. 1916.
Cloth, $79.50. Paper, $69.50. 459pp. .... Vendor G0259

3394 **RYKER/RIKER REGISTER**, edited by Conrad Burton.
Quarterly for **Ryker/Riker** families.
Subscription. $10.00/year .... Vendor G0094

3395 **THE FAMILY RECORD [MAGAZINE]: THE SACKETT, WEYGANT & MAPES FAMILIES,** by C.H. Weygant. 1897.
Cloth, $35.00. Paper, $25.00. 148pp. .... Vendor G0259

3396 **THE SACKETTS OF AMER., THEIR ANC. & DESC., 1630–1907,** by C. Weygant. 1907.
Cloth, $80.00. Paper, $70.00. 553pp. .... Vendor G0259

3397 **THE OHIO VALLEY SAFFORDS, REVISED & ENLARGED EDITION,** by R.H. Smith and S.M. Culbertson. 1932.
Cloth, $47.50. Paper, $37.50. 240pp. .... Vendor G0259

3398 **DESC. OF DAVID SAGE OF MIDDLETOWN, CONN., SECOND BRANCH,** by H.K. Sage. 1951.
Paper. $18.50. 94pp. .... Vendor G0259

3399 **GEN. RECORD OF DESC. OF DAVID SAGE OF MIDDLETOWN, CONN.,** by E.L. and C.H. Sage. 1919.
Cloth, $35.00. Paper, $25.00. 128pp. .... Vendor G0259

3400 **GEN. REC. OF DESC. OF DAVID SAGE, ONE OF THE 1ST SETTLERS OF MIDDLETON, CT., 1652,** by E. Sage. 1878.
Paper. $16.50. 82pp. .... Vendor G0259

3401 **HIST. OF THE SAGE & SLOCUM FAM. OF ENG. & AMER., INCL. ALLIED FAMS. OF MONTAGUE, WANTON (& OTHERS),** by H. Whittemore. 1908.
Paper. $18.50. 95pp. .... Vendor G0259

3402 **THE GEN. OF THE SAHLERS OF THE U.S. & OF THEIR KINSMEN, THE GRASS FAM.,** by L. Sahler. 1895.
Paper. $7.50. 38pp. .... Vendor G0259

3403 **SAINT JOHN GEN.; DESC. OF MATTHIAS OF DORCHESTER, MASS., 1634; OF WINDSOR, CT., 1640 (& WETHERSFIELD & NORWALK),** by O. Alexander. 1907.
Cloth, $89.00. Paper, $79.00. 639pp. .... Vendor G0259

3404 **SALISBURY FAM. OF ENG. & AMER.,** by E.E. Salisbury. 1885.
Cloth, $32.50. Paper, $22.50. 118pp. .... Vendor G0259

3405 **ANC. & DESC. OF SIR RICHARD SALTONSTALL, FIRST ASSOC. OF**

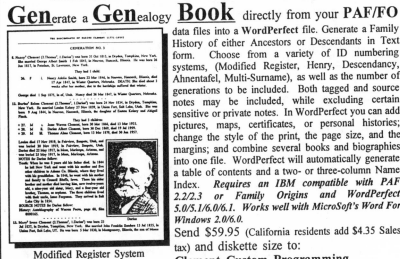
THE MASS. BAY COL. & PATENTEE OF CONN., by L. Saltonstall. 1897. Cloth, $51.50. Paper, $41.50. 277pp. .... Vendor G0259

3406 **SAMPSON FAM. (OF PENN. & OHIO)**, by L.B. Sampson. 1914. Cloth, $45.50. Paper, $35.50. 238pp. .... Vendor G0259

3407 **[Sampson]. GEN. MEM. FROM THE ARRIVAL OF THE MAYFLOWER IN 1620 TO THE PRESENT**, by J. Vinton. 1864. Paper. $21.00. 140pp. .... Vendor G0259

3408 **GEN. OF THE FAM. OF SANBORNE OR SANBORN IN ENG. & AMER., 1194–1898**, by V.C. Sanborn. 1899. Cloth, $98.00. Paper, $88.00. 709pp. .... Vendor G0259

3409 **GEN. OF THE CORTLAND CO., N.Y., BRANCH OF THE SANDERS FAM.**, by J. Sanders. 1908. Paper. $19.00. 111pp. .... Vendor G0259

3410 **ROBERT SANDFORD & HIS WIFE ANN (ADAMS) SANDFORD, WITH SOME OF THEIR DESC., 1650–1930**, by J.S. Ware. 1930. Paper. $17.50. 85pp. .... Vendor G0259

3411 **DESCENT OF COMFORT SANDS & OF HIS CHILDREN, WITH NOTES ON THE FAM. OF RAY, THOMAS, GUTHRIE (& OTHERS)**, by T. Prime. 1886. Paper. $18.00. 91pp. .... Vendor G0259

3412 **SANFORD GEN.; THE BRANCH OF WM. OF MADISON, N.Y., OF THE 6TH AMER. GEN.**, by H. Sanford. 1894.
Paper. $13.50. 70pp. .... Vendor G0259

3413 **THOMAS SANFORD, EMIGR. TO NEW ENG.: ANC., LIFE & DESC., 1632–4; ALSO SKETCHES OF FOUR OTHER PIONEER SANFORDS & SOME DESC.**, by C.E. Sanford. 2 vols. 1911.
Cloth, $195.00. Paper, $185.00. 768+840pp. .... Vendor G0259

3414 **THE SANGREY FAMILY HISTORY, DESCENDANTS OF MARY AND JOHN SANGREY**, by Abram W. Sangrey. 1989.
Paper. $24.00. 175pp. .... Vendor G0150

3415 **GEN. OF THE SANTEE FAM. IN AMER**, by E.M. Santee. 1927.
Cloth, $43.50. Paper, $33.50. 211pp. .... Vendor G0259

3416 **HIST. OF THE SAPP FAM.**, by Sapp and Stanley. 1910.
Paper. $19.00. 102pp. .... Vendor G0259

3417 **EARLY SARGENTS OF NEW ENG.**, by W. Sargent. 1922.
Paper. $10.00. 53pp. .... Vendor G0259

3418 **[Sargent]. GEN. OF THE SARGEANT FAM: THE DESC. OF WM. OF MALDEN, MASS.**, by A. Sargent. 1858.
Paper. $19.00. 108pp. .... Vendor G0259

3419 **HUGH SARGENT OF COURTEENHALL, NORTHANTS., & DESC. IN ENG.; WM. SARGENT OF MALDEN, NEW ENG., & DESC. IN AMER.**, by J. Sargent. 1895.
Cloth, $43.00. Paper, $33.00. 218pp. .... Vendor G0259

3420 **SARGENT RECORD. WILLIAM SARGENT OF NEW ENG., WITH HIS DESC. & THEIR INTERMARRIAGES, & OTHER SARGENT BRANCHES**, by E.E. Sargent. 1899.
Cloth, $59.50. Paper, $49.50. 331pp. .... Vendor G0259

3421 **[Saunders]. FOUNDERS OF THE MASS. BAY COLONY**, by S.S. Smith. 1897.
Cloth, $58.00. Paper, $48.00. 372pp. .... Vendor G0259

3422 **WM. SAUNDERS & SARAH FLAGG SAUNDERS, LATE OF CAMBRIDGE, WITH THEIR FAM. RECORD & GEN.** 1872.
Paper. $8.00. 39pp. .... Vendor G0259

3423 **A GEN. & BIOGR. RECORD OF THE SAVERY FAM. (SAVORY, SAVARY), & OF THE SEVERY FAM., (SEVERIT, SAVERY, SAVORY) DESC. FROM EARLY IMMIGR. TO NEW ENG. & PHILA.**, by A. Savary. 1893.
Cloth, $53.00. Paper, $43.00. 286pp. .... Vendor G0259

3424 **SAVERY SUPPLEMENT**, by A.W. Savary. 1905.
Paper. $11.00. 58pp. .... Vendor G0259

3425 **GEN. SKETCH OF SOME DESC. OF ROBERT SAVORY OF NEWBURY, 1656**, by F.W. Lamb. 1904.
Cloth, $55.00. Paper, $45.00. 16pp. .... Vendor G0259

3426 **SUMMARY NOTES CONCERNING JOHN SAWIN & HIS POSTERITY,** by T.E. Sawin. 1866.
Paper. $10.00. 48pp. .... Vendor G0259

3427 **GENEALOGICAL INDEX OF THE SAWYER FAMILIES OF NEW ENGLAND PRIOR TO 1900,** by Fred E. Sawyer. 1983.
Cloth, $49.50. Paper, $39.50. 394pp. .... Vendor G0259

3428 **SAWYER FAMILY OF ELLIOTSVILLE (PISCATAQUIS CO., MAINE): DESCENDANTS OF JAMES SAWYER OF GLOUCESTER, MA., & THEIR KINFOLK, THE DRAKES,** by Fred E. Sawyer. 2nd ed. 1960–1.
Paper. $19.00. 98pp. .... Vendor G0259

3429 **SAWYERS IN AMER., OR A HIST. OF THE IMMIG. SAWYERS WHO SETTLED IN NEW ENG.,** by A. Carter. 1883.
Paper. $18.00. 120pp. .... Vendor G0259

3430 **THOMAS SAXBE (1810–1860) AND HIS DESCENDANTS,** by William B. Saxbe, C.G. 1980. Indexed. Illus.
Cloth. $17.00. 147pp. .... Vendor G0328

3431 **A HIST. OF THE SAYLER FAM., BEING A COLL. OF GEN. NOTES RELATIVE TO DANIEL OF FREDERICK CO., MD., WHO CAME TO AMER. 1725–1730, & HIS DESC.,** by J.L. Sayler. 1898.
Cloth, $38.00. Paper, $28.00. 164pp. .... Vendor G0259

3432 **SAYRE FAM.; LINEAGE OF THOMAS SAYRE, A FOUNDER OF SOUTHAMPTON,** by T. Banta. 1901.
Cloth, $126.00. Paper, $116.00. 774pp. .... Vendor G0259

3433 **SAYWARD FAM.; BEING THE HIST. & GEN. OF HENRY SAYWARD OF YORK, ME, & HIS DESC.,** by C. Sayward. 1890.
Cloth, $36.50. Paper, $26.50. 183pp. .... Vendor G0259

3434 **GEN. HIST. OF THE SCARRITT CLAN IN AMERICA,** by R.E. Pearson. 2 vols. in 1. 1938–48.
Cloth, $50.00. Paper, $40.00. 265pp. .... Vendor G0259

3435 **MEMOIRS & REMINISCENCES TOGETHER WITH THE SKETCHES OF THE EARLY HISTORY OF SUSSEX CO. NJ, WITH NOTES & GENEALOGICAL RECORD OF THE SCHAEFFER, SHAVER OR SHAFER FAMILY,** by William M. Johnson. 1907.
Cloth, $39.50. Paper, $29.50. 187pp. .... Vendor G0259

3436 **SCHAEFFER/SHAEFFER/SHEAFFER SEARCH,** by Margaret E. Sheaffer and Carol M. Sheaffer, M.D. 1991. Indexed. Illus.
Contains the history and genealogy of the Levi and Mary (**Knox**) **Shaeffer** Family. Information on the Shaeffer surname and 244 Shaeffer immigrants to Colonial America. Surname and descendant charts of thirty-one Shaeffer families of Lancaster, Dauphin, Berks, Chester, Bucks, York and Lebanon counties, Pennsylvania.
Cloth. $32.00. 158pp. .... Vendor G0229

3437 **A HIST. ACCT. OF THE SCHALL/SHAULL FAM.,** by J.L.S. Lutz. 1968.
Cloth, $83.50. Paper, $73.50. 468pp. .... Vendor G0259

3438 **THE DESCENDANTS OF ENGELHARDT SCHAUBHUT (1602–1671) OF EICHEN, BADEN, GERMANY, ESPECIALLY THROUGH HIS GREAT-GREAT-GRANDSON, TOBIAS SCHAUBHUT (1762–1803), IMMIGRANT TO LANCASTER COUNTY, PENNSYLVANIA, USA,** by Rick Crume. 1995. Indexed.
Includes: **Becker, Crume, Rotzler, Shaubut.**
Paper. $9.00. 95pp. .... Vendor G0386

3439 **SCHAUFFLER CHRONICLE. ROSTER & BIOGRAPHICAL SKETCHES OF THE SCHAUFFLER FAMILY IN AMERICA: WM. GOTTLIEB SCHAUFFLER & MARY REYNOLDS SCHAUFFLER & THEIR DESCENDANTS,** by R.McE. Schauffler. 1951.
Cloth, $32.00. Paper, $22.00. 121pp. .... Vendor G0259

3440 **DESC. OF JOHN CHRISTIAN SCHELL & JOHN SCHELL OF N.Y. STATE,** by C. Denissen. 1896.
Paper. $18.00. 98pp. .... Vendor G0259

3441 **THE REV. WILLIAM SCHENK, HIS ANC. & HIS DESC.,** by A.D. Schenck. 1883.
Cloth, $35.00. Paper, $25.00. 163pp. .... Vendor G0259

3442 **SCHERMERHORN GEN. & FAM. CHRONICLES,** by R. Schermerhorn, Jr. 1914.
Cloth, $76.50. Paper, $66.50. 425pp. .... Vendor G0259

3443 **A GENEALOGY OF THE SCHLOSSER, SLUSSER & SLUSHER FAMILIES OF AMERICA 1605–1994,** compiled by Schlosser Research Associates; edited by Patricia Shaffer Frappier. 1995. Indexed.
Cloth. $35.00. 608pp. .... Vendor G0389

3444 **JOHAN GEORG SCHOFER FAMILY HISTORY, CONTAINING RECORDS OF ANTECEDENTS IN EUROPE, ACCT. OF THE MIGRATION TO AMERICA IN 1832, BIOGRAPHICAL SKETCHES OF MEMBERS OF THE FAMILY IN THIS COUNTRY,** by H.M. Schofer. 1934.
Cloth, $39.50. Paper, $29.50. 180pp. .... Vendor G0259

3445 **THE DESC. OF JACOB SCHOFF, WHO CAME TO BOSTON IN 1752 & SETTLED IN ASHBURNHAM IN 1757,** by W.H. Schoff. 1910.
Cloth, $34.50. Paper, $24.50. 163pp. .... Vendor G0259

3446 **DESC. OF JOHN PETER SCHOLL & HIS WIFE ANNA A.D. SCHOLL, & GEN. FAM. HIST. WITH A SKETCH OF PHILIP SCHOLL & DESC.,** by A.G. Scholl. 1903.
Paper. $15.00. 87pp. .... Vendor G0259

3447 **SCHOLL–SHOLL–SHULL GEN., THE COL. BRANCHES,** by J.W. Scholl. 1930.
Cloth, $137.50. Paper, $127.50. 910pp. .... Vendor G0259

3448 **SCHOPPE FAMILY GEN., 1782–1932,** by M.C. Schoppe. 1932.
Cloth, $41.00. Paper, $31.00. 208pp. .... Vendor G0259

3449 **[Schottler–Shettler]. MEMORIAL HISTORY OF DANIEL SCHOTTLER, SR & HIS FATHER-IN-LAW CRISTIAN SCHWARTZENDRUKER, SR, & JACOB & REBECCA KAUFFMAN, GRANDPARENTS OF DANIEL**

SHETTLER, JR,COMPRISING A COMPLETE FAMILY REGISTER OF LINEAL DESCENDANTS & THOSE RELATED BY INTERMARRIAGE, 1833–1910, by S.D. Guengerich. 1919.
Paper. $19.00. 119pp. . . . . Vendor G0259

3450 **THE SCHUBDREIN–SCHIBENDREIN FAMILY IN GERMANY, 1668–1751,** by Hilde Shuptrine Farley and Alfred Earl Farley, Jr. 1992. Indexed. Illus.
The ancestors of the **Shuptrine** Family from Georgia.
Paper. $18.00. 130pp. . . . . Vendor G0024

3451 **THE SCHUREMANS OF N.J.,** by R. Wynkoop. 1902.
Cloth, $34.00. Paper, $24.00. 142pp. . . . . Vendor G0259

3452 **SCHUREMAN OF N.J.,** by R. Wynkoop. 2nd ed. 1902.
Cloth, $32.00. Paper, $22.00. 144pp. . . . . Vendor G0259

3453 **SCHWARZTRAUBER, STEWART AND RELATED FAMILIES,** by Sayre Archie Schwarztrauber. 1995. Indexed. Illus.
Genealogy of **Schwarztrauber** family in America including variations: **Schwartztrauber, Swarztrauber, Swartztrauber.** With **Stewart,** other principal families: **Fouts, Hamilton, Haughey, Hussey, Judy, Penquite, Poffenberger (Poffenbarger), Redden, Sayre (Sayrs), Schneider, Sindall, Watson,** and brief treatments of twenty others. Three Mayflower, and five Revolutionary, lines. 10,300 index citations. 256 illustrations. Gateway Press.
Cloth. $34.75. xxx+1,000pp. . . . . Vendor G0454

3454 **GENEALOGY OF THE SCHWENK FAMILY,** by E.S. and J.K. Schwenk, edited by R.B. Strassburger. 1929.
Cloth, $54.50. Paper, $44.50. 282pp. . . . . Vendor G0259

3455 **GEN. REC. OF THE SCHWENKFELDER FAMS., SEEKERS OF RELIGIOUS LIBERTY WHO FLED FROM SILESIA TO SAXONY, & THENCE TO PA. IN 1731 TO 1737,** edited by S.K. Brecht. 2 vols. 1923.
Cloth, $225.00. Paper, $215.00. 1,752pp. . . . . Vendor G0259

3456 **DESC. OF WILLIAM SCOTT OF HATFIELD, MASS., 1668–1906, & OF JOHN SCOTT OF SPRINGFIELD, MASS., 1659–1906,** by O.P. Allen. 1906.
Cloth, $43.00. Paper, $33.00. 220pp. . . . . Vendor G0259

ı H ɔ

```
   SCHWARZTRAUBER,
 STEWART and RELATED
      FAMILIES
         -
 a genealogy of the
   SCHWARZTRAUBER
   family in America
```

3457 **HIST. OF THE SCOTT FAM.**, by H. Lee. 1919.
Cloth, $30.00. Paper, $20.00. 117pp. . . . . Vendor G0259

3458 **HUGH SCOTT, AN IMMIGR. OF 1670, AND HIS DESC.**, by J. Scott. 1895.
Cloth, $57.50. Paper, $47.50. 314pp. . . . . Vendor G0259

3459 **SCOTT FAM. OF SCOTLAND & STAFFORD CO., VA.**
Paper. $17.00. 86pp. . . . . Vendor G0259

3460 **SCOTT GENEALOGY**, by M.L. Holman. 1919.
Cloth, $73.50. Paper, $63.50. 410pp. . . . . Vendor G0259

3461 **THE JOHNSTON & BACON SCOTTISH CLAN HISTORIES: The Scotts**, by Jean Dunlop. (1957) reprint 1993. Illus.
Paper. $8.95. 32pp. . . . . Vendor G0011

3462 **THE SCOTCH-IRISH & CHARLES SCOTT'S DESC. & RELATED FAM.**, by O.C. Scott. 1917.
Cloth, $33.50. Paper, $23.50. 115pp. . . . . Vendor G0259

3463 **THE SCOTT FAM. OF SHREWSBURY, N.J., BEING THE DESC. OF WM. SCOTT & ABIGAIL TILTON WARNER, WITH SKETCHES OF REL. FAM.**, by A. Cole. 1908.
Paper. $14.00. 73pp. . . . . Vendor G0259

3464 **ARTHUR SCOVELL & HIS DESC. IN AMER., 1660–1900**, by J.M. Holley and H.W. Brainard. 1941.
Cloth, $55.50. Paper, $45.50. 285pp. . . . . Vendor G0259

3465 **SCOVILLE FAM. RECORDS**, by C.R. Eastman. 1910.
Paper. $15.00. 75pp. . . . . Vendor G0259

3466 **SURVEY OF THE SCOVILL(E)S IN ENG. & AMER., 700 YRS OF HIST. & GEN.**, by H. Brainerd. 1915.
Cloth, $99.00. Paper, $89.00. 586pp. . . . . Vendor G0259

3467 **GENEALOGICAL REGISTER OF DESCENDANTS OF JOHN SCRANTON OF GUILFORD, CT., WHO DIED IN THE YEAR 1671**, by E. Scranton. 1855.
Paper. $17.00. 104pp. . . . . Vendor G0259

3468 **SCRUBY—THROUGH OUR ENGLISH CHANNELS 1552–1995**, by Patricia O'Boyle. 1995. Indexed. Illus.
Rev. James **Scruby**, Cambridgeshire 1568 and his descendants: **Stockbridge, Freeman, Pepper, Newling**, more!
Paper. $40.00. 250pp. . . . . Vendor G0225

3469 **JOSEPH SEAB OF FRANKLIN COUNTY MISSISSIPPI**, by Mildred S. Ezell. 1975. Indexed. Illus.
Includes: **Seab, Nienaber, Graves, McMillan, Hunt, Combs, Jones, Seale, Hemby**.
Paper. $35.00. 306pp. . . . . Vendor G0323

3470 **HISTORY OF THE SEAMAN FAMILY IN PA., WITH GENEALOGI-CAL TABLES**, by G.S. Seaman. 1911.
Cloth, $32.00. Paper, $22.00. 135pp. . . . . Vendor G0259

3471 **SEAMANS FAM. IN AMER. AS DESC. FROM THOMAS SEAMANS OF SWANSEA, MASS., 1687**, by Lawton & Brown. 1933.
Cloth, $54.50. Paper, $44.50. 299pp. .... Vendor G0259

3472 **A REC. OF THE SEARIGHT FAM., EST. IN AMER. BY WM. SEARIGHT, WHO CAME TO LANCASTER CO., PA. ca. 1740; WITH ACCT. OF HIS DESC.**, by J.A. Searight. 1893.
Cloth, $48.50. Paper, $38.50. 242pp. .... Vendor G0259

3473 **GEN. & BIOGR. SKETCHES OF THE ANC. & DESC. OF RICHARD SEARS, THE PILGRIM**, by E.H. Sears. 1857.
Paper. $17.50. 96pp. .... Vendor G0259

3474 **THE DESC. OF RICHARD SARES (SEARS) OF YARMOUTH, MASS., 1638–1888, WITH SOME NOTICES OF OTHER FAM. BY THE NAME OF SEARS**, by S. May. 1890.
Cloth, $108.00. Paper, $98.00. 676pp. .... Vendor G0259

3475 **SEATON FAM., WITH GEN. & BIOGR.**, by O.A. Seaton. 1906.
Cloth, $78.50. Paper, $68.50. 441pp. .... Vendor G0259

3476 **SEATONS OF WESTERN PENN.**, by J.S. Crosby. 1945.
Paper. $12.50. 63pp. .... Vendor G0259

3477 **GENEALOGY OF ROBERT SEAVER OF ROXBURY, MA. & SOME DESCENDANTS**, by William B. Trask. 1872.
Paper. $11.00. 52pp. .... Vendor G0259

3478 **THE DESC. OF JACOB SEBOR, 1709–1793, OF MIDDLETOWN, CONN.**, by H. Beach. 1923.
Paper. $19.00. 109pp. .... Vendor G0259

3479 **ANC. OF DANIEL JAMES SEELY & CHARLOTTE LOUISA VAIL, WITH DESC.**, by W.P. Bacon. 1914.
Cloth, $39.50. Paper, $29.50. 185pp. .... Vendor G0259

3480 **DESCENDANTS OF JOHN SEGAR OF SOUTH KINGSTOWN, RHODE ISLAND**, by Wm. E. Wright. 1992.
Cloth. $19.00. 99pp. .... Vendor G0363

3481 **[Seitz]. A SCOTCH-IRISH CONNECTION AND A GERMAN STOW-AWAY**, by Beatrice West Seitz. 1993.
This is my husband's lineage. His mother's side goes back to **Alexanders & Clarks** in North Carolina. His grandfather was the German Stowaway. They lived in Tennessee, Iowa, Nebraska, Missouri, Arkansas, Oklahoma, and Kansas.
Paper. $15.00. 78pp. .... Vendor G0001

3482 **[Seitz]. FROM NORWAY TO THE U.S.A.**, by Beatrice West Seitz. 1992.
Illus.
This family history goes back to the 1500s in Sandsvaer, Norway. Most of the ancestors were residents of Buskerud County. The Kongsberg silver mine was a source of occupation. Many early names were—**Hedenstad, Bronstad, Myra, Gjermund, Eggar, Vettestad, Hvaal, Steg, Streng, Eid, Knive, Stenberg, Bakken, Olsen, Hanson, Gislerud**, and **Medalen.**

During the 1880s John **Gislerud**, his married sister, her husband and baby— Gulic **Hanson**—and two **Olsen** sisters came to Wisconsin. In due time the descendants spread out into Nebraska, Oregon, and other states.
Paper. $47.10. 158pp. .... Vendor G0001

3483 **SELBY FAMILIES OF COLONIAL AMERICA**, by Donna Valley Russell. 1990. Indexed. Illus.
Paper. $26.00. 200pp. .... Vendor G0126

3484 **SELDEN ANC.; A FAM. HIST.**, by G.S. Selden. 1931.
Cloth, $91.50. Paper, $81.50. 523pp. .... Vendor G0259

3485 **SELDEN & KINDRED OF VIRGINIA**, by E.M. Selden. 1941.
Cloth, $45.00. Paper, $35.00. 224pp. .... Vendor G0259

3486 **SELDENS OF VA. & ALLIED FAM.**, by M. Kennedy. 2 vols. 1911.
Cloth, $181.00. Paper, $171.00. 1,363pp. .... Vendor G0259

3487 **SELLECK AND PECK GENEALOGY**, by Wm. E. Peck. 1912.
Paper. $15.00. 74pp. .... Vendor G0259

3488 **GEN. HIST. OF THE FAM. SEMPLE FROM 1214 TO 1888**, by W.A. Semple. 1888.
Paper. $12.00. 60pp. .... Vendor G0259

3489 **SENSINEYS OF AMER. (INCL. SENSENY, SENSENIG, ETC.)**, by B. Sensening. 1943.
Cloth, $34.00. Paper, $24.00. 159pp. .... Vendor G0259

3490 **LES ANCÊTRES PATERNELS DE JOSEPH-EUGÈNE SERRÉ (1876–1959)**, by Robert Serré. 1994. Indexed. Illus.
Surname also spelled **Céré, Cerré**.
Paper. CAN $10.00. 47pp. .... Vendor G0111

3491 **MATERIALS FOR A HIST. OF THE SESSIONS FAM. IN AMER., THE DESC. OF ALEXANDER SESSIONS OF ANDOVER, MASS., 1669**, by F.C. Sessions. 1890.
Cloth, $47.50. Paper, $37.50. 252pp. .... Vendor G0259

3492 **SETONS OF SCOTLAND & AMER.**, by M. Seton. 1899.
Cloth, $78.00. Paper, $68.00. 438pp. .... Vendor G0259

3493 **SEVERANS GEN. HIST.**, by J.L. Severance. 1893.
Paper. $15.00. 91pp. .... Vendor G0259

3494 **[Sevier]. NOTABLE SOUTHERN FAMILIES, Volume IV**, by Zella Armstrong. (1926) reprint 1993.
Concerned with the genealogy of the **Sevier** family.
Paper. $26.00. 325pp. .... Vendor G0011

3495 **SEWALL FAM. OF ENG. & AMER., 1624–1857**, by E. Salisbury. 1885.
Paper. $15.00. 75pp. .... Vendor G0259

3496 **OBADIAH SEWARD OF LONG ISL., N.Y., & HIS DESC.**, by F.W. Seward, Jr. 1948.
Cloth, $54.00. Paper, $44.00. 288pp. .... Vendor G0259

3497 **SEWELLS IN THE NEW WORLD**, by Sir H.L. Duff. 1924 (England).
Cloth, $32.00. Paper, $22.00. 122pp. .... Vendor G0259

3498 **THE SEWELLS OF THE ISLE OF WIGHT [ENGLAND], WITH AN ACCT. OF SOME OF THE FAMILIES CONNECTED BY MARRIAGE**, by M.C. Owen. 1900? (England).
Cloth, $42.00. Paper, $32.00. 188+16pp. .... Vendor G0259

3499 **A RECORD OF THE SEYMOUR FAM. IN THE REV.**, by M.W. Seymour. 1912.
Paper. $8.00. 40pp. .... Vendor G0259

3500 **HIST. OF THE SEYMOUR FAM. DESC. OF RICHARD OF HARTFORD, CONN., FOR SIX GEN. WITH AMPLIFICATION OF THE LINES DERIVING FROM HIS SON JOHN OF HARTFORD**, by D. Jacobus. 1939.
Cloth, $109.50. Paper, $99.50. 662pp. .... Vendor G0259

3501 **SHAFER-HUSTON–HUSTON FAMILY HISTORY**, by F.M. Marvin. 1951.
Cloth, $82.00. Paper, $72.00. 470pp. .... Vendor G0259

3502 **"SHAKESPEAREANA GENEALOGICA": PT. I, IDENTIFICATION OF THE DRAMATIS PERSONAE IN THE HIST. PLAYS, FROM KING JOHN TO HENRY VIII, NOTES ON CHARACTERS IN MACBETH & HAMLET, PERSONS & PLACES ALLUDED TO IN SEVERAL PLAYS; PT. II, SHAKESPEARE & ARDEN FAMS. & THEIR CONNECTIONS**, by G.R. French. 1869.
Cloth, $91.00. Paper, $81.00. 546pp. .... Vendor G0259

3503 **SHANHOLTZER HISTORY AND ALLIED FAMILY ROOTS OF HAMPSHIRE COUNTY, W. VA. AND FREDERICK COUNTY, VA.**, by Wilmer L. Kerns. 1980. Indexed. Illus., 233 photographs.
Johannes **Schoenholtzer** came to Chester County, PA in 1727 from the Palatinate. Eleven generations are traced to 1980, covering most of the States. The name is also spelled **Shanholtzer, Shanholtz, Shinholts, Shinholt**, and **Shinolt**. Female lineages are traced. Index contains about 20,000 names.
Cloth. $40.00. 1,056pp. .... Vendor G0250

3504 **DESCENDANTS OF THE LEWIS RADER SHANK FAMILY**, by M. Leigh Blount and James R. Sisson. 1996. Indexed.
Cloth. $35.00. 92pp. .... Vendor G0424

3505 **THE SHANK FAMILY RECORD**, by Floyd R. Mason. 1992. Indexed.
Immigrant Michael and Mary **Shank** of PA.
Paper. $4.00. 24pp. .... Vendor G0345

3506 **SOME ANC. & DESC. OF JAMES SHANKS OF HURON CO., OHIO**, by H.S. Blaine. 1951.
Paper. $16.00. 82pp. .... Vendor G0259

3507 **SHANNON GEN., GEN. RECORD & MEMORIALS OF ONE BRANCH IN AMERICA**, by G. Hodgdon. 1905.
Cloth, $83.00. Paper, $73.00. 609pp. .... Vendor G0259

3508 **SHARP FAM., DESC. OF WM. & THOMAS OF EVESHAM, N.J. (EXTR. FROM HAINES GEN.)**. 1902.
Paper. $9.00. 46pp. .... Vendor G0259

3509 **[Sharpe]. MARY ALICE SHARPE YALDEN THOMSON & ALEXANDER BEATTY SHARPE, JR: CARTER, SHARPE & ALLIED FAMS.**, by E.E.B. Jones. 1940.
Cloth, $58.50. Paper, $48.50. 311pp. .... Vendor G0259

3510 **RECORDS OF THE SHARPE FAM. IN ENG. & AMER. FROM 1580 TO 1870**, by W.C. Sharpe. 1874.
Paper. $7.00. 34pp. .... Vendor G0259

3511 **SHARPE FAMILY MAGAZINE, VOL. I., NOS. 1–32.** 1893–6.
Cloth, $44.50. Paper, $34.50. 212pp. .... Vendor G0259

3512 **GEN. OF THE SHARPLESS FAM., DESC. FROM JOHN & JANE SHARPLES, SETTLERS NEAR CHESTER, PENN., 1682**, by G. Cope. 1887.
Cloth, $188.00. Paper, $178.00. 1,349pp. .... Vendor G0259

3513 **MEMORIALS OF THE DESC. OF WM. SHATTUCK, THE PROGENITOR OF THE FAM. IN AMER. THAT BORNE HIS NAME**, by L. Shattuck. 1855.
Cloth, $76.00. Paper, $66.00. 419pp. .... Vendor G0259

3514 **THE SHAVER FAMILY OF ROCKINGHAM COUNTY, VA**, by Lewis H. Yankey. 1991. Indexed.
Paper. $15.00. 100pp. .... Vendor G0365

3515 **JAMES SHAW FAMILY OF THE RIVER AREA FAYETTE & WASHINGTON COS. PA**, by James H. Shaw. 1988. Indexed.
Paper. $24.00. 205pp. .... Vendor G0280

3516 **SHAW RECORDS. A MEM. OF ROGER SHAW, 1594–1661**, by H.F. Farwell. 1904.
Cloth, $65.00. Paper, $55.00. 435pp. .... Vendor G0259

3517 **SHAW REC. (MA. SOLDIERS & SAILORS OF REV. WAR).** 1906.
Paper. $10.00. 48pp. .... Vendor G0259

3518 **THE FAMILY OF DANIEL SHAYS**, by Elmer S. Smail; edited by Mary Ann Nicholson. 1987. Indexed.
Paper. $11.50. 90pp. .... Vendor G0406

3519 **SHEARER–AKERS FAM., WITH "THE BRYAN LINE" THROUGH THE SEVENTH GEN.**, by J.W. Shearer. 1915.
Cloth, $35.50. Paper, $25.50. 171pp. .... Vendor G0259

3520 **SHEARMAN–SHERMAN FAM., EXTR. FROM "GEN. NOTES OF N.Y. & NEW ENG. FAMS.,"** by S.V. Talcott. 1883.
Paper. $9.00. 41pp. .... Vendor G0259

3521 **DANIEL SHED GEN.; ANC. & DESC. OF DANIEL SHED OF BRAINTREE, MASS., 1327–1920**, by F.E. Shedd, with J.G. Bartlett. 1921.
Cloth, $129.50. Paper, $119.50. 812pp. .... Vendor G0259

3522 **SHELTON GEN. EXTR. FROM CAMPBELL GEN.** 1927.
Paper. $7.00. 33pp. .... Vendor G0259

3523 **GEN. OF WM. SHEPARD OF FOSSECUT, NORTH-ANTS., ENG., & SOME DESC.**, by G. Shepard. 1886.
Paper. $12.50. 63pp. .... Vendor G0259

3524 **RALPH SHEPARD, PURITAN,** by R.H. Shepard. 1893.
Paper. $10.00. 50pp. .... Vendor G0259

3525 **GENEALOGY OF THE ALLEN SHEPPARD FAM. (DESC. OF JOHN SHEPPARD, COHANSEY NJ, 1600'S).** 1950.
Paper. $19.00. 126pp. .... Vendor G0259

3526 **CHRISTIAN STRICKLER SHERK: HIS ANCESTRY AND DESCEN-DANTS,** by Morris N. Sherk. 1994. Indexed. Illus.
Cloth. $22.00. 294pp. .... Vendor G0370

3527 **THE SHERK FAMILY,** by Thomas A. Sherk. 1982.
Cloth. $29.00. 357pp. .... Vendor G0150

3528 **SHERMAN GEN. INCL. FAM. OF ESSEX, SUFFOLK & NORFOLK, ENG.,** by T.T. Sherman. 1920.
Cloth, $86.50. Paper, $76.50. 490pp. .... Vendor G0259

3529 **DESC. OF SAMUEL SHERRILL OF EASTHAMPTON, N.Y.,** by C.H. Sherrill. 1894.
Cloth, $35.00. Paper, $25.00. 132pp. .... Vendor G0259

3530 **THOMAS SHERWOOD OF FAIRFIELD, CONN. & DESC.,** by M.B. Carlson. 1950.
Paper. $19.00. 92pp. .... Vendor G0259

3531 **REC. OF PROCEEDINGS AT THE 1ST GATHERING OF DESC. OF JOHN SHILLABER AT THE OLD HOMESTEAD, PEABODY MA, 1877.** 1877.
Paper. $9.50. 48pp. .... Vendor G0259

3532 **HIST. OF THE SHINN FAM. IN EUROPE & AMER.,** by J.H. Shinn. 1903.
Cloth, $65.00. Paper, $55.00. 434pp. .... Vendor G0259

3533 **SHIPLEY–SHEPLEY. OUR FAMILY (ALLEN, HITCHCOCK, RUTLEDGE, SHEPLEY),** by Shepley, Shepley, and Allen. n.d.
Paper. $18.00. 89pp. .... Vendor G0259

3534 **THE SHIPLEYS OF MARYLAND: A GENEALOGICAL STUDY,** prepared by committee. 1937.
Cloth, $54.00. Paper, $44.00. 281pp. .... Vendor G0259

3535 **GENEALOGY OF THE SHOBE, KIRKPATRICK & DILLING FAMS.,** rev. 1950 ed. by F.D. Shobe. (1919) rev. 1950.
Cloth, $41.00. Paper, $31.00. 182+19pp. .... Vendor G0259

3536 **SHOEMAKER FAMILY,** by T.H. Shoemaker. 1893.
Cloth, $31.00. Paper, $21.00. 112pp. .... Vendor G0259

3537 **ANNALS OF OUR COL. ANC. & THEIR DESC.; OR, OUR QUAKER FOREBEARS & THEIR POSTERITY, EMBRACING A GEN. & BIOGR. REG. OF NINE GEN. OF THE SHOTWELL FAM. IN AMER.,** by A.M. Shotwell. 1895–7.
Cloth, $54.00. Paper, $44.00. 291pp. .... Vendor G0259

3538 **AN ENGLISH ANCESTRY: AN ACCT. OF THE ANCESTRY OF ED-WARD MELVIN SHOVE & HIS SIBLINGS,** by James K. Raywalt. 1992.
Cloth, $31.00. Paper, $21.00. 149pp. .... Vendor G0259

1920 Estill County Kentucky Census
by William E. Wise and Gladys W. Wise
Contains 15,000 names
Indexed 1,000 surnames
Contact William E. Wise, 411 Elm St., Ravenna, KY 40472

3539 **THE SHRECK GEN., THE FAM. OF PAUL & BETHANY SHRECK, 1771–1954**, by C. May. 1954.
Paper. $11.00. 56pp. .... Vendor G0259

3540 **THE GEN. & HIST. OF THE SHREVE FAM. FROM 1641**, by L.P. Allen. 1901.
Cloth, $93.00. Paper, $83.00. 672pp. .... Vendor G0259

3541 **OUR FAMILIES: SHUCK, FLESHMAN, SYDENSTRICKER, SMITH, LEWIS, KINCAID, KEISTER, et. al., OF WEST VIRGINIA**, by Larry G. Shuck. 1995. Indexed.
Cloth. $43.00. 565pp. .... Vendor G0287

3542 **HIST. OF THE SHUEY FAM. IN AMER., FROM 1732 TO 1876**, by D.B. Shuey. 1876.
Cloth, $45.50. Paper, $35.50. 279pp. .... Vendor G0259

3543 **HISTORY OF THE SHUEY FAMILY IN AMERICA, 1732 TO 1919**, by D.B. Shuey. 2nd ed. 1919.
Cloth, $68.00. Paper, $58.00. 381pp. .... Vendor G0259

3544 **A HIST. SKETCH OF THE SHUFORD FAM.**, by J.H. Shuford. 1902.
Cloth, $37.50. Paper, $27.50. 156pp. .... Vendor G0259

3545 **GEO. SHUMAN FAM.; GEN. & HIST. FROM ARRIVAL IN AMER. IN 1760 TO 1913**, by W. Shuman. 1913.
Cloth, $64.00. Paper, $54.00. 341pp. .... Vendor G0259

3546 **GEN. OF THE SHUMWAY FAM. IN THE U.S.A.**, by A.A. Shumway. 1909.
Cloth, $85.00. Paper, $75.00. 478pp. .... Vendor G0259

3547 **DESCENDANTS OF WILLIAM SHURTLEFF OF PLYMOUTH & MARSHFIELD, MASS.**, by B. Shurtleff. 2 vols. 1912.
Cloth, $175.00. Paper, $165.00. 758+738pp. .... Vendor G0259

3548 **GEN. GLEANINGS OF SIGGINS & OTHER PENN. FAMS.**, by White and Maltby. 1918.
Cloth, $109.50. Paper, $99.50. 726pp. .... Vendor G0259

3549 **GEN. OF DESC. OF JOHN SILL OF CAMBRIDGE**, by G.G. Sill. 1859.
Paper. $17.50. 108pp. .... Vendor G0259

3550 **SILL FAMILY. OLD SILLTOWN: SOMETHING OF ITS HIST. & PEOPLE, BEING PRINCIPALLY A BRIEF ACCT. OF THE EARLY GEN. OF THE SILL FAMILY**, by S. Burt. 1912.
Cloth, $32.00. Paper, $22.00. 148pp. .... Vendor G0259

3551 **RICHARD SILVESTER OF WEYMOUTH, MASS. & SOME DESC. (REPR. *NEHGR*),** by A.H. Silvester.
Paper. $14.00. 71pp. .... Vendor G0259

3552 **JOHN & SUSAN SIMMONDS & SOME OF THEIR DESC. WITH RE-LATED ANC. LINES,** by F.W. Simmonds. 1940.
Cloth, $43.00. Paper, $33.00. 222pp. .... Vendor G0259

3553 **HISTORY OF OUR SIMMONS FAMILY THROUGH TEN GENERA-TIONS, & BRIEF SKETCHES OF ALLIED FAMS. OF BARTLETT, MOORE & MANN,** by M.E. Simmons. 1936.
Cloth, $48.50. Paper, $38.50. 244pp. .... Vendor G0259

3554 **HIST. OF THE SIMMONS FAM., FROM MOSES SIMMONS (SYMONSON), SHIP FORTUNE, 1621,** by L. Simmons. 1930.
Cloth, $59.00. Paper, $49.00. 315pp. .... Vendor G0259

3555 **GEN. OF ORIGINAL SIMPSON FAM. OF YORK & HANCOCK COS., ME.,** by J.S. Emery. 1891.
Paper. $10.00. 51pp. .... Vendor G0259

3556 **SIMPSONS OF RYE TOP, CUMBERLAND VAL., PENN.,** by E.S. Bladen. 1905.
Paper. $7.50. 34pp. .... Vendor G0259

3557 **BOOK OF SIMRALL: STORIES & NOTES ON FAMILY HISTORY,** by F.S. Riker. 1927.
Cloth, $41.00. Paper, $31.00. 198pp. .... Vendor G0259

3558 **THE HIST. OF THE SINCLAIR FAM. IN EUROPE & AMER. FOR 1100 YEARS,** by L.A. Morrison. 1896.
Cloth, $78.50. Paper, $68.50. 453pp. .... Vendor G0259

3559 **THE SINCLAIRS OF ENGLAND.** 1887 (London).
Cloth, $71.00. Paper, $61.00. 414pp. .... Vendor G0259

3560 **GEN. OF THE SINGLETARY-CURTIS FAM. [COMP. FROM REC. FROM MASS., N.Y., S.C. & OTHERS],** by L. Singletary-Bedford. 1907.
Paper. $19.50. 115pp. .... Vendor G0259

3561 **SINNOTT, ROGERS, COFFIN, CORLIES, REEVES, BODINE & AL-LIED FAMS.,** by M.E. Sinnott. 1905.
Cloth, $46.00. Paper, $36.00. 278pp. .... Vendor G0259

3562 **THE SIRK–ZIRK FAMILY,** by Lewis H. Yankey. 1992. Indexed.
Paper. $10.00. 45pp. .... Vendor G0365

3563 **ANCESTRY AND DESCENDANTS OF EZRA SISSON (1824–1898) AND AMELIA PLEMON (1828–1914) PLUS DESCENDANTS OF ELIHU B. GIFFORD (1830–1898) AND CATHERINE SANDOW BARROWS (1835–1917),** by Raymond L. Olson. 1991. Indexed. Includes 5 pictures.
Cloth. $23.00. 361pp. .... Vendor G0291

3564 **DESCENDANTS OF THE LUDLOW B. SISSON FAMILY,** by Sebert L. Sisson and James R. Sisson. 1995. Indexed. Illus.
Cloth. $39.00. 186pp. .... Vendor G0424

3565 **THE SKELTONS OF PAXTON, PAWHATAN CO., VA., INCL. SKETCHES OF THE FAMS. OF SKELTON, GIFFORD & CRANE**, by P.H. Baskervil. 1922.
Cloth, $32.00. Paper, $22.00. 119pp. .... Vendor G0259

3566 **DR. HENRY SKILTON & DESC.**, by J. Skilton. 1921.
Cloth, $75.00. Paper, $65.00. 412pp. .... Vendor G0259

3567 **SLACK FAMILY, MORE PARTICULARLY AN ACCT. OF THE FAMILY OF ELIPHALET SLACK & HIS WIFE ABIGAIL CUTTER: THEIR ASCENDANTS, DESCENDANTS & RELATIONS**, by W.W. Slack. 1930.
Cloth, $49.50. Paper, $39.50. 252pp. .... Vendor G0259

3568 **WM. SLADE OF WINDSOR, CONN. & HIS DESC.**, by T.B. Peck. 1910.
Cloth, $40.50. Paper, $30.50. 205pp. .... Vendor G0259

3569 **MEM. OF JOHN SLAFTER, WITH A GEN. ACCT. OF HIS DESC.**, by E.F. Slafter. 1869.
Cloth, $35.00. Paper, $25.00. 165pp. .... Vendor G0259

3570 **WM. SLATE OF WINDHAM & MANSFIELD, CONN., & SOME DESC.**, by G.O. Chapman. 1941.
Paper. $7.00. 33pp. .... Vendor G0259

3571 **DESCENDANTS OF FRANCIS SLAUGHTER OF VIRGINIA**, by Carol A. Hauk. 1995. Indexed.
Paper. $35.00. 119pp. .... Vendor G0340

3572 **HISTORY OF THE SLAYMAKER FAMILY**, by Henry C. Slaymaker. 1909, 1929.
Cloth, $59.50. Paper, $49.50. 325pp. .... Vendor G0259

3573 **HIST. OF THE SLAYTON FAM., BIOGR. & GEN.**, by A.W. Slayton. 1898.
Cloth, $59.50. Paper, $49.50. 322pp. .... Vendor G0259

3574 **THE DESCENDANTS OF LEONARD SLIPP AND ELIZABETH RYSON OF GAGETOWN, QUEENS COUNTY, NEW BRUNSWICK, CANADA, 1748–1994**, by Murray S. Thomson, David Allen, and Rick Crume. 1994. Indexed.
Includes: **Clark, MacAlpine, Merritt, Musgrove, Palmer, Pennington, Peters, Slip, Van Wart**.
Paper. $16.00. 189pp. .... Vendor G0386

3575 **A SHORT HIST. OF THE SLOCUMS, SLOCUMBS & SLOCOMBS OF AMER., GEN. & BIOGR., 1637 TO 1881**, by C.E. Slocum. 1882.
Cloth, $106.50. Paper, $96.50. 644pp. .... Vendor G0259

3576 **SLOCUM. SUPPLEMENT TO ABOVE. VOL. II.** 1908.
Cloth, $96.00. Paper, $86.00. 549pp. .... Vendor G0259

3577 **A GEN. MEMOIR OF NATHANIEL SLOSSON OF KENT, CONN. & HIS DESC., 1696–1872, WITH NATHAN SLOSSON'S DESC. TO 1896**, by D.W. Patterson. 1896.
Paper. $8.00. 38pp. .... Vendor G0259

3578 **DESC. OF EDW. SMALL OF NEW ENG. & ALLIED FAM., & TRACINGS OF ENG. ANC.**, by L. Underhill. 2nd ed. 3 vols. 1934.
Cloth, $269.00. Paper, $259.00. 1,835pp. .... Vendor G0259

3579 **GEN. OF THE SMEDLEY FAM. DESC. FROM GEO. & SARAH SMEDLEY, SETTLERS IN CHESTER CO., PA., WITH BRIEF NOTICES OF OTHER FAM.**, by G. Cope. 1901.
Cloth, $154.00. Paper, $144.00. 1,011pp. . . . . Vendor G0259

3580 **ABRAHAM AND ZERVIAH (RICKETSON) SMITH AND THEIR NINE-TEEN CHILDREN.** by Rebecca W. Hawes. 1910.
Paper. $12.00. 60pp. . . . . Vendor G0259

3581 **A GEN. HIST. OF THE DESC. OF THE REV. NEHEMIAH SMITH OF NEW LONDON CO., CONN., WITH MENTION OF HIS BROTHER JOHN & NEPHEW EDWARD, 1638–1888**, by H.A. Smith. 1889.
Cloth, $59.00. Paper, $49.00. 320pp. Vendor G0259

3582 **A MEM'L OF REV. THOMAS SMITH & HIS DESC.: A FULL GEN. RECORD, 1707–1895**, by S.A. Smith. 1895.
Cloth, $33.00. Paper, $23.00. 146pp. Vendor G0259

3583 **COMPLETE GENEALOGY OF THE DESCENDANTS OF MATTHEW SMITH OF EAST HADDAM, CT., WITH MENTION OF HIS ANCES-TORS, 1637–1890**, by Sophia S. Martin. 1890.
Cloth, $52.00. Paper, $42.00. 269pp. Vendor G0259

3584 **FAMILY TREE BOOK, GENEALOGICAL & BIOGRAPHICAL, LIST-ING THE RELATIVES OF GEN. WILLIAM ALEXANDER SMITH & OF W. THOMAS SMITH**, compiled by W. Thomas Smith. 1922.
Cloth, $57.00. Paper, $47.00. 304pp. Vendor G0259

3585 **GEN. & REMINISCENCES OF WM. SMITH & FAM.**, by M.T. Smith. 1884.
Paper. $15.00. 86pp. . . . . Vendor G0259

3586 **GENEALOGY OF THE DESCENDANTS OF ROBERT SMITH, WHO SETTLED NEAR CASTLE SHANNON, WASHINGTON CO., NOW AL-LEGHENY CO. PA, 1772**, by E.U. Smith. 1923.
Cloth, $57.50. Paper, $47.50. 311pp. Vendor G0259

3587 **HIST. & GEN. OF THE SMITHS OF "BIG SPRING PLANTATION," FREDERICK CO., VA., WITH A CHRON. OF THE DRUGAN & CARNAHAN FAMS. OF PA. & OHIO**, by B.T. Hartman. 1929.
Paper. $18.00. 101pp. . . . . Vendor G0259

3588 **JESSE SMITH, HIS ANC. & DESC.**, by L. Smith. 1909.
Cloth, $40.00. Paper, $30.00. 187pp. Vendor G0259

3589 **JOHN O.C. SMITH OF SUSSEX CO. NEW JERSEY 1760–1840 AND HIS CHILDREN WITH CHARLES D. SMITH 1799–1879, MARY ANN COOPER AND THEIR DESCENDANTS (HANCOCK CO. OHIO, MI-AMI CO., INDIANA AND BENTON CO., IOWA)**, by Ellen Brzoska. 1994. Indexed. Illus.
Cloth. $30.00. 266pp. . . . . Vendor G0127

3590 **JOHN SMITH OF ALABAMA, HIS ANC. & DESC.**, by M.O. McDavid. 1948.
Cloth, $33.00. Paper, $23.00. 189pp. Vendor G0259

3591 **LT. SAMUEL SMITH; HIS CHILDREN & ONE LINE OF DESC. & RE-LATED FAMS.**, by J.W. Hook. 1953.
Cloth, $69.50. Paper, $59.50. 381pp. .... Vendor G0259

3592 **NOTES & ILLUSTRATIONS CONCERNING THE FAM. HIST. OF JAMES SMITH OF COVENTRY [ENGLAND], (1731–1794), & HIS DESC.**, by Lady Durning-Lawrence. 1912 (England).
Cloth, $34.00. Paper, $24.00. 156pp. .... Vendor G0259

3593 **PROMINENT RHODE ISLAND "SMITHS" (EXTR. FROM "REPRE-SENTATIVE MEN & OLD FAMILIES OF R.I.").** 1908.
Paper. $18.00. 88pp. .... Vendor G0259

3594 **SMITH. COLLATERAL LINES & MAYFLOWER CONNECTIONS**, by H.S.L. Barnes. 1910.
Paper. $10.00. 51pp. .... Vendor G0259

3595 **SMITH DIGEST.** 1992.
Published quarterly. Master index. **Smiths** anywhere in the U.S. or Canada.
Subscription. $20.00/year. 70pp. per issue .... Vendor G0429

3596 **SMITH, et al (NJ), GRANT & IRONS FAMILIES OF N.J.'S SHORE COUNTIES, INCLUDING THE RELATED FAMILIES OF WILLETS & BIRDSALL**, by J.W. Hook. 1955.
Cloth, $57.50. Paper, $47.50. 280pp. .... Vendor G0259

3597 **SMITH FAMILY, BEING A POPULAR ACCT. OF MOST BRANCHES OF THE NAMES—HOWEVER SPELT—FROM THE 14TH CENT., WITH NUMEROUS PEDIGREES**, by C. Reade. 1904. (England)
Cloth, $59.50. Paper, $49.50. 324pp. .... Vendor G0259

3598 **SMITH FAM. OF PA. JOHANN FRIEDERICH SCHMIDT, 1746–1812**, by J.B. Nolan. 1932.
Cloth, $45.00. Paper, $35.00. 203pp. .... Vendor G0259

3599 **THE DESCENDANTS OF A HESSIAN SOLDIER, LORENZO FREDERICK SMITH**, by Goldie Turner May. (1985) reprint 1994. Indexed. Illus.
Cloth. $24.00. 472pp. .... Vendor G0365

3600 **WILLS OF THE SMITH FAMILIES OF N.Y. & LONG ISL., 1664–1794, WITH GEN. & HIST. NOTES**, by W.S. Pelletreau. 1898.
Cloth, $37.50. Paper, $27.50. 151pp. .... Vendor G0259

3601 **GEN. NOTES ON THE SMOCK FAM. IN AMER.**, by J.C. Smock. 1922.
Paper. $10.00. 47pp. .... Vendor G0259

3602 **SNIVELY. GEN. MEM., 1659–1882**, by W.A. Snively. 1883.
Paper. $14.00. 77pp. .... Vendor G0259

3603 **SNODGRASS FAM.**, by S.C. Scott. 1928.
Paper. $19.00. 95pp. .... Vendor G0259

3604 **HIST. OF THE FAM. OF BENJ. SNOW, A DESC. OF RICHARD SNOW OF WOBURN, MASS.**, by O. Wilcox. 1907.
Cloth, $71.50. Paper, $61.50. 385pp. .... Vendor G0259

3605 **WM. SNOW FAM. WHO LANDED AT PLYMOUTH IN 1635**, by E.H.
Snow. 1908.
Paper. $12.50. 64pp. .... Vendor G0259

3606 **THE JACOB SNYDER FAMILY (SNYDER–SNIDER)**, by Shirley C. Miller.
1995. Indexed. Illus.
Cloth. $35.00. 716pp. .... Vendor G0365

3607 **THOMAS SOLLEY & HIS DESC.**, by G.W. Solley. 1911.
Cloth, $43.50. Paper, $32.50. 217pp. .... Vendor G0259

3608 **THE ANTHONY SOUDER HISTORY 1750–1989**, by Tressie G. Souder.
1995. Indexed. Illus.
Cloth. $34.00. 566pp. .... Vendor G0365

3609 **[Soule]. A CONTRIBUTION TO THE HIST., BIOGR. & GEN. OF THE
FAM. NAMED SOLE, SOLLY, SOULE, SOWLE, SOULIS**, by G.T. Ridlon,
Sr. 2 vols. 1926.
Cloth, $187.00. Paper, $177.00. 1,180pp. .... Vendor G0259

3610 **OUTLINE OF THE SOUTHERLY–SUTHERLY–SUTHERLAND FAM-
ILY**, by Lewis H. Yankey. 1992. Indexed.
Paper. $10.00. 52pp. .... Vendor G0365

3611 **MONOGRAPHS ON THE SOUTHGATE FAM. OF SCARBOROUGH,
ME.; ANC. & DESC.**, by L. Chapman. 1907.
Paper. $14.00. 68pp. .... Vendor G0259

3612 **GEN. OF DESC. OF LAWRENCE & CASSANDRA SOUTHWICK OF
SALEM, MASS.**, by Caller and Ober. 1881.
Cloth, $89.50. Paper, $79.50. 616pp. .... Vendor G0259

3613 **A GEN. OF THE SOUTHWORTHS (SOUTHARDS), DESC. OF CON-
STANT SOUTHWORTH, WITH A SKETCH OF THE FAM. IN ENG.**, by
S.G. Webber. 1905.
Cloth, $86.50. Paper, $76.50. 492pp. .... Vendor G0259

3614 **THE SOWELL FAMILY, RANGERS & PIONEERS OF TEXAS**, by Roy
B.Young. 1996. Illus.
   Nichols—Turner—Steele—Tanner.
Cloth. $38.95. 200pp. .... Vendor G0405

3615 **SPAID GEN.; FROM THE FIRST OF THE NAME IN THIS COUNTRY
TO THE PRESENT TIME, WITH A NUMBER OF ALLIED FAMS. &
MANY HIST. FACTS**, by A.T. Secrest. 1922.
Cloth, $72.50. Paper, $62.50. 403pp. .... Vendor G0259

3616 **SPALDING MEMORIAL: GENEALOGICAL HISTORY OF EDWARD
SPALDING OF MASS. BAY, & HIS DESCENDANTS**, by S.J. Spalding.
1872.
Cloth, $101.00. Paper, $91.00. 619pp. .... Vendor G0259

3617 **SPALDING MEM. & PERSONAL REMINISCENCES, BY P. SPALDING,
& LIFE & SELECTED POEMS OF CAROLINE A. SPALDING**, by G.B.
Spalding. 1887.
Cloth, $59.50. Paper, $49.50. 324pp. .... Vendor G0259

3618 **THE SPALDING MEM.; A GEN. HIST. OF EDW. SPALDING OF VA. & MASS. BAY, & HIS DESC.**, by C. Spalding; rev. by S. Spalding. 1897. Cloth, $161.00. Paper, $151.00. 1,276pp. .... Vendor G0259

3619 **THE SPALDING REPORT. THE DESCENDANTS OF CHARLES SPALDING (1783–1856)**, by Gaynelle Jenkins Moore. 1994. Indexed. Illus. Allied families: **Belse, Miller, Simpson, Smith**, and others. Charles **Spalding** of St. Mary's Co., Maryland; Warren Co., Kentucky; and Miller Co., Missouri. Paper. $38.00. 462pp. .... Vendor G0421

3620 **THE SPARE FAM. LEONARD SPARE & HIS DESC.**, by the Spare Fam. Assoc. 1931. Cloth, $58.50. Paper, $48.50. 323pp. .... Vendor G0259

3621 **MATERIALS FOR A GEN. OF THE SPARHAWK FAM. IN NEW ENG. (REPR. ESSEX INST. HIST. COLL.)**, by C.H.C. Howard. 1892. Paper. $18.00. 113pp. .... Vendor G0259

3622 **THE ANC. OF ANNIS SPEAR, 1775–1858, OF LITCHFIELD, ME.**, by W.G. Davis. 1945. Cloth, $35.50. Paper, $25.50. 170pp. .... Vendor G0259

3623 **JOHN E. & NOAH SPEARS IN KENTUCKY, MISSOURI, KANSAS AND OKLAHOMA**, by La Roux K. Gillespie. 1987. Indexed. Illus. Paper. $35.00. 370pp. .... Vendor G0238

3624 **REC. & MEM. OF THE SPEED FAM.**, by T. Speed. 1892. Cloth, $41.00. Paper, $31.00 .... Vendor G0259

3625 **TEN GENERATIONS OF GEORGE SPEER, 1642–1942: THREE CEN-TURIES OF AMER. LIFE**, by R.C. Speer. 1942(?) Cloth, $43.50. Paper, $33.50. 205pp. typescript .... Vendor G0259

3626 **HISTORY OF THE SPEICHER, SPICHER, SPYKER FAMILY**, by P.I. Speicher. 1961. Paper. $10.00. 51pp. .... Vendor G0259

3627 **ENG. ANC. & AMER. DESC. OF RICHARD SPELMAN OF MIDDLETOWN, CT., 1700**, by F. Barbour. 1910. Cloth, $96.00. Paper, $86.00. 559pp. .... Vendor G0259

3628 **GENEALOGICAL SKETCH OF DESC. OF SAMUEL SPENCER OF PA.**, by H.M. Jenkins. 1904. Cloth, $49.00. Paper, $39.00. 253pp. .... Vendor G0259

3629 **THE MAINE SPENCERS. A HIST. & GEN., 1596–1898**, by W.D. Spencer. 1898. Cloth, $42.00. Paper, $32.00. 247pp. .... Vendor G0259

3630 **THE ANNALS OF THE FAMILIES OF CASPAR, HENRY, BALTZER & GEORGE SPENGLER, WHO SETTLED IN YORK CO. (PA.) RESPECTIVELY IN 1729, 1732, 1732, & 1751, WITH BIOGRAPHICAL & HISTORICAL SKETCHES,** by E.W. Spangler. 1896.
Cloth, $101.00. Paper, $91.00. 604pp. .... Vendor G0259

3631 **HIST. OF THE DESC. OF PETER SPICER, LANDHOLDER IN NEW LONDON, CT., AS EARLY AS 1666, & OTHERS OF THE NAME, WITH SHORT ACCTS. OF ALLIED FAMS.,** by S.S. and S.B. Meech. 1911.
Cloth, $87.00. Paper, $77.00. 610pp. .... Vendor G0259

3632 **SPICER SUPPLEMENT, A SUPPL. TO "THE DESC. OF PETER SPICER" (1911), CONTAINING ADD. & CORR.,** by S.B. Meech. 1923.
Cloth, $52.00. Paper, $42.00. 269pp. .... Vendor G0259

3633 **SPIVEY FAMILY HISTORY,** by Nathan Mathews. 1993. Indexed. Illus.
Other major family groups: **Hester, Kea/Key, Mathews, Riner, Smith, Speight,** and **Walker.**
Cloth. $40.00. 245pp. .... Vendor G0399

3634 **A FAM. RECORD OF THE DESC. OF JOHN SPOFFORD, WHO EMIGR. FROM ENG. & SETTLED AT ROWLEY, MASS., IN 1638,** by J. Spofford. 1869.
Paper. $19.00. 128pp. .... Vendor G0259

3635 **A GEN. RECORD, INCL. TWO GEN. IN FEMALE LINES OF DESC. OF JOHN SPOFFORD & ELIZABETH SCOTT, WHO SETTLED AT ROWLEY, MASS.,** by J. Spofford; edited by A.T. Spofford. 1888.
Cloth, $88.00. Paper, $78.00. 502pp. .... Vendor G0259

3636 **MEM. OF WM. SPOONER, 1637, & OF HIS DESC. TO THE 3RD GEN., OF HIS GR-GRANDSON, ELNATHAN SPOONER, & OF HIS DESC. TO 1871,** by T. Spooner. 1871.
Cloth, $46.00. Paper, $36.00. 242pp. .... Vendor G0259

3637 **RECORDS OF WM. SPOONER OF PLYMOUTH, MASS., & OF HIS DESC.,** Vol. I, by T. Spooner. 1883.
Cloth, $98.00. Paper, $88.00. 694pp. .... Vendor G0259

3638 **SPOONER SAGA—JUDAH PADDOCK SPOONER, HIS WIFE DEBORAH DOUGLAS AND THEIR DESCENDANTS—SPOONER, DOUGLAS, AND JERMAIN ANCESTRY,** by Esther Littleford Woodworth-Barnes. 1996. Indexed.
Cloth. 400pp. .... Vendor G0054

3639 **THE SPOOR FAM. (ALIAS WYBESSE) OF N.Y. STATE,** edited by H.F. Johnston.
Paper. $10.00. 54pp. .... Vendor G0259

3640 **GEN. OF THE SPOTSWOOD FAM. IN SCOTLAND & VA.,** by C. Campbell. 1868.
Paper. $9.00. 44pp. .... Vendor G0259

3641 **GENEALOGY (IN PART) OF THE SPRAGUE FAMILIES IN AMERICA, AS DESCENDED FROM EDWARD SPRAGUE OF ENGLAND, FROM 1614, WITH THE DESC. OF EDWARD SPRAGUE AND THAT OF HIS**

SON WILLIAM WHO SETTLED IN HINGHAM MA IN 1636, by A.B.R. Sprague. Rev. ed. 1905.
Paper. $10.00. 49pp. .... Vendor G0259

3642 GEN. OF THE SPRAGUES IN HINGHAM, COUNTING FROM WM. SPRAGUE, ONE OF THE 1ST PLANTERS IN MASS., WHO ARRIVED AT NAUMKEAG FROM ENG. IN 1628, by H. Sprague. 1828.
Paper. $12.50. 68pp. .... Vendor G0259

3643 HON. SETH SPRAGUE OF DUXBURY, PLYMOUTH CO., MASS.: HIS DESCENDANTS DOWN TO THE 6TH GENERATION, WITH HIS REMINISCENCES, by W.B. Weston. 1915.
Cloth, $35.00. Paper, $25.00. 134+26pp. .... Vendor G0259

3644 SPRAGUE FAM. IN AMER., by W.V. Sprague. 1913.
Cloth, $97.00. Paper, $87.00. 578pp. .... Vendor G0259

3645 PART OF THE 1940-1 SUPPLEMENT TO "SPRAGUE FAMILIES IN AMERICA" (1913), FRANCUS SPRAGUE OF DUXBURY, MASS., by W.V. Sprague. 1941.
Paper. $7.00. 35pp. typescript .... Vendor G0259

3646 THE RALPH SPRAGUE GEN., by E.G. Sprague. 1913.
Cloth, $59.50. Paper, $49.50. 322pp. .... Vendor G0259

3647 THE SPRAGUES OF MALDEN, MASS., by G.W. Chamberlain. 1923.
Cloth, $58.50. Paper, $48.50. 325pp. .... Vendor G0259

3648 A GEN. TABLE & HIST. OF THE SPRINGER FAM. IN EUROPE & N. AMER., Vol. 1., by M. Springer; rev. by E. Scribner. 1917.
Cloth, $35.00. Paper, $25.00 .... Vendor G0259

3649 SPRINGER GEN., by I.E. Springer. 1909.
Paper. $8.00. 38pp. .... Vendor G0259

3650 THE SOUTH FORK SQUIRES—LONG ISLAND, NEW YORK, by Tiger Gardiner. 1992. Indexed.
Cloth. $48.50. 411pp. .... Vendor G0339

3651 HIST. & GEN. OF THE STACKPOLE FAM., by E.S. Stackpole. 2nd ed. 1920.
Cloth, $65.50. Paper, $55.50. 352pp. .... Vendor G0259

3652 THE STACY JOURNAL, VOLUME I—ISSUES 1-4, by Barbara Stacy Mathews. 1991. Indexed. Illus.
Pictures, maps, court records, marriages.
Paper. $30.00. 135pp+index .... Vendor G0430

3653 THE STACY JOURNAL, VOLUME II—ISSUES 1-4, by Barbara Stacy Mathews. 1992. Indexed. Illus.
Pictures, maps, marriages, court records.
Paper. $30.00. 236+pp. .... Vendor G0430

3654 STAEHLING FAMILY TREE, 1598-1939, by W.E. Staehling. 1939.
Paper. $7.00. 37pp. .... Vendor G0259

3655 **SOME RECENT INVESTIGATIONS CONCERNING THE ANCESTRY OF CAPT. MILES STANDISH**, by T.C. Porteus. 1914.
Paper. $7.00. 34pp. .... Vendor G0259

3656 **STANDISHES OF AMERICA**, by M. Standish. 1895.
Cloth, $40.00. Paper, $30.00. 153pp. .... Vendor G0259

3657 **THE FAMILIES OF STANDISH OF STANDISH, LANCASHIRE, ENGLAND; & STANDISH OF DUXBURY, ARLEY, ORMSKIRK, GATHURST, CROSTON, PARK BROOK & WANTAGE; PRESCOTT OF STANDISH & PRESCOTT OF DRIBY**, by F.L. Weis. 1959.
Paper. $15.00. 77pp. .... Vendor G0259

3658 **STANLEY & ALLIED FAMILIES, VOLUME ONE**, by Alvin L. Anderson, Ph.D. 1996. Indexed.
Stanley history in England; Quaker Stanleys in colonial Virginia; five generations of descendants of James, Thomas, and John Stanley, sons of the immigrant Thomas Stanley.
Major allied families include: **Benbow, Bills, Blackburn, Bond, Butler, Cain, Carter, Cattell, Cobbs, Coffin, Cook, Coppock, Cowgill, Crew, Davis, Dicks, Dillon, Dixon, Ellyson, Foster, Fowty, Garner, Gordon, Hadley, Hale, Harris, Harrold, Harvey, Hemp, Hiatt, Hill, Hobson, Hockett/Hoggatt, Hodson, Hole, Holloway, Hunt, Hutchins, Jessup, Johnson, Jones, Kelly, Macy, Mendenhall, Meredith, Mills, Moon, Nichols, Osborn, Pearson, Reeve, Shreve, Sopher, Stuart, Thomson, Thornburg, Unthank, White, Willard, Williams, Wilson, Woody, Woolman,** and **Wright**.
Cloth. $40.00. 410pp. .... Vendor G0446

3659 **STANLEY FAMILY OF AMER. AS DESC. FROM JOHN, TIMOTHY & THOMAS STANLEY OF HARTFORD, CONN., 1636**, by I.P. Warren. 1887.
Cloth, $65.50. Paper, $55.50. 352pp. .... Vendor G0259

3660 **A RECORD, GEN., BIOGR., STATISTICAL, OF THOMAS STANTON OF CONN., & HIS DESC., 1635–1891**, by W.A. Stanton. 1891.
Cloth, $102.00. Paper, $92.00. 613pp. .... Vendor G0259

3661 **LINEAGE OF THE STANTON FAM. (GEO. STANTON, NY, 1698), EXTR. "OLDE ULSTER,"** by W. Macy.
Paper. $7.00. 34pp. .... Vendor G0259

3662 **OUR ANCESTORS, THE STANTONS**, by W.H. Stanton. 1912.
Cloth, $104.50. Paper, $94.50. 649pp. .... Vendor G0259

3663 **A HIST. OF THE STANWOOD FAM. IN AMER.**, by E.S. Bolton. 1899.
Cloth, $57.50. Paper, $47.50. 317pp. .... Vendor G0259

3664 **GENEALOGY OF THE STARBIRD–STARBARD FAMILY**, by A.A. Starbird. 1942(?)
Cloth, $37.00. Paper, $27.00. 179pp. .... Vendor G0259

3665 **STARBUCKS ALL 1635–1985, A BIOGRAPHICAL-GENEALOGICAL DICTIONARY**, by James Carlton Starbuck. 1985. Indexed.
Cloth. $25.00. 594pp. .... Vendor G0120

3666 **STARIN FAM. IN AMER. DESC. OF NICHOLAS STER (STARIN), ONE**

ALLENS OF LITTLE EGYPT BY HARDY LEE HIRAM ALLEN:

The book is 8½ x 11, weighs 4 pounds, has 450 pages, has a hard back in blue, and the title and the author's name are impressed in gold on the front and spine. The index has 33 2-column pages.

Listed are 330 first names of Allens, more than 9600 non-Allen first names, and 1300 non-Allen Family names. The book is not just about the Allen Family from the Island of Bute, Scotland; it is a representation of thousands of Families of Englishmen, Irishmen, Scotsmen, Welshmen, and a sprinkling of a variety of Europeans who had sailed across the north Atlantic seeking a better life for themselves and their descendants. Most of them landed in the Colonies of Maryland, Virginia, and the Carolinas. Waves of them as pioneers, on the Eastern Seaboard, rolled over the land, North and South, and always Westward, and spilling over on to the lands of Tennessee, Alabama, Texas, Kentucky (Territory South of the Ohio River), Indiana, Ohio, Illinois, and Missouri.

Some pioneer families pushed on into the Western Territories and settled there. Some did not stop until they reached the Pacific shores of California, Oregon, and Washington.

Mailing Address:

Corben E. Allen
8439 Terradell Street
Pico Rivera, California 90660

UNIVERSITY OF
SOUTHERN
CALIFORNIA

Mr. Corben Elko Allen
8439 Terradell St
Pico Rivera, CA 90660-5025

Standard Copy costs: $45.00
Deluxe Copy with golden edges costs: $60.00

A check or money order made out to Corben E. Allen.

OF THE EARLY SETTLERS OF FT. ORANGE (ALBANY, NY), by W.L. Stone. 1892.
Cloth, $45.00. Paper, $35.00. 233pp. .... Vendor G0259

3667 **AARON STARK FAM., SEVEN GEN. OF THE DESC. OF AARON STARK OF GROTON, CT.**, by C. Stark. 1927.
Cloth, $34.00. Paper, $24.00. 148pp. .... Vendor G0259

3668 **THE STARKEYS OF NEW ENGLAND & ALLIED FAMILIES**, by E.W. Leavitt. 1910.
Cloth, $34.00. Paper, $24.00. 149pp. .... Vendor G0259

3669 **A BRIEF GEN. HIST. OF ROBERT STARKWEATHER OF ROXBURY & IPSWICH, MASS., WHO WAS THE ORIGINAL AMER. ANC., & OF HIS DESC. IN VARIOUS LINES, 1640–1898**, by C.L. Starkweather. 1904.
Cloth, $66.00. Paper, $56.00. 356pp. .... Vendor G0259

3670 **GEN. & FAMILY MEMORIAL [OF STARLING, SULLIVANT & RE-LATED FAMS.]**, by Joseph Sullivant. 1874.
Cloth, $68.50. Paper, $58.50. 375pp. .... Vendor G0259

3671 **EARLY STARRS IN KENT & NEW ENGLAND**, by H.S. Ballou. 1944.
Cloth, $35.00. Paper, $25.00. 141pp. .... Vendor G0259

3672 **HIST. OF THE STARR FAM. OF NEW ENG., FROM COMFORT STARR OF ASHFORD, CO. KENT, ENG., WHO EMIGR. TO BOSTON (1635)**, by B. Starr. 1879.
Cloth, $99.00. Paper, $89.00. 587pp. .... Vendor G0259

3673 **GENEALOGICAL RECORD OF THE DESCENDANTS OF HENRY STAUFFER AND OTHER PIONEERS**, by A.J. Fretz. (1899) reprint 1993.
Cloth. $35.00. 371pp. .... Vendor G0150

3674 **GEN. REC. OF THE DESC. OF HENRY STAUFFER & OTHER STAUFFER PIONEERS**, by A. Fretz. 1899.
Cloth, $68.00. Paper, $58.00. 371pp. .... Vendor G0259

3675 **STAUFFER FAMILIES OF SWITZERLAND, GERMANY, AND AMERICA (INCLUDING STOUFFER AND STOVER)**, by Richard Warren Davis. 1992.
Cloth. $43.00. 201pp. .... Vendor G0150

3676 **GEN. & MEMOIRS OF CHARLES & NATHANIEL STEARNS, & THEIR DESC.**, by A.V. Wagenen. 1901.
Cloth, $93.00. Paper, $83.00. 531pp. .... Vendor G0259

3677 **GEN. & MEMOIRS OF ISAAC STEARNS & HIS DESC.**, by A.V. Wagenen. 1901.
Cloth, $107.50. Paper, $97.50. 746pp. .... Vendor G0259

3678 **GEN. OF THE STEARNS, LANES, HOLBROOK & WARREN FAM.**, by M.L. Brook. 1898.
Paper. $10.00. 59pp. .... Vendor G0259

3679 **MEM. OF THE STEARNS FAM. INCL. RECORDS OF MANY DESC.**, by W.E. Stearns. 1901.
Cloth, $33.50. Paper, $23.50. 173pp. .... Vendor G0259

3680 **GENEALOGY & HIST. OF SOME STEBBINS LINES TO 1953**, by J.A. Stebbins. 1957(?)
Cloth, $39.00. Paper, $29.00. 190pp. .... Vendor G0259

3681 **STEBBINS GENEALOGY**, by R.S. Greenlee. 2 vols. 1904.
Cloth, $186.00. Paper, $176.00. 1,386pp. .... Vendor G0259

3682 **ARCHIBALD STEELE & DESC.**, by N. Steele. 1900.
Cloth, $31.50. Paper, $21.50. 143pp. .... Vendor G0259

3683 **STEELE FAM. A GEN. HIST. OF JOHN & GEORGE STEELE (SET-TLERS OF HARTFORD, CONN., 1635–6), & THEIR DESC.; WITH AN APPENDIX RESPECTING OTHER FAM. OF THE NAME**, by D.S. Durrie. 1859.
Cloth, $33.00. Paper, $23.00. 159pp. .... Vendor G0259

3684 **A RECORD OF THE DESC. OF JOHN STEERE, WHO SETTLED IN PROVIDENCE, R.I. ABOUT 1660; WITH SOME ACCT. OF THE STEERES OF ENG.**, by J.P. Root. 1890.
Cloth, $48.00. Paper, $38.00. 224pp. .... Vendor G0259

3685 **STEGGALL FAMILY IN AMERICA: JOHN STEGGALL & SOME OF HIS DESCENDANTS, WITH BRIEF INFORMATION ON THE FAMI-LIES OF BALDRY & HASNER**, by Mary Ann [Menuey] Thies. 1993.
Cloth, $49.50. Paper, $39.50. 280pp. .... Vendor G0259

3686 **THE STEINS OF MUSCATINE [IA.]: A FAM. CHRONICLE**, by S.G. Stein. 1961.
Paper. $11.00. 53pp. .... Vendor G0259

3687 **STEINBRUGGE, VATHAVER AND VAN WORMER GENEALOGY: VOLUME I**, by John Steinbrugge. 1991. Indexed. Illus.
Computer disk. $10.00. 309pp. .... Vendor G0361

3688 **STEINBRUGGE, VATHAVER AND VAN WORMER GENEALOGY: VOLUME II**, by John Steinbrugge. 1995. Indexed.
Computer disk. $10.00. 67pp. .... Vendor G0361

3689 **GENEALOGY OF THE STEINER FAMILY IN GERMANY & AMERICA, ESPECIALLY THE DESCENDANTS OF JACOB STEINER**, by L.H. and B.C. Steiner. 1896.
Paper. $19.00. 99pp. .... Vendor G0259

3690 **A FAMILY RECORD: STEPHENS**, by Donald Lewis Osborn. 1973. Indexed.
Benjamin **Stephens** (1779–1855); Orange County, Virginia; Boone County, Kentucky; Cass County, Missouri. Intermarriages chart. Names indexed.
Paper. $7.00. 20pp. .... Vendor G0121

3691 **STEPHENS FAMILY WITH COLLATERAL BRANCHES (VOL. I OF THE AMERICAN GENEALOGICAL RECORD)**, by Edward S. Clark. 1892.
Cloth, $39.50. Paper, $29.50. 185pp. .... Vendor G0259

3692 **STEPHENSON KINSMEN. [STEPHENSON FAMILY OF COTTINGHAM, YORKSHIRE; CANADA; U.S.]**, by Wesley Petty. 1918.
Paper. $12.50. 67pp. .... Vendor G0259

3693 **THE STERLING GEN.**, by A.M. Sterling. 2 vols. 1909.
Cloth, $204.00. Paper, $194.00. 1,418pp. .... Vendor G0259

3694 **GEN. & BIOGR. SKETCH OF NAME & FAM. OF STETSON 1634–1847**, by J.S. Barry. 1847.
Cloth, $32.00. Paper, $22.00. 116pp. .... Vendor G0259

3695 **STETSON KINDRED OF AMERICA (BOOKLETS NOS. 3 & 4)**, compiled by G.W. and N.M. Stetson. 1912, 1914.
Cloth, $39.50. Paper, $29.50. 45+147pp. .... Vendor G0259

3696 **[Stevens]. A GEN. OF THE LIN. DESC. OF JOHN STEEVENS, WHO SETTLED IN GUILFORD, CONN. IN 1645**, by C.S. and C.W. Holmes. 1906.
Cloth, $36.00. Paper, $26.00. 162pp. .... Vendor G0259

3697 **ERASMUS STEVENS, BOSTON, MA., 1674–1690, & HIS DESC.**, by E.R. Stevens; rev. by W.P. Bacon. 1914.
Paper. $17.00. 116pp. .... Vendor G0259

3698 **GEN. OF THE STEVENS FAM. 1635–1891**, by F.S. Stevens. 1891.
Paper. $12.50. 63pp. .... Vendor G0259

3699 **STEVENS GEN.; BRANCHES OF THE FAM. DESC. FROM PURITAN ANC., 1650 TO PRESENT**, by E. Barney. 1907.
Cloth, $51.50. Paper, $41.50. 319pp. .... Vendor G0259

3700 **STEVENS GEN. SOME DESC. OF THE FITZ STEVENS FAM. IN ENG. & NEW ENG.**, by C.E. Stevens. 1904.
Paper. $17.00. 93pp. .... Vendor G0259

3701 **THOMAS STEVENSON OF LONDON, ENG., & HIS DESC.**, by J.R. Stevenson. 1902.
Cloth, $37.00. Paper, $27.00. 181pp. .... Vendor G0259

3702 **[Stewart]. COL. GEORGE STEUART & HIS WIFE MARGARET HARRIS: THEIR ANC. & DESC., WITH APPENDIXES OF REL. FAMS.**, by R. Stewart. 1907.
Cloth, $89.50. Paper, $79.50. 522pp. .... Vendor G0259

3703 **[Stewart]. GENEALOGICAL CLASSIFICATION BY FAMILY-GROUP CODING FOR DESCENT FROM COMMON ANCESTORS**, by Cameron R. Stewart. 2 vols. 1986. Indexed.
Vol. 1: Colonial American, Canadian, English, Scotch (**Badgerow, Sarles, Sharrard, McAlester–McMaster, Stewart**) and Norwegian: Bygland, Setesdal, and Voss (**Miltzow, Gjerde, Afdal**).
Vol. 2: 17 C. Beds-Eng./RI anc. **Wm Bentl(e)y's** descendants.
Cloth. $90.00/vol. 1,896pp. in 2 vols. plus additional 363pp.
of indexes in vol. 2. .... Vendor G0169

3704 **GEN. & BIOGR. OF THE DESC. OF WALTER STEWART OF SCOTLAND, & OF JOHN STEWART WHO CAME TO AMER. IN 1718 & SETTLED IN LONDONDERRY, N.H.**, by B.F. Severance. 1905.
Cloth, $44.00. Paper, $34.00. 226pp. .... Vendor G0259

3705 **STEWART FAMILY RECORDS**, by J.M. Seaver.
Paper. $12.50. 62pp. .... Vendor G0259

3706 **STEWART FAMILY RECORDS**, by J. Montgomery Seaver. Paper. $8.50. 65pp. .... Vendor G0011

3707 **THE JOHNSTON & BACON SCOTTISH CLAN HISTORIES: The Stewarts**, by John Stewart. (1954) reprint 1993. Illus. Paper. $8.95. 32pp. .... Vendor G0011

3708 **THE STEWARTS OF COITSVILLE: HIST. OF ROBERT & SARAH STEWART OF ADAMS CO., PA., & THEIR DESC.** 1899. Cloth, $37.50. Paper, $27.50. 198pp. .... Vendor G0259

3709 **GEN. OF THE STICHTER FAM., 1189–1902**, by J. and J.L. Stichter. 1902. Paper. $8.50. 42pp. .... Vendor G0259

3710 **STICKNEY FAM.; A GEN. OF THE DESC. OF WM. & ELIZABETH, 1637–1869**, by M.A. Stickney. 1869. Cloth, $93.00. Paper, $83.00. 534pp. .... Vendor G0259

3711 **CONTRIBUTIONS TOWARDS A GEN. OF THE (MASS.) FAM. OF STILES, DESC. FROM ROBERT, OF ROWLEY, MASS., 1659–1860**, by H.R. Stiles. 1863. Paper. $10.00. 48pp. .... Vendor G0259

3712 **HIST. OF THE KY.-MO. STILES, WITH A SKETCH OF N.J. & OTHER KINDRED**, by L.S. Pence. 1896. Paper. $9.50. 47pp. .... Vendor G0259

3713 **STILES FAM. IN AMER. GEN. OF THE CONN. FAM., ALSO THE CONN.-N.J. FAM., 1720–1894, & THE SOUTHERN (OR BERMUDA-GA.) FAM., 1635–1894, WITH CONTR. TO THE GEN. OF SOME N.Y. & PA. FAM.**, by H.R. Stiles. 1895. Cloth, $129.00. Paper, $119.00. 794pp. .... Vendor G0259

3714 **STILES FAM. IN AMER. GEN. OF THE MASS. FAM., & THE DOVER, N.H., FAM.**, by M.S. Guild. 1892. Cloth, $96.00. Paper, $86.00. 689pp. .... Vendor G0259

3715 **[Stillwell]. EARLY MEMOIRS OF THE STILWELL FAMILY, COMPRISING THE LIFE & TIMES OF NICHOLAS STILLWELL**, by Benjamin Marshall Stillwell. (1878) reprint 1995. Cloth. $50.00. 289pp. .... Vendor G0405

3716 **HISTORICAL & GENEALOGICAL RECORD OF ONE BRANCH OF THE STILLWELL FAMILY**, by DeWitt and Lamont Stilwell. (1914) reprint 1995. Indexed. Illus. Includes 1928 supplement. Cloth. $25.00. 106pp. .... Vendor G0405

3717 **HISTORY OF CAPTAIN JEREMIAH STILLWELL, ANNE STILLWELL BRITTON, ALICE STILLWELL HOLMES, MARY STILLWELL MOTT, DANIEL STILLWELL & JOHN STILLWELL**, by Dr. John E. Stillwell. (1931) reprint 1995. Indexed. Illus. Cloth. $55.00. 376pp. .... Vendor G0405

3718 **HISTORY OF CAPTAIN NICHOLAS STILLWELL, WILLIAM STILLWELL & CAPTAIN THOMAS STILLWELL**, by Dr. John E. Stillwell. (1930) reprint 1995. Indexed. Illus. Cloth. $55.00. 414pp. .... Vendor G0405

3719 **HISTORY OF CAPTAIN RICHARD STILLWELL**, by Dr. John E. Stillwell. (1930) reprint 1995. Indexed. Illus.
Cloth. $45.00. 285pp. .... Vendor G0405

3720 **HIST. OF CAPT. RICHARD STILLWELL, SON OF LT. NICHOLAS STILLWELL, & HIS DESC.**, by J. Stillwell. 1930.
Cloth, $56.00. Paper, $46.00. 285pp. .... Vendor G0259

3721 **HISTORY OF LT. NICHOLAS STILLWELL**, by Dr. John E. Stillwell. (1929) reprint 1995. Indexed. Illus.
Cloth. $35.00. 153pp. .... Vendor G0405

3722 **NOTES ON DESC. OF NICHOLAS STILLWELL; ANC. OF THE FAM. IN AMER.**, by W. Stillwell. 1883.
Paper. $12.50. 62pp. .... Vendor G0259

3723 **STILLWELL FAMILY GRANDCHILDREN**, by Roy B. Young. 1996. Illus.
The **Stillwell** family in America with emphasis on Joseph, Harold, and Walter Stillwell of Arkansas and Edward Bassett Stillwell of Oklahoma.
Bassett—Winter—Reeves—Keen.
Cloth. $38.95. 200pp. .... Vendor G0405

3724 **EARLY MEM. OF THE STILWELL FAM., COMPR. THE LIFE & TIMES OF NICHOLAS STILWELL, WITH ACCT. OF HIS BROTHERS JOHN & JASPER**, by B.M. Stilwell. 1878.
Cloth, $56.50. Paper, $46.50. 289pp. .... Vendor G0259

3725 **HIST. & GEN. RECORD OF ONE BRANCH OF THE STILWELL FAM.**, by D. Stilwell. 1914.
Paper. $17.00. 94pp. .... Vendor G0259

3726 **GEN. OF THE STIMPSON FAM. OF CHARLESTOWN, MASS., & AL-LIED LINES**, by C.C. Whittier. 1907.
Cloth, $41.00. Paper, $31.00. 206pp. .... Vendor G0259

3727 **STOCKING ANC.; DESC. OF GEO. STOCKING, FOUNDER OF THE AMER. FAM.**, by C.H.W. Stocking. 1903.
Cloth, $41.00. Paper, $31.00. 205pp. .... Vendor G0259

3728 **ANTHONY STODDARD & HIS DESC.**, by C. and E. Stoddard. 1865.
Paper. $18.50. 95pp. .... Vendor G0259

3729 **JOHN STODDARD OF NEW LONDON, CONN. & HIS DESC.**, by Stoddard and Shappee.
Paper. $19.00. 96pp. .... Vendor G0259

3730 **JOHN STODDARD OF WETHERSFIELD, CONN. & HIS DESC., 1642–1872. A GEN.**, by D.W. Patterson. 1873.
Paper. $19.00. 96pp. .... Vendor G0259

3731 **SOME OF THE ANC. OF RODMAN STODDARD, OF WOODBURY, CONN. & DETROIT, MI.**, by E. Deacon. 1893.
Paper. $16.50. 86pp. .... Vendor G0259

3732 **STODDARD FAMILY, BEING SOME ACCOUNT OF SOME OF THE DESCENDANTS OF JOHN STODDER OF HINGHAM, MA., COLONY**, by F.R. Stoddard, Jr. 1912.
Cloth, $33.00. Paper, $23.00. 148pp. .... Vendor G0259

3733 **STODDARD–SUDDUTH PAPERS**, by M.S. Stoddard. 1959/60(?)
Cloth, $55.00. Paper, $45.00. 281pp. .... Vendor G0259

3734 **THE SETTLER, JOHN STODDARD OF WETHERSFIELD, CONN. 1620–1664**, by Richard E. Stoddard; published by John H. Stoddard. 1985.
A novel based on fact about the life and family of an early settler in Connecticut.
Paper. $6.50. 107pp. .... Vendor G0319

3735 **THE STODDARD TRIBELOID—A QUARTERLY NEWSLETTER FOR THE STODDARD FAMILY ASSOCIATION**, by John H. Stoddard, Editor and Dan W. Stoddard, Archives. Annual. Illus.
Clearinghouse for surname **Stoddard, Stoddart, Stodder, Studdard**, etc.
Subscription. $10.00 per year. 8pp. per issue .... Vendor G0319

3736 **THE STODDARD TRIBELOID—NEWSLETTER OF THE STODDARD FAMILY ASSOCIATION—EVERYNAME INDEX—ISSUES 1–55, 1980–1995,** by John H. Stoddard. Feb. 1996. Indexed.
Clearinghouse for surname **Stoddard, Stoddart, Stodder, Studdard**.
80pp. estimated .... Vendor G0319

3737 **GEN. OF THE STOKES FAM., DESC. FROM THOMAS & MARY STOKES, WHO SETTLED IN BURLINGTON CO., N.J.**, by Haines and Stokes. 1903.
Cloth, $54.50. Paper, $44.50. 342pp. .... Vendor G0259

3738 **NOTES ON MY STOKES ANCESTRY**, by J. Stokes. 1937.
Paper. $12.00. 61pp. .... Vendor G0259

3739 **ANC. OF SARAH STONE, WIFE OF JAMES PATTEN OF ARUNDEL (KENNEBUNKPORT) ME.**, by W. Davis. 1930.
Cloth, $33.50. Paper, $23.50. 158pp. .... Vendor G0259

3740 **SOUVENIR OF A PART OF THE DESC. OF GREGORY & LYDIA COOPER STONE, 1634–1892**, by J.L. Stone. 1892.
Paper. $14.50. 78pp. .... Vendor G0259

3741 **STONE FAMILY HISTORY**, by J.M. Seaver.
Paper. $12.00. 59pp. .... Vendor G0259

3742 **STONE (GREGORY) ANCESTORS & DESC. OF DEA. GREGORY STONE OF CAMBRIDGE, MASS., 1320–1917**, by J.G. Bartlett. 1918.
Cloth, $117.00. Paper, $107.00. 913pp. .... Vendor G0259

3743 **STONE (SIMON), ANCESTORS & DESC. OF DEA. SIMON STONE OF WATERTOWN, MASS., 1320–1926**, by J.G. Bartlett. 1926.
Cloth, $115.00. Paper, $105.00. 811pp. .... Vendor G0259

3744 **THE FAM. OF JOHN STONE, ONE OF THE FIRST SETTLERS OF GUILFORD, CONN.**, by W.L. Stone. 1888.
Cloth, $39.00. Paper, $29.00. 192pp. .... Vendor G0259

3745 **BOOK II, OF THE FAM. OF JOHN STONE, ONE OF THE FIRST SET-TLERS OF GUILFORD, CONN.; ALSO NAMES OF ALL THE DESC. OF RUSSELL, BILLE, TIMOTHY & EBER STONE**, by T.L. Stone. 1898.
Cloth, $67.00. Paper, $57.00. 360pp. .... Vendor G0259

3746 **STONER BRETHREN: A HISTORY OF JOHN STONER (CIRCA 1705–1769) AND HIS DESCENDANTS**, by Richard R. Weber. 1993.
Cloth. $49.00. 638pp. .... Vendor G0150

3747 **ANNALS OF THE STORER FAM., TOGETHER WITH NOTES ON THE AYRAULT FAM.**, by M. Storer. 1927.
Paper. $18.50. 107pp. .... Vendor G0259

3748 **ENGLISH STORKES IN AMER.**, by C.A. Storke. 1935.
Cloth, $44.00. Paper, $34.00. 224pp. .... Vendor G0259

3749 **THE STORRS FAMILY: GENEALOGICAL & OTHER MEMORANDA**, by C. Storrs. 1886.
Cloth, $94.00. Paper, $84.00. xv+552pp. .... Vendor G0259

3750 **STOUFFER GENEALOGICAL MEMORANDA, A.D. 1630–1903.**, by K.S. Snively. 1903.
Paper. $19.00. 104pp. .... Vendor G0259

3751 **STOUT AND ALLIED FAMILIES**, by H.F. Stout. 1951.
Cloth, $139.50. Paper, $129.50. xxii+889pp. .... Vendor G0259

3752 **JAMES PINDALL STOUT AND BURTHENA S. KEMBLE—THEIR ANCESTORS AND DESCENDANTS**, by Kemble Stout. 1975. Indexed. Illus.
Paper. $20.00. 361pp. .... Vendor G0320B

3753 **STOVER GENEALOGY, BIOGRAPHY & HISTORY: A GENEALOGI-CAL RECORD OF THE DESC. OF WILLIAM STOVER, PIONEER, & OTHER STOVERS**, by B.E. Hughey. 1936.
Cloth, $49.50. Paper, $39.50. 249pp. .... Vendor G0259

3754 **STÖVER–STOEVER–STAVER–STIVER: THE ANCESTRY AND DE-SCENDANTS OF JOHANN CASPAR STOEVER**, by Vernon Stiver and Patricia Donaldson. 1992. Indexed. Illus.
Spanning over four centuries, this is the first comprehensive study of the ancestry and the descendants of two of America's early German Lutheran pastors. Six years in research and preparation, the book begins with the **Stover** progenitor in Germany and follows the lives of these two German Lutheran pastors, father and son, who came to America in 1728. It has been the recipient of state and national recognition awards.
Cloth. $50.00. 660pp. .... Vendor G0020

3755 **GENEALOGY OF THE STOWE FAMILY OF NEW ENGLAND, FROM THE MSS. OF A.G. STANLEY.** n.d.
Paper. $9.00. 44pp. typescript .... Vendor G0259

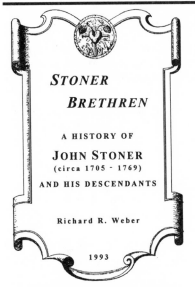

STONER BRETHREN

A HISTORY OF

JOHN STONER
(circa 1705 - 1769)

AND HIS DESCENDANTS

Richard R. Weber

1993

Verified by extensive primary evidence
Over 100 records *before* the Revolution
More than 6000 individuals, to 1993

JOHN STONER and his children, Catherine Arnold, Mary Ann Price, John (c.1730-1774), Jacob (1732-1804), David (c.1733-1820), Agnes Arnold, and Abraham (c.1744-1824), have left an astonishing trail of documents in Colonial Pennsylvania and Maryland.

With Many Allied Families, including Albaugh, Arnold, Baer/Bear, Baker, Bashor, Beery, Biggs, Bowman, Brower, Brown, Burger, Cover, Crumpacker, Danner, Diehl, Engel, Englar, Fisher, Flora/Flory, Funk, Garber, Gish, Good, Graybill, Hess, Hoover, Hyre, Johnson, Klein, Landis, Lesh, Lightner, Long, Miller, Myers, Neff, Newcomer, Noffsinger, Oller, Pfoutz, Plain, Repp, Rhoads/Rhodes, Rinehart, Roop, Royer, Sayler, Smith, Snively, Stouffer, Stover, Thomas, Ulrey, Wampler, and Wine.

BIBLIOGRAPHY   ILLUSTRATED
Premium hard cloth cover   7" x 10"
638 acid-free pages   FULLY INDEXED

Order **STONER BRETHREN** from: Richard R. Weber, 10715 Moosberger Ct., Columbia, MD 21044
Price **$45.50** (including postage)   Maryland residents please add **$2.13** sales tax

3756 **A RECORD OF THE DESC. OF SAM'L STOWELL OF HINGHAM, MASS.**, by W.H.H. Stowell. 1922.
Cloth, $149.00. Paper, $139.00. 980pp. . . . . Vendor G0259

3757 **GEN. OF THE STRANAHAN, JOSSELYN, FITCH & DOW FAM. IN N. AMER.**, by H.R. Stiles. 1868.
Paper. $19.00. 126pp. . . . . Vendor G0259

3758 **BIOGR. & HIST. SKETCHES OF THE STRANGES OF AMER. & ACROSS THE SEAS**, by A.T. Strange. 1911.
Cloth, $32.50. Paper, $22.50. 137pp. Vendor G0259

3759 **EXTRANEUS, BOOK V, STRANGE OF EASTERN AMERICA**, by John R. Mayer. rev. 2nd ed. 1995. Indexed. Illus.
Cloth, $69.50. Paper, $59.50. xviii+380pp. . . . . Vendor G0259

3760 **EXTRANEUS, BOOK X, THE ALLOWAY STRANGE**, by John R. Mayer. 2nd ed. 1994. Indexed. Illus.
Cloth, $52.00. Paper, $42.00. xvii+210pp. . . . . Vendor G0259

3761 **EXTRANEUS, BOOK XI, STRANGE OF BLISLAND**, by John R. Mayer. rev. 2nd ed. 1995. Indexed. Illus.
Paper. $84.00. xl+708pp. . . . . Vendor G0124

3762 **EXTRANEUS, BOOK XII, STRANGE OF THE CAROLINAS**, by John R. Mayer. 2nd ed. 1994. Indexed. Illus.
Paper. $58.00. xxvi+548pp. .... Vendor G0124

3763 **STRASSBURGER FAMILY & ALLIED FAMILIES OF PENNA., BEING THE ANCESTRY OF JACOB ANDREW STRASSBURGER, ESQUIRE, OF MONTGOMERY CO. PA**, by R.B. Strassburger. 1922.
Cloth, $86.50. Paper, $76.50. 520pp. .... Vendor G0259

3764 **A BOOK OF STRATTONS; BEING A COLL. OF STRATTON RECORDS FROM ENG. & SCOT., & A GEN. HIST. OF THE EARLY COL. STRATTONS IN AMER., WITH FIVE GEN. OF THEIR DESC.**, by H.R. Stratton. 2 vols. 1908–18.
Cloth, $139.00. Paper, $129.00. 910pp. .... Vendor G0259

3765 **FITHIAN STRATTON 1738–1817; PATRIOT AND PREACHER**, by Margaret E. Sheaffer and Carol M. Sheaffer, M.D. 1985. Illus.
Biographical Sketch; Fithian **Stratton**'s Bible Records; **Glenn** Family Genealogy.
Paper. $6.00. 20pp. .... Vendor G0229

3766 **[Straw]. SOME GENEALOGIES AND FAMILY RECORDS**, by A.Y. Straw. 1931.
Cloth, $56.00. Paper, $46.00. 292pp. .... Vendor G0259

3767 **STREET GENEALOGY**, by H.A. and M.A. Street. 1895.
Cloth, $79.50. Paper, $69.50. 551pp. .... Vendor G0259

3768 **A GEN. HIST. OF THE DESC. OF STEPHEN & URSULA STREETER OF GLOUCESTER, MASS., 1642, WITH AN ACCT. OF THE STREETERS OF GOUDHERST, ENG.**, by M. Streeter. 1896.
Cloth, $52.00. Paper, $42.00. 360pp. .... Vendor G0259

3769 **ALLIED FAMILIES OF DELAWARE: STRETCHER, FENWICK, DAVIS, DRAPER, KIPSHAVEN, STIDHAM**, by E.E. Sellers. 1901.
Cloth, $38.00. Paper, $28.00. 171pp. .... Vendor G0259

3770 **EARLY HISTORY OF STRICKLANDS OF SIZERGH, WITH SOME ACCT. OF THE ALLIED FAMILIES D'EYNCOURT, FLEMING, GREYSTOKE & DUNBAR**, by S.H.L. Washington. 1942.
Paper. $19.00. 100pp. .... Vendor G0259

3771 **THE STRICKLANDS OF SIZERGH CASTLE: RECORDS OF 25 GENERATIONS OF A WESTMORELAND [ENGLAND] FAMILY**, by Daniel Scott. 1908 (England).
Cloth, $56.50. Paper, $46.50. 293pp. .... Vendor G0259

3772 **FORERUNNERS. A HIST. OR GEN. OF THE STRICKLER FAM.**, by H.M. Strickler. 1925.
Cloth, $78.50. Paper, $68.50. 440pp. .... Vendor G0259

3773 **STROBRIDGE GEN. STROBRIDGE MORRISON OR MORISON STRAWBRIDGE**, by M.S.P. Guild. 1891.
Cloth, $57.50. Paper, $47.50. 318pp. .... Vendor G0259

3774 **STRONG MEN AND STRONG WOMEN: BEGINNING IN CHARD, ENGLAND**, by Jeanne Waters Strong. 1988. Indexed. Illus. Cloth. $23.00. 81pp. .... Vendor G0086

3775 **THE HIST. OF THE DESC. OF ELDER JOHN STRONG OF NORTHAMPTON, MASS.**, by B.W. Dwight. 2 vols. 1871. Cloth, $209.50. Paper, $199.50. 1,649pp. .... Vendor G0259

3776 **DESCENDANTS OF WILLIAM STROTHER OF VIRGINIA**, by Carol A. Hauk. 1995. Indexed. Paper. $35.00. 131pp. .... Vendor G0340

3777 **STROUD FAM. HIST., DESC. OF CAPT. RICHARD STROUD OF NEW LONDON, CONN.**, by H.D. Lowell. 1934. Paper. $8.50. 40pp. .... Vendor G0259

3778 **THE STRODE & STROUD FAMILIES IN ENGLAND & AMERICA**, by James S. Elston. 4 vols. 1949–1970. Cloth, $76.00. Paper, $66.00. 463pp. .... Vendor G0259

3779 **THE STROUDS. A COLONIAL FAM. OF ENG. DESC.**, by A.B. Stroud. 1918. Cloth, $49.50. Paper, $39.50. 263pp. .... Vendor G0259

3780 **GEN. HIST. OF THE DUNCAN STUART FAM. IN AMER.**, by J.A. Stuart. 1894. Cloth, $39.50. Paper, $29.50. 183pp. .... Vendor G0259

3781 **DESCENDANTS OF JOHN STUBBS OF CAPPAHOSIC, GLOUCESTER CO., VA., 1652**, by W.C. Stubbs. 1902. Paper. $19.50. 116pp. .... Vendor G0259

3782 **THE DESCENDANTS OF RICHARD STUBBS, HULL, MASS. 1642**, by Marjorie Anne Stubbs Heaney. 1984. Indexed. Illus. Cloth. Smyth sewn. $60.00. xxii+269pp. .... Vendor G0437

3783 **THE ANCESTORS AND DESCENDANTS OF ADAM STUHR**, by Virginia Ann Altaffer Stuhr. 1992. Indexed. Illus.

Immigrants from the Probstei in Holstein, they settled in Iowa 1851–65. Surnames: **Finck, Gottsch, Klindt, Ladehoff, Lage, Martens, McIntosh, Muhs, Paustian, Schick, Schneekloth, Sinjen, Stoltenberg, Stuhr, Untiedt,** and **Wiese.**
Cloth. $40.00. 600pp. .... Vendor G0027

3784 **GENEALOGY OF THE STUKEY, REAM, GROVE, CLEM & DENNISTON FAMILIES,** by E.L. Denniston. 1939.
Cloth, $99.50. Paper, $89.50. 591pp. .... Vendor G0259

3785 **THE STULTZ FAMILY OF BROCKS GAP AREA, ROCKINGHAM COUNTY, VA,** by Lewis H. Yankey. 1992. Indexed.
Paper. $13.00. 85pp. .... Vendor G0365

3786 **A GENEALOGICAL HISTORY OF THE STURGEONS OF N. AMER.,** by C.T. McCoy. 1926.
Cloth, $48.00. Paper, $38.00. 239pp. .... Vendor G0259

3787 **SOLOMON STURGES & DESC.,** by E. Buckingham. 1907.
Paper. $16.50. 84pp. .... Vendor G0259

3788 **STURGES FAM. OF MAINE,** by A.W. Sturges. 1900.
Paper. $8.00. 41pp. .... Vendor G0259

3789 **EDW. STURGIS OF YARMOUTH, MASS., 1613–1695, & HIS DESC.,** edited by R.F. Sturgis. 1914.
Paper. $18.00. 88pp. .... Vendor G0259

3790 **THE PATRIARCH OF THE VALLEY—ISAAC W. SULLIVAN,** by Emma A. Street Hively. 1977. Indexed. Illus.
Paper. $6.50. 115pp. .... Vendor G0184

3791 **MATERIALS FOR A HIST. OF THE FAM. OF JOHN SULLIVAN OF BERWICK, NEW ENG., & OF THE O'SULLIVANS OF ARDEA, IRELAND,** by T.C. Amory. 1893.
Cloth, $36.00. Paper, $26.00. 151pp. .... Vendor G0259

3792 **SAMUEL SULSER, PIONEER OF GADSDEN, ALABAMA AND ALLIED FAMILIES,** by Mildred S. Wright. 1986. Indexed. Illus.
Gartman, McCauley, Morgan, Pledger, Torbett, Totty, White.
Cloth. $35.00. 108pp. .... Vendor G0145

3793 **MEMOIR OF INCREASE SUMNER, GOV. OF MASS., BY W.H. SUMNER, WITH A GEN. OF THE SUMNER FAM.,** by W.B. Trask. 1854.
Paper. $14.00. 70pp. .... Vendor G0259

3794 **REC. OF THE DESC. OF WM. SUMNER OF DORCHESTER, MASS., 1636,** by W.S. Appleton. 1879.
Cloth, $41.50. Paper, $31.50. 209pp. .... Vendor G0259

3795 **REC. OF DESC. OF WM. SUMNER OF DORCHESTER, MASS. ADD. NOTES & CORRECTIONS TO ORIG. 1879 GEN.,** by W.S. Appleton. 1881–1902.
Paper. $8.00. 40pp. .... Vendor G0259

3796 **GEN. OF THE SURDAM FAM.,** by C.E. Surdam. 1909.
Cloth, $50.00. Paper, $40.00. 266pp. .... Vendor G0259

3797 **HISTORY OF THE SURGES–McKAY FAMILIES; ALSO ALLIED FAMS. PFLUEGER, REIBEL, BOUVILLE, BEAUNE,** by J.R. Crossman. 1991. Paper. $13.50. 60pp. .... Vendor G0259

3798 **A GEN. OF THE SUTCLIFFE–SUTLIFFE FAM. IN AMER. FROM BE-FORE 1661 TO 1903. THE DESC. OF NATHANIEL SUTCLIFFE, WITH A BRIEF ACCOUNT OF THEIR ENG. ANC. BACK TO 1500,** by B.H. Sutcliffe.
Cloth, $46.50. Paper, $36.50. 242pp. .... Vendor G0259

3799 **THE SUTCLIFFES OF HUMMELSTOWN, PENNSYLVANIA,** by Janet Snyder Welsh. 1993. Indexed. Illus.
The **Sutcliffe** history begins in 1274 in Yorkshire, England and traces Sutcliffes who settled in Pennsylvania. Allied families are **Hocker, Hoerner, Hummel,** and **McCall.**
Cloth. $25.00. 296pp. .... Vendor G0251

3800 **SUTHERLAND RECORDS,** by D. Merritt. 1918.
Paper. $15.00. 76pp. .... Vendor G0259

3801 **A HISTORY OF THE AMERICAN & PURITANICAL FAMILY OF SUTLIFF OR SUTLIFFE, SPELLED SUTCLIFFE IN ENGLAND, AND A GENEALOGY OF ALL THE DESCENDANTS THROUGH NATHANIEL SUTLIFF, JR,** by S.M. Sutliff, Jr. 1909.
Cloth, $41.00. Paper, $31.00. 199pp. .... Vendor G0259

3802 **SUTPHEN FAM. GEN. & BIOGR. NOTES,** by L.L. DeBoar. 1926.
Cloth, $37.50. Paper, $27.50. 132pp. .... Vendor G0259

3803 **SUTTON, SUTTON AND MORE SUTTONS,** by Doris Ellen Witter Bland. 1992. Indexed. Illus.
A study of the ancestors and descendants of Jonathan **Sutton** who came to Wayne County, Illinois in 1853. Mayflower and Royal lineage.
Cloth. $59.50. 699pp. .... Vendor G0387

3804 **THE DESCENDANTS OF JOHN WESLEY SUTTON 1837–1900,** by Gloria Shipp Frazier. 1995. Indexed.
From Smith County Tennessee to Greene, Montgomery, and Macoupin counties Illinois. Allied lines: **Adcock, Allen, Angelo, Bandy, Burcham, Cherry, Clawson, Fox, Kasten, Martin, Masters, Neighbors, Niles, Park, Rudanovich, Shipp, Thomas, Thompson, Waite, Weller.** Ancestors, maps, photos, documents, biographical. 8¹/₂ x 11 natural archival paper.
Cloth. $35.00. 260pp. .... Vendor G0360

3805 **SWAIN & ALLIED FAM.,** by W.C. Swain. 1896.
Cloth, $30.50. Paper, $20.50. 137pp. .... Vendor G0259

3806 **SWAIN FAMILY, JEREMIAH SWAIN OF READING, MASS., & DESC.,** by W.C. Swain. 1896.
Paper. $10.00. 52pp. .... Vendor G0259

3807 **GENEALOGY OF THE SWALLOW FAM., 1666–1910,** by Baker, North & Ellis. 1910.
Cloth, $44.50. Paper, $34.50. 217pp. .... Vendor G0259

3808 **ANC. OF ALDEN SMITH SWAN & HIS WIFE MARY ALTHEA FARWELL,** by J.C. Frost. 1923.
Cloth, $49.50. Paper, $39.50. 264pp. .... Vendor G0259

3809 **GEN. OF THE SWASEY FAM.**, by B.F. Swasey. 1910.
Cloth, $76.50. Paper, $66.50. 525pp. .... Vendor G0259

3810 **SETH SWEETSER & DESC.**, by P.S. Sweetser. 1938.
Cloth, $75.00. Paper, $65.00. 427pp. .... Vendor G0259

3811 **FAM. REGISTER OF GERRET VAN SWERINGEN & DESC.**, by H.H. Swearingen. 2nd ed. 1894.
Paper. $17.00. 85pp. .... Vendor G0259

3812 **SWETT GENEALOGY, DESC. OF JOHN SWETT OF NEWBURY, MASS.**, by E.S. Stackpole.
Paper. $18.50. 123pp. .... Vendor G0259

3813 **SWIFT FAMILY: HIST. NOTES,** compiled by K.W. Swift. 1955.
Cloth, $38.00. Paper, $28.00. 170pp. .... Vendor G0259

3814 **WILLIAM SWIFT OF SANDWICH & SOME OF HIS DESCENDANTS, 1637–1899,** by G.H. Swift. 1900.
Cloth, $39.00. Paper, $29.00. 165+15pp. .... Vendor G0259

3815 **EVENTS IN THE LIFE & HIST. OF THE SWING FAM.**, by G.S. Swing. 1889.
Cloth, $71.00. Paper, $61.00. 398pp. .... Vendor G0259

3816 **SWINT,** by Mildred S. Ezell. 1984. Indexed. Illus.
Includes: **Swint, Cartledge, Harris, Duggan, Hood, Littlefield, Bryant, Trawick.**
Paper. $40.00. 513pp. .... Vendor G0323

3817 **SYMMES MEMORIAL,** by J.A. Vinton. 1873.
Cloth, $37.50. Paper, $27.50. 184pp. .... Vendor G0259

3818 **TABER GEN.; DESC. OF THOMAS, SON OF PHILLIP TABER,** by G.L. Randall. 1924.
Cloth, $91.50. Paper, $81.50. 518pp. .... Vendor G0259

3819 **TAFT FAMILY GATHERING: PROCEEDINGS AT THE MEETING OF THE TAFT FAM. AT UXBRIDGE, MA., 1874.** 1874.
Paper. $19.00. 103pp. .... Vendor G0259

3820 **GEN. OF TAGGART FAM. OF PENN. (IN NESBIT GEN.),** by B.T. Hartman. 1929.
Paper. $16.00. 79pp. .... Vendor G0259

3821 **[Tainter]. HIST. & GEN. OF THE DESC. OF JOSPEH TAYNTER, WHO SAILED FROM ENGLAND, APR. 1638, & SETTLED IN WATERTOWN, MA.,** by D.W. Tainter. 1859.
Paper. $18.00. 94pp. .... Vendor G0259

3822 **THE ENG. ANC. OF PETER TALBOT OF DORCHESTER, MASS.**, by J.G. Bartlett. 1917.
Paper. $19.50. 116pp. .... Vendor G0259

3823 **DESCENDANTS OF RICHARD AND ELIZABETH (EWEN) TALBOTT OF POPLAR KNOWLE, WEST RIVER, ANNE ARUNDEL COUNTY, MARYLAND,** by Ida Morrison Shirk. (1927) reprint 1995. Indexed. Illus. Paper. $36.50. 569pp. .... Vendor G0011

3824 **TALCOTT PEDIGREE IN ENG. & AMER. FROM 1558–1876,** by S.V. Talcott. 1876. Cloth, $59.50. Paper, $49.50. 316pp. .... Vendor G0259

3825 **DESCENDANTS OF ROBERT TALIAFERRO OF VIRGINIA,** by Carol A. Hauk. 1995. Indexed. Paper. $45.00. 300pp. .... Vendor G0340

3826 **TALIAFERRO–TOLIVER FAMILY RECORDS,** by N.W. Sherman. 1960. Cloth, $43.50. Paper, $33.50. 242pp. .... Vendor G0259

3827 **A HIST. OF THE TALLEY FAM. ON THE DELAWARE & THEIR DESC. FROM 1686,** by G. A. Talley. 1899. Cloth, $48.00. Paper, $38.00. 252pp. .... Vendor G0259

3828 **THE HON. PELEG TALLMAN, 1764–1841. HIS ANC. & DESC.,** by W.M. Emery. 1935. Cloth, $49.00. Paper, $39.00. 260pp. .... Vendor G0259

3829 **TALMADGE, TALLMADGE & TALMAGE GEN.; THE DESC. OF THOMAS TALMADGE OF LYNN, MA., WITH AN APPENDIX INCL. OTHER FAM.,** by A. Talmadge. 1909. Cloth, $70.00. Paper, $60.00. 385pp. .... Vendor G0259

3830 **THE TANGNEY & DAY FAMILIES OF ADAMS COUNTY, WISCONSIN,** by Linda Berg Stafford. 1993. Indexed. Illus.
Winner of the 1994 Wisconsin Genealogy/Family History Book Award and 1994 Writing Awards Competition by Dallas Genealogical Society. Describes 575 families including descendants of Patrick **Tangney** and his uncle Thomas Tangney; ancestors and descendants of Rev. John **Day** [progenitor Daniel Day (c. 1700–1760) of Morris County, NJ]; and allied families from Valentin **Alt/ Ault,** Hugh **Connor,** Job **Loree,** and William **Richardson.**
Cloth. $50.00. 692pp. .... Vendor G0032

3831 **GEN. OF TANKERSLEY FAM. IN U.S.,** by C.W. Tankersley. 1895. Paper. $7.00. 31pp. .... Vendor G0259

3832 **GEN. OF THE DESC. OF THOMAS TANNER, SR., OF CORNWALL, CONN., WITH BRIEF NOTES OF SEVERAL ALLIED FAM.,** by Rev. E. Tanner. 1893. Paper. $19.00. 129pp. .... Vendor G0259

3833 **WM. TANNER OF NORTH KINGSTOWN, R.I., & HIS DESC.**, by Rev. G.C. Tanner.
$32.00. 216pp. .... Vendor G0259

3834 **WILLIAM TANNER SR. OF SO. KINGSTOWN, R.I. & HIS DESC.**, by G.C. Tanner. 1910.
Cloth, $89.50. Paper, $79.50. 516pp. .... Vendor G0259

3835 **GEN. OF THE TAPLEY FAM.**, by H. Tapley. 1900.
Cloth, $51.00. Paper, $41.00. 275pp. .... Vendor G0259

3836 **TAPPAN–TOPPAN GEN. ANC. & DESC. OF ABRAHAM TOPPAN OF NEWBURY, MA., 1606–1672**, by D. Tappan. 1915.
Cloth, $35.00. Paper, $25.00. 169pp. .... Vendor G0259

3837 **THE FAM. RECORDS OF JAMES & NANCY DUNHAM TAPPAN, OF THE 4TH GEN., FORMERLY OF WOODBRIDGE, MIDDLESEX CO., N.J.**, by P.B. Good. 1884.
Cloth, $33.00. Paper, $23.00. 136pp. .... Vendor G0259

3838 **TARLETON FAMILY**, by C.W. Tarleton. 1900.
Cloth, $46.50. Paper, $36.50. 244pp. .... Vendor G0259

3839 **A FRIENDLY HERITAGE ALONG THE DELAWARE: THE TAYLORS OF WASHINGTON CROSSING AND SOME ALLIED FAMILIES IN BUCKS COUNTY**, by Arthur E. Bye. 1959.
Cloth, $45.00. Paper, $35.00. 258pp. .... Vendor G0259

3840 **FAMILY HIST. OF ANTHONY TAYLOR OF HAMPTON, N.H., & SOME DESC., 1635–1935**, by H.M. Taylor. 1935.
Cloth, $89.50. Paper, $79.50. 530pp. .... Vendor G0259

3841 **ANTHONY TAYLOR OF HAMPTON, N.H.: ADDITIONS**, by H.M. Taylor. 1945.
Cloth, $33.50. Paper, $23.50. 134pp. .... Vendor G0259

3842 **DESCENDANTS OF JAMES TAYLOR OF VIRGINIA (ANCESTOR OF PRESIDENTS TAYLOR AND MADISON)**, by Carol A. Hauk. 1995. Indexed.
Paper. $45.00. 386pp. .... Vendor G0340

3843 **HIST. OF JOHN TAYLOR OF HADLEY, MASS., & THE GEN. OF HIS DESC.**, by Rev. E. Taylor. 1903.
Paper. $19.50. 111pp. .... Vendor G0259

3844 **DESC. OF JOHN TAYLOR OF HADLEY ; SUPPL.**, by F.L. Taylor. 1922.
Paper. $8.00. 40pp. .... Vendor G0259

3845 **DESC. OF ROBT. TAYLOR OF PA**, by A. Justice. 1925.
Cloth, $32.00. Paper, $22.00. 113pp. .... Vendor G0259

3846 **TAYLORS AND TATES OF THE SOUTH**, by Ann K. Blomquist. 1993. Indexed. Illus.
Cloth. $65.00. 986pp. .... Vendor G0374

3847 **TAYLOR FAMILY RECORDS**, by J. Montgomery Seaver.
Paper. $16.00. 80pp. .... Vendor G0259

3848 **TAYLOR GENEALOGY**, by J. Montgomery Seaver. Illus.
Paper. $8.50. 79pp. .... Vendor G0011

3849 **THE FAMILY OF JOHN HENRY TAYLOR, JR. FEATURING FAMILY
LETTERS WRITTEN DURING AND AFTER THE CIVIL WAR**, by Paula
Perkins Mortensen and Edwin Hjalmar Mortensen. 1995. Illus.
Cloth. $29.95. 136pp. .... Vendor G0258

3850 **TEALL GEN. RECORDS IN ENG. & AMER.**, by E. Dunn. 1926.
Paper. $12.50. 59pp. .... Vendor G0259

3851 **TELLMAN FAMILY HIST.**, by Jean Tellman Ketterman. 1986.
Paper. $17.00. 88pp. .... Vendor G0259

3852 **SOME TEMPLE PEDIGREES: GEN. OF THE KNOWN DESC. OF
ABRAHAM TEMPLE, WHO SETTLED IN SALEM, MA., IN 1636 [&
SOME CONNECTED FAMS.]**, by L. Temple. 1900.
Cloth, $57.50. Paper, $47.50. 316pp. .... Vendor G0259

3853 **SOME ACCT. OF THE TEMPLE FAM.**, by Temple Prime. 1887.
Paper. $18.00. 100pp. .... Vendor G0259

3854 **SOME ACCT. OF THE TEMPLE FAM.**, by Temple Prime. 2nd ed. 1894.
Paper. $19.50. 111pp. .... Vendor G0259

3855 **SOME ACCT. OF THE TEMPLE FAM.**, by Temple Prime. 3rd ed. 1896.
Cloth, $32.00. Paper, $22.00. 146pp. .... Vendor G0259

3856 **SOME ACCT. OF THE TEMPLE FAM.**, by Temple Prime. 4th ed. 1899.
Paper. $16.00. 77pp. .... Vendor G0259

3857 **TEMPLETON & ALLIED FAM. A GEN. HIST. & FAM. RECORD**, by
Y.T. Clague. 1936.
Cloth, $35.50. Paper, $25.50. 169pp. .... Vendor G0259

3858 **THE TEMPLINS OF INDIANA**, by Ronald R. Templin. 1985. Indexed. Illus.
Cloth. $35.00. 409pp. .... Vendor G0096

3859 **THE TEMPLINS OF OHIO**, by Ronald R. Templin. 1995. Indexed. Illus.
Cloth .... Vendor G0096

3860 **GEN. OF THE TENNANT FAM.: ANC. & DESC. THROUGH MANY
GENERATIONS**, by A.M. Tennant et al. 1915.
Cloth, $54.00. Paper, $44.00. 356pp. .... Vendor G0259

3861 **GEN. OF THE TENNEY FAM. & THE KENT FAM.**, by H.A. Tenney.
1875.
Paper. $15.00. 76pp. .... Vendor G0259

3862 **TENNEY FAMILY; DESC. OF THOMAS TENNEY OF ROWLEY, MASS.,
1638–1904**, by M.J. Tenney. 1904.
Cloth, $109.50. Paper, $99.50. 691pp. .... Vendor G0259

3863 **RICHMOND, WILLIAM & TIMOTHY TERRELL, COL. VIRGINIANS**,
by C.J.T. Barnhill. 1934.
Cloth, $64.00. Paper, $54.00. 339pp. .... Vendor G0259

3864 **NOTES OF TERRY FAM. IN THE U.S. MAINLY DESC. FROM SAMUEL OF SPRINGFIELD, MASS., BUT INCL. SOME DESC. FROM STEPHEN OF WINDSOR, CONN., THOMAS OF FREETOWN, MASS., ETC.**, by S. Terry. 1887.
Cloth, $54.50. Paper, $44.50. 351pp. .... Vendor G0259

3865 **TERRY TRACINGS, VOLUME 1**, by Rose Caudle Terry. 1994. Indexed. Illus.
Queries published free.
Paper. $10.45. 37pp. .... Vendor G0061

3866 **TERRY TRACINGS, VOLUME 2**, by Rose Caudle Terry. 1995. Indexed. Illus.
Queries published free. Future volumes expected or may already be completed.
Paper. $10.45. 32pp. .... Vendor G0061

3867 **AN OLD FAM.; AMER. DESC. OF PETER THACHER OF SALISBURY, MASS.** 1882.
Paper. $9.50. 48pp. .... Vendor G0259

3868 **GENEALOGY OF EPHRAIM & SARAH THAYER WITH THEIR 14 CHILDREN, FROM THE TIME OF THEIR MARRIAGE TO 1835**, by E. Thayer. 1835.
Paper. $18.00. 97pp. .... Vendor G0259

3869 **GENEALOGICAL NOTES, CONTAINING THE PEDIGREE OF THE THOMAS FAMILY OF MD., & SOME CONNECTED FAMILIES SNOWDEN, BUCKLEY, LAWRENCE, CHEW, et al**, by L.B. Thomas. 1877.
Cloth, $41.00. Paper, $31.00. 197pp. .... Vendor G0259

3870 **GEN. RECORDS & SKETCHES OF THE DESC. OF WM. THOMAS OF HARDWICK, MASS.**, by A.R. Thomas. 1891.
Cloth, $45.00. Paper, $35.00. 232pp. .... Vendor G0259

3871 **THE THOMAS BOOK, GIVING THE GEN. OF SIR RHYSAP THOMAS, K.G., THE THOMAS FAM. DESC. FROM HIM, & SOME ALLIED FAM.**, by L.B. Thomas. 1896.
Cloth, $107.00. Paper, $97.00. 648pp. .... Vendor G0259

3872 **THE THOMAS BRAND**, by Inez Taylor. 1994. Indexed. Illus.
Written by the eldest granddaughter of **Wm. Henry Thomas**, cowboy, rancher in Texas and Indian Territory, Oklahoma. It begins in Georgia with **Franklin Robert Thomas**, father of Wm. Henry, traces the family into Texas in the early '80s. It covers his ten children and their families to the present time with first-hand human-interest stories.
Cloth. $10.00. 197pp. .... Vendor G0350

3873 **THOMAS FAM. OF TALBOT CO., MD.**, by R.P. Spencer. 1914.
Paper. $8.00. 40pp. .... Vendor G0259

3874 **DESCENDANTS OF JOHN THOMPSON—1994**, by James W. Thompson. 1994. Indexed. Illus.
Scotch-Irish, English, and other families of early S.E. Pennsylvania and other areas. 1917 *Thompson Genealogy* by McAllister reprinted with 201 supplemen-

tal pages carrying some descendants to 1994. Related families: **Adams, Allen, Banks, Bell, Boal, Brown, Brownlee, Cox, Crothers, Crowther, Curran, Dibert, Dimm, Gilfillen, Greenlee, Jamison, Johnson, Keim, Marr, McAllister, Morse, Patterson, Rodgers, Schirm, Sterrett, Stuart, Wilson, Wylie, Zell.** Over 1,500 surnames.
Paper. $40.00. 540pp. .... Vendor G0159

3875 **GENEALOGY OF GORDON THOMPSON & JANE CLEMENS THOMP-SON**, by D.G. Thompson. 1940.
Paper. $16.00. 82pp. .... Vendor G0259

3876 **HIST. OF THE THOMPSON FAM. OF ENG. & N.Y.**, by G. Thompson. 1937.
Paper. $17.50. 87pp. .... Vendor G0259

3877 **JOHN THOMPSON OF CAPE GIRARDEAU, MISSOURI, AND CHRISTIAN COUNTY, KENTUCKY**, by Betty Rolwing Darnell. 1985. Indexed.
Paper. $6.00. 40pp. .... Vendor G0261

3878 **MEM. OF JAS. THOMPSON OF CHARLESTOWN, MASS., 1630–1643, & WOBURN, MASS., 1642–1682, & HIS DESC.**, by Rev. L. Thompson. 1887.
Cloth, $41.00. Paper, $31.00. 246pp. .... Vendor G0259

3879 **OUR THOMPSON FAM. IN MAINE, N.H., & THE WEST**, by C.N. Sinnett. 1907.
Cloth, $48.00. Paper, $38.00. 293pp. .... Vendor G0259

3880 **R.E.W. THOMPSON (1856–1937). NORTH CAROLINA TO ALABAMA**, by Shirley B. Adair. 1995. Indexed. Illus.
Sellers, Lawson, Carroll, Clark, Adair (related lines).
Paper. $16.50. 142pp. .... Vendor G0382

3881 **SAMUEL THOMPSON OF McMINN COUNTY, TENNESSEE AND SOME OF HIS DESCENDANTS**, by Mary Ann Morris Thompson. 1993. Indexed. Illus.
Including the related families of **Cobb, Cooke, Derrick, Lattimore**, and **Rogers.**
Cloth. $28.00. 512pp. .... Vendor G0017

3882 **THE SOLOMON AND NANCY ELLEN (BALL) THOMPSON FAMILY OF WAYNE COUNTY, WEST VIRGINIA**, by Chester E. Bartram. 1993. Indexed. Illus.
Cloth. $47.35. 300pp. .... Vendor G0183

3883 **THOMAS THOMPSON AND ANN FINNEY OF COLONIAL PENNSYL-**

VANIA AND NORTH CAROLINA. Lawrence, Closs, and John Thompson. **Allied Lines of Finney, McAllister, Buchanan, and Hart**, by Jane Gray Buchanan. 1987. Indexed. Illus.
Cloth. $37.00. 402pp. .... Vendor G0107

3884 **VIRGINIA CONNECTIONS: A GENEALOGICAL HISTORY OF THE THOMPSON–WARD FAMILY ORIGINATING IN SOUTHWEST VIRGINIA**, by Judy B. Anderson. 1992. Indexed. Illus.
Cloth. $60.00. 848pp. .... Vendor G0297

3885 **DESCENDANTS OF JOHN THOMSON, PIONEER SCOTCH COVENANTER: GEN. NOTES ON ALL KNOWN DESC. OF JOHN THOMSON OF SCOTLAND, IRELAND & PA., WITH BIOGR. SKETCHES**, by A.S. McAllister. 1917.
Cloth, $69.50. Paper, $59.50. 357pp. .... Vendor G0259

3886 **THORNBURG FAMILY OF RANDOLPH CO., IND.**, by Thornburg and Weiss. 1959.
Paper. $12.00. 60pp. .... Vendor G0259

3887 **DESCENDANTS OF JOHN THORNDIKE OF ESSEX CO., MASS.**, by M.H. Staffod. 1960.
Cloth, $64.00. Paper, $54.00. 349pp. .... Vendor G0259

3888 **DESCENDANTS OF WILLIAM THORNTON OF VIRGINIA**, by Carol A. Hauk. 1995. Indexed.
Paper. $45.00. 441pp. .... Vendor G0340

3889 **FAM. OF JAMES THORNTON**, by C.T. Adams. 1905.
Paper. $7.50. 34pp. .... Vendor G0259

3890 **THE DOZIER THORNTON LINE**, by J. Thornton. 1957.
Paper. $10.00. 52pp. .... Vendor G0259

3891 **DESCENDANTS OF JOHN THROCKMORTON OF VIRGINIA**, by Carol A. Hauk. 1995. Indexed.
Paper. $35.00. 160pp. .... Vendor G0340

3892 **DESC. OF JOHN THURBER**, by A. Thurber, Jr. 1954.
Paper. $8.00. 39pp. .... Vendor G0259

3893 **DESC. OF EDW. THURSTON, THE FIRST OF THE NAME IN THE COLONY OF R.I.**, by C. Thurston. 1868.
Paper. $14.00. 70pp. .... Vendor G0259

3894 **GEN. OF CHARLES THURSTON & RACHEL PITMAN & DESC.**, by C.M. Thurston. 1865.
Paper. $16.00. 80pp. .... Vendor G0259

3895 **THE ANC. OF WALTER M. THURSTON, GIVING SOME ACCT. OF THE FAM. OF CARROLL, DE BEAUFORT (& OTHERS)**, by J.H. and W.M. Thurston. 1894.
Paper. $18.50. 95pp. .... Vendor G0259

3896 **THURSTON GENEALOGY, 1635–1892**, by B. Thurston. 1892.
Cloth, $104.00. Paper, $94.00. 760pp. .... Vendor G0259

3897 [**Thwing**]. **A GEN., BIOGR. & HIST. ACCT. OF THE FAM.**, by W.E. Thwing. 1883.
Cloth, $42.00. Paper, $32.00. 216pp. .... Vendor G0259

3898 **HENRY TIBBETTS OF DOVER, N.H. & SOME OF HIS DESCENDANTS**, by M.T. Jarvis. 1937–41.
Cloth, $127.00. Paper, $117.00. 821pp. typescript .... Vendor G0259

3899 **TICE FAMILIES IN AMER.: THEIS, THYSSEN, TYSSEN, DEIS**, Vol. I, by J.S. Elson. 1947.
Cloth, $59.50. Paper, $49.50. 320pp. .... Vendor G0259

3900 **TIERNAN & OTHER FAMS.**, by C.B. Tiernan. 1901.
Cloth, $79.50. Paper, $69.50. 466pp. .... Vendor G0259

3901 **TIERNAN FAMILY IN MARYLAND**, by C.B. Tiernan. 1898.
Cloth, $43.50. Paper, $33.50. 222pp. .... Vendor G0259

3902 **TIFFANY FAM. GEN.**, by E.F. Wright. 1904.
Cloth, $30.00. Paper, $20.00. 92pp. .... Vendor G0259

3903 **PARTIAL REC. OF THE DESC. OF JOHN TEFFT OF PORTSMOUTH, RI, & NEARLY COMPLETE REC. OF DESC. OF JOHN TIFFT OF NASSAU, NY**, by M. Tifft. 1896.
Cloth, $36.00. Paper, $26.00. 159pp. .... Vendor G0259

3904 **"SPES ALIT AGRICOLAM" (HOPE SUSTAINS THE FARMER); THE YEARS 1225–1961 OF THE TILGHMAN (TILLMAN) & ALLIED FAM.**, by S. Tillman.
Cloth, $59.50. Paper, $49.50. 320pp. .... Vendor G0259

3905 **GEN. OF THE TILLEY FAM.**, by R.H. Tilley. 1878.
Paper. $16.00. 79pp. .... Vendor G0259

3906 **THE TILSON GEN. FROM EDMUND TILSON AT PLYMOUTH, NEW ENG., 1638–1911. ALSO BRIEF ACCT. OF WATERMAN, MURDOCK, BARTLETT, TURNER, WINSLOW, STURTEVANT, KEITH & PARRIR FAM.**, by M. Tilson. 1911.
Cloth, $101.50. Paper, $91.50. 610pp. .... Vendor G0259

3907 **ANC. OF PHOEBE TILTON, 1775–1847, WIFE OF CAPT. ABEL LUNT OF NEWBURYPORT, MA.**, by W. Davis. 1947.
Cloth, $48.50. Paper, $38.50. 257pp. .... Vendor G0259

3908 **HIST. OF THE TILTON FAM. IN AMER.**, by F.T. Tilton. Vol. I, nos. 1–8. 1927–1930.
Cloth, $43.00. Paper, $33.00. 256pp. .... Vendor G0259

3909 **GARRETT TINGEN DESCENDANTS, EARLY SETTLER OF PERSON CO., NC**, by Leallah Franklin. 1989. Indexed. Illus.
Related families: **Arrington, Brooks, Buchanan, Bullock, Carver, Clayton, Coates, Daniels, Davis, Dixon, Duncan, Elliott, Franklin, Frazier, Gentry, Hicks, Humphries, Kinton, Oakley, Satterfield, Slaughter, Yarborough**.
Cloth. $40.00. 406pp. .... Vendor G0304

3910 **TINGLEY FAMILY, BEING A REC. OF THE DESC. OF SAMUEL**

TINGLEY OF MALDEN, MA., IN THE MALE & FEMALE LINES, by R.M. Tingley. 1910.
Cloth, $137.50. Paper, $127.50. 894pp. .... Vendor G0259

3911 **TINKER FAMILY: ANCESTORS & DESCENDANTS OF JOSEPH WESCOT TINKER, ELLSWORTH ME., 1791–1868, A DESCENDANT OF JOHN TINKER OF BOSTON**, by Frederick J. Libbie. 1900.
Paper. $7.50. 36pp. .... Vendor G0259

3912 **JOHN TINKHAM IS MY NAME: ANCESTORS & CHILDREN OF JOHN TINKHAM (1789–1845); NATIVE OF ME., EARLY SETTLER OF W. N.Y., & ONE OF THE FIRST LANDOWNERS OF WAYNE CO., MI**, by Kenneth Tinkham. 1984.
Paper. $8.00. 31+xi pp. .... Vendor G0259

3913 **ANC. OF TIPPIN FAM. OF KY., WITH MAYFIELD ANC.**, by J.J. Tippin. 1940.
Paper. $8.00. 38pp. .... Vendor G0259

3914 **GEN. OF ISRAEL TISDALE & HIS DESC.**, by E.F. Tisdale. 1909.
Paper. $16.50. 82pp. .... Vendor G0259

3915 **TOBEY (TOBIE, TOBY) GEN. THOMAS OF SANDWICH & JAMES OF KITTERY, & THEIR DESC.**, by R. Tobey and C. Pope. 1905.
Cloth, $56.50. Paper, $46.50. 350pp. .... Vendor G0259

3916 **ELIZABETH TODD (BORN 1760S) OF LAWRENCE COUNTY, INDIANA IN 1820: HER DESCENDANTS**, by Nancie Todd Weber. (1991) reprint 1993. Indexed. Illus.
Circumstantial reconstruction, theorizing Elizabeth **Seip** married Andrew **Todd**, 1782, Frederick County, Maryland.
Paper. $22.00. 206pp. .... Vendor G0337

3917 **TODD GEN.; REG. OF THE DESC. OF ADAMS TODD, OF THE NAMES TODD, WHETTEN & 26 OTHERS**, by R. Greene. 1867.
Cloth, $36.00. Paper, $26.00. 160pp. .... Vendor G0259

3918 **TODD FAM. IN AMER., OR THE DESC. OF CHRISTOPHER TODD, 1637–1919**, by J.E. Todd. 1920.
Cloth, $118.00. Paper, $108.00. 721pp. .... Vendor G0259

3919 **TOERS–TUERS FAMILY**, by Howard S.F. Randolph. 1926. Indexed.
Paper. $5.00. 36pp. .... Vendor G0182

3920 **REC. OF THE ANC. & KINDRED OF THE CHILDREN OF EDW. TOMPKINS, SR., LATE OF OAKLAND, CA., WITH APPENDIX**, by E. Tompkins, Jr. 1893.
Paper. $13.00. 65pp. .... Vendor G0259

3921 **TOMKINS–TOMPKINS GEN.**, by R. and C. Tompkins. 1942.
Cloth, $109.50. Paper, $99.50. 720pp. .... Vendor G0259

3922 **HENRY TOMLINSON & DESC. IN AMER. & A FEW ADD. TOMLINSON BRANCHES**, by S. Orcott. 1891.
Cloth, $46.50. Paper, $36.50. 244pp. .... Vendor G0259

3923 **TONEY FAMILY HISTORY**, by Elma Henning and Merle Rummel. 1979.
Cloth, $79.50. Paper, $69.50. 535pp. .... Vendor G0259

3924 **TOPPING/LATHAM FAMILY HISTORY AND ALLIED FAMILIES**, by Thomas R. Topping. 1994. Indexed. Illus.
Including **Alligood, Brewer, Chilton, Ethridge, Glasgow, Satchwell, Shavender, Sillery, Wiggins, Windley**, and **Winstead**.
Cloth. $47.00. 483pp. .... Vendor G0342

3925 **A CONTRIBUTION TOWARDS A GEN. OF ALL TORREYS IN AMER., SHOWING THE DESC. FROM WM. TORREY OF ENG., 1557, TO ABNER TORREY OF WEYMOUTH, MASS., WITH AN APPENDIX**, by D. Torrey. 1890.
Cloth, $41.50. Paper, $31.50. 210pp. .... Vendor G0259

3926 **TORREY FAMS. & THEIR CHILDREN IN AMER.**, by F.C. Torrey. Vol. I. 1924.
Cloth, $68.50. Paper, $58.50. 396pp. .... Vendor G0259

3927 **TORREY FAMS. & THEIR CHILDREN IN AMER.**, Vol. II. 1929.
Cloth, $86.50. Paper, $76.50. 488pp. .... Vendor G0259

3928 **TOUSEY FAM. IN AMER.**, by T.C. Rose. 1916.
Cloth, $37.50. Paper, $27.50. 137pp. .... Vendor G0259

3929 **TOWER GENEALOGY. AN ACCT. OF THE DESC. OF JOHN TOWER OF HINGHAM, MASS.**, by C. Tower. 1891.
Cloth, $97.50. Paper, $87.50. 701pp. .... Vendor G0259

3930 **DESC. OF JONATHAN TOWLE, 1747–1822, OF HAMPTON & PITTSFIELD, N.H.**, by A. Towle et al. 1903.
Cloth, $59.00. Paper, $49.00. 312pp. .... Vendor G0259

3931 **ANC. OF LT. AMOS TOWNE OF KENNEBUNKPORT, MAINE**, by W.G. Davis. 1927.
Paper. $16.00. 81pp. .... Vendor G0259

3932 **DESC. OF WM. TOWNE, WHO CAME TO AMER. ABOUT 1630 & SETTLED IN SALEM, MA.**, by E. Towne. 1901.
Cloth, $58.50. Paper, $48.50. 379pp. .... Vendor G0259

3933 **THE TOWNE FAM. MEM.**, by E. Hubbard. 1880.
Paper. $19.50. 130pp. .... Vendor G0259

3934 **A GEN. OF THE TOWNER FAM. THE DESC. OF RICHARD TOWNER WHO CAME FROM SUSSEX CO., ENG. TO GUILFORD, CT., BEFORE 1685**, by J.W. Towner. 1910.
Cloth, $53.00. Paper, $43.00. 269pp. .... Vendor G0259

3935 **A MEMORIAL OF JOHN, HENRY & RICHARD TOWNSEND & THEIR DESCENDANTS (WITH 1969 INDEX)**, by W.A. Townsend. 1865.
Cloth, $57.00. Paper, $47.00. 233+60pp. .... Vendor G0259

3936 **ENGLISH TOWNSENDS; TANCRED CRUSADERS; TOWNSENDS OF WATERTOWN, MA.; TOWNSENDS OF HEBRON, CT. & HANCOCK, MA.**, by M.I. Townsend. 1899.
Paper. $7.50. 37pp. .... Vendor G0259

3937 **TOWNSEND MISSING LINKS.** Charles D. Townsend, Editor. 1992.
Subscription. $15.00 per year. 36pp. per issue .... Vendor G0047

3938 NOTES ON THE TOWNSEND FAM., by H. Waters. 1883.
Paper. $8.50. 43pp. .... Vendor G0259

3939 TOWNSHEND FAM. OF LYNN, IN ENG. & NEW ENG., by C.H.
Townshend. 1884.
Paper. $17.50. 138pp. .... Vendor G0259

3940 ANC. & DESC. OF LT. THOMAS TRACY OF NORWICH, CONN., 1660,
by E.E. Tracy. 1898.
Cloth, $54.00. Paper, $44.00. 294pp. .... Vendor G0259

3941 THE ANC. OF LT. THOMAS TRACY OF NORWICH, CONN., by C.S.
Ripley. 1895.
Paper. $19.00. 100pp. .... Vendor G0259

3942 TRAHAN: NICHOLAS TO GUILLAUME TO YOU, VOLUMES 1–5, by
Mitch Conover. 1993. Indexed. Illus.
    Traces the thousands of descendants of Nicholas **Trahan** and Renee **Desloges**
who were born in the later 1500s in France and of their son, Guillaume, and his
wife, Francoise **Corbineau**, who lived in the 1600s in Acadia, Canada. By the
later 1700s, descendants were in Louisiana. The Family Group Records, many
extending to 3 pages, give birth and death dates and places, parents, marriages,
children, etc. and often added paragraphs with assorted other information. Related families with the Trahans include just about every other Acadian name in
Louisiana, plus many names of other heritage.
    Volume 1 Family Groups x–xx
    Volume 2 Family Groups 1–225
    Volume 3 Family Groups 226–425
    Volume 4 Family Groups 426–625
    Volume 5 Family Groups 626–825
All volumes are hardcover. $39.00 per volume.
500+pp. per volume .... Vendor G0114

3943 DESC. OF HENRY TRAVERS OF ENG. & NEWBURY, MASS., by N.H.
Daniels. 1903.
Cloth, $35.00. Paper, $25.00. 147pp. .... Vendor G0259

**3944 JOHN TRAYNE AND SOME DESC., ESPECIALLY CHARLES JACK-
SON TRAIN, USN**, by S.T. Hand. 1933.
Cloth, $39.50. Paper, $29.50. 198pp. .... Vendor G0259

3945 DOWN SEVEN GEN. A RESCRIPT OF TREADWELL & PLATT GEN.,
by A.C. Maltbie. 1883.
Paper. $7.50. 36pp. .... Vendor G0259

**3946 [Treat]. A GEN. OF TROTT, TRATT & TREAT FOR 15 GEN. & 450
YEARS IN ENG. & AMER.**, by J. Treat. 1893.
Cloth, $90.00. Paper, $80.00. 649pp. .... Vendor G0259

**3947 TREAT FAMILY IN AMERICA, 1622–1992 (LINE OF BENJAMIN
FRANKLIN TREAT)**, by Bob Treat. 1992.
Paper. $14.00. 70pp. .... Vendor G0259

**3948 THE CAVALRY SABER: BENJ. TREAT & JOSEPH BROWN CIVIL
WAR HISTORY & LEGACY**, by Bob Treat. 1993.
Paper. $12.50. 62pp. .... Vendor G0259

3949 **HISTORY OF THE TREDWAY FAMILY**, by W.T. Tredway. 1930. Cloth, $75.00. Paper, $65.00. 14+400+18pp. .... Vendor G0259

3950 **SOME ACCT. OF THE TREE FAM. & ITS CONNECTIONS IN ENG. & AMER.**, by J. Leach. 1908. Paper. $18.00. 116pp. .... Vendor G0259

3951 **HIST. ACCT. OF THE TREGO FAM.**, by A. Shertzer. 1884. Cloth, $38.50. Paper, $28.50. 144pp. .... Vendor G0259

3952 **HIST. OF THE TREMAN, TREMAINE, TRUMAN FAM. IN AMER., WITH THE REL. FAMS. OF MACK, DEY, BOARD & AYERS. BEING A HIST. OF JOSEPH TRUMAN OF NEW LONDON, CT., (1666); RICHARD DEY OF N.Y.C. (1641); CORNELIUS BOARD OF BOARDVILLE, N.J. (1730), JOHN AYER OF NEWBURY, MA. (1635); & THEIR DESC.**, by Treman & Poole. 2 vols. 1901. Cloth. $145.00/vol. Paper, $135.00/vol. 2,129pp. .... Vendor G0259

3953 **TRIPP GEN.; DESC. OF JAMES, SON OF JOHN TRIPP**, by G.L. Randall. 1924. Cloth, $49.50. Paper, $39.50. 264pp. .... Vendor G0259

3954 **TRIPP WILLS, DEEDS & WAYS, WITH KEY TO TRIPP DESC. VIA NEW ENGLAND & ALSO NEW YORK**, compiled by Valentine Research Bureau. 1932. Cloth, $39.50. Paper, $29.50. 196pp. .... Vendor G0259

3955 **TROWBRIDGE FAM.; OR, THE DESC. OF THOMAS TROWBRIDGE, ONE OF THE FIRST SETTLERS OF NEW HAVEN, CONN.**, by F.W. Chapman. 1872.
Cloth, $81.00. Paper, $71.00. 461pp. .... Vendor G0259

3956 **TROWBRIDGE GENEALOGY: HIST. OF THE TROWBRIDGE FAM. IN AMER.**, by F.B. Trowbridge. 1908.
Cloth, $160.00. Paper, $150.00. 848pp. .... Vendor G0259

3957 **HIST. OF THE TRUBEE FAM. 1275–1894**, by H.T. Carlick. 1894.
Cloth, $40.00. Paper, $30.00. 151pp. .... Vendor G0259

3958 **TUCK GEN. ROBERT TUCK OF HAMPTON, N.H., & HIS DESC., 1638–1877**, by J. Dow. 1877.
Cloth, $35.00. Paper, $25.00. 146pp. .... Vendor G0259

3959 **GEN. & HIST. ACCT. OF DESC. OF HENRY TUCKER**, by G.H. Tucker. 1851.
Paper. $9.00. 45pp. .... Vendor G0259

3960 **GEN. OF THE TUCKER FAM., FROM VARIOUS AUTHENTIC SOURCES**, by E. Tucker. 1895.
Cloth, $75.00. Paper, $65.00. 414pp. .... Vendor G0259

3961 **THE TUCKER GEN. A RECORD OF GILBERT RUGGLES & EVELINA CHRISTINA (SNYDER) TUCKER, THEIR ANC. & DESC.**, by T.S. Morris. 1902.
Cloth, $58.50. Paper, $48.50. 305pp. .... Vendor G0259

3962 **TULEY FAM. MEMOIRS. HIST., BIOGR., & GEN. STORY OF THE TULEYS & THE FLOYD FAM. CONNECTIONS IN VA., KY. & IND.**, by W.F. Tuley. 1906.
Paper. $15.00. 75pp. .... Vendor G0259

3963 **THE TULEY FAMILY PIONEER SETTLERS OF LaPORTE COUNTY**, by William T. Tuley. 1994. Indexed. Illus.
    The story of James and Martha **Tuley** and their 10 children who came to Clinton Township, LaPorte County, Indiana in 1834.
Cloth. $25.00. 404pp. .... Vendor G0330

3964 **GENEALOGY OF THE TUNNELL FAMILY OF DELAWARE**, by James M. Tunnell, Jr. 1954.
Paper. $19.50. 100pp. .... Vendor G0259

3965 **THOMAS TUPPER & HIS DESC.**, by F.W. Tupper. 1945.
Paper. $14.00. 71pp. .... Vendor G0259

3966 **TURNER FAMILY MAGAZINE: GENEALOGICAL, HISTORICAL & BIOGRAPHICAL, VOLS. 1 & 2**, edited by Wm. M. Clemens. 1916–7.
Paper. $18.00. 95pp. .... Vendor G0259

3967 **GEN. OF THE DESC. OF HUMPHREY TURNER, WITH FAM. RECORDS**, by J. Turner. 1852.
Paper. $12.50. 64pp. .... Vendor G0259

3968 **THE "LONG JOHN" TURNER FAMILY**, by Wilson Breneman. 1993. Indexed.
Paper. $20.00. 124pp. .... Vendor G0365

3969 **TURNEYS OF FAIRFIELD COUNTY, CONNECTICUT; ASHTABULA, BROWN, LAKE, & LAWRENCE COUNTIES, OHIO; CHAUTAUQUA COUNTY, NEW YORK; TAZEWELL COUNTY, ILLINOIS; SAN LUIS OBISPO COUNTY, CALIFORNIA,** by Lynn Marks. 1996. Indexed. Descendants of David **Turney** & his wife Parthenia **Johnson** of Fairfield County, Connecticut.
Fiche only. $6.00. 160+pp. .... Vendor G0413

3970 **THE TURNLEYS: A BRIEF RECORD, BIOGRAPHIC & NARRATIVE, OF SOME TURNLEYS IN THE U.S. & EUROPE,** by P.T. Turnley. 1905.
Cloth, $56.50. Paper, $46.50. 298pp. .... Vendor G0259

3971 **DESCENDANTS OF HENRY TUTHILL 1612–1650,** compiled by Alva M. Tuttle; edited by Gwen Campbell. 1991. Indexed.
Query with SASE.
Paper. $35.00. 434pp. .... Vendor G0303

3972 **PETER TUTTLE b. 1660, ANCESTOR OF SOME SOUTHERN TUTTLES,** compiled by Alva M. Tuttle; edited by Gwen Campbell. 1995. Indexed.
Query with SASE.
Paper. $12.00. 81pp. .... Vendor G0303

3973 **"SHIPWRECK" JOHN TUTTLE, ANCESTOR OF THE NEW HAMPSHIRE TUTTLES,** compiled by Alva M. Tuttle; edited by Gwen Campbell. 1992. Indexed.
Query with SASE.
Paper. $30.00. 238pp. .... Vendor G0303

3974 **THE DESC. OF WM. & ELIZABETH TUTTLE, WHO CAME FROM OLD TO NEW ENG. IN 1635, & SETTLED IN NEW HAVEN IN 1639,** by G.F. Tuttle. 1883.
Cloth, $105.00. Paper, $95.00. 814pp. .... Vendor G0259

3975 **TUTTLE FAMILY IN AMERICA, DESCENDANTS OF SYMON OF RINGSTEAD, ENG—4 VOLS,** compiled by Alva M. Tuttle; edited by Gwen Campbell. 1990. Indexed.
Vol. I : William's sons—John and Thomas (299 pp.)
Vol. II: William's sons—Jonathan and Joseph (296 pp.)
Vol. III: William's sons—Simon and Nathaniel (287 pp.)
Vol. IV: John and Richard (248 pp.)
Query with SASE.
Paper. $30.00/vol., $120.00/set .... Vendor G0303

3976 **[TUTTLE–TUTHILL]. ONE BRANCH OF THE ELI TUTHILL FAMILY OF LIBERTY TWP. OF MICHIGAN, DESCENDANTS OF THE TUTHILL FAMILY OF SOUTHOLD & ORIENT, LONG ISL., 1640, & OF THARSTON, ENGLAND,** by Jean L. LaPorte. 1992.
Paper. $15.00. 107pp. .... Vendor G0259

3977 **DESC. OF WM. TWINING, SR., OF EASTHAM, MASS., WITH NOTES OF ENG., WELSH & NOVA SCOTIA FAMS. OF THE NAME,** by T.J. Twining. Rev. ed. 1905.
Cloth, $43.50. Paper, $33.50. 264pp. .... Vendor G0259

3978 **GEN. OF THE TWITCHELL FAM. RECORD OF THE DESC. OF THE PURITAN, BENJAMIN TWITCHELL, DORCHESTER, LANCASTER, MEDFIELD, & SHERBORN, MASS., 1632–1927,** by R.E. Twitchell. 1929. Cloth, $125.00. Paper, $115.00. 768pp. .... Vendor G0259

3979 **GEN. & BIOGR. RECORD OF ONE BRANCH OF TYER FAM., DESC. FROM JOHN TYER,** by E.T. Savery. 1894. Paper. $7.50. 35pp. .... Vendor G0259

3980 **TYLER GEN. THE DESC. OF JOB TYLER OF ANDOVER, MASS., 1619–1700,** by W.I.T. Brigham. 2 vols. 1912. Cloth, $134.00. Paper, $124.00. 891pp. .... Vendor G0259

3981 **UHLER GEN., 1735–1901,** by G.H. Uhler. 1901. Paper. $7.00. 35pp. .... Vendor G0259

3982 **JOHN UNDERHILL, CAPTAIN OF NEW ENGLAND AND NEW NETHERLAND,** by Henry C. Shelley. 1932. Indexed. Illus.
      Biography of founder of **Underhill** family of New York.
      Cloth. $20.00. 473pp. .... Vendor G0182

3983 **UNDERHILL BURYING GROUND: ACCT. OF A PARCEL OF LAND . . . AT LOCUST VAL., LONG ISLAND . . . KNOWN AS THE UNDERHILL BURYING GROUND,** compiled by D.H. and F.J. Underhill. 1924(?)
      Paper. $16.00. 79pp. .... Vendor G0259

3984 **THE UNDERHILL BURIAL GROUND,** by D. Harris Underhill and Francis J. Underhill. 1926. Illus.
      Underhill family history and inscriptions from cemetery at Locust Valley, New York.
      Cloth. $8.50. 79pp. .... Vendor G0182

3985 **ANTECEDENTS AND DESCENDANTS OF LEVI UNDERWOOD (1831–1885) AND RELATED FAMILIES,** by Dale C. Kellogg. (1965) reprint 1996. Indexed. Illus.
      1996 reprint with some corrections and additions.
      Paper. $10.00. 116pp. .... Vendor G0051

3986 **FINLEY L. UNDERWOOD AND MAHALA DOWDEN: THEIR ANCESTORS AND DESCENDANTS,** by Esther E. Gregory. 1996. Indexed. Illus.
      New research on these families: **Underwood, Blackburn, Harlan, Ewing, McBride, Thurston, Newcomb, Lantz, Hartle, Beard, Nevill, Ashford, Dowden, Gore.**
      Cloth. $50.00. 464pp. .... Vendor G0426

3987 **THE UNDERWOOD FAMILIES OF AMERICA,** by L.M. Underwood, edited by H.J. Banker. 1913. Cloth, $117.50. Paper, $107.50. 809pp. .... Vendor G0259

3988 **GEN. & FAM. HIST. OF THE UPHAMS OF CASTINE, MAINE, & DIXON, ILL., WITH GEN. NOTES OF BROOKS, KIDDER & OTHER FAM.,** by F.K. Upham. 1887. Paper. $14.00. 68pp. .... Vendor G0259

3989 **NOTICES OF JOHN UPHAM & DESC.,** by A. Upham. 1845. Paper. $18.00. 92pp. .... Vendor G0259

3990 **THE DESC. OF JOHN UPHAM OF MASS., WHO CAME FROM ENG. IN 1635 & LIVED IN WEYMOUTH & MALDEN,** by F.K. Upham. 1892. Cloth, $82.00. Paper, $72.00. 573pp. .... Vendor G0259

3991 **UPSON FAMILY IN AMERICA,** compiled by the Upson Family Assoc. 1940. Cloth, $104.00. Paper, $94.00. 624pp. .... Vendor G0259

3992 **UPTON FAM. RECORDS: BEING GEN. COLLECTIONS FOR AN UPTON FAM. HIST.,** by W.H. Upton. 1893. Cloth, $93.00. Paper, $83.00. 534pp. .... Vendor G0259

3993 **UPTON MEM. A GEN. REC. OF THE DESC. OF JOHN UPTON, OF N. READING, MA., WITH SHORT GEN. OF THE PUTNAM, STONE & BRUCE FAM.,** by J.A. Vinton. 1874. Cloth, $79.50. Paper, $69.50. 556pp. .... Vendor G0259

3994 **URANN FAM. OF NEW ENG.,** by C.C. Whittier. 1910. Paper. $12.00. 59pp. .... Vendor G0259

3995 **MEMORIAL SKETCH OF ROLAND GREENE USHER, 1823–1895, TO WHICH IS ADDED A GEN. OF THE USHER FAM. IN NEW ENG., 1638–1895,** by E.P. Usher. 1895. Cloth, $35.00. Paper, $25.00. 160pp. .... Vendor G0259

3996 **REBUILDING THE HOUSE OF USHER,** by Alma Usher Barclay. 1994. Indexed. Illus. Letters and sketches of descendants of Irish immigrant James Usher. Paper. $10.00. 74pp. .... Vendor G0423

3997 **GEN. OF THE VAIL FAM., DESC. FROM JEREMIAH VAIL, AT SALEM, MASS, 1639,** by H.H. Vail. 1902. Cloth, $68.00. Paper, $58.00. 371pp. .... Vendor G0259

3998 **MOSES VAIL OF HUNTINGTON, L.I.; HIS DESC. FROM JOSEPH VAIL, SON OF JEREMIAH OF SALEM, MA., 1640, WITH COLL. LINES,** by W.P. Vail. 1947. Cloth, $91.50. Paper, $81.50. 524pp. .... Vendor G0259

3999 **THE VALENTINES IN AMER., 1644–1874,** by T.W. Valentine. 1874. Cloth, $48.00. Paper, $38.00. 254pp. .... Vendor G0259

4000 **LINEAGE OF THE VAN AAKEN & ALLIED FAMILIES, EXTR. "OLDE ULSTER,"** by A.R. Winfield. Paper. $19.50. 112pp. .... Vendor G0259

4001 **LAMBERT JANSE VAN ALSTYNE & SOME OF HIS DESC.,** by L. Van Alstyne. 1897. Cloth, $40.00. Paper, $30.00. 142pp. .... Vendor G0259

4002 **VAN BENTHUYSEN GENEALOGY. DESC. OF PAULUS MARTENSE VAN BENTHUYSEN, WHO SETTLED IN ALBANY, N.Y., MALE & FEMALE LINES; ALSOGEN. OF CERTAIN BRANCHES OF . . . OTHER FAMS. OF DUTCH & HUGUENOT ORIGIN IN N.Y.,** by A.S. Van Benthuysen and E.M. Hall. 1953. Cloth, $99.50. Paper, $89.50. 592pp. .... Vendor G0259

4003 **GEN. OF THE VAN BRUNT FAM. OF N.Y., 1653–1867**, by T.G. Bergen. 1867.
Paper. $16.50. 79pp. .... Vendor G0259

4004 **HIST. OF CORNELIS MAESSEN VAN BUREN, WHO CAME FROM HOLLAND TO THE NEW NETHERLANDS IN 1631, & HIS DESC., INCL. THE GEN. OF THE FAMS. OF BLOOMINGDALE**, by H.C. Peckham. 1913.
Cloth, $77.50. Paper, $67.50. 431pp. .... Vendor G0259

4005 **SOME DESCENDANTS OF JAN AERTSEN VANDERBILT**, by Jean M. Rand. 1991. Indexed. Illus.
Cloth. $37.50. 322pp. .... Vendor G0210

4006 **VANDERLIP, VAN DERLIP, VANDER LIPPE FAM. IN AMER., WITH ACCT. OF VON DER LIPPE FAM. OF LIPPE, GER.**, by C. Booth. 1914.
Cloth, $50.00. Paper, $40.00. 194pp. .... Vendor G0259

4007 **VANDERLIP, VAN DERLIP, VANDER LIPPE FAMILY IN AMERICA, ALSO INCLUDING SOME ACCOUNT OF THE VON DER LIPPE FAM. OF LIPPE, GERMANY, FROM WHICH THE NORWEGIAN, DUTCH & AMERICAN LINES HAVE THEIR DESCENT**, by C.E. Booth. 1914.
Cloth, $39.00. Paper, $29.00. 188pp. .... Vendor G0259

4008 **ABRAHAM VAN DEUSEN & MANY OF HIS DESC., WITH BIOGR. NOTES**, by C.B. Benson. 1901.
Cloth, $37.50. Paper, $27.50. 182pp. .... Vendor G0259

4009 **[Van Deusen]. VAN DEURSEN FAM.**, by A. Van Deusen. 2 vols. 1912.
Cloth, $139.00. Paper, $129.00. 915pp. .... Vendor G0259

4010 **VAN DOORN FAMILY (VAN DORN, VAN DOREN, ETC.) IN HOLLAND & AMER., 1088–1908**, by A.V.D. Honeyman. 1909.
Cloth, $119.00. Paper, $109.00. 765pp. .... Vendor G0259

4011 **VAN ETTEN BEGINNINGS AND ENDINGS—MARRIAGE, OBITUARY AND CHARTED FILES**, compiled by Elwyn R. Van Etten; edited by James Lee Seidelman. 1993. Indexed.
Cloth. $23.00. 165pp. .... Vendor G0219

4012 **RECORDS OF THE VAN EVERY FAMILY, UNITED EMPIRE LOYAL-ISTS, N.Y. STATE, 1653–1784, CANADA, 1784–1947**, by Mary B. Piersol. 1947.
Cloth, $34.50. Paper, $24.50. 131pp. .... Vendor G0259

4013 **VAN HECKE AND ALLIED ANCESTRY: ANC. OF JOSINA VAN HECK, WIFE OF ROELAND DE CARPENTIER, GRANDPARENTS OF MARIA DE CARPENTIER, WIFE OF JEAN PAUL JAQUET, VICE-DIRECTOR & MAGISTRATE ON THE SOUTH RIVER OF NEE NETHERLAND, 1655–1657**, by E. Sellers. 1933.
Cloth, $35.00. Paper, $25.00. 154pp. .... Vendor G0259

4014 **GEN. OF THE VAN HOOSEAR FAM., DESC. OF RINEAR VAN HOOSEAR, AN OFFICER IN THE REV. ARMY**, by D. VanHoosear. 1902.
Cloth, $30.00. Paper, $20.00. 96pp. .... Vendor G0259

Hewick Plantation B & B
Middlesex County, Virginia
"Home of The Robinsons Since 1678"

Helen & Ed Battleson	VSH 602/615
(804) 758-4214	P.O. Box 82
(800) 484-7514 (Enter 1678)	Urbanna, VA 23175-0082

e-mail: HEWICK@AOL.COM

4015 **AN HIST. RECORD OF VanHORNE FAM. IN AMER.**, by A. VanHorne. 1888.
Paper. $16.00. 80pp. .... Vendor G0259

4016 **VAN KLEECK FAM. OF POUGHKEEPSIE, N.Y.**, by F. Van Kleeck. 1900.
Paper. $12.00. 59pp. .... Vendor G0259

4017 **AN EARLY MORAVIAN FAMILY OF TUSCARAWAS COUNTY, OHIO BORN VAN LEHN–BLICKENSDERFER**, by Betty Ellwood Kinsey. 1992.
Indexed. Illus.
Cloth. $75.00. 700pp. .... Vendor G0183

4018 **VAN NORDEN FAM., 1623–1925**, by T. Van Norden. 1923.
Paper. $15.00. 74pp. .... Vendor G0259

4019 **GEN. OF THE VAN PELT FAM.**, by E. Smith. 1913.
Cloth, $47.75. Paper, $37.75. 251pp. .... Vendor G0259

4020 **THE VAN RENSSELAERS IN HOLLAND AND AMERICA**, by Florence Van Rensselaer. 1956. Indexed. Illus.
Cloth. $14.25. 103pp. .... Vendor G0182

4021 **NOTES CONCERNING THE VanUXEM FAM. IN FRANCE AND U.S.**, by F. VanUxem. 1923.
Paper. $10.00. 49pp. .... Vendor G0259

4022 **GENEALOGICAL REC. OF THE VAN VECHTENS FROM 1638 TO 1896**, by P. Van Vechten, Jr. 1896.
Cloth, $32.00. Paper, $22.00. 117pp. .... Vendor G0259

4023 **CONDENSED GEN. OF VAN VOORHEES FAM.** 1932.
Paper. $7.00. 31pp. .... Vendor G0259

4024 **GENEALOGY OF THE VAN VOORHEES FAMILY IN AMERICA, OR THE DESCENDANTS OF STEVEN COERTE VAN VOORHEES**, by Elias W. Van Voorhis. 1888.
Cloth, $69.50. Paper, $59.50. 380pp. .... Vendor G0259

4025 **NOTES ON THE ANC. OF MAJ. WM. ROE VAN VOORHIS OF FISHKILL, DUCHESS CO., N.Y.,** by E.W. Van Voorhis. 1881. Cloth, $41.00. Paper, $31.00. 239pp. .... Vendor G0259

4026 **GEN. OF VAN WAGENEN FAM. 1650–1884,** by G. Van Wagenen. 1884. Paper. $17.50. 83pp. .... Vendor G0259

4027 **A GENEALOGY OF THE VAN WINKLE FAMILY, DESCENDANTS OF JACOB WALICHS OF HOLLAND, 1630–1993,** by James C. Van Winkle. 1994. Indexed.
Twelve generations and 8,400 Dutch **Van Winkle** descendants throughout the country in modified NGQS form. Collateral genealogy 8,000 entries. Early family history, nomenclature. Maps. Color Plate. Includes current update. 6.5" x 9". Smythe sewn. Include SASE with inquiries.
Cloth. $66.00. 1,154pp. .... Vendor G0173

4028 **GENEALOGY OF THE VAN WINKLE FAMILY: ACCOUNT OF ITS ORIGIN & SETTLEMENT IN THIS COUNTRY WITH DATA, 1630– 1913,** by Daniel Van Winkle. 1913.
Cloth, $76.50. Paper, $66.50. 433pp. .... Vendor G0259

4029 **THE VARNER NEWSLETTER,** by Janice B. Palmer. 1988. Published quarterly. Illus.
Subscription. $12.00/year. 8–10pp. .... Vendor G0418

4030 **VARNER, VERNER, WERNER FAMILIES OF AMERICA,** by Janice B. Palmer. 1995. Indexed. Illus.
The definitive book on Varners. Features 28 **Varner** lines, 134 photos, 63-page index.
Cloth. $63.00. 736pp. .... Vendor G0418

4031 **THE VARNUMS OF DRACUT, MA. HIST. OF GEO. VARNUM, HIS SON SAMUEL & GRANDSONS THOMAS, JOHN & JOSEPH, & THEIR DESC.,** by J. Varnum. 1907.
Cloth, $59.50. Paper, $49.50. 314pp. .... Vendor G0259

4032 **ABRAHAM VAUGHAN OF KY. & DESC., A FAM. TREE,** by N.V. Ragland. Paper. $10.00. 55pp. .... Vendor G0259

4033 **REMINISCENCES & GEN. RECORD OF THE VAUGHAN FAM. OF N.H., BY G. HODGDON, SUPPL. BY AN ACCT. OF THE VAUGHANS OF SOUTH WALES, WITH PAPERS REL. TO THE VAUGHANS OF N.H., TAKEN OUT OF THE RECORDS IN LONDON,** by T.W. Hancock. 1918.
Cloth, $37.00. Paper, $27.00. 179pp. .... Vendor G0259

4034 **REMINISCENCES OF THE VAUGHAN FAM., & MORE PARTICU-LARLY OF BENJAMIN VAUGHAN, LL.D., WITH A FEW ADDITIONS, A GEN. & NOTES,** by J.H. Sheppard. 1865.
Paper. $8.00. 40pp. .... Vendor G0259

4035 **VAUGHAN PIONEERS: WILLIAM & FEREBY VAUGHAN OF RUSSELL CO., VA., & THEIR DESCENDANTS,** by Lewis E. Vaughan. 1979.
Cloth, $52.00. Paper, $42.00. 359pp. .... Vendor G0259

4036 **THE VAUGHANS IN WALES & AMERICA: A SEARCH FOR THE WELSH ANC. OF WILLIAM VAUGHAN (1750–1840)**, by James E. Vaughan. Rev. ed. 1992.
Cloth, $53.00. Paper, $43.00. 270pp. . . . . Vendor G0259

4037 **AMER. LIN. VEACH & STOVER FAM.**, by R.S. Veach. 1913.
Cloth, $36.50. Paper, $26.50. 134pp. . . . . Vendor G0259

4038 **VEBLEN GEN.; AN ACCT. OF THE NORWEGIAN ANC. OF THE VEBLEN FAM. IN AMER., WHICH WAS FOUNDED BY THOMAS A. VEBLEN & HIS WIFE KARI BUNDE**, by A. Veblen. 1925.
Cloth, $33.00. Paper, $23.00. 156pp. . . . . Vendor G0259

4039 **GEN. REC. OF THE VEEDER FAM.**, by V. Leonard. 1937.
Cloth, $65.00. Paper, $55.00. 351pp. . . . . Vendor G0259

4040 **VENABLES OF VA.**, by E.M. Venable. 1925.
Cloth, $50.00. Paper, $40.00. 228pp. . . . . Vendor G0259

4041 **HISTORY OF ABRAHAM ISAACSE VER PLANCK & HIS MALE DESCENDANTS IN AMERICA**, by Wm. E. Ver Planck. 1892.
Cloth, $57.00. Paper, $47.00. 304pp. . . . . Vendor G0259

4042 **JOHN VIALL OF SWANSEY, MASS., & SOME OF HIS DESC.**, by D. Jillson.
Paper. $7.50. 37pp. . . . . Vendor G0259

4043 **GEN. OF THE VIETS FAM. WITH BIOGR. SKETCHES. DR. JOHN VIETS OF SIMSBURY, CONN., 1710, & HIS DESC.**, by F.H. Viets. 1902.
Cloth, $44.50. Paper, $34.50. 228pp. . . . . Vendor G0259

4044 **GEN. OF DESC. OF PETER VILAS**, by C. Vilas. 1875.
Cloth, $46.00. Paper, $36.00. 221pp. . . . . Vendor G0259

4045 **FAM. OF VINCENT, HIST., GEN., & BIOGR. NOTICES**, by B. Vincent.
Cloth, $40.00. Paper, $30.00. 158pp. . . . . Vendor G0259

4046 **GEN. OF THE DESC. OF JOHN VINTON OF LYNN, 1648, & SEVERAL ALLIED FAMS.**, by J. Vinton. 1858.
Cloth, $48.00. Paper, $38.00. 252pp. . . . . Vendor G0259

4047 **VINTON MEM., COMPRISING A GEN. OF THE DESC. OF JOHN VINTON OF LYNN, 1648; ALSO 1648; ALSO GEN. SKETCHES OF SEVERAL ALLIED FAM.**, by J.A. Vinton. 1858.
Cloth, $78.00. Paper, $68.00. 554pp. . . . . Vendor G0259

4048 **VISSCHER FAM. EXTR. "GEN. NOTES OF NY & NEW ENG. FAMS.,"** by S.V. Talcott. 1883.
Paper. $9.00. 45pp. . . . . Vendor G0259

4049 **VOGT AND ALLIED FAMILIES, GENEALOGICAL & BIOGRAPHICAL [ONE LINE OF DESCENT FROM AUGUST JACOB WILHELM "WILLIAM" VOGT OF W.VA.].** 1926.
Paper. $11.00. 57pp. . . . . Vendor G0259

4050 **GENEALOGICAL & HISTORICAL RECORD OF THE VORCE FAM-**

ILY IN AMERICA, WITH NOTES OF ALLIED FAMILIES, by C.M. Vorce. 1901.
Cloth, $32.00. Paper, $22.00. 110pp. .... Vendor G0259

4051 **ROBERT VOSE & HIS DESCENDANTS,** by E.F. Vose. 1932.
Cloth, $109.50. Paper, $99.50. 725pp. .... Vendor G0259

4052 **HIST. & GEN. OF THE VREELAND FAM.,** by N.G. Vreeland. 1909.
Cloth, $58.50. Paper, $48.50. 323pp. .... Vendor G0259

4053 **VROOMAN FAMILY IN AMER.: DESC. OF HENDRICK MEESE VROOMAN, WHO CAME FROM HOLLAND TO AMER. IN 1664,** by G.V. Wickersham and E.B. Comstock. 1949.
Cloth, $63.00. Paper, $53.00. 341pp. .... Vendor G0259

4054 **WADE FAM., MONONGALIA CO., VA, NOW WV,** by F. Brand. 1927.
Cloth, $86.00. Paper, $76.00. 486pp. .... Vendor G0259

4055 **WADE GEN. ACCT. OF THE ORIGIN OF THE NAME, PEDIGREES OF FAMOUS ENGLISHMEN OF THE NAME; A GEN. OF THE FAM. IN MASS. & N.J.,** by S.C. Wade. 1900.
Cloth, $69.50. Paper, $59.50. 323pp. .... Vendor G0259

4056 **INDEX TO THE 1900 WADE GEN.**
Paper. $9.50. 49pp. .... Vendor G0259

4057 **WADHAM GENEALOGY, PRECEDED BY A SKETCH OF THE WADHAM FAM. IN ENG.,** by H.W.W. Stevens. 1913.
Cloth, $107.50. Paper, $97.50. 652pp. .... Vendor G0259

4058 **250 YEARS OF THE WADSWORTH FAM. IN AMER., AN ACCT. OF THE REUNION AT DUXBURY, MASS. & A GEN. REGISTER,** by H.A. Wadsworth. 1883.
Cloth, $44.50. Paper, $34.50. 257pp. .... Vendor G0259

4059 **HIST. OF THE WAGENSELLER FAM. IN AMER. WITH KINDRED BRANCHES,** by G.W. Wagenseller. 1898.
Cloth, $44.00. Paper, $34.00. 225pp. .... Vendor G0259

4060 **JOHN WAGLE GEN.,** by L.A. Duermyer. 1947.
Paper. $10.00. 50pp. .... Vendor G0259

4061 **THOSE WHO CAME BEFORE US: WAINWRIGHTS, MAYHEWS, STUYVESANTS & OTHERS,** by J.M. Wainwright. n.d.
Cloth, $42.00. Paper, $32.00. 203pp. .... Vendor G0259

4062 **RECORDS OF THE DESC. OF THOMAS WAIT OF PORTSMOUTH, R.I.,** by J.C. Wait. 1904.
Paper. $12.50. 58pp. .... Vendor G0259

4063 **WAITE FAMILY OF MALDEN, MASS.,** by D.P. Corey. 1913.
Paper. $19.50. 129pp. .... Vendor G0259

4064 **WAKEFIELD MEM., AN HIST., GEN., & BIOGR. REGISTER OF THE NAME & FAM.,** by H. Wakefield. 1897.
Cloth, $55.00. Paper, $45.00. 367pp. .... Vendor G0259

4065 **WAKEMAN GEN., 1630–1899. HIST. OF THE DESC. OF SAM'L WAKEMAN OF HARTFORD, CT. & OF JOHN WAKEMAN, TREAS. OF NEW HAVEN COL.**, by R. Wakeman. 1900.
Cloth, $78.00. Paper, $68.00. 438pp. .... Vendor G0259

4066 **HIST. & GEN. OF THE AMER. FAM. OF WALCOTT & NOTES OF ENG. WALCOTTS**, by A. Walcott. 1925.
Cloth, $53.00. Paper, $43.00. 288pp. .... Vendor G0259

4067 **CONTINUATION OF THE WALDO GENEALOGY, 1900–1943**, by C.S. Waldo. 1943.
Cloth, $56.50. Paper, $46.50. 295pp. .... Vendor G0259

4068 **GEN. OF THE WALDO FAM.; A RECORDS OF THE DESC. OF CORNELIUS WALDO OF IPSWICH, MASS., FROM 1647 TO 1900**, by W. Lincoln. 2 vols. 1902.
Cloth, $92.50/vol. Paper, $82.50/vol. 542+578pp. .... Vendor G0259

4069 **THE GEN. & BIOGR. OF THE WALDOS OF AMER., FROM 1650 TO 1883**, by J.D. Hall, Jr. 1883.
Cloth, $34.00. Paper, $24.00. 145pp. .... Vendor G0259

4070 **GEN. OF DESC. OF TIMOTHY WALES OF CONN.**, by W.H. Whitmore. 1875.
Paper. $12.00. 56pp. .... Vendor G0259

4071 **GEN. OF THE DESC. OF JOHN WALKER OF WIGTON, SCOTLAND, WITH RECORDS OF A FEW ALLIED FAM. ALSO WAR RECORDS & SOME FRAGMENT. NOTES PERTAINING TO THE HIST. OF VA., 1600–1902**, by E. S. White. 1902.
Cloth, $101.00. Paper, $91.00. 752pp. .... Vendor G0259

4072 **LEWIS WALKER OF CHESTER VALLEY & HIS DESC., 1686–1896**, by P.W. Streets. 1896.
Cloth, $79.50. Paper, $69.50. 446pp. .... Vendor G0259

4073 **MEM. OF THE WALKERS OF OLD PLYMOUTH COL. EMBRACING GEN. SKETCHES OF JAMES OF TAUNTON, PHILIP OF REHOBOTH,**

WM. OF EASTHAM, JOHN OF MARSHFIELD, THOMAS OF BRISTOL, & THEIR DESC., by J. Walker. 1861.
Cloth, $85.00. Paper, $75.00. 479pp. .... Vendor G0259

4074 **GEN. OF WALLACE FAM. OF PA.**, by J. Wallace. 1902.
Paper. $12.50. 60pp. .... Vendor G0259

4075 **WALLACE–BRUCE & CLOSELY RELATED FAMILIES, HISTORY & GENEALOGY**, by J. Wallace. 1930.
Cloth, $69.50. Paper, $59.50. 389pp. .... Vendor G0259

4076 **WALLACE FAM. OF SCOTLAND & VA. FROM "VA. GENS."**
Paper. $10.00. 53pp. .... Vendor G0259

4077 **EVERYTHING'S RELATIVE: THE WALLACH–LIMOZIN STORY**, by Eileen Lovett Wallach. 1989. Indexed. Illus.
Cloth. $42.00. 629pp. .... Vendor G0233

4078 **DESC. OF HENRY WALLBRIDGE WHO MARRIED ANNA AMOS, DEC. 25 1688, AT PRESTON, CONN., WITH NOTES ON ALLIED FAM. OF BRUSH, FASSETT, DEWEY, FORBES, GAGER, LEHMAN, MEECH, STAFFORD, SCOTT**, by W.G. Wallbridge. 1898.
Cloth, $68.00. Paper, $58.00. 369pp. .... Vendor G0259

4079 **THE MICHIGAN WALLINS: A HISTORY, FROM STRATFORD-ON-AVON, 1791, TO WALLINWOOD-ON-THE-GRAND, 1933**, by Van A. Wallin. 1933.
Cloth, $32.00. Paper, $22.00. 129pp. .... Vendor G0259

4080 **WALTHALL FAM.**, by E. T. Walthall. 1906.
Paper. $7.50. 33pp. .... Vendor G0259

4081 **THE HOUSE OF WALTMAN & ITS ALLIED FAM.**, by L.S. LaMance. 1928.
Cloth, $50.00. Paper, $40.00. 278pp. .... Vendor G0259

4082 **WALTON FAM. RECORDS, 1598–1898, WITH INTER-MARRIAGES WITH OAKES & SATONS, & THE PROCTOR FAM.**, by J.P. Walton. 1898.
Paper. $18.00. 88pp. .... Vendor G0259

4083 **WALTZ FAM. HIST. & GEN. RECORD, DESC. OF FRED. WALTZ**, by L. Waltz. 1884.
Cloth, $36.00. Paper, $26.00. 128pp. .... Vendor G0259

4084 **DESCENDANTS OF JOHN WILSON WALWORTH AND LENORA BELLE BOODY OF EATON COUNTY, MICHIGAN**, by Victor Harold Walworth. 1984. Indexed. Illus.
Ancestry, life, and descendants of pioneer couple. 157 illustrations, 430 names.
Hardbound. 6"x 9". $7.00. 176pp. .... Vendor G0033

4085 **WALWORTHS OF AMER., FIVE CHAPTERS OF FAM. HIST., WITH ADDITIONAL CHAPTERS OF GEN.**, by C.A. Walworth. 1897.
Cloth, $50.00. Paper, $40.00. 202pp. .... Vendor G0259

4086 **JOHN WAMPLER AND MAGDALENA GARBER FAMILY RECORD**, by Floyd R. Mason.
In process .... Vendor G0345

4087 **THE WANNERS: AN EARLY LANCASTER COUNTY, PENNSYLVA-NIA MENNONITE FAMILY**, by Irma Hess Stoltzfus. 1992.
Cloth. $28.00. 228pp. .... Vendor G0150

4088 **HIST. OF THE WANTON FAM. OF NEWPORT, R. I.**, by J.R. Bartlett. 1878.
Cloth, $39.00. Paper, $29.00. 152pp. .... Vendor G0259

4089 **HIST. OF THE WANZER FAM. IN AMER., SETTLED IN NEW AMSTERDAM, 1642–1920**, by W.D. Wanzer. 1920.
Cloth, $35.00. Paper, $25.00. 121pp. .... Vendor G0259

4090 **WARBASSE HISTORY: A STUDY IN THE SOCIOLOGY OF HERED-ITY IN TWO PARTS**, by J.P. Warbasse. 1954.
Paper. $34.00. 226pp. .... Vendor G0259

4091 **[Ward]. ANDREW WARDE & HIS DESC., 1597–1910, BEING A COMP. OF FACTS RELATING TO ONE OF THE OLDEST NEW ENG. FAM., & EMBRACING MANY FAM. OF OTHER NAMES**, by G.K. Ward. Rev. ed. 1910–11.
Cloth, $86.00. Paper, $76.00. 626pp. .... Vendor G0259

4092 **THE WM. WARD GEN. HIST. OF THE DESC. OF WM. WARD OF SUDBURY, MA., 1638–1925**, by C. Martyn. 1925.
Cloth, $104.50. Paper, $94.50. 767pp. .... Vendor G0259

4093 **WARD FAM. DESC. OF WM. WARD WHO SETTLED IN SUDBURY, MA. IN 1639, WITH AN APP. OF THE NAMES OF FAM. THAT HAVE INTERMARRIED WITH THEM**, by A. Ward. 1851.
Cloth, $45.00. Paper, $35.00. 265pp. .... Vendor G0259

4094 **BRIEF HIST. OF WARDELL FAM., 1734–1910**, by G.P. Smith. Rev. ed. 1910.
Cloth, $30.00. Paper, $20.00. 104pp. .... Vendor G0259

4095 **ANC., KIN & DESC. OF JOHN WARDEN & NARCISSA DAVIE WAR-DEN, WITH REC. OF SOME OTHER BRANCHES OF WARDEN FAM. IN AMER.**, by W. Warden. 1901.
Cloth, $48.00. Paper, $38.00. 256pp. .... Vendor G0259

4096 **WARE GEN.: ROBERT WARE OF DEDHAM, MA., & HIS LINEAL DESC.**, by E. Ware. 1901.
Cloth, $63.50. Paper, $53.50. 335pp. .... Vendor G0259

4097 **WARFIELD FAM. OF MD.**, by J.D. Warfield. 1898.
Paper. $16.50. 81pp. .... Vendor G0259

4098 **GEN. OF THE WARNE FAM. IN AMER., PRINCIPALLY THE DESC. OF THOMAS WARNE 1652–1722, A PROPRIETOR OF EAST N.J.**, by G. Lobaw. 1911.
Cloth. $109.00. Paper, $99.00. 701pp. .... Vendor G0259

4099 **DESC. OF ANDREW WARNER**, by L.C. Warner and J.G. Nichols. 1919.
Cloth, $125.00. Paper, $115.00. 804pp. .... Vendor G0259

4100 **SIR THOMAS WARNER, PIONEER OF THE WEST INDIES: A CHRONICLE OF HIS FAMILY**, by A. Warner. 1933 (London).
Cloth, $36.00. Paper, $26.00. 174pp. .... Vendor G0259

4101 A GEN. OF THE DESC. OF JAMES WARREN, WHO WAS IN KITTERY, MAINE, 1652–1656, by O. Warren. 1902.
Cloth, $30.50. Paper, $20.50. 138pp. .... Vendor G0259

4102 A HIST. & GEN. OF THE WARREN FAM. IN NORMANDY, GT. BRITAIN & IRELAND, FRANCE, HOLLAND, U.S., ETC., by T. Warren 1902.
Cloth, $87.50. Paper, $77.50. 494pp. .... Vendor G0259

4103 WARREN–CLARKE GEN., A REC. OF PERSONS REL. WITHIN THE 6TH DEGREE TO THE CHILDREN OF SAMUEL DENNIS WARREN & SUSAN CLARKE, by C.W. Huntington. 1894.
Cloth, $46.00. Paper, $36.00. 238pp. .... Vendor G0259

4104 WARREN, JACKSON & ALLIED FAMS., BEING THE ANC. OF JESSE WARREN & BETSEY JACKSON, by B.W. Davis. 1903.
Cloth, $42.50. Paper, $32.50. 207pp. .... Vendor G0259

4105 SOME DESC. OF ARTHUR WARREN OF WEYMOUTH, MASS. BAY COL., by W. Foster. 1911.
Cloth, $38.50. Paper, $28.50. 209pp. .... Vendor G0259

4106 WARRENS AND RELATED FAMILIES OF NORTH CAROLINA AND VIRGINIA, by Holland D. Warren, Ph.D. 1990. Indexed. Illus.
Descendants of John and Rachel **Warren**, who lived in Old Rappahannock County, Virginia, in the seventeenth century, are discussed. Associated families are **Williams, Hackley, Rogers, Burgess, Holt, Brooks, Stone, Murdoch, Brown, Shaver, McKaughan, DeBorde**, and **Wall**.
Cloth. $48.50. 442pp. .... Vendor G0230

4107 COLONIAL [NEW ENGLAND] & EURO. ANC. OF JULIA ADELAIDE WARRINER (1853–1883), by Richard L. Dickson. 1991.
Paper. $19.50. 123pp. .... Vendor G0259

4108 WARRINER FAM. OF NEW ENG. ORIGIN, HIST. & GEN. OF WM. WARRINER OF SPRINGFIELD, MA. & HIS DESC. 1638–1898, by E. Warriner. 1899.
Cloth, $53.00. Paper, $43.00. 287pp. .... Vendor G0259

4109 EBENEZER WASHBURN; HIS ANC. & DESC., WITH SOME CONNECTED FAM. A FAM. STORY OF 700 YEARS, by G.T. Washburn. 1913.
Cloth, $43.50. Paper, $33.50. 224pp. .... Vendor G0259

4110 GEN. NOTES OF THE WASHBURN FAM. WITH A BRIEF SKETCH OF THE FAM. IN ENG., CONTAINING A FULL REC. OF THE DESC. OF ISRAEL WASHBURN OF RAYNHAM, 1755–1841, by J.C. Washburn. 1898.
Paper. $18.00. 104pp. .... Vendor G0259

4111 THE RICHARD WASHBURN FAMILY GENEALOGY; A FAMILY HISTORY OF 200 YEARS, WITH SOME CONNECTED FAMILIES, by Ada C. Haight, assisted by Frank C. Lewis. 1937.
Cloth, $149.50. Paper, $139.50. 1271pp. .... Vendor G0259

4112 SOME NOTES ON THE EVESHAM BRANCH OF THE WASHBURNE FAM., by E. Barnard. 1914.
Paper. $12.00. 60pp. .... Vendor G0259

4113 **AN EXAMINATION OF THE ENG. ANC. OF GEO. WASHINGTON; THE EVIDENCE TO CONNECT HIM WITH THE WASHINGTONS OF SULGRAVE & BRINGTON, (REPR.** *NEHGR***)**, by H.F. Waters. 1889. Paper. $10.50. 53pp. .... Vendor G0259

4114 **DESCENDANTS OF JOHN AND LAWRENCE WASHINGTON OF VIRGINIA,** by Carol A. Hauk. 1995. Indexed. Paper. $35.00. 228pp. .... Vendor G0340

4115 **PEDIGREE & HIST. OF THE WASHINGTON FAM., DERIVED FROM ODIN, FOUNDER OF SCANDINAVIA, B.C. 70, DOWN TO GEN. GEO. WASHINGTON,** by A. Welles. 1879. Cloth, $76.00. Paper, $66.00. 420pp. .... Vendor G0259

4116 **ANCESTRY OF JOSEPH WATERHOUSE, 1754–1837, OF STANDISH, ME.,** by W.G. Davis. 1949. Cloth, $31.00. Paper, $21.00. 144pp. .... Vendor G0259

4117 **THE FAMILIES OF JACOB WATERHOUSE, 1605–1676,** by Jerry E. Waterous. 1993. Cloth, $44.00. Paper, $34.00. 228pp. .... Vendor G0259

4118 **DESC. OF ROBERT WATERMAN OF MARSHFIELD, MA., THROUGH SEVEN GENERATIONS,** by D.L. Jacobus. Vol. I. 1939. Cloth, $119.00. Paper, $109.00. 818pp. .... Vendor G0259

4119 **DESCENDANTS OF ROBERT WATERMAN OF MARSHFIELD, MA., FROM 7TH GENERATION,** by Waterman and Jacobus. Vol. II. 1942. Cloth, $115.00. Paper, $105.00. 784pp. .... Vendor G0259

4120 **DESC. OF RICHARD WATERMAN OF PROVIDENCE, R.I., WITH RECORDS OF MANY OTHER FAMILY GROUPS OF THE WATERMAN NAME,** by Jacobus and Waterman. Vol. III. 1954. Cloth, $118.00. Paper, $108.00. 808pp. .... Vendor G0259

4121 **A GEN. HIST. OF THE WATERS & KINDRED FAM.,** by P.B. Waters. 1902. Cloth, $38.00. Paper, $28.00. 189pp. .... Vendor G0259

4122 **WATERS FAM. FROM "ZIMMERMAN & ALLIED FAMS."** Paper. $7.50. 34pp. .... Vendor G0259

4123 **CATALOGUE OF THOMAS WATKINS OF CHICKAHOMONY IN VA.,** by F.N. Watkins. 1899. Paper. $10.00. 50pp. .... Vendor G0259

4124 **WATKINS FAM. OF N. C., DESC. OF LEVIN WATKINS (TO ALA. & MISS.),** by W.B. Watkins. Paper. $17.50. 85pp. .... Vendor G0259

4125 **HISTORY & GENEALOGY OF THE WATSON FAMILY, DESCENDANTS OF MATTHEW WATSON WHO CAME TO AMERICA IN 1718,** by J.D. and A.A. Bemis. 1894. Cloth, $37.00. Paper, $27.00. 163pp. .... Vendor G0259

4126 **JOHN WATSON OF HARTFORD, CONN., & HIS DESC.; A GEN.,** by T. Watson. 1865. Paper. $10.00. 47pp. .... Vendor G0259

4127 **"OF SCEPTRED RACE" (WATSON GEN.)**, by A. Watson. 1910.
Cloth, $70.00. Paper, $60.00. 389pp. .... Vendor G0259

4128 **WATSON**, by Mildred S. Ezell. 1987. Indexed. Illus.
Includes: **Watson, McAllister, Bickham, Venable, Nelson, Maxey**.
Paper. $30.00. 326pp. .... Vendor G0323

4129 **WATSON, KITTREDGE, BROADWELL & ALLIED FAMILIES, GEN. & BIOGR.**, compiled for Mrs T.J Watson. 1961.
Paper. $18.00. 89pp. .... Vendor G0259

4130 **AUTOBIOGRAPHY OF GURDON WALLACE WATTLES, WITH GE-NEALOGY**, by G.W. Wattles. 1922.
Cloth, $52.00. Paper, $42.00. 268pp. .... Vendor G0259

4131 **SOME DESCENDANTS OF THOMAS WATTS AND HANNAH RUST BOGGESS**, by Fred A. Rutledge. 1995. Indexed.
Over 100 entries on **Ansley, Hightower, Knight, Smith, SoRelle**.
Paper. $40.00. 498pp. .... Vendor G0441

4132 **WATTS (WATT) IN NY & SCOTLAND, ALSO WATTER, WATTYS, WATHES, ETC. IN ENG.**, by A. Welles. 1898.
Paper. $10.00. 48pp. .... Vendor G0259

4133 **ENG. ANC. OF THE WAYNE FAM. OF PENN.**, by E.J. Sellers. 1927.
Paper. $12.00. 56pp. .... Vendor G0259

4134 **WEATHERBY GENEALOGY, 1682–1936**, by George W. Weatherby, Jr. 1936.
Paper. $19.50. 110pp. .... Vendor G0259

4135 **GARRETT WEAVER FAMILY OF WESTMORELAND & FAYETTE COS. PA**, by James H. and Coletta Shaw. 1991. Indexed.
Paper. $10.00. 91pp. .... Vendor G0280

4136 **HENRY B. WEAVER'S DESCENDANTS**, by Elizabeth W. Shirk, Eva G. Weaver, and Mary M. Weaver. 1981.
Cloth. $23.00. 342pp. .... Vendor G0150

4137 **HISTORY & GENEALOGY OF A BRANCH OF THE WEAVER FAM-ILY**, by Lucius E. Weaver. 1928.
Cloth, $115.00. Paper, $105.00. 743pp. .... Vendor G0259

4138 **RECORD OF WM. WEAVER & HIS DESC. OF ILLINOIS**, by R.I. Weaver. 1925.
Cloth, $30.00. Paper, $20.00. 106pp. .... Vendor G0259

4139 **DESC. OF ANDREW WEBBER 1763–1845**, by L. Webber. 1897.
Paper. $11.00. 55pp. .... Vendor G0259

4140 **GEN. SKETCH OF DESC. OF SEVERAL BRANCHES OF THE WEBBER FAM., WHO CAME TO NY & NEW ENG. IN THE EARLY PART OF THE 17TH CENT**, by A. Button. 1878.
Paper. $9.00. 42pp. .... Vendor G0259

4141 **GEN. OF ONE BRANCH OF THE WEBSTER FAM., FROM THOMAS WEBSTER OF ORMESBY, CO. NORFOLK, ENG.**, by P. Webster. 1894.
Paper. $9.00. 45pp. .... Vendor G0259

4142 **HIST. & GEN. OF THE GOV. JOHN WEBSTER FAM. OF CONN.**, by W.H. and M.R. Webster. 2 vols. 1915.
Cloth, $119.00/vol. Paper, $109.00/vol. 833+827pp. . . . . Vendor G0259

4143 **SOME OF THE DESC. OF JOHN WEBSTER OF IPSWICH, MASS., 1634**, by J.C. Webster. 1912.
Paper. $18.50. 92pp. . . . . Vendor G0259

4144 **LEONARD WEEKS OF GREENLAND, N. H. & DESC., 1639–1888, WITH EARLY RECORDS OF FAM. CONNECTED**, by J. Chapman. 1889.
Cloth, $35.50. Paper, $25.50. 202pp. Vendor G0259

4145 **GEN. OF THE FAM. OF GEO. WEEKES, OF DORCHESTER, MASS., 1635–1650, WITH SOME INFO. IN REGARD TO OTHER FAM. OF THE NAME, ESP. THOMAS OF HUNTINGTON, L.I.**, by R.D. Weeks. 1885.
Cloth, $69.00. Paper, $59.00. 468pp. Vendor G0259

4146 **HIST. OF THE WEIKERT FAM. FROM 1735–1930**, by E.L. Weikert, Jr. 1930.
Cloth, $67.00. Paper, $57.00. 357pp. Vendor G0259

4147 **BIOGRAPHICAL SKETCHES & FAMILY RECORDS OF THE GABRIEL WEIMER & DAVID WEIMER FAMILIES**, by L.C. Potts. 1936.
Cloth, $52.50. Paper, $42.50. 270pp. Vendor G0259

4148 **THE ANC. & DESC. OF DANIEL WEIS, "GENTLEMAN-AT-ARMS," 1629**, by F.L. Weis. 1927.
Paper. $9.00. 45pp. . . . . Vendor G0259

4149 **WEITZEL MEM., HIST. & GEN. RECORD OF DESC. OF PAUL WEITZEL OF LANCASTER, PA., 1740**, by H. Hayden. 1883.
Paper. $17.00. 81pp. . . . . Vendor G0259

4150 **PHILIP WELCH OF IPSWICH, MASS., & HIS DESC.**, by A.M. Welch. 1947.
Cloth, $66.00. Paper, $56.00. 354pp. Vendor G0259

4151 **WELCH & ALLIED FAM.**, by G.C. Weaver. 1932.
Cloth, $58.00. Paper, $48.00. 312pp. Vendor G0259

4152 **HIST. OF THE WELD FAM., FROM 1632 TO 1878**, by C.W. Fowler. 1879.
Paper. $13.50. 64pp. . . . . Vendor G0259

4153 **HIST. OF THE WELLES FAM. IN ENGLAND, WITH THEIR DERIVA- TION IN THIS COUNTRY FROM GOV. THOMAS WELLES OF CONN.**, by Welles & Clements. 1874.
Cloth, $31.50. Paper, $21.50. 127pp. Vendor G0259

4154 **HIST. OF THE WELLES FAM. IN ENG. & NORMANDY, WITH THE DERIVATION FROM THEIR PROGENITORS OF SOME DESC. IN THE U.S.**, by A. Welles. Incl. 1989 index. 1876.
Cloth, $59.50. Paper, $49.50. 317+26pp. . . . . Vendor G0259

4155 **DESC. OF THOMAS WELLMAN OF LYNN, MASS.**, by J.W. Wellman. 1918.
Cloth, $99.00. Paper, $89.00. 596pp. Vendor G0259

4156 **GEN. & HIST. OF THE WELLMANS OF NEW ENG.**, by J. Wellman. 1867.
Paper. $13.00. 66pp. .... Vendor G0259

4157 **ANC. & DESC. OF COL. DANIEL WELLS (1760–1815) OF GREEN-FIELD, MASS.**, by S.C. Wells.
Paper. $13.00. 65pp. .... Vendor G0259

4158 **GEN. OF THE WELLS FAM. & FAMS. RELATED**, by G.W. Wells-Cushing. 1903.
Cloth, $42.00. Paper, $32.00. 205pp. .... Vendor G0259

4159 **GEN. OF WELLS FAM. OF WELLS, ME**, by C. Wells. 1874.
Paper. $16.50. 81pp. .... Vendor G0259

4160 **WELLS FAMILY**, by D.W. Norris and H.A. Feldmann. 1942.
Cloth, $76.50. Paper, $66.50. 437pp. .... Vendor G0259

4161 **WM. WELLS & DESC., 1755–1909**, by F. Wells. 1909.
Cloth, $31.50. Paper, $21.50. 117pp. .... Vendor G0259

4162 **WM. WELLS OF SOUTHOLD & HIS DESC., 1638–1878**, by C.W. Hayes. 1878.
Cloth, $59.50. Paper, $49.50. 300pp. .... Vendor G0259

4163 **DIRECT ANC. OF THE LATE JACOB WENDELL OF PORTSMOUTH, N. H., WITH SKETCH OF NEW NETHERLAND SETTLEMENT 1614–1664**, by J. Stanwood. 1882.
Paper. $10.00. 49pp. .... Vendor G0259

4164 **WENDELL FAM., EXTR. FROM "GEN. NOTES OF N. Y. & NEW ENG. FAM.,"** by S.V. Talcott. 1883.
Paper. $9.00. 45pp. .... Vendor G0259

4165 **THE WENGER BOOK: FOUNDATION BOOK OF AMERICAN WENGERS, INCLUDING VARIANT[S]**, by Samuel S. Wenger, Earle K. Wenger, Sr., and Helen I. Wenger. 1978.
Cloth. $54.50. 1,248pp. .... Vendor G0150

4166 **THE WENGER BOOK INDEX**, by Jay V. Wenger. 1989.
Cloth. $37.50. 340pp. .... Vendor G0150

4167 **WENTWORTH GEN., ENG. & AMER., IN 3 VOLS.**, by J. Wentworth. 1878.
Cloth, $105.00/vol. Paper, $95.00/vol. 711, 728, 803pp. ..... Vendor G0259

4168 **REC. OF DESC. OF JOHANN JOST WENTZ**, by R. Wentz. 1884.
Paper. $18.00. 89pp. .... Vendor G0259

4169 **JOHANNES WERBEL AND HIS DESCENDANTS. THE WARVEL–WARBLE FAMILY HISTORY 1740–1991**, by Ralph W. Morton and John H. Warvel. 1991. Indexed. Illus.
The book covers twelve generations of the **Werbel, Warble, Warvel,** and related families. His fifty grandchildren lived in Maryland, Virginia, Ohio, Indiana, and Illinois. Descendants are found in most states and Canada.
Related families are: **Abbott, Allen, Amspaugh, Armentrout, Armstrong, Babcock, Baker, Beam, Bowman, Bowser, Brandon, Brenne, Brown,**

Campbell, Clark, Cluts, Crick, Davis, Davison, Dean, Eaton, Ely, Eppard, Flick, Focht, Ford, Frey/Fry/Frye, Gearhart, Gebhart, Gedling, Gephart, Gibson, Goins, Good, Graybill, Harmon, Harris, Hartle, Hartzell, Havermale, Hawkins, Hawvermale, Henninger, Hensley, Herring, Huffman, Hypes, Johnson, Johnston, Jones, Kaylor, Kershner, Kingery, Lam, Lamb, Leap, Lilly, Logan, Long, May, McVay, Michael, Miller, Monger, Morris, Peterson, Price, Richards, Rodgers, Rogers, Sellers, Shaeffer, Shafer, Shifflet, Smith, Snyder, Stump, Taylor, Thomas, Thompson, Trump, Turner, Watson, Wertz, White, Williams, Wilson, York, Young.

The book is 8¹/₂" x 11", hardbound, with 848 pages acid free paper. 20,000 names in the index. Over 100 photographs. This family history represents over twenty-five years of research and contains information that has never before been available

Cloth. $59.95. 848pp. . . . . Vendor G0022

4170 **COUNTRY CARPENTER—JOSIAH C. WERNER**, by Catherine M. Rhoads. 1991. Indexed. Illus.

Intimate glimpses into turn-of-the-century lifestyle in a rural Pennsylvania community, extracted from 1884–1920 diaries of Lydia **Werner**, wife of Josiah Werner, country carpenter. Includes connections with other German families, many from the same ancestral village, Seifertshausen: **Ackerman, Baer, Baker, Bauman, Bittner, Hay, Keidel, Stahl, Walker, Lichty, Shaulis, Smith**.

Cloth. $19.50. 128pp. . . . . Vendor G0262

4171 **LYDIA, BLACKSMITH'S DAUGHTER: LIFE OF LYDIA STAHL WERNER 1862–1920**, by Ethel M. Woelfel and Robert E. Mognet. 1994. Illus.

Book is based on diaries of Lydia and her daughter, also letters between Lydia and her carpenter husband in Somerset Co. Pennsylvania. **Hay, Stahl, Walker**, and **Werner** families included.

Paper. $12.50. 162pp. . . . . Vendor G0273

4172 **THE JOHN JACKSON & ESTHER ANN WERTS FAMILY HISTORY**, by Philip W. Allen. 1994. Indexed.

Includes descendants (**May, McCoy, Allen**, etc.) of **Werts**.

Paper. $20.00. 348pp. . . . . Vendor G0373

4173 **ANCESTORS OF SHEPERD SALISBURY WEST 1876–1937—MY WORKING NOTEBOOK**, by William Sheperd West.

West family members include: Samuel Painter 1853–1922; William S., 1829–1905; Painter, –1832. Related families include **Moore, Timmons, Warren** primarily in Sussex County, Delaware and in nearby counties on Maryland's Eastern Shore. Interesting charts, photographs, etc. planned. Your information welcome.

Cloth. $25.00. Approx. 100pp. . . . . Vendor G0308

4174 **WEST FAM. REG.; IMPORTANT LINES TRACES, 1326–1928**, by L.B. Stone. 1928.

Cloth, $87.00. Paper, $77.00. 493pp. Vendor G0259

4175 **THE WESTS AND THE RAYS AND ALLIED LINES—SOUTHERN FAMILIES FROM THE COLONIES TO TEXAS**, by Nan Overton West. 1991. Indexed. Illus.

Allies include: **Lee, Boatner, Swain, Culver, Dean, Caldwell, Grant, Culpepper, Gillespie, Egner**.
Cloth. $45.00. 475pp. .... Vendor G0244

4176 **HIST. & GEN. OF THE ANC. & DESC. OF STUKELY WESTCOTT, ONE OF THIRTEEN ORIG. PROPS. OF PROVIDENCE PLANTATION & COL OF R.I.**, by R.L. Whitman. 1932.
Cloth, $76.50. Paper, $66.50. 435pp. .... Vendor G0259

4177 **WESTCOTT. BOOK OF APPENDICES TO VOLUME I**, by Roscoe L. Whitman.
Cloth, $79.00. Paper, $69.00. 457pp. .... Vendor G0259

4178 **GEN. OF WESTERVELT FAM.**, by Westervelt and Dickinson. 1905.
Cloth, $35.00. Paper, $25.00. 175pp. .... Vendor G0259

4179 **WETMORE FAMILY OF AMER. & ITS COLLATERAL BRANCHES**, by J.C. Wetmore. 1861.
Cloth, $94.00. Paper, $84.00. 672pp. .... Vendor G0259

4180 **JOHANNES WETZLER AND HIS DESCENDANTS**, by Mary Jo Hunavy. 1993. Indexed. Illus.
Other surnames include: **Kauffman, Rowe, Rubendall, Musser, Knisley, Zimmerman, Hostetler, Heckert, Klinger, Plette**. Originating Pennsylvania Counties Lebanon, Lancaster, Dauphin, Perry, Juniata, Mifflin, Berks, Blair.
Paper. $25.00. 301pp. .... Vendor G0276

4181 **ENGLISH RECORDS OF THE WHALEY FAMILY & ITS BRANCHES IN AMER.**, by S. Whaley. 1901.
Cloth, $46.50. Paper, $36.50. 234pp. .... Vendor G0259

4182 **WHEAT GEN. A HIST. OF THE WHEAT FAM. IN AMER., WITH A BRIEF ACCT. OF THE NAME & FAM. IN ENG. & NORMANDY**, by S.C. Wheat. Vol. 1. 1902.
Cloth, $32.00. Paper, $22.00. 122pp. .... Vendor G0259

4183 **GEN. OF WHEATLEY–WHEATLEIGH FAM. HIST. OF THE FAM. IN ENG. & AMER.**, by H. Wheatley. 1902.
Cloth, $35.00. Paper, $25.00. 154pp. .... Vendor G0259

4184 **GEN. OF A BRANCH OF THE WHEELERS**, by G. Wheeler. 1908.
Paper. $12.00. 61pp. .... Vendor G0259

4185 **GEN. OF SOME OF THE DESC. OF OBADIAH WHEELER OF CONCORD, &THOMAS THAXTER OF HINGHAM**, by H.M. Wheeler. 1898.
Paper. $15.00. 74pp. .... Vendor G0259

4186 **NOTES FROM "THE WHEELER FAM. IN AMER.," TOGETHER WITH NOTES ON THE DESC. OF ELISHA WHEELER OF SUDBURY, MA.** (1930?)
Cloth, $87.00. Paper, $77.00. 506pp. typescript. .... Vendor G0259

4187 **NOTES FROM "THE WHEELER FAM. IN AMER.", TOGETHER WITH NOTES ON THE DESC. OF ELISHA WHEELER OF SUDBURY, MA. OUTLINE OF FAMS. & INDEX.** (1942?)
Cloth, $34.00. Paper, $24.00. 159pp. .... Vendor G0259

4188 **THE GEN. & ENCYCLOPEDIC HIST. OF THE WHEELER FAM. IN AMER.**, compiled by the Amer. College of Gen., dir. by A.G. Wheeler. 1914. Cloth, $179.00. Paper, $169.00. 1,273pp. .... Vendor G0259

4189 **THE WHEELER FAM. OF RUTLAND, MASS., & SOME OF THEIR ANC.**, by D.M. Wheeler. 1924. Cloth, $34.00. Paper, $24.00. 137pp. .... Vendor G0259

4190 **WHEELER & WARREN FAM., DESC. OF GEORGE WHEELER OF CONCORD 1638, & JOHN WARREN OF BOSTON 1630**, by H. Wheeler. 1892. Cloth, $35.00. Paper, $25.00. 121pp. .... Vendor G0259

4191 **WHEELOCK FAM. OF CALAIS, VT.: THEIR AMER. ANCESTRY & DESC.**, by M.W. Waite. 1940. Cloth, $36.00. Paper, $26.00. 175pp. .... Vendor G0259

4192 **[Wheelwright]. A FRONTIER FAM.**, by E.M. Wheelwright. 1894. Paper. $7.00. 35pp. .... Vendor G0259

4193 **THE WHETZEL FAMILY OF ROCKINGHAM COUNTY, VA**, by Lewis H. Yankey. 1991. Indexed. Paper. $24.00. 212pp. .... Vendor G0365

4194 **BRIEF GEN. OF THE WHIPPLE FAM.**, by J.A. Boutelle. 1857. Paper. $7.50. 36pp. .... Vendor G0259

4195 **BRIEF GEN. OF WHIPPLE FAM. WHO SETTLED IN R.I.**, by H.E. Whipple. 1873. Paper. $12.50. 63pp. .... Vendor G0259

4196 **GEN. NOTES OF THE WHIPPLE–HILL FAM., WITH FRAGMENTARY RECORDS OF OTHER FAM.**, by J.W. Hill. 1897. Cloth, $30.00. Paper, $20.00. 106pp. .... Vendor G0259

4197 **THE JOHN WHIPPLE HOUSE IN IPSWICH, MASS., & THE PEOPLE WHO HAVE OWNED & LIVED IN IT**, by T.F. Waters. 1915. Paper. $11.00. 55pp. .... Vendor G0259

4198 **WHIPPLE–WRIGHT & ALLIED FAMILIES (WHIPPLE–WRIGHT, WAGER, WARD–PELL, McLEAN–BURNETT FAMILIES), WITH RECORD OF ALLIED FAMILIES**, by Charles H. Whipple. 1917. Cloth, $32.00. Paper, $22.00. 117pp. .... Vendor G0259

4199 **WHISNANTS THROUGH THE AGES**, by Raymond C. Whisnant. 1992. Indexed. Illus. Cloth. $70.00. 534pp. .... Vendor G0183

4200 **A FAMILY HISTORY OF WHITAKER, CLOUSE, FINLEY AND CONNECTED FAMILIES**, by Blanche Whitaker Jernigan. 1993. Indexed. Illus. Cloth. $43.75. 387pp. .... Vendor G0030

4201 **THE DIARY OF JOB WHITALL, GLOUCESTER COUNTY NEW JERSEY 1775–1779**, edited by Florence Friel. 1992. Indexed.
A unique account of opposing armies on **Whitall** land —"The Battle of Red Bank"—Hundreds of area names.
Paper. $16.50. 200pp. .... Vendor G0069

4202 **DESC. OF CHASE WHITCHER OF WARREN, N. H., FOURTH IN DESC. FROM THOMAS WHITTIER OF SALISBURY (HAVERHILL), MASS.,** by W. F. Whitcher. 1907.
Cloth, $30.00. Paper, $20.00. 135pp. Vendor G0259

4203 **WHITCOMB FAM. IN AMER., A BIOGR. GEN.,** by C. Whitcomb. 1904.
Cloth, $88.00. Paper, $78.00. 621pp. Vendor G0259

4204 **A BRIEF ACCT. OF THE FAM. OF WHITE & CLARKE,** by J.C. White. 1915.
Paper. $7.50. 37pp. . . . . Vendor G0259

4205 **ANC. OF JOHN BARBER WHITE & OF HIS DESC.,** by A.L. White. 1913.
Cloth, $66.00. Paper, $56.00. 355pp. Vendor G0259

4206 **ANC. CHRONOLOGICAL RECORD OF THE WM. WHITE FAM., FROM 1607–8 TO 1895,** by T. and S. White. 1895.
Cloth, $71.00. Paper, $61.00. 393pp. Vendor G0259

4207 **DESCENDANTS OF THOMAS WHITE, SUDBURY, MASS., 1638,** by E.W. Ford. 1952.
Paper. $17.00. 93pp. . . . . Vendor G0259

4208 **DESCENDANTS OF THOMAS WHITE OF SUDBURY, MASSACHU-SETTS, VOLUME II,** by Betty King and Alice Coyle Lunn. 1992. Indexed. Illus.
Cloth. $30.00. 199pp. . . . . Vendor G0394

4209 **GEN. REC. OF THE FAM. OF WHITE,** by J. White. 1878.
Paper. $9.00. 44pp. . . . . Vendor G0259

4210 **GENEALOGY OF DESCENDANTS OF JOHN WHITE OF WENHAM & LANCASTER, MASS., 1638–1900,** Vol. I., by A.L. White. 1900.
Cloth, $125.00. Paper, $115.00. 931pp. . . . . Vendor G0259

4211 **GENEALOGY OF DESCENDANTS OF JOHN WHITE OF WENHAM & LANCASTER, MASS., 1638–1903,** Vol. II, by A.L. White. 1903.
Cloth, $123.00. Paper, $113.00. 924pp. . . . . Vendor G0259

4212 **GENEALOGY OF DESCENDANTS OF JOHN WHITE OF WENHAM & LANCASTER, MASS., 1638–1905,** Vol. III, by A.L. White. 1905.
Cloth, $115.00. Paper, $105.00. 754pp. . . . . Vendor G0259

4213 **GENEALOGY OF DESCENDANTS OF JOHN WHITE OF WENHAM & LANCASTER, MASS., 1638–1909,** Vol. IV, by A.L. White. 1909.
Cloth, $42.00. Paper, $32.00. 210pp. Vendor G0259

4214 **GEN. OF WHITE FAM.,** by J. Nichols-Vanderpool. 1899.
Cloth, $30.00. Paper, $20.00. 104pp. Vendor G0259

4215 **GENESIS OF THE WHITE FAM: A REC. OF THE WHITE FAM. BE-GINNING IN 900 AT THE TIME OF ITS WELSH ORIGIN WHEN THE NAME WAS WYNN, & TRACING THE FAM. INTO IRELAND & ENG. ALSO SCOTTS OF SCOT'S HALL, KENT, ENG,** by E.S. White. 1920.
Cloth, $65.00. Paper, $55.00. 346pp. Vendor G0259

4216 **MEMOIRS OF ELDER JOHN WHITE, ONE OF THE FIRST SETTLERS OF HARTFORD, CONN., & OF HIS DESC.,** by A. Kellogg. 1860.
Cloth, $64.00. Paper, $54.00. 340pp. . . . . Vendor G0259

4217 **NORMAN WHITE, HIS ANCESTORS & DESCENDANTS,** by E.N. White. 1905.
Cloth, $35.00. Paper, $25.00. 155pp. . . . . Vendor G0259

4218 **THE DESC. OF THOMAS WHITE OF MARBLEHEAD, & MARK HASKELL OF BEVERLY, MASS., WITH BRIEF NOTICE OF THE COOMBE FAM.,** by P. Derby. 1872.
Paper. $16.50. 82pp. . . . . Vendor G0259

4219 **THE DESC. OF WM. WHITE, OF HAVERHILL, MASS.** Gen. notices by D.A.White, 1863; additional gen. & biogr. notices, by A.F. Richards. 1889.
Paper. $16.50. 80pp. . . . . Vendor G0259

4220 **THE NICHOLAS WHITE FAM., 1643–1900,** by T.J. Lothrop. 1902.
Cloth, $73.00. Paper, $63.00. 493pp. . . . . Vendor G0259

4221 **THE WHITE GENEALOGY. A HISTORY OF THE DESCENDANTS OF MATTHEW & ELIZABETH (GIVEN) WHITE OF CO. TYRONE, IRELAND, & ALBANY, N.Y.** Orig. comp. in 1908, updated in 1951 & 1987. **VOL. I: THE LINE OF JOSEPH & ELIZABETH (WHITE) STRAIN,** by Harold Putnam White, Jr. 1991.
Cloth, $45.00. Paper, $35.00. 236pp. . . . . Vendor G0259

4222 **THE WHITE GEN. A HIST. OF THE DESC. OF MATTHEW & ELIZABETH (GIVEN) WHITE OF CO. TYRONE, IRELAND, & ALBANY, NY.** Orig. compiled in 1908; updated in 1951 & 1987. **VOL. II: THE LINE OF WILLIAM & LAURA (PUTNAM) WHITE,** by Harold Putnam White, Jr. 1988.
Cloth, $45.40. Paper, $35.50. 234pp. . . . . Vendor G0259

4223 **[White]. ABOVE, VOL. III: THE LINE OF JOHN G. & HANNAH (PUTNAM) WHITE.** 1989.
Cloth, $63.50. Paper, $53.50. 370pp. . . . . Vendor G0259

4224 **THE WHITE GENEALOGY, VOL. IV: THE LINES OF ANDREW & LILLIA (RISK) WHITE; REV. JAMES & REBECCA (WHITE) MARTIN. DESCENDANTS OF MATTHEW & ELIZABETH (GIVEN) WHITE,** by Harold P. White, Jr. 1990.
Cloth, $49.00. Paper, $39.00. 253pp. . . . . Vendor G0259

4225 **YOUR FAM.: AN INFORMAL ACCT. OF THE ANC. OF ALLEN KIRBY WHITE & EMMA CHAMBERS WHITE [INCL. WHITE, ALLEN, CHAMBERS, HAYES FAMS.],** by E. White. 1941.
Cloth, $42.00. Paper, $32.00. 196pp. . . . . Vendor G0259

4226 **WHITFIELD HISTORY AND GENEALOGY OF TENNESSEE,** by Vallie Jo Whitfield. Indexed. Illus.
Cloth. $15.00. 315pp. . . . . Vendor G0253

4227 **WHITFIELD RECORDS OF THE UNITED STATES,** by Vallie Jo Whitfield. 1996.
Cloth. $30.00. 560pp. . . . . Vendor G0253

4228 **WHITIN FAMILY HIST. NOTES,** by K.W. Swift. 1955.
Cloth, $42.00. Paper, $32.00. 216pp. .... Vendor G0259

4229 **MEM. OF REV. SAM'L WHITING & HIS WIFE ELIZABETH ST JOHN; WITH REF. TO SOME OF THEIR ENG. ANC. & AMER. DESC.,** by W. Whiting. 2nd ed. 1873.
Cloth, $63.00. Paper, $53.00. 334pp. .... Vendor G0259

4230 **NATHANIEL WHITING OF DEDHAM, MA., 1641, & FIVE GENERA-TIONS OF HIS DESC.,** by T.S. Lazell. 1902.
Paper. $16.00. 80pp. .... Vendor G0259

4231 **HIST. OF THE DESC. OF JOHN WHITMAN OF WEYMOUTH, MASS.,** by C.H. Farnam. 1889.
Cloth, $167.00. Paper, $157.00. 1,261pp. .... Vendor G0259

4232 **MEM. OF JOHN WHITMAN & HIS DESC.,** by E. Whitman. 1832.
Paper. $9.00. 44pp. .... Vendor G0259

4233 **NOTES ON THE WHITMORES OF MADELEY, ENG., & THE FARRARS & BREWERS OF ESSEX CO., MASS.,** by W.H. Whitmore. 1875.
Paper. $9.50. 47pp. .... Vendor G0259

4234 **WHITMORE GEN., RECORD OF DESC. OF FRANCIS WHITMORE OF CAMBRIDGE,** by J. Purdy. 1907.
Cloth, $40.00. Paper, $30.00. 158pp. .... Vendor G0259

4235 **ANC. OF JOHN WHITNEY, WHO EMIGRATED FROM LONDON IN 1635, & SETTLED IN WATERTOWN, MASS., THE FIRST OF THE NAME IN AMER. & THE ONE FROM WHOM A GREAT MAJORITY OF THE WHITNEYS IN THE U.S. ARE DESC.,** by H. Melville. 1896.
Cloth, $48.50. Paper, $38.50. 692pp. .... Vendor G0259

4236 **WHITNEY FAM. OF CONN. & ITS AFFILIATIONS, BEING AN AT-TEMPT TO TRACE THE DESC. OF HENRY WHITNEY, FROM 1649, TO WHICH IS PREFIXED SOME ACCT. OF THE WHITNEYS OF ENG.,** by S.W. Phoenix. 3 vols. 1878.
Cloth, $140.00/vol. Paper, $130.00/vol. 2,766pp. .... Vendor G0259

4237 **THE DESC. OF JOHN WHITNEY, WHO CAME FROM LONDON, ENG. TO WATERTOWN, MA., IN 1635,** by F. Pierce. 1895.
Cloth, $95.00. Paper, $85.00. 692pp. .... Vendor G0259

4238 **WHITON FAM. IN AMER. THE DESC. OF THOMAS WHITON (1635),** by A.S. Whiton. 1932.
Cloth, $49.00. Paper, $39.00. 258pp. .... Vendor G0259

4239 **GEN. OF THE WHITTELSEY–WHITTLESEY FAM.,** by C.B. Whittelsey. 1898.
Cloth, $63.00. Paper, $53.00. 414pp. .... Vendor G0259

4240 **A GEN. OF SEVERAL BRANCHES OF THE WHITTEMORE FAM., INCL. THE ORIGINAL WHITTEMORE FAM. OF HITCHIN, HERTS., ENG., & A BRIEF LINEAGE OF OTHER BRANCHES,** by B.B. Whittemore. 1890.
Cloth, $30.00. Paper, $20.00. 106pp. .... Vendor G0259

4241 **ANC. OF REV. WM. HOWE WHITTEMORE, BOLTON, CONN., 1800—RYE, N.Y., 1885, & OF HIS WIFE MARIA CLARK, N.Y., 1803—BROOKLYN, 1886,** by W.P. Bacon. 1907.
Cloth, $32.00. Paper, $22.50. 124pp. Vendor G0259

4242 **GEN. OF SEVERAL BRANCHES OF THE WHITTEMORE FAM.,** by B.B. Whittemore. 1893.
Cloth, $35.00. Paper, $25.00. 132pp. Vendor G0259

4243 **DESC. OF THOMAS WHITTIER & RUTH GREEN OF SALISBURY & HAVERHILL, MA.,** by C. Whittier. 1937.
Cloth, $99.00. Paper, $89.00. 594pp. Vendor G0259

4244 **MEM. OF THE WHITTLESEY FAM. IN THE U. S. (THE WHITTLESEY ASSN. PUBN.).** 1855.
Cloth, $33.00. Paper, $23.00. 131pp. Vendor G0259

4245 **WIARD FAM.,** by G.K. Collins and W.W. Wiard. 1912.
Paper. $12.00. 61pp. . . . . Vendor G0259

4246 **THE WIATT FAMILY OF VIRGINIA,** by Alexander L. Wiatt. 1980. Indexed. Illus.
The descendants of John **Wiatt**, Jr. (1732–1805) of Gloucester County, Virginia and his wife, Mary Todd, are traced with a monograph about each family member. The work also includes John's lineal descent from Adam **Wiot**, who lived in the mid-1300s in Yorkshire England, through the Rev. Haute **Wiat**, who came to America in 1619. There is also information on collateral families. These include: **Field, Carter, Todd, Cocke, Ball, Montague, Jones,** and other **Wiatt** families not descendants of John.
Cloth. $12.50. 186pp. . . . . Vendor G0137

4247 **ANCESTORS OF JAMES WICKHAM & HIS WIFE CORA PRUDENCE BILLARD,** by J.C. Frost. 1935.
Cloth, $42.50. Paper, $32.50. 207pp. Vendor G0259

4248 **GEN. OF THE WICKWARE FAM., CONTAINING AN ACCT. OF THE ORIGIN & EARLY HIST. OF THE NAME & FAM. IN ENGLAND; THE**

REC. OF JOHN WICKWARE, WHO EMIGR. TO NEW LONDON, CONN., IN 1675, & HIS DESC. IN AMER., by A.M. Wickwire. 1909.
Cloth, $47.50. Paper, $37.50. 283pp. .... Vendor G0259

4249 MEM. OF THOMAS WIGHT OF DEDHAM, WITH GEN. NOTICES OF HIS DESC., 1637–1840, by D.P. Wight. 1848.
Cloth, $37.50. Paper, $27.50. 119pp. .... Vendor G0259

4250 THE WIGHTS. THOMAS WIGHT OF DEDHAM & MEDFIELD, & HIS DESC., 1635–1890, by W. Wight. 1890.
Cloth, $68.00. Paper, $58.00. 368pp. .... Vendor G0259

4251 GEORGE WIGHTMAN OF QUIDNESSETT, R.I. (1632–1721/2) & DESC., INCL. WAITMAN, WEIGHTMAN, WHITEMAN, WHITMAN, by M.R. Whitman. 1939.
Cloth, $83.50. Paper, $73.50. 486pp. .... Vendor G0259

4252 GEN. RECORD OF THE WILBUR FAM., by A. Wilbur. 1871.
Paper. $18.50. 89pp. .... Vendor G0259

4253 [Wilbur]. THE WILDBORES IN AMER: A FAM. TREE., compiled by J.R. Wilbor and B.F. Wilbour. 5 vols. Rev. ed. 1933–8.
Cloth, $54.00/vol. Paper, $44.00/vol. 486pp. .... Vendor G0259

4254 DANIEL WILCOX OF PORTSMOUTH, R.I. & DESC., by H.F. Johnston.
Paper. $7.50. 36pp. .... Vendor G0259

4255 EDW. WILCOX OF RI & DESC., by H. Johnston.
Cloth, $35.00. Paper, $25.00. 134pp. .... Vendor G0259

4256 JOHN WILCOX OF HARTFORD, CONN. & DESC., by H.F. Johnston. 1948.
Paper. $10.00. 52pp. .... Vendor G0259

4257 WILLIAM WILCOX OF STRATFORD, CONN. & DESC., by H.F. Johnston.
Cloth, $36.00. Paper, $26.00. 138pp. .... Vendor G0259

4258 DESC. OF WILLIAM WILCOXSON, VINCENT MEIGS & RICHARD WEBB, by R.W. Wilcox. 1893.
Paper. $12.50. 83pp. .... Vendor G0259

4259 WILCOXSON & ALLIED FAMS. (WILLCOCKSON, WILCOXEN, WILCOX), by D.F. Wulfeck. 1958.
Cloth, $87.00. Paper, $77.00. 505pp. .... Vendor G0259

4260 BOOK OF THE WILDERS. THE HIST. FROM 1497 IN ENG., THE EMIGRATION OF MARTHA, A WIDOW, & HER FAM. TO MASS. BAY IN 1638, HER FAM. TO 1875 WITH A GEN. TABLE, by Rev. M. Wilder. 1878.
Cloth, $60.00. Paper, $50.00. 410pp. .... Vendor G0259

4261 WILDES FAM. OF ESSEX CO., MASS., by W. Davis. 1906.
Paper. $12.00. 61pp. .... Vendor G0259

4262 JOHN WILDRICK OF NEW JERSEY, 1707–1793; GENEALOGY OF THE DESCENDANTS OF HIS SON GEORGE WILDRICK, by W.C. Armstrong. 1933.
Paper. $14.00. 67pp. .... Vendor G0259

4263 **FAM. OF BRAY WILKINS, PATRIACH OF WILL'S HILL OF SALEM (MIDDLETON), MA.,** by W. Hill. 1943.
Cloth, $42.00. Paper, $32.00. 213pp. .... Vendor G0259

4264 **GEN. OF WILKINSON & KINDRED FAMS. (SOUTHERN BRANCH),** by M.M. Wilkinson. 1949.
Cloth, $92.50. Paper, $82.50. 546pp. .... Vendor G0259

4265 **MEM. OF THE WILKINSON FAM. IN AMER. GEN. SKETCHES OF LAWRENCE OF PROVIDENCE, RI, EDW. OF NEW MILFORD, CT., JOHN OF ATTLEBOROUGH, MA., DANIEL OF COLUMBIA CO., NY, ETC., & THEIR DESC. 1645–1868,** by I. Wilkinson. 1869.
Cloth, $99.00. Paper, $89.00. 589pp. .... Vendor G0259

4266 **THE WILKINSON BOOK,** by Patricia Wilkinson Weaver Balletta. 1994. Indexed. Illus.
History of Major General James **Wilkinson** (1757–1825). In retrograde all known progenitors are covered. Maryland, Pennsylvania, Alabama and British Royal lines are listed; including Magna Charta Sureties. **Biddle, Trudeau, Heighe, Skinner, MacKall, Storer, Morgan, Owen, Babington, Smith, Kempe, Wilkinson, Andrews, Penrose, Tompkins.**
Cloth. $75.00. 513pp. .... Vendor G0215

4267 **WILLARD MEMOIR, OR LIFE & TIMES OF MAJ. SIMON WILLARD, WITH NOTICES OF THREE GEN. OF HIS DESC., & TWO COLL. BRANCHES IN THE U.S.,** by J. Willard. 1858.
Cloth, $82.75. Paper, $72.75. 484pp. .... Vendor G0259

4268 **WILLARD GEN.; SEQUEL TO WILLARD MEMOIR,** by Willard and Walker, edited and compiled by C.H. Pope. 1915.
Cloth, $103.50. Paper, $93.50. 776pp. .... Vendor G0259

4269 **GEN. OF THE WILLCOMB FAM. OF NEW ENG. (1665–1902), TOGETHER WITH A CONDENSED HIST. OF THE TOWN OF IPSWICH, MASS.,** by O.C. Willcomb. 1902.
Cloth, $58.00. Paper, $48.00. 302pp. .... Vendor G0259

4270 **IVY MILLS, 1729–1866: WILLCOX & ALLIED FAMILIES,** by J. Willcox. 1911.
Cloth, $33.00. Paper, $23.00. 139pp. .... Vendor G0259

4271 **A UNION SOLDIER RETURNS SOUTH, THE CIVIL WAR LETTERS AND DIARY OF ALFRED C. WILLETT, 113TH OHIO VOLUNTEER INFANTRY,** edited by Charles E. Willett. 1994. Indexed. Illus.
Follows 113th OVI through war. Synopsis of family genealogy.
Cloth. $14.95. 134pp. .... Vendor G0271

4272 **THE ALFRED C. WILLETT FAMILY HISTORY,** by Charles E. Willett. 1994. Indexed. Illus.
Thomas and Ursula **Rogers** and Newman **Willett** family of England. Jacob **Snider** and Christina **Arres** family of Germany. More recent names: **Hipp, Moomaw, Redman, Catlin,** and **Harwood.**
Cloth. $40.00. 275pp. .... Vendor G0271

4273 **ANCESTORS OF MARGIE WILLEY 1877–1937—MY WORKING NOTEBOOK,** by William Sheperd West.

Willey family members include: James, 1836–1911, herein of three wives and twenty-one children; John, 1806–1877. Related families include **Saterfield, Brown, Higman**. Primarily in Sussex County, Delaware and in nearby counties of Maryland's Eastern Shore. Your information welcome. Interesting charts, photographs, etc. planned.
Cloth. $25.00. Approx. 100pp. .... Vendor G0308

4274 **ISAAC WILLEY OF NEW LONDON, CONN., & HIS DESC.**, by H. Willey. 1888.
Cloth, $38.00. Paper, $28.00. 189pp. .... Vendor G0259

4275 **ANC. OF LAWRENCE WILLIAMS. PT. I, ANC. OF HIS FATHER, SIMON BREED WILLIAMS; PT. II, ANC. OF HIS MOTHER, CORNELIA JOHNSTON**, by C. Williams. 1915.
Cloth, $53.50. Paper, $43.50. 291pp. .... Vendor G0259

4276 **DESC. OF JOHN WILLIAMS, OF NEWBURY & HAVERHILL, MA., 1600–1674**, by C. and A. Williams. 1925.
Cloth, $38.50. Paper, $28.50. 179pp. .... Vendor G0259

4277 **DESCENDANTS OF ROGER WILLIAMS BOOK I; WATERMAN LINE, WINSOR LINE**, by Dorothy Higson White and Kay Kirlin Moore. 1991. Indexed.
Paper. $28.00. 403pp. .... Vendor G0062

4278 **DESC. OF VEACH WILLIAMS OF LEBANON, CT.**, by A.H. Wright. 1887.
Cloth, $40.00. Paper, $30.00. 186pp. .... Vendor G0259

4279 **[Williams]. EXTR. FROM "HIST. OF WETHERSFIELD, CONN."** 1904.
Paper. $7.50. 38pp. .... Vendor G0259

4280 **GEN. NOTES OF THE WILLIAMS & GALLUP FAM., ESP. REL. TO THE CHILDREN OF CALEB & SABRA GALLUP WILLIAMS, DESC. OF ROBERT WILLIAMS OF ROXBURY, & CAPT. JOHN GOLLOP, SR. OF BOSTON, MASS.**, by C.F. Williams. 1897.
Cloth, $30.50. Paper, $20.50. 136pp. .... Vendor G0259

4281 **GENEALOGY OF WILLIAMS FAMILIES: WM. WILLIAMS OF NEW LONDON CO., GROTON & LEDYARD CT, & EMANUEL WILLIAMS OF TAUNTON MA**, by J.O. Williams. 1938.
Cloth, $44.00. Paper, $34.00. 215pp. .... Vendor G0259

4282 **HIST. & BIOGR. SKETCH OF THE WILLIAMS FAM. OF MASS., CONN., R.I., N.J., PENN. & MD.**
Paper. $9.00. 46pp. .... Vendor G0259

4283 **LIFE, ANC. & DESC. OF ROBERT WILLIAMS OF ROXBURY, MASS., 1607–1693, WITH BIOGR. SKETCHES**, by H. Williams. 1934.
Cloth, $43.00. Paper, $33.00. 216pp. .... Vendor G0259

4284 **ROGER WILLIAMS OF PROVIDENCE, R.I. [& DESC.]**, by B.W. Anthony and H.W. Weeden. 2 vols. 1949, 1966.
Cloth, $74.00. Paper, $64.00. 433pp. .... Vendor G0259

4285 **THE ANC. & DESC. OF EZEKIEL WILLIAMS OF WETHERSFIELD, 1608–1907**, by M.D.W. McLean. 1907.
Paper. $18.50. 92pp. .... Vendor G0259

JUST PUBLISHED

PLANTAGENET DESCENT

31 Generations
from William the Conqueror to Today

by
THOMAS R. MOORE

Hard cover, dust jacket, fully indexed, 45 pages of illustrations, 20 pages in color; xviii, 242 pages, Gateway Press, Inc. (1995), ISBN 0-9644929-0-3, $49.50

Shortly before the death of Napoleon's nemesis the Duke of Wellington, the Ulster King of Arms compiled the Registered Pedigree of Sir Richard Cooke, Secretary of State, and his wife Anne Peyton. The Registered Pedigree traced Anne Peyton's lineage back to Princess Elizabeth Plantagenet and forward to the Duke of Wellington, to his brother the Marquess Wellesley who would become the ancestor of Queen Elizabeth II, and to Frances Cooke whose son-in-law William Moore came to North America.

This brilliant book fleshes out and brings to life the 30 lineal couples from William the Conqueror and Queen Matilda in 1066, both descendants of the Emperor Charlemagne, through the royalty, nobility and gentry of England, through the Elizabethan Age, through high offices in Ireland, to William Moore who came to Canada in 1817, then down one line of his estimated 55,000 descendants alive today (with many surnames) to contemporary joyous professional and personal lives in Manhattan.

Many of us share part of the same 1,000 year history and genealogy but lack the records to know it. All, however, will revel in this human, exciting and true story.

Thomas R. Moore, the distinguished New York lawyer, author and connoisseur, received his B.A. *magna cum laude* from Yale University and his J.D. from Harvard Law School. His deep knowledge of biography, genealogy and history and his legal ability to present a story clearly and compellingly captivates his readers from beginning to end.

Order from: **Thomas R. Moore, Esq.**
1170 Fifth Avenue, Suite 2A
New York, NY 10029

$49.50 including postage

4286 **THE COMPLETE ANCESTRY OF TENNESSEE WILLIAMS**, by John A. Brayton. 1995. Impressively indexed, with slave index.

The playwright's ancestry back seventeen generations, with royal descents, and original research on the following colonial families: **Baker, Carnes, Clark, Huddlestone, Mortimer, Nickerson, Salmon**, and **Topham/Tappan** of New England; **Bellar, Bowker**, and **Evans** of Virginia; **Lawson** and **White** of North Carolina; **Cooke, Everedd** alias **Webb, Greenleaf, Lanier, Plume**, and **Purcas** of England.

Cloth. $35.00 postpaid, NC residents add 6% sales tax.

490+xxxii pp. .... Vendor G0302

4287 **THE ANCESTRY OF GEN. JAMES ROBERTSON, "FATHER OF TENNESSEE," AN ADDENDUM TO THE COMPLETE ANCESTRY OF TENNESSEE WILLIAMS**, by John A. Brayton . 1995. Impressively indexed.

Families of **Robinson** of Henrico Co., VA, and **Robertson** of NC and Middle Tennessee; **Cunningham** of Washington Co., TN; **Marks** of Prince George Co., VA.

Paper. $10.00 postpaid, NC residents add 6% sales tax.

60+viii pp. .... Vendor G0302

4288 **THE GEN. & HIST. OF THE FAM. OF WILLIAMS IN AMER., MORE PARTICULARLY OF THE DESC. OF ROBERT WILLIAMS OF ROXBURY**, by S.W. Williams. 1847.

Cloth, $76.50. Paper, $66.50. 424pp. .... Vendor G0259

4289 **THE GROVES & LAPPAN (MONAGHAN CO., IRE.) ACCT. OF A PILGRIMAGE THITHER, IN SEARCH OF THE GEN. OF THE WILLIAMS FAM.**, by J. Williams. 1889.

Paper. $13.50. 68pp. .... Vendor G0259

4290 **WILLIAMS CHRONICLE. DESC. OF THOMAS WILLIAMS OF SULLIVAN CO., N.Y., & JEFFERSON CO., PA., INCL. REL. FAMS.**, by F.H. Ehrig. 1969.

Cloth, $39.50. Paper, $29.50. 198pp. .... Vendor G0259

4291 **THE WILLIAMSON & COBB FAM. IN THE LINES OF CALEB & MARY (COBB) WILLIAMSON OF BARNSTABLE, MASS., & HARTFORD, CONN.**, by F.F. Starr. 1896.

Paper. $12.50. 66pp. .... Vendor G0259

4292 **TIMOTHY WILLIAMSON OF MARSHFIELD, MASS. (REPR. *NEHGR*)**, by G.W. Edes.

Cloth, $32.50. Paper, $22.50. 132pp. .... Vendor G0259

4293 **DESCENDANTS OF FRANCIS WILLIS OF VIRGINIA**, by Carol A. Hauk. 1995. Indexed.

Paper. $30.00. 129pp. .... Vendor G0340

4294 **HIST. OF THE WILLIS FAM. OF NEW ENG. & NJ, & THEIR ANC., TO WHICH IS ADDED A HIST. OF THE FAM. OF JOHN HOWARD OF RICHMOND, VA., & THE HARRIS & MACLEOD FAM. OF GA.**, by C. and F. Willis. 1917.

Cloth, $62.75. Paper, $52.75. 352pp. .... Vendor G0259

4295 **RECORDS OF THE WILLIS FAM. OF HAVERHILL, PORTLAND & BOSTON**, by P. Willis. 2nd ed. 1908.
Cloth, $32.50. Paper, $22.50. 130pp. .... Vendor G0259

4296 **SKETCH OF THE WILLIS FAM., FREDERICKSBURG BRANCH**, by B.C. Willis. 1909.
Cloth, $32.50. Paper, $22.50. 116pp. .... Vendor G0259

4297 **SKETCH OF THE WILLIS FAMILY OF VA., & OF THEIR KINDRED IN OTHER STATES, WITH BRIEF BIOGRAPHIES OF THE READES, WARNERS, LEWISES, BYRDS, CARTERS, ETC.**, by B.C. Willis and R.H. Willis. 1898.
Cloth, $35.00. Paper, $25.00. 160pp. .... Vendor G0259

4298 **THE GENEALOGY OF JOSHUA WILLIS**, by Mildred S. Ezell. 1994. Indexed. Illus.
Includes: **Willis, Harris, Thomason, Moreland, Birch, Malone, Nicholson, Winston.**
Paper. $20.00. 167pp. .... Vendor G0323

4299 **WILLS FAM.; DESC. OF DANIEL WHO EMIGR. TO BURLINGTON, N.J. IN 1677. EXTR. HAINES GEN.** 1902.
Paper. $10.00. 52pp. .... Vendor G0259

4300 **[Wilson]. DEAR JOHN**, by Leland E. Wilson. 1989. Indexed. Illus.
Trygstad, Benson, Wilson, Sunderhaus, Stab, Huffman, Devore, Mills, Healy.
Paper. $40.00. 304pp. .... Vendor G0347

4301 **DESCENDANTS OF JACOB WILSON OF BRAINTREE, MASSACHU-SETTS**, by Ken Stevens. 1988. Indexed.
Cloth. $24.00. x+211pp. .... Vendor G0038

4302 **DESCENDANTS OF JOHN WILSON OF WOBURN, MASSACHUSETTS**, by Ken Stevens. 1991. Indexed.
Cloth. $64.00. ix+790pp. .... Vendor G0038

4303 **EARLY HISTORY OF THE WILSON FAMILY OF KITTERY, ME.**, by F.A. Wilson. 1898.
Paper. $19.00. 98pp. .... Vendor G0259

4304 **FIVE WILSON FAMILIES FROM HARTFORD COUNTY, CONNECTI-CUT**, by Ken Stevens. 1989. Indexed.
Cloth. $24.00. ix+262pp. .... Vendor G0038

4305 **GEN. OF THE FAM. OF ELIHU PARSONS WILSON OF KITTERY, ME., b. 1769, d. 1834**, by F. Wilson. 1894.
Paper. $7.50. 38pp. .... Vendor G0259

Wilson/Willson From New England

50,000 Wilson names on file, 10,000 Wilson names in print
Send complete details and SASE for free evaluation
Ken Stevens, P.O. Box 118, Walpole, NH 03608

4306 **JOSIAH AND LYDIA WILSON AND SLASHAM VALLEY, ST. CLAIR COUNTY, ALABAMA KINFOLK,** by Mildred S. Wright. 1980. Indexed. Illus.
Baswell, Davis, Jackson, Jenkins, Jester, White.
Paper. $18.75. 94pp. .... Vendor G0145

4307 **SCOTCH WILSONS FROM CENTRAL MASSACHUSETTS,** by Ken Stevens. 1994. Indexed.
Cloth. $40.00. x+350pp. .... Vendor G0038

4308 **SCOTCH WILSONS FROM WESTERN MASSACHUSETTS,** by Ken Stevens. 1993. Indexed.
Cloth. $34.00. xi+307pp. .... Vendor G0038

4309 **GEN. & PSYCH. MEM. OF PHILIPPE WILTSEE & HIS DESC., WITH HIST. INTRO REF. TO THE WILTSEE NATION & ITS COLONIES,** by J. Wiltsee, Sr. Pt. 1. 1908.
Cloth, $58.50. Paper, $48.50. 304pp. .... Vendor G0259

4310 **THE WINCHELL GEN. THOSE BORN TO THE WINCHELL NAME IN AMER. SINCE 1635, WITH THE ORIG. & HIST. OF THE NAME IN ENG. & NOTES ON THE WINCOLL FAM.,** by N. and A. Winchell. 2nd ed. 1917.
Cloth, $97.00. Paper, $87.00. 566pp. .... Vendor G0259

4311 **JOHN WINCHESTER & ONE LINE OF HIS DESC.,** by G.R. Presson. 1897.
Paper. $9.00. 45pp. .... Vendor G0259

4312 **JOHN WINCHESTER OF NEW ENG. & SOME OF HIS DESC.,** by H.W. Cunningham. 1925.
Cloth, $31.00. Paper, $21.00. 139pp. .... Vendor G0259

4313 **WINCHESTER NOTES,** by F. Winchester. 1912.
Cloth, $68.50. Paper, $58.50. 375pp. .... Vendor G0259

4314 **WINDERS OF AMER: JOHN OF N.Y., 1674–5; THOMAS OF N.J., 1703–34; JOHN OF MD., 1665–98,** by R.W. Johnson. 1902.
Paper. $19.50. 112pp. .... Vendor G0259

4315 **WINE FAMILY IN AMER., FIRST SECTION,** by J.D. Wine. 1952.
Cloth, $96.00. Paper, $86.00. 560pp. .... Vendor G0259

4316 **HIST. & GEN. REG. OF JOHN WING OF SANDWICH, MA. & HIS DESC., 1662–1881,** by Rev. C. Wing. 1881.
Cloth, $53.00. Paper, $43.00. 340pp. .... Vendor G0259

4317 **HIST. OF THE WINGATE FAM. IN ENG. & AMER. WITH GEN. TABLES,** by C.E. Wingate. 1886.
Cloth, $54.00. Paper, $44.00. 293pp. .... Vendor G0259

4318 **GEN. OF EDW. WINSLOW OF THE MAYFLOWER & HIS DESC., FROM 1620 TO 1865,** by M.W. Bryant. 1915.
Cloth, $35.00. Paper, $25.00. 150pp. .... Vendor G0259

4319 **WINSLOW MEM. FAM. RECORDS OF THE WINSLOWS & THEIR**

DESC. IN AMER. WITH ENG. ANC. AS FAR AS KNOWN, by D.P. and F.K. Holton. 2 vols. 1877–1888.
Cloth, $185.00. Paper, $175.00. 1,270pp. .... Vendor G0259

4320 THE WINSTONS OF HANOVER COUNTY VIRGINIA AND RELATED FAMILIES 1666–1992, by Alfred S. Winston III. 1992. Indexed.
Cloth. $35.00. 901pp. .... Vendor G0003

4321 WINSTON OF VA. & ALLIED FAM., by C. Torrence. 1927.
Cloth, $88.00. Paper, $78.00. 501pp. .... Vendor G0259

4322 WINTERMUTE FAMILY HISTORY, by J.B. Wintermute. 1900.
Cloth, $63.00. Paper, $53.00. 335pp. .... Vendor G0259

4323 ANCESTORS OF HENRY ROGERS WINTHROP & HIS WIFE ALICE WOODWARD BABCOCK, by Josephine C. Frost. 1927.
Cloth, $99.50. Paper, $89.50. 595pp. .... Vendor G0259

4324 EVIDENCES OF THE WINTHROPS OF GROTON, CO. SUFFOLK, ENG. & OF FAMS. WITH WHOM THEY INTERMARRIED, by J. Muskett and R. Winthrop. 1894–1896.
Cloth, $36.00. Paper, $26.00. 176pp. .... Vendor G0259

4325 WISDOM FAMILY, by G.W. Wisdon. 1910.
Cloth, $40.00. Paper, $30.00. 231pp. .... Vendor G0259

4326 COL. JOHN WISE OF ENGLAND & VA., 1617–1695: HIS ANC. & DESC., by J.C. Wise. 1918.
Cloth, $66.00. Paper, $56.00. 355pp. .... Vendor G0259

4327 A WISWALL LINE, TEN GEN. IN DESC. FROM THOMAS WISWALL OF DORCHESTER, 1635, by C. Wiswall. 1925.
Paper. $12.00. 59pp. .... Vendor G0259

4328 WILLIAM PETER WITHERILL ANCESTORS & DESCENDANTS, PIONEER OF OHIO, by Leallah Franklin. 1988. Indexed. Illus.
Related families: **Blair, Blandin, Brand, Burd, Carter, Chamberlain, Daniels, DeVoe, Garmon, Groves, Kahley, Kayser, Leatherman, Miller, Osburn, Rideout**, and **Simons**.
Cloth. $45.00. 365pp. .... Vendor G0304

4329 WITT GENEALOGY, by F.W. Balcomb. 1943.
Paper. $8.00. 40pp. .... Vendor G0259

4330 DESC. OF WM. WITTER OF SWAMPSCOTT, MASS., 1639–1659, by G. Washburn, edited by M.T. Washburn. 1929.
Cloth, $71.00. Paper, $61.00. 394pp. .... Vendor G0259

4331 THE WITTIG FAMILY OF ROCKINGHAM COUNTY, VA, by Lewis H. Yankey. 1990. Indexed.
Paper. $13.00. 54pp. .... Vendor G0365

4332 WOLCOTT FAM. EXTR. FROM "HIST. OF WINDSOR, CONN." 1892.
Paper. $7.00. 36pp. .... Vendor G0259

4333 WOLCOTT GEN. THE FAM. OF HENRY WOLCOTT, ONE OF THE 1ST SETTLERS OF WINDSOR, CT., by C. Wolcott. 1912.
Cloth, $66.50. Paper, $56.50. 480pp. .... Vendor G0259

4334 **A GEN. OF THE LINEAL DESC. OF WM. WOOD WHO SETTLED IN CONCORD, MASS., IN 1638, CONTAINING ALSO REV. & OTHER RECORDS**, by C.W. Holmes. 1901.
Cloth, $67.50. Paper, $57.50. 365pp. Vendor G0259

4335 **DESC. OF THE BROTHERS JEREMIAH & JOHN WOOD**, by W.S. Wood. 1885.
Cloth, $48.50. Paper, $38.50. 292pp. Vendor G0259

4336 **DESC. OF TWIN BROTHERS JOHN & BENJ. WOOD**, by J.A. Wood. 1902.
Cloth, $38.00. Paper, $28.00. 187pp. Vendor G0259

4337 **THE ANC. & DESC. OF EBENEZER WOOD OF W. GOULDSBOROUGH, MAINE**, by E. Wood.
Paper. $18.00. 90pp. . . . . Vendor G0259

4338 **[Wood]. THE FIRST HUNDRED YEARS OF LAKE CO., INDIANA, AS LIVED & ACTED BY BARTLETT WOODS & FAMILY & SAM B. WOODS & FAMILY**, by Sam B. Woods. 1936.
Cloth, $69.50. Paper, $59.50. 418pp. Vendor G0259

4339 **THE WOOD FAM., SACKVILLE, N.B., BEING A GEN. OF THE LINE OF THOMAS WOOD OF ROWLEY, MASS., b. ABOUT 1634, TO JOSIAH WOOD OF SACKVILLE, N.B., b. IN 1843**, by J.A. Kibble. 1904.
Paper. $9.00. 46pp. . . . . Vendor G0259

4340 **WOOD FAMILY, FROM "FAMILY SKETCHES,"** by J.R. Wood. 1870.
Paper. $7.00. 34pp. . . . . Vendor G0259

4341 **WOOD GEN. & OTHER FAM. SKETCHES. GEN. MEMORANDA OF A BRANCH OF THE WOOD FAM. IN ENG. & AMER. ALSO SKETCHES OF REL. FAMS.**, by L.N. Wood. 1937.
Cloth, $35.00. Paper, $25.00. 130pp. Vendor G0259

4342 **YORKSHIRE TO WESTCHESTER: CHRONICLE OF THE WOOD FAMILY**, by H.B. Howe. 1948.
Cloth, $55.00. Paper, $45.00. 290pp. Vendor G0259

4343 **WOODBRIDGE RECORDS: AN ACCT. OF THE DESC. OF THE REV. JOHN WOODBRIDGE OF NEWBURY, MASS.**, by L. Mitchell. 1883.
Cloth, $45.00. Paper, $35.00. 272pp. Vendor G0259

4344 **ANNALS OF THE CLAN: A STORY FOR DESC. OF FRANCIS WOODBURY**, by A.K. Woodbury. 1932.
Paper. $19.00. 102pp. . . . . Vendor G0259

4345 **GEN. SKETCHES OF THE WOODBURY FAM., ITS INTERMAR-RIAGES & CONNECTIONS**, by C.L. Woodbury; edited by E. Woodbury. 1904.
Cloth, $47.50. Paper, $37.50. 251pp. Vendor G0259

4346 **THE DIARIES OF SAMUEL MICKLE WOODBURY, GLOUCESTER COUNTY, NEW JERSEY 1792–1829 (2 VOLS.)**, edited by Ruthe Baker. 1991. Indexed.

Thirty-seven years of local, state and national happenings, including Revolution, War of 1812, 5,000 vital statistics of South Jersey.
Paper. $63.00. 834pp. .... Vendor G0069

4347 **HIST. OF THE WOODCOCK FAM. 1692–1912**, by W.L. Woodcock. 1913.
Paper. $12.00. 62pp. .... Vendor G0259

4348 **JOHN WOODCOCK OF REHOBETH, MASS., 1647, & SOME DESC.**, by J.L. Woodcock. 1913.
Cloth, $30.00. Paper, $20.00. 144pp. .... Vendor G0259

4349 **BIOGR. HIST. & GEN. OF THE WOODLING FAM.**, by C.A. Fisher. 1936.
Paper. $8.50. 43pp. .... Vendor G0259

4350 **THE WOODMANS OF BUXTON, ME.**, by C. Woodman. 1874.
Paper. $19.50. 131pp. .... Vendor G0259

4351 **THE WOODMANS OF RHODE ISLAND—DESCENDANTS OF JOHN WOODMAN OF LITTLE COMPTON, RI**, by Helen D. Woodman. 1989. Indexed. Illus.
11 generations traced, first 3 generations resided Little Compton, Rhode Island. Family names range from **Abbey** to **Zow**. Included, but not limited to, **Anderson, Brown, Brownell, Burgess, Cook, Dingman, Grinnell, Hinchliff, Howland, Laughlin, Manchester, Pearce, Peckham, Quackenbush, Roscoe, Simmons, Van Vleet, Wilbor** and **Woodman**.
Cloth. $44.50. 400pp. .... Vendor G0208

4352 **THE WOODRUFFS OF N.J., WHO CAME FROM FORDWICH, KENT, ENG., BY WAY OF LYNN, MASS. & SOUTHAMPTON, L.I.; REV. & ENLARGED FROM "A BRANCH OF WOODRUFF STOCK,"** by F.E. Woodruff. 1909.
Cloth, $31.50. Paper, $21.50. 143pp. .... Vendor G0259

4353 **ANCESTRY OF JOHN L. WOODS**, by John L. Woods. 1988. Indexed. Illus.
Ancestral Families: **Woods, Clarke, Morton, Smith, Peden, Orchard**. Some documented more than 20 generations. 100 pictures, narrative information; family group sheets.
Cloth. $35.00. 688pp. .... Vendor G0066

4354 **WOODS–PEDEN GENEALOGY**, by John L. Woods. 1991. Indexed. Illus.
Ancestry of James **Woods**, WV Darke Co. Ohio, b. 1767, 1st of line in America, traced 8 generations to 16th-century England; mar. (2) Rebecca **Peden**, WV. Adds 70 Woods and 400 Pedens to those in ancestry of John L. Woods. Thomas **Peden** b. 1792 in Darke Co., Ohio and his descendants in Ohio and Indiana are here and are not known to be covered elsewhere.

Also covers the Lucius Chambers **Smith** and Lewis **Shedrick** families.
Cloth. $35.00. 282pp. .... Vendor G0066

4355 **ANCESTRY OF JOHN L. WOODS & WOODS–PEDEN GENEALOGY**, by John L. Woods. Indexed. Illus.
The above two items can be ordered together as a set.
Cloth. $50.00 .... Vendor G0066

4356 **THE FIRST HUNDRED YEARS OF LAKE CO., INDIANA, AS LIVED & ACTED BY BARTLETT WOODS & FAMILY & SAM B. WOODS & FAMILY**, by Sam B. Woods. 1936.
Cloth, $69.50. Paper, $59.50. 418pp. .... Vendor G0259

4357 **WOODS FAMILY OF GROTON, MASS. (EXTR. *NEHGR*)**, by H.E. Woods. 1910.
Paper. $8.50. 43pp. .... Vendor G0259

4358 **ZADOCK AND MINERVA COTTLE WOODS, MONTRAVILLE AND ISABELLA GONZALES–HIDALGO WOODS: ANCESTORS AND DE-SCENDANTS**, by Marianne Elizabeth Hall Little. 1995. Indexed. Illus.
Limited Edition; Mayflower to Texas.
Cloth, $65.00. Paper, $45.00. 100pp. .... Vendor G0264

4359 **SOME DESCENDANTS OF NATHANIEL WOODWARD, WHO CAME FROM BOSTON ABOUT 1630**, by Harold Edward Woodward. 1984. Indexed.
Cloth. $16.00. 240pp. .... Vendor G0406

4360 **DESC. OF WALTER WOODWORTH OF SCITUATE, MASS.**, by E.B. Woodworth. 1901.
Paper. $14.00. 70pp. .... Vendor G0259

4361 **FROM THE OLD COLONY OF NEW PLYMOUTH TO NEBRASKA, 1620–1920: HISTORY & GENEALOGY OF THE FAMILY OF MILDRED WOODWORTH**, by L.H. Hoppe. 1992.
Cloth, $47.50. Paper, $37.50. 248pp. .... Vendor G0259

4362 **FAMILY OF GEORGE WOOD WOOLSEY & SARAH NELSON WOOLSEY**, by Hester Woolsey Brewer. 1940.
Cloth, $32.00. Paper, $22.00. 134pp. .... Vendor G0259

4363 **FAM. RECORDS, BEING SOME ACCT. OF THE ANC. OF MY FATHER & MOTHER CHARLES W. WOOLSEY & JANE ELIZA NEWTON**, by E.W. Howland. 1900.
Cloth, $50.00. Paper, $40.00. 270pp. .... Vendor G0259

4364 **THE DESC. OF RICHARD & HANNAH HUGGINS WOOLWORTH, WHO LANDED AT NEWBURY, MASS., 1678, REMOVED TO SUFFIELD, CONN., IN 1685**, by C.R. Woolworth, assisted by J.L. Kimpton. 1893.
Cloth, $41.00. Paper, $31.00. 209pp. .... Vendor G0259

4365 **GENEALOGY OF THE WOOSTERS IN AMERICA, DESC. FROM EDW. WOOSTER, OF CT.**, by D. Wooster. 1885.
Cloth, $32.50. Paper, $22.50. 139pp. .... Vendor G0259

4366 **WE ALL BECOME FOREFATHERS . . . GENEALOGIES OF THE WOOTEN, BOYKIN, WHITAKER & BROADHURST FAMILIES**, by David Robert Wooten. 1993.
Cloth, $59.50. Paper, $49.50. 326+46pp. .... Vendor G0259

4367 **THE WORCESTER FAM.; OR, THE DESC. OF REV. WM. WORCESTER, WITH A BRIEF NOTICE OF THE CONN. WOOSTER FAM.**, by J.F. Worcester. 1856.
Cloth, $31.00. Paper, $21.00. 112pp. .... Vendor G0259

4368 **THE DESC. OF REV. WM. WORCESTER, WITH A BRIEF NOTICE OF THE CONN. WOOSTER FAM., PUB. IN 1856**, by J.F. Worcester; revised by S.A. Worcester. 1914.
Cloth, $53.50. Paper, $43.50. 292pp. .... Vendor G0259

4369 **SOME RECORDS OF PERSONS BY THE NAME OF WORDEN**, by O.N. Worden. 1868.
Cloth, $34.00. Paper, $24.00. 160pp. .... Vendor G0259

4370 **WORK FAMILY HISTORY**, by Von Gail Hamilton. (1970) reprint 1978, 1983, 1992. Indexed. Illus.
12 generations descended from Henry **Work** (1679–1738) of PA. Includes Appendix of ALL research notes not used in main part of book. Includes photos.
Cloth. $62.50. 617pp. .... Vendor G0285

4371 **WORK FAMILY HISTORY—VOL. II**, by Von Gail Hamilton. 1994. Indexed. Illus.
Companion to 1970 volume—updates, extends, and adds much new material, between 1600s and current lineages. Includes 140 photos.
Cloth. $92.50. 619pp. .... Vendor G0285

4372 **WORKMAN BRANCHES, VOLUME 1 (INCLUDING WOERTMAN & WORTMAN)**, by Rose Caudle Terry. 1993. Indexed. Illus.
Queries published free.
Paper. $10.45. 40pp. .... Vendor G0061

4373 **WORKMAN BRANCHES, VOLUME 2**, by Rose Caudle Terry. 1995. Indexed. Illus.
Queries published free. Future volumes expected or may already be completed.
Paper. $10.45. 42pp. .... Vendor G0061

4374 **THE GEN. OF THE WORTHINGTON FAM.**, by G. Worthington. 1894.
Cloth, $86.00. Paper, $76.00. 489pp. .... Vendor G0259

4375 **COLONIAL FAM. & THEIR DESC.; WRIGHT & OTHERS**, by M.B. Emory. 1900.
Cloth, $52.00. Paper, $42.00. 255pp. .... Vendor G0259

4376 **DESCENDANTS OF OWEN WRIGHT & LETITIA DOW (COLLINS) WRIGHT; JAMES WRIGHT & 1) LYDIA E. (SORRELS) WRIGHT & 2) ANNA L. (DAVENBROCK) WRIGHT**, by Evelyn W. Brown and Opal W.R. Sikes. 1991–2.
Cloth, $99.50. Paper, $89.50. 870pp. .... Vendor G0259

4377 **GENEALOGICAL & BIOGRAPHICAL NOTICES OF DESC. OF SIR JOHN WRIGHT OF KELVEDON HALL, ESSEX, ENGLAND; IN AMERICA, THOMAS WRIGHT OF WETHERSFIELD CT, 1610–1670, AND DEA. SAMUEL WRIGHT OF NORTHAMPTON MA, 1614–1665,** by Curtis Wright. 1915.
Cloth, $59.50. Paper, $49.50. 321pp. .... Vendor G0259

4378 **HIST. OF THE WRIGHT FAM., WHO ARE DESC. OF SAMUEL (1722–1789), OF LENOX, MASS., WITH LIN. BACK TO THOMAS (1610–1670), OF WETHERSFIELD, CONN.,** by W.H. Wright and G.W. Ketcham. 1913.
Cloth, $45.00. Paper, $35.00. 235pp. .... Vendor G0259

4379 **PETER WRIGHT, A FAM. RECORD,** by E. Wright. 1939.
Cloth, $35.00. Paper, $25.00. 146pp. .... Vendor G0259

4380 **SORTING SOME OF THE WRIGHTS OF SOUTHERN VIRGINIA,** by Robert N. Grant. Illus.
This is a work in process sorting the various **Wright** families of southern Virginia, focusing on the counties of Amherst, Appomattox, Bedford, Botetourt, Buckingham, Campbell, Cumberland, Franklin, Goochland, City of Lynchburg, Montgomery, Nelson, Pittsylvania, Prince Edward, Roanoke, and Rockbridge.
The work is divided into parts.The first part for each Wright family is a text with full transcription of all documents related to the family through about 1900 and evidence and arguments for identification of the family members. The second part is a descendants chart for all known descendants of the progenitor with source citations. The third part is a series of appendices listing by county through 1900 all documents of a particular type (including birth, marriage, personal property tax, census, deed, land tax, death, and probate records) and identifying the Wright person named in each record and their known Wright ancestors.
Paper. $.08 per page ordered .... Vendor G0404

4381 **THE WRIGHT ANCESTRY OF CAROLINE, DORCHESTER, SOMERSET & WICOMICO COS., MD.,** by C.W. Wright. 1907.
Cloth, $44.00. Paper, $34.00. 218pp. .... Vendor G0259

4382 **UNTANGLING SOME OF THE WRIGHTS OF BEDFORD COUNTY, VIRGINIA,** by Robert N. Grant. 1977. Indexed. Illus. with maps.
Thomas Wright (?–1763) and sons John Wright (?–1803) and Joseph Wright (?–1815) and their descendants. Related families include in part: **Asberry** or **Asbury, Brown, Corley, Drake, Greer, Hardy, Holland**(?)**, Hopper, Hurt, Mays** or **Mayse, McCormack, Meador, McGeorge, Pasley, Pate** (?)**, Scott, Simmons,** and **Wheeler.**
John Wright (?–1810) and his descendants. Related families include in part: **Bateman, Clayton, Daniel, Hardwicke, Hunter, Mayse, Waugh,** and **Worley.**
John Wright (?–1814) and his descendants. Related families include in part: **Bibb** (?)**, Pace** or **Pierce, Pullen, Watts,** and **Weekes.**
Paper. $60.00. 1,000pp. .... Vendor G0404

4383 **WRIGHT FAMILY, A GENEALOGICAL RECORD FROM 1740 TO 1914 OF THE DESCENDANTS OF PETER WRIGHT, 1740–1821,** by Fred Philo Wright. 1914.
Paper. $7.00. 35pp. .... Vendor G0259

4384 **WRIGHT FAM. MEM.**, by A.E. Mathews. 1886.
Paper. $8.50. 42pp. .... Vendor G0259

4385 **WRIGHT—400 YEARS PLUS**, by Larry Wright. 1984. Indexed. Illus.
Paper. $20.00. 308pp. .... Vendor G0358

4386 **GENEALOGICAL RECORD OF THE WURTS FAMILY: DESCEN-DANTS OF REV. JOHANNES CONRAD WIRZ, WHO CAME TO AMERICA FROM ZURICH, SWITZERLAND, IN 1734; ALSO A RECORD OF HIS ANCESTRY FROM THE 13TH CENT.**, by C.P. Wurts. 1889.
Paper. $18.00. 91pp. .... Vendor G0259

4387 **DESCENDANTS OF FRANCIS AND HAUTE WYATT OF VIRGINIA**, by Carol A. Hauk. 1995. Indexed.
Paper. $30.00. 72pp. .... Vendor G0340

4388 **THE GEN. OF THE WYATT FAM.**, by A.H. Wyatt. 1921.
Paper. $7.00. 35pp. .... Vendor G0259

4389 **WYNKOOP GEN. IN THE U.S.**, by R. Wynkoop. 1878.
Cloth, $35.00. Paper, $25.00. 130pp. .... Vendor G0259

4390 **WYNKOOP GENEALOGY IN THE U.S.A.**, by R. Wynkoop. 1904.
Cloth, $51.50. Paper, $41.50. 254pp. .... Vendor G0259

4391 **YALE FAM. DESC. OF DAVID YALE**, by E. Yale. 1850.
Cloth, $40.00. Paper, $30.00. 201pp. .... Vendor G0259

4392 **YALE GENEALOGY, & HISTORY OF WALES (WITH BIOGRAPHIES)**, by Rodney Horace Yale. 1908.
Cloth, $101.00. Paper, $91.00. 597+25pp. .... Vendor G0259

4393 **DESCENDANTS OF JACKSON M. YANCEY & ELIZABETH B. GOODE, HIS WIFE**, by L.R. Garrison. 1962.
Cloth, $32.00. Paper, $22.00. 134pp. .... Vendor G0259

4394 **YARDLEY FAM. GEN., 1402–1881**, by T. Yardley. 1881.
Cloth, $48.50. Paper, $38.50. 257pp. .... Vendor G0259

4395 **MEMORIALS OF A FAM. IN ENG. & VA., 1771–1851: YATES, ORFEUR, AGLIONBY, MUSGRAVE FAMS.**, by A.E. Terrill. 1887.
Cloth, $69.00. Paper, $59.00. 383pp. .... Vendor G0259

4396 **YATES BOOK: WM. YATES & HIS DESC. HIST. & GEN. OF WM. YATES (1772–1868), OF GREENWOOD, ME. & HIS WIFE MARTHA MORGAN, WITH HER DESC. FROM ROBERT MORGAN OF BEVERLY**, by E. Yates. 1906.
Paper. $10.00. 51pp. .... Vendor G0259

4397 **BRIEF HIST. OF THE YEAGER, BUFFINGTON, CREIGHTON, JACOBS, LEMON, HOFFMAN & WOODSIDE FAM. & THEIR COLL. KINDRED OF PA.**, by J. Yeager. 1912.
Cloth, $53.00. Paper, $43.00. 278pp. .... Vendor G0259

4398 **HIST. OF YEAGER FAM. OF PA.**, by J. Yeager.
Cloth, $32.50. Paper, $22.50. 110pp. .... Vendor G0259

4399 YEAMANS–YEAOMANS–YOUMANS GEN., by G.S. Youmans. 1946. Cloth, $35.00. Paper, $25.00. 127pp. .... Vendor G0259

4400 BEGINNING AT A PINE TREE: THE YEARLING/EARLING/EARLIN LINE, by Margaret E. Sheaffer and Carol M. Sheaffer, M.D. 1987. Indexed. Genealogies of the **Yearling, Earling, Earlin** families of southern New Jersey from the 1700s to the present. Related lines include **Malsbury, Webb, Cross, Glenn, Garroute, Howell, Horner, Meyer, Murphy**, and many others. Cloth. $20.00. 145pp. .... Vendor G0229

4401 CHRONICLE OF THE YERKES FAM., WITH NOTES ON THE LEECH & RUTTER FAM., by J.G. Leach. 1904. Cloth, $51.00. Paper, $41.00. 274pp. .... Vendor G0259

4402 FAMILY OF HESSEL P. YNTEMA, FRISIAN IMMIGRANT TO MICHIGAN, 1847, by Mary E. Yntema. 1958. Paper. $15.00. 72pp. .... Vendor G0259

4403 DESC. OF JACOB YODER, by D.A. Hostetler. 1951. Paper. $19.00. 105pp. .... Vendor G0259

4404 FOOTPRINTS OF TIME: JOSEPH YODER AND AMANDA SUNTHIMER FAMILY HISTORY, by Vesta M. Ropp. 1987. Paper. $9.00. 77pp. .... Vendor G0150

4405 YONCE FAMILIES IN THE UNITED STATES OF AMERICA, by Luther V. Yonce. 1993. Indexed. Cloth. $54.00. 560pp. .... Vendor G0183

4406 FOREVER YOUNG, VOLUME I, THE RICHARD YOUNG FAMILY OF TEXAS, by Roy B. Young. 1992. Illus. **Waggoner—Donaho**. Cloth. $38.95. 250pp. .... Vendor G0405

4407 FOREVER YOUNG, VOLUME II, THE JESSE YOUNG FAMILY, by Roy B. Young. 1994. Illus. Barnwell, SC; Amite County, MS; Claiborne Parish, LA; Caldwell, Johnson, DeWitt counties, TX. **Chaddick—Green—Garlington**. Cloth. $38.95. 250pp. .... Vendor G0405

4408 OUR YOUNG FAMILY IN AMERICA, by E.H. Young. 1947. Cloth, $58.00. Paper, $48.00. 315pp. .... Vendor G0259

4409 ROBERT JOHN YOUNG & DAISIE FRANCES DENTON; ANCESTRAL NOTES & SOME DESCENDANTS, by R.M. Young-Widdifield. 1961. Cloth, $41.00. Paper, $31.00. 160+34pp. .... Vendor G0259

4410 YOUNG FAMILIES OF THE MOHAWK VALLEY, 1710–1946, by Clifford M. Young. 1947. Cloth, $65.00. Paper, $55.00. 354pp. .... Vendor G0259

4411 YOUNG FAMILY HISTORY, by J. Montgomery Seaver. Paper. $10.00. 48pp. .... Vendor G0259

4412 THOMAS YOUNGS OF OYSTER BAY & HIS DESC., by Rev. C. Youngs. 1890. Cloth, $31.00. Paper, $21.00. 142pp. .... Vendor G0259

4413 **YOUNGS FAM. VICAR CHRISTOPHER YONGES, HIS ANC. IN ENG. & HIS DESC. IN AMERICA**, by S. Youngs, Jr. 1907.
Cloth, $58.00. Paper, $48.00. 385pp. Vendor G0259

4414 **YOUNKIN FAMILY NEWS BULLETIN**, by Donna Younkin Logan. 1990. Illus.
Surnames covered in publication include: **Younkin, Youngkin, Youngken, Yonkin, Junghen**. Family newsletter published quarterly, average issue is 20 pages. Historical family collections spanning 3 centuries of research. Subscription. $15.00/year. 80pp./yr. Vendor G0392A

4415 **THE ZAHNISERS: A HISTORY OF THE FAMILY IN AMERICA**, by Kate M. and Charles Reed Zahniser. 1906.
Cloth, $43.00. Paper, $33.00. 218pp. Vendor G0259

4416 **ZIEGLER FAMILY RECORD**, by Floyd R. Mason. 1990. Indexed. Illus.
Immigrants Philip **Ziegler** and Regina **Requel** of PA and their eight children are given thru nine generations.
Cloth. $34.00. 672pp. . . . . Vendor G0345

4417 **ZIEGLER FAMILY RECORD: COMPLETE RECORDS OF THE ZIEGLER FAMILY FROM OUR ANCESTOR, PHILIP ZIEGLER, BORN IN BERN, SWITZERLAND, IN 1734, TO 7TH AND 8TH GENERATIONS**, by J. Ziegler and D. Ziegler. 1906.
Cloth, $31.00. Paper, $21.00. 118pp. Vendor G0259

4418 **A BRANCH OF THE ZIMMERMAN OFFSPRING OF GLAUSE ZIMMERMAN . . . 12 GENERATIONS**, by Ezra and Maria Zimmerman, Ervin M. Zimmerman, and Enos N. Zimmerman. 2nd ed. 1988.
Cloth. $38.00. 1,634pp. . . . . Vendor G0150

4419 **ZIMMERMAN, WATERS & ALLIED FAMS.**, by D.E.Z. Allen. n.d.
Cloth, $36.00. Paper, $26.00. 162pp. Vendor G0259

4420 **ZINK FAMILIES IN AMERICA, INCL. MANY OF THE ARCHER, COLGLAZIER, MARSHAL, MARTIN, PERISHO, SEATON & ZIMMERLY FAMS.**, by D.Z. Kellogg. 1933.
Cloth, $71.00. Paper, $61.00. 385pp. Vendor G0259

4421 **THE THREE ZUG (ZOOK) BROTHERS OF 1742 AND THEIR MALE DESCENDANTS**, by Paul V. Hostetler. 1982.
Cloth. $21.00. 213pp. . . . . Vendor G0150

4422 **ZUG/ZUCK/ZOUCK/ZOOK GENEALOGY**, by Harry D. Zook. 1983.
Cloth. $25.00. 428pp. . . . . Vendor G0150

4423 **ZUG/ZUCK/ZOUCK/ZOOK GENEALOGY**, by Harry D. Zook. 1983. Indexed. Illus.
Five generations for male lines from all 1700–1800 immigrants.
Cloth. $20.00. 428pp. . . . . Vendor G0049

COMPILED GENEALOGIES

4424 **ALBEMARLE COUNTY IN VIRGINIA**, by Rev. Edgar Woods. (1901) reprint 1990. Indexed.
Includes brief genealogical sketches of a number of early families.
Cloth. $24.00. 412pp. .... Vendor G0011

4425 **AMERICAN ANCESTORS AND COUSINS OF THE PRINCESS OF WALES**, by Gary Boyd Roberts and William Addams Reitwiesner. 1984. Indexed. Illus.
Cloth. $14.95. 194pp. .... Vendor G0010

4426 **AMISH AND AMISH-MENNONITE GENEALOGIES**, by Hugh F. Gingerich and Rachel W. Kreider. 1986.
Includes **Berkey, Blank, Hershberger, Hochstettler, Kauffman, King, Kurtz, Mast, Miller, Schrock, Swartzentruber, Troyer, Yoder**, and **Zook**.
Cloth. $75.00. 858pp. .... Vendor G0150

4427 **ANABAPTIST-MENNONITE NAMES IN SWITZERLAND**, by Isaac Zuercher. Translated by Hannes Maria Aleman. 1988.
Names of families once registered as Anabaptist or Mennonite prior to 1800, including notes on nationality, spelling, degree of completeness, citations of surnames not included, and genealogical tips.
Paper. $9.50. 35pp. .... Vendor G0150

4428 **ANCESTRAL LINES, 3RD EDITION**, by Carl Boyer, 3rd. 1996. Indexed. Illus.
More than 175 American family lines include: **Abell** of Plymouth Colony (with noble and royal lines), **George Allen, Allsop, Althouse, Andrews, Anthony, Armington, Avery, Babcock, Ballard, Baker, Barber, Bassett, Battin, Baulstone, Bennett, Bliss, Borden, Borton, Bosworth, Bowen, Boyer, Brown, Brownell, Buffington, Bullock, Burton, Cadman, Campbell, Carpenter, Chaffee, Chandler, Chase, Cheyney, Chickering, Clute, Cobb, Coggeshall, Cooke, Cooper, Debozear, Tristram Dodge, Durfee, Eames, Evans** (with noble and royal lines), **Feller, Fish, Fiske, Fort, Fowle, Freeborn, Frost, Frye, Gardner, George, Gerritsen/Garrison, Gibbons, Gifford, Griesemer, Haines, Hale, Hancock, Hardenbergh, Harper, Haskins, Hathaway, Hazard, Heemstraat, Hickman, Hicks, Holbrook, Holloway/Holley, Holmes, Holzwarth, Howland, Hull, Hunt, Ingraham, Jefferis, Jenckes/Jenks, Kendrick, Kent, Kingsbury, Kirby, Kitchen, Kruse, Kuser, Lansing, Lawton, Leonard, Loockermans, Ludwig, Luther, Marshall, Matlack, Mendenhall, Mercer, Metselaer, Mors/Morse, Mott, Moulton, Ouderkerk, Paine, Paul(s), Peabody, Pearce, Pennell, Perry, Pitts, Potter, Quackenbos, Read, Remington, Reynolds, Rown/Rau, Rowning, Russell, Sale/Searles, Segar, Sellers, Sheever, Sheldon, Sherman, Slade, Smedley, Smith, Specht, Sprague, Strange, Strode, Talbot, Tallman, Taylor, Tefft, Thurston, Timberlake, Timm, Tisdale, Titus, Tripp, Truax/de Trieux,Tymensen, Van Antwerpen, Vandenburgh, Vanderbilt, Van der Vliet, Van Slichtenhorst, Van Vranken,**

Van Wenckum, Vinhagen, Visscher, Waeger, Walker, Warren, Watson, Webb, White, Wilbore, Wilmarth, Winthrop, Wodell and Wood.
Cloth. $63.00. Est. 1,000pp. .... Vendor G0198

4429 **ANCESTRAL ROOTS OF CERTAIN AMERICAN COLONISTS Who Came to America Before 1700.** (Formerly Ancestral Roots of Sixty Colonists Who Came to New England between 1623 and 1650). The Lineage of Alfred the Great, Charlemagne, Malcomb of Scotland, Robert the Strong, and Some of Their Descendants. Seventh Edition, by Frederick Lewis Weis. With additions and corrections by Walter L. Sheppard, Jr., and assisted by David Faris. (1992) reprint 1995. Indexed.
Cloth. $25.00. 274pp. .... Vendor G0010

4430 **ANNALS OF AUGUSTA COUNTY, VIRGINIA, From 1726 to 1871**, by Jos. A. Waddell. 2nd ed. (1901) reprint 1995. Indexed. Fldg. map.
This standard history of Augusta County, Virginia, includes numerous genealogical and biographical sketches of Augusta County families.
Paper. $35.00. 555pp. .... Vendor G0011

4431 **AUSTIN (TEXAS) COLONY PIONEERS**, by Worth Stickley Ray. (1949) reprint 1995. Indexed. Illus.
Contains biographical and genealogical sketches of the early settlers of the Texas counties of Bastrop, Fayette, Grimes, Montgomery, and Washington.
Cloth. $30.00. 378pp. .... Vendor G0010

4432 **A WORD FROM THE SOUTHEAST**, Florida & S.E. States Branch, the Monarchist League (Royal Bloodlines), edited by Dr. Lawrence Kent.
Concerned with the genealogies of the royal families of all nations. Direct inquiries require a SASE.
Annual dues are applicable .... Vendor G0448

4433 **BALTIMORE COUNTY FAMILIES, 1659–1759**, by Robert W. Barnes. 1989 (reprint 1996). Indexed.
Comprehensive genealogical data on the hundreds of families and thousands of persons who settled in the parent county in its first century.
Paper. $65.00. 924pp. .... Vendor G0011

4434 **A BIOGRAPHICAL HISTORY OF GREENE COUNTY, PENNSYLVANIA**, by Samuel P. Bates. (1888) reprint 1993.
Paper. $28.50. 338pp. .... Vendor G0011

4435 **A BIOGRAPHICAL HISTORY OF LANCASTER COUNTY [PENNSYLVANIA]: Being a History of Eminent Men of the County**, by Alexander Harris. (1872) reprint 1992.
Paper. 638pp. .... Vendor G0011

4436 **THE BLOOD ROYAL OF BRITAIN [Tudor Roll] Being a Roll of the Living Descendants of Edward IV and Henry VII, Kings of England, and James III, King of Scotland**, by The Marquis of Ruvigny and Raineval. (1903) reprint 1994. Indexed. Illus.
Cloth. $45.00. 632pp. .... Vendor G0010

4437 **[Blood Royal]. THE PLANTAGENET ROLL OF THE BLOOD ROYAL. Being a Complete Table of all the Descendants Now Living of Edward III, King of England**, by The Marquis of Ruvigny and Raineval. 4 vols. Indexed. Illus. (1905, 1907, 1908, 1911) reprint 1994.

The Clarence Volume, Containing the Descendants of George, Duke of Clarence. $50.00. 730pp.

The Anne of Exeter Volume, Containing the Descendants of Anne (Plantagenet), Duchess of Exeter. $50.00. 842pp.

The Isabel of Essex Volume, Containing the Descendants of Isabel (Plantagenet), Countess of Essex and Eu. $45.00. 698pp.

The Mortimer–Percy Volume, Containing the Descendants of Lady Elizabeth Percy, nee Mortimer. $45.00. 650pp.

Cloth . . . . Vendor G0010

4438 **THE BLOOD ROYAL OF BRITAIN** (in one volume); **THE PLANTAGENET ROLL OF THE BLOOD ROYAL** (in four volumes), by The Marquis of Ruvigny and Raineval.
See above two listings.
Cloth. $235.00/set . . . . Vendor G0010

4439 **THE BOOK OF IRISH FAMILIES Great & Small**, edited by M. O'Laughlin.
The new Hallmark series in Irish Family History, with coats of arms. Includes native & settler families found nowhere else. With families from all of Ireland. 1,800 entries.
Quality hardbound & gold stamped. $28.00. 320pp. . . . . Vendor G0455

4440 **BROCKS GAP FAMILIES VOLUME I: BIBLE, CHERRYHOLMES, FREED, HEAVNER, & AUBREY FAMILIES**, by Lewis H. Yankey. 1991. Indexed.
Paper. $17.00. 124pp. . . . . Vendor G0365

4441 **BROCKS GAP FAMILIES, VOLUME 2: FINK AND SONIFRANK FAMILIES**, by Lewis H. Yankey. 1992. Indexed.
Paper. $20.00. 152pp. . . . . Vendor G0365

4442 **BROCKS GAP MISCELLANEOUS RESEARCH, INCLUDING NOTES ON THESE FAMILIES: "HESSIAN JOHN" BAKER, MICHAEL BAKER, CAPLINGER, CUSTER, DOVE, HALTERMAN, HUPP, LAIR, LANTZ, MAY, RITCHIE, SECRIST, SIEVER, SOUDER, WEST**, by Lewis H. Yankey. 1992. Indexed.
Paper. $27.00. 285pp. . . . . Vendor G0365

4443 **BURKE'S AMERICAN FAMILIES WITH BRITISH ANCESTRY. The Lineages of 1,600 Families of British Origin Now Resident in The United States of America.** (1939) reissued 1996. Illus.
Cloth, 7" x 10" 494pp. .... Vendor G0010

4444 **BURKE'S FAMILY RECORDS,** by Ashworth P. Burke. (1897) reprint 1994. Indexed. Illus.
Traces the descent of some 300 cadet houses of the British nobility.
Paper. $50.00. 709pp. .... Vendor G0011

4445 **CAMPBELL CHRONICLES AND FAMILY SKETCHES. Embracing the History of Campbell County, Virginia 1782–1926,** by Ruth Hairston Early. (1927) reprint 1994. Indexed. Illus.
Contains a 200-page section devoted to Campbell County genealogies.
Paper. $39.95. 578pp. .... Vendor G0011

4446 **COBB COUNTY GA FAMILY TREE QUARTERLY,** edited by Mimi Jo Butler and Mary Hancock. 1991. Indexed. Illus.
Extensive Cobb County family genealogies, pictures, Bible records, and other official records.
$25.00 annually. 200pp./year .... Vendor G0313

4447 **COLONIAL ANCESTORS: WILLIAM ANDREWS, ROBERT FULLER, LAZARUS MANLEY, JOHN WHITE,** by Edward H. Little. 1991. Indexed. Illus. Book #1185.
Cloth. $34.00. 384pp. .... Vendor G0082

4448 **COLONIAL AND REVOLUTIONARY FAMILIES OF PENNSYLVANIA in Three Volumes,** by John W. Jordan. (1911) reprint 1994. Indexed.
Covers 250 Colonial and Revolutionary families.
Paper. $125.00. 1,706pp. .... Vendor G0011

4449 **COLONIAL FAMILIES OF THE SOUTHERN STATES OF AMERICA. A History and Genealogy of Colonial Families Who Settled in the Colonies Prior to the Revolution,** by Stella P. Hardy. (1958) reprint 1991. Indexed.
Cloth. $35.00. 643pp. .... Vendor G0010

4450 **COLONIAL FAMILIES OF THE UNITED STATES OF AMERICA,** by George Norbury Mackenzie. 7 vols. (1907–1920) reprint 1995. Indexed. Illus.
Treats those families who trace their ancestry back to the Colonial Period, 1607–1776. Covers 850 families and 125,000 family members.
Cloth. $300/set (each vol. also available individually).
5,019pp. .... Vendor G0010

4451 **COLONIAL VIRGINIANS AND THEIR MARYLAND RELATIVES. A Genealogy of the Tucker Family and Also Families of Allen, Blackistone, Chandler, Ford, Gerard, Harmor, Hume, Monroe, Skaggs, Smith, Stevesson, Stone, Sturman, Thompson, Ward, Yowell,** by Norma Tucker. (1994) reprint 1996. Indexed.
Paper. $25.00. 270pp. .... Vendor G0011

4452 **THE COMPENDIUM OF AMERICAN GENEALOGY. The Standard Genealogical Encyclopedia of the First Families of America,** by Frederick Adams Virkus. 7 vols. (1925–1942) reprint 1987, 1996. Indexed. Illus.
Contains the lineage records of the first families of America, with records

extending in both male and female lines from the earliest-known immigrant ancestor to the then (1925–1942) living subject of the record. Over 54,000 lineage records which list more than 425,000 names.
Cloth (Vol. 1 is paper). 6,283pp. .... Vendor G0010

4453 **COMPENDIUM OF EARLY MOHAWK VALLEY FAMILIES**, by Maryly B. Penrose. 2 vols. 1990. Indexed.
Includes a complete, concise record of every family known to have lived in New York's Mohawk Valley in the 18th and early 19th centuries.
Cloth. $75.00. 1,173pp. .... Vendor G0010

4454 **CONTRIBUTIONS FOR THE GENEALOGIES OF THE DESCENDANTS OF THE FIRST SETTLERS OF THE PATENT AND CITY OF SCHENECTADY (N.Y.), From 1662 to 1800**, by Jonathan Pearson. (1873) reprint 1982.
Cloth. $21.50. 324pp. .... Vendor G0010

4455 **EARLY FAMILIES OF EASTERN AND SOUTHEASTERN KENTUCKY AND THEIR DESCENDANTS**, by William C. Kozee. (1961) reprint 1994. Indexed. Illus.
Cloth. $45.00. 886pp. .... Vendor G0010

4456 **EARLY FAMILIES OF HERKIMER COUNTY, NEW YORK**, by William V.H. Barker. 1986. Indexed.
On pre-Revolutionary families of the area, with detailed genealogies of 87 of them.
Cloth. $25.00. 384pp. .... Vendor G0010

4457 **EARLY FAMILIES OF WALLINGFORD, CONNECTICUT. With a New Index**, by Charles Henry Stanley Davis. (1870) reprint 1995. Indexed.
Excerpted from Davis's *History of Wallingford, Conn.,* this work treats some seventy early Wallingford families.
Paper. $31.50. 363pp. .... Vendor G0011

4458 **EARLY FRIENDS FAMILIES OF UPPER BUCKS with Some Account of Their Descendants**, by Clarence V. Roberts. (1925) reprint 1995. Indexed. Illus.
Includes the genealogies of the following families: **Adamson, Ashton, Ball, Blackledge, Burson, Carr, Custard, Dennis, Edwards, Foulke, Green, Griffith, Hallowell, Heacock, Hicks, Iden, Jamison, Johnson, Kinsey, Lancaster, Lester, Levick, Lewis, Lott, McCarty, Miller, Morgan, Morris, Nixon, Penrose, Phillips, Rawlings, Roberts, Shaw, Strawn, Thomas, Thomson, Walton,** and **Zorns.**
Paper. $49.95. 680pp. .... Vendor G0011

4459 **THE EARLY SETTLERS OF NANTUCKET. Their Associates and Descendants**, by Lydia S. Hinchman. (1896) reprint 1993.
Paper. $29.95. 330pp. .... Vendor G0011

4460 **EARLY VIRGINIA FAMILIES ALONG THE JAMES RIVER. Volume I: Henrico County—Goochland County**, by Louise Pledge Heath Foley. (1974) reprint 1994. Indexed. Maps.
Paper. $18.50. 162pp. .... Vendor G0011

4461 **EARLY WESTERN AUGUSTA PIONEERS Including the Families of Cleek, Gwin, Lightner, and Warwick and Related Families of Bratton, Campbell, Carlile, Craig, Crawford, Dyer, Gay, Givens, Graham, Harper, Henderson, Hull, Keister, Lockridge, McFarland, and Moore**, by George Washington Cleek. (1957) reprint 1995. Indexed.
Paper. $37.50. 492pp. .... Vendor G0011

4462 **EAST TEXAS RELATED FAMILIES OF MUSICK, LANGSTON, PIERCE, McELROY, AND SOME OF THEIR PIONEER CONNECTIONS 1600'S–1800'S**, by Mae Gean Pettit. 1994. Indexed. Illus.
Cloth. $27.00. 247pp. .... Vendor G0402

4463 **EBENEZER BAPTIST OF ELLIS COUNTY, TEXAS; 1880–1892 CHURCH RECORDS WITH GENEALOGIES**, by Margaret B. Kinsey. 1990. Indexed. Illus.
Families: **Ball, Blocker, Borders, Burford, Cardwell, Copeland, Dennington, Farmer, Goolsby, Hall, Herndon, King, Kinsey, Leake, Miller, Nash, Power, Roberts, Smith**.
Cloth. $25.00. 338pp. .... Vendor G0307

4464 **THE EDWARD PLEASANTS VALENTINE PAPERS**, by Clayton Torrence. 4 vols. (1927) reprint 1979. Indexed.
Abstracts of 17th- and 18th-century Virginia records relating to the families of **Allen, Bacon, Ballard, Batchelder, Belson, Brassieur, Cary, Crenshaw, Dabney, Exum, Ferris, Fontaine, Gray, Hardy, Hooker, Isham, Izzard, Jordan, Langston, Lyddall, Mann, Mosby, Palmer, Pasteur, Pleasant, Povall, Randolph, Satterwhite, Scott, Smith, Valentine, Waddy, Watts, Winston, Womack, Woodson**.
Cloth. $80.00. 2,768pp. .... Vendor G0011

4465 **EMINENT WELSHMEN: A Short Biographical Dictionary of Welshmen Who Have Obtained Distinction from the Earliest Times to the Present**, by T.R. Roberts. (1908) reprint 1995. Illus.
This is a prize-winning collection of nearly 2,000 biographical essays pertaining to men and women who were either born in Wales or of Welsh descent and flourished between 1700 and 1900.
Paper. $45.00. 613pp. .... Vendor G0011

4466 **ENGLISH ORIGINS OF NEW ENGLAND FAMILIES from the *New England Historical and Genealogical Register*. First Series**. 3 vols. 1984. Indexed.
Contains hundreds of articles on the English origins of New England ancestors.
Cloth. $45.00/vol., $135.00/set. 2,550pp. .... Vendor G0010

4467 **ENGLISH ORIGINS OF NEW ENGLAND FAMILIES from the *New England Historical and Genealogical Register*. Second Series**. 3 vols. 1985. Indexed.
Covers between 750 and 1,000 immigrants, including a number for whom royal descent is generally accepted.
Cloth. $45.00/vol., $135.00/set. 3,080pp. .... Vendor G0010

4468 **FAMILIES AND KIN OF ELIAS STOCKTON, MOSES DICKEY AND**

JAMES UPCHURCH, CHEROKEE COUNTY, TEXAS, PIONEERS, by Mae Gean Pettit. 1991. Indexed. Illus.
Cloth. $20.00. 170pp. .... Vendor G0402

4469 **FAMILIES DIRECTLY DESCENDED FROM ALL THE ROYAL FAMILIES IN EUROPE (495 to 1932) & MAYFLOWER DESCENDANTS,** by Elizabeth M. Leach Rixford. (1932) reprint 1992. Indexed. Illus.
Paper. $28.00. 190pp. .... Vendor G0011

4470 **FAMILIES OF EARLY GUILFORD, CONNECTICUT,** by Alvan Talcott. (1984) reprint 1994. Indexed.
Paper. $50.00. 1,379pp. .... Vendor G0011

4471 **FAMILIES OF EARLY HARTFORD, CONNECTICUT,** by Lucius Barnes Barbour. (1977) reprint 1996. Indexed.
Contains the genealogical records of over 950 families of early Hartford, Connecticut.
Paper. $50.00. 736pp. .... Vendor G0011

4472 **FAMILIES OF EARLY MILFORD, CONNECTICUT,** by Susan Woodruff Abbott. (1979) reprint 1996. Indexed.
Contains the genealogies of approximately 300 families of early Milford, Connecticut.
Paper. $55.00. 875pp. .... Vendor G0011

4473 **THE FAMILIES OF CO. KERRY.** Maps. Illustrations.
The history/location of over 1,000 specific Kerry families. 12,000 listings.
Quality hardbound & gold stamped. $27.95. 272pp. .... Vendor G0455

4474 **FAMILIES OF WARREN, FRANKLIN AND GRANVILLE COUNTIES, NORTH CAROLINA AND VIRGINIA ANCESTRY,** by Gayle King Blankenship. 1989. Indexed. Illus.
Blackwell, Bridges, Crowshaw, Dowtin, Dymer, English, Freeman, Harris, Jeffreys, Kilby, King, Lawson, Marshall, McKinnie, Nichols, Pope, Robbins, Shearin, Tharrington, Timberlake, Watts, Wale, Wilson, Winston.
Referenced; 8¹/₂ x 11.
Cloth. $35.00. 211pp. .... Vendor G0034

4475 **FLORIDA STATE NEWSLETTER,** Huguenot Society of the Founders of Manakin in the Colony of Virginia, edited by Dr. Lawrence Kent.
Concerned with the family histories of persons who descend from any Huguenot resident of Virginia prior to 1786. Direct inquiries require a SASE.
Annual dues are applicable .... Vendor G0448

4476 **THE FOUNDERS OF ANNE ARUNDEL AND HOWARD COUNTIES, MARYLAND,** by J.D. Warfield. (1905) reprint 1991. Indexed.
Contains genealogical and biographical sketches of the founders and founding families of Anne Arundel and Howard counties.
Paper. $40.00. 599pp. .... Vendor G0011

4477 **FREDERICK COUNTY, VIRGINIA: SETTLEMENT AND SOME FIRST FAMILIES OF BACK CREEK VALLEY,** by Wilmer L. Kerns. 1995. Indexed. Illus., 46 photographs.
History of settlement and early settler families, 1730–1830. Origin, immigration, and 2–6 generations of genealogical history for each surname. Six maps show towns, streams, and mountains. Major families are **Adams, Allemong, Anderson, Babb, Bageant, Ballinger, Barrett, Bevan, Beeson, Braithwaite, Brown, Bruner, Bryan, Capper, Cather, Chapman, Clark, Coe, Dalbey, DeHaven, Dunlap, Elliott, Fisher, Good, Griffith, Grove, Harris, Harry, Haworth, Giffin, Hook, Jenkins, Johnson, Julian, Kackley, Kerns, Larrick, Lewis, Lupton, LaFollette, Lockhart, McCool, McDonald, Mellon, McKee, Malin, Marple, Mercer, Parlette, Peacemaker, Pearson, Printzler, Pugh, Purtlebaugh, Rinker, Rogers, Rosenberger, Riley, Ruble, Scarborough, Scrivener, Secrist, Shane, Shuler, Stine, Sine, Sirbaugh, Smith, Streit, Taylor, Thomas, Trowbridge, Strickling, Walker, Waln, Whitacre, White, Wickersham, Wright, Yonley**.
Cloth. $45.00. 648pp. .... Vendor G0250

4478 **FREE AFRICAN AMERICANS OF NORTH CAROLINA AND VIRGINIA Including the family histories of more than 80% of those counted as "all other free persons" in the 1790 and 1800 census. Expanded 2nd edition,** by Paul Heinegg. (1994) reprint 1995. Indexed.
Paper. $49.95. 699pp. .... Vendor G0011

4479 **FROM CAVAN TO THE CATSKILLS: AN INFORMAL HISTORY OF THE CONERTY, FINIGAN AND SMITH FAMILIES OF UPPER NEW YORK,** by Lenore Blake Stevenson. 1989. Indexed. Illus. Includes maps, genealogical charts, over 100 photographs.
The story of three families from a small area of County Cavan, Ireland, who settled in the little Catskill town of Jefferson in Schoharie County, New York. Other New York counties included are Delaware, Otsego, Albany, and Greene. Some associated families: **Brady, Champlin, Cronk, Gilbride, Horan, Lee, Mooney, Mulligan, Nesbitt, Porteus, Shannon, Utter**.
Cloth. $33.00 incl. p&h. 230pp. .... Vendor G0288

4480 **A GENEALOGICAL AND BIOGRAPHICAL HISTORY OF ALLEGHENY COUNTY, PENNSYLVANIA,** by Thomas Cushing, et al. (1889) reprint 1993. Indexed.
Paper. $43.50. 578pp. .... Vendor G0011

4481 **GENEALOGICAL AND FAMILY HISTORY OF CENTRAL NEW YORK. A Record of the Achievements of Her People in the Making of a Commonwealth and the Building of a Nation. In Three Volumes,** by William Richard Cutter. (1912) reprint 1994. Partially indexed.
Paper. $150.00. 1,612pp. .... Vendor G0011

4482 **GENEALOGICAL AND FAMILY HISTORY OF THE STATE OF CONNECTICUT. A Record of the Achievements of Her People in the Making of** a **Commonwealth and the Building of a Nation. In Four Volumes**, by William Richard Cutter, et al. (1911) reprint 1995. Partially indexed. Illus. Paper. $200.00/set. 2,842pp. .... Vendor G0011

4483 **A GENEALOGICAL AND HERALDIC HISTORY OF THE COMMONERS OF GREAT BRITAIN AND IRELAND. In Four Volumes Reprinted with the "Index to Pedigrees in Burke's Commoners," by George Ormerod**, by John Burke. (1834–1838, 1907) reprint 1996. Indexed. Illus. Paper. $200.00. 3,113pp. .... Vendor G0011

4484 **GENEALOGICAL AND MEMORIAL ENCYCLOPEDIA OF THE STATE OF MARYLAND. A Record of the Achievements of Her People in the Making of a Commonwealth and the Founding of a Nation**, by Richard Henry Spencer. 2 vols. (1919) reprint 1992. Indexed. Illus. Paper. $59.95. 756pp. .... Vendor G0011

4485 **A GENEALOGICAL AND PERSONAL HISTORY OF BUCKS COUNTY, PENNSYLVANIA**, by William W.H. Davis. 2 vols. (1905) reprint 1994. Indexed. Illus. Paper. $65.00. 751pp. .... Vendor G0011

4486 **GENEALOGICAL AND PERSONAL HISTORY OF THE UPPER MONONGAHELA VALLEY, WEST VIRGINIA**, by Bernard L. Butcher. 2 vols. (1912) reprint 1994. Indexed.
Covers some 400 families.
Paper. $80.00. 1,037pp. .... Vendor G0011

4487 **GENEALOGICAL AND PERSONAL MEMOIRS Relating to the Families of Boston and Eastern Massachusetts in Four Volumes**, by William Richard Cutter. 4 vols. (1908) reprint 1995. Partially indexed. Illus.
Contains a genealogical and biographical essay for nearly 900 main families. Contains a surname index identifying between 5,000 and 6,000 members of the main families covered.
Paper. $185.00. 2,201pp. .... Vendor G0011

4488 **GENEALOGICAL DICTIONARY OF MAINE AND NEW HAMPSHIRE**, by Sybil Noyes, Charles T. Libby, and Walter G. Davis. 5 parts in 1. (1928–39) Reissued 1996. Arranged alphabetically.
Contains extensive biographical and genealogical data on every family established in Maine and New Hampshire before 1699.
Cloth. $40.00. 795pp. .... Vendor G0010

4489 **GENEALOGICAL DICTIONARY OF RHODE ISLAND; Comprising Three Generations of Settlers Who Came Before 1690**, by John Osborne Austin; with additions & corrections by G. Andrews Moriarty (1943–1963), and a new Foreword. (1887) reprint 1995. Indexed. Large quarto.
With many families carried to the fourth generation.
Cloth. $50.00. 496pp. .... Vendor G0010

4490 **A GENEALOGICAL DICTIONARY OF THE FIRST SETTLERS OF NEW ENGLAND**, by James Savage. 4 vols. 1860–1862. Index in Vol. 4.
Vol. 1, A–C; Vol. 2, D–J; Vol. 3, K–R; Vol. 4, S–Z + index.
Cloth. $39.00/vol., $132.50/set. Index only:
$10.00 (paper). 2,541pp. .... Vendor G0259

4491 **A GENEALOGICAL DICTIONARY OF THE FIRST SETTLERS OF NEW ENGLAND**, by James Savage. 4 vols. (1860–1862) reprint 1994. With Genealogical Notes and Errata (1873) and a Cross-index (1884).
A listing of every settler who came to New England before 1692, with data on the descendants.
Cloth. $125.00. 2,541pp. .... Vendor G0010

4492 **GENEALOGICAL GUIDE TO THE FIRST SETTLERS OF AMERICA. With a Brief History of Those of the First Generation**, by William H. Whittemore. (1898–1906) reprint 1995.
Contains genealogical notices of 10,000 17th-century settlers, beginning with the letter "A" and continuing through the alphabet to the name "Ram."
Paper. $31.50. 442pp. .... Vendor G0011

4493 **GENEALOGICAL NOTES OF BARNSTABLE FAMILIES**, by Amos Otis. 2 vols. in 1. (1888, 1890) reprint 1991. Indexed.
Includes about 90 families and some 10,000 persons.
Cloth. $40.00. 536+291pp. .... Vendor G0010

4494 **GENEALOGICAL NOTES OF NEW YORK AND NEW ENGLAND FAMILIES**, by Sebastian V. Talcott. (1883) reprint 1994. Indexed.
Paper. $50.00. 786pp. .... Vendor G0011

4495 **GENEALOGICAL NOTES ON THE FOUNDING OF NEW ENGLAND**, by Ernest Flagg. (1926) reprint 1990. Illus.
Cloth. $27.50. 440pp. .... Vendor G0011

4496 **GENEALOGICAL NOTES, Or Contributions to the Family History of Some of the First Settlers of Connecticut and Massachusetts**, by Nathaniel Goodwin. (1856) reprint 1995.
Cloth. $25.00. xx+362pp. .... Vendor G0010

4497 **GENEALOGICAL RECORD OF THE DESCENDANTS OF THE SCHWENKFELDERS Who Arrived in Pennsylvania in 1733, 1734, 1736, 1737 from the German of the Rev. Balthasar Heebner and from Other Sources**, by Rev. Reuben Kriebel. (1879) reprint 1993. Indexed.
Paper. $24.50. 371pp. .... Vendor G0011

4498 **A GENEALOGICAL REGISTER OF THE FIRST SETTLERS OF NEW ENGLAND, 1620–1675**, by John Farmer; with additions and corrections by Samuel G. Drake. (1829, 1847) reprint 1994.
Cloth. $25.00. 355pp. .... Vendor G0010

4499 **GENEALOGICAL REGISTER OF PLYMOUTH FAMILIES**, by William T. Davis. (1899) reissued 1994.
Contains the names of thousands of individuals with *Mayflower* and sister-ship antecedents, with families worked through several generations, showing marriages, dates, children, and children's marriages and offspring.
Cloth. $25.00. 363pp. .... Vendor G0010

4500 **GENEALOGIES OF CONNECTICUT FAMILIES from the *New England Historical and Genealogical Register***. 3 vols. 1983. Indexed.
Includes all the family history articles on Connecticut families published in *The Register* from 1847 through 1982.
Cloth. $45.00/vol., $135.00/set. 2,402pp. .... Vendor G0010

Drake-Arrington, White-Turner, Linn-Brown and related Southern lines: Treadwell, Slade, Lacey, Harrison, Cathey, Redwine, Krider, Wood, McNair, Peden, Sandefur, Tompkins, Bennett, Hodges, Goodrich, Bechince, Williams, Bustin, Outlaw, Fox, Smith, George, Doll, and Stahle. 490 pp., casebound, charts, maps, illus., copies of orig. documents, letters, Bible records, complete-name index, $38.00.

People Named Hanes. 291 pp. casebound, 142 illus., maps, complete index. $28.00. Primarily Surry, Stokes, Forsyth, Davie Co., NC. This is a Moravian lineage. Allied lines: **Hauser, Legenauer, Zimmerman, Frey, Kerber, March, Sehner, Hinkle, Hodgin, Lassiter, Chatham, Booe, Poindexter.**

The Ancestry of Nathalie Fontaine Lyons Gray: Lyons, Nunes Miranda, Luria, Cohen, Hart, Clayland, Maffitt, Beach. 260 pp., casebound, illus., charts, index, $28.00. The first five lines are Jewish. Clayland and Maffitt are Maryland lineages. Beach is Connecticut.

The Diary of Elizabeth Dick Lindsay. Facsimile edition of diary kept by the dau. of Thomas and Jane Erwin Dick and the wife of Andrew Lindsay of Guilford County, NC, for the period 1837–1861. A detailed introduction provides the lineages. Casebound, map, illus., $25.00.

A Holmes Family of Rowan and Davidson Counties, North Carolina with Allied Lines: Haden, Heilig, Reid, Linn, Bernhardt, Snider, Pearson, Graham, White, Foushee, Ballou, Hurley, Morrison, King, Erwin, Pannill, Dillard, Knowles. 336 pp., casebound, illus., maps, complete index, $25.00.

Ancestry of Sims/Hallman Families with related lines of Jernigan, Boon, Bryan. 143 pp., soft cover, maps. $27.50.

Ancestry of Moore/Rowan Families with related lines of Fleming, Renick, Bosley, Green, Girault, Beatty, Reading, Armitage, Ryerson, Rapalje. 180 pp., soft cover. $34.00.

Please order from
Jo White Linn
P.O. Box 1948, Salisbury, NC 28145-1948
Prices include postage and handling. NC residents add 6% sales tax.

4501 **GENEALOGIES OF HADLEY [MASSACHUSETTS] FAMILIES Embracing the Early Settlers of the Towns of Hatfield, South Hadley, Amherst and Granby**, by Lucius M. Boltwood. (1905) reprint 1993. Indexed.
Contains several hundred genealogies.
Paper. 205pp. .... Vendor G0011

4502 **GENEALOGIES OF KENTUCKY FAMILIES from the *Register of the Kentucky Historical Society* and *The Filson Club History Quarterly*.** 3 vols. 1981. Indexed.
Contains 200 articles; mentions 50,000 names.
Cloth. $45.00/vol., $135.00/set. 2,665pp. .... Vendor G0010

4503 **GENEALOGIES OF LONG ISLAND FAMILIES from the *New York Genealogical and Biographical Record*.** Introduction by Henry B. Hoff, editor of the *Record*. 2 vols. 1987. Indexed.
Cloth. $45.00/vol., $90.00/set. 1,599pp. .... Vendor G0010

4504 **GENEALOGIES OF MAYFLOWER FAMILIES from the *New England Historical and Genealogical Register*.** 3 vols. 1985. Indexed.
Contains 40,000 names.
Cloth. $45.00/vol., $135.00/set. 2,929pp. .... Vendor G0010

4505 **GENEALOGIES OF NEW JERSEY FAMILIES from the *Genealogical Magazine of New Jersey*.** 2 vols. 1995. Indexed.
Includes all the compiled material (genealogies, biographies, etc.) and Bible records published in the *Genealogical Magazine of New Jersey* from its first issue through the end of Volume 65.
Cloth. $75.00/vol. 1,139, 1,087pp. .... Vendor G0010

4506 **GENEALOGIES OF PENNSYLVANIA FAMILIES from the *Pennsylvania Genealogical Magazine*.** 3 vols. 1982. Indexed. Illus.
Includes every family history article, Bible record, and genealogical fragment published in the *Pennsylvania Genealogical Magazine* from 1895 through 1980.
Cloth. $45.00/vol., $135.00/set. 2,894pp. .... Vendor G0010

4507 **GENEALOGIES OF PENNSYLVANIA FAMILIES from *The Pennsylvania Magazine of History and Biography*.** 1983. Indexed.
Contains family history articles that were published in *The Pennsylvania Magazine of History and Biography* up to 1935. Contains references to 20,000 persons.
Cloth. $45.00. 949pp. .... Vendor G0010

4508 **GENEALOGIES OF RHODE ISLAND FAMILIES from the *New England Historical and Genealogical Register*,** selected and introduced by Gary Boyd Roberts. 2 vols. 1989. Indexed.
Contains all of the articles on Rhode Island families that appeared in the *Register* since 1846.
Cloth. $95.00/set. 1,650pp. .... Vendor G0010

4509 **GENEALOGIES OF RHODE ISLAND FAMILIES from Rhode Island Periodicals.** 2 vols. 1983. Indexed.
Contains hundreds of genealogies devoted exclusively to Rhode Island.
Cloth. $45.00/vol., $90.00/set. 1,776pp. .... Vendor G0010

4510 **GENEALOGIES OF VIRGINIA FAMILIES from** *Tyler's Quarterly Historical and Genealogical Magazine.* 4 vols. 1981. Indexed. Illus.
The hundreds of family history articles are supplemented with others on Bible records, wills, etc. Vols. I & II are out of print. Vol. III: **Pinkethman–Tyler.** Vol. IV: **Walker–Yardley.**
Cloth. $45.00/vol. 892, 895pp. .... Vendor G0010

4511 **GENEALOGIES OF VIRGINIA FAMILIES from the** *William and Mary College Quarterly.* 5 vols. 1982. Indexed. Illus.
Contains hundreds of genealogies published in the *William and Mary College Quarterly* from 1892 through 1943.
Vol. I: **Adams–Clopton**; Vol. II: **Cobb–Hay**; Vol. III: **Heale–Muscoe**; Vol. IV: **Neville–Terrill**; Vol. V: Out of print.
Cloth. $45.00/vol. 944, 990, 903, 893pp. .... Vendor G0010

4512 **GENEALOGIES OF WEST VIRGINIA FAMILIES.** (1901–05) reprint 1992. Indexed.
Consists of all the family history articles that appeared in *The West Virginia Historical Magazine Quarterly* from 1901 to 1905.
Paper. $29.50. 286pp. .... Vendor G0011

4513 **GENEALOGY OF EARLY SETTLERS IN TRENTON AND EWING, "Old Hunterdon County," NEW JERSEY,** by Eli F. & William S. Cooley. (1883) reprint 1992. Indexed.
Paper. $29.50. 336pp. .... Vendor G0011

4514 **GENEALOGY OF SOME EARLY FAMILIES in Grant and Pleasant Districts, Preston County, W. Va.,** by Edward T. King. (1933) reprint 1994. Indexed.
The genealogy of some of the early families of Grant and Pleasant Districts, including **Christopher, Connor, Cunningham, King, Metheny, Ryan, Street, Thorpe, Walls, Wheeler,** and **Wolf.**
Paper. $22.50. 233pp. .... Vendor G0011

4515 **THE GEORGIANS. Genealogies of Pioneer Families,** by Jeannette Holland Austin. (1984) reprint 1986. Indexed.
A collection of 283 genealogies.
Cloth. $30.00. 479pp. .... Vendor G0010

4516 **GLEANINGS OF VIRGINIA HISTORY. An Historical and Genealogical Collection, Largely from Original Sources,** by William F. Boogher. (1903) reprint 1995. Indexed.
Includes genealogies of the families of **Anderson, Brown, Craig, Cravens, Custis, Davis, Harrison, Newman, Smith, Thomas,** and **Thompkins.**
Paper. $35.00. 443pp. .... Vendor G0011

4517 **THE GREAT HISTORIC FAMILIES OF SCOTLAND,** by James Taylor. 2 vols. in 1. 2nd ed. (1889) reprint 1995. Indexed.
A genealogical compendium of the prominent Scottish families, which traces the families from their earliest recorded origins up to the end of the 19th century.
Cloth. $55.00. 841pp. .... Vendor G0010

4518 **THE HAMMATT PAPERS: Early Inhabitants of Ipswich, Massachusetts, 1633–1700,** by Abraham Hammatt. (1880–1899) reprint 1991. Indexed.

Several hundred families are dealt with, and about 9,000 persons are cited in the new index.

Cloth. $30.00. 448pp. .... Vendor G0010

4519 **[LINEAGE BOOK OF] HEREDITARY ORDER OF DESCENDANTS OF COLONIAL GOVERNORS**, edited by Robert Glenn Thurtle. 1980. Indexed. Cloth. $25.00. 405pp. .... Vendor G0011

4520 **HISTORIC FAMILIES OF KENTUCKY**, by Thomas Marshall Green. (1889) reprint 1996. Indexed.

Traces from their origin in this country a number of Kentucky families of Scotch-Irish extraction whose ancestors immigrated to America in the early 18th century and became pioneers of the Valley of Virginia.

Paper. $27.50. 304pp. .... Vendor G0011

4521 **HISTORICAL COLLECTIONS OF HARRISON COUNTY, in the State of Ohio [Comprising *Ohio Valley Genealogies*]**, by Charles A. Hanna. (1900) reprint 1994. Indexed.

Paper. $46.50. 636pp. .... Vendor G0011

4522 **THE HISTORICAL FAMILIES OF DUMFRIESSHIRE AND THE BOR-DER WARS, Second Edition**, by C.L. Johnstone. Reprint 1996. Indexed. Illus.

More than 1,000 references to the following main Dumfriesshire families: **Armstrong, Baliol, Bell, Boswell, Bruce, Carlile/Carlyle, Carruthers, Clark, Corry, Crichton, Cummings, Douglas, Dunwiddie, Fergusson, Fleming, Gladstone, Gordon, Graham(e), Irving, Jardine, Johnstone, Kennedy, Kerr, Kirkpatrick, Laird, Maitland, Maxwell, Murray, Scott, Sharp, Stuart/ Stewart, Trumble, and Wallace.**

Paper. 213pp. .... Vendor G0011

4523 **HISTORICAL SOUTHERN FAMILIES, Volume I**, by John Bennett Boddie. (1957) reprint 1994. Indexed. Illus.

Baldwin, Barker, Boddie, Butler, Clark, De Loach, Drake, Exum, Frizzell, Gilliam, Goodrich, Harris, Harvey, Hill-Harrington, Holland, Kendrick, Killingsworth, Lawrence, Littlejohn, Lovell-Harrison-Footman, MacClamroch, McKinnie, Mallett, Norwood, Peterson, Powell, Ruffin, Salle, Sorrell, Thweatt, Whitehead, Williams.

Paper. $30.00. 385pp. .... Vendor G0011

4524 **HISTORICAL SOUTHERN FAMILIES, Volume II**, by John Bennett Boddie. (1958) reprint 1994. Indexed. Illus.

Armistead, Baber, Barlow, Barrow, Batte, Blakey, Brown, Cary, Crispe, Crocker, De Loach, Flood, Gay, George, Goffe-Prosser-Kendall, Gwaltney, Harris, Haynie, Heale-Hale, Kendall, Kendrick, Lane, Lewis, Mercer, Morris, Neville, Parsons-Thweatt, Perrymans, Reades, Reynolds, Rochelle, Stokes-Anderson, Swan, Thornton, Travers, Traverse, Travis, Tuckers, Waller, Wynn, Wynne.

Paper. $25.00. 315pp. .... Vendor G0011

4525 **HISTORICAL SOUTHERN FAMILIES, Volume III**, by John Bennett Boddie. (1959) reprint 1994. Indexed. Illus.

Allins, Arrington, Billingsley, Blackwell, Bledsoe, Boddie, Boykin, Bradford, Browns, Buchanan, Buchanan-Patton-Boyd, Clark-Anthony-Cooper, Cockerham, Cottons, Dickson, Dunlap, Evans, Figures-Figuers,

Foster, Fulgham, Giles, Harding, Harris, Haywood, Holland, Isbell, Mulholland, Mason-Watson-Woodson, Miskell, Norfleet, Northington, Norwood, Perry, Reynolds, Scarborough, Smith, Steptoe-Lawson-Edwards, Thompson, Tunstall, Williamson.

Paper. $22.50. 255pp. .... Vendor G0011

4526 HISTORICAL SOUTHERN FAMILIES, Volume IV, by John Bennett Boddie. (1960) reprint 1994. Indexed.

Allin, Arrington, Bledsoe, Browne, Boddie, Cobb, de Solms (von Solms), Dortch, Drew, Duke, Ffones, Guttery, Hardy, Harris, Haynes, Jennings, Jennings-Hill-Quincy, Jernigan, Rev. Rowland Jones, Mason-Wilson-Woodson, Meadors-Meadows, Moor, Moorman, Munger, Pennington, Poythress, Roberson-Robason, Shelley, Smith, Thomas, Treat-Thompson-Moseley-Hawkins, Washington, Winfield-Pettypool.

Paper. $23.00. 259pp. .... Vendor G0011

4527 HISTORICAL SOUTHERN FAMILIES, Volume V, by John Bennett Boddie. (1960) reprint 1994. Indexed. Illus.

Bledsoe, Boddie-Lawrence-Sanders, Cabaniss, Calhoun-Cohoon-Cahoon, Dale-Carter, Darden, Dawson, Dillard, Duke, Dunston, Ezell, Glover, Halbert-Randolph, Harrison, Heale-Hale, Heath, Huntt, Jackson, James, Joyner, Lemon, Mallory, Mason-Wilson-Woodson, Murray, Overton, Parker, Pender-Hart, Powell, Quincy-Skipworth, Randle-Randolph, Scarborough-Eagles-Norville, Soane, Sowerby-Sorsby, Strother, Stuart, Tucker, Williams, Wilson, Wynne-Tucker-Bell.

Paper. $26.00. 320pp. .... Vendor G0011

4528 HISTORICAL SOUTHERN FAMILIES, Volume VI, by John Bennett Boddie. (1962) reprint 1994. Indexed.

Battle, Baude, Boddie–Boddye–Boade–Boode–Bode, Bigod, Blow, Bourne, Bradford, Browne, Butler, Cocke, Colinsom, Cox, Drake, Duke, Griffith, Hadham, Hayes–Hays–Hay, Howard, Hunnicutt, Ive–Ivie–Ivey, Ivey, Mallet, Mann, Mixson–Mixon, Norris, Offley-Hewett, Osborne, Owen, Parham, Parva, Pharr, Prince, Pyrton, Saire De Quincy, Sanders, Sanders-Jobe-Phillips-Reynolds, Scott, Smith, Stone, Strangmen, Thompson, Thorogood, Thorpe, Tucker, Whitley-Williams, Williams, Winchester, Winn, Wykes.

Paper. $24.00. 275pp. .... Vendor G0011

4529 HISTORICAL SOUTHERN FAMILIES, Volume VII, by John Bennett Boddie. (1963) reprint 1994. Indexed.

Alderman, Alverson, Bennett, Boone, Boothe, Clayton-Orr, Dixon, Drake, Hunter, Ivy, Knott, Macon, Mehringer, Peavy, Perry, Raines, Saunders, Taylor-Chew-Downs-Brewster, Thompson, Warren, Williams.

N.b.: Pages 95–100 were omitted from Vol. VII by the author.

Paper. $25.00. 282pp. .... Vendor G0011

4530 HISTORICAL SOUTHERN FAMILIES, Volume VIII, by John Bennett Boddie. (1964) reprint 1993. Indexed. Illus.

Barham, Bathurst, Betts, Breazeales, Clayton, Dardens, Drake, Flake, Gayle, Hamblin–Hamlin, Harris, Harrison, Herring-Bell-Bowen, Hinton, Lawrence, Lothhotz, Mehringer, Porter, Taylor.

Paper. $22.50. 254pp. .... Vendor G0011

4531 **HISTORICAL SOUTHERN FAMILIES, Volume IX,** by John Bennett Boddie. (1965) reprint 1993. Indexed. Illus.

Boddie, Booth, Branch, Cooper, DeLoach, Deveny, Dickens, Ezell, Halbert, Harrison, Haynes, Hill-Hasty-Harper, Hilliard, Hilliard-Hunt, Horton, Mann, McElroy, Morrison, Ruffin, Saunders, Stovall, Warren.

Paper. $26.00. 302pp. .... Vendor G0011

4532 **HISTORICAL SOUTHERN FAMILIES, Volume X,** by John Bennett Boddie. (1966) reprint 1993. Indexed. Illus.

Allen, Allred (Aldridge), Birmingham, Bradford, Breed (Brede)-Avery-Denison-Palmer-Payson, Cole, Dobbins, Doty, Holland, Huggins, Ivy–Ivey, Jackson, Jameson, Kaigler, Kemp, Palmer, Pell, Purl, Upshur.

Paper. $24.00. 275pp. .... Vendor G0011

4533 **HISTORICAL SOUTHERN FAMILIES, Volume XI,** by John Bennett Boddie. (1967) reprint 1993. Indexed. Illus.

Albertson, Arrington, Batts, Baugh, Boat(w)right, Beeson-Grubb-Boren-Bowles, Breed, Bridger, Chipley, Collins-Smith-Ross-Wyatt-Scott-Fleete-Hawte, Cox, Hutchens, Kemp, Kline, Knight, Land, Mathews, McNulty, Pitcher-Lancaster-Douglas-George-Jordan-Booth-Jackson, Pitt, Ragan-Spence-Timmons-Hilliard-Sheffield-Singleton, Rose, Upshur, Wynn-Wynns-Wynne.

Paper. $25.00. 287pp. .... Vendor G0011

4534 **HISTORICAL SOUTHERN FAMILIES, Volume XII,** by John Bennett Boddie. (1968) reprint 1993. Indexed. Illus.

Barnett-Gentry-Dickson-Lockridge, Bennett, Cobb-Massengill-Coleman-Holtzclaw, Cureton-Jones-Heath-Rives-Massey-Baugh-Harrison-Lee-Moore, Digges, Gregory-Parsons-Stith, Montgomery-Kirk-McMurray-Briscoe-Crockett-Whitney-Mackey, Thornton-Ransdell-Cox-Atwell-Alford-Williams-Curtis.

Errata and Addenda: Blakey, Harrison, Hilliard, Jackson, Jefferson, and Ross.

Paper. $25.00. 289pp. .... Vendor G0011

4535 **HISTORICAL SOUTHERN FAMILIES, Volume XIII,** by John Bennett Boddie. (1969) reprint 1994. Indexed.

Avery, Baber–Babers, Breed, Boatright, Etheridge, Ezell, Harris, Hubbard, Montgomery, Rose, Smith, Strother, White.

Errata and Addenda: Lovelace and Parham.

Paper. $22.50. 256pp. .... Vendor G0011

4536 **HISTORICAL SOUTHERN FAMILIES, Volume XIV,** by John Bennett Boddie. (1970) reprint 1994. Indexed.

Baugh, Berry, Calvit, Clarke, Cratchett, Crook, Delke, Dowdy, Dumas, Eggleston, Elzey, Etheridge, Ezell, Fontaine, Gibson, Gordon, Halbert, Harwell, Hill, Holstead, Ijams, Ives, Johnson, Mathias, Mohun, Murray, Nash, Parham, Portlock, Powers, Rose, Seat, Stewart–Stuart, Swann, Tarpley, Veale, Woodward, Yates.

Errata and Addenda: Cobb, Blakey, Elzey-Jordan, Hubbard, and Travis-Smallwood.

Paper. $22.00. 240pp. .... Vendor G0011

4537 **HISTORICAL SOUTHERN FAMILIES, Volume XV,** by John Bennett
Boddie. (1971) reprint 1994. Indexed.
Allred, Anderson, Bigg, Cliborn, Delafields, Etheridge, Hayes–Hays, Jernigan, Matthews, Mercer, Napier, Pitman, Rose, Tate.
Errata and Addenda: **Fontaine, Jefferson, Rose,** and **Smallwood.**
Paper. $24.00. 272pp. .... Vendor G0011

4538 **HISTORICAL SOUTHERN FAMILIES, Volume XVI,** by John Bennett
Boddie. (1971) reprint 1994. Indexed.
Outlaw and allied families: **Belderlinden, Bently (Bentley), Dafnell (Davenall), Dees, Hotzheimer, Ivy (Ivey), Klingenberger, Metz, Nebel, Reynolds, Schmidt (Smith),** and **Sommer.**
Paper. $25.00. 288pp. .... Vendor G0011

4539 **HISTORICAL SOUTHERN FAMILIES, Volume XVII,** by John Bennett
Boddie. (1972) reprint 1994. Indexed.
Allred, Baylor, Bradley, Carter, Cureton, Dees (Deas), Chisholm (Chism, Chisum), Flood, Gray, Isham, Napier, Rose, Smith, Weathersbee. Descendants of Randolph **Jefferson** and Lucy (Jefferson) **Lewis.**
Errata and Addenda: **Breed.**
Paper. $22.50. 248pp. .... Vendor G0011

4540 **HISTORICAL SOUTHERN FAMILIES, Volume XVIII,** by John Bennett
Boddie. (1973) reprint 1994. Indexed.
Dees, Haynes, Massey with **Cureton** connections, **Warren** of Surry with related family **Richards.**
Paper. $22.00. 240pp. .... Vendor G0011

4541 **HISTORICAL SOUTHERN FAMILIES, Volume XIX,** by John Bennett
Boddie. (1974) reprint 1995. Indexed.
Cardwell, Carter, Cureton, Epes, Gary, Gee, Robert **Harrison, Hardyman, Harris, Hill, Humphreys, Marks, Matheny, Pitts, Rankin, Read, Sims, Sydnor, Thomas.**
Paper. $21.00. 204pp. .... Vendor G0011

4542 **HISTORICAL SOUTHERN FAMILIES, Volume XX,** by John Bennett
Boddie. (1975) reprint 1995. Indexed.

Thomas **Carter** of VA, with related families **Dale, Dymoke, Fitzalan, Kempe, Leftwich, Reno, Tipton, Skipwith; Devinny** of Huntington and Indiana Cos., PA; **Gary** of SC, MS, TX; **Kirk** with **Cureton** and **Moore** connections; John **Rose** of Brunswick Co.; **Walker** of Elizabeth City, Co.
Paper. $21.00. 201pp. .... Vendor G0011

4543 **HISTORICAL SOUTHERN FAMILIES, Volume XXI**, by John Bennett Boddie. (1976) reprint 1995. Indexed.
Adams, Abney, Buchanan, Chisholms, John **Chisum** of King's Mountain, **Ferrell, Foster** (with related families **Boyd, Johnson, Thomson**), **Hobson, McCall, Nelson, Mackie, Madison, Newton, Peacock, Winters, Woodward**.
Paper. $21.50. 226pp. .... Vendor G0011

4544 **HISTORICAL SOUTHERN FAMILIES, Volume XXII**, by John Bennett Boddie. (1978) reprint 1995. Indexed.
Conner, with related families **Eldridge, Hardaway, Hall, Moore, Morschheimer, Newbern, Pullen, White; Cornelius; Erwin; Howard** of VA, with related families **Brackett, Craig, Eppes, Harris, Moldenhauer;** Alexander **Kilpatrick** of Scotland and SC, with related families **Camp/Kemp, Clark/ Clarke, MacGillivray, McGrew; Newton** and **Wright**, with related families **Berry, Byrd, Chambless, Harrison, Robinson; Overton** of GA, with related families **Alexander, Bennett, Chambers, Crutcher, Mackey, Redditt, Topp**.
Paper. $22.50. 246pp. .... Vendor G0011

4545 **HISTORICAL SOUTHERN FAMILIES, Volume XXIII**, by John Bennett Boddie. (1980) reprint 1995. Indexed.
Bruner and **Miller** of KY; **Clements** of NC; **Eggleston** of VA; **Etheredge** and **Wright** of AL and other Southern states; **Ford, Mallory**, and **Milstead** of VA and KY; **Grubb** of PA and DE; **Miller** of SC; **Overton** of GA; Thomas **Rose** of Surry; **Ruffin** of VA, NC, TN, and MO.
Paper. $21.00. 212pp. .... Vendor G0011

4546 **HISTORY AND GENEALOGY OF THE FAMILIES OF OLD FAIRFIELD**, by Donald Lines Jacobus; with additions and corrections from *The American Genealogist*. 2 vols. in 3. (1930–1932, 1943) reprint 1991. Indexed.
Cloth. $150.00. 2,051pp. .... Vendor G0010

4547 **HISTORY AND GENEALOGY OF THE *MAYFLOWER* PLANTERS**, by Leon Clark Hills. 2 vols. in 1. (1936, 1941) reprint 1990. Indexed.
Based largely on the genealogy of *Mayflower* planter Stephen **Hopkins**; covers many *Mayflower* connections.
Cloth. $21.00. 461pp. .... Vendor G0011

4548 **HISTORY OF ANCIENT WOODBURY, CONNECTICUT**, by William Cothren. (1854) reprint 1996. Indexed. Illus.
Includes eighty-five genealogies of the families most intimately linked to the rise and progress of the town of Woodbury.
Paper. 851pp. .... Vendor G0011

4549 **A HISTORY OF CAROLINE COUNTY, VIRGINIA From Its Formation in 1727 to 1924 To Which is Appended "A DISCOURSE OF VIRGINIA" by Edward Maria Wingfield, First Governor of the Colony of Virginia**, by Marshall Wingfield. (1924) reprint 1991. Indexed. Illus.

Includes genealogies and biographical sketches of the county's prominent citizens and early inhabitants.
Cloth. 528pp. .... Vendor G0011

4550 **HISTORY OF FENTRESS COUNTY, TENNESSEE**, by Albert R. Hogue. (1916, 1920) reprint 1994. Indexed. Illus.
Includes a collection of some 350 personal and family sketches, highlighted by references to marriage, occupation, and place of residence.
Paper. $20.00. 197pp. .... Vendor G0011

4551 **A HISTORY OF HALIFAX COUNTY [VIRGINIA]**, by Wirt Johnson Carrington. (1924) reprint 1995. Indexed. Illus.
Consists almost entirely of genealogical records and includes more than 150 pages of genealogical sketches.
Paper. $39.95. 525pp. .... Vendor G0011

4552 **HISTORY OF HAVANA, N.Y. 1788–1895**, by Wayne E. Morrison, Sr. 1986. Indexed. Illus.
Family histories and portraits include **Ayres, Beardsley, Blair, Brodrick, Catlin, Clauharty, Cook, Coryell, Couch, Crawford, Decker, Fanton, Fellows, Goodwin, Henry, Hill, Hitchcock, Jackson, Lawrence, Lee, Look, Mills, Minier, Mulford, Schuyler, Skellenger, Tracy, Weller, White, Whittemore**.
Cloth. $35.00. 406pp. .... Vendor G0112

4553 **A HISTORY OF HIGHLAND COUNTY, VIRGINIA, With a New 112-Page Index to Names**, by Oren F. Morton. (1911) reprint 1994. Indexed. Illus. Maps.
Included in this book are genealogies of Highland County families.
Paper. $39.95. 532pp. .... Vendor G0011

4554 **A HISTORY OF MARLBORO COUNTY [SOUTH CAROLINA] With Traditions and Sketches of Numerous Families**, by Rev. J.A.W. Thomas. (1897, 1978) reprint 1992. Maps.
Features sketches of the following Marlboro County pioneer families: **Brown, Bruce, Carloss, Cochrane, Covington, Coxe, David, Ellerbe, Evans, Forniss, Gillespie, Henagan, Hodges, Irby, Kolb, Lee, McCall, McColl, McLaurin, McLeod, McLucas, McRae, Magee, Parker, Pearson, Pegue, Pledger, Pouncey, Rogers, Spears, Terrell, Thornwell, Thomas, Townsend**, and **Vining**.
Paper. $21.50. 325pp. .... Vendor G0011

4555 **HISTORY OF NEW PALTZ, NEW YORK, AND ITS OLD FAMILIES (FROM 1678 TO 1820)**, by Ralph LeFevre. 2nd ed. (1920) reprint 1996. Indexed.

Contains the histories of prominent New Paltz families, both Huguenot and Dutch, including **Auchmoody, Bevier, Beyo, Budd, Clearwater, Dubois, Ean, Elting, Freer, Hardenbergh, Hasbrouch, LeFevre, Low, Ronk, Relyea, Schoonmaker, Van Wagenen**, and **Wurts**.
Paper. 607pp. . . . . Vendor G0011

4556 **HISTORY OF PATRICK AND HENRY COUNTIES, VIRGINIA**, by Virginia G. Pedigo and Lewis G. Pedigo. (1933) reprint 1990. Indexed. Illus.
The first third of the book is county histories, and the rest is fine histories of no less than 110 families.
Cloth. $35.00. 400pp. . . . . Vendor G0010

4557 **THE HISTORY OF ROANE COUNTY, TENNESSEE, 1801–1870. With a New Index**, by Emma Middleton Wells. (1927) reprint 1994. Indexed.
Includes scores of family histories, with references to more than 10,000 related persons.
Paper. $29.50. 352pp. . . . . Vendor G0011

4558 **A HISTORY OF ST. MARK'S PARISH, CULPEPER COUNTY, VIRGINIA. With Notes of Old Churches and Old Families**, by Rev. Philip Slaughter. (1877) reprint 1994. Illus.
Includes genealogies of twenty-five pioneer families of the parish.
Paper. $21.00. 210pp. . . . . Vendor G0011

4559 **HISTORY OF SWEETWATER VALLEY, TENNESSEE with a New Index**, by William B. Lenoir. (1916) reprint 1994. Indexed.
Includes genealogies of fifty-five early Sweetwater families.
Paper. $34.00. 419pp. . . . . Vendor G0011

4560 **HISTORY OF THE FARM, MENDON, MONROE COUNTY 1828–1958**, by Wayne E. Morrison, Sr. 1966. Indexed. Illus.
General history and genealogy of the Zebedee **Bond**, John **Yorks**, etc. families.
Cloth. $25.00. 88pp. . . . . Vendor G0112

4561 **HISTORY OF THE OLD CHERAWS [SOUTH CAROLINA] With Notices of Families and Sketches of Individuals. With Addenda Comprising Additional Facts Concerning the Eight Pedee Counties and Sketches of the Persons for Whom They Are Named by John J. Dargan**, by Alexander Gregg. (1867, 1925) reprint 1994. Indexed. Illus.
Includes genealogical notices of early families and sketches of individuals.
Paper. $49.95. 629pp. . . . . Vendor G0011

4562 **HISTORY OF THE TOWN OF STONINGTON, CONNECTICUT with a Genealogical Register of Stonington Families**, by Richard A. Wheeler. (1900) reprint 1993. Indexed.
The genealogies generally begin with the immigrant ancestor and continue through six or seven generations in the direct line of descent.
Paper. $49.95. 754pp. . . . . Vendor G0011

4563 **HUGUENOT EMIGRATION TO VIRGINIA . . . With an Appendix of Genealogies Presenting Data of the Fontaine, Maury, Dupuy, Trabue, Marye, Chastain, Cocke, and Other Families**, by Robert Alonzo Brock. (1886) reprint 1995. Indexed.
Paper. $23.00. 255pp. . . . . Vendor G0011

Descendents of John George Ruth & Allied Families
By Ruth Bailey Allen

John George Ruth came to America on the ship Marlborough. He landed in Philadelphia 23 September 1741, and was listed as having been from Oberalben, Kusel, Germany. He was 26 years of age when he took the Oath of Allegiance to King George of England.

He settled in Slifer's Valley in northern Bucks County, Pennsylvania where many of his descendents still reside. They married into many prominent German families in the area as well as several of the Irish families. Descendents can be found in almost every state within the United States.

This new publication contains 370 pages of family information and a 46-page, every-name index. There are 30 pages of family pictures. Each generation in line of descent is recorded in a separate chapter. Chapter I covers John George Ruth and children; Chapter II, Peter Ruth and children; Chapter III, Michael Ruth and children; Chapter VIII, Fluck family; Chapter IX, Kunstman family.

Beautifully hardbound $35 plus $4.00 p&h; Georgia residents please add 5% state sales tax.

Allen's Books & Crafts, Inc. / P.O. Box 1585 / Clayton, GA 30525

4564 **HUGUENOT PEDIGREES**, by Charles Edmund Lart. 2 vols. in 1. (1924–28) reprint 1995. Indexed.
Paper. $22.50. 258pp. .... Vendor G0011

4565 **THE HUGUENOTS OR EARLY FRENCH IN NEW JERSEY**, by Albert F. Koehler. (1955) reprint 1992. Indexed.
Contains brief genealogical and biographical sketches of hundreds of early Huguenot families in the Garden State.
Paper. $8.00. 51pp. .... Vendor G0011

4566 **KE KU'AUHAU, THE GENEALOGIST. NEWSLETTER OF THE SANDWICH ISLANDS GENEALOGICAL SOCIETY.** 1992. Indexed.
Subscription. $12.00/year for 6 issues. 10–12pp./issue ...... Vendor G0154

4567 **KING AND QUEEN COUNTY, VIRGINIA**, by Rev. Alfred Bagby. (1908) reprint 1990. Indexed. Illus.
One-third of this county history is devoted to genealogical sketches and family records compiled from the primary sources of King and Queen County. Also includes biographical sketches.
Cloth. $23.50. 402pp. .... Vendor G0011

4568 **THE MAGNA CHARTA BARONS AND THEIR AMERICAN DESCENDANTS [1898]. Together with the Pedigrees of the Founders of the Order of Runnemede**, by Charles H. Browning. (1898) reprint 1991. Indexed. Illus.
Cloth. $32.50. 463pp. .... Vendor G0011

4569 **MAGNA CHARTA BARONS AND THEIR DESCENDANTS [1915]**, by Charles H. Browning. (1915) reprint 1991. Indexed. Illus.
Cloth. $31.50. 366pp. .... Vendor G0011

4570 **THE MAGNA CHARTA SURETIES, 1215. The Barons Named in the Magna Charta, 1215 and Some of Their Descendants Who Settled in America, 1607–1650. Fourth Edition**, by Frederick Lewis Weis and Arthur Adams. With additions and corrections by Walter L. Sheppard, Jr. (1991) reprint 1993. Indexed.
Cloth. $20.00. 196pp. .... Vendor G0010

4571 **MASSACHUSETTS AND MAINE FAMILIES. In the Ancestry of Walter Goodwin Davis (1885–1966): A reprinting, in Alphabetical Order by Surname, of the Sixteen Multi-Ancestor Compendia (plus *Thomas Haley of Winter Harbor and His Descendants*) compiled by Maine's Foremost Genealogist, 1916–1963,** by Walter Goodwin Davis; with an introduction by Gary Boyd Roberts. 3 vols. (1916–1963) reprint 1996. Indexed.

Covers the entire known American and usually some English ancestry of each of Davis's sixteen great-great-grandparents: 1. Nicholas **Davis**, 1753–1832, of Limington, Maine; 2. Charity **Haley**, 1755–1800, wife of Nicholas Davis; 3. Joseph **Waterhouse**, 1754–1837, of Standish, Maine; 4. Lydia **Harmon**, 1755–1858, wife of Joseph Waterhouse (1924); 5. Joseph **Neal**, 1769–c.1835, of Litchfield, Maine (1945); 6. Sarah **Johnson**, 1775–1824, wife of Joseph Neal; 7. Annis **Spear**, 1775–1858, of Litchfield, Maine; 8. Sarah **Hildreth**, 1773–1857, wife of Annis Spear; 9. Dudley **Wildes**, 1759–1820, of Topsfield, Massachusetts; 10. Bethia **Harris**, 1748–1833, wife of Dudley Wildes; 11. Abel **Lunt**, 1769–1806, of Newbury, Massachusetts ; 12. Phoebe **Tilton**, 1775–1847, wife of Abel Lunt; 13. James **Patten**, 1747?–1817, of Arundel (Kennebunkport), Maine; 14. Sarah **Stone**, wife of James Patten; 15. Amos **Towne**, 1737–1793, of Arundel (Kennebunkport), Maine; 16. Sarah **Miller**, 1755–1840, wife of Amos Towne.

Cloth. $50.00/vol., $135.00/set. 2,300pp. . . . . Vendor G0010

4572 **MEMOIRS OF THE EARLY PIONEER SETTLERS OF OHIO, with Narratives of Incidents and Occurrences,** by S.P. Hildreth. (1854) reprint 1995.

This work consists of biographical sketches of the early settlers of Washington County.

Paper. $35.00. 539pp. . . . . Vendor G0011

4573 **MERION IN THE WELSH TRACT with Sketches of the Townships of Haverford and Radnor. Historical and Genealogical Collections Concerning the Welsh Barony in the Province of Pennsylvania Settled by the Cymric Quakers in 1682,** by Thomas Allen Glenn. (1896) reprint 1994. Partially indexed. Illus.

Detailed genealogies or extensive genealogical notes can be found on some 25 main families.

Paper. $32.50. 394pp. . . . . Vendor G0011

4574 **NEWBERRY COUNTY, SOUTH CAROLINA: Historical and Genealogical Annals,** by George Leland Summer. (1950) reprint 1995. Indexed.

Includes genealogies of some seventy pioneer families of Newberry County.

Paper. $37.50. 483pp. . . . . Vendor G0011

4575 **NEW ENGLAND COLONIAL FAMILIES, VOL. 1: Brown Families of Bristol Counties, Massachusetts and Rhode Island, from the Immigrants to the Early Nineteenth Century [and] Descendants of Jared Talbot of the South Purchase of Taunton, Now Dighton, Massachusetts,** by Helen H. Lane, Elaine Varley, and Carl Boyer, 3rd. 1981. Indexed.

Cloth. $14.50. 219pp. . . . . Vendor G0198

4576 **NEW ENGLAND FAMILIES, GENEALOGICAL AND MEMORIAL. Third Series,** by William Richard Cutter. 4 vols. (1915) reprint 1996. Indexed. Illus.

Includes nearly 1,000 *additional* New England genealogical and biographical essays not found in the First Series.

Paper. $200.00. 2,395pp. . . . . Vendor G0011

4577 **NEW JERSEY BIOGRAPHICAL AND GENEALOGICAL NOTES**, by William Nelson. (1916) reprint 1995. Indexed.

Contains 224 biographies of colonial New Jerseymen, many of which contain extensive genealogies.

Paper. $21.50. 222pp. .... Vendor G0011

4578 **NEW YORK'S FINGER LAKES PIONEER FAMILIES ESPECIALLY TOMPKINS COUNTY**, by Helen F. Lewis. 1991. Indexed.

Includes: **Bower, Brown, Buck, Case, Davenport, Drake, Gibbs, Lewis, Snyder, Teeter**.

Cloth. $71.45. 403pp. .... Vendor G0450

4579 **NOTABLE SOUTHERN FAMILIES, Volume I**, by Zella Armstrong. (1918) reprint 1993.

Genealogies of the families of **Armstrong, Banning, Blount, Brownlow, Calhoun, Deaderick, Gaines, Howard, Key, Luttrell, Lyle, McAdoo, McMillan, Phinizy, Polk, Sevier, Shields, Stone, Turnley**, and **Van Dyke**.

Paper. $23.00. 247pp. .... Vendor G0011

4580 **NOTABLE SOUTHERN FAMILIES, Volume II**, by Zella Armstrong. (1922) reprint 1993.

Genealogies of the families of **Bean, Boone, Borden, Bryan, Carter, Davis, Donaldson, Hardwick, Haywood, Holliday, Hollingsworth, Houston, Johnston, Kelton, Magill, Rhea, Montgomery, Shelby, Vance, Wear**, and **Williams**.

Paper. $28.50. 377pp. .... Vendor G0011

4581 **NOTABLE SOUTHERN FAMILIES, Volume III**, by Zella Armstrong. (1926) reprint 1993.

Genealogies of the families of **Armstrong ("Trooper"), Cockrill, Duke, Elston, Lea, Park, Parkes**, and **Tunnell**.

Paper. $28.50. 369pp. .... Vendor G0011

4582 **THE OLD FAMILIES OF SALISBURY AND AMESBURY, MASSACHU-SETTS**, by David W. Hoyt. (1897–1919) reprint 1996. Indexed.

Includes the genealogies of more than 300 families, each traced through at least five or six generations.

Paper. $65.00. 1,097pp. .... Vendor G0011

4583 **OLD FAMILIES OF STATEN ISLAND**, by J.J. Clute. (1877) reprint 1990.

Contains genealogical information on eighty early Staten Island families.

Cloth. $15.00. 103pp. .... Vendor G0011

4584 **THE OLD FREE STATE. A Contribution to the History of Lunenburg County and Southside Virginia**, by Landon C. Bell. 2 vols. (1927) reprint 1995.

This work identifies the early pioneers and settlers of the territory and traces approximately 20,000 Southside residents both in original records and in separately prepared genealogies.

Paper. $95.00. 1,267pp. .... Vendor G0011

4585 **OLD KENT: THE EASTERN SHORE OF MARYLAND**, by George A. Hanson. (1876) reprint 1996. Indexed. Illus.

This standard history of the area includes genealogies of early Eastern Shore families.

Paper. 383pp. .... Vendor G0011

4586 **OLD KING WILLIAM HOMES AND FAMILIES. An Account of Some of the Old Homesteads and Families of King William County, Virginia, from Its Earliest Settlement**, by Peyton Neale Clarke. (1897) reprint 1995. Indexed. Illus.

Contains genealogical sketches of seventy-five early King William County families and their descendants, including a lengthy history of the **Edwards** family, the descendants of Ambrose Edwards of Cherry Grove.

Paper. $21.50. 211pp. .... Vendor G0011

4587 **ONE HUNDRED AND SIXTY ALLIED FAMILIES**, by John Osborne Austin. (1893) reprint 1982. Indexed.

On the families of New England settlers, many of whom migrated to Rhode Island.

Cloth. xxi+288pp. .... Vendor G0010

4588 **THE ORDER OF THE FOUNDERS AND PATRIOTS OF AMERICA REGISTER [OF] LINEAGES OF ASSOCIATES, 1896–1993. In Four Volumes**. 1994. Partially indexed.

Cloth. $225.00. 3936pp. .... Vendor G0011

4589 **OUR CHEROKEE-DELAWARE HERITAGE**, compiled by Mary Smith Witcher; edited by Fay Louise Smith Arellano. 1994. Indexed. Illus.

Includes affiliated lines of: **McDaniel, Arthur, Ward, Blevins, Courvoisier, Frierson, Lunday, Ketchum, Connor**.

Soft binding. $30.00. 309pp. .... Vendor G0393

4590 **PEDIGREES OF SOME OF THE EMPEROR CHARLEMAGNE'S DE-SCENDANTS, Volume I**, by von Redlich. (1941) reissued 1996. Indexed.

Contains more than fifty lines of descent from the Emperor Charlemagne.

Cloth. $25.00. 320pp. .... Vendor G0010

4591 **PEDIGREES OF SOME OF THE EMPEROR CHARLEMAGNE'S DE-SCENDANTS, Volume II**, by Langston and Buck. (1974) reissued 1996. Indexed.

Contains more than seventy-five lines of descent from the Emperor Charlemagne.

Cloth. $35.00. 516pp. .... Vendor G0010

4592 **PEDIGREES OF SOME OF THE EMPEROR CHARLEMAGNE'S DE-SCENDANTS, Volume III**, by J. Orton Buck, Jr., and Timothy Field Beard. (1978) reissued 1996. Indexed.

Contains more than eighty-five lines of descent of living people from the Emperor Charlemagne. Each section of the book is headed with the name of the immigrant ancestor through whom descent from Charlemagne is traced, followed by all family names in the line of descent in America. Also contains a chapter called "A Glimpse of Emperor Lothair," by Prof. James Allen Cabaniss, and a list of corrections to Volume II.

Cloth. $30.00. 389pp. .... Vendor G0010

4593 **PENNSYLVANIA GENEALOGIES Chiefly Scotch-Irish and German**, by William Henry Egle. 2nd ed. (1896) reprint 1994. Indexed.

Concerned primarily with families which, for the most part, settled in the extreme regions of colonial Chester County.

Paper. $49.95. 798pp. .... Vendor G0011

FIVE GENERATIONS
PROJECT PUBLICATIONS
Published by General Society
of Mayflower Descendants
MAYFLOWER FAMILIES GENEALOGIES
THROUGH FIVE GENERATIONS
(All books listed below are hard cover)

This series traces descendants of the Pilgrims down through the fifth generation to the birth of the sixth generation children. They are carefully researched and contain the best documented genealogical data that is available.

___ Volume One: Lucy M. Kellogg, FASG, Editor, Three families
    FRANCIS EATON - by Lee D. van Antwerp, MD, CG
    SAMUEL FULLER - by Arthur H. and Katharine W. Radasch
    WILLIAM WHITE -by Robert M. Sherman, FASG, & Ruth W. Sherman, FASG
    includes addendum & Revised Index .... $ 20.00
___ Volume Two: Robert M. Sherman, FASG, Editor, Three families
    JAMES CHILTON - by Robert M. Sherman, FASG and Verle D. Vincent
    RICHARD MORE - by Robert S. Wakefield, FASG, and Lydia R.D. Finlay
    THOMAS ROGERS - by Alice W.A. Westgate
    includes addendum .... $ 25.00
___ Volume Four, Second Edition
    EDWARD FULLER - by Bruce Campbell MacGunnigle, CG .... $ 25.00
___ Volume Five: Two families
    EDWARD WINSLOW - by Ruth C. McGuyre and Robert S. Wakefield, FASG
    JOHN BILLINGTON - by Harriet W. Hodge .... $ 20.00
___ Volume Six
    STEPHEN HOPKINS - by John D. Austin, FASG .... $ 35.00
___ Volume Seven
    PETER BROWN - by Robert S. Wakefield, FASG .... $ 20.00
___ Volume Eight
    DEGORY PRIEST .... $ 20.00
    compiled by Mrs. Charles Delmar Townsend, Robert S. Wakefield FASG,
    Margaret Harris Stover; Edited by Robert S. Wakefield FASG

Please send order to: **MAYFLOWER FAMILIES**
                        P.O. Box 3297, Plymouth, MA 02361

PLEASE INDICATE SELECTIONS ON APPROPRIATE LINES ABOVE.

NAME _____

Address _____

City _____ State _____ Zip _____

Postal Rates	Total Order
US orders:	
$0 - $12 $3.00	MA residents, please
$13 and over $4.00	add 5% Sales Tax
Canada (US funds) $6.00	
Foreign (US funds) $7.00	Shipping
	Total Enclosed

4594 **PENOBSCOT PIONEERS VOL. ONE: ALLEY, BAKEMAN, SMART**, by Philip Howard Gray. 1992. Indexed. Book #1315.
Cloth. $39.00. 160pp. .... Vendor G0082

4595 **PENOBSCOT PIONEERS, VOL. TWO: BRAY, CLOSSON, HOWARD**, by Philip Howard Gray. 1992. Indexed. Book #1398.
Cloth. $39.00. 160pp. .... Vendor G0082

4596 **PENOBSCOT PIONEERS, VOL. THREE, BILLINGS, GRAY, HERRICK**, by Philip Howard Gray. 1993. Indexed. Book #1443.
Cloth. $39.00. 192pp. .... Vendor G0082

4597 **PENOBSCOT PIONEERS, VOL. FOUR: EATON, HASKELL, MARCHANT, RAYNES**, by Philip Howard Gray. 1994. Indexed. Book #1528.
Cloth. $39.00. 192pp. .... Vendor G0082

4598 **PENOBSCOT PIONEERS, VOL. FIVE: BUNKER, PENDLETON, POMEROY, VEASEY**, by Philip Howard Gray. 1995. Indexed. Book #1629.
Cloth. $39.00. 224pp. .... Vendor G0082

4599 **PIONEER FAMILIES OF FRANKLIN COUNTY, VIRGINIA**, by Marshall Wingfield. (1964, 1992) reprint 1996. Indexed.
Includes the following families: **Akers, Bernard, Boone, Booth, Bowman, Brodie, Brown, Cahill, Callaway, Carper, Claiborne, Cooper, Craghead, Davis, Dillard, Dillon, Dudley, Early, Ferguson, Finney, Fishburn, Glass, Goode, Greer, Hancock, (Thomas) Hancock, Harper, Hill, Hook, Hopkins, (Charles) Hopkins, James, Jamison, Laprade, Lavinder, Lee, McNiel, Marshall, Martin, Mitchell, Montgomery, Motley-Martin, Naff (Naeff, Knaff), Nelson, Peters, Pinkard, Powell-Payne, Price, Prillaman, Prunty, Ross, Saunders, Swanson-Muse, Taliaferro, Tate, Tinsley, Turner, Walker, Webster, and Wingfield.**
Paper. 373pp. .... Vendor G0011

4600 **PIONEERS AND MAKERS OF ARKANSAS**, by Josiah H. Shinn. (1908) reprint 1991. Indexed.
Includes genealogies of the following Arkansas families: **Brilhart, Coffman/ Cuffman, Davis, Desha, Fletcher, Garland, Hall, Johnson, Kaufman, Lafferty, Lindsey, Martin, Newton, Rector/Rechtor/Richter, Watkins,** and **Wilson.**
Cloth. $27.00. 423pp. .... Vendor G0011

4601 **PIONEER SETTLERS OF GRAYSON COUNTY, VIRGINIA. With a New Index**, by Benjamin Floyd Nuckolls. (1914) reprint 1994. Indexed.
Paper. $23.00. 219pp. .... Vendor G0011

4602 **THE PIONEERS OF MAINE AND NEW HAMPSHIRE, 1623–1660**, by Charles Henry Pope. (1908) reprint 1994.
Contains genealogical notices on 1,000 early settlers of Maine and New Hampshire.
Paper. $23.50. 263pp. .... Vendor G0011

4603 **THE PLANTAGENET ANCESTRY. Being Tables Showing Over 7,000 of the Ancestors of Elizabeth (Daughter of Edward IV and Wife of Henry VII) the Heiress of the Plantagenets**, by Lt.-Col. W.H. Turton. (1928) 1993. Indexed.
Cloth. $50.00. 274pp, quarto .... Vendor G0010

4604 **POCAHONTAS' DESCENDANTS. A Revision, Enlargement and Extension of the List as Set Out by Wyndham Robertson in His Book** *Pocahontas and Her Descendants* **(1887)**, by Stuart E. Brown, Jr., Lorraine F. Myers, and Eileen M. Chappel. (1985, 1992) reprint 1994. Indexed. Illus.
Combined with two volumes of corrections and additions.
Cloth. $50.00. 716pp. .... Vendor G0010

4605 **THE PROMINENT FAMILIES OF THE UNITED STATES OF AMERICA**, by Arthur Meredyth Burke. (1908) reprint 1991. Indexed.
Includes hundreds of pedigrees, each beginning with the subject living at the turn of this century and showing his descent from the earliest known forebearer.
Cloth. $35.00. 510pp. .... Vendor G0010

4606 **RED RIVER SETTLERS. Records of the Settlers of Northern Montgomery, Robertson, and Sumner Counties, Tennessee**, by Edythe Rucker Whitley. (1980) reprint 1995. Indexed.
Includes ninety-five genealogies of Red River families.
Paper. $18.50. 189pp. .... Vendor G0011

4607 **REGISTER . . . OF THE EARLY SETTLERS OF KINGS COUNTY, LONG ISLAND, N.Y., from Its First Settlement by Europeans to 1700**, by Teunis G. Bergen. (1881) reprint 1994. Indexed.
Contains genealogies of the 17th-century pioneers of Kings County, most of whom were of Dutch or, to a lesser extent, British origin.
Paper. $35.00. 452pp. .... Vendor G0011

4608 **ROANE COUNTY, WEST VIRGINIA FAMILIES, Excerpted from** *History of Roane County*, **West Virginia from the Time of its Exploration to A.D. 1927**, by William H. Bishop. (1927) reprint 1995.
Includes hundreds of genealogical and historical essays of pioneer families of Roane County.
Paper. $21.50. [431–704]pp. .... Vendor G0011

4609 **ROYAL AND NOBLE FAMILIES OF MEDIEVAL EUROPE**, by Gayle King Blankenship. 1993. Indexed. Illus.
For anyone with ties to medieval royalty of Europe (including **Alfred the Great & Charlemagne**) or the nobility of France & England; not a lineage book; presented as families with children; many biographies; all are **Ligon, Batte**, or **Mallory** ancestors. Referenced; $8^{1}/_{2}$ x 11; 16.6 pitch.
Cloth. $45.00. 365pp. .... Vendor G0034

4610 **THE ROYAL DESCENTS OF 500 IMMIGRANTS to the American Colonies or the United States Who Were Themselves Notable or Left Descendants Notable in American History**, by Gary Boyd Roberts. 1993. Indexed.
Cloth. $45.00. 700pp. .... Vendor G0010

4611 **ROYALTY FOR COMMONERS. The Complete Known Lineage of John of Gaunt, Son of Edward III, King of England, and Queen Philippa**, by Roderick W. Stuart. Rev. 2nd ed. 1995. Indexed.
Cloth. $30.00. 277pp. .... Vendor G0010

4612 **SHENANDOAH VALLEY PIONEERS AND THEIR DESCENDANTS: A History of Frederick County, Virginia from its Formation in 1738 to 1908, Compiled Mainly from Original Records of Old Frederick County, now Hampshire, Berkeley, Shenandoah, Jefferson, Hardy, Clarke, Warren,**

Morgan, and Frederick. Indexed Edition, by T.K. Cartmell. (1908, 1963) reprint 1995. Indexed.

Contains several hundred detailed genealogical and biographical sketches of early families of old Frederick County. Includes genealogical accounts of Shenandoah pioneers Joist **Hite**, Daniel **Morgan**, and others.

Paper, 8¹/₂" x 11". $57.50. vii+572pp. . . . . Vendor G0011

4613 **SIX COLUMBIANA COUNTY, OHIO, PIONEER FAMILIES. FAMILY 1. WILLIAM FETTERS (1794–1857) AND MARY B. LEECH: ANCESTORS AND DESCENDANTS**, by William Brooke Fetters. 1991. Indexed. Illus.

Major families: **Vetter/Fetters** (Germany, New Jersey, Pennsylvania, Ohio), **Madoeri/Madera** (Switzerland, New Jersey), **Jung/Young** (Germany, Pennsylvania), **Hayes** (Wales, Pennsylvania), and **David/Davies/Davis** (Wales, Pennsylvania).

Cloth. $27.50. 258pp. . . . . Vendor G0206

4614 **SIX COLUMBIANA COUNTY, OHIO, PIONEER FAMILIES. FAMILY 2. JOHN WEBB (c1754–1824) AND ELIZABETH MONTGOMERY: ANCESTORS AND DESCENDANTS**, by William Brooke Fetters. 1993. Indexed. Illus.

Major families: **Webb** (Pennsylvania, Maryland, Ohio), **Montgomery** (Maryland), **Hurford** (England, Pennsylvania).

Cloth. $27.50. 250pp. . . . . Vendor G0206

4615 **SIX COLUMBIANA COUNTY, OHIO, PIONEER FAMILIES. FAMILY 3. SAMUEL SMITH (1765–1855) AND SARAH BISHOP: ANCESTORS AND DESCENDANTS**, by William Brooke Fetters. 1994. Indexed. Illus.

Major families: **Smith** (New Jersey, Pennsylvania, Virginia, Ohio), **Scott** (England, Pennsylvania), **Bond** (England, Pennsylvania), **Parker** (England), **Whitaker/Whitacre** (England, Pennsylvania, Virginia, Ohio), **Hulme** (England, Pennsylvania), **Palmer** (England, Pennsylvania), **Bishop** (Maryland, Pennsylvania).

Cloth. $33.00. 503pp. . . . . Vendor G0206

4616 **SIX COLUMBIANA COUNTY, OHIO, PIONEER FAMILIES. FAMILY 4. BALTZER YOUNG (1760–1845) AND MARY ELIZABETH BUSS**, by William Brooke Fetters. 1995. Indexed. Illus.

Major families: **Jung/Young** (Pennsylvania, Ohio), **Buss/Boose** (Pennsylvania, Maryland), **Dentler** (Pennsylvania).

Cloth. $27.50. 247pp. . . . . Vendor G0206

4617 **SKETCHES OF SOME OF THE FIRST SETTLERS OF UPPER GEORGIA, OF THE CHEROKEES, AND THE AUTHOR. Revised and Corrected Edition with an Added Index**, by George R. Gilmer. (1926, 1965) reprint 1995. Indexed. Illus.

Includes genealogies of the following main families: **Andrew, Barnett, Bibb, Campbell, Clark, Crawford, Dooly, Gilbert, Gilmer, Grattan, Hart, Harvie, Johnson, Lewis, Long, Mathews, McGehee, Meriwether, Strother**, and **Taliaferro**.

Paper. $35.00. 463pp. . . . . Vendor G0011

4618 **SOME PROMINENT VIRGINIA FAMILIES**, by Louise Pecquet du Bellet.
4 vols. (1907) reprint 1994. Illus.
Contains hundreds of family histories.
Paper. $135.00. 1,715pp. .... Vendor G0011

4619 **[Sons and Daughters of the Pilgrims]. LINEAGES OF MEMBERS OF
THE NATIONAL SOCIETY OF THE SONS AND DAUGHTERS OF THE
PILGRIMS.** 2 vols. (1929, 1953) reprint 1988. Indexed.
Volume I includes the lineages of all members of the Society from 1909 to
1928; Volume II includes lineages of members who joined the Society between
1929 and 1952.
Cloth. $75.00. 1,004 pp. .... Vendor G0010

4620 **[Sons and Daughters of the Pilgrims]. SIXTEEN HUNDRED LINES TO
PILGRIMS. National Society of the Sons and Daughters of the Pilgrims**,
edited by Mary E. Mayo. (1982) reprint 1996. Indexed.
Covers the lineage records of 1,500 members new to the Society from 1953
to 1981.
Cloth. $75.00. 1,048pp. .... Vendor G0010

4621 **SOUTHEASTERN MICHIGAN PIONEER FAMILIES ESPECIALLY
LENAWEE COUNTY**, by Helen F. Lewis. 1994. Organized alphabetically.
Cloth. $75.45. 426pp. .... Vendor G0450

4622 **SOUTHEASTERN MICHIGAN PIONEER FAMILIES ESPECIALLY
LIVINGSTON COUNTY**, by Helen F. Lewis. 1995. Organized alphabetically.
Cloth. $53.45. 302pp. .... Vendor G0450

4623 **SOUTHERN COLUMBIA COUNTY, NEW YORK FAMILIES, A GENE-
ALOGY**, by Arthur C.M. Kelly. 1996. Indexed.
Cloth. $42.00. 227pp. .... Vendor G0450

4624 **SOUTHOLD CONNECTIONS. Historical and Biographical Sketches of
Northeastern Long Island**, by Judy Jacobson. (1991) reprint 1992. Indexed.
Maps.
Examines the early families and history of the North Fork of Long Island,
New York and presents genealogies on seventeen families who settled there
during the 17th and 18th centuries.
Paper. $16.50. 113pp. .... Vendor G0011

4625 **SOUTHSIDE VIRGINIA FAMILIES, Volume I**, by John Bennett Boddie.
(1955) reprint 1996. Indexed. Illus.
Contains lineages of the following families from the early counties of Isle of
Wight, Prince George, and Surry: **Allen, Bailey, Ballard, Barker-Bradford-
Taylor, Batte, Bell, Bennett-Pierce, Bishop-Stokes, Blunt, Boyce-Scott-Tatum,
Braswell, Briggs, Browne, Burges, Cato, Champion, Clark, Cocke, Cooke,
Corker, Dixon, Eaton, Faulcon, Flake, Fort, Goodrich, Gordon, Graves-
Hancock, Hamblin-Hamlin, Hancock, Hill, Hines, Howle, Irwin, Jennings-
Hill, Johnston, Jones, Jordan, Lanier, Lewis, Long, Massengill, Norfleet,
Overton-Harris-Day, Pitt, Plummer, Rudulph, Sitgreaves, Sledge, Smith,
Sweeney, Tyrus, Weldon, West**, and **Whitmel**.
Paper. $31.50. 390pp. .... Vendor G0011

4626 **SOUTHSIDE VIRGINIA FAMILIES, Volume II**, by John Bennett Boddie. (1956) reprint 1996. Indexed. Illus.

Contains lineages of the following families from the early counties of Isle of Wight, Surry, and Sussex: **Arrington, Bailey, Barham, Barker, Branch, Chappell, Cloud, Cocer, Cofer, Coffer, Coker, Collier, Copher, Darden–Durden, Edmunds, Foliot, Green, Gurgany, Hargrave, Hart, Harvin, Herbert, Hill, Holt, Judkins, Lane, Lucas, McKain, Macon, Mann, Norwood, Perry, Philips, Rogers, Sorrell-Earle-Warren, Stover, Taylor, Tyas–Tyus, Westbrook**, and **Worsham-Marshall.**
Paper. $29.50. 298pp. .... Vendor G0011

4627 **THIS OLD MONMOUTH OF OURS**, by William S. Hornor. (1932) reprint 1990. Indexed.

Treats nearly 100 early Monmouth County families.
Cloth. $30.00. 444pp. .... Vendor G0011

4628 **THREE HUNDRED COLONIAL ANCESTORS AND WAR SERVICE— Their Part in Making American History from 495 to 1934 Bound with Supplement, Supplement II, and Supplement II, Concluded**, by Elizabeth M. Leach Rixford. (1934, 1938, 1943, 1944) reprint 1991. Indexed. Illus.

Treats nearly 150 different lines touching on more than 5,000 ancestors.
Paper. $35.00. 425pp. .... Vendor G0011

4629 **TIDEWATER VIRGINIA FAMILIES**, by Virginia Lee Hutcheson Davis. 1990. Indexed.

Covering 375 years, this book sets forth the genealogical history of some forty families who have their roots in Tidewater Virginia.
Cloth. 730pp. .... Vendor G0010

4630 **VIRGINIA FAMILIES OF LOUISA, HANOVER AND MONROE COUNTIES**, by Gayle King Blankenship. 1991. Indexed. Illus.

Archey, Corker, Durvin, Greene, Hall, Higginson, Hudson, Kersey, Shirey, Sifford, Stanley, Strong, Tate, Ward, Wash, Watkins, Wheeler. Referenced; 8½ x 11.
Cloth. $37.00. 274pp. .... Vendor G0034

4631 **VIRGINIA GENEALOGIES. A Genealogy of the Glassell Family of Scotland and Virginia, Also of the Families of Ball, Brown, Bryan, Conway, Daniel, Ewell, Holladay, Lewis, Littlepage, Moncure, Peyton, Robinson, Scott, Taylor, Wallace, and Others of Virginia and Maryland**, by Horace Edwin Hayden. (1891) reprint 1996. Indexed.
Paper. $49.95. 777pp. .... Vendor G0011

4632 **VIRGINIA HISTORICAL GENEALOGIES**, by John Bennett Boddie. (1954) reprint 1996. Indexed. Illus.

Contains the lineages of about fifty families, the main branches of which were located in Virginia, Maryland, and the Carolinas. Genealogies of the following families are given: **Allen, Aston, Barker-Bradford-Taylor, Berkeley-Ligon-Norwood, Binns, Butler, Claiborne, Clark, Colclough, Crafford, Crayfford-Crafford, Davis, Doniphan, Eldridge, Flood, Godwyn, Gray, Gregg, Griffis, Grigsby, Harris, Haynes, Jones, Mallory, Mason, Moore, Mumford-DeJarnette-Perryman, Newton, Norwood, Pace, Peche-Cornish-Everard-Mildmay-Harcourt-Crispe, Reade, Ruffin, Sledge, Smith, Sowerby-**

Sorsby, Stone-Smallwood-Smith, Stover, Thomas, Travis, Warren, Woodliffe, Wynne, and Wythe.
Paper. 384pp. .... Vendor G0011

4633 **WELSH FOUNDERS OF PENNSYLVANIA**, by Thomas Allen Glenn. 2 vols. in 1. (1911, 1913) reprint 1991. Indexed. Illus.
Cloth. $31.50. 356pp. .... Vendor G0011

4634 **YARMOUTH, NOVA SCOTIA, GENEALOGIES. Transcribed from the** *Yarmouth Herald*, by George S. Brown. 1993. Indexed.
Data on New England families who migrated to Nova Scotia around the time of the Revolutionary War, which appeared in Mr. Brown's articles in the *Yarmouth Herald* between 1896 and 1910.
Cloth. $60.00. 956pp. .... Vendor G0010

Surname Index

Abbe, 1
Abbey, 1–2, 4351
Abbot, 3
Abbott, 4–7, 385, 4169
Abee, 1232
Abell, 8–9, 4428
Abercrombie, 10
Abernathy, 2763
Abey, 1232
Abney, 4543
Abraham, 2557
Ackerman, 553, 4170
Adair, 11–12, 494, 3880.
　See also ad p. 37
Adami, 766
Adams, 13–27, 39, 68,
　218, 1266, 2297, 3164,
　3874, 4477, 4511, 4543
Adamson, 4458
Adcock, 3804
Addington, 28
Adkins, 398, 1266, 1460,
　2141
Adler, 1448
Afdal, 3703
Agee, 29, 385
Aglionby, 4395
Agnew, 30–31, 2962,
　3284
Ainsworth, 32
Akers, 33, 1460, 3519,
　4599
Albaugh. *See* ad p. 315
Albee, 34
Albertson, 4533
Albrecht, 35
Albright, 35–36, 2563,
　3108
Albrite, 36
Alcott, 1596
Alden, 37–43, 1483
Alderman, 4529
Aldrich, 44, 540
Aldridge, 1447, 4532

Aldworth, 45
Alexander, 46–52, 2608,
　2734, 3481, 4544
Alford, 4534
Alfred the Great, 4429,
　4609
Alger, 53–54
Alison, 76
Allan, 70
Allemong, 4477
Allen, 55–72, 75, 479,
　540, 881, 1062, 1183,
　1682, 1939, 2157, 2329,
　2445, 3164, 3168, 3533,
　3804, 3874, 4169, 4172,
　4225, 4428, 4451, 4464,
　4532, 4625, 4632. *See*
　also ad p. 307
Allerton, 73
Alley, 1460, 4594
Alleyne, 276
Alligood, 3924
Allin, 63, 70, 4525–26
Alling, 74–75
Allison, 76–77
Allon, 70
Alloway, 3760
Allred, 2181, 4532, 4537,
　4539
Allsop, 4428
Allsup, 671
Allyn, 74, 78–79
Alston, 80
Alstons, 80
Alt, 3830
Alten, 81
Althouse, 4428
Alverson, 4529
Alvord, 82, 540, 611
Amadowne, 83
Amazeen, 1533
Ames, 84, 1213
Amidon, 1682
Amis, 669

Amiss, 1965
Amory, 85
Amos, 86
Amspaugh, 4169
Anderson, 87–90, 211,
　254, 789, 1917, 2108,
　2144, 2608, 3145, 4351,
　4477, 4516, 4524, 4537
Andrew, 91, 4617
Andrews, 92–96, 218,
　2445, 4266, 4428, 4447
Andrus, 97
Angell, 99
Angelo, 3804
Ankeny, 100
Ansley, 4131
Anthon, 101
Anthony, 102, 384, 1070,
　3164, 4428, 4525
Antisell, 103
Antrim, 104
Applegate, 2721
Appler, 105
Appleton, 106, 172, 2131
Archer, 3177, 4420
Archey, 4630
Arden, 3502
Ardery, 107
Arellano, 2546
Arey, 108
Armentrout, 4169
Armington, 109, 4428
Armistead, 110–11, 4524
Armitage. *See* ad p. 383
Arms, 112, 1533
Armstrong, 113–14,
　2557, 2788, 3164, 4169,
　4522, 4579, 4581
Arndt, 115
Arnold, 39, 116–18,
　1795, 1804, 2043, 2448.
　See also ad p. 315
Arres, 4272
Arrington, 3909, 4525–

Numbers refer to book numbers that appear in the left-hand column of pages 1–403.

26, 4533, 4626. *See also* ad p. 383
Arroyo, 119
Arthur, 2875, 4589
Asberry, 4382
Asbury, 4382
Asfordby, 273
Ashcraft, 120
Asher, 2449
Ashford, 3986
Ashley, 121
Ashman, 1429
Ashton, 4458
Ashworth, 2708
Askew, 122
Aspinwall, 123
Asselstine, 1292
Asseltyne, 1292
Aston, 4632
Atchisons, 211
Aten, 2788
Atherton, 3108
Atkey, 509. *See also* ad p. 59
Atkins, 124
Atkinson, 1266, 1682, 2445
Atlee, 125
Atte Wode, 129
Atwater, 126–28
Atwell, 4534
Atwood, 129
Aubrey, 4440
Auchincloss, 130
Auchmoody, 4555
Augur, 131
Aull, 132
Ault, 3830
Austin, 133–34, 1917, 2137
Autry, 135
Auxier, 136
Averell, 137
Avery, 137–44, 218, 280, 4428, 4532, 4535
Awbrey, 2466
Axford, 145
Axtell, 146
Ayer, 2935. *See also* ad p. 153
Ayers, 3952
Aylsworth, 147

Aymar, 148
Ayres, 149–51, 4552

Babb, 152, 4477
Babbidge. *See* ad p. 153
Babbitt, 153
Babcock, 154–57, 2000, 4169, 4323, 4428
Baber, 4524, 4535
Babers, 4535
Babington, 4266
Bache, 1090
Bachilar, 240
Bachiler, 2297
Backenstoss, 158
Backus, 159–60
Bacon, 161–63, 1598, 1682, 1805, 4464
Badger, 164
Badgerow, 3703
Badgley, 795
Baer, 165, 4170. *See also* ad p. 315
Bageant, 4477
Bahl, 1307
Baierschmidt, 255
Baierschmitt, 255
Bailey, 166–69, 500, 2144, 2166, 2962, 3155, 3387, 4625, 4626. *See also* ad p. 15
Bailleul, 257
Baillie. *See* ad p. 15
Baird, 170, 1398, 1431
Bakeman, 171, 4594
Baker, 172–74, 254, 299, 1905, 2144, 2724, 2926, 3305, 4169–70, 4286, 4428, 4442. *See also* ad p. 315
Bakken, 3482
Balch, 175–77
Balcombe, 178
Baldridge, 3284
Baldry, 3685
Baldwin, 179–80, 1682, 2296, 4523
Balew, 344–45
Baliol, 4522
Balis, 2144
Ball, 181–89, 275, 1556, 1800, 3882, 4246, 4458, 4463, 4631

Ballamy, 299
Ballangee, 398
Ballard, 190–93, 1447, 1508, 4428, 4464, 4625. *See also* ad p. 153
Ballinger, 4477
Ballou, 194, 344–45. *See also* ad p. 383
Ballow, 385
Baltzer, 3630
Bandy, 3804
Bangs, 195
Banker, 196
Bankor, 196
Banks, 197, 1246, 3137, 3874
Banning, 198, 4579
Banta, 199
Barbee, 2845
Barber, 200–204, 4428
Barbor, 2962
Barbour, 2962
Barclay, 205, 1090
Barcroft, 206
Bard, 207
Barger, 208
Bargman, 2815
Bargy, 2935
Barham, 4530, 4626
Barker, 209–10, 1682, 1917, 4523, 4625–26, 4632
Barkley, 211, 2307
Barksdale, 212
Barlow, 213, 2724, 4524
Barnard, 214, 2028
Barnes, 215–18, 540, 1051, 1195, 1437, 2315, 3108. *See also* ad p. 19
Barnett, 4534, 4617
Barney, 219–20
Barnhart, 221
Barr, 222–23
Barrett, 224, 299, 1596, 2570, 4477
Barrow, 3164, 4524
Barrows, 1278, 1541, 3563
Barry, 225–26, 1795
Barse, 1693
Bartelt, 3107
Bartholomew, 227

Bartlett, 228–31, 2370, 2603, 3553, 3906
Barton, 232
Bartow, 233
Bartram, 1460, 2141
Bascom, 234, 1682
Bashforth, 1805
Bashor. *See* ad p. 315
Bass, 39, 235, 2708, 3145
Bassett, 236–37, 608, 3723, 4428
Bastin, 1266
Baswell, 4306
Basye, 238, 817
Batchelder, 239–40, 4464
Batcheller, 240
Bateman, 4382. *See also* ad p. 153
Bates, 241–44, 634, 1051, 2296, 2487
Bathurst, 4530
Battaile, 245
Batte, 385, 4524, 4609, 4625
Batten, 246
Battey, 247
Battin, 2297, 4428
Battle, 248, 4528
Batts, 4533
Baude, 4528
Baugh, 4533–34, 4536
Baughman, 249–50, 1804
Baulstone, 4428
Bauman, 251, 4170
Bauscher, 441
Bausher, 441
Baxter, 252–54
Bayerschmitt, 255
Bayeux, 259
Bayle, 2763
Bayles, 256
Bayley, 166, 257. *See also* ad p. 15
Baylis, 258
Baylor, 4539
Bayly. *See* ad p. 15
Bayne, 259
Baynes, 259
Beach, 260–61. *See also* ad p. 383

Beachy, 3057
Beal, 262
Beale, 263–65
Beales, 421
Beall, 87, 218, 536
Beam, 4169
Beaman, 266
Bean, 267, 4580
Bear, 268, 1768. *See also* ad p. 315
Bearce, 3226
Beard, 170, 269–70, 3986
Beardsley, 271–72, 544, 4552
Beasley, 1712, 2608
Beatty, 273–74, 940. *See also* ad p. 383
Beauchamp, 275
Beaune, 3797
Beavens, 218
Beavers, 2662
Bechince. *See* ad p. 383
Bechtol, 2716
Beck, 276, 1795, 2306
Becker, 2307, 2935, 3438
Beckham, 277
Beckley, 278
Beckwith, 279–81, 1596, 2081
Bedon, 282
Bedwell, 283
Beebe, 218, 284–87
Beery, 288–89. *See also* ad p. 315
Beeson, 290, 4477, 4533
Beggs, 291, 2369
Beharrell, 292
Beidler, 293
Beierschmitt, 255
Beiler, 3057
Beisel, 294
Beissel, 294
Bekesby, 362
Belcher, 295
Belden, 296
Belderlinden, 4538
Belew, 344–45
Belieu, 344–45
Bell, 297–98, 530, 3874, 4522, 4527, 4530, 4625

Bellamy, 299. *See also* ad p. 27
Bellar, 4286
Belleville, 300
Bellew, 344–45
Bellhouse, 301
Bellingham, 2191
Bellows, 302
Belse, 3619
Belser, 303
Belson, 4464
Belt, 2979
Belue, 344–45
Bement, 218
Bemis, 304
Benbow, 479, 3658
Bender, 3057
Benedict, 305
Benjamin, 306
Bennage, 307
Bennetch, 307
Bennett, 211, 308–12, 1652, 2296, 4428, 4529, 4534, 4544, 4625. *See also* ad p. 383
Benson, 313–15, 688, 1278, 4300
Bent, 316
Bentley, 317, 2708, 3703, 4538
Bently, 3703, 4538
Benton, 318
Bereman. *See* ad p. 153
Beresford, 3378
Bergen, 62, 319
Bergey, 320
Bergundthal, 2206
Berkeley, 321, 4632
Berkey, 322, 4426
Bernard, 323, 2202, 4599
Bernhardt. *See* ad p. 383
Berrey, 324
Berry, 324, 688, 4536, 4544
Berryman, 1447
Bertine, 325
Bertolet, 326
Bertram, 2905
Besbedge, 354
Bess, 2043
Besse, 1278

Numbers refer to book numbers that appear in the left-hand column of pages 1–403.

Bessellieu, 2933
Bestman, 327
Bettenhausen, 2307
Betts, 328–29, 4530
Bevan, 4477
Beverley, 330. *See also* ad p. 29
Beverly, 86
Bevier, 331, 4555
Bevill, 1515
Beville, 332
Bevins, 1800
Beyo, 4555
Beyrer, 641
Bibb, 333, 4382, 4617
Bible, 4440
Bickham, 4128
Bicknell, 334–35, 2181
Biddle, 336–37, 4266
Bidwell, 338
Bierce, 339
Biersmith, 255
Bigelow, 340
Bigg, 4537
Bigge, 1682
Biggs. *See* ad p. 315
Bignold, 341
Bigod, 4528
Bigsby, 362
Bilieu, 344–45
Bill, 342
Billard, 4247
Bille, 3745
Billing, 343
Billings, 39, 343, 4596
Billingsley, 4525
Billington. *See* ad p. 397
Billopp, 1321
Bills, 3658
Bilyeu, 344–45
Bines, 299
Binford, 346–47
Bingeman, 1233
Bingham, 275, 348–51, 1803
Binion, 385
Binney, 352
Binns, 4632
Birch, 4298
Bird, 353, 2081
Birdsall, 1061, 3596
Birdsell, 3392

Birkhead, 970
Birmingham, 4532
Bisbee, 354
Bishop, 355–58, 548, 608, 1035, 4615, 4625
Bispham, 359
Bissell, 360
Bittner, 361, 4170
Bixby, 362, 881
Black, 473, 662, 1221, 1307
Blackburn, 363, 1800, 3658, 3986
Blackhall, 364
Blackistone, 4451
Blackledge, 4458
Blackman, 365
Blackstock, 122
Blackstone, 366–68, 4474, 4525
Blackwell, 367–68
Blades, 500
Blair, 369–76, 1398, 4328, 4552. *See also* ad p. 33
Blaisdell, 839
Blake, 377–81, 649, 1210
Blakemore, 3156
Blakeney, 382–83
Blakeslee, 2636
Blakey, 384, 4524, 4534, 4536
Blanchard, 1278, 3021
Bland, 554
Blandin, 4328
Blank, 3057, 4426
Blankenship, 385, 1800
Blassingame, 688
Blatchford, 386
Blatchley, 2773
Blauvelt, 387
Blazer, 388
Bledsoe, 530, 4525–27
Blethen, 389
Blevins, 2875, 4589
Blickensderfer, 390, 4017
Blish, 391
Bliss, 392–93, 1596, 4428
Blissit, 3164
Bliven, 394
Blocker, 4463
Blodgett, 395

Blood, 396–97
Bloss, 398, 1278
Blott, 1682
Blount, 500, 4579
Blow, 4528
Blue, 344–45
Blunston, 2466
Blunt, 4625
Boade, 4528
Boal, 3874
Board, 3952
Boardman, 399–400, 1656, 2344
Boatner, 4175
Boat(w)right, 4533, 4535
Bock, 401, 2306
Bockenhauers, 2307
Boddie, 1885, 4523, 4525–28, 4531
Boddye, 4528
Bode, 4528
Bodine, 3561
Boehm, 3387
Bogaert, 405
Bogardus, 402–3, 1496
Bogart, 404–5
Bogert, 406–7
Boggess, 4131. *See also* ad p. 283
Boggs, 557, 2181
Bogue, 408, 2296
Bohlander, 409
Bohnsack, 2307
Bohren, 2206
Bohrer, 410
Boileau, 344–45
Boing, 677
Boit, 411
Bolich, 2306
Bolles, 412
Bolling, 413, 494. *See also* ad p. 37
Bolton, 414–16
Bomberger, 417
Bomholt, 1429
Bonafield, 2157
Bonar, 544
Bond, 418–22, 1210, 3658, 4560, 4615
Bon Durant, 2845
Bonner, 254
Bonney, 1828
Bontecou, 423

Bontrager, 3057
Boode, 4528
Boodey, 424
Boody, 4084
Booe. *See* ad p. 383
Booker, 2931
Boon. *See* ad p. 383
Boone, 425–26, 2684,
  3035, 3305, 4529, 4580,
  4599
Boose, 4616
Booth, 398, 427–29, 885,
  1278, 2141, 4531, 4533
Boothe, 427, 540, 4529,
  4599
Borah, 410
Borchert, 3360
Borden, 430–31, 4428,
  4580
Borders, 432, 4463
Boren, 2295–96, 4533
Borer, 410
Borlase, 433
Borneman, 434
Borthwick, 435
Borton, 4428
Bosley. *See* ad p. 383
Bostwick, 436–37, 3392
Boswell, 4522
Bosworth, 438–40, 4428
Bosworth–Perry, 3052
Bottorff, 2296
Boucher, 441
Boughton, 442
Bourne, 4528
Bousher, 441
Boutcher, 3376
Bouton, 442
Boutwell, 2570
Bouville, 3797
Bovey, 1795
Bowden, 443
Bowditch, 444
Bowdoin, 445
Bowen, 446–48, 669,
  677, 1454, 4428, 4530.
  See also ad p. 153
Bower, 449, 4578
Bowie, 450–51
Bowker, 4286
Bowlby, 452

Bowler, 453
Bowles, 4533
Bowman, 251, 454, 1635,
  1768, 4169, 4599. *See
  also* ad p. 315
Bowne, 455, 1364
Bowser, 456, 4169
Bowsher, 441
Bowyer, 673
Box, 535
Boyce, 457
Boyd, 458–59, 473, 1405,
  2296–97, 2979, 4525,
  4543
Boyden, 460–61
Boydstun, 462, 2032
Boyce, 4625
Boyer, 463, 2838, 4428
Boyersmith, 255
Boyington, 466
Boyken, 500
Boykin, 4366, 4525
Boylan, 464
Boyle, 465
Boynton, 466–68
Bozarth, 2315
Bozeman, 469
Brace, 470
Bracken, 471
Brackenbury, 472
Brackett, 473–74, 4544
Bradbury, 475, 2944
Bradford, 476–78, 1061,
  1352, 4525, 4528, 4532,
  4625, 4632
Bradham, 479
Bradhurst, 480
Bradlee, 481
Bradley, 481–86, 4539
Bradstreet, 1829
Bradt, 487–88
Brady, 2962, 4479
Brainerd, 489–90, 1829
Braithwaite, 4477
Braley, 491
Bran, 603
Branch, 385, 2256, 4531,
  4626
Brand, 4328
Brandon, 4169
Brandt, 2474

Branham, 3164
Branner, 492
Brasher, 2296
Brasier, 2449
Brassieur, 4464
Braswell, 649, 2582,
  4625
Brattle, 493
Bratton, 4461
Braun, 574
Brawley, 494. *See also* ad
  p. 37
Brawner, 3305
Bray, 299, 495, 4595
Breazeales, 4530
Breck, 496
Breckenridge, 1803
Brede, 4532
Breed, 4532–33, 4535,
  4539
Breeden, 497
Breeding, 497
Breese, 498–99
Breitenbecker, 2935
Breland, 500
Breneman, 501
Brenne, 4169
Brenneman, 502, 3057
Brenner, 503
Brent, 504, 3305
Brents, 3305
Brereton, 789
Breseman, 3360
Brett, 505
Bretz, 506
Brevard, 494. *See also* ad
  p. 37
Brewbaker, 566–67
Brewer, 325, 507, 3924,
  4233
Brewster, 508–9, 2107,
  4529. *See also* ad p. 59
Breymann, 3164
Bridge, 510–11
Bridger, 4533
Bridges, 512, 4474
Bridgman, 513, 966,
  1682
Briggs, 514–15, 574,
  1210, 4625
Brigham, 516–18

Numbers refer to book numbers that appear in the left-hand column of pages 1–403.

Bright, 519–20
Brilhart, 4600
Brillhart, 521
Brinckerhoff, 523
Brindle, 2028
Bringhurst, 522
Brinkley, 524
Brinkman, 525
Briscoe, 4534
Bristol, 526
Britton, 527, 3717
Broadhurst, 480, 1623,
　4366
Broadway, 479
Broadwell, 4129
Brock, 479, 528, 2074,
　2213
Brockett, 529
Brockman, 323, 530–31
Brockway, 532
Brodie, 4599, 4599
Brodnax, 533
Brodrick, 4552
Brogdon, 479
Bromley, 534
Bronsdon, 535
Bronson, 218
Bronstad, 3482
Brook, 970, 3108
Brooke, 536
Brookfield, 53–38
Brookhiser, 2724
Brooks, 539–42, 970,
　1429, 1682, 1712, 3909,
　3988, 4106
Brookshire, 1447
Brosius, 543
Brothers, 544
Broughton, 545, 1352
Broussard, 546
Brower, 3287. *See also*
　ad p. 315
Brown, 211, 218, 254,
　283, 547–60, 1210,
　1266, 1473, 1533, 1556,
　1669, 1682, 1768, 1795,
　1939, 2022, 2256,
　2296–97, 2563, 2563,
　2639, 2708, 2713, 3164,
　3342, 3874, 3948, 4106,
　4169, 4273, 4351, 4382,
　4428, 4477, 4516,
　4524–25, 4554, 4575,

4578, 4599, 4631. *See
also* ads pp. 315, 383,
and 397
Browne, 561–62, 1352,
　2325, 4526, 4528, 4625
Brownell, 563, 4351,
　4428
Browning, 564, 2708
Brownlee, 3874
Brownlow, 4579
Brownrigg, 2358
Brubacher, 565–67
Brubaker, 566–67
Bruce, 568–70, 2721,
　3993, 4522, 4554
Brumbach, 571
Brumby, 494. *See also* ad
　p. 37
Brumfield, 572
Bruner, 573–74, 4477,
　4545
Bruning, 1531
Brunner, 573–74
Brush, 4078
Bryan, 4477, 4580, 4631.
　See also ad p. 383
Bryant, 479, 575, 2297,
　3816
Buchanan, 576–78, 3883,
　3909, 4525, 4543
Buck, 540, 579–80, 4578
Buckingham, 581–82,
　3029
Buckley, 3869
Buckman, 583
Bucknam, 583
Buckner, 554
Budd, 584–85, 855, 2445,
　4555
Buehler, 2838
Buell, 586
Buffington, 4397, 4428
Buffum, 540
Buford, 587
Bulkeley, 588–89, 1714
Bull, 590–92
Bullard, 309, 593, 594
Bullen, 595
Bulloch, 596
Bullock, 3909, 4428
Bunds, 673
Bunker, 597–601, 3164,
　4598

Bunting, 602
Burbank, 603
Burbeck, 2466
Burbeen, 604
Burch, 122
Burcham, 3804
Burchett, 2923
Burd, 4328
Burdick, 605
Burdue, 2724
Bure, 621
Burford, 385, 4463
Burger. *See* ad p. 315
Burges, 4625
Burgess, 479, 606–8,
　4106, 4351
Burgner, 609
Burhans, 610
Burk, 35, 2563
Burke, 611
Burkhead, 970
Burkholder, 612, 1768
Burleigh, 613
Burley, 613
Burling, 1364
Burlingame, 1682
Burlingham, 2957, 3029
Burmeister, 2307
Burnap, 614
Burnett, 614–16, 2137,
　2575, 2708, 4198
Burnham, 617–18, 845,
　2721
Burns, 2763
Buroker, 1210
Burr, 619–21
Burrage, 622
Burrill, 623, 3075
Burris, 649
Burritt, 1440
Burrus, 530
Burson, 4458
Burt, 624, 1682
Burton, 625–26, 2315,
　4428
Burwell, 627
Buschur, 1429
Bush, 628, 1693
Bushman, 3360
Bushnell, 629–30
Buss, 4616
Bussman, 3107

Bustin. *See* ad p. 383
Butler, 211, 254, 473, 631–37, 1398, 1682, 3658, 4523, 4528, 4632
Butt, 1266
Butter, 638
Butters, 638
Buttolph. *See* ad p. 153
Butts, 639, 789, 1266
Butz, 1307
Byam, 3226
Bye, 640
Byerly, 641
Byersmith, 255
Byington, 466
Byler, 3057
Byram, 642
Byrd, 643–44, 668, 1768, 2043, 4297, 4544
Byrn, 1515
Byrne, 554
Bywaters, 3217
Byxbee, 362

Cabaniss, 4527
Cabell, 645
Cable, 560
Cabot, 646
Caddy, 1210
Cadman, 4428
Cady, 647, 1869
Cagle, 211
Cahill, 4599
Cahoon, 648, 4527
Cain, 649, 1210, 2144, 2295–96, 3658
Caldwell, 650–52, 688, 911, 4175
Cale, 653
Calef, 654
Calhoun, 655–56, 2296, 2714, 4527, 4579
Calkins, 657
Call, 658
Callahan, 833
Callaway, 4599
Calthorpe, 659
Calthrop, 659
Calverts, 660
Calvin, 661
Calvit, 4536

Calwell, 911
Cambe, 662
Camby, 662
Cameron, 663, 2788
Camp, 4544
Campbell, 181, 664–72, 1391, 1768, 2028, 2358, 4169, 4428, 4461, 4617
Campster, 1062
Canaday, 673
Canby, 662
Candee, 674
Canfield, 675, 2234
Canning, 3387
Cannon, 16, 676
Cansler, 2043
Canterbury, 677
Cantine, 678
Cantrell, 679–81
Cantrill, 681
Capen, 39, 682
Caplinger, 683, 4442
Capper, 4477
Capron, 684
Card, 3164
Cardwell, 4463, 4541
Carey, 2296, 2875
Carhart, 685
Carlile, 4461, 4522
Carloss, 4554
Carlton, 2724
Carlyle, 4522
Carman, 1266
Carnahan, 1405, 3587
Carnes, 4286
Carney, 686
Carothers, 669
Carpenter, 509, 662, 687–91, 4428. *See also* ad p. 59
Carper, 4599
Carr, 692–93, 1266, 1289, 4458
Carraway, 649
Carrell, 694, 1895
Carrier, 696
Carrington, 1623
Carroll, 122, 695, 3880, 3895
Carruth, 697
Carruthers, 4522

Carson, 2608
Carter, 16, 330, 367, 494, 541, 698–704, 1035, 1460, 2933, 3509, 3658, 4246, 4297, 4328, 4527, 4539, 4541–42, 4580. *See also* ad p. 37
Cartledge, 3816
Carver, 680, 705–6, 1662, 3909
Carwithen, 1682
Cary, 707–12, 4464, 4524
Case, 713–14, 4578
Casey, 275, 715–16
Caspar, 3630
Cass, 1803, 3164
Cassel, 717–19
Cassell, 2488
Cassity, 71
Castleberry, 3235
Castor, 720
Caswell, 1682
Cate, 721
Cates, 721. *See also* ad p. 283
Catesby, 1367
Cathcart, 1623
Cather, 4477
Cathey, 122. *See also* ad p. 383
Catlett, 722, 1367
Catlin, 4272, 4552
Cato, 4625
Catt, 723
Cattell, 724, 3658
Caudy, 662
Caverly, 725
Caves, 1795
Cecil, 2684
Cerré, 3490
Cessna, 726–27
Chace, 728
Chadbourn, 729
Chadbourne, 729
Chaddick, 4407
Chadwick, 730
Chafee, 731
Chaffee, 731–33, 2346, 4428
Chaffin, 734
Challenor, 1804

Chamberlain, 735–36, 1210, 2144, 4328
Chamberlin, 735–36
Chambers, 3108, 4225, 4353–55, 4544
Chambless, 4544
Champion, 533, 737, 1693, 3265, 4625
Champlin, 4479
Chancellor, 738, 3293
Chandler, 677, 739–41, 2980, 4428, 4451
Channon, 1682
Chapin, 742–46, 1596
Chaplin, 747
Chapman, 748–50, 1800, 4477
Chappelear, 751
Chappell, 457, 752, 4626
Charland, 2652
Charlemagne, 673, 1519, 3095, 4429, 4590–92, 4609
Charles, 1800
Charney–Urso, 1061
Chase, 276, 753–55, 1918, 4428
Chastain, 385, 4563
Chatham. *See* ad p. 383
Chauncey, 756
Chavers, 757
Cheavens, 1221
Cheesman, 246
Cheever, 758
Chenault, 2107–8
Cheney, 759–60, 1682
Chenoweth, 761–63, 2449
Cherry, 3804
Cherryholmes, 4440
Chesebrough, 764
Chester, 2371
Chew, 2295–96, 3869, 4529
Cheyney, 4428
Chickering, 4428
Child, 765–66
Childe, 765
Childress. *See* ad p. 211
Childs, 765–66, 1398
Chilton, 181, 3924. *See also* ad p. 397
Chipley, 4533

Chipman, 767–69, 3021
Chipp, 770
Chisholm, 4539, 4543
Chism, 4539
Chisolm, 771
Chisum, 4539, 4543
Chittenden, 772, 1278
Chivington, 773
Choate, 774
Chouteau, 775
Chrisman, 1768
Christlieb, 776
Christmas, 1662
Christopher, 4514
Christophers, 777–78
Chunn, 258
Church, 779–82
Churchill, 783–84
Chute, 785
Cilley, 786
Claflin, 787
Claghorn, 788
Claiborne, 789–90, 4599, 4632
Claibourne, 1532
Clap. *See* ad p. 153
Clapp, 35, 74, 791, 2563, 2842
Clark, 69, 218, 266, 279, 792–98, 800, 804, 1035, 1398, 1795, 1839, 1939, 2296, 2487, 2557, 2734, 3481, 3574, 3880, 4169, 4241, 4286, 4477, 4522–23, 4525, 4544, 4617, 4625, 4632
Clarke, 793, 795, 799–805, 1526, 2188, 3164, 4103–4, 4353, 4536, 4544
Clarkson, 806. *See also* ad p. 153
Clason, 807
Classon, 807
Clauharty, 4552
Clauson, 807
Clawson, 807–8, 3804
Clay, 809, 1690
Clayland. *See* ad p. 383
Claypole, 1027
Claypoole, 1027
Clayton, 3909, 4382, 4529–30

Clearwater, 4555
Cleaveland, 813
Cleaver, 181, 308
Cleek, 4461
Cleghorne, 788
Clem, 3784
Clemens, 810, 1804, 2935
Clement. *See* ad p. 153
Clements, 811, 4545
Clemmer, 2869
Clemons, 2028
Clepper, 2093
Cleveland, 812–13
Cliborn, 4537
Clifford, 1533, 2708
Cline, 2594
Clinton, 814
Clokey, 2979
Clope, 1152
Clopton, 4511
Closson, 807, 4595
Cloud, 4626
Clough, 815–16, 2931
Clouse, 4200
Cloyd, 817
Cluff, 1623
Clute, 4428
Cluts, 4169
Coaldwell, 652
Coates, 818–19, 3909
Cobb, 820, 1405, 2708, 3881, 4291, 4428, 4511, 4526, 4534, 4536
Cobbs, 3658
Coburn, 2724
Cocer, 4626
Cochran, 2962
Cochrane, 821, 4554
Cock, 934
Cockburn, 822
Cocke, 385, 789, 1367, 4246, 4528, 4563, 4625
Cockerham, 4525
Cockey, 2297
Cockman, 823
Cockrill, 4581
Cocks, 934
Codman, 824
Cody, 825, 3164
Coe, 473, 826–27, 4477
Cofer, 4626

Coffenberry, 832
Coffer, 4626
Coffey, 828
Coffin, 829–31, 1027, 2296, 3561, 3658
Coffinberry, 832
Coffman, 833, 4600
Coffyn, 831
Coggeshall, 834, 4428
Coggin, 1440
Coggins, 457
Cognate, 2177
Cogswell, 835. *See also* ad p. 153
Cohen. *See* ad p. 383
Cohoon, 4527
Coit, 836
Coker, 479, 4626
Colbrook, 980
Colburn, 837–38
Colby, 839–40
Colclough, 4632
Colcord, 841
Coldwell, 652
Cole, 842–46, 1398, 4532
Cole–Malone, 2979
Coleman, 847–49, 1035, 1623, 1800, 2838, 4534
Coles, 846, 850, 2445
Colgate, 851
Colglazier, 4420
Colinsom, 4528
Collacutt, 299
Collamer, 852
Collier, 853, 4626
Collin, 854
Collins, 662, 855–56, 1695, 4376, 4533
Colt, 857
Colton, 858
Coltrane, 859
Colver, 860–61
Colvin, 862, 1682
Combs, 1246, 3469
Comee, 863
Comey, 863
Comly, 864–65
Compton, 181
Comstock, 866–68
Conable, 977–78
Conant, 869–71

Condit, 872
Condra, 662
Cone, 873, 1839
Conerty, 4479
Congdon, 874–75, 1905, 2329
Conger, 876
Conkwright, 1447
Conley, 2600
Connable, 977–78
Connelly, 3164
Conner, 4544
Connet, 877
Connor, 3830, 4514, 4589
Conrad, 878, 1768
Convers, 881
Converse, 879–81, 2779
Conway, 882–83, 1556, 4631
Conwell, 2830
Conyers, 1885
Cooch, 78
Cook, 500, 884, 1210, 1398, 1693, 1804, 1939, 2028, 2296, 3658, 4351, 4552
Cooke, 118, 885–87, 3881, 4286, 4428, 4625
Cool, 843
Coolbaugh, 888
Cooley, 889–91
Coolidge, 892–93
Coombe, 4218
Coombs, 894
Coons, 895
Cooper, 557, 896, 3164, 3589, 4428, 4525, 4531, 4599
Cope, 2729
Copeland, 500, 897, 4463
Copher, 4626
Copley, 2141
Coppage, 898–99
Coppedge, 898–99
Coppock, 3658
Corbett, 479, 900
Corbin, 901–2, 3217
Corbineau, 3942
Corbould, 903
Corder. *See* ad p. 283

Cordis, 3021
Cordray, 16
Cordry, 16
Corey, 1352
Corker, 4625, 4630
Corley, 4382
Corlies, 2445, 3561
Corliss, 904
Cornelius, 905, 4544
Cornell, 62, 906
Cornewall, 907
Cornish, 299, 908, 4632
Cornwall, 540, 909
Corry, 910–11, 4522
Corson, 912
Cortelyou, 62
Corwin, 913
Corwine, 913
Cory, 914–19. *See also* ad p. 77
Coryell, 4552
Coskrey, 479
Coté, 920
Cottle, 921, 1623, 4358
Cotton, 922, 1682, 1829
Cottons, 4525
Cottrell, 339
Couch, 74, 4552
Coulston, 308
Coursen, 923
Courtney, 662, 673
Courvoisier, 4589
Coutant, 325
Coutts, 857
Covell, 1623
Cover. *See* ad p. 315
Covert, 924–25
Covington, 926, 4554
Cowan, 2596. *See also* ad p. 283
Cowden, 927
Cowdery, 928
Cowdray, 928
Cowdrey, 928
Cowgill, 3658
Cowles, 846, 929
Cowperthwaite, 2445
Cox, 930–34, 1808, 1939, 2137, 2296, 2980, 3305, 3874, 4528, 4533, 4534
Coxe, 935, 2297, 4554

Coyle, 2325
Crabtree, 2141
Crafford, 4632
Craft, 936
Crafts, 936, 1682
Craghead, 4599
Cragin, 937
Craig, 938–39, 1344, 2962, 4461, 4516, 4544
Crain, 211, 500
Crall, 940
Cramer, 2315
Cramton, 2329
Crandall, 394, 941–42
Crane, 943, 1398, 3565
Crapo, 944
Cratchett, 4536
Craven, 457, 1768
Cravens, 4516
Crawford, 945, 4461, 4552, 4617
Crayfford, 4632
Creecy, 479
Creed, 1768
Crego, 946
Creighton, 62, 4397
Crell, 940
Crenshaw, 947, 4464
Cresap, 948
Cressey, 949
Cresswell, 950
Creswell, 951
Crew, 3658
Crewe, 16
Crews, 1895
Crichton, 4522
Crick, 4169
Crider, 952
Crim, 1895
Crippen, 953
Crippin, 953
Crispe, 4524, 4632
Crispell, 954
Criswell, 950–51
Critchett, 2639
Crocker, 955–56, 1152, 4524
Crockett, 957–59, 4534
Cromwell, 761, 960
Crone, 961
Cronk, 4479
Crook, 4536

Crosby, 962–64, 1990
Crosland, 965
Cross, 966, 1646, 1682, 4400
Crothers, 3874
Crow, 967
Crowder, 1401
Crowe, 968
Crowshaw, 4474
Crowther, 3874
Crudup, 1885
Cuffman, 4600
Crumb, 969
Crume, 970–71, 3438
Crummer, 972
Crumpacker. *See* ad p. 315
Crutcher, 4544
Cryfer, 441
Culberson, 973
Culbertson, 973
Cully, 1152
Culp, 2311–12
Culpepper, 4175
Culver, 860–61, 4175
Cumbe, 662
Cumming, 1690
Cummings, 974–76, 1035, 4522
Cunditt, 872
Cunnabell, 977–78
Cunningham, 1210, 2675, 4287, 4514
Cunreds, 2323
Curd, 680
Cureton, 4534, 4539–42
Curran, 3874
Currier, 979
Curry, 2449
Curtin, 980–1
Curtis, 983, 1591, 1682, 2445, 3108, 3560, 4534
Curtiss, 982–83, 1440, 1776
Curwen, 913, 984
Curwin, 913
Cushing, 985–86
Cushman, 987–89
Custard, 4458
Custer, 181, 990, 2310, 4442
Custis, 991, 4516

Cutcheon, 2639
Cuthbert, 992
Cuthbertson, 993
Cutler, 994–95
Cutter, 996, 3567
Cutts, 997
Céré, 3490

Dabinott, 1682
Dabney, 998, 2787, 4464
Dafford, 3376
Dafnell, 4538
Daggett, 1130, 1623
Dague, 449, 999
Dailey, 1000
Dakin, 1001
Dalbey, 4477
Dale, 4527, 4542
Dallas, 1002
Dall'ava, 1003
Dallenbach, 1004
Dallenback, 1004
Dalrymple, 1005
Damon, 1006–7
Dana, 1008–10
Dance, 1011
Danckwart, 2307
Danforth, 1012
Daniel, 1013, 1230, 1556, 4382, 4631
Daniels, 181, 500, 1014–15, 3909, 4328
Danner. *See* ad p. 315
Darby, 1016, 1623
Darcy, 1144
Darden, 4527, 4530, 4626
Dare, 509, 1017–19. *See also* ad p. 59
Darling, 802, 1141
Darlington, 1020–21
Darnall, 1022
Darneal, 1022
Darnell, 1022–23
Darnielle, 1022
Darnold, 1022, 3359
Dart, 1024
Dashiell, 16
Davenall, 4538
Davenbrock, 4376
Davenport, 673, 1025–26, 1804, 2297, 4578

David, 4554, 4613
Davidson, 494, 1027, 1047, 2158. *See also* ad p. 37
Davies, 4613
Davis, 16, 385, 540, 671, 1028–45, 1210, 1567, 1706, 1768, 1795, 1939, 2296–97, 2488, 2563, 2721, 3164, 3373, 3658, 3769, 3909, 4169, 4306, 4516, 4571, 4580, 4599–4600, 4613, 4632. *See also* ad p. 153
Davison, 1046–47, 1768, 1808, 2158, 4169
Davisson, 1047
Dawes, 1048, 1522, 3021
Dawley, 1346
Daws, 1049
Dawson, 1050–51, 4527. *See also* ad p. 153
Day, 218, 256, 1052–54, 1596, 3830, 4625
Dayton, 1055
Deacon, 1056
Deaderick, 4579
Dean, 1057–61, 1682, 1917, 2256, 2603, 4169, 4175
Dearing, 1062, 1071
DeArmond, 1063. *See also* ad p. 90
Deas, 4539
De Beaufort, 3895
DeBoard, 1266
DeBord, 1266
DeBorde, 4106
Debozear, 4428
De Bradehurst, 480
DeCamp, 1064–65
DeCarpentier, 1067
De Carpentier, 1066, 4013
Decher, 1068
Decherd, 1068
Dechert, 1068
De Chiel, 16
Deckard, 1068
Decker, 1068, 1768, 4552
Deckert, 1068
De Cou, 1069

Dedman, 1070
Deem, 971
Deen, 2093
Deering, 1071
Dees, 4538–40
DeForest, 2724
De Forest, 1072
De Franchimont, 1078
De Fronsac, 1430
DeGraffenried, 1073
DeHaven, 308, 1074–75, 4477. *See also* ad p. 91
De Hinnidal, 1929
Deis, 3899
DeJarnette, 4632
Delacy, 2325
Delafield, 4537
De La Fontaine, 1415
De La Mater, 1076
Deland, 1077
De Lannoy, 1078
Delano, 1078
Delawder, 2013
Delke, 4536
DeLoach, 500, 4531
De Loach, 4523–24
DeMaranville, 1079
Demarest, 1080
Deming, 1081
De Motte, 62
Denio, 1082
Denis, 2587
Denison, 296, 1083–84, 4532
Denman, 1085
Denney, 1086, 2662
Dennington, 4463
Dennis, 299, 1210, 2144, 4458
Dennison, 1087
Denniston, 3784
Denny, 1088, 2028
Denson, 1885
Dentler, 4616
Denton, 4409
dePeyster. *See* ad p. 153
Depriest, 3266
Derby, 1089
De Rham, 1090
Derien, 677
Derr, 1210, 2144

Derrick, 3881
Derthick, 1091
Deschler, 3387
Desha, 4600
Deskins, 1800
Desloges, 3942
des Marest, 1080
De Solms, 4526
De Trieux, 4428
Detwiller, 1307
Deveaux, 1092
Devendorf, 1093
Devenish, 1094
Deveny, 4531
Dever, 3107
Devinny, 4542
Devoe, 4328
Devore, 4300
Dewees, 181
Dewey, 1095, 1412, 3029, 4078
Dewing, 1096
DeWolf, 1097, 1693
Dexter, 1098–1100
Dey, 3952
Dibble, 1101
Dibert, 3874
Dick. *See* ad p. 383
Dickens, 4531
Dickerman, 1102
Dickerson, 2684
Dickey, 1103–4, 4468
Dickie, 752
Dickinson, 122, 1105
Dicks, 3658
Dickson, 530, 1115, 2137, 3164, 4525, 4534
Diehl. *See* ad p. 315
Diehm, 1106
Dietz, 1849
Digges, 4534
Dikeman, 1209
Dill, 1682
Dillard, 4527, 4599. *See also* ad p. 383
Dille, 1107
Dillenbach, 2935
Diller, 2308
Dilling, 3535
Dillinger, 2297, 2980
Dillingham, 650–51

Numbers refer to book numbers that appear in the left-hand column of pages 1–403.

Dillman, 2023
Dillon, 3658, 4599
Dilworth, 2296
Dimm, 3874
Dimmock, 1682
Dimon, 1108
Dimond, 1108
Dingman, 4351
Dings, 1109
Dinkey, 1405
Dinsmoor, 1111
Dinsmore, 1110–11
Dinwiddie, 1112
Disk, 1635
Ditto, 2296
Dittoe, 1795
Dix, 144, 3360
Dixon, 1113–14, 1785, 2297, 3658, 3909, 4529, 4625
Dixson, 1115
Doak, 1116–17
Doan, 2369
Doane, 1118
Dobbin, 2724
Dobbins, 2763, 4532
Dockstader, 3164
Dod, 1119
Dodd, 1119–20
Dodds, 1121
Dodge, 1122–27, 4428
Dodson, 1128, 2575
Doe, 1129
Doggett, 1130
Dolan, 2587
Doll. *See* ad p. 383
Dommerich, 1131
Donaho, 4406
Donald, 1132–33
Donaldson, 1134, 4580
Done, 1118
Doniphan, 4632
Don Levi, 1188
Donnell, 1135
Donner, 1136
Doolittle, 540, 1137–40
Dooly, 4617
Dorland, 1141
Dorlon–an, 1141
Dorman, 1142
Dorsett, 670, 1143

Dorsey, 1144
Dortch, 4526
Doten, 1145
Dotson, 1128, 1800
Doty, 1145–46, 4532
Doude, 1147
Douglas, 1148–50, 3108, 3638, 4522, 4533
Dove, 1151, 2013, 4442
Dow, 3757
Dowd, 1147
Dowden, 3986
Dowdy, 4536
Downen, 1152
Downer, 1153
Downey, 1154
Downing, 1682
Downs, 4529
Dowse, 1155
Dowtin, 4474
Dozier, 2582
Drake, 325, 1156–59, 2721, 4382, 4523, 4528–30, 4578. *See also* ad p. 383
Drake–Brockman, 531
Draper, 1160, 3769
Dreisbach, 2838
Drew, 4526
Drinkwater, 1161
Driver, 1162
Dromgold, 1851
Drugan, 3587
Drury, 1163–64
Druva, 540
Dryer, 1165
Dubois, 4555
Dudley, 1166–72, 1829, 4599
Duffield, 1266
Dufour, 1173
Duggan, 3816
Duke, 1174–75, 1515, 4526–28, 4581
Dulany, 1176
Dumas, 4536
Dummer, 3181
Dumont, 2672
Dunaway, 1177
Dunbar, 1006, 1178
Duncan, 1179–81, 2596, 3909

Duncklee, 1182
Dungan, 694, 799, 2297
Dunham, 1183–86
Dunks, 1341
Dunlap, 1187, 2684, 4477, 4525
Dunlavey, 1188
Dunlevy, 1188
Dunn, 385, 2108
Dunnell, 1189
Dunster, 1190
Dunston, 4527
Dunwiddie, 4522
Dunwoody, 1191
Dupree, 122
Dupuy, 1192–93, 4563
Durand, 1194–95
Durden, 4626
Durfee, 1196–97, 4428
Durkee, 635
Durland, 1141
Durnell, 1022
Durtschi, 2206
Durvin, 4630
Dusenbury, 1198
Dustin, 1199–1200
Duston, 1199–1200
Dutton, 1201–2
Duval, 1203
Duyckinck, 1204
Dwiggins, 2296
Dwight, 1205, 3029
Dwinell, 1189
Dyck, 3107
Dyckman, 1207–9
Dyer, 299, 1206, 1210–11, 2144, 4461
Dykeman, 1209
Dymer, 4474
Dymoke, 4542
Dymont, 1108

Eager, 1212
Eagles, 4527
Eagon, 2245
Eames, 1213, 4428
Ean, 4555
Earle, 1214–15, 3284, 4626
Earlin, 4400
Earling, 4400
Early, 1216–18, 4599

Easley, 500, 1219–21
Eastburn, 1222–23
Easterbrook, 1294
Easterday, 449
Eastlick, 2684
Eastman, 1224
Easton, 1225
Eaton, 1226–28, 4169, 4597, 4625. *See also* ad p. 397
Eberhart, 1229
Eberwein, 1230
Eberwine, 1230
Eby, 1231–33
Eck, 1234
Eckert, 3387
Eddy, 1235–37
Edgerly, 1238
Edmonds, 1239
Edmunds, 4626
Edson, 1240–44
Edwards, 1245–48, 1682, 4458, 4525, 4586
Eels, 1249
Ege, 1250
Eggar, 3482
Eggleston, 4536, 4545
Egle, 274
Egner, 4175
Ehle, 1251
Eichelberger, 1252
Eicher, 1253
Eid, 3482
Eisenhart, 1254
Ela, 1255
Elbridge, 45
Elder, 107, 1256–57, 3145
Eldredge, 1258, 2336
Eldridge, 4544, 4632
Elgin, 1220
Eliot, 1259–62
Elkins, 3222
Elkinton, 1263, 2445
Eller, 1264, 1987
Ellerbe, 4554
Elliot, 1265
Elliott, 1266, 1776, 2788, 3909, 4477
Ellis, 1267–70, 2192,

2232, 2724, 3107, 3265, 3288
Ellsworth, 1271
Ellyson, 3658
Elmer, 1272
Elmore, 1272–73
Elston, 1274, 4581
Elswick, 2450
Elting, 4555
Elton, 1345
Elwell. *See* ad p. 211
Ely, 280, 1275–77, 4169
Elzey, 4536
Emerson, 12, 1278–82, 1682
Emery, 1283
Emmerton, 1284
Emmons, 1285, 3164
Endress, 230
Engel. *See* ad p. 315
Englar. *See* ad p. 315
Engle, 1286
English, 4474
Eno, 1287
Ensign, 1288
Epes, 3167, 4541
Epler, 1289
Eppard, 4169
Eppes, 4544
Erb, 1290
Ernst, 325, 2721
Erving, 445
Erwin, 1291, 4544. *See also* ad p. 383
Esh, 3057
Esselstyne, 1292
Esseltine, 1292
Esslinger, 1293
Estabrook, 1294
Estep, 62
Esterbrook, 1294
Estes, 1295
Etheredge, 1296, 4545
Etheridge, 4535–37
Ethridge, 2647, 3924
Eubanks, 2213
Evans, 1297, 2710, 4286, 4428, 4525, 4554. *See also* ad p. 153
Evelyn, 1298
Everard, 4632

Everedd, 4286
Everenden, 1299
Everest, 1300
Everett, 1042, 1301
Everly, 1303–4
Ewell, 1556, 4631
Ewen, 3823
Ewing, 1289, 1302, 1305–6, 1768, 3986
Exum, 4464, 4523
Eyer, 2935
Eyerman, 1307–8
Ezell, 4527, 4531, 4535–36

Fahnestock, 1309–10
Fair, 1895
Fairbanks, 1311
Fairchild, 138, 144, 1312
Fairfax, 554, 1313
Fairfield, 1314
Fairman, 1315
Falconer, 3177
Fales, 1316
Fancher, 1317
Fanning, 1318
Fant, 1319
Fanton, 4552
Farlee, 1377
Farley, 1320–21, 1377, 1440
Farman, 1425
Farmer, 1322, 4463
Farnham, 1323
Farnsworth, 1324
Farr, 1325, 2449
Farrar, 4233
Farrell, 540
Farren, 1326
Farrington, 2296, 3035, 3306
Farwell, 1327–28, 3808
Fassett, 1412, 4078
Fast, 3107
Fauconnier, 1329, 3177
Faulcon, 4625
Faulconer, 1330–31
Faulkner, 1332
Fauntleroy, 1333
Fauss, 1442
Favill, 1334

Numbers refer to book numbers that appear in the left-hand column of pages 1–403.

Fawcett, 258
Fawley, 1335
Faxon, 1336
Fay, 1337–38
Feake, 74
Featherstone, 299, 1339
Feezle, 2013
Feherman, 1377
Feke, 1473
Felch, 1340
Feldhausen, 1341
Fell, 1342
Feller, 4428
Fellows, 1343–46, 2647, 4552
Felt, 1347–48
Felton, 1349–51
Fennell, 540
Fenner, 1352
Fenton, 1353–54
Fenwick, 3769
Fergus, 1359
Ferguson, 398, 1246, 1355–59, 1460, 1795, 2141, 2563, 4599
Fergusson, 1359–60, 4522
Ferrell, 4543
Ferrier, 1361
Ferrill, 1804
Ferrin, 1326
Ferris, 1362, 1662, 4464
Fessenden, 2944, 3022
Fetters, 4613
Few, 2297
Ffones, 4526
Fick, 3392
Fidler, 2708
Field, 1363–67, 1805, 2152, 4246
Fielden, 1368
Fielder, 1808
Fields, 1246
Figuers, 4525
Figures, 4525
Fillmore, 1369
Fillow, 1370
Finch, 1795, 1917
Finck, 3783
Fingon, 1371
Finigan, 4479
Fink, 4441

Finley, 2108, 4200
Finnell, 1372
Finney, 1804, 2734, 3883, 4599
Finster, 2935
Fischer, 1373
Fiscus, 673
Fish, 1374, 1380, 1447, 3164, 4428
Fishback, 1375
Fishburn, 4599
Fisher, 181, 1376–79, 3057, 4477. *See also* ad p. 315
Fiske, 1380–81, 1471, 4428
Fissell, 961
Fitch, 962, 1382–85, 3757
Fite, 1386
Fitts, 1387
Fitz, 1387
Fitzalan, 4542
Fitzhugh, 1388
FitzRandolph, 1389
Fitz Randolph, 1390
Fiveash, 2600
Flagg, 1391–93
Flake, 4530, 4625
Flanders, 1394
Flaningham, 1395
Fleek, 1396–97
Fleete, 4533
Flegg, 1392
Fleming, 1398–99, 4522. *See also* ad p. 383
Fleshman, 3541
Fletcher, 241, 1400–1, 1682, 4600
Flick, 4169
Flickinger, 1402
Flint, 1403–4
Flippin, 2808
Flippo. *See* ad p. 283
Flood, 4524, 4539, 4632
Flora. *See* ad p. 315
Flory, 1405. *See also* ad p. 315
Flower, 1352, 1682
Floyd, 1266, 1406–7, 3962
Floyd–Jones, 1407

Fluck, 3387. *See also* ad p. 393
Focht, 4169
Fogg, 1408–10
Fogge, 1410
Fogle, 1210, 2144
Foley, 1411
Folger, 1623
Foliot, 4626
Follett, 1412
Folsom, 1413–14
Folts, 2935
Fontaine, 1415, 4464, 4536–37, 4563
Foote, 78, 218, 367, 494, 1416–18. *See also* ad p. 37
Footman, 4523
Forbes, 1419–20, 4078
Forbush, 1419
Ford, 1421–24, 1905, 2137, 2842, 4169, 4451, 4545. *See also* ad p. 153
Fordney, 1433–34
Foreman, 649, 1425
Foresman, 696
Forman, 1425–26
Forney, 2763
Forniss, 4554
Forrest, 1427, 1533
Forsha, 2788
Forst, 1428
Forst–Boul, 1428
Forsthoff, 1429
Forsyth, 1430, 1431
Forsythe, 1431
Fort, 1432, 2256, 4428, 4625
Fortinet, 1434
Fortineux, 1433–34
Fortna, 1433–34
Fortney, 1220, 1433–34
Fortune, 2763
Fosdick, 1435–36
Foss, 1391
Fosselmann, 1437
Foster, 1438–41, 2652, 3000, 3658, 4525, 4543
Foulke, 4458
Fouse, 1442
Foushee. *See* ad p. 383
Fouts, 3453

Fowle, 1443, 4428
Fowler, 509, 1444–46, 1795, 3164. *See also* ad p. 59
Fowty, 3658
Fox, 789, 1447–51, 2724, 3804. *See also* ad p. 383
Foxcroft, 16
Frache, 1452
Frame, 1431
Franceis, 1465, 1469
Francis, 662, 1453
Francisco, 1454
Francus, 1465, 1469
Frank, 181, 3164, 3387
Franklin, 1447, 1455, 3909
Fraser, 1456–59
Frasher, 1460
Frasure, 1460
Frazer, 2933
Frazier, 859, 1062, 1460, 2153, 3909
Freeborn, 2297, 4428
Freed, 4440
Freeman, 608, 1278, 1461, 3164, 3468, 4474
Freer, 4555
Freese, 1462
French, 891, 1463–69, 3108
Fretz, 1470
Frey, 4169. *See also* ad p. 383
Friend, 449
Frierson, 4589
Frisbee, 1471
Frisbie, 1471
Frisbye, 1471
Frizzell, 16, 4523
Frost, 1472–76, 4428
Frothingham, 1477
Fry, 1478, 2245, 4169
Frye, 1479, 4169, 4428
Fuchs, 1448
Fugate, 557
Fulgham, 2763, 4525
Fulk, 1480
Full, 2346
Fullenkamp, 1429

Fuller, 662, 1482–89, 1828, 4447. *See also* ad p. 397
Fullerton. *See* ad p. 153
Fulp, 1895
Fulton, 1490–91
Funck, 1492
Funk, 1492. *See also* ad p. 315
Furhman, 2369
Furtney, 1433–34
Fussell, 500
Fusselman, 1437

Gaar, 1517
Gaddy, 3145
Gade, 1608
Gage, 494, 1493, 1494, 2252. *See also* ad p. 37
Gager, 4078
Gah, 574
Gaines, 1495, 1768, 4579
Galbreath, 2600
Gale, 1496–97
Gallagher, 1795
Galland, 1429
Galley, 1498
Gallop, 2192
Gallup, 1499, 4280
Gamage, 1500
Gamble, 1501, 2721
Gammill, 649
Gantz, 500
Gar, 1517
Garber, 1502–4, 4086. *See also* ad p. 315
Gardener, 1509, 3021
Gardiner, 1505–6, 1509
Gardinier, 2935
Gardner, 1006, 1507–13, 1682, 2307, 4428. *See also* ad p. 153
Garland, 1514, 2563, 2931, 4600
Garlington, 4407
Garmon, 4328
Garner, 1509, 1515, 3376, 3658
Garnett, 1516, 2931
Garr, 1517
Garret, 2466

Garrett, 1518, 2979
Garrigues, 1519
Garrison, 4428
Garroute, 4400
Garst, 1520
Gartman, 3792
Garvin, 3305
Gary, 1521, 4541–42
Gascho, 3057
Gaskill, 2445
Gaston, 494, 3235. *See also* ad p. 37
Gates, 1048, 1522–25
Gaudern, 1608
Gaudie, 1608
Gaulding, 385
Gaumer, 62
Gaunt, 608
Gavin, 2652
Gawdy, 1608
Gawkroger, 1682
Gay, 494, 4461, 4524. *See also* ad p. 37
Gayle, 4530
Gaylord, 218
Gearhart, 4169
Gebhart, 4169
Gedling, 4169
Gedney, 1526
Gee, 457, 1527, 4541
Geer, 1528
Gehman, 1997
Geiger, 1529, 2708
Geist, 1530
Geldart, 1543
Gelette, 2232
Genning, 1531
Gentry, 1532, 3909, 4534
George, 384, 1246, 4428, 4524, 4533. *See also* ad p. 383
Gephart, 4169
Gerade, 1533
Gerard, 2931, 4451
Gernhardt, 1534
Gerould, 1535
Gerran, 2256
Gerritsen, 4428
Getzendanner, 574
Gibbel, 1536
Gibbons, 4428

Numbers refer to book numbers that appear in the left-hand column of pages 1–403.

Gibbs, 1537–38, 3164, 3293, 4578. *See also* ad p. 283
Gibson, 384, 479, 1180, 1533, 1539, 2721, 4169, 4536
Giddings, 1540
Giffem, 2888
Giffen, 2888
Giffin, 4477
Gifford, 1541–42, 1808, 2186, 3563, 3565, 4428
Gilbert, 280, 4617
Gilbride, 4479
Gildart, 1543
Gildersleeve, 1544
Gile, 1681
Giles, 1545, 4525
Gilfillen, 3874
Gilkison, 832
Gill, 1546
Gillespie, 1547–48, 4175, 4554
Gilliam, 4523
Gilliland, 927
Gillman, 1549
Gillson, 1550
Gilman, 1549, 1551, 2891
Gilmer, 1552, 4617
Gilmor, 1553
Gilmore, 2093
Gilmour, 668
Gimbel, 1061
Gingerich, 3057
Ginther, 3066
Girault. *See* ad p. 383
Girvan, 3164
Gish. *See* ad p. 315
Gislerud, 3482
Gist, 1554
Given, 4221–22, 4224
Givens, 4461
Gjerde, 3703
Gjermund, 3482
Gladding, 1555
Gladstone, 4522
Glann, 3164
Glarmorgan, 2774
Glasby, 2721
Glasgow, 3924
Glass, 4599

Glassell, 1556, 4631
Glasson, 51
Glazener, 2596
Glazier, 560, 662
Gleason, 1557
Glen, 1558
Glenn, 1662, 3765, 4400
Glick, 3057
Glidden, 377, 1559
Glidewell, 548
Glover, 1560–61, 4527
Gnaege, 1562
Goad, 1563
Goble, 1564, 1804
Godbey, 1266
Goddard, 1565
Goding, 1566
Godley, 1846
Godwyn, 4632
Goecke, 323
Goeke, 1429
Goff, 1567
Goffe, 4524
Goins, 4169
Golder, 74
Goldthwait, 1568
Goldthwaite, 1569
Goltry, 71
Gonzales, 4358
Good, 4169, 4477. *See also* ad p. 315
Good Cow, 2546
Goodale, 86
Goode, 1570, 4393, 4599
Goodell, 1571, 2724
Goodenough, 1572
Goodenow, 1572
Goodfellow, 1573
Goodhue, 1574
Goodnow, 1572
Goodrich, 1575, 1596, 4523, 4625. *See also* ad p. 383
Goodridge, 1576–77
Goodwin, 385, 669, 1578–85, 1623, 2860, 4552
Goodyear, 1586
Gookin, 1587–88
Gooll, 3180
Goolsby, 4463
Gorby, 1589

Gordey, 1590
Gordon, 1591–93, 1768, 3658, 4522, 4536, 4625
Gordy, 16
Gore, 3986
Gorham, 1594–95
Gorton, 668, 1596–97
Gosnold, 1598
Goss, 1038, 1599, 2365
Gott, 1600
Gottsch, 3783
Gottshall, 1601
Gould, 1545, 1602–4
Gourdin, 1605
Gourlay, 1606
Gove, 1607
Gow, 686
Gowdy, 1608
Goyette, 2274
Grace, 1609
Graf, 1610
Grafton, 1611, 3021
Graham, 86, 1612–14, 4461, 4522. *See also* ad p. 383
Grahame, 4522
Granberry, 1615
Granger, 1616
Grannis, 1617–18
Grant, 500, 669, 1619–23, 3036, 3596, 4175
Granville, 1624
Grattan, 4617
Graves, 1625–34, 1804, 3469, 4625
Gray, 802, 1635–38, 3021, 3306, 4464, 4539, 4596, 4632. *See also* ad p. 383
Graybeal, 2488
Graybill, 4169. *See also* ad p. 315
Grayson, 1639
Greaves, 1629–30
Greeley, 1640
Greely, 1640
Green, 181, 1641–44, 1650, 1682, 2186, 2299, 4243, 4407, 4458, 4626. *See also* ad p. 383
Greenaway, 299
Greenberry, 2297
Greene, 1645–52, 4630

Greenhill, 789
Greenlaw, 1653
Greenleaf, 1654–56, 4286
Greenlee, 1657–58, 3874
Greenough, 1659
Greenwood, 1660–61
Greer, 1662, 4382, 4599
Gregg, 4632
Gregory, 299, 789, 1663, 4534
Gregson, 2449
Greider, 2317–20
Gresham, 1664
Gridley, 3029
Griesemer, 4428
Griffin, 1693
Griffing, 1665–66
Griffis, 4632
Griffith, 1918, 3164, 4458, 4477, 4528
Griffiths, 3134
Griggs, 1667, 1682, 3145
Grigsby, 4632
Grimes, 1668
Grimm, 449
Grimmett, 1669
Grinnell, 4351
Grippen, 953
Griscom, 3355
Griscomb, 3355
Griswold, 1670–71
Groff, 1672
Groo, 1676
Groughbrough, 2207
Grout, 1673–74
Grove, 3784, 4477
Grover, 3164
Groves, 1675, 4328
Grow, 1676
Growdon, 1677
Grubb, 4533, 4545
Grundy, 2931
Guelph, 1678
Guest, 2672
Guild, 1679–81
Guile, 1681
Guilford, 1682
Gulath, 1428
Gulath–Schwarz, 1428
Gulick, 62
Gunn, 1531

Gunnison, 1683
Gurgany, 4626
Gurley, 1684
Gurry, 540
Gustafson, 555
Gustin, 1685
Gustine, 1686
Guthrie, 49, 1687–88, 3411
Guttery, 4526
Gwaltney, 4524
Gwin, 4461
Gwyn, 1689
Gwynn, 1689
Gwynne, 1689

Habersham, 1690
Hacker, 299
Hackley, 4106
Hackstaff, 2641
Haden, 384. *See also* ad p. 383
Hadham, 4528
Hadley, 1691–92, 1939, 3658
Hafer, 181
Haff, 62, 940, 1693
Hafford, 1278
Hagen, 2815
Haggard, 1447
Haight, 1652, 2044–47
Hain, 1694
Haines, 1695–98, 1829, 4428
Haise, 1827
Hakes, 1699–1700
Halbert, 1701, 4527, 4531, 4536
Hale, 1596, 1702–5, 3658, 4428, 4524, 4527
Haley, 1210, 1447, 1706–7, 4571
Hall, 533, 540, 1278, 1339, 1682, 1708–15, 2842, 3164, 3293, 4463, 4544, 4600, 4630. *See also* adp. 153
Hallet, 1716
Hallett. *See* ad p. 153
Hallman. *See* ad p. 383
Hallock, 1717–18

Hallowell, 1719–20, 4458
Halsey, 1721
Halstead, 1722
Halterman, 2013, 4442
Ham, 299, 1723
Hamblen, 3156
Hambleton, 1724
Hamblin, 4530, 4625
Hamilton, 1246, 1553, 1725–27, 3164, 3453
Hamlin, 1728–31, 4530, 4625
Hammer, 1732, 3035
Hammond, 1733–35, 1846, 2297, 3160
Hampton, 1736
Hanaford, 1737
Hance, 1808
Hancock, 385, 1738, 2176, 2349, 4428, 4599, 4625
Handerson, 1739
Handley, 2181, 2708
Haner, 1804
Hanes. *See* ad p. 383
Haney, 1740
Hanford, 1682, 1741
Hanna, 1553, 1768
Hannum, 1742–43
Hansen, 2324
Hanson, 3482
Hapgood, 1744
Harbaugh, 1745
Harbough, 1746
Harcourt, 74, 4632
Hard, 1795
Hardaway, 4544
Hardenbergh, 1747, 4428, 4555
Hardie, 1750
Hardiman, 1061
Harding, 1748–49, 4525
Hardwick, 4580
Hardwicke, 4382
Hardy, 649, 1027, 1750, 2369, 3021, 4382, 4464, 4526
Hardyman, 4541
Hare, 2296
Hargrave, 4626
Haring, 62, 2488

Numbers refer to book numbers that appear in the left-hand column of pages 1–403.

Harlan, 1751, 2708, 3986
Harman, 1752–53
Harmon, 1753–54, 2144, 4169, 4571
Harmor, 4451
Harper, 1755, 2787, 4428, 4461, 4531, 4599
Harpster, 441
Harrington, 1756–57, 4523
Harris, 118, 385, 494, 634, 1532, 1758–63, 2713, 2931, 3164, 3658, 3702, 3816, 4169, 4294, 4298, 4474, 4477, 4523–26, 4530, 4535, 4541, 4544, 4571, 4625, 4632. *See also* ads pp. 37 and 153
Harrison, 1764–71, 2845, 4516, 4523, 4527, 4530–31, 4534, 4541, 4544. *See also* ad p. 383
Harrold, 421, 3658
Harry, 4477
Hart, 218, 1772–76, 2724, 3164, 3883, 4617, 4626. *See also* ad p. 383
Hartings, 1429
Hartle, 3986, 4169
Hartman, 1777–79, 4358
Hartmann, 1778–79
Hartt, 1780
Hartwell, 1781
Hartzell, 4169
Hartzler, 1890–91
Harvard, 1782
Harvey, 1783–86, 3658, 4523
Harvie, 4617
Harvin, 4626
Harwell, 4536
Harwood, 1682, 1787–89, 4272
Hasbrouch, 4555
Hasbrouck, 1790–91
Hase, 1827
Haskell, 1471, 1792–93, 2413, 2570, 4218, 4597
Haskin, 1794
Haskins, 1795, 4428

Hasner, 3685
Hass, 3066
Hastings, 25, 1796
Hasty, 4531
Haswell, 3021
Hatch, 211, 1797–99, 2842
Hatfield, 1800–2, 2240
Hathaway, 728, 1803, 4428
Hatherly, 1682
Haughey, 2296, 3453
Haughton, 1804–5
Hauser, 673. *See also* ad p. 383
Haven, 1806–7
Havens, 1808
Havermale, 4169
Haviland, 1061, 1809
Hawes, 1246, 1810–11
Hawker, 1812
Hawkins, 258, 1813, 2186, 3265, 4169, 4526
Hawks, 1533
Hawksby, 1154
Hawley, 1682, 1814, 2244
Haworth, 4477
Hawte, 4533
Hawvermale, 4169
Hay, 1815, 4170–71, 4511, 4528
Hayden, 1490, 1816–19
Haydon, 1820
Hayes, 218, 1821–27, 4225, 4528, 4537, 4613
Hayford, 1828
Haygood, 670
Hayley, 548
Haynes, 1682, 1829–30, 4526, 4531, 4540, 4632. *See also* ad p. 283
Haynie, 1831, 4524
Hays, 1832, 2157, 4528, 4537
Hayton, 2369
Hayward, 1833
Haywood, 4525, 4580
Hazard, 1364, 1834, 3316, 4428. *See also* ad p. 153
Hazelton, 1835
Hazen, 1836, 2721

Heacock, 4458
Heale, 4511, 4524, 4527
Healy, 4300
Heard, 2089, 2845
Hearn, 16, 2990
Hearne, 122, 1837
Heath, 1719, 1838–40, 2724, 4527, 4534
Heatwole, 961, 1841
Heavner, 4440
Heckert, 4180
Heckman, 606
Hedenstad, 3482
Hedges, 2721
Heemstraat, 4428
Hees, 1827
Heeter, 2369
Heffner, 2202
Hegeman, 2488
Heifner, 2144
Heighe, 4266
Heilig. *See* ad p. 383
Heinecke, 1842–43
Heiner, 1926. *See also* ad p. 355
Heist, 218
Heller, 1307, 1777, 3066
Helm, 2962
Helmboldt, 2307
Helmer, 1844
Helwig, 1845
Hemby, 649, 1846, 3469
Hemenway, 1847–49
Heminger, 1239
Hemp, 3658
Hemphill, 494, 1768. *See also* ad p. 37
Hempstead, 1850
Henagan, 4554
Hench, 1851
Henckel, 1852
Hendershot, 1853
Henderson, 540, 1854–58, 2734, 3164, 3362, 4461
Hendrick, 1859, 1885
Hendrickson, 1860, 2307
Henkel, 1768, 1861
Henley, 1862, 2349
Henninger, 4169
Henry, 1515, 1863–69, 2137, 3630, 4552

Hensel, 2144
Henshaw, 1930
Hensley, 4169
Henton, 1768
Hepburn, 1870
Hepple, 2905
Herbert, 4626
Herbold, 540
Hereford. *See* ad p. 283
Hericke, 1882–83
Herkimer, 1871
Herndon, 1872–79, 3035, 4463
Herr, 1880–81
Herrick, 1682, 1882–84, 4596. *See also* ad p. 153
Herring, 1768, 1885, 4169, 4530
Hersey, 2928
Hershberger, 3057, 4426
Hershey, 1886–88
Hertzler, 1889–91
Hess, 1437, 1892. *See also* ad p. 315
Hesser, 662
Hester, 1893–95, 2299, 3633
Heverly, 1896
Hewes, 1897
Hewett, 662
Hewitt, 509, 662, 1898, 2487, 4528. *See also* ad p. 59
Heydon, 1899
Heyl, 2043
Hiatt, 2296, 3658
Hibbard, 1805, 1900–2
Hickman, 4428
Hickok, 1795, 1903
Hickoks, 1903
Hicks, 299, 1904–5, 2137, 3909, 4428, 4458
Hidalgo, 4358
Hiddleston, 1591
Hiestand–Moore, 374
Hiester, 1906
Higby, 1061, 1907
Higgins, 1908–10
Higginson, 1911, 4630
Hight, 2044–47
Hightower, 1062, 2845, 4131
Higleys, 1912
Higman, 4273
Hilbert, 540
Hildebrand, 1913, 2574
Hildreth, 1914–15, 4571
Hill, 1916–19, 2296–97, 2358, 3658, 4196, 4523, 4526, 4531, 4536, 4541, 4552, 4599, 4625, 4626
Hillhouse, 1920
Hilliard, 1885, 4531, 4533–34
Hillman, 1623, 1921
Hills, 1922–23
Hillsman, 2763
Hinchliff, 4351
Hinckley, 1924
Hindman, 2557
Hinds, 1925
Hinegardner, 2245
Hiner, 1926. *See also* ad p. 355
Hines, 4625
Hinkle, 1768. *See also* ad p. 383
Hinkson, 2296
Hinman, 1927–28
Hinsch, 2721
Hinsdale, 1929
Hinsdill, 1803
Hinshaw, 1930–31, 1939
Hinton, 4530
Hipp, 4272
Hiscock, 509. *See also* ad p. 59
Hitchcock, 1932, 3533, 4552
Hite, 1768, 1933, 4612
Hiveley, 221
Hjelm, 677, 2962
Hoadley, 1934
Hoag, 1935
Hoagland, 1936
Hoar, 1682, 1937
Hobart, 1938
Hobbs, 12, 1905, 2297
Hobson, 1939, 2186, 3658, 4543
Hochstatter, 2935
Hochstedler, 1940
Hochstetler, 1941–42
Hochstettler, 4426
Hocker, 3799
Hockett, 421, 3658
Hodgdon, 1947
Hodge, 479, 1943
Hodges, 1507, 1944–45, 2315, 2763, 4554. *See also* ads pp. 162, 383
Hodgin. *See* ad p. 383
Hodgkins, 1946
Hodsdon, 1947
Hodson, 3658
Hoehn, 2307
Hoerner, 3799
Hoffelbauer, 1948
Hoffman, 1061, 1949, 4397
Hoge, 2245
Hogg, 2488
Hoggatt, 3658
Hogle. *See* ad p. 163
Holbrook, 2297, 2842, 3678, 4428
Holcomb, 1950–52
Holcombe, 1950, 1953
Holdeman, 1954
Holden, 1955
Holder, 1956
Holdredge, 2888
Hole, 3658
Holladay, 479, 1957, 4631
Holland, 1958–59, 2918, 3021, 4382, 4523, 4525, 4532
Holley, 4428
Holliday, 4580
Hollingsworth, 1768, 1960–61, 4580
Hollister, 1962
Hollon, 1963
Holloway, 181, 1964–66, 3658, 4428
Hollyday, 1556
Hollyman, 1967
Holman, 1968
Holmes, 280, 392, 1545, 1623, 1969–72, 3717, 4428. *See also* ad p. 383

Numbers refer to book numbers that appear in the left-hand column of pages 1–403.

Holstead, 4536
Holt, 1973–74, 4106, 4626
Holtgrieve, 1531
Holtzclaw, 1975, 4534
Holway, 1976
Holzhausen, 2021
Holzwarth, 4428
Honaker, 1977–79
Honeyman, 1980
Honeywell, 1981–83
Honyman, 1980
Hood, 1191, 1984–85, 2448, 3816
Hooe, 1986
Hook, 1987, 2245, 4477, 4599
Hooke, 1988
Hooker, 1989, 4464
Hoomes, 789
Hooper, 1935, 1990–91
Hooser, 1460
Hoover, 449, 2023, 2055–57. *See also* ad p. 315
Hope, 669
Hopkins, 1992–95, 2826, 4547, 4599. *See also* ad p. 397
Hopper, 1768, 4382
Hopwood, 2297
Horan, 4479
Hord, 1996, 2089
Hormel, 2307
Horn, 2307
Hornby. *See* ad p. 211
Horne, 802
Horner, 4400
Horning, 1997
Horsford, 1998
Horton, 1999–2004, 4531
Hosford, 1998, 2005
Hoshal, 2006
Hoskins, 1682, 2007
Hosmer, 219, 2008–11
Hostetler, 4180
Hottel, 2012
Hottinger, 2013
Hotzheimer, 4538
Hough, 2014–16
Houghtaling, 3168
Houghton, 2017–20

House, 1705, 2021–22
Houser, 2023, 3035
Houston, 1768, 2024–25, 2093, 2108, 2608, 4580
Hovey, 2026, 3036
Howard, 1768, 2027, 2028–33, 2297, 2763, 4294, 4528, 4544, 4579, 4595
Howe, 1182, 2034–36
Howell, 3222, 4400
Howes, 2037–38
Howland, 1596, 2039–42, 4351, 4428
Howle, 4625
Hoy, 557
Hoying, 323
Hoyle, 2043
Hoyt, 2044–50
Hubbard, 540, 1685, 1829, 2051–52, 4535–36
Hubbell, 2053–54
Huber, 2055–57
Huckins, 1737, 2058
Huckleberry, 1289
Huddlestone, 4286
Hudson, 2465, 4630
Huff, 2014–16
Huffman, 4169, 4300
Hufford, 2059
Huggins, 494, 4532. *See also* ad p. 37
Hughes, 1391, 1447, 2060–63, 2763
Huidekoper, 2064
Huit, 1682
Huling, 2065
Hull, 2066–68, 4428, 4461. *See also* ads pp. 173 and 211
Hulme, 4615
Hume, 2069, 4451
Hummel, 1777, 3799
Humphrey, 1266, 2690
Humphreys, 1679, 2070–73, 4541
Humphries, 2074, 3909
Hungerford, 2075–76
Hunneman, 1980
Hunnewell, 1983
Hunnicutt, 4528
Hunsicker, 2077

Hunt, 74, 325, 421–22, 2078–80, 2295–96, 3469, 3658, 4428, 4531
Hunter, 2081, 2596, 4382, 4529
Hunting, 2082
Huntington, 845, 2083–84
Huntley, 2085
Hunton, 2087–88, 3293
Huntoon, 2086–88
Huntt, 4527
Huntting, 2082
Huntton, 2088
Hupp, 4442
Hurd, 2089, 2845
Hurford, 4614
Hurlbut, 2090
Hurley. *See* ad p. 383
Hurst, 2091
Hurt, 4382
Huse, 2092
Huson, 2093
Hussey, 2608, 3453
Huston, 2093, 3501
Hutchens, 2095, 2098, 2100, 4533
Hutchin, 2095
Hutchings, 2094–95, 2098, 2100
Hutchins, 2094–2100, 3658
Hutchinson, 2101–5, 2465
Hutchison, 3108
Huxley, 3164
Hvaal, 3482
Hyatt, 2450
Hyde, 2106
Hynes, 2107–8
Hypes, 4169
Hyre. *See* ad p. 315

Ide, 2109
Iden, 4458
Ijams, 4536
Imbrie, 2110
Inaebnit, 2206
Ingalls, 2111–12
Ingels, 817
Ingersoll, 2113–14, 3145
Ingham, 2115

Ingli, 3360
Inglis, 16
Ingpen, 2116
Ingraham, 2117, 4428
Ingram, 2118
Innes, 2119
Irby, 4554
Ireland, 2120–21
Ireton, 2122–24
Irish, 2125–27
Irons, 3596
Irvine, 596, 2128–29
Irving, 4522
Irwin, 2130, 2996, 4625
Isaac, 2131
Isbell, 2132, 4525
Isham, 2133–34, 4464, 4539
Israel, 1659
Ive, 4528
Ives, 2135, 4536
Ivey, 4528, 4532, 4538
Ivie, 4528
Ivy, 4529, 4532, 4538
Izzard, 4464

Jackson, 385, 540, 789, 1246, 1297, 2136–41, 2708, 4104, 4306, 4527, 4532, 4533–34, 4552
Jacobs, 4397
Jacoby, 2142
Jagers, 649
James, 503, 530, 1086, 2143–45, 4527, 4599
Jameson, 939, 1785, 2146, 4532
Jamison, 3874, 4458, 4599
Janes, 1431, 1682, 2147
Jaquet, 1066, 4013
Jaquett, 2148
Jaquith, 2149
Jardine, 4522
Jarrett, 1719
Jarvis, 2150
Jay, 2151
Jaycocks, 1918
Jayroe, 479
Jefferies, 911
Jefferis, 1862, 4428

Jefferson, 2152, 4534, 4537, 4539
Jeffreys, 4474
Jeffries, 574, 911
Jelke, 2153
Jenckes, 4428
Jenkins, 1006, 2154, 4306, 4477
Jenks, 2155, 4428
Jennings, 2156–58, 2380, 2931, 4526, 4625
Jerauld, 1535
Jermain, 3638
Jernigan, 122, 4526, 4537. *See also* ad p. 383
Jesse, 2159
Jessop, 2296
Jessup, 2160, 3658
Jester, 4306
Jett, 1062
Jewell, 2161
Jewett, 2162, 3160
Jillson, 1550
Jinings, 2157
Jobe, 4528
Jocelyn, 2163
Johnes, 2164
Johnson, 71, 218, 479, 500, 533, 540, 560, 662, 677, 1246, 1825, 1939, 2165–74, 2186, 2245, 2600, 2708, 3164, 3353, 3658, 3874, 3969, 4169, 4458, 4477, 4536, 4543, 4571, 4600, 4617. *See also* ad p. 315
Johnston, 385, 500, 2173, 2175–76, 4169, 4275, 4580, 4625
Johnstone, 4522
Jolliffe, 2177
Jones, 16, 218, 385, 479, 789, 817, 1297, 1367, 1407, 1805, 1939, 2178–92, 2456, 3164, 3293, 3469, 3658, 4169, 4246, 4526, 4534, 4625, 4632
Jones–Peterson, 3058
Jordan, 1682, 2193, 2734,

4464, 4533, 4536, 4625
Jordon, 1768
Joseph, 1027
Joslin, 2163, 2940. *See also* ad p. 153
Joslyn, 2163
Josselyn, 2163, 3757
Joy, 2194–95
Joyner, 4527
Joys, 2474
Judd, 2196
Judkins, 1623, 4626
Judy, 3453
Julian, 1770, 4477
Jung, 4613, 4616
Junghen, 4414
Junkins, 2197
Justice, 1800, 2199
Justis, 2198–99
Justus, 2198–99

Kachlein, 1307
Kackley, 4477
Kagy, 2200
Kahley, 4328
Kaigler, 4532
Kandel, 2201
Karch, 2202
Karr, 2788
Kassel, 718
Kasten, 3804
Kathan, 2203
Katterhenry, 3107
Kauffman, 2204–5, 3057, 3449, 4180, 4426
Kaufman, 2204–6, 4600
Kaufmann, 2206
Kavanaugh, 2713
Kaylor, 4169
Kayser, 4328
Kea, 3633
Kearfott, 2247
Kearns, 2207
Keasey, 832
Keck, 2208–10
Keeler, 3333
Keen, 2211–14, 3235, 3723
Keenan, 540
Keene, 2215

Numbers refer to book numbers that appear in the left-hand column of pages 1–403.

Keeney, 86
Keep, 2216
Keese, 2217
Keezells, 1768
Keidel, 4170
Keim, 3874
Keinadt, 2308
Keister, 3541, 4461
Keith, 1431, 2218, 3906
Kelker, 1431, 2219
Keller, 1210, 2220–21, 3168
Kelley, 2222
Kellogg, 2223, 2724
Kelly, 479, 2224–25, 2708, 3658
Kelsey, 2226–28, 3145
Kelso, 1357
Kelton, 4580
Kemball, 2259
Kemble, 2229, 2259, 3752
Kembolde, 2259
Kemmerer, 2230
Kemp, 500, 2231, 4533, 4544
Kempe, 4266, 4542
Kemper, 181
Kendall, 2232–33, 3226, 4524
Kendrick, 4428, 4523–24
Kenfield, 2234
Kennan, 2235
Kennedy, 677, 2236–41, 3376, 4522
Kennerly, 1768
Kent, 2242–45, 3861, 4428
Kenworthy, 1805
Kenyon, 1646, 2246
Keplinger, 683
Keppler, 3359
Kerber. *See* ad p. 383
Kerchival, 971
Kerfoot, 2247
Kerley, 2248, 2488
Kerns, 4477
Kerr, 1266, 3164, 4522
Kersey, 2296, 4630
Kershner, 4169
Kessen, 1429
Kester, 3132

Ketchum, 4589
Ketterman, 2249
Key, 2250, 3633, 4579
Keyes, 1391, 2251–52
Kicker, 2253
Kidd, 673
Kidder, 2254–55, 2940, 3988
Kigh, 2256
Kilbourn, 2257
Kilby, 4474
Kile, 2325
Kilker, 323
Killingsworth, 2575, 4523
Killoran, 540
Kilmer, 2258
Kilpatrick, 4544
Kimball, 2259–63
Kimber, 2264
Kimberly, 2265
Kimble, 2229
Kincaid, 3541
Kindred, 2423
King, 1862, 2181, 2266–70, 3057, 4426, 4463, 4474, 4514. *See also* ad p. 383
Kingery, 4169
Kingman, 2271
Kingsbury, 2272–73, 4428
Kingsley, 2274
Kinnear, 2275
Kinney, 1682
Kinsey, 2276–77, 4458, 4463
Kinsman, 2278
Kinton, 3909
Kintzy, 2277
Kip, 2279–80
Kiplinger, 1049
Kipshaven, 3769
Kirby, 1682, 2281, 4428
Kirk, 2282–83, 4534, 4542
Kirkbride, 2284
Kirkpatrick, 3284, 3535, 4522
Kistler, 2285
Kitchen, 4428
Kite, 2286
Kittredge, 2287, 4129

Klapp, 35
Klein. *See* ad p. 315
Kleinhans, 1531, 2915
Klindt, 3783
Kline, 4533
Klingenberger, 4538
Klinger, 2288, 4180
Klinglesmith, 970
Knaff, 4599
Knapp, 2289–90
Knaus, 808
Kneeland, 2291
Kneisly, 2292
Knepper, 2293
Knickerbacker, 2294
Kniffen, 3392
Knight, 1682, 2295–97, 4131, 4533
Knisely, 2298, 4180
Knive, 3482
Knott, 2299, 4529
Knowles, 1431, 1682, 2300. *See also* ad p. 383
Knowlton, 540, 1682, 2301–2
Knox, 494, 666, 2303–5, 3436. *See also* ad p. 37
Koch, 308, 2306
Koelliker, 2219
Koger, 2709, 3389
Kohlhagen, 2307
Koiner, 2308–9
Kolb, 2310–12, 4554
Kolliker, 1431
Kool, 843
Koolock, 2313
Koon, 895
Koontz, 1768, 2708
Koppelmann, 2307
Kothe, 2314
Kramer, 2315
Kratz, 2316
Krehe, 2322
Kreider, 2317–20
Krekler, 2321
Krider. *See* ad p. 383
Krogh, 88
Kruse, 4428
Kuechmann, 2322
Kugler, 2721
Kuhn, 895

Kulp, 2311–12
Kunders, 2323
Kunstman, 3387. *See also*
ad p. 393
Kuntz, 895
Kunzman, 181
Kurtz, 4426
Kurz, 1136
Kuser, 4428
Kyhl, 2324
Kyle, 2325
Kyn, 2211, 2214

Lacey. *See* ad p. 383
Lacy, 2326
Ladd, 2296, 2327, 3371
Ladehoff, 3783
Lafeit, 385
Lafferty, 4600
Lafollette, 4477
Lage, 3783
Lain, 2348
Lair, 4442
Laird, 4522
Lake, 2328–29
Lakin, 1682
Lam, 4169
Lamar, 1635
Lamb, 1682, 2330–32,
4169
Lambert, 2333–34, 2708,
3376
Lamborn, 2335
Laminack, 2662
Lamont, 2336
Lampton, 2337
Lamson, 2338–39
Lancaster, 211, 2340–42,
4458, 4533
Land, 2448, 4533
Landis, 1888, 2343. *See
also* ad p. 315
Landon, 2344
Lane, 144, 1481, 2345–
49, 4524, 4626
Lanes, 3678
Lang, 2962
Langaker, 2478
Langdon, 218
Langston, 2563, 4462,
4464

Lanier, 479, 4286, 4625
Lankford, 1062
Lannard, 2377
Lansing, 2350, 4428
Lantz, 2351–52, 3986,
4442
Lapham, 2353–54
Lapp, 3057
Laprade, 4599
Large, 2297
Larimer, 2355
Larkin, 2439
Larned, 2377
Larrick, 4477
LaRue, 1795
Lasher, 2356–57
Laskin, 1682
Lassiter. *See* ad p. 383
Latham, 2297, 2358,
3222, 3924
Lathrop, 2359–60, 3021,
3164
Lattimore, 3881
Lauder, 2361
Lauffer, 2362
Laugharn, 3164
Laughlin, 2363, 4351
Lauterbach, 673
Lavender, 479
Lavinder, 4599
Lawrence, 1062, 2364–
70, 2721, 3869, 4523,
4527, 4530, 4552
Lawson, 789, 2371, 2931,
3880, 4286, 4474, 4525
Lawton, 4428
Layne, 2348, 2372
Lazell, 2373
Lea, 2374, 4581
Leach, 2375
Leadbetter, 2376
Leake, 2256, 4463
Leap, 4169
Leaphart, 3164
Learnard, 2377
Learned, 1682, 2377
Leatherman, 4328
Leavell, 1965
Leavens, 2378
Leavenworth, 2379
Leavitt, 2380–81

Le Baron, 2382
Le Bosquet, 731
Lechmere, 2383
LeConte, 2384
Ledlow, 1712
Lee, 218, 271, 280, 1246,
1431, 2295–96, 2385–
93, 2596, 4175, 4479,
4534, 4552, 4554, 4599.
See also ad p. 162
Leech, 4401, 4613
Leese, 2394
Leete, 2395–96
LeFevre, 4555
LeFevres, 2397
Lefferts, 2398
Leffingwell, 2399
Leftwich, 2400, 4542
Legare, 2401
Legenauer. *See* ad p. 383
Legh, 2402
LeGrand, 2403
Lehman, 2404, 4078
Leibensperger, 1437
Leidy, 3164
Leighton, 2405–7
Leitch, 3383
Leland, 2408
Le Maitre, 1076
Lemon, 4397, 4527
Lent, 2409
Lenthall, 1249
Lentz, 2935
Lenz, 2410
Lenzen, 1429
Leonard, 2411–14, 2983,
4428
Lerned, 2377
LeRoy, 325
Lesh. *See* ad p. 315
Leslie, 2415–16
Lester, 4458
LeStrange, 2417
Letcher, 2108
Lett, 2141
Leverett, 2418
Levering, 308, 1074,
2419, 2420
Levick, 4458
Levings, 2378
Lewis, 218, 398, 479,

Numbers refer to book numbers that appear in the left-hand column of pages 1–403.

1278, 1556, 1646,
2421–31, 2575, 3145,
3293, 3541, 4297, 4458,
4477, 4524, 4539, 4578,
4617, 4625, 4631
L'Hommedieu, 2432
Libby, 2433
Lichty, 4170
Liger, 3392
Lightfoot, 1367, 2434
Lightner, 4461. *See also*
ad p. 315
Ligon, 385, 2435–36,
4609, 4632
Lilley, 2636
Lillie, 2437
Lilly, 4169
Limesi, 2444
Limozin, 4077
Lincoln, 1768, 2438–41
Lindbergh, 2788
Lindeseie, 2444
Lindley, 3376
Lindopp, 1623
Lindsay, 1635, 2442,
2448. *See also* ad p.
383
Lindsey, 4600. *See also*
ad p. 283
Lingenfelter, 3164
Linn, 2443. *See also* ad
p. 383
Linton, 2962
Linville, 1895
Linzee, 2444
Lippincott, 2445–46
Lippitt, 1682
Lipscomb, 789
Litchfield, 2447
Littell, 2448–51
Littig, 2452
Little, 144, 832, 2451,
2453–54
Littlefield, 2455, 3816
Littlefields, 608
Littleford, 2456
Littlejohn, 2358, 4523
Littlepage, 1556, 4631
Livengood, 1062
Livermore, 2457
Livezey, 2458–59
Livingston, 2460–62
Lliff, 2463

Lloyd, 2464–66
Loar, 2467
Lobdell, 1682, 2468
Lobden, 2468
Lockard, 2788
Locke, 1918, 2469–70
Lockhart, 4477
Lockridge, 4461, 4534
Lockwood, 1408, 2471
Loesch, 2472
Logan, 325, 673, 1768,
2473, 2721, 4169
Logue, 680
Loker, 1682
Lomax, 2295–97
Lomen, 2474
Lomonaco, 677
London, 2475
Long, 1682, 2157, 2476–
77, 4169, 4617, 4625.
See also ad p. 315
Longacre, 2478
Longenecker, 2478
Longfellow, 1268
Longyear, 2479
Loockermans, 4428
Look, 4552
Loomis, 1596, 2480–81,
2494
Loos, 2482
Lord, 1061, 1278, 1440,
2334, 2483–84
Loree, 3830
Loring, 1805, 2485
Lothhotz, 4530
Lothrop, 144, 2360, 2486
Lott, 2487–88, 4458. *See
also* ad p. 255
Loucks, 2489
Loud, 2490
Loughry, 2491
Lound, 385
Lounsberry, 2731
Lounsbury, 1809
Love, 662, 1246, 2492–
94, 2652
Lovejoy, 2495
Lovekyn, 2505
Lovelace, 4535
Loveland, 2496
Lovell, 4523
Lovewell, 2497

Lovvorn, 2662
Low, 4555
Lowe, 1460, 1800, 2297,
2498. *See also* ad p.
153
Lowell, 2499
Lower, 2500
Lowndes, 2501
Lowry, 2502
Lucas, 1128, 2503, 4626
Luckey, 116
Luckyn, 2505
Ludlam, 74
Ludlow, 74, 2721
Ludlum, 74
Ludwig, 2504, 4428
Luers, 62
Lujan, 2546
Luken, 1719
Lukin, 2505
Lum, 673, 2506
Lumas, 2507
Lunday, 2875, 4589
Lunde, 2520
Lundy, 2508
Lunt, 2509–10, 3907,
4571
Lupton, 4477
Luria. *See* ad p. 383
Lush. *See* ad p. 211
Luther, 2511, 4428
Luttrell, 3217, 4579
Lybarger, 2512
Lyddall, 4464
Lyford, 2513
Lyle, 2514–15, 4579
Lyman, 1278, 1352,
1682, 1803, 2516, 2517
Lyme, 2402
Lynch, 2518–19
Lynde, 445
Lyon, 2521–23, 2708
Lyons. *See* ad p. 383
Lytle, 2451

Mabery, 2157
Mabvie, 1471
MacAlpine, 3574
MacClamroch, 4523
MacClaughry, 2628
MacCutcheon, 2638
MacDonald 1133, 1135,
2524–25

Mace, 662
MacFarlan, 2644, 2646
MacFarland, 2646
MacFarlane, 2646
MacFarlin, 2646
MacGillivray, 4544
MacGregor, 2526
Mack, 2527–28, 3952
Mackall, 4266
MacKay, 2369, 2529
Mackclothlan, 787
MacKenzie, 2530–31
Mackey, 4534
Mackie, 4543
Mackintosh, 2532
Macklin, 3108
Maclay, 2533
Maclean, 2534
MacLeod, 2535–37, 4294
MacMillan, 2538
MacNeil, 2539
Macomb, 2540
Macomber, 394, 2541
Macon, 4529, 4626
MacQueen, 2542
Macrae, 2543
Macy, 1591, 2544, 3658
Maddy, 2545
Mader, 1429
Madera, 4613
Madison, 4543
Madoeri, 4613
Maes, 2546
Maese, 2546
Maffitt. *See* ad p. 383
Magee, 16, 4554
Magill, 2547, 4580
Magoffin, 2650
Maham, 2614
Main, 156, 2548
Maine, 2548
Maitland, 4522
Makepeace, 2549
Male, 299
Malick, 2682
Malin, 4477
Mallet, 2550
Mallett, 4523, 4528
Mallory, 385, 2551, 4527,
    4545, 4609, 4632
Malone, 2552, 4298

Maloney, 1396, 1397
Malsbury, 4400
Maltbie, 2553
Maltby, 2553–54
Maltman, 863
Manchester, 4351
Mandigo, 2772
Maner, 500
Manire, 2575
Manley, 4447
Manly, 2555
Mann, 2256, 2556, 3553,
    4464, 4528, 4531, 4626
Manner, 2557
Manning, 2558–59. *See
    also* ad p. 153
Mansel, 2825
Mansell, 2825
Mansfield, 2560, 2724
Manson, 2744
Manter, 1623
Mapes, 3394
Marbury, 2103
March, 1682, 3387. *See
    also* ad p. 383
Marchant, 4597
Marcum, 385
Margeson, 2561
Mariana, 677
Maris, 2562
Mark, 299
Markham, 2569
Marks, 970–71, 4287,
    4541
Markwith, 2563
Marple, 4477
Marquis, 2256
Marr, 3874
Marrow, 2694
Marsh, 1533, 2564–67
Marshal, 4420
Marshall, 299, 817, 1431,
    1623, 1682, 1805, 1939,
    2568–70, 2608, 4428,
    4474, 4599, 4626
Marshfield, 3339
Marston, 2571–73. *See
    also* ad p. 153
Martens, 3107, 3783
Martense, 3393
Martin, 132, 1431, 1679,

1803, 2296, 2574–83,
    2662, 2815, 2962, 3164,
    3804, 4224, 4420,
    4599– 4600
Martín, 2546
Martínez, 2546
Martz, 1768
Marvin, 2584–87
Marye, 4563
Mason, 1070, 2589–95,
    2708, 4525–27, 4632
Massengill, 4534, 4625
Massey, 2596, 3376,
    4534, 4540
Mast, 2597, 3057, 4426
Masters, 3804
Matheny, 677, 4541
Mather, 2598
Matheson, 2599
Mathews, 2600, 3633,
    4533, 4617
Mathias, 4536
Mathis, 479
Matlack, 2601, 4428
Matoaka, 3104–5
Matson, 2684
Matteson, 2602, 2708
Matthews, 1939, 2603,
    4537
Maudlin, 2296
Maull, 2604
Maulsby, 2605
Maunsell, 2824–25
Maupin, 2713
Mauran, 2606
Maury, 1415, 4563
Mauzy, 1768
Maxet, 2107
Maxey, 4128
Maxson, 2607
Maxwell, 688, 2608–9,
    4522
May, 1061, 1247, 1589,
    2610–11, 3021, 4169,
    4172, 4442
Mayall, 2297
Maybee, 2349
Maydew, 2612
Mayer, 2613
Mayes, 1246
Mayham, 2614

Numbers refer to book numbers that appear in the left-hand column of pages 1–403.

Mayhew, 4061
Mayhugh, 2615
Maynard, 1460, 2297, 2617
Mays, 4382
Mayse, 1623, 4382
McAdoo, 4579
McAlester, 3703
McAllister, 2618, 3874, 3883, 4128
McBride, 3986
McCabe, 2619
McCall, 2620–21, 3799, 4543, 4554
McCallister, 2684
McCallum, 1918, 2622–23
McCardell, 2838
McCarty, 2449, 2624–25, 4458
McCauley, 3792
McClanahan, 2626
McClary, 2627, 2639
McClatchy, 2787
McClaughry, 2628
McClean, 1971
McClenahan, 2629
McClendon, 2630
McClintock, 1812
McClung, 2631
McClure, 2632, 3362
McColl, 4554
McColley, 1776
McComb, 1685
McCombs, 911
McConnell, 2633
McCool, 4477
McCord, 2157
McCormack, 4382
McCormick, 540, 673, 2634
McCown, 677
McCoy, 1800, 1803, 2298, 2635, 4172
McCray, 2636, 2664
McCuiston, 2674
McCulloch, 2358
McCullough, 1795, 1905, 2608, 2637, 2734
McCutchan, 2638
McCutchen, 2638
McCutcheon, 2638–39

McCutchin, 2638
McDaniel, 2640, 4589
McDilda, 2600
McDonald, 2524–25, 4477
McDonough, 2641
McDowell, 1658, 2642
McElfresh, 662
McElroy, 2643, 4462, 4531
McEwen, 62
McFadden, 494. *See also* ad p. 37
McFarlan, 2644
McFarland, 1905, 2645, 4461
McFarlane, 2646
McFaffey, 2647
McGaffin, 2650
McGavock, 2648
Mcgee, 16
McGee, 1635, 1795
McGehee, 230, 649, 4617
McGeorge, 4382
McGiffin, 2650
McGill, 2547, 2649
McGinnis, 2449
McGlathery, 308
McGoffin, 2650
McGregor, 3311
McGrew, 4544
McGriffin, 107
McGuffin, 671, 2650
McGuire, 1795, 2651
McHargue, 2448
McIlraith, 2652
McIntire, 2653–55
McIntosh, 2107, 3783
McIntyre, 2708
McKain, 4626
McKaughan, 4106
McKay, 2656, 3797
McKean, 2657
McKee, 1210, 2108, 2144, 2658, 4477
McKeen, 3036
McKelvey, 2659
McKinley, 2660
McKinnie, 4474, 4523
McKinstry, 2661
McKisson, 3164
McKnight, 479

McKnitt, 494. *See also* ad p. 37
McLaurin, 4554
McLean, 4198
McLendon, 2630, 2662, 3164
McLeod, 4554
McLucas, 4554
McMaster, 3703
McMasters, 2355
McMath, 2663
McMicken, 2721
McMillan, 1905, 2329, 3280, 3469, 4579
McMorris, 2664
McMurray, 4534
McMurtrey, 2157
McNair, 2665–68. *See also* ad p. 383
McNary, 2669
McNear, 2665, 2667, 2670
McNeil, 1264
McNeill, 2671
McNeir, 2665, 2667
McNiel, 4599
McNulty, 4533
McNutt, 107
McPike, 2672
McQueen, 2673
McQuesten, 2674
McQuiston, 2674
McRae, 4554
McVay, 4169
McWhorter, 1266
McWilliams, 181, 673, 1768
McWillie, 2675
Mead, 1408, 2676–77
Meade, 2678
Meador, 4382
Meadors, 4526
Meadows, 677, 4526
Means, 1030
Mears, 2679. *See also* ad p. 283
Medalen, 3482
Medley, 2081
Meech, 4078
Meek, 1035, 1795, 2680
Mehringer, 4529–30
Meier, 2835

Meigs, 2681, 4258
Mellick, 2682
Mellon, 2144, 4477
Mendelsohn, 2683
Mendelssohn, 2683
Mendenhall, 422, 2296, 3658, 4428
Menkel, 2815
Menton, 1434
Mercer, 2684, 4428, 4477, 4524, 4537
Meredith, 1795, 2295–96, 3658
Meriam, 2685
Merick, 2689
Meriet, 2692
Merivale, 2686
Meriwether, 2425, 2687, 4617
Merriam, 2688
Merrick, 2689
Merrill, 1278, 2690
Merriman, 2691
Merritt, 2692–93, 3574
Merrow, 2694
Merry, 2694
Merryman, 2695, 2979
Merwin, 2696–97
Mesick, 2698
Messenger, 1860
Metcalf, 1762
Metheny, 4514
Metselaer, 4428
Metz, 4538
Meyer, 2699, 2700–1, 3107, 3164, 4400
Michael, 4169
Michelet, 2702
Michell. *See* ad p. 173
Mickley, 2702
Middlebrook, 2703
Miedema, 2704
Mildmay, 4632
Miles, 2705–6, 2775
Milk, 2707
Milks, 2707
Millanges, 2723
Millard, 1682
Milleman, 2708
Millemon, 2708
Miller, 86, 218, 1503,

1795, 2487, 2594, 2709–22, 3057, 3108, 3306, 3619, 4169, 4328, 4426, 4458, 4463, 4545, 4571. *See also* ad p. 315
Millerman, 2708
Millermon, 2708
Milligan, 1210
Milliken, 2723
Millikin, 2723
Milliman, 2708, 2724
Millingas, 2723
Millis, 1635, 2725
Mills, 419, 422, 1813, 2296, 2726–29, 3164, 3658, 4300, 4552
Milone, 1795
Milstead, 4545
Miltzow, 3703
Minear, 2730
Miner, 156, 1230, 2731
Minich, 1437
Minier, 4552
Minnich, 449
Minor, 2732
Minot, 1596, 2733
Miskell, 4525
Mitchell, 1596, 2734–36, 2980, 3164, 3392, 4599
Mixon, 4528
Mixson, 4528
Moeder, 1429
Moelich, 2682
Moffat, 2737
Mohler, 2738
Mohun, 4536
Moldenhauer, 4544
Molyneux, 2739
Moncure, 2740, 4631
Money, 394
Monfort, 911
Monger, 2820, 4169
Mongold, 2741
Mongor, 2820
Monk, 3306
Monnet, 2742
Monroe, 1768, 1918, 2743, 4451
Monsell, 2824
Monson, 2744

Montague, 2745–47, 3401, 4246
Montfort, 911, 2358
Montgomery, 2748–51, 4534, 4580, 4599, 4614
Mooar, 2752
Mood, 2753
Moody, 2754
Moomaw, 4272
Moon, 3658
Moone, 2297
Mooney, 4479
Mooneyhan, 1062
Moor, 2755, 4526
Moore, 218, 670, 1246, 1768, 1862, 2448, 2662, 2721, 2756–62, 3095, 3107, 3155, 3553, 4173, 4461, 4534, 4542, 4544, 4632. *See also* ad p. 383
Moorman, 2296, 4526
Moors, 2752
Moragne, 2763
Moran, 2764–65
More, 2766–67. *See also* ad p. 397
Morehead, 2769, 2788, 3293
Morehouse, 2554, 2768
Moreland, 4298
Morey, 1762, 2770
Morgan, 554, 1481, 1596, 1770, 2191, 2346, 2771–75, 3164, 3792, 4266, 4396, 4458, 4612. *See also* ad p. 231
Morgen. *See* ad p. 231
Morgin. *See* ad p. 231
Morison, 2785
Morrell, 2776
Morrill, 2777
Morris, 286, 677, 856, 1719, 2296, 2778–84, 3306, 4169, 4458, 4524
Morrison, 2785–87, 4531. *See also* ad p. 383
Morrow, 2788–89
Mors, 4428
Morschheimer, 4544
Morse, 2790–91, 2968, 3874, 4428

Numbers refer to book numbers that appear in the left-hand column of pages 1–403.

Mortimer, 4286, 4437
Morton, 2792–97, 4353
Mosby, 4464
Moseley, 385, 540, 1431, 2296, 2798, 4526
Moses, 1431, 2256, 2799, 2800
Mosher, 2801
Motley, 4599
Mott, 2802–3, 3717, 4428
Moulinier, 1809
Moulton, 230, 1278, 2269, 2804–7, 4428
Mount, 2808
Mountjoy, 181
Mousall, 540
Mower, 2809
Mowry, 118, 2810–13
Moyer, 2699
Muckler, 891
Muckridge, 2563
Mudge, 2814
Mueller, 2815
Muhs, 3783
Muir, 3305
Mulford, 918, 4552
Mulholland, 4525
Muller, 274, 2935
Mulligan, 4479
Mullin, 2816
Mumford, 2817, 4632
Muncy, 2818
Mundy, 2819
Munford, 181
Munger, 2820, 4526
Munro, 2743, 2821–23, 2828
Munsell, 2824–25
Munsey, 2826
Munsill, 2824
Munson, 218, 2744, 2827
Murdoch, 4106
Murdock, 2828, 3906
Murphy, 662, 2829, 4400
Murray, 274, 325, 2830–31, 4522, 4527, 4536
Muscoe, 4511
Muse, 4599
Musgrave, 2144, 2832, 4395
Musgrove, 3574

Musick, 1800, 2574, 4462
Musser, 2833, 4180
Mussey, 2721
Mybird, 1074
Myers, 677, 2834–35. See also ad p. 315
Mygatt, 2836
Mylin, 2837
Mynatt, 2763
Myra, 3482
Myrick, 2689

Naef, 2849
Naf, 2847
Naeff, 4599
Naff, 4599
Nagel, 2838
Nagle, 2296
Nail, 2843
Naille, 2843
Napier, 398, 789, 1460, 4537, 4539
Nash, 2839–40, 2943, 4463, 4536
Nason, 1814
Navarre, 2841
Nave, 275
Nazelrod, 2013
Neal, 218, 2165, 2842–43, 3389, 4571
Neale, 2844
Nealeigh, 2563
Nebel, 4538
Neblett, 2845
Needham, 553, 2846
Neff, 449, 2847–49. See also ad p. 315
Neighbors, 3804
Neilson, 2708
Nell, 2850
Nelms, 2118
Nelson, 330, 2851–54, 2941–42, 4128, 4543, 4599
Nesbit, 2855
Nesbitt, 1785, 4479
Nesper, 1531
Nesselrodt, 2013
Neufang, 2306
Nevill, 3986
Neville, 2574, 2856, 4511, 4524

Nevin, 2857
Nevius, 2858
Newbaker, 2859
Newbern, 4544
Newberry, 2860
Newbold, 864
Newby, 2296
Newcomb, 2861–62, 3986
Newcomer. See ad p. 315
Newell, 673, 1682, 2863
Newgate, 445
Newhall, 551, 2864
Newling, 3468
Newman, 1768, 4516
Newsom, 3164
Newton, 2865–68, 4363, 4543–44, 4600, 4632
Nice, 2869
Nicholas, 2870
Nicholls, 2871
Nichols, 1600, 1693, 2448, 2872, 3164, 3614, 3658, 4474
Nicholson, 4298
Nicholson–Adams, 2873
Nickels, 1623
Nickerson, 4286
Nicks, 2296
Nicolet, 2874
Nidiffer, 2875
Niel, 2843
Nienaber, 3469
Niles, 1061, 3804
Niven, 2876
Nix, 2875
Nixon, 4458
Noble, 668, 1795, 2877–78
Noe, 1447
Noffsinger. See ad p. 315
Norfleet, 4525, 4625
Norris, 2298, 2879–81, 4528
North, 2882–83
Northington, 4525
Northrop, 2884
Northrup, 2884
Norton, 1035, 1596
Norville, 4527
Norwood, 4523, 4525, 4626, 4632

Nothstein, 2885
Nourse, 2886
Nowlin, 2887
Noyes, 2888–91
Null, 2843
Nunes Miranda. *See* ad p. 383
Nunn, 2892
Nusberger, 2307
Nutter, 931
Nutting, 2893
Nye, 608, 2894
Nyssen, 62

Oak, 2895
Oake, 2895, 4082
Oakes, 2256
Oakley, 3909
Oberholtzer, 2896–97
O'Brien, 2898
Odell, 2899
Odenbaugh, 2245
Odiorne, 2900
Odom, 500
Oehler, 1136
Oehlman, 2721
Oetjen, 3164
Offley, 4528
Ogden, 662, 2901–4
Ogilbay, 2608
Ogilvee, 2608
Ogilvie, 2608
Ogilvy, 2608
Ogle, 2905–6
Oglethorpe, 122
Olcott, 2907–8
Old, 2838
Oldham, 2713
Oldwiler, 1289
Olin, 2909–10
Oliver, 299, 1447, 2101, 2439
Oller. *See* ad p. 315
Olmstead, 1596
Olmsted, 2664, 2912–14
Olney, 2911
Olsen, 3482
Olson, 2915. *See also* ad p. 283
O'Meagher, 2916
Onderdonk, 2917

Onstine, 662
Op Den Graeff, 1074
Opdyck, 2918
Opdycke, 2918
Opdyke, 2918
Orchard, 4353
Ordway, 2919
Orfeur, 4395
Orgek, 540
Orme, 3305–6
Ormsby, 2920
Orr, 1795, 4529
Orton, 2921
Orvis, 2922
Osborn, 1808, 2141, 2296, 2923, 3035, 3658
Osborne, 2924, 4528
Osburn, 4328
Osgood, 1364, 2192, 2925. *See also* ad p. 153
Oster, 1307
Osterhoudt, 628
Ostrander, 3168
Otis, 2926–28
Otstot, 2929
Otstott, 2929
Ott, 62, 1768
Ouderkerk, 3164, 4428
Ousley, 2208
Outh, 274
Outlaw. *See* ad p. 383
Overby, 70
Overton, 89, 2930–31, 4527, 4544, 4545, 4625
Owen, 87, 669, 2708, 2724, 2932–34, 4266, 4528
Owens, 70, 3164
Owings, 2788
Oyer, 2935–36

Pabodie, 3002
Pabody, 3002
Paca, 2937
Pace, 4382, 4632
Pack, 479
Packard, 2938
Packwood, 662
Page, 330, 1691, 2603,

2939–46. *See also* ad p. 245
Paige, 2940
Paine, 2947–53, 2999, 4428, 4599
Painter, 218, 2980
Palgrave, 2954
Palmer, 2955–57, 3574, 4464, 4532, 4615
Pancoast, 2958–59
Pannill. *See* ad p. 383
Paradise, 421
Pardee, 2960
Parham, 4528, 4535–36
Park, 138, 144, 2961–62, 3804, 4581
Parke, 336–37, 1471, 2465, 2963–65
Parker, 1515, 1682, 1712, 2074, 2966–73, 4527, 4554
Parkes, 3164, 4581
Parkhurst, 2974
Parks, 2964
Parlee, 2975
Parlette, 4477
Parlin, 2976
Parmley, 3389
Parr, 1623, 2977
Parrir, 3906
Parrish, 1447, 2978–80
Parry, 1278, 2191
Parshall, 2981–82
Parsons, 1868, 2979, 2983–84, 4524, 4534
Parthemore, 2985
Partridge, 2986–87
Parva, 4528
Pasley, 4382
Pasteur, 4464
Patch, 1682
Pate, 181, 1623, 4382
Patrick, 911
Patten, 2988–89, 3739, 4571
Patterson, 458, 2990–92, 3874
Patton, 1770, 4525
Paul, 1719, 2993–94, 4428
Paulk. *See* ad p. 261

Numbers refer to book numbers that appear in the left-hand column of pages 1–403.

Paull, 2995–96
Pauls, 4428
Paustian, 3783
Pawling, 1074
Paxton, 2997
Paybody, 3002
Payn, 2951
Payne, 2951, 2998–99
Payson, 4532
Peabody, 1596, 3000–2, 4428
Peacemaker, 4477
Peacock, 4543
Peak, 3003
Peake, 3003
Pearce, 299, 3004, 4351, 4428
Pearl, 3005
Pearsall, 3006
Pearse, 3079
Pearson, 540, 3007–10, 3658, 4477, 4554. *See also* ad p. 383
Pease, 3011–14
Peaslee, 3015
Peavy, 4529
Peche, 4632
Peck, 1693, 2943, 2966, 3016–17, 3487
Peckham, 3018, 4351
Pedan, 530
Peden (Paden), 4353–55. *See also* ad p. 383
Peebles, 1635
Peffley, 3019
Peffly, 3019
Pefley, 3019
Pegue, 4554
Peira, 2574
Peirce, 500, 3020–22, 3079
Pell, 4198, 4532
Pelt, 3023
Pelton, 3024
Pember, 3025
Pemberton, 1268, 2465
Pembleton, 3027
Pence, 961, 3026
Pender–Hart, 4527
Pendleton, 2941–42, 3027–28, 3293, 4598
Penfield, 3029

Pengry, 3030
Penn, 1733, 3031–33
Pennell, 4428
Penney, 3034
Pennington, 3035–36, 3574, 4526
Pennock, 1795, 3037
Pennypacker, 3038
Penquite, 3453
Penrose, 4266, 4458
Pepper, 3468
Pepperrell, 3039
Percy, 4437
Perdue, 385
Perine, 3048
Peringer, 2684
Perisho, 4420
Perkins, 3040–45
Perkio, 677
Perley, 2944, 3046, 3122
Perney, 3047
Peroney, 3047
Peroni, 3047
Perpont, 3081
Perrin, 3048–49, 3177
Perrine, 3048
Perry, 494, 608, 1006, 1246, 1278, 1460, 1646, 1682, 1885, 3050–52, 4428, 4525, 4529, 4626. *See also* ad p. 37
Perryman, 4524, 4632
Pers, 3079
Pershing, 3053
Peters, 553, 3054–56, 3574, 4599
Petersheim, 3057
Peterson, 2721, 2815, 3058, 4169, 4523
Petker, 3107
Pettigrew, 2619
Pettingell, 3059
Pettit, 1812
Pettypool, 4526
Peyton, 3060, 4631
Pfeiffer, 3061
Pfieffer, 2144
Pflueger, 3797
Pfoutz. *See* ad p. 315
Pharr, 4528
Phelix, 1918
Phelps, 1266, 1440, 3062–63

Philbrick, 3064
Philbrook, 3064
Phileo, 1370
Philips, 3065, 4626
Philipse, 3164
Phillips, 46, 1800, 1939, 2081, 2137, 2487–88, 3065–70, 3164, 4458, 4528. *See also* ad p. 255
Philo, 1370
Phinizy, 4579
Phinney, 1828, 3071
Phippen, 608
Phoenix, 3072
Pickel, 3073
Pickenpaugh, 1210, 2144
Pickens, 2734
Pickering, 931, 1768, 3074–75
Pierce, 509, 540, 1682, 3076–79, 4382, 4462, 4625
Pierpont, 1884, 3080–81
Pierrepont, 3081
Pierson, 3010, 3082–83
Piety, 3084
Piggin, 1623
Pike. *See* ad p. 153
Pilcher, 669
Pildner, 1352
Pile, 3035
Pillsbury, 3085–86
Pilsbery, 3086
Pinckney, 1917
Pinkard, 4599
Pinkethman, 4510
Pinkham, 3087
Pinney, 1244
Piper, 3088
Pitcher, 4533
Pitchford, 2315
Pitman, 3089–90, 3894, 4537
Pitman–Goldthwait, 1568
Pitner, 1377
Pitt, 4533, 4625
Pitts, 2296, 3091–92, 4428, 4541
Plain. *See* ad p. 315
Plaisted, 3093
Plant, 3094
Plantagenet, 3095, 4437–

38, 4603. *See also* ad p. 359

Plantner. *See* ad p. 283

Platt, 144, 832, 1682, 3096–97, 3945

Platts, 1682, 3160

Player, 479

Pleasant, 4464

Pledger, 3792, 4554

Plemon, 3563

Plette, 4180

Plimpton, 3098

Plough, 1230

Plowman, 3099

Plumb, 3100

Plume, 4286

Plumer, 3101–2

Plumley, 2296

Plummer, 3102, 4625

Plumpton, 3098

Plunketts, 3103

Plympton, 3098

Pocahontas, 494, 3104–5, 4604. *See also* ad p. 37

Poe, 3106

Poetker, 3107

Poettcker, 3107

Poffenbarger, 3453

Poffenberger, 3453

Pogue, 3108. *See also* ad p. 261

Poindexter, 2931. *See also* ad p. 383

Polhemus, 62

Polk, 3108–9, 4579. *See also* ad p. 261

Pollock, 3108, 3110. *See also* ad p. 261

Pomeroy, 3111–13, 4598

Pomroy, 2365

Pond, 2966, 3114–15

Poole, 3116

Poore, 3117

Poorman, 3118

Pope, 2074, 3119–20, 4474

Pordage, 445

Porter, 181, 2734, 2855, 3121–25, 3164, 3362, 4530

Porterfield, 3126

Porteus, 4479

Portlock, 4536

Post, 3127

Potker, 3107

Potter, 218, 509, 540, 3128, 4428. *See also* ad p. 59

Pottker, 3107

Potts, 3129–31

Pouncey, 4554

Pound, 3132

Povall, 4464

Powell, 669, 2021, 2191, 2256, 2721, 3133–35, 4523, 4527, 4599

Power, 3136, 4463

Powers, 2107, 3136–37, 4536

Poythress, 457, 4526

Prather, 71, 662

Pratt, 3138–43

Preble, 3144

Predmore, 1210, 2144

Prehn, 3145

Prentice, 2684, 3146–47

Prentiss, 3146

Presbrey, 3148

Prescott, 1268, 1682, 1737, 3149–50, 3657

Preston, 236, 2176, 3151–52

Price, 677, 680, 1768, 2979, 3036, 3153–56, 4169, 4599

Prichard, 3157

Priest, 3158. *See also* ad p. 397

Prillaman, 4599

Prime, 3159–61

Prince, 1431, 2213, 3162, 3235, 4528

Prindle, 3163

Prine, 3048

Pringle, 3163

Printup, 3164

Printzler, 4477

Prior, 3165

Probst, 1437

Proctor, 2558, 3166–67, 4082

Proper, 3168

Propper, 3168

Prosser, 4524

Proute, 3169

Prouty, 3169

Provost, 3170

Prudden, 3171

Prunty, 4599

Pryor, 3165

Puckett, 2296, 2369, 3172

Puffer, 3173

Pugh, 3174, 4477

Pulfiser, 3175

Pullen, 1682, 4382, 4544

Punchard, 3176

Purcas, 4286

Purcell, 3310

Purdy, 3177

Purl, 4532

Purtlebaugh, 4477

Pusey, 2980

Puthoff, 1429

Putman, 3164

Putnam, 3178–80, 3993, 4222–23

Puttenham, 3179

Pyldren, 3181

Pyles, 398, 1128

Pymme, 1623

Pyncheon, 3029

Pyrton, 4528

Quackenbos, 4428

Quackenbush, 4351

Quarles, 2763

Quattlebaum, 3182

Queen, 398

Quick, 62, 3183

Quimby, 3184–85

Quinby, 3184–85

Quincy, 3186, 4526–27

Quinn, 3164

Radcliffe, 2296

Ragan, 4533

Ragin, 479

Ragland, 673, 3187

Raines, 4529

Rainier, 3188

Rakestraw, 3189

Ralph, 1682, 2144

Numbers refer to book numbers that appear in the left-hand column of pages 1–403.

Ralston, 1210, 2144, 2245, 2296
Rambo, 308, 1074, 2557
Ramey, 662
Ramge, 2144
Ramsay, 1431
Ramsburg, 574
Ramsdell, 3190
Ramsey, 1431, 3191
Rand, 3192
Randall, 931, 3193–96
Randle, 4527
Randolph, 330, 1390, 2941–42, 3197–98, 4464, 4527
Randsdell, 4534
Rankin, 2596, 3199, 4541
Ransom, 70, 1682, 3200
Rantzen, 2307
Rapalje, 62. *See also* ad p. 383
Rapier, 1431
Ratcliff, 2013
Rathbone, 3201–3
Ratliff, 1800
Ratts, 2449
Rau, 4428
Rauenzabner, 3204
Ravenel, 3205
Rawle, 3206
Rawlings, 4458
Rawlins, 3207, 3345
Rawson, 3208–10
Ray, 3411, 4175
Rayl, 2296
Raymond, 3211–16
Raynes, 4597
Read, 107, 2763, 3217–19, 3232–34, 4428, 4541
Reade, 3220–21, 3226, 3229, 3231, 4297, 4524, 4632
Reading, 3222. *See also* ad p. 383
Reagin, 2256
Ream, 3784
Rechtor, 4600
Rector, 4600
Redden, 3453
Redditt, 4544
Redfearn, 3223
Redfield, 3224

Redington, 3225
Redman, 4272
Red Track, 2546
Redwine. *See* ad p. 383
Reece, 1939
Reed, 1804, 2245, 3226–34
Reeder, 181, 1377
Reese, 3107
Reeve, 3658
Reeves, 544, 3561, 3723
Reibel, 3797
Reichard, 401
Reid, 12, 1322, 2213, 2256, 3233–35. *See also* ad p. 383
Reif, 3236
Reiff, 2296–97, 3236
Reiley, 1210
Reitz, 3237
Relyea, 4555
Remick, 3238
Remington, 4428
Remsberg, 574
Renaud, 325
Renfro, 1669
Renick. *See* ad p. 383
Rennolds, 3254
Reno, 4542
Rentz, 1429
Repp. *See* ad p. 315
Requa, 3239
Requel, 4416
Resseguie, 3240
Revell, 1275
Rex, 3241
Rexford, 3242
Reyersz, 3393
Reyerszen, 3393
Reynolds, 1800, 3243–55, 3375, 4428, 4524–25, 4528, 4538
Rhea, 4580
Rhoades, 1917
Rhoads, 181. *See also* ad p. 315
Rhodes, 3256. *See also* ad p. 315
Rhorer, 2023
Rice, 218, 494, 3168, 3257–59. *See also* ad p. 37
Rich, 479, 1976, 3260–63

Richard, 1090
Richards, 181, 540, 2144, 3264–65, 4169, 4540
Richardson, 418, 540, 2157, 3266–69, 3830
Richey, 688, 3270
Richie, 2450
Richmond, 1682, 3271–74
Richter, 4600
Ricketson, 3275–76, 3580
Ricketts, 2721
Ricks, 3277–78
Riddell, 3279
Riddle, 3279–80
Riddlesdale, 1466
Rideout, 4328
Ridgeway, 3281, 3294
Ridgill, 479
Ridgway, 3281
Ridley, 3279
Ridlon, 3279
Ried, 3227
Riedl, 2202
Rief, 3236
Rieff, 2297, 3236
Riehl, 3057
Rieth, 3227
Rife, 3236
Riffe, 3236
Riggleman, 3282
Riggs, 3283–85
Rigsbee, 1895
Riker, 3394
Riland, 3286
Riley, 2081, 4477. *See also* ad p. 153
Rima, 2935
Rindler, 1429
Rinehart, 3287. *See also* ad p. 315
Riner, 3633
Ring, 3107, 3288
Ringstad, 2474
Rinker, 4477
Rinkle, 2935
Ripley, 218, 3289
Risk, 4224
Risley, 3290
Ritchey, 2450
Ritchie, 2450, 3373, 4442

Ritt, 3227
Rivers, 479
Rives, 457, 3291, 4534
Rix, 3292
Rixey, 3293
Roach, 2192, 3294
Roark, 3295
Robards, 3296
Robason, 4526
Robbins, 1682, 3297–99, 4474
Robe, 1431
Roberd, 3300
Roberdeau, 3300
Roberson, 4526
Robert, 1291. *See also* ad p. 283
Roberts, 1697, 2369, 2445, 2608, 2757, 2980, 3294, 3301–7, 4458, 4463
Robertson, 1357, 1460, 2931, 3164, 3306, 3308–12, 4287
Robeson, 2157, 3313
Robesoume, 16
Robin, 3299
Robins, 3299
Robinson, 330, 494, 608, 1712, 1813, 2093, 3164, 3314–28, 4287, 4544, 4631. *See also* ad p. 37
Robson, 2369
Roby, 3329
Rochelle, 4524
Rochester, 1128
Rockefeller, 3330–32
Rockwell, 2679, 3333–35
Rockwood, 3336
Rodgers, 479, 3874, 4169
Rodman, 325, 3337
Roessel, 1307
Rogers, 421, 1278, 1596, 1682, 2192, 2731, 2842, 3164, 3338–42, 3561, 3881, 4106, 4169, 4272, 4477, 4554, 4626. *See also* ad p. 397
Rogge, 2452
Rohrbach, 3343
Rohrbough, 3344
Rolfe, 494, 3104–5. *See*

also ad p. 37
Rolfes, 323
Rollins, 3207, 3345
Rolwing, 3346
Romer, 3347
Rongnion, 3376
Ronk, 4555
Roome, 3348
Roop. *See* ad p. 315
Roosevelt, 3349
Root, 218, 1682, 3350
Roots, 3350
Roper, 3351
Roscoe, 4351
Rose, 3352, 4533, 4535–37, 4539, 4542, 4545
Roseboom, 3353
Rosenberger, 4477
Rosenkrans, 3354
Rosenkranz, 2487
Ross, 398, 2855, 3355–57, 4533–34, 4599
Rossi, 1003
Rotch, 3358
Roth, 3359
Rothenberger, 3360
Rotzler, 3438
Round, 3361
Rounds, 3361
Rouse, 3362
Routson, 3204
Rowan. *See* ad p. 383
Rowe, 2662, 4180
Rowell, 3363
Rowland, 2721
Rowlee, 3364
Rowley, 3365
Rowlison, 773
Rown, 4428
Rowning, 4428
Roy, 2574, 3366
Royer, 3367. *See also* ad p. 315
Rubendall, 4180
Ruberson, 2296
Ruble, 4477
Rucker, 677, 3368
Rudanovich, 3804
Rudd, 3369
Rudt, 3227
Rudulph, 4625

Ruehling, 1136
Ruffin, 4523, 4531, 4545, 4632
Rugg, 3370
Ruggles, 2970, 3371
Rulifson, 3372
Rulison, 3372
Runion, 3373, 3376
Runkle, 3374
Runnels, 3375
Runyan, 553, 773, 3376
Runyon, 1800, 3376
Rushton, 1804
Rusling, 3377
Russell, 122, 669, 1939, 2487, 2684, 3021, 3378–84, 3745, 4428
Rust, 1531, 3385–86. *See also* ad p. 283
Ruth, 3387. *See also* ad p. 393
Rutledge, 3388, 3533. *See also* ad p. 283
Rutter, 4401
Ryan, 3389, 4514
Ryder, 3390
Ryedale, 3279
Ryerse, 3391–93
Ryerson, 3391–93. *See also* ad p. 383
Ryerss, 3393
Ryker, 3394
Ryson, 3574
Ryves, 3291

Sabin, 382
Sackett, 3395–96
Safford, 1278, 1412, 3397
Sage, 3398–3401
Sahler, 3402
Sailer, 181
Saint John, 3403
Saire De Quincy, 4528
Sale, 4428
Salisbury, 3404
Salle, 4523
Salmon, 4286
Saltonstall, 3405
Sampson, 3406–7
Sanborn, 3408

Numbers refer to book numbers that appear in the left-hand column of pages 1–403.

Sanborne, 3408
Sanches, 2546
Sandefur. *See* ad p. 383
Sandercock, 299
Sanders, 299, 1662, 2144, 2721, 3409, 4527–28
Sanderson, 1352
Sandford, 3410
Sands, 3411
Sanford, 260, 2888, 3412–13
Sangrey, 3414
Santee, 3415
Sapp, 673, 3416
Sares, 3474
Sargeant, 3418
Sargent, 3417–19, 3420
Sarles, 3703
Satchwell, 3924
Saterfield, 4273
Saton, 4082
Satterfield, 3909
Satterly, 1813
Satterwhite, 4464
Saunders, 3421–22, 4529, 4531, 4599
Saur, 574
Savary, 3423
Savery, 3423–24
Savory, 3423, 3425
Sawin, 3426
Sawyer, 3427–29. *See also* ad p. 283
Saxbe, 3430
Saxon, 2708
Sayler, 3431. *See also* ad p. 315
Sayre, 2721, 3432, 3453. *See also* ad p. 153
Sayrs, 3453
Sayward, 3433
Scalf, 398
Scarborough, 4477, 4525, 4527
Scarritt, 3434
Schaeffer, 1307, 3435–36
Schall, 3437
Schaubhut, 3438
Schauer, 980
Schauffler, 3439
Schell, 3440
Schenk, 2935, 3441

Schermerhorn, 3164, 3442
Schibendrein, 3450
Schick, 3783
Schirm, 3874
Schliemann, 2307
Schlosser, 3443
Schmidt, 1090, 3598, 4538
Schneekloth, 3783
Schneider, 494, 1307, 3453. *See also* ad p. 37
Schoenholtzer, 3503
Schofer, 3444
Schoff, 3445
Scholl, 3446–47
Schoonmaker, 4555
Schoppe, 3448
Schottler, 3449
Schouppe, 1061
Schrock, 3057, 4426
Schubdrein, 3450
Schulte, 2815
Schumacher, 2307
Schureman, 3451–52
Schuyler, 1871, 4552
Schwartzendruker, 3449
Schwartztrauber, 3453
Schwarztrauber, 3453. *See also* ad p. 289
Schwenk, 3454
Schwenkfelder, 3455
Scoggan, 1905
Scoggin, 2575
Scott, 457, 1553, 1596, 1800, 2296, 3108, 3164, 3456–63, 3635, 4078, 4215, 4382, 4464, 4522, 4528, 4533, 4615, 4625, 4631
Scovell, 3464
Scovill, 3466
Scoville, 218, 3465–66
Scranton, 3467
Scribner, 1431
Scrivener, 4477
Scruby, 3468
Scull, 1719
Seab, 3469
Seacord, 325
Seagraves, 3164
Seale, 649, 3469
Seaman, 3470

Seamans, 3471
Searight, 3472
Searles, 4428
Sears, 3473–74
Seat, 4536
Seaton, 2449, 3475–76, 4420
Seaver, 3477
Seawright, 911
Sebor, 3478
Secrist, 4442, 4477
Sedgley, 603
Sedgwick, 2269
Seely, 786, 3479
Seemann, 2307
Segar, 1646, 3480, 4428
Sehner. *See* ad p. 383
Seip, 3916
Seitz, 3481–82
Selby, 1805, 3306, 3483
Selden, 3484–86
Self, 1221
Sell, 422
Sellards, 398
Sellars, 2622
Selleck, 3487
Sellers, 3880, 4169, 4428
Semple, 3488
Sensenig, 3489
Senseny, 3489
Sensineys, 3489
Serré, 3490
Serven, 843
Sessions, 3491
Seton, 3492
Severans, 3493
Severe, 1035
Severit, 3423
Severy, 3423
Sevier, 3494, 4579
Sewall, 1268, 3495
Seward, 3496
Sewell, 3497–98
Sewits, 1307
Seymour, 3499–3500
Shadbolt, 74
Shadinger, 1481
Shaeffer, 3436, 4169
Shafer, 3435, 3501, 4169
Shakespeare, 3502
Shane, 4477
Shanholtz, 3503

Shanholtzer, 3503
Shank, 3504, 3505
Shanks, 3506
Shannon, 1635, 3507, 4479
Sharp, 1532, 1695, 3508, 4522
Sharpe, 3509, 3510–11
Sharples, 3512
Sharpless, 3512
Sharrard, 3703
Shattuck, 2445, 3513
Shaubut, 3438
Shaulis, 4170
Shaull, 3437
Shavender, 3924
Shaver, 3435, 3514, 4106
Shaw, 1278, 2269, 2933, 3515–17, 4458
Shays, 3518
Sheaffer, 3436
Shearer, 3519
Shearin, 4474
Shearman, 3520
Shed, 3521
Shedrick, 4354
Sheever, 4428
Sheffield, 4533
Shelby, 4580
Sheldon, 1682, 4428
Shelley, 1682, 4526
Shelly, 2296
Shelton, 668, 3522
Shepard, 1174, 1682, 1803, 2947, 3523–24. *See also* ad p. 153
Shepherd, 1685, 3389
Shepley, 1805, 3533
Sheppard, 3525
Sherk, 3526–27
Sherman, 921, 2647, 3520, 3528, 4428
Sherouse, 2600
Sherrill, 3529
Sherwood, 3073, 3530
Shettler, 3449
Shields, 2450, 2563, 3164, 4579
Shifflet, 4169
Shillaber, 3531
Shinault, 671

Shinholt, 3503
Shinholts, 3503
Shinn, 2445, 3532
Shinolt, 3503
Shipley, 2575, 3533–34
Shipman, 1377
Shipp, 2369, 2931, 3804
Shirey, 4630
Shiveley, 1391
Shobe, 3535
Shockey, 2708
Shockley, 311
Shoemaker, 3536
Shoff, 2734
Sholl, 3447
Shore, 1939
Short, 2296
Shotwell, 3537
Shove, 3538
Shreck, 3539
Shreve, 2307, 3540, 3658
Shuck, 2708, 3541
Shuey, 3542–43
Shuford, 3544
Shugart, 2296
Shuler, 4477
Shull, 3447
Shults, 3164
Shumaker, 2449
Shuman, 3545
Shumway, 3546
Shuptrine, 1770, 3450
Shurtleff, 3547
Sibley, 540
Siever, 4442
Sifford, 4630
Siggins, 3548
Sigourney, 634
Sikes, 2081
Sill, 3549–50
Sillery, 3924
Silvester, 3551
Simmonds, 3552
Simmons, 2192, 3553–54, 4351, 4382
Simons, 1210, 4328
Simonton, 1027, 3235
Simpson, 3555–56, 3619
Simrall, 3557
Sims, 1662, 4541. *See also* ad p. 383

Sinclair, 3558–59
Sindall, 3453
Sinderson, 540
Sine, 4477
Singletary, 3560
Singleton, 4533
Sinjen, 3783
Sinks, 1062
Sinn, 574
Sinnott, 2587, 3561
Sirbaugh, 4477
Sirk, 3562
Sisson, 3563–64
Sitgreaves, 4625
Skaggs, 4451
Skellenger, 4552
Skelton, 3565
Skilton, 3566
Skinner, 4266
Skipwith, 3156, 4542
Skipworth, 4527
Slack, 3567
Slade, 1083, 3568, 4428. *See also* ad p. 383
Slafter, 3569
Slate, 3570
Slaughter, 3571, 3909
Slaymaker, 3572
Slayton, 3573
Sledge, 3306, 4625, 4632
Slemons, 1391
Sliger, 2563
Slingsby, 1804
Slip, 3574
Slipp, 3574
Sloan, 688
Slocomb, 3575
Slocum, 3401, 3575–76
Slocumb, 3575
Slosson, 3577
Slusher, 3443
Slusser, 3443
Slye, 2931
Small, 608, 2186, 3308, 3578
Smallwood, 4536–37, 4632
Smart, 171, 500, 2110, 4594
Smedley, 3579, 4428
Smith, 41, 62, 218, 280,

Numbers refer to book numbers that appear in the left-hand column of pages 1–403.

283, 398, 473, 540,
677, 680, 817, 1210,
1266, 1291, 1367, 1440,
1460, 1662, 1682, 1759,
1768, 1795, 1800, 1803,
1862, 1939, 2141, 2180,
2245, 2724, 3164, 3371,
3541, 3580–3600, 3619,
3633, 4131, 4169–70,
4266, 4353–54, 4428,
4451, 4463–64, 4477,
4479, 4516, 4525–26,
4528, 4533, 4535,
4538–39, 4615, 4625,
4632. *See also* ads pp.
315 and 383
Smithers, 3035
Smock, 3601
Smucker, 3057
Snider, 3606, 4272. *See
also* ad p. 383
Snidow, 3054
Snively, 2608, 3602. *See
also* ad p. 315
Snodgrass, 3603
Snow, 891, 3604–5
Snowden, 671, 3869
Snyder, 3606, 3961,
4169, 4578
Soane, 2152, 4527
Sole, 3609
Solley, 3607
Solly, 3609
Somerby, 805
Somers, 1297
Sommer, 4538
Sonifrank, 4441
Sopher, 3658
SoRelle, 4131
Sorrell, 4523, 4626
Sorrels, 4376
Sorsby, 4527, 4632
Souder, 3608, 4442
Soule, 3609
Soulis, 3609
Southard, 3613
Southerland, 280
Southerly, 3610
Southern, 16
Southgate, 3611
Southwick, 3612
Southworth, 3613
Sowash, 62

Sowder, 2209
Sowell, 1862, 3614
Sowerby, 4527, 4632
Sowle, 3609
Spackman, 2244
Spaid, 3615
Spain, 211
Spainhower, 673
Spalding, 3616–19
Spare, 3620
Sparhawk, 3621
Sparr, 49
Spear, 1278, 3622–23,
4571
Spears, 4554
Specht, 4428
Speed, 3624
Speer, 3625
Speicher, 3626
Speight, 3633
Spelman, 3627
Spence, 4533
Spencer, 3628–29
Spengler, 3630
Spicer, 3631–32
Spicher, 3626
Spivey, 2600, 3633
Spofford, 3634–35
Spooner, 3636–38
Spoor, 3639
Spotswood, 3640
Sprague, 3641–47, 4428
Springer, 3648–49
Spry, 299
Spyker, 3626
Squires, 3650
St. John, 4229
Stab, 4300
Stackpole, 3651
Stacy, 3652–53
Stacye, 1275
Staehling, 3654
Stafford, 500, 4078
Stahl, 4170–71
Stahle. *See* ad p. 383
Standish, 3655–57
Stanfield, 2297
Stanley, 2295–96, 2575,
2773, 3658–59, 4630
Stanton, 2888, 3660–62
Stanwood, 3663
Staples, 2582

Starbard, 3664
Starbird, 3664
Starbuck, 1895, 2296,
3665
Starin, 3666
Stark, 1918, 3667
Starke, 2582
Starkey, 3668
Starkweather, 3669
Starling, 3670
Starr, 2107, 3671–72
Stauffer, 3673–75
Staver, 3754
Stearns, 1682, 3676–79
Stebbins, 2172, 3680–81
Steel, 961
Steele, 1352, 3614,
3682–83
Steelman, 1070
Steere, 3684
Steevens, 3696
Steg, 3482
Stegall, 2299
Steggall, 3685
Stein, 3686
Steinbrugge, 3687–88
Steiner, 3689
Stellmach, 1352
Stenberg, 3482
Stephens, 3389–91
Stephenson, 2369, 3692
Steptoe, 4525
Ster, 3666
Sterling, 16, 3693
Stern, 2644
Sternbergh, 3164
Sternburgh, 3164
Sterns, 3164
Sterrett, 3874
Stetson, 3694–95
Stetzel, 2684
Steuart, 3702
Stevens, 1278, 3696–
3700
Stevenson, 3701
Stevesson, 4451
Steward, 1061, 2144
Stewart, 181, 385, 662,
688, 911, 1246, 1257,
3035, 3108, 3453,
3702–8, 4522, 4536.
See also ad p. 283

Stichter, 3709
Stickney, 3710
Stidham, 3769
Stierwalt, 2449
Stiles, 1690, 3711–14
Stillwell, 2213, 3715–23
Stilwell, 3715, 3724–25
Stimpson, 3726
Stimson, 2188
Stine, 4477
Stingley, 2608
Stipe, 2662
Stith, 4534
Stiver, 3754
Stobo, 596
Stockbridge, 3468
Stocker, 3066
Stocking, 3727
Stockton, 384, 4468
Stoddard, 1682, 3728–36
Stoddart, 3735–36
Stodder, 3732, 3735–36
Stoessel. *See* ad p. 341
Stoever, 3754
Stokely, 1431
Stoker, 1264
Stokes, 548, 1719, 2445, 3737–38, 4524, 4625
Stoltenberg, 3783
Stoltzfus, 3057
Stone, 1905, 2887, 3305, 3739–45, 3993, 4106, 4451, 4528, 4571, 4579, 4632. *See also* ad p. 153
Stoneking, 2144
Stoner, 3746. *See also* ad p. 315
Storer, 3747, 4266
Storke, 3748
Storm, 574, 2448
Storrs, 3749
Story, 1055, 1258
Stouffer, 3675, 3750. *See also* ad p. 315
Stough, 1893
Stoughton, 2852
Stout, 62, 961, 2144, 3751–52
Stovall, 4531
Stover, 3675, 3753, 4037, 4626, 4632. *See also* ad p. 315
Stöver, 3754
Stow, 1682
Stowe, 3755
Stowell, 3756
Strain, 4221
Stranahan, 3757
Strange, 3758–62, 4428
Strangmen, 4528
Strassburger, 3763
Stratton, 1862, 2618, 3764–65
Straw, 3766
Strawbridge, 3773
Strawn, 441, 4458
Street, 3767, 4514
Streeter, 3768
Streit, 4477
Streng, 3482
Stretcher, 3769
Strickland, 3770–71
Strickler, 3772
Strickling, 4477
Strieber, 1778–79
Strihl, 574
Stripp, 540
Strobridge, 3773
Strode, 3778, 4428
Strong, 2724, 3774–75, 4630
Strother, 2176, 3776, 4527, 4535, 4617
Stroud, 3777–79
Stuart, 911, 3658, 3780, 3874, 4522, 4527, 4536
Stubbs, 2186, 3781–82
Studdard, 3735–36
Study, 2296
Stuhr, 3783
Stukes, 479
Stukey, 3784
Stultz, 3785
Stump, 4169
Sturgeon, 3786
Sturges, 3787–88
Sturgis, 3789
Sturm, 574, 2448
Sturman, 4451
Sturtevant, 3906
Stutzman, 1940
Stuyvesant, 4061
Sudduth, 3733
Sullivan, 3790–91
Sullivant, 3670
Sulser, 3792
Sumlar, 1623
Summerfield, 1454
Summitt, 1431
Sumner, 1278, 2272, 3793–95. *See also* ad p. 153
Sunderhaus, 4300
Sunthimer, 4404
Supplee, 181, 308, 1074
Surdam, 3796
Surges, 3797
Sutcliffe, 3798–99, 3801
Sutherland, 3610, 3800
Sutherlin, 2763
Sutherly, 3610
Sutliff, 3801
Sutliffe, 3798, 3801
Sutor, 2962
Sutphen, 3802
Sutton, 1171, 1220, 3803–4
Swain, 3805–6, 4175
Swallow, 3807
Swan, 544, 3808, 4524
Swann, 4536
Swanson, 4599
Swartzentruber, 3057, 4426
Swartztrauber, 3453
Swarztrauber, 3453
Swasey, 3809
Swazey, 3194
Swearingen, 2788, 3811
Sweeney, 4625
Sweet, 2296
Sweetser, 3810
Swett, 1805, 3812
Swickard, 449
Swift, 2297, 3813–14
Swinehart, 449
Swing, 3815
Swingley, 509, 680
Swint, 3816
Switzer, 961
Sybrant, 766
Sydenstricker, 3541

Numbers refer to book numbers that appear in the left-hand column of pages 1–403.

Sydnor, 4541
Sykes, 2256
Symmes, 3817
Symonson, 3554

Tabb, 1367
Taber, 540, 3818
Tackett, 3376
Taft, 1679, 1682, 1968, 3819
Taggart, 2855, 3820
Tailer, 2852
Tainter, 3821
Talbot, 3822, 4428, 4575
Talbott, 3823
Talcott, 3824
Taliaferro, 669, 1367, 3825–26, 4599, 4617
Talley, 3827
Tallmadge, 3829
Tallman, 3828, 4428
Talmadge, 3829
Talmage, 3829
Tamblyn, 299
Tangney, 3830
Tankersley, 3831
Tannehill, 211
Tanner, 385, 3362, 3614, 3832–34
Tapley, 3835
Tapp, 817
Tappan, 3836–37, 4286
Tarleton, 3305, 3838
Tarpley, 4536
Tate, 3846, 4537, 4599, 4630
Tatum, 422, 457, 4625
Tay, 1682
Taylor, 330, 394, 1266, 1939, 2108, 2349, 2448, 3108, 3142, 3839–49, 4169, 4428, 4477, 4529–30, 4625–26, 4631–32
Taynter, 3821
Teall, 3850
Tebbs, 554
Tedrow, 441
Teeter, 4578
Tefft, 3903, 4428
Tellman, 3851
Temple, 2329, 3852–56
Templeton, 3857

Templin, 3858–59
Tenley, 1431
Tennant, 3860
Tenney, 3861–62
Terrell, 3863, 4554
Terrill, 4511
Terry, 1061, 3864–66
Thacher, 3867
Thallaug, 2915
Tharrington, 4474
Thaxter, 4185
Thayer, 2763, 3868
Theaker, 2734
Theis, 3899
Thiesen, 3107
Thomas, 274, 574, 867, 1291, 2295–96, 2315, 2708, 3293, 3411, 3804, 3869–73, 4169, 4458, 4477, 4516, 4526, 4541, 4554, 4632. *See also* ads pp. 315 and 325
Thomason, 4298
Thompkins, 4516
Thompson, 12, 789, 1061, 1460, 1737, 1776, 1795, 1862, 1939, 2052, 2141, 2413, 2449, 2488, 2888, 3376, 3804, 3874–84, 4169, 4451, 4525–26, 4528–29. *See also* ad p. 153
Thomson, 3658, 3885, 4458, 4543
Thornbrough, 2297
Thornburg, 3658, 3886
Thorndike, 3887
Thorne, 74
Thornhill, 500
Thornton, 3360, 3888–90, 4524, 4534
Thornwell, 4554
Thorogood, 4528
Thorpe, 4514, 4528
Throckmorton, 3891
Thurber, 3892
Thurston, 500, 1682, 3893–96, 3986, 4428
Thweatt, 4523–24
Thwing, 3897
Thyssen, 3899
Tibbetts, 1481, 2346, 3898

Tice, 3899
Tidwell, 2621
Tiernan, 3900–1
Tiffany, 3902
Tifft, 3903
Tilden, 2842
Tilghman, 3904
Tilley, 3905
Tillinghast, 203
Tillman, 3904
Tilson, 3906
Tilton, 1369, 1808, 3907–8, 4571
Timberlake, 4428, 4474
Timberman, 3108
Timm, 4428
Timmons, 4173, 4533
Tingen, 3909
Tingley, 3910
Tinker, 3911
Tinkham, 3912
Tinsley, 4599
Tippin, 3913
Tipton, 2979, 4542
Tisdale, 2192, 3914, 4428
Titcomb, 1268
Titterington, 2557
Titus, 4428
Tobey, 3915
Tobie, 3915
Tobin, 677
Toby, 2853, 3915
Todd, 1367, 1447, 2557, 2596, 3916–18, 4246
Toers, 3919
Toliver, 3826
Tolson, 557
Tomkins, 3921
Tomlinson, 479, 1055, 3922
Tompkins, 3920–21, 4266. *See also* ad p. 383
Toney, 2450, 3923
Toothaker, 1481
Tope, 449
Topham, 4286
Topp, 4544
Toppan, 3836
Topping, 3924
Torbett, 3792, 1776
Torres, 2546

Torrey, 381, 3925–27
Tottingham, 1496
Totty, 3792
Tousey, 3928
Tower, 1006, 3929
Towle, 3930
Towne, 3931–33, 4571
Towner, 3934
Townsend, 3935–38, 4554
Townshend, 3939
Trabue, 4563
Tracy, 3940–41, 4552
Trahan, 3942
Train, 3944
Trammell, 670, 2256, 3389
Tratt, 3946
Travers, 3943, 4524
Traverse, 4524
Travis, 533, 4524, 4536, 4632
Trawick, 3816
Trayne, 3944
Treadwell, 3945. *See also* ad p. 383
Treat, 3946–48, 4526
Tredway, 3949
Tree, 3950
Trefethen, 1533
Trego, 3951
Tremaine, 3952
Treman, 3952
Trent, 494, 789, 2369. *See also* ad p. 37
Treweek, 299
Trickey, 1062
Trimble, 2955
Triplett, 3376
Tripp, 2487, 2639, 3953–54, 4428
Trolinder, 1062
Trott, 3946
Trotter, 2596
Trowbridge, 1266, 3955–56, 4477
Troyer, 2815, 4426
Truax, 4428
Trubee, 3957
Trudeau, 4266
Truman, 3952

Trumble, 4522
Trumbull, 2487
Trump, 4169
Trygstad, 4300
Tubb, 670
Tuck, 2299, 3958
Tucker, 299, 662, 1291, 1401, 3959–61, 4451, 4527–28
Tuckers, 4524
Tuers, 3919
Tuley, 3962–63
Tull, 2192
Tunnell, 3964, 4581
Tunstall, 4525
Tupper, 3965
Turfler, 3341
Turner, 258, 330, 2400, 3614, 3906, 3966–68, 4169, 4599. *See also* ad p. 383
Turney, 3969
Turnley, 3970, 4579
Tuthill, 3971, 3976
Tuttle, 218, 1447, 3378, 3971–76
Twining, 3977
Twisden, 2842
Twiss, 1152
Twitchell, 3978
Tyas, 4626
Tyer, 3979
Tyler, 3980, 4510
Tymensen, 4428
Tyrus, 4625
Tyssen, 3899
Tyus, 4626

Uhler, 3981
Ulrey. *See* ad p. 315
Umble, 3057
Umpleby, 1795
Underhill, 1364, 1473, 3982–84
Underwood, 3985–87
Unthank, 3658
Untiedt, 3783
Upchurch, 4468
Updike, 2918
Upham, 3988–90
Upshur, 4532–33

Upson, 1682, 3991
Upton, 473, 1408, 3992–93
Urann, 3994
Usher, 3995–96
Usry, 3164
Utrich, 540
Utter, 4479

Vail, 3479, 3997–98
Valentine, 3999, 4464
Valleaux, 1329
Van Aaken, 4000
Van Alstyne, 4001
Van Antwerpen, 4428
Van Benthuysen, 4002
Van Blarcum, 1795
Vanblaricom, 2684
Van Brunt, 4003
Van Buren, 4004
Vance, 4580
Van Cleve, 3305
Vandenburgh, 4428
Van Der Vliet, 4428
Van Derlip, 4006–7
Vander Lippe, 4006–7
Vanderbeek, 62
Vanderbilt, 4005, 4428
Vanderlip, 4006–7
Vandersaal, 1842–43
Vanderveer, 62
Van Deursen, 4009
Van Deusen, 4008–9
Van Doorn, 4010
Van Doren, 4010
Van Dorn, 4010
Van Dyke, 4579
Van Etten, 4011
Van Every, 4012
Vanhorne, 4015
Van Heck, 4013
Van Hecke, 4013
Van Hoosear, 4014
Van Kleeck, 4016
Van Lehn, 4017
Van Lehn–Blickensderfer, 4017
Van Lent, 2409
Van Metre, 1174
Van Nice, 62
Van Norden, 4018

Numbers refer to book numbers that appear in the left-hand column of pages 1–403.

Van Nostrand, 74
Vannoy, 1264
Van Noy, 1264, 1652
Van Patten, 3265
Van Pelt, 4019
Van Rensselaer, 4020
Van Slichtenhorst, 4428
Van Sweringen, 3811
Van Tassel, 3347
VanUxem, 4021
Van Vechtens, 4022
Van Vleet, 4351
Van Voorhees, 4023–24
Van Voorhis, 4025
Van Vranken, 4428
Van Wagenen, 4026,
 4555
Van Wart, 3574
Van Wenckum, 4428
Van Wie, 3164
Van Winkle, 4027–28
Van Wormer, 3164,
 3687–88
Varn, 500
Varner, 4029–30
Varney, 1800, 2926
Varnum, 4031
Vathaver, 3687–88
Vaughan, 2466, 4032–36
Veach, 4037
Veale, 4536
Veasey, 4598
Veblen, 4038
Veeder, 4039
Vehorn, 323
Veitenheimer, 1061
Veloz, 119
Venable, 4040, 4128
Venner, 299
Verdery, 3164
Vermilyea, 325
Verner, 4030
Ver Planck, 4041
Vestal, 1939
Vetter, 4613
Vettestad, 3482
Viale, 1003
Viall, 4042
Vickers, 1770, 2296
Viele, 2294
Viets, 4043
Vigil, 2546

Vilas, 4044
Vincent, 325, 4045
Vinhagen, 4428
Vining, 4554
Vinton, 4046–47
Visscher, 4048, 4428
Vivion, 1447
Vogt, 4049
Von Alten, 81
Von Der Lippe, 4006–7
Von Solms, 4526
Vorce, 4050
Vorsthoven, 1429
Vosburgh, 1776
Vose, 4051
Voskuhl, 1429
Vreeland, 3284, 4052
Vrooman, 4053

Waddy, 4464
Wade, 1682, 4054–56
Wadham, 4057
Wadsworth, 3378, 4058
Waeger, 4428
Wagenbreth, 1136
Wagener, 1307
Wagenseller, 4059
Wager, 4198
Wages, 2754
Waggoner, 4406
Waggonman, 2173
Wagle, 4060
Wahl. *See* ad p. 341
Wainwright, 4061
Wait, 2107, 4062
Waite, 3804, 4063
Waitman, 4251
Wakefield, 4064
Wakeman, 4065
Walcott, 4066
Waldo, 4067–69
Waldon, 1496
Waldron, 2926
Wale, 4474
Wales, 4070
Walford, 1533
Walichs, 4027
Walk, 2256
Walker, 1352, 2557,
 2721, 2941–42, 3164,
 3633, 4071–73, 4170–
 71, 4428, 4477, 4510,
 4542, 4599

Walkerley, 1805
Wall, 500, 1266, 4106
Wallace, 1405, 2713,
 4074, 4076, 4522, 4631
Wallace–Bruce, 4075
Wallach, 4077
Wallbridge, 2865, 4078
Waller, 4524
Wallin, 4079
Walling. *See* ad p. 153
Walls, 4514
Waln, 4477
Walter, 100
Walters, 16, 1210, 2144
Walthall, 4080
Waltman, 4081
Walton, 86, 4082, 4458
Waltz, 4083
Walworth, 4084–85
Wampler, 4086. *See also*
 ad p. 315
Wanner, 4087
Wanton, 3401, 4088
Wanzer, 4089
Warbasse, 4090
Warble, 4169
Ward, 16, 211, 540, 826,
 1682, 2721, 2875, 3884,
 4091–93, 4198, 4451,
 4589, 4630
Warde, 4091
Wardell, 4094
Warden, 4095
Ware, 1246, 1408, 4096
Warfield, 299, 4097
Warham, 1682
Warne, 4098
Warner, 218, 1464, 1490,
 1776, 1803, 3463,
 4099–4100, 4297. *See
 also* ad p. 153
Warren, 144, 311, 340,
 3678, 4101–6, 4173,
 4190, 4428, 4529, 4531,
 4540, 4626, 4632
Warriner, 4107–8
Warvel, 4169
Warwick, 534, 4461
Wash, 4630
Washburn, 4109–11
Washburne, 4112
Washington, 330, 494,

4113–15, 4526. *See also* ad p. 37

Waterhouse, 4116–17, 4571

Waterman, 3906, 4118–20

Waters, 16, 89, 2558, 4121–22, 4419

Wathes, 4132

Watkins, 4123–24, 4600, 4630

Watson, 554, 670, 1429, 1768, 3164, 3453, 4125–29, 4169, 4428, 4525

Watt, 4132

Watter, 4132

Wattles, 4130

Watts, 3222, 4131–32, 4382, 4464, 4474. *See also* ad p. 283

Wattys, 4132

Waugh, 4382

Way, 2296

Waybright, 677

Wayne, 608, 4133

Wear, 4580

Weatherby, 4134

Weathersbee, 4539

Weaver, 961, 2297, 4135–38

Webb, 78, 1460, 2141, 2684, 2838, 3272, 4258, 4286, 4400, 4428, 4614

Webber, 4139–40

Weber, 2833

Webster, 218, 1061, 1440, 2582, 4141–43, 4599

Weekes, 4145, 4382

Weeks, 4144–45

Weightman, 4251

Weikert, 4146

Weimer, 4147

Weis, 4148

Weitzel, 1437, 4149

Welby, 1328

Welch, 603, 2032, 4150–51

Weld, 4152

Weldon, 4625

Welker, 1264

Wellcome, 603

Weller, 3804, 4552

Welles, 4153–54

Wellman, 1460, 2141, 4155

Wellmans, 4156

Wells, 299, 1970–72, 2299, 2487, 4157–62

Wellwood, 3369

Welschans, 2297

Wendell, 4163–64

Wenger, 4165–66

Wentworth, 4167

Wentz, 308, 1074, 4168

Werbel, 4169

Werley, 361

Werner, 4030, 4170–71

Werts, 62, 4172

Wertz, 4169

Wesel, 2918

Wesley, 1266

Wessel, 3164

Wessels, 3164

West, 3021, 4173–75, 4442, 4625

Westall, 3145

Westbrook, 4626

Westcott, 4176–77

Westervelt, 2901, 4178

Westfall, 3145

Westphal, 2307

Wetmore, 4179

Wetzler, 4180

Weygant, 3394

Whaley, 74, 2724, 4181

Whalley, 1195

Wharton, 2450, 2763, 3199

Wheat, 2990, 4182

Wheatleigh, 4183

Wheatley, 4183

Wheeler, 144, 1210, 2144, 2450, 4185–90, 4382, 4514, 4630

Wheelers, 4184

Wheelock, 4191

Wheelwright, 4192

Whetten, 3917

Whetzel, 4193

Whipple, 1071, 3070, 4194–98

Whisnant, 4199

Whitacre, 4477, 4615

Whitaker, 2448–49, 4200, 4366, 4615

Whitall, 4201

Whitcher, 4202

Whitcomb, 4203

White, 385, 1905, 2245, 2272, 2297, 2842, 3658, 3792, 4169, 4204–25, 4286, 4306, 4428, 4447, 4477, 4535, 4544, 4552. *See also* ads pp. 383 and 397

Whitehead, 4523

Whitely, 2369

Whiteman, 4251

Whitfield, 2558, 4226–27. *See also* ad p. 355

Whitin, 4228

Whiting, 330, 540, 4229–30

Whitley, 4528

Whitman, 144, 4231–32, 4251

Whitmel, 4625

Whitmore, 4233–34

Whitney, 4235–37, 4534

Whiton, 4238

Whitsitt, 384

Whittelsey, 4239

Whittemore, 4240–42, 4552

Whitten, 1623

Whittier, 4202, 4243

Whittlesey, 4239, 4244

Whitworth, 2931

Whorton, 2763

Wiard, 4245

Wiat, 4246

Wiatt, 1367, 4246

Wichert, 2307

Wicker, 1895

Wickersham, 4477

Wickes, 1473

Wickett, 299

Wickham, 4247

Wickware, 4248

Widmer, 1061

Numbers refer to book numbers that appear in the left-hand column of pages 1–403.

Widrig, 2935
Wiens, 3107
Wier, 688
Wiese, 3783
Wiggins, 3924
Wight, 4249–50
Wightman, 280, 4251
Wilbor, 4351
Wilbore, 1682, 4428
Wilbur, 4252–53
Wilcox, 4254–57, 4259
Wilcoxen, 4259
Wilcoxson, 4258–59
Wildbore, 4253
Wilder, 1805, 4260
Wildes, 4261, 4571
Wildrick, 4262
Wilds, 662
Wiley, 1210, 1635, 2144
Wilkerson, 308
Wilkey, 2256
Wilkins, 4263
Wilkinson, 49, 649, 1805, 4264–66
Willard, 1268, 3658, 4267–68
Willcockson, 4259
Willcomb, 4269
Willcox, 2587, 4270
Willcutts, 2296
Willets, 3596
Willett, 723, 4271–72
Willey, 4273–74
Williams, 218, 280, 283, 330, 422, 500, 1070, 1352, 1768, 1939, 2487, 2608, 2708, 2721, 2763, 3164, 3392, 3658, 4106, 4169, 4275–90, 4523, 4527–29, 4534, 4580. *See also* ads pp. 162 and 383
Williamson, 1768, 1800, 2141, 4291–92, 4525
William the Conqueror, 3095
Willis, 1682, 4293–98
Wills, 222–23, 299, 500, 4299
Willson, 789. *See also* ad p. 361
Wilmarth, 4428
Wilson, 688, 1460, 2141,

2299, 2603, 2721, 2763, 3164, 3658, 3874, 4169, 4300–8, 4474, 4526–27, 4600. *See also* ad p. 361
Wilton, 1682
Wiltsee, 4309
Winchell, 4310
Winchester, 4311–13, 4528
Wincoll, 4310
Winder, 16
Winders, 4314
Windley, 3924
Wine, 4315. *See also* ad p. 315
Winfield, 4526
Wing, 218, 2297, 4316
Wingate, 4317
Wingfield, 2256, 4599
Winn, 4528
Winship, 845
Winslow, 1596, 2296, 3906, 4318–19. *See also* ad p. 397
Winstead, 3924
Winston, 4298, 4320–21, 4464, 4474
Winter, 3723
Wintermute, 4322
Winters, 3359, 4543
Winthrop, 1473, 1682, 4323–24, 4428
Wiot, 4246
Wirz, 4386
Wisdom, 4325
Wise, 2721, 4326
Wiswall, 4327
Withee, 2346
Witherill, 4328
Withers, 1291
Witherstine, 317
Withington, 2838
Witt, 4329
Witten, 2684
Witter, 67, 4330
Wittig, 4331
Wodell, 4428
Woertman, 4372
Wolcott, 4332–33
Wolf, 2298, 4514
Wollam, 2144
Womack, 2369, 4464

Wood, 163, 1027, 1061, 2731, 3306, 4334–42, 4428. *See also* ad p. 383
Woodbridge, 4343
Woodbury, 1682, 4344–46. *See also* ad p. 153
Woodcock, 4347–48
Woodford, 1682
Woodhull, 2721
Woodlee, 2575
Woodley, 1768
Woodliffe, 4632
Woodling, 4349
Woodman, 4350–51
Woodmansey, 1682
Woodruff, 218, 1034, 4352
Woods, 557, 1210, 1778–79, 2256, 2329, 2713, 3306, 4338, 4353–58
Woodside, 4397
Woodson, 4464, 4525–27
Woodward, 540, 4359, 4536, 4543
Woodworth, 1006, 4360–61
Woody, 3658
Woolley, 2445
Woolman, 3658
Woolsey, 4362–63
Woolworth, 4364
Wooster, 4365, 4367–68
Wootan, 671
Wooten, 4366
Wootten, 16
Worcester, 4367–68
Worden, 608, 4369
Work, 4370–71
Workman, 1895, 4372–73
Worley, 12, 385, 4382
Worsham, 4626
Worth, 1719
Worthington, 4374
Wortman, 71, 4372
Wratchford, 2013
Wright, 680, 1623, 1682, 2708, 2842, 3145, 3164, 3658, 4198, 4375–85, 4477, 4544–45
Wriston, 2157
Wurts, 4386, 4555
Wyant, 1429

Wyatt, 2582, 2845, 4387–88, 4533
Wybesse, 3639
Wykes, 4528
Wylie, 3874
Wymer, 62
Wynkoop, 4389–90
Wynn, 4524, 4533
Wynne, 2557, 4524, 4527, 4533, 4632
Wynns, 4533
Wythe, 4632

Yadon, 2208
Yaklin, 1429
Yale, 1195, 4391–92
Yancey, 1768, 4393
Yankey, 2013
Yarborough, 3909
Yardley, 4394, 4510
Yates, 4395–96, 4536
Yeager, 4397–98
Yeamans, 4399
Yeaomans, 4399
Yearling, 4400

Yeilding, 2763
Yelf, 509. *See also* ad p. 59
Yeoman, 1623
Yerian, 1437
Yerkes, 3222, 4401
Yntema, 4402
Yocum, 181
Yoder, 2815, 3057, 4403–4, 4426
Yonce, 4405
Yonges, 4413
Yonkin, 4414
Yonley, 4477
York, 4169
Yorks, 4560
Yost, 3108
Youmans, 2349, 4399
Young, 540, 662, 1431, 1496, 2763, 4169, 4406–11, 4613, 4616
Youngken, 4414
Youngkin, 4414
Younglove, 1278
Youngman, 2838

Youngs, 4412–13
Younkin, 4414
Yowell, 4451

Zahniser, 4415
Zehr, 3057
Zeislof, 1437
Zell, 3874
Zeller, 2815
Ziegler, 4416–17
Zielley, 3164
Zimmerly, 4420
Zimmerman, 574, 3362, 4180, 4418–19. *See also* ad p. 383
Zimms, 554
Zink, 4420
Zirk, 3562
Zook, 3057, 4421–23, 4426
Zorns, 4458
Zouck, 4422–23
Zow, 4351
Zuck, 4422–23
Zug, 4421–23

Index to Advertisers

Allen's Books & Crafts, Inc., 393
Allen, Corben E., 307
Allie Pink Genealogical Research,
   Inc., 365
Bales, Miriam, 207
Barnes, Fred W., 19
Beers, Donna, 15
Blair, Edward P., 33
Brawley, Dorothy P., 37
Brewster, Marcus V., 59
Burgess, Jane F., 109
Clement Custom Programming, 285
Cory, Al B., 77
d'Armand, Virginia Carlisle, 90
DeHaven Club, 91
Dudley-Higham, Mary, Genesis
   Publications, 27
Family Tree Sleuths, 303
Finnell, Arthur Louis, 127
Gateway Press, 81
Hazard, Mary J., 153
Heart of the Lakes Publishing, 187
Hewick Plantation B & B, 337
Hogle, Francis M., Jr., 163
Hull, Robert E., 173, 211
International Forum, 255
Kaufman, Dr. Frank L. & Odette J.,
   237
Kinship, 379

Komives, Ralph, 317
Lineage Search Associates, 231, 261
Linn, Jo White, 383
Lomar Research, 217
Madigan's Books, 119
Mayflower Families, 397
Moore, Thomas R., Esq., 359
W.E. Morrison & Co., 103
Moulton, Joy Wade, 269
Neimeyer, David, 331
Nowell, Mary, 365
Origins, 389
Plumley, Boyd, 321, 391
Ross Research, 195
Rutherford, Dolores C., 162, 245
Rutledge, Fred, 283
Schwarztrauber, Sayre A., 289
Stevens, Ken, 361
Stoddard, John H., 313
Taylor, Inez, 325
Tennessee Valley Publishing, 135
Thomas Turner Association, 29
Tidewater Virginia Families, 181
UMI, 295
Wahl's Discoveries, 341
Weber, Richard R., 315
Whitfield Books, 355
Williams, James E., 375
Wise, William E., 297

REFERENCE